The World Economic Factbook

2002/2003

10th edition

Euromonitor International plc 60-61 Britton Street, London EC1M 5UX

The World Economic Factbook

The World Economic Factbook 2002/2003

10th edition

Researched and published by:

EUROMONITOR plc
60-61 Britton Street
London EC1M 5UX
United Kingdom
Telephone: +44 207-251-8024
Fax: +44 207-608-3149

EUROMONITOR INTERNATIONAL INC
122 South Michigan Avenue
Suite 1200
Chicago
Illinois 60603, USA
Tel: + 1 312 922 1115
Fax: +1 312 922 1157

EUROMONITOR INTERNATIONAL (Asia) Pte Ltd
3 Lim Teck Kim Road
#08-02 Singapore Technologies Building
Singapore 088934

Tel: + 65 6429 0590
Fax: + 65 6324 1855

E-mail: info@euromonitor.com

http://www.euromonitor.com

British Library Cataloguing in Publication Data
A CIP catalogue record for this book is available from the British Library

ISBN 1 84264-234 0

Printed in Great Britain by Antony Rowe Ltd., Chippenham, Wiltshire

Contents

Introduction

Introduction

The World Economic Factbook 2002/2003 (10th edition) represents a unique compilation of hard-to-get political and economic information on 204 countries of the world, laid out in a concise and above all completely regular format which allows not only ease of access but also the maximum degree of comparability.

Countries are arranged in alphabetical order, with each country presented as a two-page section, the first page of which is a textual summary while the second contains statistical information for the years 1999 to 2001, organised according to a regular grid.

The information is supplemented by a series of specially commissioned maps showing the different continents with the location of each country.

Rankings

The uniformity of coverage is a key feature of the book. The individual country sections have been designed in order to allow the compilation of a series of unique rankings, showing the relative position for each country measured by a variety of criteria, such as geographical area, population, inflation, GDP, and so on. Thus each country can be ranked from 1 to 204 to show its relative position according to a wide variety of different benchmarks.

In order to compile the rankings it has been necessary to standardise and convert the basic data in many cases, particularly where economic material is concerned. It is inevitable that fluctuations in exchange rates and inflation have caused a considerable amount of distortion to the basic data, and as a result the rankings may contain some anomalies, although the editors have taken every care to cross-check the listings.

Where no data was available for the ranking criteria in each case some individual countries have been omitted.

Country Coverage

The 204 countries covered in this Handbook include all of the states for which standardised data is available. Excluded are micro-states such as the Vatican or San Marino, where no significant amount of comparable data is available, and where most of the economic data is in any case subsumed within the economy of a larger state (ie Italy in both of these cases).

Sources and Methodology

This book is the result of an extensive research programme carried out during the early part of 2002, involving contact with a wide-ranging set of sources and contacts to gather together as much comprehensive material as possible.

The data have been drawn wherever possible from national sources, including official figures from national statistical agencies. This primary data has been supplemented where necessary from multilateral sources such as the International Monetary Fund, United Nations, International Labour Organisation, and so on. (See below for further details by sector). In addition information has been drawn from the national press and specialist publications, or collated from Euromonitor's extensive international statistical database.

The availability of data is inevitably somewhat uneven, since some countries are far better documented than others. In many cases figures were unavailable for the latest year from published sources, and it has therefore been necessary in these cases to include estimates based on the best available external data. It was also necessary in many cases to undertake some degree of standardisation of the available data, since the information presented by some countries does not conform reliably with the international norms; there would, after all, be no point in attempting any international comparisons or rankings without having first established a high degree of standardisation.

Euromonitor estimates have mainly been used for 2001 economic data where official figures were unavailable. Data have been compiled using a mathematical model, which is based on data from national statistical agencies and calculated by taking into account economic and inflationary trends, current spending trends, demographic patterns, and so on. Political events and statistical material have been updated as far as September 2002 wherever possible.

Subject Coverage and Definitions

Inflation
This refers to annual average inflation, and is based mainly on figures provided by the *International Monetary Fund*.

Exchange rate
This refers to annual average official exchange rates, and is drawn mainly from figures provided by the *International Monetary Fund*.

GDP
Data for gross domestic product have been drawn wherever possible from national statistical sources, supplemented with data collected by the *International Monetary Fund* or, where necessary, Euromonitor estimates for the latest year.

GDP growth rate figures have also been included wherever they are reliably available. They refer, as one would suppose, to the rate of overall economic growth, which is recorded by a country after stripping out the distorting effects of inflation. There is, however, more to this apparently simple task than meets the eye. In some countries, notably those where no proper statistical information has been available since perhaps 1990, it was felt that the foundation for such an estimate was not available, and real growth figures have accordingly been omitted. In certain high-inflation countries, on the other hand, the distortions caused by fluctuating currencies sometimes become so extreme that even the best and most accurate information from independent sources fails to produce a satisfactory result; in these cases, Euromonitor estimates have been supplied.

Consumption
These figures, which refer to private final consumption expenditure, have also been drawn wherever possible from national statistical sources, supplemented with data collected by the *International Monetary Fund* or, where necessary, Euromonitor estimates for the latest year.

Tourism Receipts and Spending
Tourism receipts refers to revenue from foreign nationals, ie payments from visitors within the destination country and to the national carriers, while tourism expenditure refers to the reciprocal expenditure by that country's nationals in foreign countries, as collected by government agencies such as national statistical bodies and customs and excise bodies.

The main sources for this section have been national statistics, supplemented wherever necessary by data from the *World Tourism Organisation* and the *Organisation for Economic Co-operation and Development*.

Demographic Data
Population figures, drawn principally from UN data, refer to estimates at mid-year. Birth rates refer to live births per '000 inhabitants in the given year. Figures for number of households, and average household size, are generally based on the latest official census material.

Foreign Trade
Import and export data refer to trade in goods and services, and are mainly sourced from *IMF Direction of Trade Statistics*. Figures refer to imports cif (cost, insurance and freight) and exports fob (free on board). Percentages of imports and exports for major export destinations and import sources are provided for the leading four major trading partners in each case.

Per capita and dollar conversions
Data for each year have been converted to US dollars, for the sake of ranking and comparability, using the exchange rate quoted on each page. The relevant rate for back years is used for previous years' data. Similarly, per capita calculations are based on population figures for preceding years each time, to arrive at an accurate three-year trend.

Disclaimer
Every effort has been made to ensure accuracy, and great care has been taken during the compilation of ***The World Economic Factbook 2002/2003***, but it is possible that omissions and errors may have occurred, for which Euromonitor cannot accept responsibility.

1

Maps

■ Europe

1 SLOVENIA
2 CROATIA
3 BOSNIA-HERZEGOVINA
4 SERBIA
4a Vojvodina
4b Kosovo
5 MONTENEGRO
6 MACEDONIA

■ Middle East and Asia

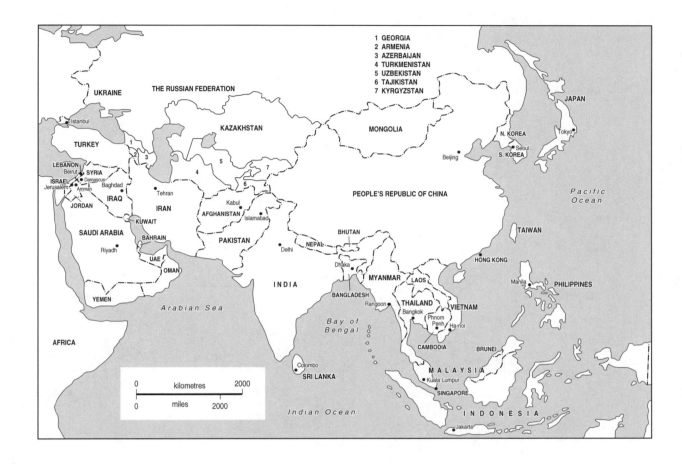

Africa

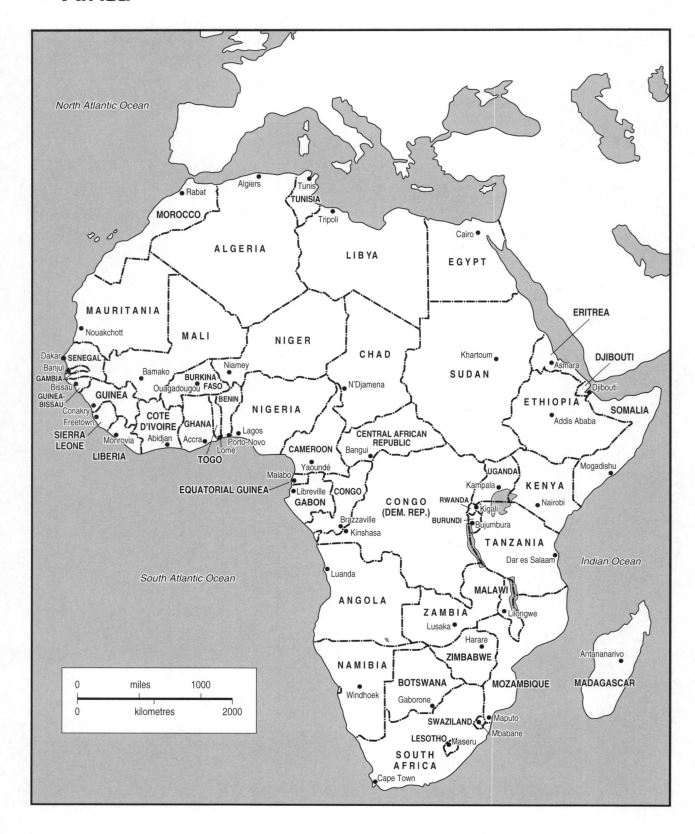

■ Oceania

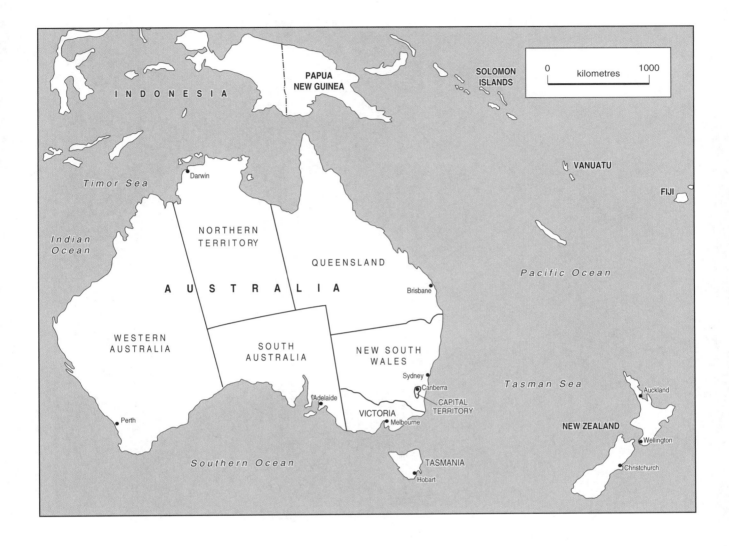

North and Central America

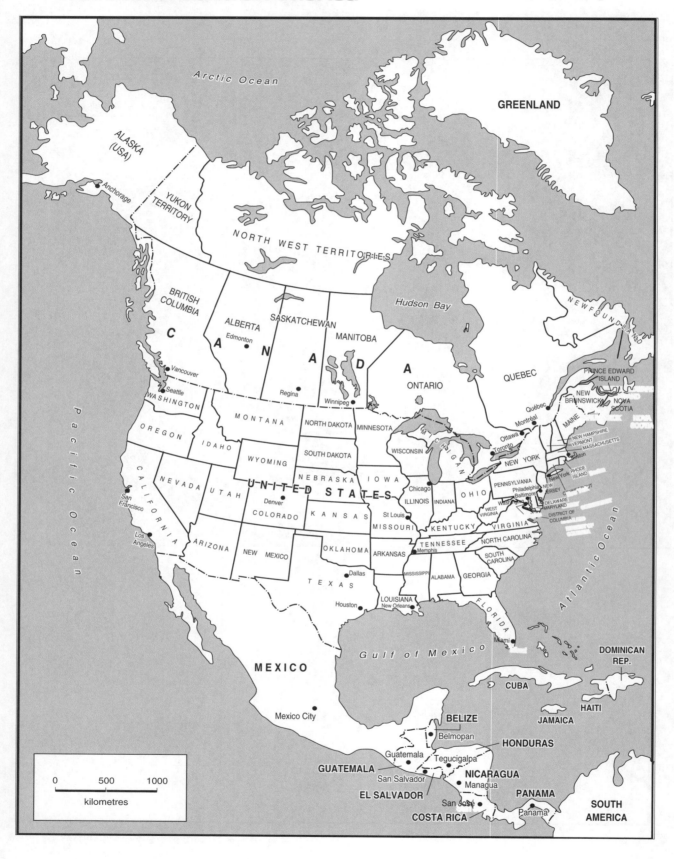

■ South America

Comparative World Rankings

Ranking by Area (km^2)

1	Russia	17,075,400		54	Morocco	458,730
2	Canada	9,922,385		55	Sweden	449,790
3	China	9,597,000		56	Uzbekistan	447,400
4	USA	9,363,130		57	Iraq	438,445
5	Brazil	8,511,965		58	Paraguay	406,750
6	Australia	7,682,300		59	Zimbabwe	390,310
7	India	3,166,830		60	Japan	369,700
8	Argentina	2,777,815		61	Germany	356,840
9	Kazakhstan	2,717,300		62	Congo-Brazzaville	342,000
10	Sudan	2,505,815		63	Finland	337,030
11	Saudi Arabia	2,400,900		64	Malaysia	332,965
12	Algeria	2,381,745		65	Vietnam	329,565
13	Congo, Democratic Republic	2,345,410		66	Norway	323,895
14	Mexico	1,972,545		67	Côte d'Ivoire	322,465
15	Indonesia	1,919,445		68	Poland	312,685
16	Libya	1,759,540		69	Italy	301,245
17	Iran	1,648,000		70	Philippines	300,000
18	Mongolia	1,565,000		71	Burkina Faso	274,122
19	Peru	1,285,215		72	Oman	271,950
20	Chad	1,284,000		73	Gabon	267,665
21	Angola	1,246,700		74	New Zealand	265,150
22	Mali	1,240,140		75	Ecuador	263,950
23	Niger	1,186,410		76	Guinea	245,855
24	South Africa	1,184,825		77	United Kingdom	244,755
25	Colombia	1,138,915		78	Ghana	238,305
26	Bolivia	1,098,575		79	Romania	237,500
27	Mauritania	1,030,700		80	Laos	236,725
28	Ethiopia	1,023,050		81	Uganda	236,580
29	Egypt	997,739		82	Guyana	214,970
30	Tanzania	939,760		83	Belarus	207,595
31	Nigeria	923,850		84	Kyrgyzstan	198,500
32	Venezuela	912,045		85	Senegal	196,720
33	Namibia	824,295		86	Uruguay	186,925
34	Pakistan	803,940		87	Syria	185,680
35	Mozambique	784,755		88	Cambodia	181,000
36	Turkey	779,450		89	Tunisia	164,150
37	Zambia	752,615		90	Suriname	163,820
38	Chile	751,625		91	Nicaragua	148,000
39	Myanmar	678,030		92	Bangladesh	144,000
40	Afghanistan	636,265		93	Tajikistan	143,100
41	Somalia	630,000		94	Nepal	141,415
42	Central African Republic	624,975		95	Greece	131,985
43	Ukraine	603,700		96	North Korea	122,310
44	Madagascar	594,180		97	Cuba	114,525
45	Kenya	582,645		98	Benin	112,620
46	Botswana	575,000		99	Honduras	112,085
47	France	543,965		100	Liberia	111,370
48	Yemen	527,968		101	Bulgaria	110,910
49	Thailand	514,000		102	Guatemala	108,890
50	Spain	504,880		103	Iceland	102,820
51	Turkmenistan	488,100		104	South Korea	98,445
52	Cameroon	465,500		105	Malawi	94,080
53	Papua New Guinea	462,840		106	Eritrea	93,679

107	Hungary	93,030
108	Portugal	91,630
109	French Guiana	91,000
110	Jordan	90,650
111	Serbia and Montenegro	88,361
112	Azerbaijan	86,600
113	Austria	83,855
114	Czech Republic	78,864
115	Panama	78,515
116	United Arab Emirates	75,150
117	Sierra Leone	72,325
118	Georgia	70,000
119	Ireland	68,895
120	Sri Lanka	65,610
121	Lithuania	65,300
122	Latvia	64,589
123	Togo	56,785
124	Croatia	56,538
125	Bosnia-Herzegovina	51,129
126	Costa Rica	50,900
127	Slovakia	49,035
128	Dominican Republic	48,440
129	Bhutan	46,620
130	Estonia	45,226
131	Denmark	43,075
132	Switzerland	41,285
133	Netherlands	41,160
134	Guinea-Bissau	36,125
135	Taiwan	35,990
136	Moldova	33,700
137	Belgium	30,520
138	Lesotho	30,345
139	Armenia	29,800
140	Solomon Islands	29,790
141	Albania	28,750
142	Equatorial Guinea	28,050
143	Burundi	27,835
144	Haiti	27,750
145	Rwanda	26,330
146	Macedonia	25,713
147	Kuwait	24,280
148	Djibouti	23,000
149	Belize	22,965
150	El Salvador	21,395
151	Israel	20,770
152	Slovenia	20,254
153	New Caledonia	19,105
154	Fiji	18,330
155	Swaziland	17,365
156	Vanuatu	14,765
157	Bahamas	13,865
158	Qatar	11,435
159	Jamaica	11,425
160	Gambia	10,690
161	Lebanon	10,400

162	Cyprus	9,250
163	Puerto Rico	8,960
164	Brunei	5,765
165	Trinidad and Tobago	5,130
166	Cape Verde	4,035
167	French Polynesia	3,940
168	Western Samoa	2,840
169	Luxembourg	2,585
170	Réunion	2,510
171	Mauritius	1,865
172	Comoros	1,860
173	Guadeloupe	1,780
174	Martinique	1,079
175	Hong Kong, China	1,062
176	Netherlands Antilles	993
177	Sao Tomé e Príncipe	964
178	Dominica	751
179	Tonga	699
180	Kiribati	684
181	Bahrain	661
182	St Lucia	616
183	Singapore	616
184	Seychelles	455
185	Guam	450
186	Antigua	442
187	Barbados	430
188	St Vincent & the Grenadines	389
189	Grenada	345
190	Malta	316
191	Maldives	298
192	St Kitts	261
193	Cayman Islands	259
194	American Samoa	197
195	Aruba	193
196	Liechtenstein	160
197	British Virgin Islands	153
198	Anguilla	91
199	Bermuda	54
200	Tuvalu	25
201	Nauru	21
202	Macau	16
203	Gibraltar	5
204	Monaco	2

Ranking by Mid-Year Population 2001 ('000)

1	China	1,287,867.7		54	Syria	16,845.0
2	India	1,026,877.6		55	Madagascar	16,820.0
3	USA	275,306.4		56	Kazakhstan	16,131.5
4	Indonesia	214,236.8		57	Netherlands	16,030.1
5	Brazil	166,112.5		58	Cameroon	15,935.4
6	Pakistan	160,250.9		59	Côte d'Ivoire	15,338.0
7	Russia	144,336.1		60	Chile	15,211.3
8	Bangladesh	129,087.3		61	Angola	13,575.0
9	Japan	127,013.6		62	Ecuador	12,995.7
10	Nigeria	122,696.6		63	Burkina Faso	12,639.0
11	Mexico	101,109.8		64	Mali	11,725.0
12	Germany	81,884.0		65	Malawi	11,580.0
13	Vietnam	81,750.0		66	Niger	11,405.0
14	Philippines	78,330.3		67	Guatemala	11,385.3
15	Iran	67,896.0		68	Cuba	11,200.5
16	Turkey	65,287.7		69	Cambodia	11,180.0
17	Ethiopia	65,063.0		70	Somalia	10,893.0
18	Egypt	63,294.1		71	Serbia and Montenegro	10,689.5
19	Thailand	61,991.9		72	Greece	10,546.3
20	United Kingdom	59,545.9		73	Belgium	10,266.1
21	France	59,267.7		74	Czech Republic	10,265.5
22	Italy	57,647.8		75	Belarus	10,087.4
23	Congo, Democratic Republic	54,106.0		76	Hungary	10,045.5
24	Ukraine	48,680.9		77	Portugal	10,032.8
25	South Korea	47,873.7		78	Senegal	9,940.0
26	Myanmar	45,620.5		79	Zambia	9,705.0
27	South Africa	43,949.1		80	Tunisia	9,549.9
28	Colombia	39,805.6		81	Sweden	8,872.3
29	Spain	39,504.9		82	Rwanda	8,670.0
30	Poland	38,695.7		83	Dominican Republic	8,495.4
31	Argentina	37,031.8		84	Bolivia	8,328.7
32	Tanzania	34,785.0		85	Bulgaria	8,109.1
33	Sudan	30,975.0		86	Azerbaijan	8,108.0
34	Canada	30,733.8		87	Austria	8,092.5
35	Algeria	30,385.1		88	Chad	7,959.0
36	Morocco	28,702.9		89	Haiti	7,959.0
37	Peru	26,305.5		90	Guinea	7,581.0
38	Venezuela	24,862.6		91	Switzerland	7,188.8
39	Iraq	24,339.0		92	Hong Kong, China	7,018.3
40	Uzbekistan	24,306.2		93	Burundi	6,917.5
41	North Korea	24,064.6		94	Honduras	6,485.5
42	Nepal	23,918.5		95	Benin	6,410.0
43	Uganda	23,085.0		96	El Salvador	6,319.4
44	Malaysia	22,880.8		97	Israel	6,235.1
45	Taiwan	22,469.5		98	Tajikistan	6,195.2
46	Afghanistan	22,420.6		99	Libya	5,835.0
47	Saudi Arabia	22,353.6		100	Paraguay	5,496.5
48	Romania	22,300.3		101	Georgia	5,454.4
49	Ghana	21,104.0		102	Laos	5,428.8
50	Mozambique	20,615.0		103	Slovakia	5,408.9
51	Yemen	19,401.0		104	Denmark	5,359.8
52	Australia	19,182.8		105	Jordan	5,284.3
53	Sri Lanka	18,821.6		106	Finland	5,189.5

107	Sierra Leone	5,010.0
108	Togo	4,853.0
109	Papua New Guinea	4,803.9
110	Nicaragua	4,694.4
111	Kyrgyzstan	4,693.8
112	Turkmenistan	4,563.1
113	Croatia	4,532.3
114	Norway	4,514.1
115	Moldova	4,380.0
116	Eritrea	4,092.0
117	Bosnia-Herzegovina	4,052.0
118	Puerto Rico	3,942.0
119	New Zealand	3,884.4
120	Ireland	3,839.2
121	Armenia	3,812.3
122	Costa Rica	3,797.7
123	Central African Republic	3,726.0
124	Lithuania	3,699.3
125	Liberia	3,592.0
126	Albania	3,469.8
127	Lebanon	3,395.0
128	Singapore	3,274.5
129	Uruguay	3,274.5
130	Kenya	3,185.0
131	United Arab Emirates	3,087.7
132	Congo-Brazzaville	2,973.0
133	Panama	2,855.7
134	Mauritania	2,815.0
135	Oman	2,695.0
136	Mongolia	2,662.6
137	Jamaica	2,641.0
138	Latvia	2,391.6
139	Kuwait	2,292.0
140	Lesotho	2,248.0
141	Bhutan	2,122.8
142	Macedonia	2,033.4
143	Slovenia	1,961.5
144	Namibia	1,783.0
145	Botswana	1,669.0
146	Estonia	1,424.8
147	Gambia	1,374.0
148	Trinidad and Tobago	1,310.0
149	Gabon	1,289.0
150	Guinea-Bissau	1,263.0
151	Zimbabwe	1,257.0
152	Mauritius	1,182.0
153	Swaziland	1,063.0
154	Guyana	873.0
155	Fiji	816.1
156	Cyprus	762.3
157	Comoros	735.0
158	Réunion	715.0
159	Djibouti	657.0
160	Bahrain	632.7
161	Qatar	620.0

162	Macau	475.7
163	Guadeloupe	475.0
164	Equatorial Guinea	474.0
165	Cape Verde	447.0
166	Solomon Islands	443.3
167	Luxembourg	442.3
168	Suriname	422.0
169	Martinique	404.0
170	Malta	384.2
171	Brunei	328.3
172	Bahamas	317.0
173	Maldives	285.9
174	Iceland	284.5
175	Barbados	272.0
176	Belize	249.5
177	French Polynesia	235.1
178	Netherlands Antilles	222.0
179	New Caledonia	214.3
180	French Guiana	195.0
181	Vanuatu	190.3
182	Western Samoa	179.7
183	Guam	167.7
184	St Lucia	158.0
185	Sao Tomé e Príncipe	153.0
186	St Vincent and the Grenadines	117.0
187	Aruba	111.0
188	Tonga	100.0
189	Grenada	94.0
190	Kiribati	85.0
191	Seychelles	77.0
192	American Samoa	72.0
193	Dominica	71.0
194	Antigua	70.0
195	Bermuda	66.0
196	Cayman Islands	40.0
197	St Kitts	38.0
198	Monaco	34.0
199	Liechtenstein	33.8
200	Gibraltar	25.0
201	British Virgin Islands	22.0
202	Nauru	13.0
203	Tuvalu	12.0
204	Anguilla	8.0

Ranking by Population Density, Latest Year (persons/km^2)

1	Macau	29,895.5	54	Nepal	168.5
2	Monaco	17,000.0	55	Sao Tomé e Príncipe	158.0
3	Hong Kong, China	7,139.6	56	Antigua	157.3
4	Singapore	5,395.2	57	Cayman Islands	151.9
5	Gibraltar	2,500.0	58	British Virgin Islands	142.8
6	Bermuda	1,322.2	59	Tonga	137.5
7	Malta	1,197.0	60	China	137.4
8	Bangladesh	996.5	61	Gambia	137.1
9	Maldives	967.7	62	Armenia	135.1
10	Bahrain	917.1	63	Czech Republic	132.9
11	Nauru	660.8	64	Nigeria	126.3
12	Barbados	632.8	65	Denmark	126.1
13	Mauritius	628.6	66	Albania	125.8
14	Taiwan	588.4	67	Kuwait	125.7
15	Aruba	580.1	68	Poland	123.7
16	South Korea	481.9	69	Malawi	123.0
17	Netherlands	471.5	70	Thailand	120.8
18	Puerto Rico	444.0	71	Indonesia	117.2
19	Tuvalu	406.7	72	Uganda	117.0
20	Martinique	372.7	73	Kiribati	116.0
21	American Samoa	360.1	74	Slovakia	112.4
22	Rwanda	351.3	75	Cape Verde	110.7
23	Japan	348.4	76	Portugal	109.5
24	India	342.2	77	Hungary	108.9
25	Lebanon	331.4	78	France	107.6
26	Comoros	329.6	79	Guatemala	106.4
27	Belgium	312.5	80	St Kitts	105.6
28	El Salvador	308.1	81	Serbia and Montenegro	104.6
29	Guam	307.0	82	Cuba	102.2
30	Israel	304.6	83	Austria	97.8
31	St Vincent and the Grenadines	298.1	84	Slovenia	97.7
32	Sri Lanka	292.0	85	Romania	97.0
33	Haiti	291.8	86	Dominica	94.7
34	Réunion	285.5	87	Azerbaijan	93.1
35	Guadeloupe	279.8	88	Ghana	92.7
36	Grenada	277.4	89	Syria	91.6
37	Netherlands Antilles	276.7	90	Togo	89.1
38	Burundi	269.3	91	Anguilla	87.9
39	Philippines	259.3	92	Turkey	85.2
40	St Lucia	257.8	93	Ukraine	84.6
41	Trinidad and Tobago	254.7	94	Cyprus	82.2
42	Vietnam	249.0	95	Greece	81.8
43	United Kingdom	247.0	96	Croatia	80.9
44	Jamaica	243.4	97	Bosnia-Herzegovina	80.7
45	Germany	229.6	98	Spain	79.1
46	Liechtenstein	208.8	99	Georgia	78.2
47	Pakistan	204.6	100	Costa Rica	75.1
48	North Korea	200.9	101	Lesotho	73.8
49	Italy	195.7	102	Bulgaria	73.6
50	Switzerland	181.4	103	Sierra Leone	71.2
51	Dominican Republic	176.9	104	Myanmar	69.6
52	Seychelles	171.7	105	Malaysia	67.9
53	Luxembourg	170.1	106	Morocco	64.6

107	French Polynesia	64.6		162	Uruguay	18.8
108	Egypt	63.9		163	Somalia	17.4
109	Cambodia	63.8		164	Finland	17.0
110	Western Samoa	63.8		165	Equatorial Guinea	16.9
111	Brunei	62.7		166	Solomon Islands	16.0
112	Tunisia	61.7		167	Norway	14.7
113	Swaziland	61.6		168	New Zealand	14.4
114	Ethiopia	59.1		169	Paraguay	14.0
115	Uzbekistan	58.9		170	Argentina	13.6
116	Honduras	58.7		171	Sudan	13.0
117	Jordan	58.0		172	Zambia	13.0
118	Benin	57.9		173	Vanuatu	13.0
119	Lithuania	56.6		174	Algeria	12.7
120	Qatar	56.3		175	Oman	12.6
121	Iraq	55.6		176	New Caledonia	11.8
122	Ireland	55.4		177	Belize	10.9
123	Senegal	51.6		178	Angola	10.9
124	Mexico	50.9		179	Papua New Guinea	10.7
125	Belarus	48.8		180	Saudi Arabia	10.2
126	Côte d'Ivoire	48.2		181	Turkmenistan	9.6
127	Ecuador	46.5		182	Mali	9.4
128	Burkina Faso	46.2		183	Niger	8.9
129	Bhutan	45.6		184	Congo-Brazzaville	8.7
130	Guinea-Bissau	44.8		185	Russia	8.6
131	Fiji	44.8		186	Bolivia	7.8
132	Tajikistan	44.2		187	Chad	6.3
133	Iran	42.1		188	Kazakhstan	6.0
134	Eritrea	40.5		189	Central African Republic	6.0
135	Tanzania	39.3		190	Kenya	5.6
136	Nicaragua	39.2		191	Gabon	5.0
137	Latvia	38.7		192	Guyana	4.4
138	Panama	38.7		193	Canada	3.3
139	Colombia	38.0		194	Libya	3.3
140	United Arab Emirates	37.5		195	Botswana	2.9
141	Yemen	36.7		196	Iceland	2.8
142	South Africa	35.6		197	Mauritania	2.7
143	Afghanistan	34.7		198	Suriname	2.7
144	Cameroon	34.2		199	Australia	2.5
145	Estonia	33.8		200	French Guiana	2.2
146	Liberia	32.2		201	Namibia	2.2
147	Bahamas	31.7		202	Mongolia	1.7
148	Zimbabwe	31.0				
149	Guinea	30.8				
150	USA	30.2				
151	Djibouti	28.3				
152	Madagascar	28.3				
153	Venezuela	27.9				
154	Mozambique	26.3				
155	Kyrgyzstan	24.5				
156	Congo, Democratic Republic	23.9				
157	Laos	23.7				
158	Sweden	21.5				
159	Chile	20.4				
160	Peru	20.4				
161	Brazil	20.0				

Ranking by Child Population, Latest Year (% aged 0-14)

1	Uganda	49.7	54	Belize	40.7
2	Niger	48.3	55	Cambodia	40.7
3	Liberia	48.2	56	Gambia	40.7
4	Mali	48.0	57	Sudan	40.6
5	Yemen	47.9	58	Nicaragua	40.6
6	Congo, Democratic Republic	47.8	59	Cape Verde	40.3
7	Somalia	47.8	60	Saudi Arabia	40.2
8	Zambia	47.7	61	Lesotho	40.1
9	Angola	47.6	62	Tajikistan	40.1
10	Burkina Faso	47.4	63	Haiti	39.8
11	Malawi	47.2	64	Bolivia	39.5
12	Benin	46.8	65	Libya	39.4
13	Burundi	46.3	66	Gabon	39.4
14	Rwanda	46.2	67	Paraguay	39.3
15	Congo-Brazzaville	46.1	68	Jordan	38.6
16	Ethiopia	46.0	69	Papua New Guinea	38.6
17	Togo	45.9	70	Western Samoa	38.1
18	Chad	45.8	71	Egypt	37.2
19	Tanzania	45.8	72	Uzbekistan	37.2
20	Senegal	45.0	73	Turkmenistan	37.2
21	Oman	44.9	74	Philippines	35.8
22	Mozambique	44.8	75	Iran	35.8
23	Guinea	44.7	76	El Salvador	35.4
24	Kenya	44.4	77	Bangladesh	34.9
25	Eritrea	44.3	78	Kyrgyzstan	34.8
26	Madagascar	44.2	79	Tonga	34.5
27	Côte d'Ivoire	44.2	80	American Samoa	34.5
28	Sierra Leone	44.1	81	Kiribati	34.5
29	Afghanistan	44.0	82	Tuvalu	34.5
30	Ghana	44.0	83	Seychelles	34.5
31	Mauritania	43.9	84	Sao Tomé e Príncipe	34.5
32	Laos	43.8	85	Algeria	34.3
33	Cameroon	43.8	86	Mongolia	34.2
34	Swaziland	43.5	87	South Africa	34.1
35	Guatemala	43.5	88	St Vincent and the Grenadines	34.0
36	Comoros	43.4	89	Malaysia	33.8
37	Nigeria	43.2	90	Venezuela	33.6
38	Equatorial Guinea	43.2	91	India	33.6
39	Botswana	42.9	92	Ecuador	33.3
40	Central African Republic	42.8	93	Lebanon	33.3
41	Solomon Islands	42.7	94	French Polynesia	32.9
42	Maldives	42.7	95	Guam	32.9
43	Syria	42.7	96	Peru	32.9
44	Guinea-Bissau	42.6	97	Costa Rica	32.9
45	Bhutan	42.5	98	Dominican Republic	32.8
46	Zimbabwe	42.3	99	Mexico	32.7
47	Iraq	42.0	100	Vietnam	32.7
48	Namibia	41.9	101	Azerbaijan	32.6
49	Pakistan	41.5	102	Suriname	32.3
50	Honduras	41.4	103	Colombia	32.1
51	Djibouti	41.3	104	Brunei	32.1
52	Vanuatu	41.2	105	Morocco	32.1
53	Nepal	40.8	106	Jamaica	32.0

107	Albania	31.9		162	USA	21.2
108	Fiji	31.1		163	Cuba	21.0
109	Panama	31.1		164	Taiwan	20.7
110	Guyana	31.0		165	Bosnia-Herzegovina	20.4
111	St Lucia	30.8		166	Australia	20.4
112	Bahrain	30.4		167	Norway	20.0
113	Indonesia	30.4		168	Serbia and Montenegro	19.9
114	Guadeloupe	30.2		169	Croatia	19.9
115	Grenada	30.2		170	Poland	19.6
116	French Guiana	30.2		171	Lithuania	19.4
117	Cayman Islands	30.2		172	Slovakia	19.3
118	Anguilla	30.2		173	United Kingdom	19.0
119	Antigua	30.2		174	Luxembourg	19.0
120	Dominica	30.2		175	Canada	19.0
121	Aruba	30.2		176	Liechtenstein	18.8
122	Bermuda	30.2		177	Belarus	18.6
123	British Virgin Islands	30.2		178	Netherlands	18.6
124	Turkey	29.9		179	Denmark	18.6
125	New Caledonia	29.8		180	Sweden	18.3
126	Tunisia	29.6		181	Romania	18.1
127	St Kitts	28.9		182	Finland	18.1
128	Israel	28.6		183	Monaco	18.0
129	Réunion	28.3		184	France	18.0
130	Bahamas	28.3		185	Gibraltar	18.0
131	Chile	28.3		186	Russia	17.9
132	Brazil	28.0		187	Ukraine	17.6
133	Myanmar	27.7		188	Belgium	17.6
134	North Korea	27.6		189	Estonia	17.4
135	Argentina	27.6		190	Switzerland	17.3
136	Trinidad and Tobago	27.5		191	Latvia	17.0
137	Kazakhstan	27.2		192	Hungary	16.9
138	Qatar	26.6		193	Austria	16.7
139	Mauritius	26.3		194	Portugal	16.4
140	United Arab Emirates	26.1		195	Czech Republic	16.2
141	Sri Lanka	26.0		196	Hong Kong, China	16.2
142	Netherlands Antilles	25.4		197	Slovenia	15.8
143	Moldova	25.2		198	Germany	15.6
144	Thailand	24.8		199	Bulgaria	15.4
145	Puerto Rico	24.8		200	Greece	14.9
146	China	24.4		201	Spain	14.9
147	Kuwait	24.2		202	Japan	14.6
148	Armenia	23.9		203	Italy	14.3
149	Uruguay	23.8				
150	Cyprus	23.1				
151	Martinique	23.0				
152	Iceland	22.9				
153	New Zealand	22.7				
154	Macau	22.6				
155	Macedonia	22.2				
156	Georgia	22.1				
157	Barbados	22.0				
158	Singapore	22.0				
159	Ireland	21.6				
160	South Korea	21.5				
161	Malta	21.5				

Ranking by Elderly Population, Latest Year (% aged 65+)

1	Italy	18.0		54	Martinique	10.8
2	Greece	17.7		55	Puerto Rico	10.2
3	Japan	17.3		56	Macedonia	10.1
4	Sweden	17.3		57	Liechtenstein	10.0
5	France	17.2		58	Israel	9.9
6	Spain	17.0		59	Argentina	9.7
7	Belgium	16.9		60	Cuba	9.7
8	Germany	16.6		61	Armenia	9.3
9	Bulgaria	16.4		62	Taiwan	8.7
10	Portugal	15.6		63	Bosnia-Herzegovina	8.3
11	Switzerland	15.4		64	Moldova	7.9
12	Austria	15.4		65	Netherlands Antilles	7.5
13	United Kingdom	15.4		66	Singapore	7.4
14	Hungary	15.2		67	South Korea	7.3
15	Norway	15.1		68	Kazakhstan	7.3
16	Finland	15.0		69	Chile	7.2
17	Latvia	14.9		70	Jamaica	7.1
18	Denmark	14.8		71	China	7.0
19	Estonia	14.7		72	Macau	6.9
20	Slovenia	14.3		73	Aruba	6.7
21	Luxembourg	14.2		74	Guadeloupe	6.7
22	Ukraine	14.2		75	French Guiana	6.7
23	Gibraltar	14.1		76	Cayman Islands	6.7
24	Monaco	14.1		77	Anguilla	6.7
25	Serbia and Montenegro	13.9		78	Antigua	6.7
26	Czech Republic	13.8		79	Bermuda	6.7
27	Georgia	13.8		80	British Virgin Islands	6.7
28	Lithuania	13.7		81	Dominica	6.7
29	Netherlands	13.6		82	Grenada	6.7
30	Belarus	13.4		83	Sri Lanka	6.7
31	Romania	13.2		84	Trinidad and Tobago	6.5
32	American Samoa	13.0		85	Benin	6.5
33	Sao Tomé e Príncipe	13.0		86	Réunion	6.4
34	Tonga	13.0		87	Tunisia	6.4
35	Tuvalu	13.0		88	Albania	6.2
36	Seychelles	13.0		89	Mauritius	6.1
37	Kiribati	13.0		90	Kyrgyzstan	6.0
38	Russia	12.8		91	Thailand	6.0
39	Uruguay	12.7		92	Gabon	5.9
40	Bahamas	12.6		93	Azerbaijan	5.7
41	USA	12.6		94	Lebanon	5.7
42	Canada	12.5		95	Panama	5.6
43	Poland	12.4		96	Turkey	5.5
44	Malta	12.4		97	Guam	5.5
45	Australia	12.3		98	North Korea	5.4
46	Croatia	12.3		99	Vietnam	5.3
47	New Zealand	11.8		100	New Caledonia	5.3
48	Iceland	11.8		101	Brazil	5.3
49	Slovakia	11.5		102	Suriname	5.3
50	Cyprus	11.3		103	Costa Rica	5.2
51	Ireland	11.2		104	St Lucia	5.1
52	Hong Kong, China	10.9		105	Morocco	5.1
53	Barbados	10.9		106	South Africa	5.0

107	Peru	4.9	162	Cambodia	3.1
108	Algeria	4.9	163	Sudan	3.1
109	Myanmar	4.9	164	Ghana	3.1
110	Mexico	4.8	165	Iraq	3.1
111	Ecuador	4.8	166	Nigeria	3.1
112	El Salvador	4.8	167	Solomon Islands	3.0
113	Colombia	4.7	168	Papua New Guinea	3.0
114	India	4.7	169	Syria	3.0
115	Fiji	4.7	170	Libya	3.0
116	Indonesia	4.6	171	Gambia	3.0
117	Cape Verde	4.6	172	Kenya	3.0
118	Uzbekistan	4.6	173	Sierra Leone	2.9
119	Western Samoa	4.5	174	Madagascar	2.9
120	Dominican Republic	4.5	175	Liberia	2.9
121	Tajikistan	4.5	176	Afghanistan	2.9
122	Venezuela	4.5	177	Angola	2.9
123	Iran	4.4	178	Ethiopia	2.9
124	Turkmenistan	4.3	179	Côte d'Ivoire	2.9
125	Belize	4.3	180	Eritrea	2.8
126	St Vincent and the Grenadines	4.3	181	Bahrain	2.8
127	French Polynesia	4.3	182	Congo, Democratic Republic	2.8
128	Malaysia	4.2	183	Zimbabwe	2.8
129	Lesotho	4.1	184	Burundi	2.7
130	Guinea-Bissau	4.1	185	Guinea	2.7
131	Guyana	4.1	186	Swaziland	2.7
132	St Kitts	4.1	187	Malawi	2.7
133	Bhutan	4.1	188	Comoros	2.6
134	Bolivia	4.0	189	Burkina Faso	2.6
135	Philippines	4.0	190	Tanzania	2.6
136	Mongolia	4.0	191	Senegal	2.5
137	Equatorial Guinea	4.0	192	Jordan	2.5
138	Central African Republic	3.9	193	Oman	2.5
139	Haiti	3.8	194	Niger	2.5
140	Namibia	3.8	195	Somalia	2.4
141	Mali	3.7	196	Botswana	2.4
142	Cameroon	3.6	197	Yemen	2.4
143	Nepal	3.6	198	Rwanda	2.4
144	Guatemala	3.6	199	Zambia	2.2
145	Maldives	3.5	200	Uganda	2.2
146	Paraguay	3.5	201	Qatar	1.8
147	Honduras	3.5	202	Kuwait	1.5
148	Chad	3.4	203	United Arab Emirates	1.1
149	Egypt	3.4			
150	Vanuatu	3.3			
151	Laos	3.3			
152	Brunei	3.3			
153	Mozambique	3.3			
154	Congo-Brazzaville	3.2			
155	Djibouti	3.2			
156	Bangladesh	3.2			
157	Pakistan	3.2			
158	Mauritania	3.2			
159	Nicaragua	3.2			
160	Saudi Arabia	3.2			
161	Togo	3.1			

Ranking by Birth Rate 2001 (per '000)

1	Niger	55.2		54	Jordan	33.2
2	Liberia	54.2		55	Lesotho	33.1
3	Somalia	51.9		56	Nicaragua	32.9
4	Angola	51.2		57	Ghana	32.9
5	Uganda	50.6		58	Papua New Guinea	32.8
6	Mali	49.7		59	Vanuatu	32.3
7	Yemen	49.4		60	Botswana	31.3
8	Sierra Leone	49.2		61	Bolivia	31.1
9	Chad	48.5		62	Honduras	30.9
10	Afghanistan	47.4		63	Haiti	30.9
11	Congo, Democratic Republic	47.3		64	Bangladesh	30.5
12	Burkina Faso	46.8		65	Paraguay	30.0
13	Malawi	45.5		66	Syria	29.8
14	Guinea-Bissau	44.6		67	Cape Verde	29.7
15	Congo-Brazzaville	44.3		68	French Guiana	28.9
16	Ethiopia	44.0		69	Western Samoa	28.3
17	Guinea	44.0		70	Grenada	27.4
18	Mauritania	43.7		71	Guam	27.2
19	Burundi	43.4		72	American Samoa	27.0
20	Equatorial Guinea	43.2		73	Philippines	27.0
21	Mozambique	42.4		74	Kiribati	26.9
22	Rwanda	42.2		75	Libya	26.7
23	Madagascar	42.1		76	Turkmenistan	26.6
24	Zambia	42.1		77	Belize	26.0
25	Benin	41.5		78	El Salvador	25.9
26	Sao Tomé e Príncipe	41.5		79	Tajikistan	25.3
27	Nigeria	40.0		80	Morocco	25.3
28	Togo	39.1		81	South Africa	25.1
29	Eritrea	39.1		82	Fiji	25.0
30	Djibouti	38.6		83	India	24.8
31	Tanzania	38.5		84	Tonga	24.6
32	Solomon Islands	38.5		85	Myanmar	24.5
33	Senegal	38.1		86	Algeria	24.0
34	Central African Republic	38.0		87	Egypt	24.0
35	Comoros	38.0		88	Ecuador	23.8
36	Gambia	38.0		89	Dominican Republic	23.6
37	Gabon	37.6		90	Malaysia	23.5
38	Pakistan	36.9		91	Venezuela	23.3
39	Laos	36.7		92	Peru	23.2
40	Cameroon	36.6		93	St Lucia	23.0
41	Cambodia	36.2		94	Colombia	22.8
42	Oman	35.8		95	Mexico	22.8
43	Zimbabwe	35.7		96	Mongolia	22.7
44	Côte d'Ivoire	35.5		97	Guyana	22.3
45	Bhutan	35.4		98	Costa Rica	22.2
46	Namibia	35.2		99	Uzbekistan	22.1
47	Nepal	34.9		100	Tuvalu	22.0
48	Guatemala	34.8		101	St Kitts	22.0
49	Iraq	34.5		102	Iran	21.8
50	Kenya	34.4		103	Indonesia	21.0
51	Sudan	34.2		104	Kyrgyzstan	21.0
52	Saudi Arabia	34.1		105	Turkey	20.9
53	Swaziland	33.9		106	French Polynesia	20.8

107	Panama	20.8
108	Jamaica	20.5
109	Vietnam	20.4
110	Brunei	20.3
111	New Caledonia	20.3
112	Israel	20.2
113	Bahamas	20.0
114	Brazil	19.5
115	Lebanon	19.3
116	Argentina	19.2
117	Seychelles	19.0
118	Suriname	18.8
119	Albania	18.7
120	Tunisia	18.6
121	Chile	18.6
122	St Vincent and the Grenadines	18.5
123	Thailand	18.5
124	Nauru	18.4
125	Kuwait	18.4
126	Réunion	18.2
127	Qatar	18.0
128	North Korea	17.5
129	Sri Lanka	17.3
130	Uruguay	17.1
131	Dominica	16.8
132	Kazakhstan	16.5
133	Bahrain	16.5
134	Guadeloupe	16.3
135	Antigua	16.2
136	Mauritius	16.0
137	Anguilla	15.9
138	United Arab Emirates	15.8
139	British Virgin Islands	15.7
140	Netherlands Antilles	15.5
141	Puerto Rico	15.3
142	China	15.1
143	Ireland	15.0
144	Taiwan	14.9
145	Iceland	14.1
146	Azerbaijan	14.1
147	New Zealand	14.0
148	Martinique	13.7
149	Trinidad and Tobago	13.6
150	Cyprus	13.4
151	USA	13.4
152	Cayman Islands	13.2
153	South Korea	13.2
154	Australia	12.9
155	Aruba	12.8
156	Gibraltar	12.8
157	Barbados	12.4
158	Luxembourg	12.3
159	France	12.3
160	Liechtenstein	12.2
161	Macedonia	12.2
162	Singapore	12.2
163	Cuba	12.0
164	Malta	12.0
165	Norway	11.8
166	Moldova	11.7
167	Croatia	11.5
168	Serbia and Montenegro	11.4
169	Denmark	11.3
170	Bermuda	11.2
171	Canada	11.1
172	Portugal	11.1
173	United Kingdom	10.9
174	Netherlands	10.9
175	Georgia	10.6
176	Romania	10.4
177	Slovakia	10.3
178	Armenia	10.1
179	Monaco	10.1
180	Finland	10.1
181	Belgium	10.0
182	Bosnia-Herzegovina	9.9
183	Hong Kong, China	9.8
184	Poland	9.7
185	Macau	9.6
186	Japan	9.4
187	Lithuania	9.1
188	Belarus	9.1
189	Greece	9.0
190	Hungary	9.0
191	Switzerland	9.0
192	Spain	9.0
193	Czech Republic	8.8
194	Austria	8.7
195	Italy	8.7
196	Estonia	8.7
197	Russia	8.6
198	Sweden	8.6
199	Germany	8.5
200	Slovenia	8.4
201	Ukraine	8.3
202	Bulgaria	7.9
203	Latvia	7.8

Ranking by Average Household Size 2001 (persons)

1	Kuwait	8.40	54	Fiji		5.28
2	Tuvalu	7.99	55	Nigeria		5.27
3	Saudi Arabia	7.86	56	Grenada		5.27
4	Pakistan	7.61	57	Madagascar		5.23
5	Gabon	7.12	58	Vietnam		5.19
6	Bosnia-Herzegovina	6.58	59	Azerbaijan		5.15
7	Algeria	6.47	60	Turkmenistan		5.12
8	Solomon Islands	6.44	61	Kyrgyzstan		5.11
9	Nauru	6.30	62	Mauritius		5.11
10	Swaziland	6.23	63	New Caledonia		5.10
11	United Arab Emirates	6.18	64	Mali		5.10
12	Jordan	6.16	65	Haiti		5.06
13	Rwanda	6.13	66	Liberia		5.03
14	Guam	6.12	67	Philippines		5.03
15	Sudan	6.11	68	Mongolia		5.02
16	North Korea	6.05	69	Aruba		5.01
17	Congo-Brazzaville	6.04	70	Djibouti		4.99
18	Togo	6.03	71	Netherlands Antilles		4.98
19	Niger	6.00	72	Panama		4.97
20	India	5.96	73	Ecuador		4.96
21	Malawi	5.95	74	Afghanistan		4.95
22	Comoros	5.92	75	Suriname		4.94
23	Seychelles	5.91	76	Armenia		4.93
24	Réunion	5.87	77	Syria		4.93
25	Burundi	5.86	78	Western Samoa		4.92
26	Sierra Leone	5.86	79	Tonga		4.91
27	Papua New Guinea	5.83	80	Puerto Rico		4.91
28	Ghana	5.83	81	Bahamas		4.89
29	Anguilla	5.83	82	Jamaica		4.86
30	Kiribati	5.82	83	St Lucia		4.86
31	Senegal	5.77	84	Guadeloupe		4.83
32	Vanuatu	5.71	85	Trinidad and Tobago		4.79
33	Uzbekistan	5.69	86	Venezuela		4.77
34	Mozambique	5.64	87	Guatemala		4.77
35	French Polynesia	5.63	88	Namibia		4.76
36	Yemen	5.63	89	Tunisia		4.76
37	French Guiana	5.62	90	Peru		4.76
38	Lesotho	5.61	91	Libya		4.75
39	Maldives	5.50	92	Honduras		4.74
40	Central African Republic	5.45	93	Ethiopia		4.73
41	Sri Lanka	5.45	94	Qatar		4.71
42	Sao Tomé e Príncipe	5.44	95	Dominican Republic		4.69
43	Guinea	5.43	96	Guyana		4.67
44	Laos	5.37	97	Barbados		4.66
45	Bangladesh	5.37	98	Cayman Islands		4.65
46	Iraq	5.36	99	Paraguay		4.64
47	Tanzania	5.36	100	Brunei		4.64
48	Uganda	5.34	101	Bhutan		4.60
49	Gambia	5.34	102	Malaysia		4.57
50	Chad	5.32	103	Martinique		4.56
51	Morocco	5.31	104	Angola		4.55
52	Iran	5.31	105	Côte d'Ivoire		4.55
53	Guinea-Bissau	5.30	106	Tajikistan		4.54

107	British Virgin Islands	4.54
108	Egypt	4.54
109	Burkina Faso	4.52
110	Kenya	4.50
111	St Kitts	4.49
112	Cambodia	4.47
113	Lebanon	4.46
114	Bermuda	4.46
115	South Africa	4.44
116	Mexico	4.40
117	El Salvador	4.38
118	Nepal	4.36
119	Georgia	4.35
120	Cape Verde	4.31
121	Colombia	4.30
122	Dominica	4.30
123	St Vincent and the Grenadines	4.21
124	Equatorial Guinea	4.18
125	Zambia	4.17
126	American Samoa	4.15
127	Benin	4.13
128	Mauritania	4.11
129	Bolivia	4.10
130	Turkey	4.08
131	Indonesia	4.04
132	Kazakhstan	4.04
133	Costa Rica	4.02
134	Botswana	3.98
135	Moldova	3.97
136	Cuba	3.97
137	Thailand	3.93
138	Chile	3.81
139	Cameroon	3.81
140	Bahrain	3.81
141	Congo, Democratic Republic	3.79
142	Gibraltar	3.76
143	Oman	3.72
144	Zimbabwe	3.66
145	China	3.64
146	Argentina	3.61
147	Nicaragua	3.51
148	Israel	3.49
149	Singapore	3.48
150	Brazil	3.47
151	Albania	3.42
152	Taiwan	3.39
153	South Korea	3.36
154	Antigua	3.32
155	Ireland	3.28
156	Hong Kong, China	3.27
157	Macau	3.24
158	Belarus	3.23
159	Malta	3.18
160	Spain	3.17
161	Myanmar	3.13

162	Slovenia	3.09
163	Greece	3.03
164	Luxembourg	2.96
165	Romania	2.92
166	New Zealand	2.88
167	Croatia	2.88
168	Poland	2.88
169	Cyprus	2.86
170	Russia	2.81
171	Czech Republic	2.79
172	Portugal	2.74
173	Bulgaria	2.73
174	Belize	2.72
175	Japan	2.70
176	Slovakia	2.69
177	Hungary	2.68
178	Ukraine	2.63
179	USA	2.63
180	Lithuania	2.62
181	Italy	2.61
182	Australia	2.60
183	Uruguay	2.60
184	Liechtenstein	2.57
185	Canada	2.56
186	Austria	2.48
187	France	2.45
188	United Kingdom	2.45
189	Estonia	2.45
190	Latvia	2.45
191	Belgium	2.42
192	Iceland	2.34
193	Netherlands	2.33
194	Switzerland	2.28
195	Finland	2.26
196	Monaco	2.23
197	Norway	2.17
198	Denmark	2.15
199	Germany	2.15
200	Sweden	2.03

Ranking by Urban Population, Latest Year (% of total population)

1	Bermuda	100.0		53	Suriname	74.8
2	Cayman Islands	100.0		54	Colombia	74.8
3	Gibraltar	100.0		55	Norway	74.7
4	Hong Kong, China	100.0		56	Mexico	74.6
5	Monaco	100.0		57	Trinidad and Tobago	74.3
6	Nauru	100.0		58	Jordan	74.2
7	Singapore	100.0		59	Belarus	73.8
8	Guadeloupe	99.7		60	Lithuania	73.8
9	Macau	98.8		61	Latvia	73.4
10	Kuwait	97.6		62	Estonia	73.3
11	Belgium	97.3		63	Peru	72.9
12	Martinique	95.1		64	Brunei	72.7
13	Iceland	93.2		65	Ukraine	71.6
14	Qatar	92.7		66	Réunion	71.4
15	Bahrain	92.5		67	Dominica	71.3
16	Luxembourg	91.9		68	Netherlands Antilles	70.7
17	Uruguay	91.5		69	Armenia	70.3
18	Israel	91.3		70	Bulgaria	70.0
19	Malta	90.7		71	Czech Republic	67.7
20	Lebanon	90.0		72	Italy	67.1
21	Argentina	89.6		73	Hungary	66.5
22	United Kingdom	89.5		74	Tunisia	66.0
23	Netherlands	89.4		75	Poland	65.7
24	Bahamas	88.8		76	Finland	65.6
25	Libya	87.9		77	Dominican Republic	65.6
26	Germany	87.7		78	Austria	64.8
27	Venezuela	87.4		79	Seychelles	64.5
28	New Zealand	86.8		80	Bolivia	64.4
29	United Arab Emirates	85.9		81	Mongolia	64.0
30	Denmark	85.7		82	Switzerland	63.3
31	Saudi Arabia	85.7		83	Cape Verde	63.3
32	Oman	85.0		84	Congo-Brazzaville	63.1
33	Chile	85.0		85	Ecuador	63.1
34	Australia	84.7		86	Macedonia	62.4
35	Djibouti	83.5		87	Iran	62.1
36	Sweden	83.4		88	British Virgin Islands	61.9
37	South Korea	82.4		89	Slovakia	61.3
38	Gabon	81.8		90	Georgia	61.2
39	Brazil	81.3		91	North Korea	60.5
40	Japan	79.0		92	Greece	60.3
41	French Guiana	78.4		93	Algeria	60.1
42	New Caledonia	77.8		94	Philippines	59.4
43	Russia	77.8		95	Ireland	58.8
44	Spain	77.7		96	Mauritania	58.7
45	Taiwan	77.5		97	Romania	57.9
46	USA	77.3		98	Croatia	57.9
47	Canada	77.2		99	Azerbaijan	57.7
48	Iraq	77.2		100	Cyprus	57.3
49	France	75.8		101	Malaysia	57.3
50	Puerto Rico	75.6		102	Paraguay	56.7
51	Cuba	75.5		103	Jamaica	56.6
52	Turkey	75.2		104	Panama	56.6

105	Kazakhstan	56.6		160	Togo	33.9
106	Nicaragua	56.4		161	Comoros	33.8
107	St Vincent and the Grenadines	55.9		162	Guinea	33.5
108	Morocco	55.8		163	Tanzania	33.3
109	Moldova	55.1		164	Kyrgyzstan	33.3
110	Syria	55.0		165	Gambia	33.2
111	Belize	54.8		166	China	32.6
112	Honduras	53.5		167	Namibia	31.3
113	French Polynesia	53.3		168	Congo, Democratic Republic	30.8
114	Tuvalu	53.2		169	Mali	30.7
115	American Samoa	52.8		170	Madagascar	30.3
116	Slovenia	52.3		171	India	28.8
117	Botswana	50.7		172	Lesotho	28.8
118	South Africa	50.6		173	Myanmar	28.2
119	Barbados	50.6		174	Somalia	28.0
120	Fiji	50.2		175	Tajikistan	27.5
121	Cameroon	49.7		176	Swaziland	26.7
122	Equatorial Guinea	49.3		177	Malawi	25.8
123	Costa Rica	48.1		178	Bangladesh	25.1
124	Senegal	48.0		179	Chad	24.2
125	El Salvador	47.0		180	Guinea-Bissau	24.2
126	Côte d'Ivoire	46.9		181	Laos	24.1
127	Sao Tomé e Príncipe	46.9		182	Sri Lanka	24.0
128	Egypt	46.0		183	Liechtenstein	23.0
129	Liberia	45.6		184	Afghanistan	22.4
130	Turkmenistan	45.0		185	Thailand	22.0
131	Nigeria	44.2		186	Western Samoa	21.7
132	Zambia	43.8		187	Niger	21.1
133	Portugal	43.5		188	Vanuatu	20.3
134	Bosnia-Herzegovina	43.3		189	Solomon Islands	20.3
135	Benin	43.1		190	Vietnam	19.9
136	Albania	42.2		191	Eritrea	19.1
137	Indonesia	41.9		192	Burkina Faso	19.1
138	Central African Republic	41.7		193	Ethiopia	18.1
139	Mauritius	41.6		194	Papua New Guinea	17.7
140	Mozambique	41.2		195	Cambodia	16.3
141	Guatemala	40.0		196	Uganda	14.6
142	Kiribati	39.7		197	Anguilla	12.3
143	Guam	39.5		198	Nepal	12.3
144	Ghana	39.0		199	Burundi	9.3
145	Guyana	38.8		200	Bhutan	7.4
146	Tonga	38.6		201	Rwanda	6.3
147	Grenada	38.4				
148	St Lucia	38.1				
149	Pakistan	37.6				
150	Sierra Leone	37.3				
151	Antigua	37.1				
152	Sudan	37.0				
153	Uzbekistan	36.9				
154	Haiti	36.3				
155	Zimbabwe	36.0				
156	Yemen	35.7				
157	Angola	34.7				
158	St Kitts	34.3				
159	Kenya	34.0				

Ranking by GDP Growth Rate 2001 (%)

1	Equatorial Guinea	46.50		54	Georgia	4.50
2	Mozambique	12.90		55	Lithuania	4.50
3	Turkmenistan	10.00		56	Bangladesh	4.50
4	Tajikistan	10.00		57	Uzbekistan	4.50
5	Ukraine	9.10		58	Bulgaria	4.50
6	Azerbaijan	9.00		59	India	4.30
7	Kazakhstan	9.00		60	Jordan	4.20
8	Chad	8.90		61	Croatia	4.20
9	Ethiopia	7.90		62	Greece	4.10
10	Armenia	7.50		63	Belarus	4.10
11	China	7.30		64	Sao Tomé e Príncipe	4.00
12	Qatar	7.20		65	Moldova	4.00
13	Botswana	7.10		66	Vanuatu	4.00
14	Albania	7.00		67	Ghana	4.00
15	Latvia	7.00		68	Cyprus	4.00
16	Mauritania	6.70		69	Nigeria	4.00
17	Mauritius	6.70		70	Guinea-Bissau	4.00
18	Madagascar	6.70		71	Tuvalu	4.00
19	Oman	6.50		72	Hungary	3.80
20	Eritrea	6.40		73	Czech Republic	3.60
21	Morocco	6.30		74	Algeria	3.50
22	Rwanda	6.20		75	Grenada	3.50
23	Ireland	6.00		76	Syria	3.50
24	Bhutan	5.90		77	Suriname	3.40
25	Benin	5.80		78	Pakistan	3.40
26	Gambia	5.80		79	Philippines	3.40
27	Senegal	5.70		80	Yemen	3.30
28	Burkina Faso	5.70		81	Slovakia	3.30
29	Bosnia-Herzegovina	5.60		82	Bahrain	3.30
30	Sierra Leone	5.40		83	Burundi	3.30
31	Sudan	5.30		84	Egypt	3.30
32	Cambodia	5.30		85	Congo-Brazzaville	3.30
33	Cameroon	5.30		86	Indonesia	3.20
34	Romania	5.30		87	Angola	3.20
35	Nepal	5.30		88	Slovenia	3.00
36	Ecuador	5.20		89	Jamaica	3.00
37	Laos	5.20		90	Nicaragua	3.00
38	Luxembourg	5.10		91	Cape Verde	3.00
39	Tanzania	5.10		92	Dominican Republic	3.00
40	Iran	5.10		93	Tonga	3.00
41	Niger	5.10		94	Lesotho	2.90
42	Zambia	5.00		95	Guinea	2.90
43	Estonia	5.00		96	Spain	2.80
44	United Arab Emirates	5.00		97	Malawi	2.80
45	Tunisia	5.00		98	Chile	2.80
46	Western Samoa	5.00		99	Venezuela	2.70
47	Russia	5.00		100	Namibia	2.70
48	Kyrgyzstan	5.00		101	Togo	2.70
49	Maldives	4.90		102	Kuwait	2.70
50	Uganda	4.90		103	Honduras	2.50
51	Myanmar	4.80		104	Belize	2.50
52	Vietnam	4.70		105	New Zealand	2.40
53	Trinidad and Tobago	4.50		106	Australia	2.40

107	Bermuda	2.40
108	Cayman Islands	2.30
109	Brunei	2.30
110	Saudi Arabia	2.20
111	United Kingdom	2.20
112	South Africa	2.20
113	Iceland	2.10
114	Djibouti	2.00
115	France	2.00
116	South Korea	2.00
117	Macau	2.00
118	El Salvador	2.00
119	Panama	2.00
120	Comoros	1.90
121	New Caledonia	1.80
122	Guatemala	1.80
123	Italy	1.80
124	Thailand	1.80
125	Anguilla	1.80
126	St Kitts	1.80
127	American Samoa	1.80
128	French Polynesia	1.60
129	Swaziland	1.60
130	Central African Republic	1.60
131	Portugal	1.60
132	Kiribati	1.50
133	Canada	1.50
134	Brazil	1.50
135	Colombia	1.50
136	Aruba	1.50
137	Gabon	1.50
138	Norway	1.40
139	Guam	1.40
140	Lebanon	1.30
141	Switzerland	1.30
142	USA	1.20
143	Sweden	1.20
144	Poland	1.10
145	Belgium	1.10
146	Netherlands	1.10
147	Mongolia	1.10
148	Kenya	1.10
149	Nauru	1.10
150	Bolivia	1.00
151	Austria	1.00
152	Denmark	0.90
153	Guyana	0.80
154	Paraguay	0.80
155	Finland	0.70
156	Libya	0.60
157	Germany	0.60
158	St Lucia	0.50
159	Costa Rica	0.40
160	Malta	0.40
161	Sri Lanka	0.40

162	St Vincent and the Grenadines	0.30
163	Malaysia	0.30
164	Peru	0.20
165	Mali	0.10
166	Hong Kong, China	0.10
167	Fiji	0.00
168	Netherlands Antilles	0.00
169	Mexico	-0.30
170	Japan	-0.40
171	Antigua	-0.60
172	Israel	-0.60
173	Côte d'Ivoire	-0.90
174	Seychelles	-1.00
175	Bahamas	-1.00
176	Haiti	-1.70
177	Taiwan	-1.90
178	Barbados	-2.10
179	Singapore	-2.10
180	Solomon Islands	-3.00
181	Uruguay	-3.10
182	Papua New Guinea	-3.40
183	Argentina	-3.70
184	Congo, Democratic Republic	-4.00
185	Macedonia	-4.60
186	Iraq	-6.00
187	Turkey	-6.20
188	Zimbabwe	-8.40

Ranking by GDP 2001 (US$ million)

1	USA	10,208,125.0	54	Hungary	46,945.7
2	Japan	4,148,647.4	55	Nigeria	41,372.4
3	Germany	1,846,090.5	56	Puerto Rico	40,910.7
4	United Kingdom	1,424,094.0	57	Romania	39,714.2
5	France	1,306,155.4	58	Ukraine	37,587.7
6	China	1,170,574.3	59	Kuwait	35,565.3
7	Italy	1,088,652.3	60	Morocco	33,492.4
8	Canada	699,992.3	61	Vietnam	31,075.4
9	Mexico	617,817.1	62	Libya	28,950.4
10	Spain	581,820.2	63	Kazakhstan	22,390.0
11	Brazil	502,508.4	64	Dominican Republic	21,383.5
12	India	473,388.0	65	Cuba	20,649.3
13	Myanmar	425,305.0	66	Guatemala	20,645.1
14	South Korea	422,166.9	67	Croatia	20,443.3
15	Netherlands	380,062.6	68	Tunisia	20,003.3
16	Iran	378,733.8	69	Slovakia	19,948.4
17	Australia	357,140.6	70	Luxembourg	19,516.5
18	Russia	309,926.8	71	Oman	19,334.2
19	Taiwan	282,239.0	72	Slovenia	18,810.4
20	Argentina	269,611.8	73	Uruguay	18,588.6
21	Switzerland	246,945.7	74	Ecuador	17,828.0
22	Belgium	227,216.0	75	Costa Rica	17,026.4
23	Sweden	209,821.3	76	Lebanon	16,709.0
24	Austria	188,545.1	77	Qatar	16,553.3
25	Poland	176,313.3	78	Sri Lanka	15,664.3
26	Denmark	167,076.1	79	El Salvador	13,965.7
27	Saudi Arabia	166,692.7	80	Bulgaria	13,027.4
28	Norway	163,711.7	81	Sudan	12,512.6
29	Hong Kong, China	161,870.0	82	Belarus	12,167.4
30	Turkey	148,339.0	83	Lithuania	12,021.8
31	Indonesia	145,307.8	84	Brunei	11,763.8
32	Venezuela	124,948.5	85	Uzbekistan	11,497.0
33	Finland	119,850.9	86	Kenya	10,500.5
34	Greece	116,818.1	87	Côte d'Ivoire	10,410.6
35	Thailand	114,774.0	88	Panama	10,238.0
36	South Africa	112,335.7	89	Angola	9,471.5
37	Israel	110,472.3	90	Zimbabwe	9,195.2
38	Portugal	109,406.1	91	Tanzania	9,119.3
39	Ireland	101,546.3	92	Cyprus	9,035.8
40	Egypt	91,236.8	93	Jordan	8,829.5
41	Singapore	88,228.0	94	Yemen	8,740.6
42	Malaysia	87,540.0	95	Cameroon	8,622.2
43	Syria	81,975.4	96	Trinidad and Tobago	8,412.2
44	Colombia	81,453.0	97	Bahrain	8,045.2
45	Philippines	71,438.0	98	Bolivia	7,959.8
46	United Arab Emirates	67,488.1	99	Jamaica	7,812.9
47	Chile	66,450.6	100	Latvia	7,569.5
48	Pakistan	58,006.9	101	Iceland	7,528.8
49	Czech Republic	56,423.9	102	Paraguay	7,014.4
50	Algeria	54,858.1	103	Macau	6,432.8
51	Peru	54,046.5	104	Ethiopia	6,267.9
52	New Zealand	49,486.5	105	Nepal	5,987.0
53	Bangladesh	46,973.1	106	Honduras	5,751.5

107	Uganda	5,730.7
108	Azerbaijan	5,689.6
109	Turkmenistan	5,443.7
110	Estonia	5,367.9
111	Botswana	5,341.1
112	Ghana	5,301.2
113	Guadeloupe	5,255.8
114	Bahamas	4,923.0
115	Senegal	4,633.2
116	Gabon	4,621.0
117	Madagascar	4,566.1
118	Laos	4,381.0
119	Mauritius	4,279.7
120	Albania	4,133.6
121	Bosnia-Herzegovina	4,023.4
122	Congo, Democratic Republic	3,876.0
123	Haiti	3,643.1
124	Zambia	3,641.0
125	Malta	3,568.3
126	Mozambique	3,553.1
127	Macedonia	3,449.9
128	Cambodia	3,302.0
129	New Caledonia	3,159.9
130	Georgia	3,138.4
131	Namibia	3,100.1
132	Papua New Guinea	2,915.3
133	Guinea	2,881.6
134	Congo-Brazzaville	2,876.9
135	Martinique	2,792.6
136	Bermuda	2,757.7
137	Mali	2,586.3
138	Netherlands Antilles	2,545.8
139	Nicaragua	2,535.5
140	Barbados	2,498.0
141	Benin	2,395.0
142	Burkina Faso	2,328.5
143	Armenia	2,115.0
144	Niger	1,908.6
145	Malawi	1,826.2
146	French Polynesia	1,811.3
147	Rwanda	1,723.9
148	Equatorial Guinea	1,706.2
149	Fiji	1,635.7
150	Chad	1,603.4
151	Moldova	1,581.3
152	Kyrgyzstan	1,465.7
153	Guam	1,392.9
154	Cayman Islands	1,324.0
155	Togo	1,258.6
156	Swaziland	1,237.5
157	Tajikistan	1,084.0
158	Liechtenstein	1,049.3
159	Mongolia	1,029.9
160	Aruba	979.6
161	Central African Republic	977.6

162	Lesotho	810.2
163	British Virgin Islands	792.8
164	Belize	786.0
165	Sierra Leone	749.0
166	Eritrea	724.4
167	St Lucia	724.1
168	French Guiana	704.4
169	Burundi	689.2
170	Antigua	662.2
171	Guyana	654.5
172	Seychelles	617.7
173	Maldives	581.3
174	Djibouti	574.2
175	Cape Verde	564.1
176	Suriname	544.3
177	Bhutan	506.2
178	Mauritania	488.4
179	Grenada	434.1
180	American Samoa	405.5
181	Gambia	384.6
182	St Kitts	343.0
183	St Vincent and the Grenadines	337.4
184	Solomon Islands	307.0
185	Gibraltar	287.2
186	Dominica	276.7
187	Guinea-Bissau	245.0
188	Western Samoa	243.2
189	Vanuatu	227.0
190	Comoros	220.1
191	Nauru	178.0
192	Tonga	130.4
193	Anguilla	70.8
194	Sao Tomé e Príncipe	47.7
195	Kiribati	43.0
196	Tuvalu	5.3

Ranking by GDP per capita 2001 (US$)

1	Luxembourg	44,123.6	54	South Korea	8,818.4
2	Bermuda	41,784.0	55	Guam	8,305.0
3	USA	37,079.1	56	Seychelles	8,021.6
4	Norway	36,266.9	57	French Polynesia	7,703.7
5	British Virgin Islands	36,037.5	58	Saudi Arabia	7,457.1
6	Brunei	35,828.1	59	Zimbabwe	7,315.2
7	Switzerland	34,351.5	60	Argentina	7,280.5
8	Cayman Islands	33,101.1	61	Oman	7,174.1
9	Japan	32,663.0	62	Martinique	6,912.3
10	Denmark	31,172.1	63	Trinidad and Tobago	6,421.5
11	Liechtenstein	31,087.0	64	Mexico	6,110.4
12	Singapore	26,944.0	65	Uruguay	5,676.8
13	Qatar	26,698.9	66	American Samoa	5,631.4
14	Iceland	26,467.0	67	Iran	5,578.1
15	Ireland	26,449.7	68	Czech Republic	5,496.5
16	United Kingdom	23,915.9	69	Venezuela	5,025.6
17	Netherlands	23,709.3	70	Libya	4,961.5
18	Sweden	23,649.1	71	Lebanon	4,921.7
19	Austria	23,298.7	72	Syria	4,866.5
20	Finland	23,094.9	73	Hungary	4,673.3
21	Hong Kong, China	23,063.9	74	Grenada	4,617.8
22	Canada	22,776.0	75	St Lucia	4,582.7
23	Germany	22,545.2	76	Poland	4,556.4
24	Belgium	22,132.7	77	Croatia	4,510.6
25	France	22,038.2	78	Costa Rica	4,483.3
26	United Arab Emirates	21,857.3	79	Chile	4,368.5
27	Italy	18,884.5	80	Dominica	3,896.7
28	Australia	18,617.8	81	Malaysia	3,825.9
29	Israel	17,717.8	82	Estonia	3,767.5
30	Bahamas	15,530.0	83	Slovakia	3,688.1
31	Kuwait	15,517.3	84	Mauritius	3,620.7
32	New Caledonia	14,746.7	85	French Guiana	3,612.4
33	Spain	14,727.8	86	Equatorial Guinea	3,599.5
34	Nauru	13,690.7	87	Panama	3,585.1
35	Macau	13,522.7	88	Gabon	3,585.0
36	New Zealand	12,739.9	89	Kenya	3,296.9
37	Bahrain	12,715.7	90	Lithuania	3,249.8
38	Taiwan	12,561.0	91	Botswana	3,200.2
39	Cyprus	11,853.2	92	Latvia	3,165.0
40	Gibraltar	11,488.7	93	Belize	3,150.3
41	Netherlands Antilles	11,467.6	94	Brazil	3,025.1
42	Greece	11,076.7	95	Jamaica	2,958.3
43	Guadeloupe	11,064.8	96	St Vincent and the Grenadines	2,883.8
44	Portugal	10,904.8	97	South Africa	2,556.0
45	Puerto Rico	10,378.2	98	Dominican Republic	2,517.1
46	Slovenia	9,589.6	99	Turkey	2,272.1
47	Antigua	9,460.3	100	El Salvador	2,210.0
48	Myanmar	9,290.1	101	Russia	2,147.3
49	Malta	9,288.5	102	Tunisia	2,094.6
50	Barbados	9,183.8	103	Peru	2,054.6
51	St Kitts	9,025.3	104	Colombia	2,046.3
52	Anguilla	8,853.6	105	Maldives	2,032.8
53	Aruba	8,824.8	106	Fiji	2,004.3

107	Thailand	1,851.4
108	Cuba	1,843.6
109	Guatemala	1,813.3
110	Algeria	1,805.4
111	Romania	1,780.9
112	Namibia	1,738.7
113	Macedonia	1,696.6
114	Jordan	1,670.9
115	Bulgaria	1,606.5
116	Egypt	1,441.5
117	Kazakhstan	1,388.0
118	Ecuador	1,371.8
119	Western Samoa	1,353.6
120	Tonga	1,304.4
121	Suriname	1,289.7
122	Paraguay	1,276.2
123	Cape Verde	1,261.9
124	Belarus	1,206.2
125	Vanuatu	1,193.0
126	Turkmenistan	1,193.0
127	Albania	1,191.3
128	Morocco	1,166.9
129	Swaziland	1,164.2
130	Bosnia-Herzegovina	992.9
131	Congo-Brazzaville	967.7
132	Bolivia	955.7
133	Philippines	912.0
134	China	908.9
135	Honduras	886.8
136	Djibouti	874.0
137	Sri Lanka	832.3
138	Laos	807.0
139	Ukraine	772.1
140	Guyana	749.7
141	Azerbaijan	701.7
142	Angola	697.7
143	Solomon Islands	692.6
144	Côte d'Ivoire	678.7
145	Indonesia	678.3
146	Papua New Guinea	606.9
147	Georgia	575.4
148	Armenia	554.8
149	Cameroon	541.1
150	Nicaragua	540.1
151	Kiribati	505.9
152	Uzbekistan	473.0
153	Senegal	466.1
154	India	461.0
155	Haiti	457.7
156	Yemen	450.5
157	Tuvalu	442.0
158	Sudan	404.0
159	Mongolia	386.8
160	Vietnam	380.1
161	Guinea	380.1

162	Zambia	375.2
163	Benin	373.6
164	Bangladesh	363.9
165	Pakistan	362.0
166	Moldova	361.0
167	Lesotho	360.4
168	Nigeria	337.2
169	Kyrgyzstan	312.3
170	Sao Tomé e Príncipe	311.9
171	Comoros	299.4
172	Cambodia	295.3
173	Gambia	279.9
174	Madagascar	271.5
175	Central African Republic	262.4
176	Tanzania	262.2
177	Togo	259.3
178	Ghana	251.2
179	Nepal	250.3
180	Uganda	248.2
181	Bhutan	238.5
182	Mali	220.6
183	Chad	201.5
184	Rwanda	198.8
185	Guinea-Bissau	194.0
186	Burkina Faso	184.2
187	Eritrea	177.0
188	Tajikistan	175.0
189	Mauritania	173.5
190	Mozambique	172.4
191	Niger	167.3
192	Malawi	157.7
193	Sierra Leone	149.5
194	Burundi	99.6
195	Ethiopia	96.3
196	Congo, Democratic Republic	71.6

Ranking by Inflation Rate 2001 (% increase)

1	Congo, Democratic Republic	299.0	54	Tonga	7.0
2	Angola	152.6	55	Kyrgyzstan	6.9
3	Zimbabwe	76.7	56	Brazil	6.8
4	Belarus	61.3	57	Guinea	6.8
5	Iraq	60.0	58	Togo	6.8
6	Turkey	54.4	59	Iceland	6.7
7	Suriname	50.2	60	Mexico	6.4
8	Tajikistan	38.6	61	Seychelles	6.2
9	Ecuador	37.0	62	Philippines	6.1
10	Romania	34.5	63	Sierra Leone	6.0
11	Ghana	32.9	64	Estonia	5.8
12	Malawi	27.2	65	South Africa	5.7
13	Uzbekistan	27.2	66	Poland	5.5
14	Zambia	22.5	67	Macedonia	5.3
15	Russia	21.5	68	Tanzania	5.2
16	Nigeria	18.9	69	Netherlands	5.1
17	Haiti	16.7	70	Bhutan	5.0
18	Eritrea	15.1	71	British Virgin Islands	5.0
19	Myanmar	15.0	72	Comoros	5.0
20	Turkmenistan	15.0	73	Fiji	5.0
21	Sri Lanka	14.2	74	Guinea-Bissau	5.0
22	Venezuela	12.5	75	Jamaica	5.0
23	Chad	12.4	76	Madagascar	5.0
24	Equatorial Guinea	12.0	77	Mali	5.0
25	Ukraine	12.0	78	Sudan	5.0
26	Yemen	11.9	79	Croatia	4.9
27	Iran	11.7	80	Czech Republic	4.7
28	Indonesia	11.5	81	Georgia	4.7
29	Costa Rica	11.0	82	Mauritania	4.7
30	Moldova	9.8	83	Uganda	4.6
31	Honduras	9.7	84	Côte d'Ivoire	4.4
32	Sao Tomé e Príncipe	9.3	85	Mauritius	4.4
33	Papua New Guinea	9.3	86	Portugal	4.4
34	Namibia	9.2	87	Uruguay	4.4
35	Hungary	9.2	88	Australia	4.4
36	Mozambique	9.0	89	South Korea	4.3
37	Dominican Republic	8.8	90	Algeria	4.1
38	Guatemala	8.7	91	Niger	4.0
39	Slovenia	8.4	92	Gambia	4.0
40	Kazakhstan	8.4	93	Ireland	4.0
41	Nicaragua	8.3	94	Nauru	4.0
42	Mongolia	8.2	95	Netherlands Antilles	3.9
43	Burundi	8.0	96	Benin	3.8
44	Colombia	8.0	97	India	3.8
45	Laos	7.8	98	Pakistan	3.8
46	Lesotho	7.8	99	El Salvador	3.8
47	Paraguay	7.7	100	Cape Verde	3.7
48	Bulgaria	7.5	101	Greece	3.7
49	Swaziland	7.5	102	Maldives	3.7
50	Slovakia	7.3	103	Chile	3.6
51	Botswana	7.2	104	Rwanda	3.5
52	Kiribati	7.1	105	Bosnia-Herzegovina	3.3
53	Solomon Islands	7.0	106	Central African Republic	3.3

107	Spain	3.2
108	Albania	3.1
109	Norway	3.0
110	Burkina Faso	3.0
111	Senegal	3.0
112	Malta	2.9
113	American Samoa	2.9
114	Bermuda	2.9
115	Nepal	2.9
116	Aruba	2.9
117	Armenia	2.9
118	USA	2.8
119	Anguilla	2.8
120	Cameroon	2.8
121	French Polynesia	2.8
122	Luxembourg	2.7
123	Italy	2.7
124	New Zealand	2.7
125	Finland	2.6
126	Gabon	2.6
127	Sweden	2.6
128	Canada	2.5
129	Grenada	2.5
130	Kuwait	2.5
131	New Caledonia	2.5
132	St Lucia	2.5
133	Trinidad and Tobago	2.5
134	Latvia	2.5
135	Belgium	2.4
136	Egypt	2.4
137	Germany	2.4
138	Guyana	2.4
139	Austria	2.3
140	Barbados	2.2
141	United Arab Emirates	2.2
142	Denmark	2.1
143	St Kitts	2.1
144	United Kingdom	2.1
145	Guam	2.0
146	Vanuatu	2.0
147	Peru	2.0
148	Cyprus	2.0
149	Tunisia	1.9
150	Bangladesh	1.8
151	Brunei	1.8
152	Djibouti	1.8
153	Dominica	1.8
154	France	1.8
155	Jordan	1.8
156	Panama	1.8
157	Tuvalu	1.8
158	Thailand	1.7
159	Bolivia	1.6
160	Azerbaijan	1.5
161	Western Samoa	1.5

162	Malaysia	1.4
163	Lithuania	1.3
164	Belize	1.2
165	Israel	1.1
166	Macau	1.1
167	Antigua	1.0
168	Bahamas	1.0
169	Singapore	1.0
170	Switzerland	1.0
171	Syria	1.0
172	St Vincent and the Grenadines	0.9
173	Kenya	0.8
174	China	0.7
175	Morocco	0.5
176	Vietnam	0.1
177	Lebanon	0.0
178	Taiwan	0.0
179	Bahrain	-0.2
180	Congo-Brazzaville	-0.5
181	Cambodia	-0.6
182	Japan	-0.7
183	Qatar	-0.7
184	Argentina	-1.1
185	Saudi Arabia	-1.4
186	Hong Kong, China	-1.6
187	Oman	-2.6
188	Ethiopia	-7.1
189	Libya	-8.5

Ranking by Total Imports 2001 (US$ million)

1	USA	1,180,150.0		54	Egypt	12,755.9
2	Germany	486,294.0		55	Algeria	12,435.0
3	Japan	350,095.0		56	Morocco	11,387.2
4	United Kingdom	320,973.0		57	Luxembourg	11,022.9
5	France	292,533.0		58	Nigeria	10,748.4
6	China	243,567.0		59	Pakistan	10,206.0
7	Italy	234,382.0		60	Slovenia	10,143.5
8	Canada	231,876.8		61	Tunisia	10,055.3
9	Hong Kong, China	202,252.0		62	Croatia	9,044.0
10	Netherlands	194,461.0		63	Bangladesh	8,154.0
11	Belgium	176,811.0		64	Belarus	8,049.0
12	Spain	153,607.0		65	Peru	7,646.9
13	Mexico	147,742.4		66	Dominican Republic	7,506.2
14	South Korea	141,098.0		67	Kuwait	7,324.4
15	Singapore	116,000.0		68	Lebanon	7,293.5
16	Taiwan	107,274.0		69	Bulgaria	7,230.0
17	Switzerland	77,070.5		70	Costa Rica	6,564.3
18	Malaysia	74,384.0		71	Kazakhstan	6,445.0
19	Austria	70,413.8		72	Lithuania	6,281.0
20	Brazil	64,508.8		73	Sri Lanka	6,100.0
21	Australia	63,886.1		74	Guatemala	5,606.8
22	Sweden	62,670.2		75	Libya	5,440.9
23	Thailand	62,057.7		76	Ecuador	5,299.2
24	Ireland	50,622.4		77	Oman	5,291.2
25	India	50,533.0		78	Cuba	4,958.6
26	Poland	50,275.1		79	Qatar	4,671.6
27	Turkey	46,340.6		80	Jordan	4,423.0
28	Denmark	45,047.8		81	Syria	4,332.4
29	Russia	41,237.0		82	Estonia	4,279.8
30	United Arab Emirates	40,259.4		83	Bahrain	4,262.8
31	Portugal	37,965.5		84	Cyprus	3,937.9
32	Czech Republic	36,504.0		85	El Salvador	3,865.8
33	Hungary	33,682.0		86	Angola	3,863.2
34	Norway	32,955.1		87	Trinidad and Tobago	3,672.3
35	Israel	31,434.9		88	Uruguay	3,525.1
36	Philippines	31,358.1		89	Latvia	3,504.5
37	Saudi Arabia	31,223.0		90	Jamaica	3,330.8
38	Indonesia	31,170.0		91	Kenya	3,214.8
39	Finland	30,443.8		92	Panama	2,963.5
40	Greece	28,547.0		93	Ghana	2,949.5
41	South Africa	28,405.1		94	Honduras	2,917.6
42	Puerto Rico	28,143.2		95	Zimbabwe	2,777.4
43	Argentina	20,311.0		96	Uzbekistan	2,715.0
44	Iran	18,543.0		97	Malta	2,592.3
45	Venezuela	18,022.0		98	Myanmar	2,461.0
46	Chile	17,233.8		99	Côte d'Ivoire	2,405.4
47	Vietnam	16,000.0		100	Macau	2,386.3
48	Ukraine	15,775.0		101	Yemen	2,354.8
49	Romania	15,560.9		102	Bosnia-Herzegovina	2,340.0
50	Slovakia	14,686.0		103	Mauritius	2,327.8
51	New Zealand	13,346.9		104	Iceland	2,256.3
52	Iraq	12,900.0		105	Sudan	2,192.7
53	Colombia	12,833.6		106	Paraguay	2,175.2

107	Turkmenistan	2,105.0
108	Nicaragua	1,776.4
109	Bolivia	1,760.0
110	Tanzania	1,750.3
111	Azerbaijan	1,725.0
112	Macedonia	1,688.0
113	Bahamas	1,678.5
114	Uganda	1,593.5
115	Senegal	1,577.6
116	Cambodia	1,476.0
117	Ethiopia	1,400.5
118	Cameroon	1,399.3
119	Netherlands Antilles	1,361.6
120	Albania	1,308.0
121	Nepal	1,235.0
122	Congo-Brazzaville	1,135.3
123	Papua New Guinea	1,072.8
124	Mozambique	1,047.9
125	Swaziland	1,032.0
126	Brunei	1,030.0
127	Namibia	1,028.7
128	Haiti	1,013.0
129	Barbados	988.3
130	New Caledonia	983.0
131	Moldova	897.0
132	Armenia	890.0
133	Gabon	877.1
134	Zambia	791.1
135	Aruba	784.6
136	Tajikistan	775.0
137	Guinea	701.0
138	Georgia	684.0
139	Lesotho	680.6
140	Madagascar	670.4
141	Malawi	661.9
142	Mali	656.7
143	Burkina Faso	655.8
144	Benin	650.6
145	Chad	617.2
146	Fiji	584.0
147	Guyana	583.9
148	Botswana	568.9
149	Afghanistan	512.0
150	Suriname	476.2
151	Kyrgyzstan	475.0
152	Mongolia	461.0
153	Niger	439.5
154	Laos	437.0
155	Antigua	419.3
156	Belize	408.8
157	Maldives	396.0
158	St Lucia	384.7
159	Seychelles	381.9
160	Mauritania	376.8
161	Togo	354.8

162	Djibouti	308.6
163	Congo, Democratic Republic	289.5
164	Rwanda	249.7
165	Equatorial Guinea	240.0
166	Cape Verde	223.7
167	Grenada	220.7
168	Gambia	207.4
169	Bhutan	203.0
170	Sierra Leone	194.8
171	St Vincent and the Grenadines	185.9
172	St Kitts	179.9
173	Dominica	153.0
174	Central African Republic	148.1
175	Burundi	139.3
176	Western Samoa	129.0
177	Solomon Islands	108.0
178	Tonga	94.0
179	Vanuatu	80.0
180	Guinea-Bissau	71.7
181	Kiribati	36.0
182	Sao Tomé e Príncipe	28.5

Ranking by Total Exports 2001 (US$ million)

1	USA	730,803.0		54	Romania	11,385.0
2	Germany	570,522.0		55	Slovenia	9,251.0
3	Japan	403,496.0		56	Pakistan	9,209.0
4	France	292,503.0		57	Kazakhstan	8,750.0
5	United Kingdom	267,349.0		58	Greece	8,693.0
6	China	266,620.0		59	Qatar	8,427.0
7	Canada	259,858.0		60	Luxembourg	8,157.0
8	Italy	243,376.0		61	Libya	7,812.0
9	Netherlands	216,099.0		62	Oman	7,439.0
10	Hong Kong, China	189,894.0		63	Belarus	7,428.0
11	Belgium	187,981.0		64	Morocco	7,116.0
12	Mexico	158,547.0		65	Peru	7,092.0
13	South Korea	150,439.0		66	Angola	7,009.0
14	Taiwan	122,505.0		67	Tunisia	6,492.0
15	Singapore	121,751.0		68	Bangladesh	6,300.0
16	Spain	115,155.0		69	Bahrain	5,545.0
17	Russia	100,653.0		70	Bulgaria	5,099.0
18	Malaysia	88,521.0		71	Costa Rica	5,010.0
19	Ireland	83,335.0		72	Trinidad and Tobago	4,964.0
20	Switzerland	78,066.0		73	Sri Lanka	4,817.0
21	Sweden	75,140.0		74	Croatia	4,659.0
22	Saudi Arabia	74,622.0		75	Lithuania	4,583.0
23	Austria	66,652.0		76	Ecuador	4,495.0
24	Thailand	64,223.0		77	Syria	4,357.0
25	Australia	63,387.0		78	Egypt	4,128.0
26	Brazil	58,223.0		79	Côte d'Ivoire	4,054.0
27	Norway	57,638.0		80	Brunei	3,727.0
28	Indonesia	56,716.0		81	Yemen	3,677.0
29	United Arab Emirates	46,447.0		82	Estonia	3,305.0
30	Denmark	45,608.0		83	Uzbekistan	2,655.0
31	India	43,611.0		84	Gabon	2,596.0
32	Finland	41,706.0		85	Turkmenistan	2,560.0
33	Poland	36,092.0		86	Guatemala	2,466.0
34	Czech Republic	33,369.0		87	Armenia	2,460.0
35	Iran	33,176.0		88	Macau	2,300.0
36	Puerto Rico	32,699.0		89	Botswana	2,291.0
37	Philippines	32,664.0		90	Jordan	2,180.0
38	Venezuela	31,462.0		91	Uruguay	2,069.0
39	Hungary	30,498.0		92	Latvia	2,001.0
40	Israel	29,409.0		93	Malta	1,917.0
41	South Africa	29,284.0		94	Zimbabwe	1,873.0
42	Turkey	28,537.0		95	Congo-Brazzaville	1,854.0
43	Argentina	26,655.0		96	Papua New Guinea	1,813.0
44	Portugal	23,933.0		97	Kenya	1,797.0
45	Nigeria	20,223.0		98	Iceland	1,773.0
46	Chile	17,440.0		99	Cameroon	1,773.0
47	Ukraine	16,265.0		100	Myanmar	1,760.0
48	Kuwait	16,179.0		101	Cuba	1,753.0
49	Vietnam	15,100.0		102	Mauritius	1,745.0
50	Algeria	13,958.0		103	Cambodia	1,531.0
51	New Zealand	13,726.0		104	Ghana	1,432.0
52	Slovakia	12,691.0		105	Honduras	1,318.0
53	Colombia	12,257.0		106	Bolivia	1,285.0

107	Jamaica	1,225.0
108	El Salvador	1,214.0
109	Equatorial Guinea	1,166.0
110	Macedonia	1,155.0
111	Dominican Republic	1,075.0
112	Senegal	999.0
113	Cyprus	975.0
114	Namibia	949.0
115	Azerbaijan	927.0
116	Panama	911.0
117	Zambia	889.0
118	Guinea	877.0
119	Lebanon	870.0
120	Sudan	856.0
121	Swaziland	812.0
122	Bosnia-Herzegovina	799.0
123	Paraguay	776.0
124	Mali	740.0
125	Tanzania	687.0
126	Nepal	646.0
127	Nicaragua	606.0
128	Tajikistan	580.0
129	Moldova	570.0
130	Kyrgyzstan	560.0
131	New Caledonia	554.0
132	Ethiopia	544.0
133	Fiji	495.0
134	Liberia	479.0
135	Guyana	478.0
136	Uganda	457.0
137	Bahamas	445.0
138	Benin	427.0
139	Suriname	402.0
140	Malawi	399.0
141	Madagascar	373.0
142	Mozambique	361.0
143	Congo, Democratic Republic	359.0
144	Laos	336.0
145	Georgia	320.0
146	Martinique	307.0
147	Niger	304.0
148	Mauritania	300.0
149	Albania	294.0
150	Mongolia	250.0
151	Barbados	228.0
152	Togo	226.0
153	Chad	197.0
154	Burkina Faso	175.0
155	Belize	166.0
156	Central African Republic	160.0
157	Lesotho	154.0
158	Haiti	141.0
159	Bhutan	140.0
160	Seychelles	134.0
161	St Lucia	103.0

162	Bermuda	90.0
163	Rwanda	85.0
164	Solomon Islands	84.0
165	Maldives	76.0
166	Guinea-Bissau	72.0
167	Afghanistan	66.0
168	Dominica	56.0
169	Antigua	52.0
170	Cape Verde	51.0
171	St Vincent and the Grenadines	41.0
172	Burundi	39.0
173	Grenada	32.0
174	Aruba	30.0
175	St Kitts	28.0
176	Kiribati	24.0
177	Gambia	18.0
178	Sierra Leone	16.0
179	Western Samoa	16.0
180	Vanuatu	15.0
181	Djibouti	13.0
182	Tonga	13.0
183	Sao Tomé e Príncipe	8.0

Ranking by Tourism Receipts 2001 (US$ million)

1	USA	68,447.7		54	Finland	1,253.0
2	France	29,283.2		55	Jamaica	1,106.2
3	Spain	27,391.5		56	Costa Rica	895.8
4	Italy	24,439.2		57	Iran	891.4
5	United Kingdom	19,251.7		58	Bulgaria	867.6
6	Germany	14,358.5		59	Venezuela	830.7
7	China	14,313.9		60	Chile	794.3
8	Austria	11,010.3		61	Colombia	792.0
9	Canada	9,146.3		62	Lebanon	748.0
10	Mexico	8,203.7		63	Barbados	718.6
11	Poland	8,050.8		64	Panama	689.8
12	Greece	7,510.7		65	Aruba	688.5
13	Switzerland	7,077.5		66	Peru	683.5
14	Australia	6,708.1		67	Malta	608.1
15	Hong Kong, China	6,463.7		68	Guatemala	556.9
16	Russia	6,297.3		69	Slovakia	553.0
17	South Korea	6,293.8		70	Estonia	551.1
18	Netherlands	6,217.1		71	Tanzania	542.0
19	Singapore	6,162.3		72	Romania	531.3
20	Turkey	5,522.6		73	Uruguay	526.4
21	Belgium	5,377.7		74	Jordan	518.7
22	Thailand	4,940.3		75	Mauritius	493.3
23	Portugal	4,587.1		76	Lithuania	461.8
24	Argentina	4,252.6		77	Bermuda	448.3
25	Ireland	3,836.0		78	Vietnam	430.8
26	Sweden	3,704.5		79	Kazakhstan	411.7
27	Denmark	3,558.2		80	Cayman Islands	407.1
28	Indonesia	3,473.9		81	Bahrain	364.1
29	Ukraine	3,415.2		82	Martinique	341.1
30	Egypt	3,326.9		83	Guadeloupe	338.9
31	Croatia	3,302.0		84	Georgia	338.6
32	Hungary	3,136.9		85	Kenya	320.9
33	Taiwan	3,013.1		86	Ecuador	294.3
34	Czech Republic	2,995.4		87	Antigua	271.8
35	India	2,790.8		88	French Polynesia	266.1
36	Japan	2,736.4		89	Fiji	254.6
37	Brazil	2,637.5		90	British Virgin Islands	251.0
38	Malaysia	2,515.0		91	Latvia	246.8
39	Puerto Rico	2,399.2		92	St Lucia	233.7
40	Dominican Republic	2,274.1		93	Namibia	202.6
41	Norway	1,954.0		94	El Salvador	199.0
42	Cyprus	1,841.5		95	Gibraltar	192.5
43	South Africa	1,779.3		96	Iceland	192.5
44	Macau	1,769.5		97	Botswana	191.4
45	Morocco	1,757.3		98	Trinidad and Tobago	191.0
46	Israel	1,652.6		99	Honduras	187.6
47	Philippines	1,648.8		100	Sri Lanka	186.8
48	New Zealand	1,592.1		101	Paraguay	182.6
49	Bahamas	1,575.0		102	Kuwait	178.4
50	Cuba	1,462.8		103	Ghana	178.0
51	Tunisia	1,371.6		104	Bolivia	171.0
52	Syria	1,299.6		105	Senegal	164.3
53	Slovenia	1,263.1		106	Cambodia	162.0

107	Laos	125.6
108	Zimbabwe	125.0
109	Azerbaijan	119.7
110	Turkmenistan	117.3
111	Nepal	112.4
112	Uganda	105.1
113	Belize	98.6
114	Madagascar	96.6
115	Oman	95.4
116	Nigeria	95.0
117	Seychelles	90.1
118	Côte d'Ivoire	77.2
119	St Kitts	73.3
120	Nicaragua	72.1
121	Pakistan	70.3
122	Yemen	68.0
123	Grenada	60.9
124	Suriname	60.4
125	St Vincent and the Grenadines	56.8
126	Haiti	55.8
127	Albania	54.7
128	Zambia	53.3
129	Anguilla	51.6
130	Bangladesh	49.4
131	Guyana	46.7
132	Vanuatu	42.6
133	Gambia	42.2
134	Myanmar	36.5
135	Dominica	35.2
136	Benin	35.1
137	Western Samoa	34.0
138	Papua New Guinea	33.6
139	Burkina Faso	33.2
140	Moldova	33.1
141	Mali	32.7
142	Swaziland	32.4
143	Algeria	28.0
144	Mauritania	27.4
145	Belarus	26.4
146	Ethiopia	26.0
147	Lesotho	25.3
148	Mongolia	19.5
149	Niger	18.4
150	Malawi	18.4
151	Libya	16.6
152	Macedonia	16.4
153	Cape Verde	16.2
154	Comoros	14.7
155	Uzbekistan	10.0
156	Gabon	9.3
157	Bhutan	9.0
158	Tonga	8.2
159	Angola	8.0
160	Congo-Brazzaville	7.9
161	Armenia	7.8

162	Solomon Islands	6.3
163	Sudan	5.9
164	Kyrgyzstan	5.1
165	Sierra Leone	5.1
166	Togo	4.8
167	Guinea	3.3
168	Burundi	0.7

World Economic Database

Afghanistan

Area (km^2)   636,265

Currency   Afghani (= 100 puls)

Location   Afghanistan divides the Middle East from the Indian subcontinent. It borders on China in the northeast, Pakistan in the east and south, Iran in the west and the former Soviet Union republics of Turkmenistan Uzbekistan and Tajikistan in the north. It is this central location that has largely accounted for the successive invasions of the country over the centuries. The capital is Kabul.

Head of State   Hamid Karzai (2002)

Head of Government   Hamid Karzai (2002)

Ruling Party   The government is led by a loose coalition of Pushtuns, Tajiks and other ethnic groups with strong support from the international community.

Political Structure   Afghanistan remains a divided country. Various faction leaders, in particular the mainly-Tajik Northern Alliance, have immense power behind the scenes. According to the Bonn Agreement, negotiated at the beginning of 2002, the country's loya jirga, has the power to approve key personnel in the government as well as its structure.

Last Elections   The loya jirga, a group of 1,500 delegates from across the country, met in June 2002 and chose Karzai as president for the next 18 months. Karzai then selected his cabinet which was eventually approved by the loya jirga, with a few changes.

Political Risk   The present government has very little influence or control outside of Kabul and occasional fighting, both among Afghans or involving allied forces, continues. No effective national military is expected to be in place for several years. In the meantime, local warlords exercise considerable influence. Taliban resisters continue their rearguard actions. The assassination of vice-president Haji Abdul Qadir in July 2002 was shocking and rocked the new government. It may well prompt a change in strategy for the allied forces in Afghanistan.

International Disputes   The country's leaders are disappointed with the flows of financial and material aid that the West has provided so far and the central government is frequently in danger of running out of money. The new government estimates that just training the armed forces will cost about US$135 million a year. Foreign donors will have to foot the bill and have generally been reluctant to do so. Altogether, foreign aid is suppose to amount to US$4.5 billion in 2002-2007, with US$1.8 billion being made available in 2002. The allies think they should have a considerable say over how this money is to be spent but the government has its own plans.

Economy   Any assessment of recent economic performance is necessarily tentative since the underlying information base is extremely weak. Estimates made early in 2001 placed Afghanistan's per capita income at about US$300, for a population of 23 million, giving an aggregate GDP of about US$6.9 billion. However, this is likely to have declined substantially during the past year. Current assessments of assistance start from the assumption of a per capita GDP of only US$200 in 2001. According to the latest available estimates, the bulk of national production consists of agriculture and forestry products (53%), followed by mining and light industry (28%), trade (8%) and construction (6%). Transport, communications and services account for the remaining 5%. These estimates exclude the illegal cultivation of poppy and the production of narcotics, which are known to be major sources of income.

Main Industries   Agriculture is the mainstay of the economy. Most Afghans used to be settled farmers, herders, or both. In more recent years, opium replaced wheat as the country's main crop. Recent information suggests that poppy cultivation fell significantly over most of 2001 but may have resumed in recent months. Meat and fruits are the other main products. Traditional production of food crops, primarily wheat and livestock products, has been severely affected by three consecutive years of drought, which has considerably reduced irrigation coverage. Agricultural production has also been affected by the shortage of quality seeds and fertilizers. The restoration of traditional agriculture and food security over the medium term will be difficult. Extensive mining clearing and rehabilitation of irrigation systems will have to be combined with mobile livestock extension, the rehabilitation of the road system and a policy regime that encourages traditional agriculture. Mining and light industry constitute the second major sector of the economy after agriculture. Among manufactured products, carpets, leather goods, and gold and silver jewellery are the main items. With the restoration of political and economic stability, production of these goods should recover fairly quickly. Afghanistan is believed to have substantial hydrocarbon reserves, both oil and gas, in the north. Exploration started in 1967 with collaboration from the former Soviet Union, but ended with the Soviet withdrawal in 1989. With the restoration of peace, prospects for the resumption of hydrocarbon exploration are good, as well as for the transit flow of oil and gas from the Central Asian republics to India and Pakistan, on the basis of foreign capital. The mining sector is also underdeveloped but has the most potential for growth. Afghanistan has silver, copper, iron, gold, chrome, lapis lazuli and talc.

Energy   Afghanistan's proven and probable natural gas reserves are estimated to be up to five trillion cubic feet. Production, however, has been declining since the mid-1970s. At its peak, Afghanistan supplied 70-90% of its natural gas output to the Soviet Union's gas grid. Now, all production is for domestic consumption. The country's power grid was virtually destroyed prior to the defeat of the Taliban. In the past, Afghanistan has received much of its electricity from Uzbekistan, but payment problems forced Uzbekistan to reduce power exports.

	1999	2000	2001
Inflation (% change)	12.0	15.3	
Exchange rate (per US$)	3,000.00	3,000.00	3,000.00
Interest rate			
GDP (% real growth)			
GDP			
GDP (US$ million)			
GDP per capita (US$)			
Consumption			
Consumption (US$ million)			
Consumption per capita (US$)			
Population, mid-year ('000)	21,353.8	21,923.5	22,420.6
Birth rate (per '000)	47.5	47.5	47.4
Death rate (per '000)	21.8	21.7	21.9
No. of households ('000)	4,289.7	4,479.2	4,464.2
Total exports (US$ million)	120.0	130.0	66.0
Total imports (US$ million)	380.0	450.0	512.0
Tourism receipts (US$ million)			
Tourist spending (US$ million)			

Average household size 2001 (persons)	4.95				
Urban population 2001 (%)	22.4				
Age analysis (%) (2001)	*0-14*	44.0	*15-64* 53.1	*65+*	2.9
Population by sex (%) (2001)	*Male*	51.3	*Female* 48.7		
Life expectancy (years) (2001)	*Male*	42.4	*Female* 42.9		
Infant mortality (deaths per '000 live births) (2001)	165.3				
Adult literacy (%) (1997)	34.7				

TRADING PARTNERS

Major export destinations 2001 (% share)

PAKISTAN	29.7
INDIA	13.9
GERMANY	8.2
FINLAND	7.9

Major import sources 2001 (% share)

PAKISTAN	20.0
SOUTH KOREA	14.1
KAZAKHSTAN	9.6
KENYA	7.0

Albania

Area (km^2) 28,750

Currency Lek (= 100 quindarka)

Location Albania is situated on the eastern Adriatic coast, with the former Yugoslavian provinces of Montenegro, Serbia and Macedonia marking its northern and eastern boundaries and with Greece to the south. Southern Albania faces the Greek island of Corfu across the Straits of Corfu. The climate is temperate and warm in summer with little rainfall. The capital is Tirana.

Head of State President Rexhep Mejdani

Head of Government Prime Minister Fatos Nano (2002)

Ruling Party The Social Democrats lead a coalition with three minor parties.

Political Structure Albania is run under an executive Presidency answerable to a 140-member People's Assembly elected by popular vote. The president is elected for a 5-year term by parliament. The People's Assembly has 155 members, elected for 4-year terms, 115 members in single-seat constituencies and 40 members elected through proportional representation.

Last Elections The Socialist Party took 42% of the vote and won 71 seats in the 140-member parliament in elections held in June/July 2001. Along with the seats won by their centre-left coalition partners, this was enough to allow the Socialists to remain in power. Ex-Prime Minister, Fatos Nano, returned to the office, replacing Ilir Meta in July 2002.

Political Risk Corruption is thought to be rife. Albania continues to have a bad reputation as a transit point for smuggled drugs, often imported from Kosovo, and for trafficking in illegal migrants. Weapons proliferation is a significant problem, following the war in Kosovo.

International Disputes Albania was due to start negotiations with the EU in 2002 on a "stability and association agreement" similar to the ones signed with Croatia and Macedonia, in the hope of eventually obtaining membership. Corruption issues within the government and other problems have forced a delay in the talks.

Economy Albania enjoyed growth of 7% in 2001. GDP is expected to increase by 6.5% in 2002 and 7% in 2003. Inflation was 3.1% in 2001 and should be about 3% in 2002 and 2003. Albania was Europe's poorest country for many years, but has been replaced by Moldova. The country now has the highest rate of growth in the Balkans, albeit from a low base. Albania's government has a genuine desire to create a market economy but has had to address other problems - crime and corruption - before coming to terms with the economic issues. Some of the recent growth is simply a rebound from the financial crisis in 1997, when half the public's savings were wiped out in a series of pyramid banking schemes. Grinding poverty is still pervasive; per capita GDP is no more than US$1,000, only about 8% of the level in neighbouring Greece. Despite these efforts, the black market continues to thrive. Albania's richest people are its drug barons and traffickers in human cargo.

Main Industries With the help of Western aid, the Albanians have modernised their main port at Durees. The government is still hoping to receive enough aid to build new electricity and rail links to Kosovo and Macedonia and to improve existing roads. The country's tiny tourist industry should show some growth over the next few years as more visitors seek out its unspoiled southern coast, which is only a short trip by boat from Corfu. Foreign investors are also beginning to return. They include a Greek-Norwegian consortium that has bought the country's first mobile-phone network. Most firms, however, are tiny and industry is continually plagued by power cuts. Remittances from the 500,000 Albanians, working abroad, mainly in Greece, is valued at US$500 million a year and is increasingly invested in small businesses rather than helping unemployed relatives at home. Albania possesses significant mineral resources, which include some of the world's richest deposits of chrome, molybdenum and copper, as well as nickel and limestone. A copper-mining concession has been bought by an American group. Agriculture is geared to meet domestic needs, with wheat, maize, potatoes and fruit being the main crops. Farm output rose, thanks to the almost total privatisation of agricultural land, where about 60% of the population live. Smuggling flourishes and is still probably one of the biggest income-earning activities.

Energy Albania has the second-largest amount of oil reserves in the Balkans, after Romania, and there is some international investment going into the country's energy projects. Exploration is active, but none of the new projects are producing yet. One foreign-operated field which is already in production expects initial peak production of 15,000 barrels per day (bbl/d). Albania presently imports more than half its modest energy needs.

	1999	2000	2001
Inflation (% change)	0.4	0.0	3.1
Exchange rate (per US$)	137.69	143.71	143.49
Interest rate (% per annum, lending rate)	21.6	22.1	19.7
GDP (% real growth)	7.3	7.8	7.0
GDP (Million units of national currency)	506,205.0	539,210.0	593,103.0
GDP (US$ million)	3,676.4	3,752.1	4,133.6
GDP per capita (US$)	1,079.1	1,091.8	1,191.3
Consumption (Million units of national currency)	329,801.2	357,188.2	409,692.3
Consumption (US$ million)	2,395.2	2,485.5	2,855.3
Consumption per capita (US$)	703.0	723.2	822.9
Population, mid-year ('000)	3,407.0	3,436.7	3,469.8
Birth rate (per '000)	20.1	19.4	18.7
Death rate (per '000)	5.5	5.4	5.4
No. of households ('000)	998.5	1,001.4	994.8
Total exports (US$ million)	352.0	261.0	294.0
Total imports (US$ million)	903.0	1,070.0	1,308.0
Tourism receipts (US$ million)	41.3	46.1	54.7
Tourist spending (US$ million)	10.3	10.5	9.6

Average household size 2001 (persons)	3.42				
Urban population 2001 (%)	42.2				
Age analysis (%) (2001)	*0-14*	31.9	*15-64*	61.9	*65+* 6.2
Population by sex (%) (2001)	*Male*	49.5	*Female*	50.5	
Life expectancy (years) (2001)	*Male*	70.7	*Female*	76.5	
Infant mortality (deaths per '000 live births) (2001)	25.7				
Adult literacy (%) (1997)	85.0				

TRADING PARTNERS

Major export destinations 2001 (% share)		Major import sources 2001 (% share)	
ITALY	66.8	ITALY	35.1
GREECE	16.8	GREECE	25.5
GERMANY	5.3	TURKEY	6.1
USA	2.3	GERMANY	5.4

■ **Algeria**

Area (km^2) 2,381,745

Currency Algerian dinar (= 100 centimes)

Location Algeria, one of the largest countries in Africa, occupies most of the western Mediterranean coast of North Africa, and faces Spain and Italy across the Mediterranean at a distance of no more than 150km. It is bordered to the west by Morocco and Mauritania, to the south by Mali and Niger, and to the east by Tunisia and Libya. The climate is warm and has a dry desert character. The capital is Algiers.

Head of State Abdelaziz Bouteflika (1999)

Head of Government Ali Benflis (2000) National Liberation Front (FLN)

Ruling Party The National Democratic Rally (RND) leads the government in a coalition with the FLN and several smaller parties.

Political Structure The president is elected for a 5-year term by the people. Parliament has two chambers. The National People's Assembly) has 380 members, elected for a 5-year term in multi-seat constituencies by proportional representation. Eight seats in the national assembly are reserved for Algerians abroad. The National Council has 144 members, 96 members elected by communal councils and 48 members appointed by the president.

Last Elections Presidential elections were held in April 1999 but six of the seven candidates withdrew, citing massive fraud. In that election, Bouteflika of the RND took 74% of the vote. Elections to the National Assembly were held in May 2002. The FLN won 199 seats while the RND took 47 seats. The Movement of the Society for Peace, an Islamic party, captured 39 seats with the remainder being scattered among several minor parties. All recent elections have been boycotted by the two Berber parties, the Front of Socialist Forces and Rally for Culture and Democracy.

Political Risk The government's popularity has sunk to a low level, with widespread allegations of corruption. The decade of violence that followed the army's cancellation of the 1992 election - which would have brought moderate Islamists to power - has left 150,000 dead. Meanwhile, Western governments are anxious to avoid an Islamic takeover of a country that provides 40% of Europe's natural gas needs. Approximately 70% of the population is under 30 years of age and official unemployment exceeds 30%. Algeria is gradually becoming two separate entities. In the heavily populated north, opposition to the government is strongest. In this Algeria, factories do not work, people are jobless and living standards deteriorate. The second Algeria is the oil- and gas-rich section, including the desert south, which is run by the oil companies.

International Disputes Algeria has been in conflict with Morocco (and initially Mauritania as well) over occupation of the Western Sahara territories which were controlled by Spain until 1976. In the past, Algerian terrorists were frequently charged with bombings in France and opposed their country's ties with Paris. The frequency of those attacks has declined sharply, however.

Economy GDP grew by 3.5% in 2001 while prices rose by 4.1%. Growth in 2002 is expected to be around 2.3% and improve to 3.4% in 2003. Inflation should be about 5.6% in 2002 and fall to 4.4% in 2003. The slightly higher rates of growth enjoyed in more recent years caused the country's foreign reserves to rebound sharply (to nearly US$18 billion by late 2001, compared to US$12 billion at the end of 2000). External debt fell to the lowest level in a decade and the current account balance has improved dramatically. Given the decline in oil prices, however, these positive trends are beginning to show signs of reversing, with a significant budget deficit, for instance, now expected in 2002. Continued economic, social and political problems for Algeria include: high unemployment (around 30%, and apparently rising, labour unrest; a large black market (possibly 20% of the country's GDP) and continued weakness in the non-oil economy. International authorities are urging the government to proceed with privatisation and banking reforms, while lowering tariffs aimed at protecting domestic industry and reducing dependence on hydrocarbons. In the meantime, the economy is plagued by state inefficiencies and corruption.

Main Industries Agriculture accounts for 12% of GDP with most farming being limited to the coastal regions where wheat, maize and sugar beet are grown. A severe drought hurt the agricultural sector in 2000, and massive flooding struck northern Algeria in November 2001, killing 800 and causing an estimated US$300 million in damage. Algeria remains highly dependent on oil and natural gas exports, which account for more than 90% of Algerian export earnings, and about 30% of GDP. The country also has a substantial petrochemical and fertiliser industry. There are a number of other downstream, oil-using industries, as well as plants producing steel, paper products, metal manufactures and even motor vehicles. Together, oil and gas revenues make up 60% of the state budget. Most non-oil industries are located in the northern part of the country. Few of these industries are profitable and most are operating with considerable excess capacity.

Energy Algeria is considered to be under-explored although significant oil and gas discoveries have been made over the last few years. The government hopes to increase crude oil production capacity significantly but that will require large amounts of foreign capital and expertise. The goal is to double the number of companies operating in Algeria by 2005. Official estimates of Algeria's proven oil reserves remain at 9.2 billion barrels but recent discoveries will push that figure upward. Algeria expects a sharp increase in crude oil exports due to a rapid shift towards domestic natural gas consumption and planned increases in oil production.

	1999	2000	2001
Inflation (% change)	2.6	0.3	4.1
Exchange rate (per US$)	66.57	75.26	77.22
Interest rate (% per annum, lending rate)	10.0	10.0	9.5
GDP (% real growth)	3.2	2.4	3.5
GDP (Billion units of national currency)	3,168.0	4,011.8	4,235.9
GDP (US$ million)	47,586.2	53,306.0	54,858.1
GDP per capita (US$)	1,606.3	1,775.2	1,805.4
Consumption (Billion units of national currency)	1,745.2	1,856.9	2,075.8
Consumption (US$ million)	26,215.1	24,672.8	26,883.5
Consumption per capita (US$)	884.9	821.6	884.8
Population, mid-year ('000)	29,625.3	30,028.7	30,385.1
Birth rate (per '000)	25.0	24.5	24.0
Death rate (per '000)	5.6	5.5	5.4
No. of households ('000)	4,542.2	4,638.9	4,732.0
Total exports (US$ million)	12,010.2	14,159.0	13,957.5
Total imports (US$ million)	8,676.9	10,681.0	12,435.0
Tourism receipts (US$ million)	21.0	20.2	28.0
Tourist spending (US$ million)	139.0	152.0	92.2

Average household size 2001 (persons)		6.47				
Urban population 2001 (%)		60.1				
Age analysis (%) (2001)	*0-14*	34.3	*15-64*	60.9	*65+*	4.9
Population by sex (%) (2001)	*Male*	51.4	*Female*	48.6		
Life expectancy (years) (2001)	*Male*	68.4	*Female*	71.4		
Infant mortality (deaths per '000 live births) (2001)		44.7				
Adult literacy (%) (1999)		60.2				

TRADING PARTNERS

Major export destinations 2001 (% share)

ITALY	21.8
FRANCE	13.9
SPAIN	13.2
USA	13.2

Major import sources 2001 (% share)

FRANCE	31.5
USA	9.6
ITALY	8.5
GERMANY	6.5

American Samoa

Area (km^2)   197

Currency   US dollar (US$ = 100 cents)

Location   American Samoa is a cluster of islands within the Samoan group, to the east of the state of Western Samoa. Apart from Tutuila, Tau, Aunu'u, Ofu, Olosega and Rose, American Samoa includes the more northerly Swain's Island, which is closer to Tokelau, a dependent territory of New Zealand. The climate is warm, with limited rainfall but occasional danger of cyclones. The capital is Pago Pago.

Head of State   President George W. Bush (2000)

Head of Government   Governor: Tauese P. Sunia (1996)

Ruling Party   None.

Political Structure   American Samoa is an unincorporated territory of the US, whose executive authority rests in the Governor, appointed for a 4-year term. The Legislature has two chambers. The House of Representatives has 21 members, elected for a 2-year term, 20 in single-seat constituencies and one by a public meeting on Swain's Island. The Senate has 18 members, elected for a 4-year term by and from the chiefs of the islands. One observer is sent to the US Congress in Washington.

Last Elections   Elections to the legislature were last held in November 2000 when only non-partisans were elected. In gubernatorial elections held at the same time, Tauese Sunia was re-elected with 51% of the vote.

Political Risk   With a modestly wealthy population and a stable political structure, American Samoa poses little risk to businesses and investors. However, the reorientation of US defence interests to focus on the war on terrorism and the Asian mainland raises some doubts that Washington will continue to provide the islands with aid over the longer term.

International Disputes   The island has no international disputes.

Economy   American Samoa is a traditional Polynesian economy where more than 90% of the land is communally owned. The islands are highly dependent on the US, which provides about a third of the government's budget. GDP should grow by no more than 1.5% in 2002. Unemployment is high - typically 15-16% and over half the population lives below the poverty line. American Samoa receives certain tax advantages and some immunity from US import restrictions. Average per capita income is about US$3,200 per year. Attempts by the government to develop a larger and broader economy are restrained by Samoa's remote location, its limited transportation and its devastating hurricanes. Tourism is a promising area for development but has been hurt first by the financial crisis in Asia and more recently by the slowdown in some parts of the world economy and the fears of terrorism.

Main Industries   Fishing - primarily tuna fishing and tuna canning - is the most important economic activity in American Samoa and the main source of income. Fishing operations employ a third of the workforce and account for more than 90% of exports, which are valued at US$250-300 million per annum. The main agricultural products are bananas, coconuts, vegetables, taro, breadfruit, yams, copra, pineapples and papayas; dairy farming is also important. There are two large American-owned canneries that comprise the greater part of the country's industrial base. With no natural mineral resources and limited scope for manufacturing exports, the country depends heavily on fishing and agriculture. Smallholders producing crops such as yams and pineapples own the greater part of the farmland. The tourist sector has also added a number of new hotels and hopes to attract more Japanese visitors.

Energy   American Samoa has at least twice as much generating capacity it actually needs at present. Apart from geothermal sources and natural resources such as timber, the country has ready access to oil supplies from the US.

	1999	2000	2001
Inflation (% change)	2.2	2.7	2.9
Exchange rate (per US$)	1.00	1.00	1.00
Interest rate			
GDP (% real growth)	1.3	2.5	1.8
GDP (Million units of national currency)	367.7	387.1	405.5
GDP (US$ million)	367.7	387.1	405.5
GDP per capita (US$)	5,571.2	5,692.2	5,631.4
Consumption (Million units of national currency)	247.5	249.7	263.1
Consumption (US$ million)	247.5	249.7	263.1
Consumption per capita (US$)	3,750.1	3,671.7	3,654.4
Population, mid-year ('000)	66.0	68.0	72.0
Birth rate (per '000)	27.5	27.2	27.0
Death rate (per '000)	3.8	3.7	3.7
No. of households ('000)	15.6	16.4	17.1
Total exports (US$ million)			
Total imports (US$ million)			
Tourism receipts (US$ million)			
Tourist spending (US$ million)	66.0	68.0	72.0

Average household size 2001 (persons)		4.15				
Urban population 2001 (%)		52.8				
Age analysis (%) (2001)	0-14	34.5	15-64	52.5	65+	13.0
Population by sex (%) (2001)	Male	51.6	Female	48.4		
Life expectancy (years) (2001)	Male	71.0	Female	80.1		
Infant mortality (deaths per '000 live births) (2001)		9.2				
Adult literacy (%)						

TRADING PARTNERS

Major export destinations 2001 (% share)		Major import sources 2001 (% share)	
AUSTRALIA	95.5	SOUTH KOREA	35.7
WESTERN SAMOA	2.6	AUSTRALIA	27.9
NEW ZEALAND	0.6	NEW ZEALAND	17.4
JAPAN	0.5	JAPAN	11.8

◼ Angola

Area (km^2) 1,246,700

Currency New kwanza (Kw = 100 lwei)

Location Angola lies on the western (Atlantic) coast of southern Africa. It is bounded in the south by Namibia, in the east and north by the Democratic Republic of the Congo (formerly Zaire), and in the east by Zambia. The capital is Luanda.

Head of State President José Eduardo dos Santos

Head of Government José Eduardo dos Santos

Ruling Party The People's Movement for the Liberation of Angola - Worker's Party (MPLA-PA) leads a coalition.

Political Structure After more than 21 years of armed conflict, virtually all national institutions have been destroyed. In 1998, dos Santos did away with the post of Prime Minister, creating a parallel ministry of defence within the office of the presidency and sacked a number of political figures who might have threatened his monopoly on power. In essence, the president is in total control of the government, though his forces have no influence whatsoever in the countryside.

Last Elections Elections were last held in October 1992, when the government of the ruling MPLA-PA faced competition for the first time from opposition parties. The MPLA-PA received more than 60% of the national vote - though much less in many rural areas. The UNITA rebels, who won the remaining 40%, denounced the result as a sham and reopened the war.

Political Risk Angola's savage civil war began back in the 1970s and finally appears to be winding down. In February 2002, the leader of the rebel forces known as UNITA, was shot dead and the rebel army began to unravel. Since 1990, the war has made more than three million Angolans homeless with hundreds of thousands more being killed. In March 2002, a peace agreement was signed between the government and UNITA; it appeared to hold in the ensuing months.

International Disputes Angola has seen two UN-sponsored "peace processes" collapse in the past ten years. Cynics reserve judgements about the new developments. In the meantime, the UN maintains its sanctions.

Economy GDP grew at the relatively modest pace of 3.2% in 2001 while Angola experienced one of the highest rates of inflation in the world - 153%. Even if the war is over, rebuilding Angola will be arduous. The country's fields are mined, its buildings have been blasted to rubble and its people have struggled so long to avoid being killed that they have had little chance to learn the skills that the country so desperately needs. There are few jobs in Angola and even fewer that pay better than pillage. Both the ex-guerrillas and the government's own soldiers still live by looting, often with the approval of commanders who do not wish to pay them. Angola is potentially one of the richest countries in southern Africa but civil war and economic mismanagement have now made it one of the poorest on the continent. More than three quarters of the population live below the poverty line. The situation is worst in Luanda, which has become home to over 40% of Angolans as a result of wartime displacement.

Main Industries Angola is the second largest oil producer in sub-Saharan Africa after Nigeria. Most of this oil comes from offshore fields. A number of oil analysts believe that new discoveries could soon make the country Africa's leading producer. The economy is highly dependent on offshore oil which accounts for over 40% of GDP and as much as 90% (approximately US$3.5 billion annually) of government revenues. The sector has very few linkages to other sectors of the economy. The bulk of the country's oil earnings have been spent to fight the civil war but the government has kept the defence budget secret. Thus, little is known about what happens to a vast chunk of the US$3-5 billion a year that Angola receives in oil receipts. In times past, agriculture accounted for 12-15% of GDP and employed almost 60% of the workforce. For several years, however, the government has followed a policy of systematically emptying the countryside of people in order to starve UNITA into submission. In mid-2002, farming was carried out on no more than 2% of the country's land. Sporadic water supplies, yearly outbreaks of cholera and the abysmal condition of the roadways are other complications that have contributed to the sharp fall in agricultural output. In peacetime, bananas, coffee, palm products and timber are the sector's main exports while maize, cassava and potatoes are grown for domestic consumption.

Energy Angola is sub-Saharan Africa's second largest oil producer behind Nigeria, with the majority of its crude production located offshore. Crude reserves also are located onshore around the city of Soyo, offshore in the Kwanza Basin north of Luanda and offshore of the northern coast. Crude oil production averaged 746,000 barrels per day (bbl/d) in 2000 and the level is expected to rise in the future. The major foreign oil companies operating in Angola are ChevronTexaco, TotalFinaElf and ExxonMobil. Cabinda produces about 70% of Angola's oil and accounts for nearly all of its foreign exchange earnings. Political tensions are high in some areas of Cabinda as separatist groups demand a greater share of oil revenue There are plans to build a second refinery with most of its production being exported to regional markets.

	1999	2000	2001
Inflation (% change)	248.2	325.0	152.6
Exchange rate (per US$)	2.79	10.04	22.06
Interest rate (% per annum, lending rate)	80.3	103.2	96.0
GDP (% real growth)	3.3	3.0	3.2
GDP (Trillion units of national currency)		0.1	0.2
GDP (US$ million)	6,088.4	8,858.5	9,471.5
GDP per capita (US$)	484.2	687.9	697.7
Consumption			
Consumption (US$ million)			
Consumption per capita (US$)			
Population, mid-year ('000)	12,572.9	12,878.0	13,575.0
Birth rate (per '000)	51.1	51.2	51.2
Death rate (per '000)	19.8	19.6	19.3
No. of households ('000)	2,805.5	2,828.6	2,927.6
Total exports (US$ million)	5,344.0	6,275.0	7,008.9
Total imports (US$ million)	3,267.0	3,516.0	3,863.2
Tourism receipts (US$ million)	4.1	5.2	8.0
Tourist spending (US$ million)	31.3	60.3	53.1

Average household size 2001 (persons)	4.55				
Urban population 2001 (%)	34.7				
Age analysis (%) (2001)	*0-14*	47.6	*15-64*	49.6	*65+* 2.9
Population by sex (%) (2001)	*Male*	49.6	*Female*	50.4	
Life expectancy (years) (2001)	*Male*	44.2	*Female*	46.8	
Infant mortality (deaths per '000 live births) (2001)	119.9				
Adult literacy (%) (1997)	45.0				

TRADING PARTNERS

Major export destinations 2001 (% share)

USA	48.3
CHINA	10.6
FRANCE	9.8
BELGIUM	8.2

Major import sources 2001 (% share)

SOUTH KOREA	22.6
PORTUGAL	14.5
SOUTH AFRICA	12.3
USA	9.0

Anguilla

Area (km^2) 91

Currency East Caribbean dollar (EC$ = 100 cents)

Location Anguilla is located at the northern limit of the Leeward Islands group, north of St Kitts and to the east of the British Virgin Islands and Puerto Rico. The island is built on coral and is entirely low-lying. The climate is equable, with occasional threat from hurricanes. The capital is The Valley.

Head of State HM Queen Elizabeth II

Head of Government Osbourne Fleming (2000)

Ruling Party Anguilla National Alliance (ANA) and Anguilla Democratic Party (ADP) form a coalition.

Political Structure As a Dependent Territory of the UK, ultimate sovereignty rests with the British monarch, although in practice the Chief Minister governs. Until 1980, Anguilla was technically a part of St Christopher (St Kitts)/Nevis/Anguilla, but this proved to be an unhappy union and the Anguillans repudiated the St Kitts administration. The 1982 Constitution came into operation in May 1990. The House of Assembly has 11 members, 7 members elected for a 5-year term in single-seat constituencies, 2 ex officio members and 2 nominated members.

Last Elections General elections were held in March 2000. The Anguilla National Alliance won 3 seats, the ADP won 2 seats and the AUP took the remaining two seats.

Political Risk Despite its relatively low level of income, Anguilla is generally regarded as politically safe. However, the vulnerability of the climate to droughts and/or hurricanes has highlighted some potential for poverty-related unrest in the recent past.

International Disputes There are no international disputes.

Economy GDP is estimated to have risen by just 1.8% in 2001 while inflation was 2.8%. The economy grew very slowly for more than a decade. Each year more inhabitants leave the island in search of better jobs elsewhere. The government's priorities are to develop the services sector - mainly tourism and financial services. The number of visitors fell in 2001 but is expected to recover. The island's financial services sector faces numerous problems. Anguilla has few natural resources, and the economy depends heavily on high-class tourism, remittances from Anguillans employed in other countries and grants from the British Government.

Main Industries Anguilla's burgeoning tourist industry dominates the economy, eclipsing all traditional activities such as farming and fishing. Hotel construction drives the accompanying development of infrastructure. Farming is for subsistence purpose and consists mainly of small holdings. Productivity in this sector is very low. The agricultural products include peas, corn, sweet potatoes; sheep, goats, pigs, cattle and poultry. Major export crops are lobster, fish, livestock and salt. The island aspires to be a domicile for offshore banks, trusts and international business companies. However, problems of inadequate regulation and charges of money laundering have plagued the sector. The licences of all but one offshore bank have been cancelled.

Energy The bulk of Anguilla's energy derives from oil, most of it imported from Venezuela. Firewood and geothermal resources are other sources of fuel.

	1999	2000	2001
Inflation (% change)	2.1	2.5	2.8
Exchange rate (per US$)	2.70	2.70	2.69
Interest rate			
GDP (% real growth)	2.9	2.2	1.8
GDP (Million units of national currency)	174.4	182.7	190.2
GDP (US$ million)	64.6	67.7	70.8
GDP per capita (US$)	8,076.2	8,460.2	8,853.6
Consumption (Million units of national currency)	120.6	123.2	129.7
Consumption (US$ million)	44.7	45.6	48.3
Consumption per capita (US$)	5,581.9	5,706.0	6,037.0
Population, mid-year ('000)	8.0	8.0	8.0
Birth rate (per '000)	16.6	16.2	15.9
Death rate (per '000)	5.9	5.9	5.8
No. of households ('000)	1.3	1.4	1.4
Total exports (US$ million)			
Total imports (US$ million)			
Tourism receipts (US$ million)	58.2	61.1	51.6
Tourist spending (US$ million)			

Average household size 2001 (persons)		5.83			
Urban population 2001 (%)		12.3			
Age analysis (%) (2001)	*0-14*	30.2	*15-64* 63.0	*65+*	6.7
Population by sex (%) (2001)	*Male*	49.3	*Female* 50.7		
Life expectancy (years) (2001)	*Male*	73.5	*Female* 79.3		
Infant mortality (deaths per '000 live births) (2001)		18.7			
Adult literacy (%)					

▪ Antigua

Area (km²) 442

Currency East Caribbean dollar (EC$ = 100 cents)

Location Antigua, along with Barbuda (25 miles to Antigua's north) forms part of the Leeward Islands in the Eastern Caribbean. Also included in the Leeward Islands is the uninhabited islet of Redonda (25 miles southwest of Antigua). The capital is St John's.

Head of State HM Queen Elizabeth II

Head of Government Lester Bird

Ruling Party The Antigua Labour Party (ALP) leads the government.

Political Structure Antigua is a member of the British Commonwealth and the British monarch is the titular head of state. In practice, the Prime Minister appoints the British Governor. Legislative authority is vested in the 17-member parliament and a 17-member Senate (Upper House) which is appointed by the governor-general.

Last Elections In March 1999, elections to the 17-member House of Representatives resulted in another win for the ALP, which has held power since 1976. The ALP claimed 12 seats (up from 11 in the previous administration) while the opposition United National Democratic Party took 4 seats. The remaining seat went to the Barbuda People's Movement. Lester Bird was again named Prime Minister.

Political Risk Despite fairly high standards of living, the government has been plagued by periodic charges of corruption, money laundering and drug dealing. Most the accusations revolve around the Bird family and the ALP which, together, have dominated island politics (with one brief break) since the 1940s. A US government report warned that Antigua's government was under threat from wealthy individuals who had used their influence to weaken the island's money laundering and offshore business legislation. A British government report has uncovered links with Colombian drug dealers, and suspicious arms shipments were discovered in late 1998. These charges have fuelled the drive for separation on the part of Barbuda. The Barbudians maintain that in the original agreement with the UK the relationship would be reviewed after five years but that Antigua refuses to consider other arrangements.

International Disputes Antigua has frequently criticised for its lax banking regulations and has agreed to take additional measures against money laundering through its offshore financial sector.

Economy Antigua's economy contracted by 0.6% in 2001 while inflation was about 1%. Unemployment rose in 2001 and now exceeds 6%. In 2001, the central government's overall deficit is estimated to have risen to 12% of GDP, because of delays in implementing revenue measures and a boost in expenditures related to increased public employment and higher capital spending. However, the overall deficit of the consolidated public sector declined to 7.5% of GDP, reflecting efforts to improve the operating performance of public enterprises. The government is actively promoting its policy and social benefits and tax concessions to alleviate poverty. Critics argue that these policies are really intended to enrich supporters of the ALP and the Bird family. Investment in public projects is increasing rapidly, however.

Main Industries Tourism accounts for almost three quarters of GDP and is the driving force for the development of the country's infrastructure. The sector has ample capacity, but existing facilities require much refurbishment and other improvements in quality. The number of visitors fell markedly in 2001. Farming suffers from recurrent droughts and soil erosion. The agriculture sector's share of GDP is declining and in 2002 amounted to just over 5%. Sugar, maize, fruit and vegetables are grown for domestic consumption, and bananas and coconuts for export. The country also has considerable mineral resources, including limestone and clay, but these have never been developed, partly for environmental reasons. The financial services sector is small but growing. Despite the introduction of more stringent laws governing banking practices, the island is still suspected of money laundering and subject to much international pressure.

Energy Nearly all of Antigua's energy needs are met through imports. Oil from Venezuela is refined in Trinidad and Tobago and then supplied to Antigua. There are opportunities to develop geothermal energy but little capital is available for development.

	1999	2000	2001
Inflation (% change)	1.6	2.0	1.0
Exchange rate (per US$)	2.70	2.70	2.70
Interest rate (% per annum, lending rate)	12.1	11.4	11.5
GDP (% real growth)	3.2	2.5	-0.6
GDP (Million units of national currency)	1,758.1	1,786.6	1,788.0
GDP (US$ million)	651.1	661.7	662.2
GDP per capita (US$)	9,718.4	9,730.8	9,460.3
Consumption (Million units of national currency)	711.3	780.1	785.4
Consumption (US$ million)	263.4	288.9	290.9
Consumption per capita (US$)	3,931.7	4,248.8	4,155.5
Population, mid-year ('000)	67.0	68.0	70.0
Birth rate (per '000)	16.9	16.5	16.2
Death rate (per '000)	5.9	5.9	5.9
No. of households ('000)	20.4	20.5	20.6
Total exports (US$ million)	37.8	47.8	52.3
Total imports (US$ million)	414.1	435.6	419.3
Tourism receipts (US$ million)	291.5	312.1	271.8
Tourist spending (US$ million)			

Average household size 2001 (persons)		3.32				
Urban population 2001 (%)		37.1				
Age analysis (%) (2001)	*0-14*	30.2	*15-64*	63.0	*65+*	6.7
Population by sex (%) (2001)	*Male*	49.2	*Female*	50.8		
Life expectancy (years)						
Infant mortality (deaths per '000 live births) (2001)		19.0				
Adult literacy (%)						

TRADING PARTNERS

Major export destinations 2001 (% share)

GERMANY	54.9
FRANCE	35.9
SPAIN	2.2
UNITED KINGDOM	1.4

Major import sources 2001 (% share)

FRANCE	21.9
USA	17.3
POLAND	10.0
DENMARK	8.4

■ Argentina

Area (km^2) 2,777,815

Currency Peso argentino (P = 100 centavos = 10,000 australes)

Location Argentina is the second largest state in South America and occupies most of the continent south of the Tropic of Capricorn and east of the Andes. With its only coastline facing the Atlantic, Argentina's terrain varies from the vast prairies of the north to the mountains of the east and the sub-Antarctic south. The capital is Buenos Aires.

Head of State Eduardo Duhalde (2002)

Head of Government Eduardo Duhalde (2002)

Ruling Party The government is led by the Justicialist Party (JP).

Political Structure A new constitution was introduced in August 1994 which effectively cemented the country's departure from the military system that ran the country in the 1960s and 1970s. Argentina comprises a Federal District, 23 provinces and the National Territory of Tierra del Fuego, all of which enjoy varying degrees of autonomy. The executive president is elected every six years, answering to a 257-seat Chamber of Deputies and a 72-seat Senate.

Last Elections Parliamentary elections were held in October 2001. In the Chamber of Deputies the JP won 116 seats, the Alliance took 88 seats and the Alternative for a Republic of Equals received 17 seats. The remainder were spread among smaller parties. In the Senate, the JP won 40 seats and the Alliance won 21 seats. Other seats were dispersed among several parties.

Political Risk Duhalde was chosen as an unelected president after riots toppled Fernando de la Rua and ended Argentina's decade-long policy of fixed exchange rates. Now, Duhalde, himself, has called for early elections. Negotiations with the IMF continue to drag on as the economy slips closer to economic disaster. Few, if any countries have ever faced such a complete economic collapse as could befall Argentina.

International Disputes Argentina's relations with the US have become strained since the collapse of the exchange rate. Argentinian politicians see Washington as uninterested and unwilling to offer constructive assistance. Relations with the UK are much improved since the Falklands war, while Argentina has settled its 150-year-old dispute with Chile over three islands in the far south (Picton, Lennox and Nueva).

Economy Real GDP contracted by 3.7% in 2001 and is expected to decline by another 12.5% in 2002 before the recession ends. In 2003, the economy should grow by about 1.5%. Prices fell by 1% in 2001 but expected to rise by nearly 27% in 2002. In 2003, the rate of inflation is forecast to rise even further to 32.5%. The government's failure to implement any of the reforms wanted by international institutions has exasperated lenders. The most crucial of these proposed reforms are the repeal of two populist anti-bank laws, and especially, strict measures to cut public spending that are mainly aimed at provincial governors. Duhalde has argued that these moves would entail, among other consequences, the sacking of 400,000 public employees in the provinces. The result, if this is true, would make it impossible to get any support in Congress. What is clear is that the government has failed to tackle the country's near-fatal fiscal weaknesses. Argentina's tax system is inefficient and tax evasion is rampant. The country collects just 21% of GDP in taxes, while in Brazil the corresponding figure is 30%. Even worse, until 2001 the country operated under a system created 150 years ago which guaranteed the provinces an automatic share of revenues collected by the central government. By the end of 2001, these and other miscalculations led to a run on the country's banks. Argentinians withdrew around US$15 billion from local banks. To save many banks, the government was forced to limit cash withdrawals. That move, however, dealt a deadly blow to the informal service economy which operates purely on cash. The situation remains far too confused for economists to speculate about the length of time needed for the country to recover. Once the exchange rate is stabilised, Argentinians will certainly repatriate some of the US$100 billion or more they have moved abroad. Restoring public trust in government will take much longer, however. Argentina's long-standing fiscal weaknesses must be fixed and the banking system must be repaired.

Main Industries In comparison with other parts of the economy, agricultural output has remained buoyant with good harvests for both wheat and maize. The country's favourable climate and fertile soils have traditionally made Argentina a leading agricultural power. However, the sector has been squeezed by lower international prices, higher domestic costs and the collapse of the banking system at home. A third of local farmers have gone broke, while the rest have accumulated total debt of around US$10 billion. In manufacturing, the Argentinian auto sector is a key player but is heavily dependent on the Brazilian market for exports. Automobile exports were just beginning to recover from a sharp fall in foreign demand in 2001 but have now begun to fall once again. Tourism generates US$4 billion per year in foreign exchange. While that is roughly 15% of the country's total exports, it is still a decline from the US$5 billion earned as recently as 1998.

Energy Argentina has around 3.1 billion barrels of proven oil reserves and is the region's fourth largest oil producer, behind Venezuela, Mexico and Brazil. The country is also the region's third largest oil consumer, after Mexico and Brazil. Argentina's production increased rapidly throughout the 1990s, allowing exports to grow from negligible levels in the 1980s to exceed 400,000 barrels per day in the late 1990s. Although the country is widely considered to be too mature to offer significant exploration potential, there are opportunities for further development of existing reserves. Most of Argentina's oil is produced in two onshore basins, Neuquén in western Argentina, and Golfo San Jorge in the southeast. A new hydrocarbons law is expected to make Argentina's oil and gas sectors more attractive to international companies. The law will increase the regulatory power of provincial governments, shifting power away from the central government in Buenos Aires.

	1999	2000	2001
Inflation (% change)	-1.2	-0.9	-1.1
Exchange rate (per US$)	1.00	1.00	1.00
Interest rate (% per annum, lending rate)	11.0	11.1	27.7
GDP (% real growth)	-3.4	-0.8	-3.7
GDP (Million units of national currency)	283,523.0	284,204.0	269,477.0
GDP (US$ million)	283,664.8	284,346.2	269,611.8
GDP per capita (US$)	7,852.3	7,773.6	7,280.5
Consumption (Million units of national currency)	193,570.9	192,294.0	181,262.2
Consumption (US$ million)	193,667.7	192,390.2	181,352.9
Consumption per capita (US$)	5,361.1	5,259.7	4,897.2
Population, mid-year ('000)	36,124.9	36,578.4	37,031.8
Birth rate (per '000)	19.6	19.4	19.2
Death rate (per '000)	7.9	7.8	7.8
No. of households ('000)	10,028.2	10,142.9	10,257.6
Total exports (US$ million)	23,333.0	26,409.0	26,655.0
Total imports (US$ million)	25,508.0	25,243.0	20,311.0
Tourism receipts (US$ million)	4,990.5	4,922.5	4,252.6
Tourist spending (US$ million)	4,107.0	2,332.8	1,718.6

Average household size 2001 (persons)	3.61				
Urban population 2001 (%)	89.6				
Age analysis (%) (2001)	*0-14*	27.6	*15-64*	62.7	*65+* 9.7
Population by sex (%) (2001)	*Male*	49.0	*Female*	51.0	
Life expectancy (years) (2001)	*Male*	70.4	*Female*	77.5	
Infant mortality (deaths per '000 live births) (2001)	20.5				
Adult literacy (%) (1998)	96.5				

TRADING PARTNERS

Major export destinations 2001 (% share)   **Major import sources 2001 (% share)**

BRAZIL	26.4	BRAZIL	31.2
USA	10.4	USA	18.2
CHILE	10.3	GERMANY	4.7
SPAIN	3.8	ITALY	3.8

▦ Armenia

Area (km^2) 29,800

Currency Dram (= 100 luma)

Location Geographically, the Republic of Armenia occupies the southwestern sector of the land mass known as Transcaucasia, and borders Turkey and Iran in the south; politically, it spans the gulf between the former Soviet Union and the Islamic states of the Middle East. Armenia was formed as a protective haven for members of the Armenian church from all parts of the region. The capital is Yerevan.

Head of State President Robert Kocharian (1998)

Head of Government Andranik Markaryan (2000)

Ruling Party The government is formed by a coalition of minority parties and non-partisans.

Political Structure Armenia declared its unilateral independence from the Soviet Union in 1990, a decision confirmed by a national referendum later that year when 94% voted in favour. Armenia's executive President is elected by popular vote and serves a 4-year term. The National Assembly has 131 members, elected for a 4-year term.

Last Elections In parliamentary elections held in May 1999, the opposition Unity bloc claimed a surprisingly large share of the vote (42%). Presidential elections held in March 1998 gave the presidency to the country's standing Prime Minister, Robert Kocharian, despite the strong showing of Armenia's former Communist Party. Kocharian took 61% of the vote, compared to 39% for his rival. Western observers expressed doubts about the accuracy of the result but refrained from lodging any serious objections.

Political Risk If Armenia's long-standing dispute with Azerbaijan can be resolved, the prospects of stability should improve greatly. For the time being, Armenia's transport links and borders cannot be regarded as secure but the outlines of the tentative agreement would address this problem. Kocharian engineered the downfall of his predecessor, Ter-Petrosian, precisely because the latter suggested that Armenia might be flexible on some of the issues in dispute with Azerbaijan.

International Disputes Armenia's dispute with neighbouring Azerbaijan over the sovereignty of Nagorno-Karabakh has still not been resolved despite US efforts. However, the Armenians have agreed to give Azerbaijan back six of the seven regions they captured. Nagorno-Karabakh and the adjacent Lachin region that links it to Armenia would be granted self-governing status. Azerbaijan would be compensated with an international protected road, linking it to Nakhichevan. Armenia has uneasy relations with Turkey, where ethnic Armenian militants seek the creation of their own Armenian state.

Economy GDP grew by 7.5% in 2001 and is forecast to increase by 6% in both 2002 and 2003. Inflation was 3.4% in 2001 and should fall to 3% in 2002 and 2003. In more recent years, Armenia has begun a slow recovery following the collapse of the Soviet Union and the effects of Armenia's 6-year war with Azerbaijan over Nagorno-Karabakh. The country's unemployment rate dropped from 11.7% in 2000 to 10.5% in 2001. Armenia's small- and medium-sized enterprises, most of which have already been privatised, are the main sources of much of the country's economic growth. At its current growth rate, by 2005, Armenia's absolute GDP will reach the same level as in 1991, the year that the Soviet Union and its central economic planning system collapsed. Armenia's new 3-year economic programme for 2001-2003 focuses on policies that would reduce fiscal vulnerabilities and ensure sustained and rapid economic growth as the cornerstone for its efforts to combat poverty. Under the programme, the gross official reserves of the central bank will be maintained at around three and a half months of imports. The external position is expected to strengthen due to foreign direct investment in the export sector, production by new or newly privatised firms, and anticipated private inflows.

Main Industries Agriculture accounts for about a third of GDP and is the backbone of the Armenian economy. Farmers produce grain, sugar beet, potatoes and other vegetables, as well as grapes and other fruit. Cattle, sheep and pigs are the main forms of livestock. Industry accounts for another 32% of GDP. Traditionally, most operations in this sector have been under the control of the state but the number of privately-owned farms now exceeds state-run farms, thanks to the government's privatisation programme which is showing results. In industry, over 70% of large enterprises and 80% of small enterprises have been privatised. The government has also imposed a system to monitor the financial operation of state-owned firms on a regular basis. Industrial activity is limited to basic manufactures and suffers from power shortages. There is a 4-year economic programme aimed at modernising decaying infrastructure, refurbishing electric power plants and generally reforming the economy in a market-oriented direction. Armenia is a member (along with Albania, Azerbaijan, Bulgaria, Georgia, Greece, Moldova, Romania, Russia, Turkey and Ukraine) of the Black Sea Economic Cooperation, or BSEC. The group has set up a Black Sea and Balkan regional economic centre to help coordinate energy strategies, such as finding the best locations for pipelines through the region.

Energy Armenia has no oil production and is completely dependent on imports of refined products. Since there are no petroleum product pipelines into the country, all imports must be transported either by railcars or trucks. Most of Armenia's estimated 13,000 barrels per day in petroleum product imports comes from Georgia. The country's hopes of becoming an important part of an energy trans-shipment system are opposed by Azerbaijan and Turkey. Because Armenia does not expect to benefit substantially from the east-west pipelines that are in development, it is cultivating closer ties with Iran in order to diversify its energy sources. In addition, Armenia and Iran are developing a natural gas pipeline to connect the two countries, with the pipeline possibly continuing further northwards to connect to Georgia and then to the Russian pipeline system.

	1999	2000	2001
Inflation (% change)	0.7	-0.8	2.9
Exchange rate (per US$)	535.06	539.53	555.08
Interest rate (% per annum, lending rate)	38.8	31.6	26.7
GDP (% real growth)	3.3	6.0	7.5
GDP (Billion units of national currency)	987.1	1,035.9	1,174.0
GDP (US$ million)	1,844.9	1,920.0	2,115.0
GDP per capita (US$)	485.1	504.1	554.8
Consumption (Billion units of national currency)	951.6	985.8	1,107.6
Consumption (US$ million)	1,778.4	1,827.2	1,995.4
Consumption per capita (US$)	467.6	479.7	523.4
Population, mid-year ('000)	3,802.9	3,808.8	3,812.3
Birth rate (per '000)	10.7	10.4	10.1
Death rate (per '000)	7.3	7.4	7.4
No. of households ('000)	757.8	772.8	788.1
Total exports (US$ million)	929.2	1,745.0	2,460.0
Total imports (US$ million)	799.7	881.9	890.0
Tourism receipts (US$ million)	7.6	8.3	7.8
Tourist spending (US$ million)	34.0	37.8	44.9

Average household size 2001 (persons)	4.93					
Urban population 2001 (%)	70.3					
Age analysis (%) (2001)	*0-14*	23.9	*15-64*	66.8	*65+*	9.3
Population by sex (%) (2001)	*Male*	48.6	*Female*	51.4		
Life expectancy (years) (2001)	*Male*	70.0	*Female*	76.0		
Infant mortality (deaths per '000 live births) (2001)	15.7					
Adult literacy (%) (1997)	98.8					

TRADING PARTNERS

Major export destinations 2001 (% share)		Major import sources 2001 (% share)	
RUSSIA	18.0	IRAN	12.3
BELGIUM	12.2	RUSSIA	9.2
USA	12.2	USA	7.6
IRAN	11.7	BELGIUM	7.2

Aruba

Area (km²) 193

Currency Aruban guilder

Location Aruba is located in the Leeward Islands chain within the Caribbean Sea, about 70km west of Curacao, the capital island of the Netherlands Antilles and no more than 30km north of the Venezuelan coast. The country enjoys a warm tropical climate, with relatively little susceptibility to hurricanes. The capital is Oranjestad.

Head of State HM Queen Beatrix (Netherlands)

Head of Government Nelson Oduber (2001)

Ruling Party The government is formed by People's Electoral Movement (MEP).

Political Structure Aruba is an overseas territory of the Netherlands. It was formerly part of the Netherlands Antilles but became a separate political entity in January 1986. In 1990, Aruba requested and received from the Netherlands cancellation of the agreement that would have automatically given independence to the island in 1996. The Parliament has 21 members, elected for 4-year terms by proportional representation. The prime minister and deputy prime minister are elected by parliament for 4-year terms.

Last Elections Parliamentary elections were held in September 2001. The MEP took 12 seats while the Aruban People's Party won 6 seats. Smaller parties won the remainder.

Political Risk Aruba has one of the highest per capita incomes in the Caribbean region, but the island's delicate balance of political power remains a source of concern.

International Disputes Relations with the Netherlands Antilles have been strained since Aruba became a separate entity within the Dutch empire. The Netherlands Antilles once derived considerable revenues from Aruba's tourism activity and its economy has suffered since the breakaway.

Economy GDP rose by 1.5% in 2001 while inflation was 2.9%. Since beginning its operations in 1986, the Central Bank of Aruba has successfully preserved the fixed exchange rate to the U.S. dollar - its primary monetary policy objective - supported by a strong foreign reserve position. However, despite efforts to liberalise the monetary policy framework, the array of policy instruments has remained essentially limited to credit limits, moral persuasion and liquidity reserve requirements. In 2001, the public deficit widen to about 2.5% of GDP, reflecting the cost of the universal coverage health system introduced in January 2001, increased public employment and subdued revenue as the tax windfall from the temporary measures fades away. Growth remains constrained by the island's small labour force. Unemployment is less than 1% and there are many unfilled jobs, despite sharp rises in wage rates in recent years. The tourism sector provided the main impetus for growth in the past, but officials are now trying to control the pace of the sector's development. The island has one of the highest per capita incomes in the Caribbean region, thanks mainly to its oil activities. Meanwhile, the scope for developing the financial services sector has been limited by bilateral agreements with the US designed to prevent tax evasion. In the future, economic growth in Aruba will depend on increased capacity utilisation and moves to further upgrade the quality of tourism.

Main Industries The island's small agricultural sector produces aloes and raises livestock. Fishing also generates some income but the land is poorly adapted to farming. Tourism is a major earner of income and provides most employment opportunities. Offshore banking and oil refining and storage are the other mainstays of the economy. The island hosts large numbers of visitors from the Netherlands, the US, Venezuela, Canada and other Caribbean countries. The rapid growth of the tourism sector over the last decade has had positive spillover effects for other parts of the economy. Construction has boomed, with hotel capacity rising many fold. Officials would like to slow growth of the tourist sector because it is putting great strains on social services and other parts of the economy. The island has no fresh water supplies and every litre has to be imported.

Energy Aruba has no oil deposits but does have some of the largest oil refining capacity in the Caribbean as well as substantial storage capacity. The bulk of the country's oil supplies come from other islands in the Netherlands Antilles group.

	1999	2000	2001
Inflation (% change)	2.3	4.0	2.9
Exchange rate (per US$)	1.79	1.79	1.79
Interest rate (% per annum, lending rate)	13.1	12.1	12.1
GDP (% real growth)	1.9	2.6	1.5
GDP (Million units of national currency)	1,597.3	1,679.3	1,753.4
GDP (US$ million)	892.3	938.1	979.6
GDP per capita (US$)	9,105.4	9,108.2	8,824.8
Consumption (Million units of national currency)	1,073.6	1,112.7	1,154.7
Consumption (US$ million)	599.8	621.6	645.1
Consumption per capita (US$)	6,120.2	6,035.3	5,811.5
Population, mid-year ('000)	98.0	103.0	111.0
Birth rate (per '000)	13.5	13.2	12.8
Death rate (per '000)	6.1	6.1	6.1
No. of households ('000)	19.2	20.6	22.0
Total exports (US$ million)	29.2	25.8	29.8
Total imports (US$ million)	782.1	802.6	784.6
Tourism receipts (US$ million)	782.0	773.3	688.5
Tourist spending (US$ million)	122.0	143.8	160.9

Average household size 2001 (persons)	5.01					
Urban population (%)						
Age analysis (%) (2001)	*0-14*	30.2	*15-64*	63.0	*65+*	6.7
Population by sex (%) (2001)	*Male*	49.4	*Female*	50.6		
Life expectancy (years) (2001)	*Male*	75.3	*Female*	82.1		
Infant mortality (deaths per '000 live births) (2001)	5.3					
Adult literacy (%)						

TRADING PARTNERS

Major export destinations 2001 (% share)		Major import sources 2001 (% share)	
COLOMBIA	28.8	NETHERLANDS	11.4
NETHERLANDS	25.3	UNITED KINGDOM	6.8
PANAMA	20.4	NETHERLANDS ANTILLES	3.2
VENEZUELA	8.7	VENEZUELA	2.8

Australia

Area (km^2)   7,682,300

Currency   Australian dollar (A$ = 100 cents)

Location   Some 3,680km from its eastern tip to its western extreme, Australia is the world's second largest island. The country lies about 1,000km from New Zealand, and about 500km south of Indonesia. Thus its climate ranges from the subtropical in the north to the significantly colder regions of the south. The capital is Canberra.

Head of State   HM Queen Elizabeth II

Head of Government   John Howard (1996)

Ruling Party   The Liberal Party (LP) leads a coalition with the National Party (NP).

Political Structure   Australia is a federation of six states and two territories (Northern Territory and Capital Territory of Canberra), each of which exercises considerable autonomy over its own affairs. The country's central affairs are run by a Cabinet which answers to a 148-member House of Representatives, elected for a term of three years, and an elected 76-member Senate with 12 seats drawn from the various parliaments of the states and territories. The question of Australia's status in the Commonwealth emerged as a key issue during the previous administration but in November 1999, Australians voted to retain its membership, with Queen Elizabeth as their head of state.

Last Elections   Elections to the House of Representatives took place in November 2001. The LP won 68 seats, the Australian Labour Party (ALP) took 65 seats and the NP won 13 seats. The remainder were spread among smaller parties. Elections to the Senate occurred at the same time and the ALP claimed 28 seats while the ruling coalition took 34 seats. Smaller parties won the remainder. Howard, the leader of the coalition, was re-appointed as prime minister.

Political Risk   After years of acrimonious debate about reforming the tax schedule and labour market, Australians have belatedly recognised that they face some equally serious problems as a result of their country's ageing population. A report released by the government in 2002 warns that over the next 20 years "new sources of labour will dry up". A low birth rate combined with the impending retirement of baby boomers is the source of the problem. The government has failed to achieve a long sought reconciliation with its indigenous people. Relations between the white and aboriginal communities are very tense and there is a heated debate among minority leaders about the effects of welfare benefits. Support for a formal treaty between indigenous and non-indigenous Australians is growing slowly but this issue will not be resolved for several years.

International Disputes   Relations with Indonesia are strained because the latter country acts as a transit point for illegal immigrants and asylum-seekers destined for Australia. These tensions will gradually be repaired but Canberra is unlikely to re-establish the very close relations with Jakarta that it maintained in the 1990s. Australia's relations with Papua New Guinea have often been tense but appear to be improving now that the situations in East Timor and Bougainville are being resolved. The country's greatest fear is a refugee exodus from one of the trouble spots or from Indonesia itself. Canberra also contests a compensation claim by Nauru, in respect of allegations that it stripped that country of its phosphate reserves without making provision for any secondary economic activity there.

Economy   Real GDP grew by 2.4% in 2001 and should increase by 3.9% in 2002. Growth is forecast to be 4% in 2003. Meanwhile, inflation was 4.4% in 2001 and will fall to 2.3% in both 2002 and 2003. Business investment is expected to be the main driver over the next couple of year. The investment impetus, however, will begin to wane by 2004. The economic upswing in recent years has been accompanied by solid employment gains and a substantial reduction in unemployment to a low of 6%, which is near to the OECD estimate of the structural unemployment rate. Over the medium term, efforts to raise the rate of national savings must receive the highest priority. The government is likely to push for significant fiscal consolidation and measures to promote private saving in order to reduce the dependence on foreign capital. Public saving may also have to be cut back in view of the long-term pressures on the budget from the ageing of the population.

Main Industries   The structure of the Australian economy changed dramatically during the country's long period of high growth. The main result of this development has been a marked fall in the share of the manufacturing sector of GDP. Finance, business services and communications are believed to account for up to a third of total economic growth experienced over the 10 years to 2001. Traditionally, growth has been driven primarily by domestic demand but there appears to have been a marked slowdown in this component since the turn of the 21st Century. Meanwhile, the manufacturing sector continues to move from the processing of agricultural and mineral raw materials into more sophisticated types of products and markets. Despite this economic transformation, Australia continues to be one of the world's major producers of commodities. A large agricultural sector specialises in wheat and sheep rearing, and together, these two activities account for more than half of the sector's export revenues. Australia also has vast amounts of natural resources. It has approximately 30% of the world's recoverable uranium and is a major producer of copper, iron ore, manganese, nickel, lead, limestone and gemstones. In addition, Australia is a major player in world energy markets.

Energy   Australia is a significant energy producer, and one of the few OECD countries that is a net energy exporter. Coal is Australia's largest export commodity, and accounts for 44% of the country's total energy needs. Australia is also a net exporter of natural gas. However, the country is becoming increasingly dependent upon foreign oil. A rapidly expanding economy and declining domestic oil production have led some observers to forecast an energy supply crisis in the decade from 2002-2011. In addition, stagnating foreign investment, an undersized natural gas market and difficulty transmitting electricity across the country have led the government, industry leaders and international observers to call for a new long-term energy strategy. Most of the country's 1.8 billion barrels of oil reserves are located offshore. It also has approximately 30% of the world's recoverable uranium.

	1999	2000	2001
Inflation (% change)	1.5	4.5	4.4
Exchange rate (per US$)	1.55	1.72	1.93
Interest rate (% per annum, lending rate)	7.5	8.8	8.1
GDP (% real growth)	4.8	3.2	2.4
GDP (Million units of national currency)	607,140.0	653,398.0	690,510.0
GDP (US$ million)	391,715.9	378,818.8	357,140.6
GDP per capita (US$)	20,913.4	19,973.0	18,617.8
Consumption (Million units of national currency)	369,859.0	396,102.7	416,469.6
Consumption (US$ million)	238,626.4	229,647.4	215,403.4
Consumption per capita (US$)	12,740.1	12,108.0	11,229.0
Population, mid-year ('000)	18,730.4	18,966.6	19,182.8
Birth rate (per '000)	13.2	13.0	12.9
Death rate (per '000)	7.2	7.3	7.3
No. of households ('000)	7,216.0	7,286.0	7,347.3
Total exports (US$ million)	56,079.5	63,870.4	63,386.7
Total imports (US$ million)	69,157.7	71,530.9	63,886.1
Tourism receipts (US$ million)	7,525.0	8,050.9	6,708.1
Tourist spending (US$ million)	5,792.0	5,259.8	4,344.2

Average household size 2001 (persons)	2.60				
Urban population 2001 (%)	84.7				
Age analysis (%) (2001)	*0-14*	20.4	*15-64*	67.3	*65+* 12.3
Population by sex (%) (2001)	*Male*	49.8	*Female*	50.2	
Life expectancy (years) (2001)	*Male*	76.3	*Female*	81.9	
Infant mortality (deaths per '000 live births) (2001)	5.0				
Adult literacy (%) (1997)	99.0				

TRADING PARTNERS

Major export destinations 2001 (% share)

JAPAN	19.3
USA	9.7
SOUTH KOREA	7.8
CHINA	6.2

Major import sources 2001 (% share)

USA	18.4
JAPAN	13.0
CHINA	8.8
GERMANY	5.7

Austria

Area (km^2)   83,855

Currency   Euro (= 100 cents)

Location   Austria occupies a strategic position in the centre of Western Europe, bordering on Germany and the Czech and Slovak Republics in the north, Italy and Slovenia in the south, and Switzerland in the west. The climate is temperate, but becomes very cold in winter because of the high altitude. The capital is Vienna.

Head of State   President Thomas Klestil (July 1998)

Head of Government   Wolfgang Schüssel (2000)

Ruling Party   The centre-right Austrian People's Party (ÖVP) leads a coalition with the right-wing Freedom Party (FPÖ).

Political Structure   The Republic of Austria was formed in 1955 following the end of the post-war administration by the Western allies. It consists of nine provinces, which have little autonomy. The country has a non-executive president who is elected every six years by popular vote, and a bicameral Federal Assembly with a 183-member Nationalrat and a 63-member Bundesrat, or Upper House. Both bodies are elected for four years at a time. Austria became a full member of the EU in January 1995.

Last Elections   Austria's "Grand Coalition" between the Social Democratic Party (SPÖ) and the ÖVP was finally dismantled in parliamentary elections held in 2000. Jorg Haider, the controversial leader of the FPÖ, is excluded from the new government but is thought to be very influential behind the scenes. Thomas Klestil, Austria's popular president, was re-elected to a second 6-year term in April 1998.

Political Risk   Austria controls more than a third of the EU's external borders with countries seeking EU membership. No country will benefit more from the opportunities of enlargement. However, no other country will be affected to the same extent by the potential problems of immigration. Austria is home to Europe's most successful far right-wing leader. Jorg Haider and his Freedom Party have been campaigning for the far right for a number of years. Haider's support has ranged from 22-27% over the past 10 years. Currently, the Freedom Party (though not Haider) is part of the ruling coalition. Haider's Nazi ties and his outspoken opposition to immigrants, the EU and other causes have often led Austria into conflict with other EU members. A majority of Austrians are concerned about the growing numbers of immigrants in the country. Haider has exploited these fears but the issue is a much wider one in Austrian society. Opinion polls suggest that support for EU enlargement is closely tied to this issue. Vienna's East European allies are disappointed with the cautious approach.

International Disputes   Austria's disputes with the EU about the views of the country's right-wing minority partner in the coalition have been smoothed over. Austria has occasional disagreements which arise with the Italian authorities over the sovereignty of Trentino-Alto-Adige, a predominantly German-speaking part of Italy occupied by German and Austrian forces in the 1940s.

Economy   GDP grew by just 1% in 2001 but the rate should rise to 1.3% in 2002 and 2.9% in 2003. Inflation was 2.3% in 2001 and will fall to 1.8% in 2002 and 1.6% in 2003. So far, it appears that the economy has not yet embarked on a path of higher trend growth despite Austria's EU accession in 1995 and the fact that the market transition of Eastern European countries eliminated many entry barriers for Austrian exporters and importers. The growth of private consumption has slowed as consumer price inflation increased, mainly due to higher oil prices and the weakening of the exchange rate. Employment has continued to rise but at a decelerating rate with unemployment even increasing in 2001. Wide-ranging structural reforms announced by the government include putting the pension system on a fiscally sustainable base, increasing the efficiency of the public sector, tightening the targeting of social benefits, improving incentives in the labour market, opening network industries to competition and lifting the performance of the education system. Over the next few years, the government intends to address two broad problem areas in an effort to boost the country's growth potential. First, plans for budgetary consolidation have been delayed for too long, and a distortionary fiscal stop-and-go policy adopted instead. Similarly, the need for a significant public sector reform was deferred in the 1990s and must now be tackled. Secondly, Austria delayed reform of its regulatory framework. This decision was understandable, since the existing framework successfully supported high economic growth during earlier times of relatively modest structural change. However, reaping positive growth effects from increased international integration and more rapid technological change requires a more thorough reform in product and labour markets favouring market-determined outcomes and higher structural flexibility.

Main Industries   Austria's recent slowdown can be attributed in part to the performance of the tourist sector, which is the country's largest single industry and biggest foreign-exchange earner. The industry has been in decline as vacationers become richer and seek out more exotic locations. Because vacations in Austria are expensive, the country also loses out to other European sites. Tourism is trying to regroup by offering high-quality niche products, including elaborate new theme parks. Industry accounts for around 30% of GDP and benefits from a rate of capital investment that is one of the highest in the world. The sector also enjoyed one of the highest rates of productivity growth during the 1990s but this trend is going to slow in the 10 years to 2010. Agriculture makes up just 1% of GDP with farming activities being relatively inefficient and fragmented. The country's traditional industrial strengths are in engineering and metals - both of which are low growth, cyclical industries. Firms producing automated machine tools and automobile components are highly competitive in international markets but many other parts of the sector are not. An inefficient services sector accounts for a large share of GDP and has made modest gains in more recent years. However, further deregulation and liberalisation is badly needed.

Energy   Austria's energy sector is in the midst of a period of restructuring as the EU presses for full deregulation of the energy sector. Utilities, in particular, face enormous challenges if they are to fend off the interest of competitors. Both the oil and gas and the electricity sectors are too small to survive on their own in an open European market. The fear in Austria is that the local energy sector will be taken over by powerful German neighbours.

	1999	2000	2001
Inflation (% change)	0.9	1.1	1.1
Exchange rate (per US$)	0.94	1.09	1.12
Interest rate (% per annum, lending rate)	5.6	6.4	
GDP (% real growth)	2.8	3.0	1.0
GDP (Million units of national currency)	196,658.0	204,843.0	210,706.0
GDP (US$ million)	209,688.6	177,930.7	188,545.1
GDP per capita (US$)	25,938.6	22,001.2	23,298.7
Consumption (Million units of national currency)	113,135.7	119,459.0	1.0
Consumption (US$ million)	120,632.1	103,764.5	109,450.5
Consumption per capita (US$)	14,922.3	12,830.5	13,524.9
Population, mid-year ('000)	8,084.0	8,087.3	8,092.5
Birth rate (per '000)	9.5	9.1	8.7
Death rate (per '000)	10.0	10.0	10.0
No. of households ('000)	3,243.0	3,266.0	3,301.0
Total exports (US$ million)	64,107.0	64,296.1	66,651.7
Total imports (US$ million)	69,532.9	69,073.7	70,413.8
Tourism receipts (US$ million)	12,533.0	12,501.2	11,010.3
Tourist spending (US$ million)	9,803.0	11,217.7	11,049.8

Average household size 2001 (persons)	2.48				
Urban population 2001 (%)	64.8				
Age analysis (%) (2001)	*0-14*	16.7	*15-64*	67.8	*65+* 15.4
Population by sex (%) (2001)	*Male*	48.6	*Female*	51.4	
Life expectancy (years) (2001)	*Male*	75.2	*Female*	81.3	
Infant mortality (deaths per '000 live births) (2001)	5.0				
Adult literacy (%)					

TRADING PARTNERS

Major export destinations 2001 (% share)		Major import sources 2001 (% share)	
GERMANY	32.5	GERMANY	43.7
ITALY	8.9	ITALY	6.7
SWITZERLAND	5.2	HUNGARY	5.1
USA	5.1	NETHERLANDS	4.6

■ Azerbaijan

Area (km^2)   86,600

Currency   Manat (M = 100 gopik). The rouble is still in use, but is gradually being phased out.

Location   The Republic of Azerbaijan lies in the eastern Transcaucasian region, bordering the Caspian Sea from Grozny to Baku. It includes the autonomous provinces of Nagorny-Karabakh (mainly Armenian in character) and Nakhichevan, which was obtained from Iran recently. The capital is Baku.

Head of State   President Heidar Aliev (June 1993)

Head of Government   Artur Rasi-Zade (1996)

Ruling Party   Yeni Azerbaycan Partiyasi (YAP)

Political Structure   Azerbaijan was one of the last states to declare its independence from the Soviet Union. The move came in August 1991 and was later confirmed by a 99.6% vote in a referendum. The president is elected by the people for a 5-year term. The National Assembly has 125 members, 100 members elected for a 5-year term in single-seat constituencies and 25 members elected by proportional representation. In practice, Azerbaijan aligns itself more closely with Russia than do other countries in this volatile region.

Last Elections   Elections to the National Assembly took place in January 2001 and were dominated by members of the Yeni Azerbaycan Partiyasi (YAP), which took 75 seats. All the remaining seats were widely scattered among several parties. Aliev was first installed as president in 1993 after a military-backed coup.

Political Risk   Political dissent in Azerbaijan is vigorously suppressed. Violence and rebellion in the ethnically Armenian enclave of Nagorno-Karabakh and the Autonomous Region of Nakhichevan remain close to the surface but recent efforts to resolve the problems in these regions have reduced tensions. Azerbaijan entered into a Transcaucasus-EU Pact in 1996 that also includes Armenia and Georgia and is intended to help stabilise this explosive region. The Pact offers trade concessions and access to certain EU loans in return for democratic and economic reforms.

International Disputes   Continued uncertainty over the Caspian Sea's legal status is hindering oil and natural gas development. The Caspian Sea littoral states - Azerbaijan, Iran, Kazakhstan, Russia and Turkmenistan - thus far have failed to agree on a plan to divide up the sea's resources, including the oil-rich seabed. Azerbaijan, along with Russia and Kazakhstan, has advocated the establishment of maritime boundaries based on an equidistant division of the sea, but Iran and Turkmenistan disagree. There is more progress on Azerbaijan's dispute with neighbouring Armenia over the sovereignty of Nagorno-Karabakh. During US-sponsored meetings in April 2001, the Armenians agreed to give Azerbaijan back six of the seven regions they captured. Nagorno-Karabakh and the adjacent Lachin region that links it to Armenia would be granted self-governing status. Azerbaijan would be compensated with an international protected road, linking it to Nakhichevan. Azerbaijan remains wary of Russia, in part because of the military support Russia has extended to Armenia.

Economy   Azerbaijan's economy has performed impressively in the past two years with GDP, growing by 7.4% in 1999 and 11.1% in 2000. In the short term, growth is expected to remain strong. GDP is forecast to rise by 9% in 2001 and 8.5% in 2002 and 2003. Hyperinflation existed during the early 1990s but prices actually fell in 1999 by more than 8% and rose by just 1.8% in 2000. The outlook is for prices to rise by a mere 1.5% in 2001 and by 2.4% and 3.3% in 2002 and 2003, respectively. Domestic investment recovered in 2001. Foreign investment inflows (primarily in the oil and gas sector), which currently account for 56% of total gross domestic investment, are estimated to have climbed to about US$700 million during 2001. Despite strong economic growth and improved investment, there is no indication of improvement in the employment situation: unemployment is now estimated to have risen to 18%, because much of the economic growth has been in capital-intensive areas that create few jobs. Government revenues (excluding the State Oil Fund), which rose in nominal terms on account of the strong GDP growth, still fell short of budget targets. As a result, revenues relative to GDP declined to 18% in 2001 from 18.6% in the previous year. Foreign capital remained the major source of deficit financing.

Main Industries   Agricultural output increased by around 11% in 2001 because of higher grain production resulting from an expansion in the area under cultivation. The oil and gas sector is the most important part of the economy, accounting for almost 30% of GDP. It continued to grow only slowly, due mainly to a sluggish rise in production. Some major investment activities are expected to begin in 2002, which will help boost economic activity. They include the start of phase one of the full development of the Azeri-Chirag-Guneshi oil field and the construction of the Baku-Tbilisi-Erzurum gas pipeline. To promote non-oil trade activities, the government will likely allow a quicker depreciation of the manat. The backbone of the manufacturing sector is a number of heavy industries that were developed more than 20 years ago. The more important of these are steel, aluminium and cement. However, production has suffered badly as a result of the near-cessation of raw material supplies from other parts of the former Soviet Union. Baku, Azerbaijan's largest city and port, could become a major regional transportation and communications hub for the Trans-Caucasus and Central Asian republics.

Energy   Following Azerbaijan's independence in 1991, the country's oil production continued to decline, falling to 180,000 barrels per day in 1997. Yet, with Azerbaijan's 1.2 billion barrels of proven oil reserves, as well as enormous possible reserves in undeveloped offshore Caspian fields, international investors and multinational energy companies have been returning to the country. Since 1996, over US$4 billion has been invested in the country's oil sector. The government expects investment in the country's oil sector to surpass US$60 billion in the next few years. As a result of this inflow of capital, the country's decline in oil production has been halted. In 2001, Azerbaijan posted its fourth consecutive annual increase in its average oil production, as output rose to 311,200 barrels per day. Over 80% of Azerbaijan's oil production currently comes from offshore, with a significant percentage coming from a shallow-water section, located 60 miles off the Azeri coast.

	1999	2000	2001
Inflation (% change)	-8.5	1.8	1.5
Exchange rate (per US$)	4,120.17	4,474.15	4,656.58
Interest rate (% per annum, lending rate)	19.5	19.7	19.7
GDP (% real growth)	7.4	11.1	9.0
GDP (Billion units of national currency)	18,875.0	23,565.0	26,494.0
GDP (US$ million)	4,581.1	5,266.9	5,689.6
GDP per capita (US$)	573.6	654.7	701.7
Consumption (Billion units of national currency)	13,497.8	13,933.6	15,625.2
Consumption (US$ million)	3,276.0	3,114.3	3,355.5
Consumption per capita (US$)	410.2	387.1	413.9
Population, mid-year ('000)	7,986.8	8,045.3	8,108.0
Birth rate (per '000)	15.1	14.5	14.1
Death rate (per '000)	6.2	6.2	6.2
No. of households ('000)	1,553.4	1,560.9	1,556.3
Total exports (US$ million)	929.2	897.4	927.1
Total imports (US$ million)	1,360.0	1,390.0	1,725.0
Tourism receipts (US$ million)	81.0	109.2	119.7
Tourist spending (US$ million)	481.0	542.6	641.6

Average household size 2001 (persons)	5.15				
Urban population 2001 (%)	57.7				
Age analysis (%) (2001)	*0-14*	32.6	*15-64*	61.7	*65+* 5.7
Population by sex (%) (2001)	*Male*	49.0	*Female*	51.0	
Life expectancy (years) (2001)	*Male*	68.3	*Female*	75.2	
Infant mortality (deaths per '000 live births) (2001)	33.4				
Adult literacy (%) (1996)	99.6				

TRADING PARTNERS

Major export destinations 2001 (% share)		Major import sources 2001 (% share)	
ITALY	57.2	TURKEY	16.1
ISRAEL	7.1	RUSSIA	9.3
GEORGIA	4.5	GERMANY	5.8
SPAIN	4.4	USA	4.6

Bahamas

Area (km^2)   13,865

Currency   Bahamian dollar (B$ = 100 cents)

Location   The Bahamas are made up of some 700 islands in the Atlantic Ocean, of which 30 are inhabited. They extend from just off the coast of Florida (US) to within a short distance of Cuba and Haiti. The capital is Nassau.

Head of State   HM Queen Elizabeth II

Head of Government   Perry Christie (2002)

Ruling Party   The government is formed by the Progressive Liberal Party (PLP).

Political Structure   The Bahamas are an independent member of the British Commonwealth with a British-appointed governor-general who exercises only nominal powers. The Prime Minister and his Cabinet are answerable to a 40-member House of Assembly (Lower House of Parliament) and to a 16-member Senate. Elections to the House of Assembly are normally held every five years while members of the Senate are appointed.

Last Elections   Elections to the House of Assembly were held in May 2002. The PLP, led by Perry Christie, took 29 seats, the Free National Movement won 7 and the remainder went to non-partisans.

Political Risk   Native Bahamians are fearful of the continued influx of illegal immigrants. As many as 30,000 Haitians now live in the country illegally and their presence is placing great strains on the social system. Diseases such as AIDS and tuberculosis often remain unchecked because illegal immigrants fear going to the authorities. The high rate of violent crime is another serious problem.

International Disputes   The government is still contesting OECD pressures to open up its financial system to greater scrutiny by overseas tax authorities, arguing that it would be asked to agree to a greater degree of transparency than some OECD members. The country remains a major transhipment point for drugs.

Economy   GDP fell by 1% in 2001 while inflation was running at about 1%. The present administration's policy of gradual fiscal consolidation has been a key factor in turning the economy around. The deficit of the central government narrowed from over 3% of GDP in 1997 to an estimated 0.2% of GDP in 2001. This was achieved through an increase in tourism taxes, the elimination of some import duty exemptions and a reduction in both current and capital outlays. Public officials concede that the main challenge for the period ahead will be to build on current accomplishments by maintaining a prudent fiscal stance, enhancing competitiveness and pressing ahead with pending structural reforms. Additional efforts will probably be needed to strengthen central government savings to ensure an adequate level of public investment to sustain growth. The government is seeking to reduce the workweek from 48 to 40 hours, establish a minimum wage, introduce health and safety requirements, and codify practices regarding severance payments and the settlement of labour disputes. Overall growth prospects will depend heavily on the fortunes of the tourism sector and continued income growth in the US, which accounts for the majority of tourist visitors.

Main Industries   The tourist sector is the heart of the economy but suffered severely after the events of 11 September 2001. Occupancy levels dropped to as low as 30% in the first few weeks after the attacks, and important investments were put on hold. Tourist numbers have now recovered, although many hotel workers are still on a part-time basis. The financial sector, which is the other cornerstone of the economy, saw several significant changes in 2001/2002. The government took important steps to address international concerns about the supervision of the offshore financial centre, money laundering and tax practices. To that end, parliament enacted a comprehensive body of legislation, which is being implemented. The authorities also intend to privatise the telephone company and will begin to open the telecommunications sector to private competition. This step will be followed by the privatisation of the electricity corporation. Manufacturing and agriculture together contribute less than 10% of GDP and show little growth, despite government incentives aimed at those sectors.

Energy   Most of the country's energy needs are met by imports of oil and gas, or by natural materials such as firewood. All electricity generation is derived from thermal plants.

© Euromonitor International 2002

	1999	2000	2001
Inflation (% change)	1.3	1.6	1.0
Exchange rate (per US$)	1.00	1.00	1.00
Interest rate (% per annum, lending rate)	6.4	6.0	6.0
GDP (% real growth)	5.9	5.0	-1.0
GDP (Million units of national currency)	4,546.0	4,899.0	4,923.0
GDP (US$ million)	4,546.0	4,899.0	4,923.0
GDP per capita (US$)	15,055.0	15,957.7	15,530.0
Consumption (Million units of national currency)	2,179.6	2,270.4	2,304.3
Consumption (US$ million)	2,179.6	2,270.4	2,304.3
Consumption per capita (US$)	7,218.3	7,395.4	7,269.1
Population, mid-year ('000)	302.0	307.0	317.0
Birth rate (per '000)	20.6	20.3	20.0
Death rate (per '000)	6.9	7.0	7.0
No. of households ('000)	61.8	62.8	64.7
Total exports (US$ million)	450.0	399.9	444.7
Total imports (US$ million)	1,910.9	1,730.0	1,678.5
Tourism receipts (US$ million)	1,503.0	1,815.7	1,575.0
Tourist spending (US$ million)	309.0	302.6	310.1

Average household size 2001 (persons)	4.89					
Urban population 2001 (%)	88.8					
Age analysis (%) (2001)	*0-14*	28.3	*15-64*	59.1	*65+*	12.6
Population by sex (%) (2001)	*Male*	49.7	*Female*	50.3		
Life expectancy (years) (2001)	*Male*	65.1	*Female*	73.8		
Infant mortality (deaths per '000 live births) (2001)	17.5					
Adult literacy (%) (1997)	95.8					

TRADING PARTNERS
Major export destinations 2001 (% share)   **Major import sources 2001 (% share)**

USA	36.0	USA	35.2
FRANCE	15.6	SOUTH KOREA	17.4
GERMANY	14.3	ITALY	8.0
SPAIN	12.1	SINGAPORE	5.6

Bahrain

Area (km^2)   661

Currency   Bahraini dinar (BD = 1,000 fils)

Location   Bahrain is made up of a group of islands located in the midst of the Gulf, about 24km off the eastern coast of Saudi Arabia. The main urban centre is on Bahrain Island, but the country's airport is located on the island of Muharraq. The capital is Manama.

Head of State   Sheikh Hamad ibn 'Isa Al Khalifah (1999)

Head of Government   Sheikh Khalifa bin Al Khalifa

Ruling Party   There are no political parties in Bahrain.

Political Structure   Bahrain is an absolute monarchy in which traditional consultative procedures, involving senior figures in the tribal hierarchy, are preferred to a formal parliamentary system. In addition, a 30-member Consultative Council was established and met for the first time in 1993. The Council, which has only limited powers, is charged with handling certain political matters. Sunni families rule the country, although a majority of the population are Shiites who feel politically and economically disenfranchised. In March 1999, Sheikh Khalifa bin Sulman Al Khalifa died suddenly and was replaced by his eldest son, Sheikh Hamad ibn 'Isa Al Khalifah The previous ruler's brother is Prime Minister.

Last Elections   Bahrain's constitution provides for a 30-member National Assembly elected by popular mandate but there have been no elections in the country since the Assembly was forcibly dissolved in 1975, allegedly for interfering with the system of government. The Khalifa family holds half the cabinet posts and its members chair most public sector organisations. The Royal Family, however, has set out a plan for evolution and tentatively set national elections for 2004.

Political Risk   The level of violence and unrest in the country rose in more recent years. Bahrain's Shia majority deeply resent the influence of the Sunni sect which accounts for only about 30% of the total population.

International Disputes   The whole territory of Bahrain is technically claimed by Iran, although that claim has not been formally stated since 1979. The government of Bahrain asserts that both Iran and Syria are tacitly supporting and encouraging the internal disturbances, although the two countries vehemently deny this. The island is also of international significance because it is the headquarters of the US navy's Fifth Fleet in the Gulf. Bahrain's relations with Iraq have been strained since US warplanes use the island as a base to patrol parts of the Iraqi no-fly zone.

Economy   Bahrain's economy grew by 3.3% in 2001 while prices declined by 0.2%. Whatever the rate of growth, it is clear that the economy is not keeping pace with the annual 3% rise in population, most of which consists of expatriates. In the 10 years to 2001, the country's population rose by 31%. The government states that unemployment is at 2.5% but the actual figure is much higher. Unofficial estimates put the figure at 15-30%. Most Bahrainis work in the public sector, but it is clear that many cannot find work. In addition, the expatriates send much of their earnings abroad. In a typical year, remittances are about US$1 billion. The capital drain is compounded by the practice of wealthy Bahrainis, who prefer to keep the bulk of their money abroad. In mid-2002, between US$15 and US$20 billion was invested overseas. Not surprisingly, the country is short of cash. Total government domestic and foreign debt stands at 30% of GDP. This is not high by the region's standards but it has almost doubled since 1996. The island also receives revenues in the form of gifts of Saudi crude oil and cash and handouts from Kuwait and Abu Dhabi. However, it has done nothing to curb the rising cost of expatriate remittances or the share of recurrent expenditures in the budget.

Main Industries   The country's economy depends heavily on the oil industry, but it also is an important centre for financial services and banking. Oil prices affect Bahrain's economy both directly, as revenues, and indirectly, due to banking and export links to neighbouring Persian Gulf countries which depend on oil revenues. The island's principal activity is the extraction of oil from its own fields, along with the processing of other countries' oil at its Sipra refinery. Nine years after it joined the World Trade Organisation and just a year before the end of its transition period, all the island's main industries are still firmly in the hands of the state. Hidden subsidies distort the viability of local industries, creating uncertainties that keep investors away. So far, the government has partially privatised just 14 companies and only one, Bahrain Aluminium, is a large one. Agriculture is of marginal importance, although there are fishing industries and pearl culture. Bahrain has had more success in attracting international banks with tax-haven facilities. The offshore banking sector presently has assets in excess of US$90 billion.

Energy   Bahrain has proven oil reserves of only 148 million barrels, all in one field - Awali. The Awali field was discovered in 1932, and was the first oilfield developed in the Persian Gulf. It is currently is producing around 35,000 barrels per day (bbl/d) of crude oil. Production peaked at more than 75,000 bbl/d in the early 1970s, but the field is now nearing depletion. More important than crude oil production, however, is Bahrain's refining industry. The country has a refinery south of Manama with a capacity of 248,900 bbl/d.

	1999	2000	2001
Inflation (% change)	-1.3	-0.7	-0.2
Exchange rate (per US$)	0.38	0.38	0.38
Interest rate (% per annum, commercial lending rate)	11.9	11.7	10.8
GDP (% real growth)	4.3	5.3	3.3
GDP (Million units of national currency)	2,489.3	2,996.9	3,025.0
GDP (US$ million)	6,620.5	7,970.5	8,045.2
GDP per capita (US$)	10,506.9	12,918.1	12,715.7
Consumption (Million units of national currency)	1,378.4	1,411.8	1,463.2
Consumption (US$ million)	3,666.0	3,754.8	3,891.4
Consumption per capita (US$)	5,818.0	6,085.6	6,150.5
Population, mid-year ('000)	630.1	617.0	632.7
Birth rate (per '000)	17.9	17.2	16.5
Death rate (per '000)	3.6	3.6	3.7
No. of households ('000)	162.6	162.1	169.7
Total exports (US$ million)	4,140.4	5,703.5	5,544.7
Total imports (US$ million)	3,697.6	4,633.5	4,262.8
Tourism receipts (US$ million)	408.0	395.5	364.1
Tourist spending (US$ million)	630.1	617.0	632.7

Average household size 2001 (persons)	3.81					
Urban population 2001 (%)	92.5					
Age analysis (%) (2001)	0-14	30.4	15-64	66.7	65+	2.8
Population by sex (%) (2001)	Male	57.1	Female	42.9		
Life expectancy (years) (2001)	Male	71.9	Female	76.1		
Infant mortality (deaths per '000 live births) (2001)	14.5					
Adult literacy (%) (1997)	86.2					

TRADING PARTNERS
Major export destinations 2001 (% share)   **Major import sources 2001 (% share)**

INDIA	8.7	SAUDI ARABIA	30.1
USA	4.8	USA	12.8
JAPAN	2.4	UNITED KINGDOM	6.7
SAUDI ARABIA	2.1	GERMANY	5.2

▪ **Bangladesh**

Area (km^2)   144,000

Currency   Taka (= 100 poisha)

Location   Bangladesh is a low-lying and densely populated territory lying in the Bay of Bengal between India and Myanmar. The country occupies most of the delta of the river Ganges, and has a tropical and humid climate. The capital is Dhaka.

Head of State   President Lajuddin Ahmed (2002)

Head of Government   Khaleda Zia (2001)

Ruling Party   The government is formed by a coalition led by the Bangladesh Nationalist Party (BJD).

Political Structure   Bangladesh is an independent member of the Commonwealth, with an executive President elected by parliament. National Parliament has 330 members, 300 members elected for a 5-year term in single-seat constituencies and 30 women elected by the parliamentarians.

Last Elections   Parliamentary elections were held in October 2001. The BJD won 191 seats and the Awami League won 62 seats. The remainder were spread among several smaller parties. Zia was then appointed as the new Prime Minister. In September 2002, parliament endorsed the nomination of Lajuddin Ahmed as president of the country.

Political Risk   Poverty remains pervasive and social and political unrest is widespread. The level of violence is escalating in the dispute between the two major political parties. Each year, thousands of people lose their lives in flooding which costs the country billions of dollars. Agriculture, which accounts for 22% of GDP, frequently suffers from flooding and typhoons. The country's foreign exchange reserves are dangerously low and efforts to close or privatise large firms are vigorously opposed.

International Disputes   Relations with India, Bangladesh's largest and most powerful neighbour, have generally been positive although not without strains. The two countries disagree over the ownership of an island formed in the Hariabhanga Delta. Flooding in Bangladesh, a phenomenon believed by many Bangladeshis to originate largely in India, has aggravated tensions. A 30-year water-sharing agreement for the Ganges was signed in December 1996, ending a 25-year dispute. Bangladesh still has several issues to be resolved with Pakistan from the 1971 war for independence. They include the division of assets from the pre-1971 period and the status of more than 250,000 non-Bengali Muslims (known as "Biharis") remaining in Bangladesh, but seeking resettlement in Pakistan.

Economy   GDP is expected to rise by 3.9% in 2002 and 4% in 2003. Meanwhile, inflation is expected to be 3.8% in 2002 and 5.3% in 2003. The global economic slowdown and developments following the events of 11 September 2001 in the US have diminished the country's growth prospects. The resulting setback in export-oriented manufacturing and loss of investor confidence are also adversely affecting key production and services sectors such as trade and transport, banking, insurance, ports and shipping. Moreover, the sharp deceleration in export growth over recent months is also leading to considerably slower import growth, with negative consequences for the government's revenue intake. The loss of employment in the sectors immediately affected by the global slowdown, including garments in particular, is likely to be substantial with adverse consequences for poverty reduction. Between July and December 2001, about 1,200 garment factories closed and an estimated 350,000 workers in the garment industry lost their jobs. Higher unemployment will also make it harder for the Government to achieve its goal of reducing income poverty by 25% by 2005, from the levels that prevailed in 2000. Progress remains elusive because of political conflicts, the slow pace of reforms and the government's extensive involvement in most industries.

Main Industries   The economy's recent performance was underpinned by an exceptional crop harvest and a rebounding industry sector. Favourable weather, the increased use of high-yielding varieties of crops, extended irrigation and the ready availability of agricultural inputs such as seeds, fertiliser and fuel at lower prices contributed to a record 26.8 million tonnes of food grain production in 2001. This represents a 7.6% increase over the previous year and was over two million tonnes more than domestic requirements (calculated at 455 grams per person per day). Despite the record, the overall growth rate of the agriculture sector declined to 3.1% from 7.4% in 2000, due to a high base for comparison following several years of successive bumper crop harvests. Industry sector growth improved to 7.2% in 2001 from 6.2% in 2000, due mainly to stronger manufacturing. Increasing to 6.3% from 4.8% in 2000, manufacturing expansion was underpinned by a rise in domestic demand and a rapid strengthening in the export-oriented garment industry. The output of domestic market-oriented industries, including food processing, chemicals, cement and small-scale industries, also rose considerably. Greater availability of bank credit to the private sector and higher imports of raw materials and machinery also supported manufacturing growth. Value added in 2001 in electricity, gas and water supply together grew by a robust 7.4% compared with 6.8% in the preceding year, partly reflecting greater manufacturing activity. Growth in construction, however, rose marginally to 8.7% from 8.5% in 2000 because of an oversupply of commercial buildings and apartments.

Energy   Bangladesh has small reserves of oil and coal, but potentially very large natural gas resources. Commercial energy consumption is around 71% natural gas, with the remainder almost entirely oil. Only around 18% of the population (25% in urban areas and 10% in rural areas) has access to electricity, and per capita commercial energy consumption is among the lowest in the world. Non-commercial energy sources, such as wood, animal wastes and crop residues, are estimated to account for over half of the country's energy consumption. Consumption of wood for fuel has contributed to deforestation and other environmental problems in Bangladesh. The World Bank has estimated that Bangladesh loses around US$1 billion per year due to power outages and unreliable energy supplies.

	1999	2000	2001
Inflation (% change)	6.4	2.3	1.8
Exchange rate (per US$)	49.09	52.14	55.81
Interest rate (% per annum, commercial lending rate)	14.1	15.5	15.8
GDP (% real growth)	5.4	5.5	4.5
GDP (Billion units of national currency)	2,283.9	2,451.7	2,621.4
GDP (US$ million)	46,529.4	47,020.0	46,973.1
GDP per capita (US$)	372.9	370.4	363.9
Consumption (Billion units of national currency)	1,707.1	1,838.5	1,979.9
Consumption (US$ million)	34,778.8	35,260.3	35,478.4
Consumption per capita (US$)	278.7	277.8	274.8
Population, mid-year ('000)	124,773.8	126,947.1	129,087.3
Birth rate (per '000)	31.0	30.7	30.5
Death rate (per '000)	9.4	9.1	8.9
No. of households ('000)	23,480.3	23,853.0	24,134.8
Total exports (US$ million)	5,458.0	6,399.0	6,300.0
Total imports (US$ million)	7,694.4	8,359.9	8,154.0
Tourism receipts (US$ million)	50.0	64.9	49.4
Tourist spending (US$ million)	212.0	224.4	221.4

Average household size 2001 (persons)	5.37				
Urban population 2001 (%)	25.1				
Age analysis (%) (2001)	*0-14*	34.9	*15-64*	61.9	*65+* 3.2
Population by sex (%) (2001)	*Male*	51.2	*Female*	48.8	
Life expectancy (years) (2001)	*Male*	59.9	*Female*	60.1	
Infant mortality (deaths per '000 live births) (2001)	71.3				
Adult literacy (%) (1997)	38.9				

TRADING PARTNERS

Major export destinations 2001 (% share)		Major import sources 2001 (% share)	
USA	29.6	INDIA	13.1
GERMANY	10.3	SINGAPORE	9.1
UNITED KINGDOM	8.5	CHINA	8.5
FRANCE	5.4	JAPAN	7.9

■ Barbados

Area (km^2) 430

Currency Barbados dollar (BD$ = 100 cents)

Location Barbados, the most easterly of the Caribbean islands, is some 30km long and 20km wide. With its pleasant climate (subject to occasional storms in the autumn months), it has proved popular as a tourist venue. The capital is Bridgetown.

Head of State HM Queen Elizabeth II

Head of Government Hon. Owen Arthur (September 1994)

Ruling Party Barbados Labour Party

Political Structure Barbados, an independent member of the Commonwealth, has a 28-seat House of Assembly whose members are elected by universal suffrage for a term of five years, and a 21-member Senate. Queen Elizabeth II is represented by a governor-general who appoints the Prime Minister on the advice of Parliament. Barbados is likely to change its political status in the next few years, removing the Queen of England as head of state and converting itself to a republic with an elected president.

Last Elections General elections to the House of Assembly were held in January 1999 when the Barbados Labour Party (BLP) of Owen Arthur took 26 seats in the 28-seat Assembly. The Democratic Labour Party (DLP) of L. Erskine Sandiford was badly defeated, gaining only two seats in the Assembly. The National Democratic Party, a DLP splinter group, failed to win any seats.

Political Risk The economy, although performing reasonably well, is vulnerable to external shocks. The main export sectors are relatively inefficient and face increasingly intense competition. The island has also lost much of its US market share to Mexico as a result of the North American Free Trade Agreement (NAFTA). Like many other Caribbean countries, Barbados has suffered as the US has cut back on foreign aid to the region. Worst of all is the rise in drug trafficking and the increased use of drugs on the island.

International Disputes Barbados's banks have come under pressure in more recent years to employ stricter regulations to prevent money laundering. To a large extent, they have complied. Barbados is used as a transhipment point for drugs.

Economy GDP contracted by 2.1% in 2001 while prices rose by 2.2%. The main reasons for the contraction was the sharp drop in tourism in late 2001. The unemployment rate edged upward in 2001 and now exceeds 8.5%. The central government deficit remains at about 1.5% of GDP, as gains in income tax revenue have been offset by shortfalls in other taxes (particularly the value added tax). The external current account deficit continues to rise, due mainly to a continued strong demand for imports of consumer and capital goods and a decline in key exports. Authorities continue to implement a prudent incomes policy and have extended through 2001 the social pact signed by representatives of business and labour. This pact maintains the link between productivity and wages and includes safeguards concerning issues of job security and training. Barbados, honouring its WTO commitments, has replaced non-tariff barriers with protective tariffs ranging from 20% to over 200%. The authorities intend to reduce tariffs annually to reach WTO ceiling levels by 2004.

Main Industries During the 1990s, economic activity in Barbados shifted towards services, notably tourism and offshore financial services, while sugar exports declined as an important source of foreign exchange earnings. There has been strong growth in construction for tourism projects and public investment in infrastructure, although the number of tourist arrivals was stagnating before the events of 11 September 2001. In the last quarter of 2001, the number of tourist arrivals fell by 30% relative to the same period in 2000. A contraction in manufacturing reflects strong regional and extra-regional competition as Barbados gradually liberalises trade. Industrial production centres on the processing of raw materials such as sugar cane or crude oil. However, the sector also includes rum distillers, chemicals, electronic goods, clothing and various assembly processes that are operated in collaboration with US firms. Government authorities expect tourism will continue to be the mainstay of the economy, but are optimistic about achieving more balanced growth, citing foreign exchange earning activities outside tourism - in particular, offshore business and financial services.

Energy Barbados has about 2.5 million barrels of proven reserves and produces small amounts of natural gas. Oil production for 2001 totalled 1,000 bbl/d. The country plans to expand production to 3,000 bbl/d in the next few years and has begun to employ horizontal-drilling techniques in the country's fields. The island, along with the Dominican Republic, Haiti and Jamaica, is party to the San Jose pact under which Mexico and Venezuela supply crude oil and refined products on favourable terms.

	1999	2000	2001
Inflation (% change)	1.6	2.5	2.2
Exchange rate (per US$)	2.00	2.00	2.00
Interest rate (% per annum, lending rate)	9.4	10.2	9.6
GDP (% real growth)	1.3	3.1	-2.1
GDP (Million units of national currency)	4,862.0	5,229.0	4,996.0
GDP (US$ million)	2,431.0	2,614.5	2,498.0
GDP per capita (US$)	9,031.8	9,683.3	9,183.8
Consumption (Million units of national currency)	3,205.8	3,545.0	3,458.2
Consumption (US$ million)	1,602.9	1,772.5	1,729.1
Consumption per capita (US$)	5,955.2	6,564.8	6,356.9
Population, mid-year ('000)	269.2	270.0	272.0
Birth rate (per '000)	12.7	12.5	12.4
Death rate (per '000)	8.1	8.0	7.9
No. of households ('000)	56.6	58.0	57.8
Total exports (US$ million)	263.8	272.4	227.6
Total imports (US$ million)	1,108.1	1,156.1	988.3
Tourism receipts (US$ million)	677.0	863.1	718.6
Tourist spending (US$ million)	91.5	97.8	79.3

Average household size 2001 (persons)	4.66					
Urban population 2001 (%)	50.6					
Age analysis (%) (2001)	*0-14*	22.0	*15-64*	67.1	*65+*	10.9
Population by sex (%) (2001)	*Male*	48.0	*Female*	52.0		
Life expectancy (years) (2001)	*Male*	74.3	*Female*	79.3		
Infant mortality (deaths per '000 live births) (2001)	11.2					
Adult literacy (%) (1997)	97.6					

TRADING PARTNERS

Major export destinations 2001 (% share)

USA	15.0
UNITED KINGDOM	11.7
TRINIDAD AND TOBAGO	11.0
JAMAICA	7.8

Major import sources 2001 (% share)

USA	42.0
TRINIDAD AND TOBAGO	16.3
UNITED KINGDOM	8.0
JAPAN	4.2

Belarus

Area (km^2)   207,595

Currency   Rouble

Location   Belarus (Byelorussia, or White Russia), lies in the far west of the former Soviet Union. It borders on Poland in the west, Lithuania and Latvia in the north, and Ukraine in the south. The country is a large and swampy plain that is served by several major rivers, including the Pripyat, which forms the upper reaches of the Dnepr. The capital is Minsk.

Head of State   President Aleksandr Lukashenko (July 1994)

Head of Government   Henadz Navitski (2001)

Ruling Party   The government is formed by non-partisans, loyal to the president.

Political Structure   Belarus declared its independence from the old USSR in August 1990. The National Assembly has two chambers. The House of Representatives has 110 members chosen in single-seat constituencies and elected for 4-year terms. The Council of the Republic has 64 members, 56 members indirectly elected and 8 members appointed by the president.

Last Elections   Elections to the House of Representatives took place in October 2000 when 81 non-partisans were voted in. The remaining seats were widely dispersed among numerous parties. Lukashenko was re-elected as president in September 2001 with 76% of the vote.

Political Risk   Lukashenko is believed to be planning a referendum to change the constitution to let him rule until 2015. Belarus has returned to Soviet-era authoritarian practices but behind the scenes, Moscow appears to be trying to disentangle itself from Lukashenko in order to support his rival. Russia is also putting increased financial pressure on the country - apparently hoping for a new economic bargain that leaves Russia in control of its neighbour's lucrative potash industry and bits of the energy industry.

International Disputes   Belarus has been accused of profiteering by delivering ex-Cold War arms to countries across the world, including many impoverished African states, as well as to groups supporting terrorism.

Economy   GDP grew by 4.1% in 2001 but the pace will slow to 1.5% in 2002 and 2.3% in 2003. Inflation was 61% in 2001 but should fall to 34% in 2002 and 22.4% in 2003. Measured output growth, especially in 2001, masks an underlying weakening of economic activity, as suggested by the rising levels of inventories, non-cash transactions and domestic arrears, the low level of profits and investment, and sagging competitiveness. The external current account improved markedly during 2000-2001, turning into a surplus of US$240 million (4.5% of GDP) at end-June 2001, partly owing to a strong export performance during the first quarter. Gross reserves increased during 2000-2001, but still cover less than one month of imports. In 2001, the authorities appeared to have made headway in further liberalising the foreign exchange market, stabilising the exchange rate and reducing inflation; they also took steps to liberalise prices and initiate other structural reforms. At the same time, a policy of raising wages to unaffordable levels during an election year undermined progress achieved in stabilisation. Real wages rose steadily during 2000-2001. This policy had a negative impact on enterprise profitability, investment and the budget. After a significant tightening of fiscal policy in 2000, fiscal developments in 2001 were shaped by efforts to cut expenditures to offset increases in budgetary wages. While the consolidated fiscal deficit (cash basis) was limited to 0.6% of GDP in 2000, it rose to 1.8% in 2001. A climate hostile to business inhibits foreign investment. Inflation and unemployment are other serious problems that go unchecked.

Main Industries   Agricultural accounts for almost a quarter of GDP, industry for about two fifths and services the remainder. Agricultural output has been declining for several years. Forestry and agriculture, notably potatoes, grain, peat and cattle, are important sources of income and employment. Most of the country's industries are dependent on imports for their raw materials and intermediate supplies. In fact, as much as 90% of the republic's raw materials are imported from Russia, a situation which has given rise to difficulties. These establishments date back to the country's Soviet past and are still state owned. Engineering, machine tools, agricultural equipment, chemicals, motor vehicles and some consumer durables such as watches, televisions and radios are all prominent state-run industries. Many of the products they produce are out of date and inferior to Western versions. Privatisation of enterprises controlled by the central government has virtually ceased. Only about 10% of all enterprises that were under central government control have been privatised. Bank fragility remains a major obstacle to macroeconomic stabilisation. Some steps were made to initiate structural reforms during 2001, but the outstanding agenda remains large. In particular, the authorities made major headway in foreign exchange liberalisation and started to dismantle the extensive system of price controls. In addition, a new investment code was adopted in October 2001, providing new safeguards for domestic and foreign investment.

Energy   Belarus has a small oil industry which produces around 37,000 bbl/d of oil each year. The country has 198 million barrels of oil in proven reserves, but the lack of political and economic reform in the past decade has hindered any investment to boost production. Belarusnafta, the state-owned oil production monopoly, estimates that active oil deposits may last for another 17 years, with more difficult deposits (eg those with a water content of over 80% or with high viscosity) lasting for 34 years. Although oil consumption in Belarus fell sharply in more recent years, the country still must import nearly 80% of its oil. Most of this comes from Russia. Oil exported from Russia via Belarus (approximately 50% of Russia's net oil exports go through Belarus) is not subject to export duties due to the Russian-Belarusian Union agreement, which, along with high oil prices in 1999 and 2000, contributed to a significant increase in the amount of oil flowing through the pipeline and to Belarusian refineries.

	1999	2000	2001
Inflation (% change)	293.8	168.9	61.3
Exchange rate (per US$)	248.80	876.75	1,390.00
Interest rate (% per annum, lending rate)	51.0	67.7	47.0
GDP (% real growth)	3.4	5.8	4.1
GDP (Trillion units of national currency)	3.0	9.1	16.9
GDP (US$ million)	12,162.9	10,408.4	12,167.4
GDP per capita (US$)	1,196.0	1,026.3	1,206.2
Consumption (Trillion units of national currency)	1.7	5.0	8.9
Consumption (US$ million)	6,673.3	5,655.9	6,414.1
Consumption per capita (US$)	656.2	557.7	635.9
Population, mid-year ('000)	10,169.2	10,141.3	10,087.4
Birth rate (per '000)	9.2	9.1	9.1
Death rate (per '000)	13.6	13.8	13.9
No. of households ('000)	3,137.2	3,142.3	3,148.2
Total exports (US$ million)	5,909.0	7,331.0	7,428.0
Total imports (US$ million)	6,674.0	8,574.0	8,049.0
Tourism receipts (US$ million)	13.0	17.9	26.4
Tourist spending (US$ million)	116.0	99.7	95.1

Average household size 2001 (persons)	3.23				
Urban population 2001 (%)	73.8				
Age analysis (%) (2001)	*0-14*	18.6	*15-64*	67.9	*65+* 13.4
Population by sex (%) (2001)	*Male*	46.7	*Female*	53.3	
Life expectancy (years) (2001)	*Male*	62.8	*Female*	74.4	
Infant mortality (deaths per '000 live births) (2001)	12.0				
Adult literacy (%) (1997)	99.5				

TRADING PARTNERS

Major export destinations 2001 (% share)

RUSSIA	53.1
LATVIA	6.6
UKRAINE	5.7
LITHUANIA	3.7

Major import sources 2001 (% share)

GERMANY	20.3
UKRAINE	9.8
POLAND	6.2
LITHUANIA	5.1

Belgium

Area (km^2)   30,520

Currency   Euro (= 100 cents)

Location   Belgium lies on the northwestern coast of continental Europe, facing the North Sea some distance north of the English Channel. The land is largely flat and low-lying, although there are some mineral-bearing hills to the east. Belgium's excellent road and rail communications make it an obvious choice for the administrative centre of the EU. The climate is moderate with mild winters. The capital is Brussels.

Head of State   HM King Albert II (1993)

Head of Government   Guy Verhofstadt (1999)

Ruling Party   A multiparty coalition leads the country.

Political Structure   Belgium is a constitutional monarchy in which the monarch has often been required to mediate and to propose governments. There is a 150-seat Chamber of Representatives, normally elected for four years, and a 184-member Senate. Four reforms since the 1970s have transformed Belgium from a unitary into a federal state. The result is a federation of three "regions": Flanders, Wallonia and Brussels-Capital, overlaid with three languages - Flemish, French and German. Each has its own parliament.

Last Elections   General elections were held in June 1999. The right-leaning Liberal Party took 24% of the vote and 41 seats. The Christian Democrats won 20% and 32 seats, while the Socialists received 20% of the vote and 33 seats. The far-right Flemish Vlaams Blok took almost 10% of the vote and won 15 seats.

Political Risk   Belgium needs to reform its inefficient bureaucracy and police to defuse tensions between the Dutch-speaking north and the French-speaking south. Reforms are also needed as part of a response to political scandals in recent years. The gradual transfer of power from federal to regional institutions continues to create tensions and uncertainty. Flemish leaders argue that their region subsidises poorer Wallonia, particularly through the social security system. To a varying degree, Flemish political parties want greater fiscal and budgetary autonomy. Some have also proposed that the social security system be broken up - easing the funding burden on Flanders, but imposing serious financial strains on Wallonia. Brussels, itself, generates 35% of the country's corporate taxes and hopes to negotiate a more favourable arrangement for the dispersal of tax receipts. As devolution continues, the country's future shape is at stake and some constitutional experts predict that it will gradually become a confederation of two largely autonomous states.

International Disputes   Intense rivalries between Dutch and French speakers have periodically broken out into inter-communal violence, although both France and the Netherlands have been careful not to get involved.

Economy   GDP grew by just 1.1% in 2001 and is expected to rise by only 0.9% in 2002. Growth in 2003, however, should be 3.2%. Inflation was 2.4% in 2001 and will fall to 1.1% in 2002 and 1.2% in 2003. The recent contraction was primarily due to a sharp fall in private consumption, but the more fundamental shift behind this drop was a worsening international climate. The rise in oil prices and relatively unaccommodating monetary conditions in the euro area were other factors that worsened the decline. Surprisingly, both exports and imports experienced an absolute contraction as well. Unemployment was not significantly affected but is expected to creep up in 2002 and 2003. Despite the downturn, the government will continue to pursue a policy of fiscal consolidation in order to further reduce the country's high debt-to-GDP ratio. The budgetary plan for 2001-2005 calls for the general government budget surplus to rise from 0.2% of GDP in 2001 to 0.7% in 2005. Meanwhile, the debt-to-GDP ratio should fall from 106% of GDP in 2001 to less than 90% in 2005. These targets assume that annual growth is 2.5% per year during this period. That assumption, of course, will not be met in 2002. The country's programme of tax reform has been stretched out over a longer period (2001-2004) than originally intended. As outlined by the government, it will represent a tax cut of BEF135 billion (or a little over 1% of GDP). Its primary aim is to alleviate the tax burden on labour income, especially on lower wage incomes.

Main Industries   Belgium's industrial sector accounts for almost a third of GDP. The bulk of this sector is in Wallonia in the south and east of the country, where a predominantly French-speaking population once operated a massive coal mining and steel manufacturing industry. Long the country's industrial powerhouse, Wallonia is now undergoing a painful conversion process and its economic performance lags far behind that of high-tech Flanders. Heavy industry in Wallonia is steadily contracting, leaving behind large pockets of unemployment. In services, the pressure on Belgium's financial and banking sector persists, as many policy makers work to restructure and consolidate the sector in order to better compete in Europe's markets. Belgium's farming sector was already weakened by the "dioxin-in-food" crisis in 1999 and fortunately was spared from the foot and mouth disease that hurt neighbouring countries in 2001. However, the finances of farmers and food manufacturers remain precarious.

Energy   Belgium's energy markets have been open to competition but only for large industrial clients. However, officials are keen to speed up the pace of liberalisation and have pushed through price cuts for residential consumers and small and medium-sized businesses. Competition among suppliers is also gathering pace. The country's consumption of nuclear energy is among the highest in Europe, accounting for almost a tenth of all primary use. This is about the same as solid fuels, in which the country once specialised. Crude oil accounts for almost half of the total energy consumption.

       © Euromonitor International 2002

	1999	2000	2001
Inflation (% change)	0.9	1.1	1.1
Exchange rate (per US$)	0.94	1.09	1.12
Interest rate (% per annum, lending rate)	6.7	8.0	8.5
GDP (% real growth)	3.0	4.0	1.1
GDP (Million units of national currency)	235,548.0	248,340.0	253,917.0
GDP (US$ million)	251,155.9	215,712.9	227,216.0
GDP per capita (US$)	24,565.4	21,055.8	22,132.7
Consumption (Million units of national currency)	119,874.2	128,620.7	1.0
Consumption (US$ million)	127,817.3	111,722.4	118,973.5
Consumption per capita (US$)	12,501.7	10,905.3	11,589.0
Population, mid-year ('000)	10,224.0	10,244.8	10,266.1
Birth rate (per '000)	10.4	10.2	10.0
Death rate (per '000)	9.9	9.9	9.9
No. of households ('000)	4,209.1	4,237.8	4,260.7
Total exports (US$ million)	178,961.0	187,847.0	187,981.0
Total imports (US$ million)	164,617.0	176,965.0	176,811.0
Tourism receipts (US$ million)	7,039.0	5,552.2	5,377.7
Tourist spending (US$ million)	10,057.0	10,619.4	8,718.8

Average household size 2001 (persons)	2.42				
Urban population 2001 (%)	97.3				
Age analysis (%) (2001)	*0-14* 17.6		*15-64* 65.6		*65+* 16.9
Population by sex (%) (2001)	*Male* 48.9		*Female* 51.1		
Life expectancy (years) (2001)	*Male* 75.5		*Female* 81.7		
Infant mortality (deaths per '000 live births) (2001)	4.0				
Adult literacy (%) (1998)	99.0				

TRADING PARTNERS
Major export destinations 2001 (% share)   **Major import sources 2001 (% share)**

FRANCE	17.6	NETHERLANDS	16.8
GERMANY	16.8	GERMANY	16.6
NETHERLANDS	11.8	FRANCE	12.9
UNITED KINGDOM	9.7	UNITED KINGDOM	7.9

Belize

Area (km^2)   22,965

Currency   Belize dollar (BZ$ = 100 cents)

Location   Belize lies on the Caribbean coast of Central America, bounded in the north by Mexico and in the south and west by Guatemala. The coastal areas are mainly swamp, although inland they rise to meet the Maya mountain range. The country has a subtropical climate and is subject to hurricanes in the autumn months. The capital is Belmopan.

Head of State   HM Queen Elizabeth II

Head of Government   Said Musa (1998)

Ruling Party   People's United Party (PUP)

Political Structure   Belize, an independent member of the Commonwealth since 1981, has a bicameral National Assembly. The country's 29-member House of Representatives is elected by popular vote for a 5-year term, while its 8-member Senate is appointed by the governor-general. The possibility of political union with Dominica, St Lucia and St Vincent and the Grenadines has been discussed.

Last Elections   Elections to the House of Representatives were held in August 1998. The PUP took 59% of the vote and won 26 of the 29 seats. The remaining seats are held by members of the United Democratic Party.

Political Risk   The country's delicate political balance is a cause for concern.

International Disputes   Relations with Guatemala are occasionally tense when politicians in the latter country refer to Guatemala's claims on a large chunk of the land area of the Belize. The claim dates back to the Spanish era when Guatemala ruled this area. Guatemala's 1945 Constitution treats Belize as its 23rd department but the claim had been dormant for years.

Economy   Growth slowed in 2001 with GDP increasing by just 2.5% while inflation was 1.2%. Belize's small economy is based on agriculture, agro-based industry and merchandising, with tourism and construction assuming greater importance. Growth has been sluggish for more than a decade. The government's priorities are to boost public spending on infrastructure and housing, reduce taxes and promote tourism and foreign direct investment. To restrain the growth in public external debt, several public enterprises are being privatised. The current account deficit now exceeds 8% of GDP, owing to the higher prices of capital imports and fuel. The privatisation programme will continue both as a means to generate resources for the government's investment programme as well as to strengthen the economy's competitiveness. Because Belize is heavily dependent upon imports, international borrowing and foreign investment (which requires the repatriation of profits), the availability of hard currency is watched closely.

Main Industries   Agriculture is the dominant sector in Belize, accounting for 16% of GDP and employing more than 40% of the workforce. Bananas, coca, citrus, sugarcane, fish, cultured shrimp and fruit are the major products, while bananas, citrus fruits and sugar cane are grown for export. Sugar, the chief crop, accounts for more than one third of exports, but tourism is the major foreign-exchange earner. Citrus production is rising sharply and officials hope this will be a major foreign-exchange earner in the future. Fishery products, especially lobsters and conches, are exported to the US. The manufacturing sector is small with most almost all firms geared solely to the domestic market. The main manufacturing activities consist of garment production, food processing and construction Altogether, industry makes up about 29% of GDP. The country has no railway system and this factor hinders the development of exports and economic progress in general. Belize has good prospects for the development of a thriving tourist industry but needs investment in this field and better planning. Offshore financial services are relatively new to the country, but show a significant potential for growth. Over 6,000 offshore businesses and trusts have been registered in Belize. An offshore banking act has been added to the growing legal infrastructure for offshore services and a money-laundering (prevention) act has been passed. Belize expects as many as 300,000 tourists in 2002, up from 24,000 in the first three quarters of 2001.

Energy   Belize meets almost all its energy requirements from imports of oil and natural gas. The country has no known oil deposits but has signed an agreement with an American firm which has agreed to search for oil. The country's electricity monopoly wants to build a hydropower dam on the environmentally-sensitive Macal River and this has created a controversy. At present, all of the country's electricity is derived from thermal power plants.

	1999	2000	2001
Inflation (% change)	-1.2	0.6	1.2
Exchange rate (per US$)	2.00	2.00	2.00
Interest rate (% per annum, lending rate)	16.3	16.0	15.5
GDP (% real growth)	3.7	9.7	2.5
GDP (Million units of national currency)	1,376.0	1,515.0	1,572.0
GDP (US$ million)	688.0	757.5	786.0
GDP per capita (US$)	2,915.3	3,143.2	3,150.3
Consumption (Million units of national currency)	883.7	1,109.9	1,155.7
Consumption (US$ million)	441.8	555.0	577.8
Consumption per capita (US$)	1,872.2	2,302.7	2,316.0
Population, mid-year ('000)	236.0	241.0	249.5
Birth rate (per '000)	27.4	26.7	26.0
Death rate (per '000)	4.4	4.4	4.3
No. of households ('000)	86.2	88.6	92.2
Total exports (US$ million)	166.1	194.3	166.4
Total imports (US$ million)	366.2	450.4	408.8
Tourism receipts (US$ million)	112.0	104.5	98.6
Tourist spending (US$ million)	24.0	31.2	27.4

Average household size 2001 (persons)		2.72				
Urban population 2001 (%)		54.8				
Age analysis (%) (2001)	0-14	40.7	15-64	55.0	65+	4.3
Population by sex (%) (2001)	Male	50.4	Female	49.6		
Life expectancy (years) (2001)	Male	72.9	Female	75.7		
Infant mortality (deaths per '000 live births) (2001)		30.5				
Adult literacy (%) (1997)		75.0				

TRADING PARTNERS

Major export destinations 2001 (% share)   **Major import sources 2001 (% share)**

USA	40.2	USA	41.4
UNITED KINGDOM	19.6	MEXICO	9.7
JAPAN	13.7	JAPAN	6.0
NETHERLANDS	3.9	NETHERLANDS ANTILLES	5.2

Benin

Area (km²) 112,620

Currency CFA franc (= 100 centimes)

Location Benin, one of the poorest countries in Africa, is located on the West African coastline with the Gulf of Guinea to the south. The country is bounded by Togo in the west, Burkina Faso and Niger in the north and Nigeria in the east. The capital is Porto Novo.

Head of State President Mathieu Kerekou (1996)

Head of Government Mathieu Kerekou (1996)

Ruling Party A multiparty coalition has been formed.

Political Structure Benin's transition to multiparty democracy began in 1991 when the first elections were held under the terms of the 1990 Constitution. In practice, all power rests with the president who is elected by universal suffrage for a 5-year term, and answers to the 83-seat National Assembly (itself elected for a 4-year term). The president has organised a multiparty coalition, although splits and defections are commonplace in Benin politics.

Last Elections Parliamentary elections were held in March 1999. The Parti de la renaissance du Bénin received 23% of the vote and took 27 seats. The Parti du renouveau démocratique took 12% of the vote and 11 seats while the Front d'action pour le renouveau et le développement gained 10 seats with only 5% of the vote. The remaining seats were divided among minor parties. Presidential elections were held in March 2001 when Mathieu Kerekou, was re-elected with 84% of the vote. Opposition candidates, including ex-president Nicéphore Soglo. Kerekou, boycotted the final round of the elections.

Political Risk Benin serves as a transhipment point for narcotics associated with Nigerian trafficking organisations with most of the drugs destined for Western Europe. The government is weak and there is a danger that drug groups will increase their influence. The country's limited political maturity is a constant source of uncertainty and instability.

International Disputes There are no international disputes.

Economy Benin's economy grew by 5.8% in 2001 and prices increased by 3.8%. GDP is expected to grow by about 4.4% in 2002. The government's overall fiscal balance remains in surplus thanks largely to grants and loans, though revenues also rose marginally. Authorities have made serious efforts to strengthen the tax administration, streamline the tax system and improve controls on tax exemptions. Total government spending remains high - more than 18% of GDP - with outlays for education and health rising rapidly. Despite the attempts at financial stringency, economic growth does not match rates of population increase, meaning that per capita standards of living are deteriorating. International authorities are pressing Benin to open all sectors to private investment so as to broaden and strengthen the country's economic base.

Main Industries Benin's economy is primarily agricultural. The most important crop is cotton but production slumped for several years before recovering in 2001. Analysts fear that another poor performance in the cotton sector will have broad repercussions on the rest of the economy. Authorities have launched a major reorganisation of the cotton sector to bolster its long-term competitiveness. Other agricultural products include corn, sorghum, cassava (tapioca), yams, beans, rice, palm oil, peanuts; and poultry and livestock. The country's parched soil will not normally support conventional fruit or vegetable crops. The manufacturing sector consists mainly of textiles, cigarettes, beverages, food, construction materials and petroleum and is geared almost exclusively to serving the domestic market. In the industrial sphere, the government has opened public enterprises to private sector participation. Authorities have sold a majority of the capital of the publicly-owned petroleum distribution system and implemented a flexible mechanism for adjusting retail prices of petroleum products. Commercial and transport activities make up nearly 40% of GDP, but are extremely vulnerable to market conditions in Nigeria There are deposits of gold, chrome and iron, although these are of only limited size. Oil has been extracted since the early 1980s, but again the scale of the deposits is not large.

Energy Benin derives virtually all of its almost negligible energy requirements from imported oil and gas resources. It had no hydroelectric plants to produce electricity in mid-2002.

	1999	2000	2001
Inflation (% change)	0.3	4.2	3.8
Exchange rate (per US$)	615.70	711.98	733.04
Interest rate			
GDP (% real growth)	4.7	5.8	5.8
GDP (Billion units of national currency)	1,469.9	1,605.4	1,755.7
GDP (US$ million)	2,387.4	2,254.9	2,395.0
GDP per capita (US$)	399.6	369.8	373.6
Consumption (Billion units of national currency)	1,155.2	1,259.2	1,344.2
Consumption (US$ million)	1,876.3	1,768.5	1,833.7
Consumption per capita (US$)	314.0	290.1	286.1
Population, mid-year ('000)	5,975.0	6,097.0	6,410.0
Birth rate (per '000)	42.2	41.9	41.5
Death rate (per '000)	12.8	12.7	12.5
No. of households ('000)	1,467.5	1,475.8	1,526.6
Total exports (US$ million)	422.2	392.1	426.5
Total imports (US$ million)	749.1	613.1	650.6
Tourism receipts (US$ million)	34.4	31.4	35.1
Tourist spending (US$ million)	7.5	6.8	6.0

Average household size 2001 (persons)	4.13				
Urban population 2001 (%)	43.1				
Age analysis (%) (2001)	*0-14*	46.8	*15-64* 46.8	*65+*	6.5
Population by sex (%) (2001)	*Male*	49.3	*Female* 50.7		
Life expectancy (years) (2001)	*Male*	52.3	*Female* 55.6		
Infant mortality (deaths per '000 live births) (2001)	82.7				
Adult literacy (%) (1997)	33.9				

TRADING PARTNERS

Major export destinations 2001 (% share)		Major import sources 2001 (% share)	
INDIA	20.6	CHINA	36.1
BRAZIL	13.4	FRANCE	14.5
ITALY	12.7	GERMANY	3.6
INDONESIA	6.4	ITALY	3.5

Bermuda

Area (km^2) 54

Currency Bermudian dollar (BD$ = 100 cents)

Location Bermuda comprises a group of some 150 small islands, of which 20 are inhabited. The group lies in the Western Atlantic, over 900km off the coast of South Carolina. The climate is variable, with a susceptibility to hurricanes during the autumn. The capital is Hamilton.

Head of State HM Queen Elizabeth II

Head of Government Jennifer Smith (1998)

Ruling Party Progressive Labour Party (PLP)

Political Structure Bermuda, a British Dependent Territory, has a 40-member House of Assembly which exercises legislative authority and is elected by universal suffrage for a term of five years. There is also an 11-member Senate whose members are nominated by the Governor. The Governor also appoints the Prime Minister, on the basis of advice from the House of Assembly, and the Premier then appoints his own Cabinet. There has been intense discussion about the possibility of declaring independence from the UK, but in August 1995 the government lost a referendum on the subject.

Last Elections General elections were held in November 1998. The PLP received 54% of the vote and 26 of the 40 seats in the Assembly. The United Bermuda Party won 46% of the vote and the remaining 14 seats. The PLP, which supports total independence from the UK, greatly improved its representation in the Assembly.

Political Risk Black Bermudians make up 60% of the population but are often left out of the economy. There is a growing debate over employment levels, remuneration in the business sector and the granting of work permits to white expatriate workers. Businesses deny that they discriminate but the issue is becoming a very sensitive one.

International Disputes The issue of political independence is a perennial one which is never very far below the surface. A referendum on the matter was rejected in 1995 but a majority of voters are now believed to support the call for independence. So far, political parties have steered clear of the question However, young, disaffected Bermudians are likely to raise the matter again, and if unemployment should continue to rise, they will gain more supporters.

Economy Bermuda's economy is among the most affluent in the Atlantic/Caribbean nexus but remains vulnerable to any recession in North America. GDP increased by 2.4% in 2001 while inflation was 2.9%. Unemployment is low, though the number of jobs being created is rising very slowly. The significance of tourism is nevertheless crucial, since no other activity has the same employment potential. Competition is fierce, but the island's planners have begun to pay more attention to matching the quality of its tourism product to the premium it charges. The island's tax and regulatory system has made it an attractive base for insurers since the 1950s. Companies pay no tax on their profits or their investment income, allowing them to build up reserves for future losses more quickly. Sophisticated telecommunications, the island's proximity (900km) to the US and new laws designed to strengthen confidence in the financial sector are some of the reasons for Bermuda's success. The government has failed to restrain labour costs while productivity growth has lagged.

Main Industries Bermuda enjoys one of the highest per capita incomes in the world, having successfully exploited its location by providing financial services for international firms and luxury tourist facilities for 360,000 visitors annually. The tourist industry, which accounts for an estimated 28% of GDP, attracts 84% of its business from North America. Agriculture is severely limited by a lack of suitable land. The industrial sector is small, although over 60% of all non-tourist activity is the result of international business. Manufacturing tends to centre on perfumes, flowers and pharmaceuticals. About 80% of food needs are imported. International business contributes over 60% of Bermuda's economic output; the failed independence vote in late 1995 can be partially attributed to Bermudian fears of scaring away foreign firms. Government economic priorities are the further strengthening of the tourist and international financial sectors. Bermuda's economy is a high-cost one, a characteristic due in part to the need to import everything from fuel to food.

Energy Like most of its counterparts in the Atlantic, Bermuda is entirely dependent on imports of oil and gas for its energy needs.

	1999	2000	2001
Inflation (% change)	2.0	2.7	2.9
Exchange rate (per US$)	1.00	1.00	1.00
Interest rate			
GDP (% real growth)	4.3	2.9	2.4
GDP (Million units of national currency)	2,476.6	2,617.2	2,757.7
GDP (US$ million)	2,476.6	2,628.8	2,757.7
GDP per capita (US$)	38,696.6	40,442.7	41,784.0
Consumption (Million units of national currency)	1,832.1	1,844.5	1,924.4
Consumption (US$ million)	1,832.1	1,852.6	1,924.4
Consumption per capita (US$)	28,626.6	28,502.2	29,157.0
Population, mid-year ('000)	64.0	65.0	66.0
Birth rate (per '000)	11.9	11.6	11.2
Death rate (per '000)	7.2	7.2	7.2
No. of households ('000)	14.2	14.6	15.0
Total exports (US$ million)	83.7	85.0	90.2
Total imports (US$ million)			
Tourism receipts (US$ million)	536.7	488.3	448.3
Tourist spending (US$ million)			

Average household size 2001 (persons)	4.46					
Urban population 2001 (%)	100.0					
Age analysis (%) (2001)	*0-14*	30.2	*15-64*	63.0	*65+*	6.7
Population by sex (%) (2001)	*Male*	49.4	*Female*	50.6		
Life expectancy (years) (2001)	*Male*	75.1	*Female*	79.1		
Infant mortality (deaths per '000 live births) (2001)	7.0					
Adult literacy (%)						

TRADING PARTNERS

Major export destinations 2001 (% share)		Major import sources 2001 (% share)	
FRANCE	73.6	KAZAKHSTAN	23.6
USA	4.5	FRANCE	19.2
UNITED KINGDOM	4.4	ITALY	7.5
NORWAY	4.1	GERMANY	6.5

▥ Bhutan

Area (km^2)   46,620

Currency   Ngultrum (Ng = 100 chetrum)

Location   Bhutan is a small and sparsely populated state located in the Himalayan mountain range, between India and Tibet, which is part of China. The mountainous character of the landscape precludes all possibility of intensive agriculture, forcing much of the workforce to seek employment abroad. The capital is Thimphu.

Head of State   HM King Jigme Singye Wangchuk

Head of Government   Lyonpo Jigmi Thinley (1998)

Ruling Party   There are no legal political parties in Bhutan.

Political Structure   The Kingdom of Bhutan is a hereditary limited monarchy in which the King shares power with the Council of Ministers, the National Assembly and the chief priest of the Buddhist religion in Bhutan. The 150-member National Assembly includes 105 elected representatives and 45 appointed members. After nearly a century of absolute rule by a monarchy, King Jigme Singye Wangchuk took a step towards increased political participation by recently giving the legislature the right to remove him from leadership and to appoint his cabinet. An income tax also was introduced for the first time.

Last Elections   There are no general elections in Bhutan. The 105 elective delegates to the National Assembly are elected in their various constituencies when the need arises and are not allowed to represent political groups.

Political Risk   With one of the lowest per capita incomes in the world, and one of the most impenetrable political systems, Bhutan has little real attraction for Western businesses. The agricultural sector employs over 75% of the workforce and is frequently subject to flooding.

International Disputes   Bhutan's relations with neighbouring Nepal have been strained by the latter's accusations of human rights offences against 100,000 ethnic Nepalese residing in Bhutan. The army has occasionally crossed the border into India in pursuit of pro-democracy activists.

Economy   Growth has been strong in recent years and this trend is expected to continue during the short term, with increases in GDP of around 6.5% in 2002 and 2003. Inflation should be around 4.5% in 2002 and rise to 5.2% in 2003. The government used to pursue a prudent fiscal policy, maintaining current expenditures at a level that could be completely financed by domestic revenues. However, the fiscal deficit rose steeply in recent years and reached over 5% in 2001, though some favourable factors are expected to mitigate the fiscal constraints. These include the fact that domestic revenues will probably strengthen as a result of the commissioning of major hydropower plants over the coming months, the likely upward revision of power export tariffs and the introduction of a personal income tax in 2002. Given that monetary policy has to be geared to supporting the exchange rate peg with the Indian rupee, inflation and interest rates have to be kept in line with those in India and therefore the scope of monetary policy is substantially limited. The economy is, other than tourism, relatively well insulated from the direct effects of global economic volatility, although it is vulnerable to the effects of major developments in India.

Main Industries   The industrial sector grew by 8% in 2001, despite a disappointing performance by mining and manufacturing. The services sector grew by 6.3%, buoyed by the transport and communications subsectors. However, tourism, which registered double-digit growth in the 1990s, performed poorly as a result of slower tourist arrivals following the events of 11 September 2001, poor weather conditions earlier in the year and logistics difficulties with air transport from overseas. Agriculture, traditionally the slowest sector, stayed at 4.8% growth due to stable livestock production and to strong forestry output offsetting disappointing crop production and exports of fruits and horticultural products. Electricity and related construction will continue to boost the industry sector, while private sector development will determine the prospects for mining and manufacturing. The services sector will also benefit from an expected recovery in tourism.

Energy   Bhutan does not produce or consume much energy, but it has hydroelectric power potential and is a hydropower exporter (to India). Around 98% of Bhutan's energy consumption is met by biomass - mainly fuel wood. Bhutan's coal industries provide the greater part of the Kingdom's modest energy needs.

	1999	2000	2001
Inflation (% change)	6.8	4.8	5.0
Exchange rate (per US$)	43.06	44.94	47.19
Interest rate			
GDP (% real growth)	5.9	6.1	5.9
GDP (Million units of national currency)	18,810.0	21,481.0	23,885.0
GDP (US$ million)	436.9	478.0	506.2
GDP per capita (US$)	218.0	231.6	238.5
Consumption (Million units of national currency)	10,067.0	11,329.0	12,695.3
Consumption (US$ million)	233.8	252.1	269.0
Consumption per capita (US$)	116.7	122.1	126.7
Population, mid-year ('000)	2,003.6	2,063.9	2,122.8
Birth rate (per '000)	35.8	35.6	35.4
Death rate (per '000)	9.3	9.1	8.8
No. of households ('000)	443.2	455.2	464.4
Total exports (US$ million)	132.0	140.0	140.0
Total imports (US$ million)	237.0	245.0	203.0
Tourism receipts (US$ million)	9.0	8.1	9.0
Tourist spending (US$ million)	2,003.6	2,063.9	2,122.8

Average household size 2001 (persons)	4.60				
Urban population 2001 (%)	7.4				
Age analysis (%) (2001)	*0-14*	42.5	*15-64*	53.4	*65+* 4.1
Population by sex (%) (2001)	*Male*	50.5	*Female*	49.5	
Life expectancy (years) (2001)	*Male*	61.3	*Female*	63.8	
Infant mortality (deaths per '000 live births) (2001)	57.2				
Adult literacy (%) (1997)	44.2				

Bolivia

Area (km^2)   1,098,575

Currency   Boliviano (= 100 centavos)

Location   Bolivia, a landlocked republic located in central South America, is bordered by Brazil in the north and east, by Argentina and Paraguay in the south, and by Chile and Peru in the west. Its mountainous terrain, though well stocked with minerals, makes for poor farming. There are, however, some 20,000km of navigable rivers. La Paz is the seat of government while Sucre is the legal capital and seat of judiciary.

Head of State   Gonzalo Sanchez de Lozada (2002)

Head of Government   Gonzalo Sanchez de Lozada (2002)

Ruling Party   The centre-right Nationalist Revolutionary Movement (MNR) leads a coalition with the Movimiento Izquierda Revolucionaria (MIR).

Political Structure   The president and the vice president are elected for a 5-year term by the people (1st round) or parliament (2nd round). The National Congress has two chambers. The Chamber of Deputies has 130 members, elected for a 5-year term by proportional representation. The Chamber of Senators has 27 members, elected for a 5-year term by proportional representation.

Last Elections   Elections held in July 2002 produced no clear winner but Gonzalo Sanchez de Lozada was confirmed as president in August by the parliament. He defeated Evo Morales, the leader of a long-running campaign to thwart US-led efforts to wipe out coca leaf production. In elections to the National Congress held at the same time, the MNR and the MIR, together took two thirds of the seats while Morales' Party, the Socialist Movement, won the remaining third.

Political Risk   A wave of crime has swept the country since 1999. Even worse is the evidence that police officers themselves have been actively engaged in violent crime. Vigilante groups have begun to respond and there is much talk of reform, but little action. These problems are compounded by the social unrest among coca growers, farmers, public sector workers and the unemployed. Corruption is also widespread.

International Disputes   The US-backed programme to eradicate coca production is highly unpopular. In 2000 and 2001, protestors demanded more public investment in rural areas and an end to the coca eradication scheme. In spring 2001, blockades were regularly halting traffic on many of the country's major highways around the capital, La Paz. Bolivia has had better results in improving relations with neighbours. It has defused a dispute with Peru over that country's annexation of a piece of land representing Bolivia's main outlet to the Pacific. Relations with Chile are complicated by a similar issue dating from 1884, when Chile seized the Bolivian port of Antofagasta and left the country landlocked. A Bolivian proposal for the return of the city has been rejected. Bolivia is an associate partner of the Mercosur and a member of the Andean Pact. Owing to these arrangements, the country is becoming an increasingly important transport hub within the continent.

Economy   Bolivia's GDP rose by only 1% in 2001 but growth of 3.6% is expected in 2002 and an increase of 3.4% is forecast for 2003. Inflation was 1.6% in 2001 and should be around 2% in 2002 and 2003. Foreign direct investment in Bolivia peaked in 1999, as privatisation brought in record revenues of about US$1 billion. Investment is expected to be about half that amount for 2001 and 2002, with increased activity in the oil and gas sectors as the driving force. Meanwhile, unemployment is rising and the real value of wages is falling. Bolivia's weak economy owes much to its larger neighbours - Argentina, Brazil and Peru. But officials have not handled their problems well. The government was slow to recognise that two of its major policies - coca eradication and a reform of customs procedures - removed several hundred million dollars from the informal economy, in which many unskilled workers make their living. The government's options are constrained by a budget deficit that is nearly 4% of GDP. The deficit has been pushed up by the high cost of pension reform but most of it is financed by foreign aid. Prospects for some parts of the economy are improving but the problem is that that these areas of growth are capital-intensive and generate very few jobs.

Main Industries   Bolivia's agricultural sector accounts for 15% of GDP. Programmes to boost productivity and encourage exports have had some positive effects, but productivity is low. Exports of non-traditional products, such as soya, have increased. Subsistence farmers produce rice, barley, oats, wheat and sugar cane, but coca and cocaine are the dominant crops. The major export crops (aside from coca) are rubber, cotton and herbs. Industry contributes 30% to GDP and depends mainly on mining activities. In the industrial sector, the government has pushed through an aggressive programme of privatisation. Rather than pay the government for their stakes, the buyers are required to make investment pledges in the privatised businesses. There are hopes that increased natural gas exports to neighbouring Brazil, currently in the grips of a critical energy shortage, could help boost Bolivia's economic conditions. Meanwhile, Bolivia is considering expanding its natural gas exports to include liquefied natural gas, which could be shipped worldwide from a port in Chile. Mining is the single largest sector in the country and accounts for more than half of all exports. Bolivia is one of the world's largest producers of tin and has deposits of copper, lead, silver, zinc, antimony, wolfram and gold in considerable quantity.

Energy   In 2001, Bolivia's total proven oil reserves amounted to 396.5 million barrels (an increase of 265 million barrels since 2000). Bolivia is relatively self sufficient in oil, consuming an estimated 40,000 barrels per day, slightly more than it produced (around 38,900 barrels per day), during 2001. Almost all crude oil produced in Bolivia is for domestic consumption, except for a small amount that is exported to Chile through the Sica-Arica pipeline.

	1999	2000	2001
Inflation (% change)	2.2	4.6	1.6
Exchange rate (per US$)	5.81	6.18	6.61
Interest rate (% per annum, lending rate)	35.4	34.6	20.1
GDP (% real growth)	0.4	2.4	1.0
GDP (Million units of national currency)	48,267.0	51,261.0	52,590.0
GDP (US$ million)	8,304.1	8,289.9	7,959.8
GDP per capita (US$)	1,043.6	1,018.1	955.7
Consumption (Million units of national currency)	37,210.1	39,052.2	40,526.0
Consumption (US$ million)	6,401.8	6,315.5	6,133.9
Consumption per capita (US$)	804.6	775.6	736.5
Population, mid-year ('000)	7,956.9	8,142.5	8,328.7
Birth rate (per '000)	32.3	31.7	31.1
Death rate (per '000)	8.8	8.6	8.4
No. of households ('000)	1,933.8	1,985.1	2,023.9
Total exports (US$ million)	1,051.2	1,229.5	1,284.8
Total imports (US$ million)	1,755.1	1,829.7	1,760.0
Tourism receipts (US$ million)	179.0	205.9	171.0
Tourist spending (US$ million)	165.0	182.9	171.0

Average household size 2001 (persons)	4.10				
Urban population 2001 (%)	64.4				
Age analysis (%) (2001)	*0-14*	39.5	*15-64*	56.5	*65+* 4.0
Population by sex (%) (2001)	*Male*	49.8	*Female*	50.2	
Life expectancy (years) (2001)	*Male*	63.8	*Female*	64.8	
Infant mortality (deaths per '000 live births) (2001)	58.4				
Adult literacy (%) (1997)	83.6				

TRADING PARTNERS

Major export destinations 2001 (% share)		Major import sources 2001 (% share)	
BRAZIL	22.1	BRAZIL	25.8
COLOMBIA	14.1	ARGENTINA	18.9
USA	13.9	USA	14.7
SWITZERLAND	13.0	CHILE	9.8

■ Bosnia-Herzegovina

Area (km^2)   51,129

Currency   Marka

Location   Bosnia-Herzegovina lies in the centre of the former territory of Yugoslavia, with its eastern borders alongside Serbia and the western edge against Croatia. The mountainous interior gives way to a stretch of coastline in the southwest running down to the city of Dubrovnik. The capital is Sarajevo.

Head of State   Halid Genjac (2000), Zivko Radisic (1998) and Jozo Krizanovic (2000)

Head of Government   Zlatko Lagumdzija (2001)

Ruling Party   The government is formed by a coalition of several parties.

Political Structure   The country has a rotating collective presidency of three, representing each of the three ethnic groups. There is a bicameral parliament consisting of the House of Representative (42 members) and the House of Peoples (15 members), two thirds of whose members are elected from the Moslem-Croat Federation and one third from the Serbian Republic. A valid majority requires at least one third of the members representing each entity. The Federation and the Serbian Republic have their own parliaments. Western governments have a "high representative" who can dismiss officials he deems to be impeding the peace process.

Last Elections   Presidential elections were held in September 1998. Zivko Radisic won the Serbian office with 51.2% of the vote. Alija Izetbegovic took the Muslim office with 87% of the vote while Ante Jelavic won the Croatian presidency with 53% of the vote. Izetbegovic later died and was replaced by Genjac. Jelavic was also subsequently replaced. Elections to the House of Representatives were last held in November 2000. The Party of Democratic Action won 8 seats, the Social Democratic Party won 9 and the Serb Democratic Party took 6. Seven other parties are represented in the House.

Political Risk   In 2002, the 51% of the country run jointly by Bosnians and Croats, the Croat Democratic Union, launched a campaign for Croat rights which saw Croat leaders threaten to declare autonomy. Rioting later broke out against peacekeeping forces. There has also been violence in Republika Srpska, directed mainly at Muslims.

International Disputes   A successful conclusion to the trial of Slobodan Milosevic could help to strengthen the highly unstable situation in the tiny country. The apprehension of other high-profile war criminals such as Radovan Karadzic would also help to calm the political scene. Muslims, who totalled 44% of Bosnians before the war, received only 27% of the land after the peace agreement and remain unhappy. Croats, who make up 17% of the population, were able to keep a quarter of the land.

Economy   Bosnia's GDP grew by 5.6% in 2001 while prices rose by 3.3%. After several years of double-digit growth rates, the slowdown in 2001 was particularly disappointing. The slump was particularly marked in the Republika Srpska, where output grew by just 2%. The slowdown - which is partly due to lower aid-financed reconstruction spending - marks the end of the post-war economic rebound. Industrial production is still less than half its pre-war level and measured unemployment remains high at 40%. Strong export growth and a reduction in aid-financed imports helped reduce the external current account deficit in 2001. While the deficit remains large, it continues to be financed mainly by non-debt creating flows, primarily grants. Debt cancellation in 2001 helped lower the external debt burden: the external public debt ratio declined to 54% of GDP at end-2001. In 2001, the two entities started to reverse fiscal imbalances that had worsened in previous years. Fiscal discipline was improved in both entities. The net accumulation of arrears was halted in spite of lower-than-anticipated external assistance and some arrears were repaid, although public sector wages rose more than planned. Tax and structural fiscal reforms moved ahead in 2001. A reform of the sales tax brought full harmonisation of indirect taxes and was a step towards creating a single economic space. The reform also eliminated virtually all sales tax exemptions, and significantly reduced the effective indirect tax rates. However, work on a VAT remains stalled.

Main Industries   Bosnia-Herzegovina's economy relied almost exclusively on agriculture before the war and this sector is even more dominant today. However, large tracts of land remain in dispute between the different ethnic groups and between different families. Cronyism and corruption are hindering the development of private enterprise. The process of privatisation is handicapped by the existence of at least 14 different privatisation agencies in the country. On the positive side, the banking system strengthened in 2001, giving hope for the funding of businesses, Advisers on privatisation say that many managers are enthusiastic about escaping from state control and finding new owners. Other observers point to the large grey economy - 50-60% of GDP by some estimates - as proof that Bosnians are entrepreneurs at heart, if only the system could accommodate them.

Energy   The country has no energy resources of its own and relies on imports.

	1999	2000	2001
Inflation (% change)	3.2	5.4	3.3
Exchange rate (per US$)	1.84	2.12	2.19
Interest rate (% per annum, lending rate)	24.3	30.5	
GDP (% real growth)	10.0	5.9	5.6
GDP (Million units of national currency)	8,300.0	11,300.0	8,800.0
GDP (US$ million)	4,518.0	5,319.3	4,023.4
GDP per capita (US$)	1,163.7	1,339.2	992.9
Consumption			
Consumption (US$ million)			
Consumption per capita (US$)			
Population, mid-year ('000)	3,882.4	3,972.0	4,052.0
Birth rate (per '000)	10.2	10.1	9.9
Death rate (per '000)	7.6	7.8	7.9
No. of households ('000)	556.2	599.4	645.8
Total exports (US$ million)	518.0	675.0	799.0
Total imports (US$ million)	2,431.0	2,290.0	2,340.0
Tourism receipts (US$ million)	21.0		
Tourist spending (US$ million)	3,882.4	3,972.0	4,052.0

Average household size 2001 (persons)	6.58				
Urban population 2001 (%)	43.3				
Age analysis (%) (2001)	*0-14*	20.4	*15-64*	71.3	*65+* 8.3
Population by sex (%) (2001)	*Male*	49.9	*Female*	50.1	
Life expectancy (years) (2001)	*Male*	71.1	*Female*	76.5	
Infant mortality (deaths per '000 live births) (2001)	14.2				
Adult literacy (%)					

TRADING PARTNERS

Major export destinations 2001 (% share)		Major import sources 2001 (% share)	
ITALY	28.9	CROATIA	21.3
GERMANY	15.0	SLOVENIA	15.4
CROATIA	14.8	GERMANY	14.0
AUSTRIA	10.1	ITALY	13.3

Botswana

Area (km^2) 575,000

Currency Pula (P = 100 thebe)

Location Botswana is a landlocked territory in central southern Africa. It is bounded by South Africa in the south and east, by Zimbabwe in the northeast, and by Namibia in the west and north. There is also a short northern border with Zambia. The country has a varied climate, ranging from the swamplands of the Okavango and Limpopo to the deserts of the Kalagadi. The capital is Gaborone.

Head of State President Festus Mogae (1998)

Head of Government Ian Khama (1998)

Ruling Party Botswana Democratic Party (BDP)

Political Structure Botswana is an independent member of the Commonwealth with an executive president who is elected by universal suffrage for a term of five years. Legislative power is vested in the National Assembly, which has 47 members. Of these, 40 members are elected for a 5-year term in single-seat constituencies, 4 members co-opted by the elected members and 2 members ex officio and the Speaker (if elected from outside Parliament).

Last Elections Legislative elections were held in October 1999, when the ruling BDP was returned to power with 54% of the vote and 33 seats in the National Assembly. Most of the remaining seats went to the Botswana National Front (BNF). The BDP has held power without a break since independence but is losing its influence in urban areas to the BNF. Although the government spends freely in the towns, its supporters are mostly rural Batswana - a group of eight ethnic clans defined by the constitution as the "majority tribe". Unlike other ethnic groups, this majority tribe is officially represented in a special chamber and their presence helps to preserve the government's core support.

Political Risk The greatest threat to Botswana's prosperity is the AIDS pandemic. The country has one of the highest infection rates in the world with about 38% of its population infected. Life expectancy is only 40 years. The government, however, has been commended by international experts for its positive attitude toward the problem and its efforts to slow the disease's progress.

International Disputes There have been some tensions with Namibia over the sovereignty of the tiny island of Kasikili on the Lobe River. This issue was referred to the International Court of Justice.

Economy Abundant resources, coupled with sound macroeconomic policies, have enabled Botswana to record some of the highest growth rates in the world over the past 30 years. GDP grew by 7.1% in 2001 and prices increased by 7.2%. Botswana boasts one of the best economic records of any country in southern Africa. The World Bank ranked it as the fastest-growing country between 1966 and 1997. Good management of natural assets is the difference between Botswana and many of its African peers. The country presently enjoys a per capita income of US$2,800 and has foreign reserves of US$6.3 billion. Revenues from diamonds have helped to achieve a 74% literacy rate and strong road and telecommunications infrastructure. The country's market-friendly environment and investments in education are other factors that have contributed to growth. Monetary policy has tightened as interest rates rose and the growth of credit to the private sector has slowed. Unemployment remains a problem, running at more than 20% of the labour force. The country's development plan places a great emphasis on diversification, which is considered critical for generating employment, alleviating poverty and reducing income inequality. Botswana's strong external position provides considerable flexibility to pursue these objectives. The public enterprise sector is being restructured through privatisation.

Main Industries Botswana is one of the world's largest diamond producers. Diamonds account for more than one third of GDP, 70% of export earnings and about two thirds of the central government's revenue. Mining and government services are the other foundations and together represent over half of the country's GDP. Manufacturing, on the other had, accounts for just 5% of GDP and has performed poorly in recent years. One of the biggest blows to manufacturing was the closure of its vehicle export business in 2001. Vehicle exports accounted for US$144 million of the country's export earnings and 48% of all manufacturing exports. Privatisation promises to bring more revenues over the next few years. The biggest intended sell-off is the country's telecommunications firm. Agricultural is the main employer with cattle herding contributing over 85% of total farming production. This activity has suffered in recent years as a result of recurrent disease in cattle herds. Aside from cattle farming, the land is generally too dry to permit much arable crop production. The government continues to pursue policies aimed at diversification of the economy but with only modest success.

Energy Botswana's coal resources, together with natural fuels such as brushwood, account for most of its needs. A sizeable proportion of its electricity is of hydroelectric origin, although some of this is imported.

	1999	2000	2001
Inflation (% change)	6.9	7.9	7.2
Exchange rate (per US$)	4.62	5.10	5.84
Interest rate (% per annum, lending rate)	14.6	15.3	15.8
GDP (% real growth)	6.1	8.7	7.1
GDP (Million units of national currency)	23,366.0	27,240.0	31,198.0
GDP (US$ million)	5,052.8	5,339.3	5,341.1
GDP per capita (US$)	3,161.3	3,291.8	3,200.2
Consumption (Million units of national currency)	6,936.8	7,824.5	9,477.4
Consumption (US$ million)	1,500.0	1,533.7	1,622.5
Consumption per capita (US$)	938.5	945.5	972.2
Population, mid-year ('000)	1,598.3	1,622.0	1,669.0
Birth rate (per '000)	32.6	32.0	31.3
Death rate (per '000)	19.6	21.1	22.7
No. of households ('000)	416.2	407.3	402.1
Total exports (US$ million)	2,162.1	2,506.0	2,290.6
Total imports (US$ million)	2,214.5	2,468.7	568.9
Tourism receipts (US$ million)	234.0	223.4	191.4
Tourist spending (US$ million)	143.0	162.7	137.1

Average household size 2001 (persons)	3.98					
Urban population 2001 (%)	50.7					
Age analysis (%) (2001)	*0-14*	42.9	*15-64*	54.6	*65+*	2.4
Population by sex (%) (2001)	*Male*	48.8	*Female*	51.2		
Life expectancy (years) (2001)	*Male*	38.3	*Female*	37.8		
Infant mortality (deaths per '000 live births) (2001)	68.7					
Adult literacy (%) (1997)	74.4					

◼ Brazil

Area (km²) 8,511,965

Currency Real (= 100 centavos)

Location Brazil, the largest country in South America, occupies some two thirds of the continent's entire Atlantic coast and has a wide range of climatic conditions, from the humid equatorial states of the north to the cooler and drier south. Much of the country is made up of dense tropical forest and jungle, and apart from the capital, Brasilia, there are no settlements of any size in the interior of the country.

Head of State President Fernando Henrique Cardoso (1995)

Head of Government President Fernando Henrique Cardoso

Ruling Party Brazilian Social Democratic Party (PSDB) leads a 4-party coalition.

Political Structure Brazil has an executive president who is elected by popular mandate for a term of four years and is answerable to a bicameral National Congress which has two chambers. The Chamber of Deputies is composed of 513 members, elected for a 4-year term by proportional representation. The Federal Senate has 81 members, elected for 8-year terms, with elections every four years for alternately one third and two thirds of the seats. Originally barred from seeking a second term, Cardoso pushed through a constitutional amendment in 1997 that allowed him to run again in 1998.

Last Elections In October 1998, Cardoso won a second term as president when he narrowly defeated Lula da Silva of the leftwing Workers Party. In Congressional elections held at the same time, the Liberal Front Party (LFP) took 106 seats in the Chamber of Deputies and 20 in the Senate. The PSDB won 99 seats in the Chamber and 16 in the Senate. The Brazilian Democratic Movement (PMDB), which generally supports Cardoso, won 82 votes in the Chamber and 27 in the Senate. These figures mean little, however, since no fewer than 18 different political parties are represented in Congress and operate without any real form of party discipline.

Political Risk In the summer of 2002, Brazil's currency, the real, fell to its lowest level since the introduction of the Real Plan in 1994. In the wake of the debacle in Argentina, investors are extremely reluctant to put more money into the region. The situation is further complicated by the coming election in October 2002. This combination of political risk and fragile fiscal fundamentals puts extreme pressure on industry. Even if the country quickly regains stability, the affair will have highlighted the fragility of the reforms put into place by the current government. Meanwhile, social problems remain serious. Crime is rampant in most urban areas and the country's largest cities are some of the most dangerous in the world. Drugs, unemployment and bad policing are behind the crime wave. The country's distribution of income is the most inequitable in the world.

International Disputes Brazil has a long-standing disagreement with Argentina over the use of waterways for power generation but has moderated its objections now that both countries are members of Mercosur. In the north, Brazil's relations with Guyana and Suriname are sometimes strained by guerrilla activity. Brazil, along with Argentina, has occasionally intervened in the domestic political scene in Paraguay (another member of Mercosur) to shore up the country's fragile democracy.

Economy Brazil's GDP rose by a meagre 1.5% in 2001 and is expected to grow by 2.5% in 2002 and 3.5% in 2003. Inflation was 6.8% in 2001 but should fall to 6.1% in 2002 and 3.9% in 2003. The current account deficit in 2001 reached US$23.2 billion, almost entirely financed by net inflows of FDI. The events of 11 September 2001 were followed by a sharp depreciation of the real, a rise in bond spreads and a significant fall in the stock market index. Brazil's currency lost about a quarter of its value during the first nine months of 2002, most of it in July of that year. The government has made some progress on its agenda of structural reform. A constitutional amendment introducing explicit taxation in domestic markets of petroleum products was approved by Congress in December, 2001. Progress has been made as well in the privatisation of federalised state banks, with the auctions of two banks which were finalised in December 2001and January 2002, respectively. The government is attempting to address its energy problems by attracting more foreign investment to the energy sector and by promoting increased supply in the medium and long term.

Main Industries Brazil has a vibrant agricultural sector. The growth of farm output was 3.5% in 2001 and in 2002 output is expected to increase by 4.3%. The sector's stellar performance has helped to keep inflation under control. Brazil is the world's top producer of orange juice, sugar cane and coffee. It ranks second in world production of soya and meat (beef and poultry) and third for fruits and corn. Agri-business accounts for over a quarter of total GDP. The country also has an abundance of mineral deposits (for example, bauxite, iron ore, manganese, chrome, lead, zinc, tungsten and nickel). Brazil's industrial base is one of the largest and most diversified of any emerging economy. The country's big manufacturers include producers of automobiles, consumer electronics, computers and software, and heavy industries making everything from steel to planes. With the stagnation of government activities as a result of the steps taken to curtail expenditure, services expanded only moderately. Tourism is another sector with great potential though it has never lived up to its potential, relying too heavily on local visitors rather than international tourists. The country has built up a streamlined and competitive private sector but growth will only be strong if policy makers manage to further reduce the country's underlying economic imbalances.

Energy Brazil contains the second largest oil reserves in South America (after Venezuela), at 8.1 billion barrels. Although Brazil continues to strive for self-sufficiency in oil production, it is unlikely that the country will reach this goal within the next few years. Production has been rising steadily since the early 1990s, topping 1.5 million barrels per day in 2000. The offshore Campos Basin, north of Rio de Janeiro, is the country's most prolific production area. Brazil's oil consumption is estimated at nearly two million barrels per day. In 2001, an electricity shortage forced the government to introduce emergency measures to cut consumption by 20%. A combination of factors contributed to the problem including a failure to expand grid limits, partial privatisation and Californian-style bungling of tariffs. To modernise, Brazil will need an estimated US$38 billion worth of investment in its energy sector.

	1999	2000	2001
Inflation (% change)	4.9	7.0	6.8
Exchange rate (per US$)	1.81	1.83	2.36
Interest rate (% per annum, lending rate)	80.4	56.8	57.6
GDP (% real growth)	0.8	4.4	1.5
GDP (Trillion units of national currency)	1.0	1.1	1.2
GDP (US$ million)	531,136.3	593,779.7	502,508.4
GDP per capita (US$)	3,282.9	3,621.8	3,025.1
Consumption (Trillion units of national currency)	0.6	0.7	0.8
Consumption (US$ million)	352,700.4	401,980.9	341,072.7
Consumption per capita (US$)	2,180.0	2,451.9	2,053.3
Population, mid-year ('000)	161,790.3	163,947.5	166,112.5
Birth rate (per '000)	19.9	19.7	19.5
Death rate (per '000)	7.1	7.0	7.0
No. of households ('000)	46,306.3	47,278.7	48,583.1
Total exports (US$ million)	48,011.0	55,085.5	58,222.6
Total imports (US$ million)	51,674.7	58,531.9	64,508.8
Tourism receipts (US$ million)	3,994.0	3,405.3	2,637.5
Tourist spending (US$ million)	3,059.0	4,610.5	3,253.4

Average household size 2001 (persons)	3.47				
Urban population 2001 (%)	81.3				
Age analysis (%) (2001)	*0-14*	28.0	*15-64*	66.7	*65+* 5.3
Population by sex (%) (2001)	*Male*	49.4	*Female*	50.6	
Life expectancy (years) (2001)	*Male*	64.4	*Female*	72.3	
Infant mortality (deaths per '000 live births) (2001)	39.0				
Adult literacy (%) (1997)	84.0				

TRADING PARTNERS

Major export destinations 2001 (% share)

USA	23.2
ARGENTINA	11.1
GERMANY	5.2
NETHERLANDS	4.2

Major import sources 2001 (% share)

USA	24.6
ARGENTINA	12.1
GERMANY	8.0
JAPAN	4.5

British Virgin Islands

Area (km^2) 153

Currency US dollar (US$ = 100 cents)

Location The British Virgin Islands lie in the Eastern Caribbean, to the east of Puerto Rico and northeast of St Kitts and Nevis. Only about 16 of the 60-plus islands administered by Britain (as distinct from those run by the US) are inhabited. All except the coral island of Anegada are hilly or mountainous. The capital is Road Town.

Head of State HM Queen Elizabeth II

Head of Government Ralph T. O'Neal (1995)

Ruling Party Virgin Islands Party

Political Structure The British Virgin Islands, a UK Crown Colony, are governed to a large extent by the local assembly (Legislative Council), despite the presence of a Governor appointed by the Crown who formally presides over an Executive Council. The Legislative Council has 15 members, 13 members elected for a 4-year term in single-seat constituencies, one ex officio member and one speaker chosen from outside the council.

Last Elections General elections were held in May 1999. The ruling Virgin Islands Party took 38% of the vote and seven seats in the Legislative Council. The National Democratic Party received 37% of the vote and five council seats. Ralph O'Neal was returned as head of the government.

Political Risk With a high standard of living and a successful upmarket tourist industry, the British Virgin Islands pose little political risk. A high level of political security complements the extensive tax haven facilities on offer in the islands.

International Disputes The islands have been under pressure from OECD to allow greater transparency in the dealings of the financial sector with international business companies. More stringent regulations have been imposed in 2001 and 2002.

Economy GDP grew by less than 3% in 2001 while prices rose by around 5%. The economy, one of the most prosperous in the Caribbean, is highly dependent on tourism but the sector performed poorly in 2001. The government's efforts to diversify the financial sector beyond its traditional base of focusing on international business companies has yielded encouraging, but far from spectacular results. However, more than 90% of government revenues are still derived from international business companies. There is some discussion of changing the laws governing these entities but officials insist that the proposals are not in response to international action on tax havens.

Main Industries Agriculture accounts for only 2% of GDP and industry contributes just 6%. Agriculture is a minor activity consisting mainly of livestock. Poor soils limit the islands' ability to meet domestic food requirements but there is some cultivation of fruit and vegetables and fish are exported. Industry centres on the processing of agricultural products, especially rum manufacturing, although there is a stone quarry and a paint factory. The economy is nevertheless one of the most stable and prosperous in the Caribbean. Income and wealth depend on tourism, which generates an estimated 45% of the national income. Unlike most other tourist destinations, the country did not suffer significantly from the effects of 11 September 2001. The British Virgin Islands are also home to over 140,000 international business companies and the number is growing steadily. The islands are regarded as the world capital for setting up international business companies. However, these opaque identities have raised the concerns of regulators in Western nations. The government is actively trying to broaden the financial sector to include new areas such as insurance and mutual funds. The islands' small number of expensive resorts is complemented by a growing number of others aimed at the mass market.

Energy The islands have no domestic sources of energy and rely entirely on imports.

	1999	2000	2001
Inflation (% change)	6.1	5.4	5.0
Exchange rate (per US$)	1.00	1.00	1.00
Interest rate			
GDP (% real growth)	4.4	3.2	
GDP (Million units of national currency)	677.9	737.4	792.8
GDP (US$ million)	677.9	737.4	792.8
GDP per capita (US$)	32,281.1	35,113.0	36,037.5
Consumption (Million units of national currency)	422.7	438.1	480.2
Consumption (US$ million)	422.7	438.1	480.2
Consumption per capita (US$)	20,130.2	20,859.7	21,825.6
Population, mid-year ('000)	21.0	21.0	22.0
Birth rate (per '000)	16.4	16.1	15.7
Death rate (per '000)	5.1	5.1	5.1
No. of households ('000)	4.7	4.6	4.6
Total exports (US$ million)			
Total imports (US$ million)			
Tourism receipts (US$ million)	273.2	324.1	251.0
Tourist spending (US$ million)			

Average household size 2001 (persons)		4.54				
Urban population 2001 (%)		61.9				
Age analysis (%) (2001)	*0-14*	30.2	*15-64*	63.0	*65+*	6.7
Population by sex (%) (2001)	*Male*	49.3	*Female*	50.7		
Life expectancy (years) (2001)	*Male*	74.8	*Female*	76.6		
Infant mortality (deaths per '000 live births) (2001)		19.1				
Adult literacy (%)						

Brunei

Area (km^2) 5,765

Currency Brunei dollar (S = 100 sen)

Location The Sultanate of Brunei lies on the northwestern coast of the island of Borneo and is surrounded on all sides by Malaysian territory. The country has a humid and tropical climate. The capital is Bandar Seri Begawan.

Head of State HM Sultan Sir Muda Hassanal Bolkiah Mu'izzadin Waddaulah

Head of Government HM Sultan Sir Muda Hassanal Bolkiah Mu'izzadin Waddaulah

Ruling Party There are no legal political parties.

Political Structure Brunei achieved full independence from the UK in 1984 and is ruled by an executive monarch, the Sultan, in whose hands all legal powers are vested. The Sultan is assisted by a Council of Ministers, a Religious Council and a Privy Council. However, part of the Constitution has been revoked since 1962, when massive protests developed, and a state of emergency was declared which has yet to be revoked. The Sultan disbanded the Legislative Council in 1984 and now rules by decree.

Last Elections There are no elections in Brunei.

Political Risk A financial dispute within the royal family has been resolved and no major risks now exist.

International Disputes The whole territory of Brunei is subject to an old claim by Malaysia that has remained dormant for some time. Brunei is also one of several countries making a claim for the sovereignty of the Spratly Islands.

Economy Brunei's small, wealthy economy is a mixture of foreign and domestic entrepreneurship, government regulation and welfare measures, and village tradition. It is almost totally supported by exports of crude oil and natural gas, with revenues from the hydrocarbons sector accounting for over 50% of GDP, around 80-90% of exports, and 75-90% of government revenues. GDFP grew by about 2.3% in 2001 while prices rose by around 1.8%. Per capita GDP is far above most other developing countries (although sharply down from its high point around 1980), and substantial income from overseas investment supplements income from domestic sources. The government provides for all medical services and subsidises food and housing. Expatriates - mainly engaged in the oil and gas industries - account for over 40% of the workforce. The Brunei Investment Agency, which at one point was worth around US$110 billion, has now fallen in value to an estimated US$30-40 billion. Brunei's main economic problems include rising unemployment (especially among recent college graduates), huge state subsidies, a civil service which employs around 75% of Brunei's workforce, extensive state economic controls, a chronic (and worsening) budget deficit, a small tax base and a heavy reliance on the hydrocarbons sector.

Main Industries Brunei's income is almost entirely derived from its oil and gas resources, which account for around 70% of annual revenues in a typical year and employees two-fifths of the workforce. Farming is largely limited to yams, bananas and cassava, mainly for the domestic market, but there are also considerable stocks of hardwoods, which are exported. Agriculture accounts for only 5% of GDP. There are very few industries other than those related to oil and gas. The government had hoped to develop a financial centre, based on the country's policy of low taxation and banking secrecy. This ambition, however, is likely to be strongly opposed by Western countries. Brunei would like to diversify away from hydrocarbons into areas like tourism (the country boasts unspoiled tropical forests, beaches, shipwrecks, the world's largest palace and gilded mosques, among other things) and energy-intensive industries like petrochemicals, oil refining and aluminium smelting.

Energy Brunei contains proven crude oil reserves of 1.35 billion barrels and produces 173,000 barrels per day (of mainly low-sulphur crude oil), plus around 22,000 barrels per day of natural gas liquids. This is down from production of around 270,000 barrels per day in 1980. Crude oil production peaked in 1979 at about 240,000 barrels per day, but was cut back deliberately to extend life of the fields and to improve recovery rates. Brunei has seven offshore oil fields. Major customers for Brunei's oil include Japan, South Korea, Singapore, Taiwan and Thailand. In November 2000, Brunei signed an agreement with China to export 10,000 barrels per day, the first time Brunei has exported to mainland China. In 2001, Brunei launched its first deepwater petroleum exploration areas, and competitive bidding will be allowed for the first time.

	1999	2000	2001
Inflation (% change)	1.0	1.6	1.8
Exchange rate (per US$)	1.69	1.72	1.79
Interest rate			
GDP (% real growth)	-1.0	1.7	2.3
GDP (Million units of national currency)	19,587.5	20,239.3	21,077.5
GDP (US$ million)	11,556.3	11,740.0	11,763.8
GDP per capita (US$)	36,672.9	36,496.5	35,828.1
Consumption (Million units of national currency)	13,559.9	13,542.9	14,099.1
Consumption (US$ million)	8,000.2	7,855.7	7,869.0
Consumption per capita (US$)	25,387.6	24,421.3	23,966.0
Population, mid-year ('000)	315.1	321.7	328.3
Birth rate (per '000)	21.2	20.7	20.3
Death rate (per '000)	3.1	3.1	3.2
No. of households ('000)	69.4	70.1	70.4
Total exports (US$ million)	2,216.0	3,552.0	3,727.0
Total imports (US$ million)	1,034.0	1,111.0	1,030.0
Tourism receipts (US$ million)			
Tourist spending (US$ million)	315.1	321.7	328.3

Average household size 2001 (persons)	4.64				
Urban population 2001 (%)	72.7				
Age analysis (%) (2001)	*0-14*	32.1	*15-64* 64.6	*65+*	3.3
Population by sex (%) (2001)	*Male*	52.3	*Female* 47.7		
Life expectancy (years) (2001)	*Male*	74.0	*Female* 78.7		
Infant mortality (deaths per '000 live births) (2001)	9.4				
Adult literacy (%) (1997)	90.1				

TRADING PARTNERS
Major export destinations 2001 (% share)   **Major import sources 2001 (% share)**

JAPAN	46.4	SINGAPORE	33.9
SOUTH KOREA	12.4	MALAYSIA	23.3
USA	11.6	USA	8.6
THAILAND	10.6	UNITED KINGDOM	7.1

▨ Bulgaria

Area (km^2)　110,910

Currency　Lev (= 100 stotinki)

Location　With its southern borders meeting Turkey, Greece, Macedonia and Serbia, and its northern border meeting Romania, Bulgaria has been exposed to a wide range of cultures. The climate is equable, with low rainfall especially along the popular Black Sea coast. The capital is Sofia.

Head of State　Georgi Parvanov (2002)

Head of Government　Simeon Saxe-Coburg (2001)

Ruling Party　The National Movement for Simenon II leads a coalition.

Political Structure　The new constitution provides for a 240-seat parliament which is directly elected for a 4-year term. The president is also directly elected but most power rests with the Prime Minister who is generally leader of the dominant party.

Last Elections　Presidential elections held in November 2001 brought Georgi Parvanov of the Bulgarian Socialist Party to power. He received 54% of the vote. In parliamentary elections occurring in July 2001, the National Movement won 120 seats, soundly defeating the United Democratic Forces which took 51 seats. The Coalition for Bulgaria took the remaining seats. Simenon, the former King of Bulgaria, was then named Prime Minister.

Political Risk　Bulgaria's reform-minded government lacks cohesion and influence. Moreover, public impatience is mounting because the government has not successfully delivered on promises to cut taxes and boost spending on social programmes. So far, the government has managed to press forward with its reforms but it must do much more to satisfy social needs or voters will turn away and the country's prospects for accession to the EU will be jeopardised.

International Disputes　The country has improved its bilateral relations with several Balkan neighbours. Bulgaria's long-running disputes with Macedonia have finally been resolved. This should remove most of the barriers that have delayed more than 20 bilateral agreements in recent years. Relations with Turkey look to improve now that disagreements over the demarcation of part of the border have been resolved. A free-trade agreement between the two countries came into force in 1999 and economists predict that Turkish investment in the country will rise quickly during the coming decade.

Economy　GDP increased by 4.5% in 2001 and should grow by another 4% in 2002. In 2003, growth is forecast at 5%. Inflation was 7.5% in 2001 and should be about 4.5% in 2002. In 2003, prices are forecast to rise by 3.5%. The government plans to maintain a balanced budget over the medium term by gradually reducing the budget deficit. The purpose is to bring down the public debt-to-GDP ratio. The personal income tax will also be lowered by raising the threshold for the non-taxable income bracket by more than expected inflation. At the same time, officials are taking steps to broaden the tax base in order to move toward a more efficient system that also satisfies EU requirements and improves revenue collection. Total employment has been falling since 1997 because the large contractions in the public sector have not been fully offset by gains in the private sector. Job creation in the private sector has been sluggish owing to the Russian crisis in late 1998 and the conflict in Kosovo in 1999 but also because the restructuring process in many privatised companies sold as part of management-employee buyouts has lagged behind. In addition, more than half the unemployed have been out of work for more than a year. Sofia must quickly act to revamp its labour policies or risk a loss of support for the overall programme of liberalisation and reform.

Main Industries　Agriculture accounts for a fifth of GDP and its share is growing. Bulgaria has the potential to become a major agricultural supplier for all of Central Europe but foreign investment is badly needed. Agriculture, along with the country's food processing industries, supply a wide range of cereal crops, as well as fruit, vegetables and wine. About a quarter of the labour force works in agriculture but productivity is low. At the time of writing, the economy was mainly driven by rapid growth in the services sector. Tourism holds promise, especially sites along the Black Sea coast. Almost all of this industry has been privatised and the government has boosted its funding for this sector. More than two thirds of the state's assets other than infrastructure have been privatised and a number of loss-making state enterprises have been eliminated. Banking supervision has improved markedly. Bulgaria has deposits of iron, coal and limestone that have yet to be developed. There is also a possibility of oil in the Black Sea. Bulgaria is restructuring its energy sector in hopes of attracting private investors and reducing the country's dependence on nuclear energy. Several thermal power plants have been privatised as well as a number of small hydroelectric plants.

Energy　Bulgaria has small indigenous oil reserves and produced only 1,000 bbl/d of oil in 2000. With the transition to a market economy and the end of favourable Eastern bloc prices for Soviet oil, Bulgarian oil consumption decreased by more than 50% since 1989. However, domestic demand has picked up in the past four years, with consumption rising to 121,000 bbl/d in 2001. Solid fuels account for half of Bulgaria's energy requirements, with oil and natural gas imports from Russia making up most of the remainder. The country has ambitious plans to supply gas to western and southern Europe with the help of American, European and Turkish investments.

	1999	2000	2001
Inflation (% change)	2.6	10.4	7.5
Exchange rate (per US$)	1.84	2.12	2.18
Interest rate (% per annum, lending rate)	12.8	11.5	11.1
GDP (% real growth)	2.4	5.8	4.5
GDP (Million units of national currency)	22,776.4	25,453.6	28,461.0
GDP (US$ million)	12,402.9	11,987.9	13,027.4
GDP per capita (US$)	1,511.6	1,469.5	1,606.5
Consumption (Million units of national currency)	18,752.6	20,246.4	22,617.0
Consumption (US$ million)	10,211.7	9,535.5	10,352.4
Consumption per capita (US$)	1,244.6	1,168.9	1,276.6
Population, mid-year ('000)	8,204.9	8,158.0	8,109.1
Birth rate (per '000)	8.0	7.9	7.9
Death rate (per '000)	14.6	14.7	14.9
No. of households ('000)	2,988.4	2,992.0	2,992.3
Total exports (US$ million)	4,006.0	4,825.0	5,099.0
Total imports (US$ million)	5,515.0	6,507.0	7,230.0
Tourism receipts (US$ million)	932.0	762.3	867.6
Tourist spending (US$ million)	524.0	567.9	446.7

Average household size 2001 (persons)	2.73				
Urban population 2001 (%)	70.0				
Age analysis (%) (2001)	0-14	15.4	15-64	68.2	65+ 16.4
Population by sex (%) (2001)	Male	48.6	Female	51.4	
Life expectancy (years) (2001)	Male	67.1	Female	74.8	
Infant mortality (deaths per '000 live births) (2001)	15.0				
Adult literacy (%) (1997)	98.1				

TRADING PARTNERS

Major export destinations 2001 (% share)

ITALY	15.1
GERMANY	9.6
GREECE	8.8
TURKEY	8.2

Major import sources 2001 (% share)

RUSSIA	20.1
GERMANY	15.4
ITALY	9.7
FRANCE	6.1

Burkina Faso

Area (km^2) 274,122

Currency CFA franc (= 100 centimes)

Location Burkina Faso, the former Upper Volta, is a landlocked state in northwest Africa, which is bounded in the north and west by Mali, in the east by Niger, and in the south by Côte d'Ivoire, Ghana, Benin and Togo. The country's especially arid climate and hard soil makes farming difficult. The capital is Ouagadougou.

Head of State President Blaise Compaoré (1991)

Head of Government Kadre Désiré Ouedraogo (1996) resigned June 1997

Ruling Party Congress for Democracy and Progress (CDP) leads a coalition.

Political Structure Burkina Faso, which was known until 1984 as Upper Volta, has an executive president who is elected by universal suffrage for a 7-year term. The National Assembly consists of 111 members and is also elected by universal suffrage. Members serve 5-year terms. There is also a House of Representatives made up of 178 members appointed for 3-year terms.

Last Elections Presidential elections were last held in November 1998 when Blaise Compaoré won with more than 87% of the vote. Elections to the National Assembly were held in May 2002. The CDP won 57 seats in the National Assembly. The main other parties are the centrist Alliance for Democracy and Federation-African Democratic Rally which won 17 seats and the social democratic Party for Democracy and Progress/Socialist Party which took 10 seats.

Political Risk The restoration of multiparty democracy has not removed the threat of continued social unrest. The government is becoming increasingly corrupt and little interested in economic development. Poverty is widespread.

International Disputes The government's support for rebels in Sierra Leone led to tensions with Western nations but the rupture may soon be repaired now that the war is over.

Economy Burkina Faso saw growth of 5.7% in 2001 with inflation of 3%. The fiscal situation remains precarious but the stronger growth in 2001 should help. A number of revenue-raising measures have been adopted in order to meet deficit targets. The country's main challenge is to move ahead with its reform programme, so as to create the conditions for sustainable and equitable growth and durable poverty reduction. Structural reforms focus on the adoption of an automatic pricing policy for petroleum products in line with international prices, pursuit of the reform of the cotton sector and completion of the privatisation programme. Modest efforts have been made to strengthen the country's public finances and widen its revenue base, but there has been little progress in attempts to scale back public spending or alter its composition.

Main Industries One of the poorest countries in the world, landlocked Burkina Faso has a high population density, few natural resources and a fragile soil. About 90% of the population is engaged in (mainly subsistence) agriculture which is highly vulnerable to variations in rainfall. Industry remains dominated by unprofitable government-controlled corporations. Agriculture accounts for a third of GDP but is prone to drought. Animal husbandry is the main source of farming income. The recent increase in import prices, particularly of oil products, and a sharp decline in workers' remittances have been a drag on all sectors of the economy. The government's attempts to spur agricultural progress by deregulating production of rice and sugar, eliminating non-tariff barriers to trade and restructuring the cotton sector have been only half-heartedly implemented. Industry remains dominated by unprofitable government-controlled corporations. The main manufactured products are cotton lint, beverages, agricultural processing, soap, cigarettes and textiles. The financial situation of the banking system has continued to improve. Burkina Faso has some mineral deposits that are being actively mined. These include gold, copper, bauxite, manganese and graphite.

Energy The bulk of Burkina Faso's very modest fuel requirements are met by natural resources such as brushwood. In the absence of coal deposits, oil remains the main source of thermally generated energy.

	1999	2000	2001
Inflation (% change)	-1.1	-0.2	3.0
Exchange rate (per US$)	615.70	711.98	733.04
Interest rate			
GDP (% real growth)	6.2	2.2	5.7
GDP (Billion units of national currency)	1,518.0	1,561.0	1,706.9
GDP (US$ million)	2,465.5	2,192.5	2,328.5
GDP per capita (US$)	210.8	183.7	184.2
Consumption (Billion units of national currency)	1,162.9	1,206.6	1,281.2
Consumption (US$ million)	1,888.7	1,694.7	1,747.8
Consumption per capita (US$)	161.5	142.0	138.3
Population, mid-year ('000)	11,693.7	11,937.0	12,639.0
Birth rate (per '000)	46.7	46.8	46.8
Death rate (per '000)	17.2	16.8	16.4
No. of households ('000)	2,638.4	2,638.5	2,726.5
Total exports (US$ million)	254.9	213.0	174.7
Total imports (US$ million)	578.9	550.1	655.8
Tourism receipts (US$ million)	39.7	32.0	33.2
Tourist spending (US$ million)			

Average household size 2001 (persons)	4.52					
Urban population 2001 (%)	19.1					
Age analysis (%) (2001)	*0-14*	47.4	*15-64*	49.9	*65+*	2.6
Population by sex (%) (2001)	*Male*	49.6	*Female*	50.4		
Life expectancy (years) (2001)	*Male*	46.3	*Female*	48.3		
Infant mortality (deaths per '000 live births) (2001)	89.9					
Adult literacy (%) (1997)	20.7					

TRADING PARTNERS

Major export destinations 2001 (% share)

SINGAPORE	14.6
ITALY	13.5
COLOMBIA	8.6
FRANCE	7.1

Major import sources 2001 (% share)

COTE D'IVOIRE	25.6
FRANCE	24.4
TOGO	4.8
BELGIUM	3.9

Burundi

Area (km^2) 27,835

Currency Burundi franc (= 100 centimes)

Location The tiny landlocked republic of Burundi is located to the northeast of Tanzania, with Rwanda to the north and the Democratic Republic of the Congo (formerly Zaire) to the west. It lies along the rivers that feed into Lake Tanganyika further south. The climate is tropical, although there is an ample supply of water available from the rivers. The capital is Bujumbura.

Head of State Major Pierre Buyoya (July 1996)

Head of Government Pascal-Firmin Ndimira

Ruling Party All political parties were banned following Buyoya's coup d'état in July 1996.

Political Structure De facto Burundi is in de facto state of civil war. The National Assembly has 81 members, elected for a 5-year term by proportional representation with a 5% barrier. In July 1998, the Assembly was reformed into the National Transition Assembly, whereby 40 additional members were appointed, belonging to political parties and civil society.

Last Elections Buyoya's representatives hold 65 seats in the National Transition Assembly. The last elections were held in 1993 prior to the coup. In that poll, Sylvestre Ntibantunganya was confirmed as head of state. He led an uneasy coalition between the Tutsi-dominated Uprona Party and the mainly Hutu Frodebu Party. The break-up of the coalition contributed to the subsequent coup d'état. In July 1998, 40 additional members were appointed, belonging to political parties and civil society.

Political Risk More than 600,000 people died in the country's ethnic war and over 6% of the population was displaced. Malaria continues to be a serious problem, while violence and drought have caused severe food shortages.

International Disputes Although the violence in the neighbouring Democratic Congo has abated, Burundi is still under pressure because of the influx of refugees.

Economy Burundi's GDP increased by 3.3% in 2001 while prices rose by 8%. The economy remains in a desperate situation with exports depressed and the threat of violence stalling investment. The persistent decline in foreign exchange reserves and the further accumulation of external arrears, in conjunction with the absence of corrective measures and minimal international assistance has forced the rationing of foreign exchange. The financing requirements of the government are met largely by an accumulation of external arrears and domestic bank borrowing.

Main Industries Burundi is a landlocked, resource-poor country with an underdeveloped manufacturing sector. The economy is predominantly agricultural with roughly 90% of the population dependent on subsistence agriculture. Its economic health depends on the coffee crop, which accounts for 80% of foreign exchange earnings, but cotton and tea were sold on the international markets until the civil war disrupted production. The ability to pay for imports rests largely on the vagaries of the climate and the international coffee market. Only one in four children go to school, and one in nine adults has HIV/AIDS. Foods, medicines and electricity remain in short supply. The government maintains a number of restrictions on foreign financial obligations and transfers that hamper both importers and exporters. There has been some prospecting for minerals, and major deposits of zinc have been located. However, their difficult location would make them uneconomic to extract, even if there were no civil war.

Energy The greater part of Burundi's very modest energy needs is met by solid fuels such as coal, or by natural fuels such as brushwood. Hydroelectric power accounts for virtually all of its limited electricity consumption.

	1999	2000	2001
Inflation (% change)	7.9	24.3	8.0
Exchange rate (per US$)	563.56	720.67	830.35
Interest rate (% per annum, commercial lending rate)	15.2	15.8	16.8
GDP (% real growth)	-0.8	0.1	3.3
GDP (Million units of national currency)	402,519.0	489,035.0	572,316.0
GDP (US$ million)	714.2	678.6	689.2
GDP per capita (US$)	108.1	101.4	99.6
Consumption (Million units of national currency)	386,157.0	474,498.0	473,594.0
Consumption (US$ million)	685.2	658.4	570.4
Consumption per capita (US$)	103.7	98.3	82.5
Population, mid-year ('000)	6,608.6	6,695.0	6,917.5
Birth rate (per '000)	43.2	43.3	43.4
Death rate (per '000)	21.1	21.0	20.9
No. of households ('000)	1,116.5	1,142.0	1,156.8
Total exports (US$ million)	54.3	50.0	38.5
Total imports (US$ million)	118.1	147.9	139.3
Tourism receipts (US$ million)	1.0	0.8	0.7
Tourist spending (US$ million)	8.3	11.4	9.5

Average household size 2001 (persons)	5.86				
Urban population 2001 (%)	9.3				
Age analysis (%) (2001)	*0-14*	46.3	*15-64*	51.0	*65+* 2.7
Population by sex (%) (2001)	*Male*	48.9	*Female*	51.1	
Life expectancy (years) (2001)	*Male*	39.8	*Female*	41.4	
Infant mortality (deaths per '000 live births) (2001)	113.2				
Adult literacy (%) (1997)	44.6				

TRADING PARTNERS

Major export destinations 2001 (% share)		Major import sources 2001 (% share)	
SWITZERLAND	22.5	SAUDI ARABIA	12.6
GERMANY	13.3	BELGIUM	11.0
KENYA	12.0	FRANCE	9.7
JAPAN	5.9	TANZANIA	8.7

Cambodia

Area (km^2)   181,000

Currency   Riel (R = 100 sen)

Location   Cambodia, the former Kampuchea, is located at the centre of the Indochinese peninsula with Vietnam to the south and east, Laos to the north and Thailand to the northwest. Its access to the sea is through a 300-kilometre stretch of land adjoining the Gulf of Thailand. Most of the country is near-impenetrable jungle. The climate is tropical and extremely humid. The capital is Phnom-Penh.

Head of State   King Norodom Sihanouk

Head of Government   Hun Sen

Ruling Party   The Cambodian People's Party (CPP) leads a coalition with its main rival, the royalist United National Front party, known as Funcinpec.

Political Structure   The State of Cambodia resumed its traditional title in 1990, having been known since the late 1970s as Kampuchea or Democratic Kampuchea. Prince Ranariddh, the leader of Funcinpe, was ousted in a coup in 1997. The National Assembly has 122 members, elected for a 5-year term by proportional representation.

Last Elections   Hun Sen claimed victory in the July 1998 elections, defeating the royalist Funcinpe Party and its leader Prince Norodom Ranariddh. The CPP claims to have won 64 of the 122 seats in the National Assembly that were contested, with Funcinpec taking 43 seats.

Political Risk   Cambodia's experiment with democracy has been difficult. The country is still recovering from more than 20 years of war and international isolation. It has made significant progress in improving the quality of life of the population in the 10 years to 2001. However, the government - together with donors - needs to do more. Some indicators are still among the worst in Asia. For example, an estimated 36% of the population still live below the poverty line. Poverty remains concentrated in rural areas, where an estimated 90% of poor people live. Economic expansion in recent years has centred on rapid growth in textile production and exports, mainly in urban areas. For the benefits of this growth to reach the rural poor, significant investment is necessary to restore the physical infrastructure.

International Disputes   Cambodia and Vietnam have several areas of dispute. These include their maritime boundary in the Gulf of Thailand and Phnom Penh's objections to illegal immigration from Vietnam. The country's relations with Thailand reflect a century of tension. Thailand supported the Khmer Rouge rebels during their decade-long struggle to regain control and criticise the Cambodians for drug-running practices and military incursions.

Economy   GDP has been growing at rates of 5-6% in recent years but the pace of growth could slow slightly over the next couple of years. Growth is expected to be about 4.5% this year and rise to 6.1% in 2003. Meanwhile, the country has been experiencing deflation but prices should resume their rise in 2003. Cambodia's trade balance continued to improve, to an estimated surplus of US$55 million in 2001 from a deficit of US$198 million in 2000. Total exports grew to US$1.53 billion from US$1.33 billion over this period. While this growth rate is less than in 2000, it still reflects healthy external demand for Cambodian exports, led by strong growth in garments. The current account deficit of 6.6% of GDP is financed through official transfers and capital inflows in the form of concessional loans and FDI. FDI was estimated to be US$120 million in 2001. Public finances are weak as the government makes the transition between taxes on international trade to broader measures such as VAT. Concessional loans and grants are widely used to finance the capital needs of the country, which are extensive given two decades of war and neglect by the international community. The government is committed to maintaining fiscal stability with both revenues and expenditures scheduled to increase gradually as a proportion of GDP. It is also taking further steps to reorient spending toward the priority sectors of health, education, agriculture and rural infrastructure, while reducing the share of expenditures on the military. By 2003, revenues should increase to around 13% of GDP with expenditures expected to rise to 17%. Although the domestic cost of labour is quite low, exporters are often at a disadvantage due to the high costs of doing business, the country's poor infrastructure and the strong US dollar (since most costs are denominated in US dollars).

Main Industries   In 2000, the industry sector (and in particular the garments subsector) led economic growth because agriculture suffered from flooding, and growth in services was muted. In 2001, economic developments were more balanced. The agriculture sector, which accounts for 32% of the economy, grew by 5% in 2001, despite localised flooding along the Mekong River and droughts in the north and northwest. Growth in industry, recently dominated by garments, slowed to a rate of 12%. The services sector registered an increase of 1.9%, with tourism continuing to play an important role. The rate of expansion in the agriculture sector is of particular concern, given that over 80% of the population live in rural areas and depend largely on agriculture for their livelihoods. Labour market statistics show that wages for unskilled workers in Phnom Penh were stagnant or declining in 2001, highlighting the difficulty that the labour market faces in absorbing new entrants.

Energy   Cambodia's best chance to achieve some measurable improvement in living standards is that one of the energy consortiums exploring off its coast will find oil and/or gas. Preliminary wells proved the existence of hydrocarbons but it is still uncertain that these are available in commercial quantities. Most of the country's energy needs are met either from coal or natural fuels such as firewood. Its electricity production, however, is almost 40% derived from hydroelectric power plants.

	1999	2000	2001
Inflation (% change)	4.0	-0.8	-0.6
Exchange rate (per US$)	3,807.83	3,840.75	3,916.33
Interest rate (% per annum, lending rate)	17.6	17.3	16.5
GDP (% real growth)	6.9	5.4	5.3
GDP (Billion units of national currency)	11,646.4	11,923.0	12,931.5
GDP (US$ million)	3,058.5	3,104.3	3,302.0
GDP per capita (US$)	285.4	283.6	295.3
Consumption (Billion units of national currency)	5,487.8	6,083.4	6,810.9
Consumption (US$ million)	1,441.2	1,583.9	1,739.1
Consumption per capita (US$)	134.5	144.7	155.6
Population, mid-year ('000)	10,715.6	10,945.3	11,180.0
Birth rate (per '000)	37.1	36.6	36.2
Death rate (per '000)	10.7	10.7	10.6
No. of households ('000)	2,500.2	2,472.2	2,424.4
Total exports (US$ million)	980.0	1,327.0	1,531.0
Total imports (US$ million)	1,212.0	1,525.0	1,476.0
Tourism receipts (US$ million)	190.0	180.3	162.0
Tourist spending (US$ million)	8.0	12.3	10.8

Average household size 2001 (persons)	4.47				
Urban population 2001 (%)	16.3				
Age analysis (%) (2001)	*0-14*	40.7	*15-64*	56.2	*65+*	3.1
Population by sex (%) (2001)	*Male*	48.6	*Female*	51.4	
Life expectancy (years) (2001)	*Male*	53.8	*Female*	58.6	
Infant mortality (deaths per '000 live births) (2001)	76.6				
Adult literacy (%) (1997)	66.0				

TRADING PARTNERS

Major export destinations 2001 (% share)

USA	64.2
UNITED KINGDOM	9.8
GERMANY	7.6
FRANCE	2.7

Major import sources 2001 (% share)

THAILAND	23.4
SINGAPORE	18.6
HONG KONG, CHINA	13.2
CHINA	7.7

▪ Cameroon

Area (km^2)   465,500

Currency   CFA franc (= 100 centimes)

Location   Cameroon lies on the West African Atlantic coast facing south-westwards into the Gulf of Guinea. With Nigeria to the west, Gabon, Equatorial Guinea and Congo to the south, and the Central African Republic and Chad to the east and northeast, it has a tropical but dry climate. The capital is Yaoundé.

Head of State   President Paul Biya (1982)

Head of Government   Peter Mafany Musonge Mafani (1996)

Ruling Party   The Rassemblement Démocratique du Peuple Camerounais (RDPC) leads a coalition.

Political Structure   Cameroon was a 1-party socialist state from 1964 (when all but the ruling party were banned) until 1992. Under the 1990 Constitution, the executive president is elected by popular mandate for a 7-year term. Members of the 180-member National Assembly are elected for a 5-year term by popular mandate. In December 1995 a new constitution was approved, with provisions included to increase the president's term from five to seven years with a maximum presidential tenure of two terms.

Last Elections   Presidential elections held in October 1997 returned Biya to power. He claimed to have won over 90% of the vote but international observers put the turnout at 30%. Biya stood without opposition, leaving foreigners with little basis to criticise the results. In practice, the president continues to rule by decree. Elections to the national assembly were held at the same time and the RDPC won 109 seats. No percentage of the total vote was reported.

Political Risk   Cameroon is under international pressure to manage its oil revenues with more transparency. There are few democratic foundations in the Cameroon, but Biya has made modest efforts at democratic appeasement. He advocates a new democratic structure and has drawn the main opposition leaders into talks. The division between the country's English and French-speaking population is an uneasy one. Donor countries frequently express concerns about the lack of progress on human rights.

International Disputes   Cameroon and Nigeria claim the Bakassi peninsula, a 1,000-square-kilometer area in the Gulf of Guinea that is believed to contain significant oil reserves. Several oil discoveries have been made on the peninsula and its adjoining waters, but at present operations in the disputed area have been suspended. Clashes between security forces of the two countries have occurred, and each country maintains a significant force in the area.

Economy   Cameroon's GDP increased by 5.3% in 2001 and should grow by 4.6% in 2002. In 2003, growth is forecast at 4.9%. Prices rose by 2.8% in 2001 and are expected to increase by 2.9% in 2002. Inflation should be about 2.5% in 2003. Cameroon's external position has strengthened considerably in more recent years. In the budget area, progress has been made in realising fiscal sustainability through the strengthening of the collection of both oil and non-oil revenues. A weak expenditure management system has also been strengthened. Other improvements are mainly the result of the government's implementation of several structural reforms in compliance with IMF and World Bank agreements. The country's growth prospects depend on its success in increasing investment (both domestic and foreign), raising the domestic tax revenue base, rebuilding infrastructure and implementing structural reforms that will bolster its external competitiveness.

Main Industries   Cameroon's economy is less dominated by petroleum than many other national economies in West Central Africa, although petroleum products constitute more than half of total exports. After petroleum, agriculture is the most significant sector in Cameroon's economy, providing employment for about 60% of the population. Timber, coffee and cocoa are the country's principal non-oil exports. The country faces many serious problems, however, owing mainly to an unfavourable climate for business enterprises. Many farms are extremely small but the government hopes to develop larger-scale agro-industrial complexes that will boost productivity. Industrial development centres on bauxite, with a large aluminium smelter at Edéa. There is also an oil refinery which processes part of Cameroon's crude oil production. Other industries include food processing, light consumer goods, textiles and lumber. In the structural area, important reforms were launched, including a large-scale privatisation programme, and significant actions were taken to liberalise Cameroon's energy and transport sectors.

Energy   While Cameroon's oil production is predicted to steadily decline, its refinery capacity and its position as the terminus of the 225,000-barrels-per-day export pipeline from Chad could transform the country into a significant oil transport centre. The total cost of field development and construction of pipeline and export facilities is estimated at US$3-3.5 billion. The country is presently sub-Saharan Africa's fifth largest oil producer with crude oil production of 84,800 barrels per day (bbl/d). Cameroon's crude oil output is expected to fall to between 50,000 bbl/d and 60,000 bbl/d by 2005.

	1999	2000	2001
Inflation (% change)	2.9	0.8	2.8
Exchange rate (per US$)	615.70	711.98	733.04
Interest rate (% per annum, lending rate)	22.0	22.0	20.7
GDP (% real growth)	4.4	4.2	5.3
GDP (Billion units of national currency)	5,406.0	5,827.5	6,320.4
GDP (US$ million)	8,780.3	8,184.9	8,622.2
GDP per capita (US$)	594.1	542.6	541.1
Consumption (Billion units of national currency)	4,317.4	4,498.4	4,669.2
Consumption (US$ million)	7,012.2	6,318.2	6,369.7
Consumption per capita (US$)	474.4	418.8	399.7
Population, mid-year ('000)	14,780.4	15,085.0	15,935.4
Birth rate (per '000)	37.2	36.9	36.6
Death rate (per '000)	14.7	14.7	14.6
No. of households ('000)	3,962.1	3,960.5	4,079.8
Total exports (US$ million)	1,600.6	1,635.0	1,772.9
Total imports (US$ million)	1,317.6	1,205.0	1,399.3
Tourism receipts (US$ million)			
Tourist spending (US$ million)			

Average household size 2001 (persons)	3.81					
Urban population 2001 (%)	49.7					
Age analysis (%) (2001)	*0-14*	43.8	*15-64*	52.6	*65+*	3.6
Population by sex (%) (2001)	*Male*	49.6	*Female*	50.4		
Life expectancy (years) (2001)	*Male*	49.3	*Female*	50.6		
Infant mortality (deaths per '000 live births) (2001)	80.9					
Adult literacy (%) (1997)	71.7					

TRADING PARTNERS

Major export destinations 2001 (% share)		Major import sources 2001 (% share)	
ITALY	24.5	FRANCE	29.7
SPAIN	13.7	NIGERIA	12.3
FRANCE	12.0	USA	9.9
CHINA	8.0	GERMANY	6.5

Canada

Area (km^2) 9,922,385

Currency Canadian dollar (C$ = 100 cents)

Location Extending some 3,000 miles from the Pacific Ocean in the west to the Arctic Atlantic in the east, Canada occupies virtually the entire northern half of the North American continent. The capital is Ottawa.

Head of State HM Queen Elizabeth II

Head of Government Jean Chrétien (1993)

Ruling Party The Liberal Party leads the government.

Political Structure Canada comprises a federation of 12 provinces and territories, each of which exercises considerable political autonomy over its own affairs. The Northwest Territories are to be divided so as to create an Indian territory, to be known as Nunavut. The province of Québec, which is French-speaking, narrowly rejected a referendum on secession from the Federation in 1995. Parliament consists of the House of Commons in Ottawa with 301 elected members from individual constituencies and the Senate which has 12 members appointed by the Prime Minister. A governor-general represents the monarch.

Last Elections Elections to the House of Commons were held in November 2000. The Liberal Party took 172 seats while the Reform Conservative Alliance won 66 seats. Others seats were scattered among numerous parties.

Political Risk A perennial question in Canadian politics is when the country's separatists will once again pose a challenge to unity. In 1995, just over 49% of voters in Quebec opted for independence. Federalists are pleased that the issue has dropped out of the headlines but supporters vow to push for a new referendum when the time is right. Roughly 40% of Quebeckers are separatists. English-speaking Canadians are also opposed and believe Quebec has used the threat of secession to extort special concessions from the state government.

International Disputes Canada has no significant territorial disputes. Relations with the EU, Japan and the US are occasionally strained by disputes over fishing rights. Disagreements with Canada's giant neighbour to the south are frequent but rarely fundamental. Issues that the two countries have battled over in the past decade include attempts to limit Canadian advertising content in American magazines, a running debate over Canada's "cultural rights", American influence in Canada's financial markets and concerns about the loss of skilled Canadians who are lured away by higher-paying US jobs. Most recently, the two countries have tangled over Canada's timber exports to the US and the charge that unfair subsidies are driving the trade. Such issues emerge every few years, especially in periods when growth is slowing.

Economy The Canadian economy grew by 1.5% in 2001 and is expected to increase by 2.5% in 2002. In 2003, growth should be up to 3.6%. Inflation was 2.5% in 2001 and will fall to 0.9% in 2002 and 1.8% in 2003. After ending the 1990s with a very strong performance, underpinned by the sound macroeconomic and structural policies put in place during the decade, the Canadian economy has slowed substantially. The downturn in large part has reflected the weaker US economy, which has reduced growth in Canada's exports and contributed to a slowdown in private investment. In addition, consumption growth has moderated, owing to a fall in real income growth, a softening in the job market and an associated fall in consumer confidence. Given its proximity and close integration with the US, Canada has been significantly affected in the aftermath of the terrorist attacks. The impact on the Canadian economy has included a significant disruption of commercial traffic in the Canada-US border area, a decline in business confidence and interruptions in activities such as air travel and tourism. The slowing in economic activity in recent quarters has led to a decline in resource utilisation. Labour shortages have diminished, with the unemployment rate rising from 7% at the beginning of 2001 to around 8% in December-January. Capacity utilisation in the non-farm goods-producing sector fell sharply, largely reflecting a downturn in manufacturing.

Main Industries Canada's economy has been shifting away from being primarily resource-based, and now boasts a larger portion of manufacturing and high-technology industries. However, the economic slowdown in North America has had a disproportionate impact on Canada's high-technology industries. Agriculture accounts for less than 5% of GDP but the sector's exports provide an important boost to the economy. A rebound in commodity prices is the major reason for the strong performance of farming exports since 2000. The industrial sector makes up almost 80% of GDP but is suffering from the effects of a weak US economy. The auto industry has experienced layoffs and production halts due to lower demand while businesses in the information and communications technology have shrunk. These developments are worrying because the latter two industries accounted for a quarter of total manufacturing output in 2000 and a fifth of output growth in that year. In the mineral sector, Canada is the world's largest producer of zinc and uranium and has substantial reserves of nickel, potash, cobalt, silver and gold.

Energy Canada has proven conventional oil reserves of 4.4 billion barrels, a 152 million barrel increase over estimates in 2001 levels. Oil production averaged 2.8 million barrels per day in 2001, with estimated consumption of two million barrels. The province of Alberta, located in western Canada, is by far the country's leading oil producer. While Alberta's light oil reserves are declining (the province now contains an estimated 45% of the country's light oil reserves), there are huge oil sands deposits. Meanwhile, projects and potential projects in other provinces are shifting the oil industry focus to include the eastern and northern parts of the country. Some analysts estimate that the region off Canada's east coast could hold upwards to 20 trillion cubic feet of gas. The 26-year ban on oil and gas exploration along Canada's West Coast continues. Although there is great potential in the West Coast, environmental groups continue to oppose such development. The Canadian oil industry is also in the midst of consolidation, reducing the number of active companies. Two of the largest companies, Alberta Energy and PanCanadian, began merger discussions in 2002. If the deal goes through, the new company reportedly will become the largest independent North American producer.

	1999	2000	2001
Inflation (% change)	1.8	2.7	2.5
Exchange rate (per US$)	1.49	1.49	1.55
Interest rate (% per annum, lending rate)	6.4	7.3	5.8
GDP (% real growth)	5.1	4.4	1.5
GDP (Million units of national currency)	975,263.0	1,056,010.0	1,084,120.0
GDP (US$ million)	656,420.1	711,065.2	699,992.3
GDP per capita (US$)	21,535.4	23,320.3	22,776.0
Consumption (Million units of national currency)	520,758.3	551,132.4	564,286.9
Consumption (US$ million)	350,506.7	371,105.5	364,347.6
Consumption per capita (US$)	11,499.2	12,170.9	11,854.9
Population, mid-year ('000)	30,480.9	30,491.3	30,733.8
Birth rate (per '000)	11.6	11.4	11.1
Death rate (per '000)	7.4	7.5	7.6
No. of households ('000)	11,790.0	11,900.0	11,964.1
Total exports (US$ million)	238,446.0	276,635.0	259,858.0
Total imports (US$ million)	220,183.0	244,786.0	231,876.8
Tourism receipts (US$ million)	10,171.0	11,194.0	9,146.3
Tourist spending (US$ million)	11,345.0	12,733.3	10,236.8

Average household size 2001 (persons)	2.56				
Urban population 2001 (%)	77.2				
Age analysis (%) (2001)	*0-14*	19.0	*15-64*	68.4	*65+* 12.5
Population by sex (%) (2001)	*Male*	49.6	*Female*	50.4	
Life expectancy (years) (2001)	*Male*	76.1	*Female*	81.7	
Infant mortality (deaths per '000 live births) (2001)	5.2				
Adult literacy (%) (1998)	99.0				

TRADING PARTNERS

Major export destinations 2001 (% share)

USA	87.1
JAPAN	2.1
UNITED KINGDOM	1.3
CHINA	1.0

Major import sources 2001 (% share)

USA	64.1
JAPAN	4.2
CHINA	3.6
MEXICO	3.6

Cape Verde

Area (km^2) 4,035

Currency Escudo (Esc = 100 centavos)

Location Cape Verde, one of the smallest African states, consists of two groups of islands (known as the Windward and Leeward Islands) off the Atlantic coast of West Africa, some 500km west of Senegal. The capital is Praia.

Head of State Pedro Verona Rodrigues Pires (2001)

Head of Government José Maria Neves (2001)

Ruling Party The government is formed by the African Party of Independence of Cape Verde (PAICV).

Political Structure The Republic of Cape Verde became independent from Portugal in 1985 and quickly established itself as a 1-party state with a socialist orientation. Under the 1990 Constitution the country has an executive president, elected by popular mandate for a 5-year term. He answers to a 72-member National Assembly, also elected for five years.

Last Elections Elections to he National Assembly were held in January 2001 when the PAICV received 47% of the votes and 40 seats. The Movement for the Democracy won 40% of the votes and 30 seats. Presidential elections occurred in February 2001. Pires received just over 50% of the vote, narrowly defeating Carlos Alberto Wahnon de Carvalho Veiga.

Political Risk As elsewhere in Africa, the resumption of multiparty politics has opened up the potential for foreign assistance. Cape Verde, however, is extremely poor and its political institutions especially fragile.

International Disputes There are no international disputes.

Economy Growth of GDP fell to 3% in 2001 while inflation was 3.7%. After several years of strong growth, Cape Verde's economy has weakened. The slowdown is putting increasing pressure on the budget. Expenditure restraint, coupled with a tighter monetary policy, is critical. The government has also been forced to ration foreign exchange and this caused a loss of confidence in the currency. Optimists find encouragement in the government's modest achievements with its programme of privatisation and the decision to liberalise trade.

Main Industries Cape Verde's low per capita GDP reflects a poor natural resource base, including serious water shortages exacerbated by cycles of long-term drought. The economy is service-oriented, with commerce, transport and public services accounting for almost 70% of GDP. Although nearly 70% of the population lives in rural areas, the share of agriculture in GDP in 1998 was only 13%. Only the farms in the country's irrigated valleys are reliable producers of basic foodstuffs. The main agricultural products are bananas, corn, beans, sweet potatoes, sugarcane, coffee and peanuts. About 90% of food must be imported. The fishing potential, mostly lobster and tuna, is not fully exploited. Cape Verde annually runs a high trade deficit, financed by foreign aid and remittances from emigrants; remittances constitute a supplement to GDP of more than 20%. Cape Verde has very little domestic industry of any importance, the main activities revolving around the processing of agricultural raw materials (flour milling, rum manufacture, garment production, fish processing) and ship repair. Industry accounts for 18% of GDP but the sector's only exports are hides and shoes. The mining industry centres on the extraction of pozzuolana, a volcanic rock, and the production of sea salt, which is obtained by an evaporation process.

Energy Cape Verde is entirely dependent on imported energy supplies, mainly in the form of oil and natural gas. All electricity is produced by thermal power stations.

	1999	2000	2001
Inflation (% change)	4.4	-2.4	3.7
Exchange rate (per US$)	102.70	115.88	123.21
Interest rate (% per annum, lending rate)	12.0	11.9	12.8
GDP (% real growth)	8.6	6.8	3.0
GDP (Million units of national currency)	60,388.0	64,680.0	69,501.0
GDP (US$ million)	588.0	558.2	564.1
GDP per capita (US$)	1,397.9	1,304.2	1,261.9
Consumption (Million units of national currency)	30,271.4	35,341.0	37,051.2
Consumption (US$ million)	294.8	305.0	300.7
Consumption per capita (US$)	700.7	712.6	672.7
Population, mid-year ('000)	420.6	428.0	447.0
Birth rate (per '000)	30.9	30.3	29.7
Death rate (per '000)	6.1	6.0	5.8
No. of households ('000)	102.8	99.2	101.4
Total exports (US$ million)	47.0	49.0	51.0
Total imports (US$ million)	224.7	215.0	223.7
Tourism receipts (US$ million)	23.0	16.0	16.2
Tourist spending (US$ million)	19.2	20.9	21.7

Average household size 2001 (persons)		4.31				
Urban population 2001 (%)		63.3				
Age analysis (%) (2001)	*0-14*	40.3	*15-64*	55.0	*65+*	4.6
Population by sex (%) (2001)	*Male*	46.2	*Female*	53.8		
Life expectancy (years) (2001)	*Male*	66.6	*Female*	72.4		
Infant mortality (deaths per '000 live births) (2001)		51.4				
Adult literacy (%) (1997)		71.0				

TRADING PARTNERS

Major export destinations 2001 (% share)

PORTUGAL	52.7
UNITED KINGDOM	25.6
USA	10.6
FRANCE	6.1

Major import sources 2001 (% share)

PORTUGAL	48.1
NETHERLANDS	9.1
ITALY	5.6
FRANCE	5.3

Cayman Islands

Area (km^2)   259

Currency   Cayman Islands dollar (CI$ = 100 cents)

Location   The Cayman Islands lie in the Caribbean, about 230km south of Cuba and 300km northwest of Jamaica. The climate is consistently warm, with only light rainfall. The capital is George Town.

Head of State   HM Queen Elizabeth II

Head of Government   Governor Peter Smith (1999)

Ruling Party   There are no formal political parties in the Cayman Islands, though some exist in practice. A "National Team" governs.

Political Structure   The Cayman Islands were a dependency of Jamaica until 1962 and have been a UK Dependent Territory ever since. There has been no serious move to replace the system created by the 1972 Constitution, which awards all executive power to the Governor and the 8-member Executive Council (of which four members are elected by the Legislative Assembly, with the Governor and the other three ex officio members). The Legislative Assembly has 18 members, of whom 3 are officials and the other 15 are elected by universal suffrage for a term of five years. A move introduced in 1987 granted resident Cayman Islanders certain electoral privileges over immigrants.

Last Elections   Elections to the Legislative Assembly were last held in November 2000, when all the candidates presented themselves as independents.

Political Risk   Generally, personalities rather than issues dominate in Caymanian politics but there is a movement to introduce political parties to the territory. The Islands' status as a dependent territory and their relatively high level of per capita income yield a stable economic and political system.

International Disputes   Financial regulations have been tightened but the government refuses to aid "fishing expeditions" by other countries hoping to catch tax dodgers.

Economy   Affluence is high, thanks to the considerable revenues derived from tourism, import duties and other fee incomes and the operations of the financial sector. However, growth of GDP fell to 2.3% in 2001 while inflation exceeded 3%. More than 75% of the economy is service-based, principally financial services and tourism. Today, the Caymans are home to more than 580 banks, the biggest offshore centre for structured debt transactions and second only to Luxembourg as a home for fund (mainly hedge fund) administrators. The number of registered companies increased by 17% in 2001 and is now almost 60,000. The figure represents one-and-a-half companies per person. The currency is often stronger than the US dollar, a factor which periodically impacts on the tourism sector.

Main Industries   Tourism is the main source of income in the Caymans, with a wide range of facilities on offer. Tourist revenues are also the primary source of funding for the country's development. The sector accounts for about three quarters of all economic activity and employs a third of the workforce. There were more than 100,000 visitors in 2000 but the number plummeted in 2001. A majority of tourist arrivals (close to 70%) are passenger visits from cruise ships. Tourism, however, has reached its saturation point. The planned construction of several large resorts is now raising concerns about the environmental impact of such large-scale development. The islands' financial services industry has been under constant pressure to stop money laundering and has imposed stringent new regulations. International offshore funds, attracted by a complete absence of income tax or other corporate taxes, are the driving force for growth in this sector. Both fund management and structured debt business are growing at more than 10% per year but the pace of growth slumped markedly in 2002. Meanwhile, the insurance business has doubled in size. The total assets of Cayman Islands' banks exceed US$500 billion, making it the world's fifth largest banking centre.

Energy   All of the country's energy requirements are imported, with oil predominating. All electricity generation is derived from thermal stations.

© Euromonitor International 2002

	1999	2000	2001
Inflation (% change)	2.2	2.7	
Exchange rate (per US$)	0.82	0.80	0.82
Interest rate			
GDP (% real growth)	3.6	3.0	2.3
GDP (Million units of national currency)	978.6	1,035.2	1,088.6
GDP (US$ million)	1,200.3	1,290.7	1,324.0
GDP per capita (US$)	32,440.3	33,966.7	33,101.1
Consumption (Million units of national currency)	523.8	535.6	573.8
Consumption (US$ million)	642.5	667.8	697.8
Consumption per capita (US$)	17,364.7	17,574.2	17,445.8
Population, mid-year ('000)	37.0	38.0	40.0
Birth rate (per '000)	13.9	13.6	13.2
Death rate (per '000)	4.9	4.9	4.9
No. of households ('000)	7.8	8.2	8.4
Total exports (US$ million)			
Total imports (US$ million)			
Tourism receipts (US$ million)	526.6	607.2	407.1
Tourist spending (US$ million)	37.0	38.0	40.0

Average household size 2001 (persons)	4.65					
Urban population 2001 (%)	100.0					
Age analysis (%) (2001)	*0-14*	30.2	*15-64*	63.0	*65+*	6.7
Population by sex (%) (2001)	*Male*	49.9	*Female*	50.1		
Life expectancy (years)						
Infant mortality (deaths per '000 live births) (2001)	5.7					
Adult literacy (%)						

■ Central African Republic

Area (km^2) 624,975

Currency CFA franc (= 100 centimes)

Location The Central African Republic is located in the geographic centre of the continent. It borders on Congo and the Democratic Republic of the Congo (formerly Zaire) in the south, Chad in the north, Sudan in the east and Cameroon in the west. Although there are important watercourses in the east of the country, much of the rest is semi-desert, and climatic conditions are dry tropical. The capital is Bangui.

Head of State President Ange-Felix Patasse (1993)

Head of Government Anicet Georges Dologuele (1999)

Ruling Party Central African People's Liberation Party leads a 4-party coalition.

Political Structure Talks to restore multiparty democracy were held in 1993 and 1994 following the collapse of the "Grand National Debate" during 1992. Under the present version of the constitution the people elect the president for a 6-year term. The National Assembly consists of 109 members, elected for a 5-year term in 3- and 4-seat constituencies.

Last Elections In presidential elections held in September 1999, Patasse received 52% of the vote and was returned to office. The latest elections to the National Assembly took place in December 1998. The Central African People's Liberation Party took 47 seats with the remainder spread among several minor parties.

Political Risk In June 2001, the government - with much Libyan support - turned back an attempted coup by rebel soldiers. Another uprising was put down in November 2001, again with Libyan support. The Central African Republic is plagued by recurrent violence and political disagreements. Problems stem from corruption that has become commonplace and ethnic rivalries. Over 30,000 emigrated in 2001/2002.

International Disputes Relations between the president and France are poor. Libyan soldiers keep the peace in the country and the opposition regards them as the "new colonialists".

Economy Growth of GDP fell to 1.6% in 2001 and prices rose by 3.3%. Measures implemented in 2001 and the last quarter of 2000 have helped the authorities regain a measure of control over public finances. A key challenge facing the authorities is to raise revenue collection. The revenue ratio in the Central African Republic remains one of the lowest in sub-Saharan Africa and constrains the functioning of the central administration. The authorities have responded by implementing measures to strengthen tax and customs administrations and streamlining the tax system. The agenda for structural reform is focused on measures designed to improve economic efficiency and increase growth potential. A tiny domestic market prevents the development of many manufacturing operations and related activities. Other barriers to development include the country's landlocked position, a poor transportation system, a largely unskilled workforce and a legacy of misdirected macroeconomic policies.

Main Industries Subsistence agriculture, together with forestry, remains the backbone of the economy of the Central African Republic, with more than 70% of the population living in outlying areas. The agricultural sector generates half of GDP. Cattle herding is the major activity, although cotton and coffee are other important commodities. The small industrial sector consists mainly of sawmills, breweries, textiles, footwear, and the assembly of bicycles and motorcycles. The privatisation of petroleum distribution has been completed and the national oil company was sold in 2001. Authorities are also planning to place the large public companies in the electricity and telecommunications sectors under private management, and to divest or liquidate the remaining public enterprises. Mining provides much of the impetus for the economy, with diamonds, gold, uranium, copper and manganese being extracted in the west of the country. In the late 1980s, the mineral sector provided half of GDP but its share has declined over the past 15 years.

Energy The country has no domestic sources of energy, relying entirely on imports.

	1999	2000	2001
Inflation (% change)	-1.5	3.0	3.3
Exchange rate (per US$)	615.70	711.98	733.04
Interest rate (% per annum, lending rate)	22.0	22.0	20.7
GDP (% real growth)	3.5	2.6	1.6
GDP (Million units of national currency)	647,296.0	685,344.0	716,607.0
GDP (US$ million)	1,051.3	962.6	977.6
GDP per capita (US$)	295.1	266.3	262.4
Consumption (Million units of national currency)	384,056.2	428,711.0	454,084.1
Consumption (US$ million)	623.8	602.1	619.5
Consumption per capita (US$)	175.1	166.6	166.3
Population, mid-year ('000)	3,563.1	3,615.0	3,726.0
Birth rate (per '000)	38.9	38.5	38.0
Death rate (per '000)	18.9	18.8	18.7
No. of households ('000)	655.1	662.8	680.5
Total exports (US$ million)	163.4	148.0	160.4
Total imports (US$ million)	163.6	144.0	148.1
Tourism receipts (US$ million)			
Tourist spending (US$ million)			

Average household size 2001 (persons)	5.45					
Urban population 2001 (%)	41.7					
Age analysis (%) (2001)	*0-14*	42.8	*15-64*	53.3	*65+*	3.9
Population by sex (%) (2001)	*Male*	48.3	*Female*	51.7		
Life expectancy (years) (2001)	*Male*	42.7	*Female*	46.0		
Infant mortality (deaths per '000 live births) (2001)	94.9					
Adult literacy (%) (1997)	42.4					

TRADING PARTNERS

Major export destinations 2001 (% share)		Major import sources 2001 (% share)	
BELGIUM	53.1	FRANCE	24.1
KAZAKHSTAN	9.0	CAMEROON	12.1
SPAIN	8.5	SPAIN	4.1
PAKISTAN	7.5	GERMANY	3.2

Chad

Area (km²) 1,284,000

Currency CFA franc (= 100 centimes)

Location Chad, one of the largest and most sparsely populated countries in Africa, is located in central North Africa. Libya is to the north, Sudan to the east, and Niger and Cameroon to the west. The Central African Republic borders on the country's more fertile southern regions. The climate is dry tropical, with little rainfall. The capital is N'Djaména.

Head of State President Idriss Déby (2001)

Head of Government Nagoum Yamassoum (1999)

Ruling Party The Patriotic Salvation Movement (MPS) leads a 3-party coalition.

Political Structure The president is elected for a 5-year term by the people. The National Assembly has 155 members, elected for a 4-year term in 25 single-member constituencies and 34 multi-member constituencies. The president can serve a maximum of two 5-year terms in office.

Last Elections Elections to the National Assembly took place in April 2002. The MPS won 112 seats, the Rally for Democracy and Progress took 10 seats and the remainder were scattered among several smaller parties. Elections for president occurred in May 2001 when Déby was easily re-election with 63% of the vote.

Political Risk Unrest in Chad is widespread. Rebel groups maintain bases in the mountains from which they attack government troops. The government stepped up its campaign against the rebels in 2001, using US$25 million for new weapons that had been paid as an advance for oil royalties. Some members of the government remained mired in a scandal over counterfeiting. The president is harshly criticised, both at home and abroad.

International Disputes The US has supported international loans to Chad on the condition that the revenue generated from projects is used for health and education. When it was revealed that Chad was using the funds to purchase arms, the country was told that its debt would not be reduced as part of the international debt moratorium. Chad and Libya have a dispute about several islands in Lake Chad. Finally, there is disagreement about international boundaries in the vicinity of Lake Chad, the lack of which has led to border incidents in the past. The International Court has made a ruling that must be ratified by Cameroon, Chad, Niger and Nigeria.

Economy Chad's economy made an impressive recovery in 2001, growing by 8.9%. Inflation was 12.4% in that year. The strong rate of growth was mainly because of the acceleration of the construction of the Chad-Cameroon pipeline. Fiscal policies followed a broadly prudent path and progress in structural reforms was close to targets. Notwithstanding the overall progress, advances in certain areas have been less than anticipated. Revenue collection, in particular, weakened in the second half of 2001. The external current account deficit (excluding official transfers) widened from 16% of GDP in 2000 to an estimated 42% in 2001, owing to higher imports related to the investment in the energy sector. A large part of the current account deficit was financed by foreign direct investment. Net official foreign exchange reserves increased in the third quarter to reach CFA18 billion, partially reversing a decline in the first half of the year. The structure of expenditure was somewhat unfavourable, with defence spending slightly higher than envisaged as a result of increased rebel activity in the North. Rapid development of the country's major natural resources (petroleum, uranium and kaolin) appears to offer the only prospects for economic improvement in this country.

Main Industries Chad's economy is dominated by the agricultural sector, which accounts for over 45% of GDP and employs roughly 80% of the population. Cotton, the major cash crop, accounts for 60% of Chad's exports. Agricultural production slipped in 2001 owing to extreme weather conditions, a shortfall in external financing and a sharp decline in the world market price of cotton. Cotton is grown in the south of the country, while cattle herding, the other main source of foreign revenues, is conducted in the central regions. Consumer prices increased sharply in 2001, reflecting mainly the impact of food shortages, but prices started declining in the last quarter of the year as food supplies improved. The industrial sector accounts for only a small portion of GDP. The major industries are simple ones such as textiles, meatpacking, beer brewing, soap, cigarettes and construction materials. The financial sector's health remained good, with all but one bank complying with the main prudential ratios at the end of 2001. Chad is rich in natural and mineral resources. Currently, only deposits of sodium carbonate and kaolin are utilised commercially. Deposits of other minerals have been discovered in Chad, including gold, bauxite, tin, tungsten, titanium, iron ore and petroleum. Chad possesses substantial proven oil reserves and has received backing from the World Bank for a US$3.7 billion project in the south, plus a pipeline to transport the oil to the Cameroon coast.

Energy With its large undeveloped oil reserves, Chad has the potential to become a significant energy producer. Construction is currently underway on a 650-mile pipeline which will allow Chad to export 225,000 barrels per day of crude by the middle of the decade. The total cost of field development and construction of the pipeline and export facilities is estimated to be US$3.5 billion. The pipeline consists of two primary components, development of the oil fields and construction of the pipeline and export facilities. Chad's downstream oil sector is currently totally dependent on petroleum product imports from neighbouring Nigeria and Cameroon.

	1999	2000	2001
Inflation (% change)	-8.4	3.7	12.4
Exchange rate (per US$)	615.70	711.98	733.04
Interest rate (% per annum, lending rate)	22.0	22.0	20.7
GDP (% real growth)	2.3	1.0	8.9
GDP (Million units of national currency)	962,858.0	1,002,371.0	1,175,334.0
GDP (US$ million)	1,563.8	1,407.9	1,603.4
GDP per capita (US$)	208.5	184.0	201.5
Consumption (Million units of national currency)	387,708.0	432,802.1	544,113.5
Consumption (US$ million)	629.7	607.9	742.3
Consumption per capita (US$)	84.0	79.5	93.3
Population, mid-year ('000)	7,499.5	7,651.0	7,959.0
Birth rate (per '000)	48.4	48.5	48.5
Death rate (per '000)	19.3	19.1	18.8
No. of households ('000)	1,426.4	1,439.0	1,477.0
Total exports (US$ million)	201.6	192.7	197.1
Total imports (US$ million)	315.9	322.8	617.2
Tourism receipts (US$ million)			
Tourist spending (US$ million)			

Average household size 2001 (persons)	5.32					
Urban population 2001 (%)	24.2					
Age analysis (%) (2001)	*0-14*	45.8	*15-64*	50.8	*65+*	3.4
Population by sex (%) (2001)	*Male*	49.7	*Female*	50.3		
Life expectancy (years) (2001)	*Male*	44.8	*Female*	47.2		
Infant mortality (deaths per '000 live births) (2001)	117.7					
Adult literacy (%) (1997)	50.3					

TRADING PARTNERS

Major export destinations 2001 (% share)		Major import sources 2001 (% share)	
PORTUGAL	27.7	USA	35.2
GERMANY	15.0	FRANCE	24.3
USA	7.2	CAMEROON	7.4
FRANCE	6.5	NIGERIA	4.5

Chile

Area (km^2)   751,625

Currency   Chilean peso (P = 100 centavos)

Location   Although never more than about 200km wide, Chile occupies the greater part of South America's Pacific coastline, with Argentina to its east over the Andes mountains and Peru and Bolivia to the north. In the south its Tierra del Fuego regions are sub-Antarctic in character. The extraordinary range of climatic conditions that result is one of the most striking features of the country. The capital is Santiago.

Head of State   President Ricardo Lagos Escobar (2000)

Head of Government   President Ricardo Lagos Escobar (2000)

Ruling Party   The Christian Democratic Party leads a broad-based coalition of Parties for Democracy.

Political Structure   An executive president serves a 6-year term. The National Congress) has two chambers - a 48-member Senate and a 117-member Chamber of Deputies, elected for four years.

Last Elections   In presidential elections held in January 2000, Lagos took 51% of the vote. He defeated Joaquín Lavín Infante, who received 49%. Congressional elections were held in December 2001. The coalition led by Lagos took 51 seats while the Independent Democratic Union gained 35 seats. The remainder of the seats were dispersed among various other parties.

Political Risk   Chile's armed services urgently need modernisation but the government's latest effort to accomplish that has made the task harder. In 2000, Lagos promised to scrap the peculiar arrangement under which Chile's armed forces receive an off-budget allocation from Codelco, the state-owned copper company, to finance purchases of equipment. The agreement transfers 10% of Codelco's export returns directly to the armed forces. In 2002, Lagos reversed himself and agreed to purchase a number of F-16s from the US at a cost of US$660 million. The decision will absorb all the available funds from Codelco until 2009. Many suspect that the decision was influenced by Chile's current negotiations for a free-trade treaty with the US. For the armed services, the decision is bad news because, although the air force needs planes, the navy needs ships even more. By 2010, the entire surface fleet will be obsolete. Ships are badly needed to protect fisheries and control drug trafficking, while Chile's relations with its neighbours are good and there may little need for attack aircraft. The distribution of income in Chile poses an entirely different problem. Almost a quarter of citizens live below the poverty line and the country's richest 10% have incomes that are 15 times greater than those of the poorest 10%. Because of the gap, social tensions are rising.

International Disputes   Chile has an ongoing disagreement with Bolivia about that country's demand for the restoration of access to the Pacific Ocean. Chile and Argentina have solved most their border disputes, paving the way for closer cooperation between the two economies.

Economy   GDP grew by 2.8% in 2001 and the economy should strengthen, growing by 3% in 2002 and by 6% in 2003. Inflation was 3.6% in 2001 and is expected to be 2.3% in 2002. In 2003, prices are forecast to rise by 3%. Chile has maintained a very open trade regime and has continued with the unilateral phased reduction of its uniform external tariff rate, now down to 8%. Authorities recently intensified trade agreement negotiations with the US and have concluded an agreement with the EU. In 2001, Chile introduced a new system of unemployment insurance. Officials are also addressing unemployment problems with temporary programmes, including a scheme to support rescheduling of small and medium-sized enterprises' debt. With tighter fiscal controls, the combined public sector deficit is projected to narrow moderately to less than 2% of GDP by the end of 2002. Despite general success, the country's level of unemployment remains high. Many analysts believe that it is important that the government do more in this area. Authorities are under pressure to ensure that any new labour market reform measures do not introduce rigidities that would limit the economy's ability to generate employment. There is much support for a policy of granting adjustments to the minimum wage where this will help to boost employment.

Main Industries   Despite frequent efforts to diversify, the mining sector remains the backbone of Chile's economy, accounting for 40% of export revenues. Codelco, the giant state-owned copper firm, is the dominant firm but there are other large mining operations. The government is trying to redress Chile's dependence on copper and mining in general by channelling more capital into non-traditional areas such as seafood and wine. Manufacturing has faired well in recent years as the private sector took hold. Most firms are either small or of medium size but nevertheless have rapidly won new foreign markets, with processed fruits and vegetables and fine wines becoming important foreign-exchange earners. Chile's agricultural sector depends on livestock rearing in the plateau and extensive crop farming in the central region. Products such as tomato paste, wine, shoes and textiles are expected to benefit as the pattern of trade changes to reflect Chile's new associate membership in Mercosur. Chile has been privatising major government holdings since the 1970s. The last two major companies to remain under state control are the oil company, Empresa Nacional de Petróleo, and the copper company, Codelco, Chile's largest company.

Energy   Chile has only 150 million barrels of proven oil reserves and produced 17,000 barrels per day (bbl/d) in 2001. Domestic production is only 6% of total consumption. The country also has natural gas reserves of 3.5 trillion cubic feet and produces about 69 billion cubic feet of gas each year. The energy sector is largely in private hands. Chile's electricity sector has served as a model for subsequent privatisations throughout the world and is improving its efficiency and reliability. The recent opening of Chile's gas sector has helped to satisfy growing demand in the industrial and power-generating sectors.

	1999	2000	2001
Inflation (% change)	3.3	3.8	3.6
Exchange rate (per US$)	508.78	535.47	634.94
Interest rate (% per annum, lending rate)	12.6	14.8	11.9
GDP (% real growth)	-1.0	4.4	2.8
GDP (Billion units of national currency)	37,164.0	40,436.0	42,192.0
GDP (US$ million)	73,045.8	75,515.5	66,450.6
GDP per capita (US$)	4,928.3	5,028.4	4,368.5
Consumption (Billion units of national currency)	22,106.2	24,181.2	25,131.7
Consumption (US$ million)	43,449.8	45,159.1	39,581.3
Consumption per capita (US$)	2,931.5	3,007.0	2,602.1
Population, mid-year ('000)	14,821.7	15,017.8	15,211.3
Birth rate (per '000)	19.3	19.0	18.6
Death rate (per '000)	5.6	5.7	5.7
No. of households ('000)	3,834.9	3,938.2	3,970.8
Total exports (US$ million)	15,615.6	18,158.0	17,439.9
Total imports (US$ million)	15,137.4	18,107.0	17,233.8
Tourism receipts (US$ million)	894.0	960.6	794.3
Tourist spending (US$ million)	806.0	865.2	683.6

Average household size 2001 (persons)	3.81					
Urban population 2001 (%)	85.0					
Age analysis (%) (2001)	*0-14*	28.3	*15-64*	64.5	*65+*	7.2
Population by sex (%) (2001)	*Male*	49.5	*Female*	50.5		
Life expectancy (years) (2001)	*Male*	72.8	*Female*	78.8		
Infant mortality (deaths per '000 live births) (2001)	12.2					
Adult literacy (%) (1997)	95.2					

TRADING PARTNERS

Major export destinations 2001 (% share)

USA	18.3
JAPAN	12.5
UNITED KINGDOM	6.0
BRAZIL	5.5

Major import sources 2001 (% share)

ARGENTINA	18.7
USA	17.6
BRAZIL	8.8
CHINA	6.1

China

Area (km^2) 9,597,000

Currency Renminbi (RMB = 100 fen)

Location Occupying the entire 5,000-km spread from the Sea of Japan and the East China Sea in the east to the Afghan border in the west, China has one of the longest international boundaries in the world. In the north and northwest, its border is shared with Mongolia, Russia, Tajikistan, Kyrgyzstan and Kazakhstan. In the west, it meets Afghanistan and Pakistan, while India, Nepal, Bhutan, Myanmar, Laos and Vietnam lie to the south. The capital is Beijing.

Head of State President Jiang Zemin (1993)

Head of Government Zhu Rongji (1998)

Ruling Party Chinese Communist Party.

Political Structure China's 1992 constitution vests all legislative authority in the 3,000-member National People's Congress, which is elected every five years. The Congress, however, meets only once a year, and the Communist Party undertakes most political decisions.

Last Elections In March 1998, Zhu was elected Premier, replacing Li Peng, who had served two 5-year terms. At the same time, the legislature approved a major government reform package eliminating or merging 15 ministries (reducing the total number from 40 to 29) and abolishing four million government jobs over the next three years (cutting the bureaucracy in half).

Political Risk There is growing uncertainty about the future of the Communist Party in China. The need for reform is a universal sentiment but reforms that include direct challenges to the party's rule are still not on the table. On the economic front, there is a growing likelihood that the policies Beijing has used to stimulate growth in recent years will not be as useful in the future. Policy makers must find ways to support the private sector and to strengthen the regulatory system. If some remedy is not found soon, growth will slow to levels which could threaten the social and political fabric of the country. Meanwhile, the government has separatist movements to contend with in Tibet and Xinjiang.

International Disputes Many Chinese strategists worry about what they see as the encirclement of their country by US power in the wake of the 11 September 2001 attacks. China is also surrounded by 14 states with some borders still in dispute. Russia is wracked by domestic troubles and its new partnership with NATO has increased concerns in Beijing. Japan is regarded as bent on regional domination. No relations are more difficult than those with Taiwan, however. Beijing's rhetoric is harsh, but if it chose to go to war with Taiwan (and presumably the US), the country would lose two of its major trading partners and sources of foreign capital, as well as risking domestic political stability. China has several territorial disputes with other regional states involving the potentially hydrocarbon-rich Spratly Islands, which are claimed by Beijing.

Economy China's rate of growth has been exceptionally high during the past decade but gradually falling. Real GDP is forecast to rise by around 7% in 2002 and 7.4% in 2003. Prices will rise by a negligible amount in 2002 and increase by 1.5% in 2003. Due to increasing incomes, retail sales strengthened by 10.1% in 2001, a slightly higher rate than in 2000. Purchasing power stayed largely in the hands of urban residents, as the government increased salaries for civil servants and pensions for government retirees twice during 2001. Expansionary fiscal policy continued in 2001: Ø150 billion in government bonds were issued and a large proportion of the proceeds were targeted to support western region development. To minimise the adverse impact of the slowdown in the global economy, the government adopted several measures in 2001 to encourage exports. In May 2001, Beijing published its new 10-year poverty strategy. In it, the government designated 592 key counties for poverty reduction development work. Over the longer run, China's history of robust economic growth and its accession to the World Trade Organisation should make the country more attractive to foreign investors.

Main Industries The agricultural sector did not fare as well as other parts of the economy in 2001. Owing to a severe drought and a decrease in the planted area, farm output grew by only 2.8% in 2001. Although agriculture is no longer the dominant sector, the government gives farming a high priority. Over 900 million people live in rural China and their contentment is essential to national stability. In 2000, the sector experienced one of the worst droughts in a century with output of grain being sharply curtailed. Rice is the main food crop, but tea, sugar, cotton and fibre crops are all important cash earners. The profitability of both private and state-owned enterprises has improved as a result of increased demand and reform measures such as debt-equity swaps. The services sector has also shown improvements, recording impressive rates of growth in 2000 and 2001. Meanwhile, the government continues to pressure the military to relinquish its control over many businesses. Despite progress, the state still dominates large chunks of the economy. The Chinese themselves admit that the military controls as many as 18,000 businesses in the country. This is a major source of corruption. Each year, around US$2.5 billion is diverted from the state into personal bank accounts.

Energy China is expected to surpass Japan as the second largest world oil consumer within the next decade and reach a consumption level of 10.5 million bbl/d by 2020, making it a major factor in the world oil market. China's petroleum industry has undergone major changes in recent years. In 1998, the Chinese government reorganised most state-owned oil and gas assets into two vertically integrated firms - the China National Petroleum Corporation (CNPC) and the China Petrochemical Corporation (Sinopec). This created two regionally focused firms, CNPC in the north and west, and Sinopec in the south, though CNPC is still tilted toward crude oil production and Sinopec toward refining. Experts estimate that Beijing will have to import 40% of its oil by the 2010 - up from less than 20% today. Recent discoveries in the west and northwest of the country proved disappointing, both in terms of the size of reserves and the high cost. Planners therefore intend to diversify sources of supply toward diplomatic allies such as Russia, the republics of Central Asia, Africa and Latin America. Beijing must also find efficient suppliers to keep costs down. This means that China cannot do without Middle East production.

	1999	2000	2001
Inflation (% change)	-1.4	0.3	0.7
Exchange rate (per US$)	8.28	8.28	8.28
Interest rate (% per annum, lending rate)	5.9	5.9	5.9
GDP (% real growth)	7.1	8.0	7.3
GDP (Billion units of national currency)	8,205.4	8,940.4	9,688.9
GDP (US$ million)	991,199.8	1,079,948.1	1,170,574.3
GDP per capita (US$)	781.0	844.5	908.9
Consumption (Billion units of national currency)	3,963.3	4,173.6	4,559.2
Consumption (US$ million)	478,759.8	504,149.1	550,828.7
Consumption per capita (US$)	377.2	394.2	427.7
Population, mid-year ('000)	1,269,205.0	1,278,768.0	1,287,867.7
Birth rate (per '000)	15.6	15.3	15.1
Death rate (per '000)	7.0	7.0	7.0
No. of households ('000)	341,530.0	351,420.0	353,289.4
Total exports (US$ million)	195,150.0	249,297.0	266,620.0
Total imports (US$ million)	165,788.0	225,094.0	243,567.0
Tourism receipts (US$ million)	14,098.0	14,432.8	14,313.9
Tourist spending (US$ million)	10,864.0	8,639.5	9,798.8

Average household size 2001 (persons)	3.64				
Urban population 2001 (%)	32.6				
Age analysis (%) (2001)	*0-14*	24.4	*15-64*	68.7	*65+* 7.0
Population by sex (%) (2001)	*Male*	50.8	*Female*	49.2	
Life expectancy (years) (2001)	*Male*	68.8	*Female*	73.1	
Infant mortality (deaths per '000 live births) (2001)	38.4				
Adult literacy (%) (1997)	82.9				

TRADING PARTNERS

Major export destinations 2001 (% share)   **Major import sources 2001 (% share)**

USA	24.8	JAPAN	15.2
HONG KONG, CHINA	18.9	HONG KONG, CHINA	14.7
JAPAN	15.0	USA	9.1
GERMANY	4.1	SOUTH KOREA	8.2

Colombia

Area (km^2) 1,138,915

Currency Colombian new peso (NP = 100 centavos)

Location Colombia forms the geographical link between Central and South America. Meeting the Isthmus of Panama in the west, it is bordered on the south and east by Ecuador, Peru, Venezuela and Brazil, and has coastlines on both the Caribbean and the Pacific. Its climate is warm and temperate in the coastal strip, but arid in the inland plateau. The capital is Bogotá.

Head of State President Alvaro Uribe Velez (2002)

Head of Government President Alvaro Uribe Velez (2002)

Ruling Party The government is formed by the Colombian Conservative Party (PCC), the Liberal Party of Colombia (PLC) and non-partisans.

Political Structure Colombia has an executive president who answers to a 102-member Senate and a House of Representatives with 161 elected members. Constitutional reform has been under way for many years, but in practice the issue has been repeatedly overshadowed by concerns about the eradication of the gangs who operate the drug trade.

Last Elections In presidential elections held in May 2002, the independent candidate Alvaro Uribe Velez won in the first round 53% of the vote. The main other contender was Horacio Serpa of the Liberal Party who took 32% of the vote. Elections to the House were held in March 2002. The PLC won 54 seats followed by the PCC which took 21 seats. The remainder of the seats went to numerous smaller parties.

Political Risk The government has been unable to bring the country's 36-year long battle with insurgents to a halt. Until recently, however, Colombia's armed conflicts were remote from major population centres. That is no longer true. Even before the collapse of talks in February 2002, the Armed Forces of Colombia, the largest of the guerrilla groups, had started to bring the war to the cities with bombings and political kidnappings. The guerrillas' strategy seems to be that a firm line against them can be undermined if they show the public that the country's armed forces cannot protect them. Though strengthened by American military aid, the armed forces are hopelessly overstretched in trying to contain the guerrillas.

International Disputes The Americans want Colombia's left-wing guerrillas to be defeated and are generous in their military support. There is no such aid intended to curb the right-wing paramilitary groups. Yet it is the latter groups that are the most deeply involved in the drugs industry. The situation is a very complicated one and there is no sign that the influence of the drug-traffickers, guerrillas or paramilitaries is waning. Together, they control some US$200 billion of assets and their domination of Colombian society is as strong as ever.

Economy GDP grew by just 1.5% in 2001 but the economy should pick up in the short term. Growth of 2.5% is expected in 2002 and an increase of 3.3% is forecast for 2003. Inflation was 8% in 2001. It will fall to 7.1% in 2002 and 5.3% in 2003. The public sector deficit is expected to fall to about 2.6% of GDP in 2002, down from 5.6% in 1999. There are also plans to reform the pension system, a move which should reduce pressure on fiscal policy. Although the country's financial system remains weak, authorities continue to take steps to improve the soundness of many banks through restructuring and the imposition of higher standards. The programme of privatisation of banks will continue with several more scheduled for sale during 2002 and 2003. In last quarter of 2001, the government also launched a programme to reform labour markets. One goal is to address the problem of unemployment. At present, the inflexibility of labour markets, coupled with the country's high payroll taxes, is producing a shift in employment to the informal sector. More than 50% of all employment is now in the informal activities.

Main Industries Colombia currently is weathering difficult political and economic conditions. However, improved US and Latin American economic outlooks for the second half of 2002 are likely to have positive implications for the Colombian economy. Additionally, higher world oil prices provide a significant boost to Colombian export earnings, as oil is Colombia's top export product (followed by coal and then coffee in 2001). Oil accounted for about 25% of government revenues in 2001. Farming is the mainstay of the Colombian economy with production of coffee, sugar, bananas, cotton and meat. Coffee is grown by 400,000 farmers, mainly smallholders who employ a similar number of labourers. Coffee prices fell, however, with the advent of new, low-cost producers (for example, Vietnam and Brazil) and many Colombian farmers are losing money. In the manufacturing sector, the country's large conglomerates produce everything from soft drinks to glass, televisions and textiles. Many firms borrowed heavily in the recent past and are now in trouble. The government took over three banks and liquidated others. Further shake-ups in the still fragile financial system are expected. Investment in transportation infrastructure accounts for more than 15% of all public and private sector investment, most of it going to the rehabilitation and construction of new roads. Colombia has vast and still under-exploited reserves of minerals including coal and oil and deposits of gold, silver, copper, nickel, iron ore, platinum, bauxite, gypsum, limestone, phosphates, sulphur and uranium.

Energy Colombia has about 1.75 billion barrels of proven oil reserves, down from 2001 estimates of 1.97 billion barrels. Potential oil reserves are much larger. Estimates indicate that, without new discoveries, Colombia could become a net oil importer in the medium term. Colombia's oil production declined in 2001 to 616,000 barrels per day (bbl/d), after reaching an all-time high of 826,000 bbl/d in 1999. The Colombian government owns the country's hydrocarbon reserves. Oil and natural gas development is regulated by state oil company Empresa Colombiana de Petroleos (Ecopetrol) and the Energy and Mines Ministry. The government took measures since 2000 to make the investment climate friendlier to foreign oil companies. Ecopetrol's mandatory share in joint ventures was reduced from 50% to 30%, and a sliding royalty scale is in the process of being established. Royalties had been fixed at 20%, but the new upper limit will be 20%. The lower limit will be 5%, with production field size as the rate-determining factor.

	1999	2000	2001
Inflation (% change)	10.9	9.2	8.0
Exchange rate (per US$)	1,756.23	2,087.90	2,299.63
Interest rate (% per annum, lending rate)	25.8	18.8	20.7
GDP (% real growth)	-4.1	2.8	1.5
GDP (Billion units of national currency)	149,042.2	169,704.0	187,311.8
GDP (US$ million)	84,864.9	81,279.7	81,453.0
GDP per capita (US$)	2,198.5	2,073.1	2,046.3
Consumption (Billion units of national currency)	98,472.9	112,987.6	115,502.4
Consumption (US$ million)	56,070.6	54,115.4	50,226.5
Consumption per capita (US$)	1,452.6	1,380.3	1,261.8
Population, mid-year ('000)	38,600.6	39,205.9	39,805.6
Birth rate (per '000)	23.8	23.3	22.8
Death rate (per '000)	6.0	6.1	6.3
No. of households ('000)	8,602.9	9,114.0	9,233.6
Total exports (US$ million)	11,576.4	13,040.4	12,257.0
Total imports (US$ million)	10,658.6	11,538.8	12,833.6
Tourism receipts (US$ million)	928.0	845.1	792.0
Tourist spending (US$ million)	1,078.0	1,042.8	904.0

Average household size 2001 (persons)	4.30				
Urban population 2001 (%)	74.8				
Age analysis (%) (2001)	*0-14*	32.1	*15-64*	63.2	*65+* 4.7
Population by sex (%) (2001)	*Male*	49.6	*Female*	50.4	
Life expectancy (years) (2001)	*Male*	68.7	*Female*	75.1	
Infant mortality (deaths per '000 live births) (2001)	27.0				
Adult literacy (%) (1997)	90.9				

TRADING PARTNERS

Major export destinations 2001 (% share)		Major import sources 2001 (% share)	
USA	43.7	USA	32.4
VENEZUELA	10.2	VENEZUELA	8.3
ECUADOR	3.6	JAPAN	5.5
GERMANY	3.5	BRAZIL	5.0

Comoros

Area (km^2) 1,860

Currency Comoros franc (= 100 centimes)

Location The Comoros are an archipelago of islands in the Indian Ocean, situated between Mozambique and the island of Madagascar. They retain both French and Islamic cultural traditions - with the latter becoming more important in recent years. The climate is tropical and many islands are heavily forested. The capital is Moroni.

Head of State Hamada Madi (2002) (acting head of state)

Head of Government Bianrifi Tarmidi (1999)

Ruling Party Rassemblement National pour la Développement (RND).

Political Structure The president is elected for a 6-year term by the people. The Federal Assembly has 42 members, elected for a 5-year term in single-seat constituencies.

Last Elections The presidential elections held in April 2002 were marred by violence and a boycott by two of the three candidates and one of the archipelago's three main islands. Later, the election commission cancelled the election and refused to release the results. Parliament has been dissolved.

Political Risk Comoros has had difficulty in achieving political stability, having endured 18 coups or attempted coups since achieving independence from France in 1975. In 1997, the islands of Anjouan and Moheli declared their independence from Comoros.

International Disputes The Comoros claims French-administered Mayotte.

Economy GDP grew by only 1.9% in 2001, while inflation was 5%. One of the world's poorest countries, the Comoros' three islands have inadequate transportation links, a young and rapidly increasing population, and few natural resources. The low educational level of the labour force contributes to a subsistence level of economic activity, high unemployment, and a heavy dependence on foreign grants and technical assistance. Per capita income in some parts of the county is only US$30 and unemployment is near 90%. Political turmoil, including the conflict over the independence of the two islands, Anjouan and Moheli, has occasionally disrupted government services for extended periods of time. The deficit in the balance of payments has been erased as a result of a large increase in private transfers from the Comorian community living abroad. Some progress had been made in strengthening tax administration but further efforts in this regard are essential. A return to sustained growth would require determined implementation of structural policy reforms aimed at improving efficiency and competitiveness, including an accelerated programme of privatisation and gradual trade liberalisation. International donors have pledged money to help reduce the Comoros' high population growth rate but very little to improve the standard of living. The country remains highly dependent on its trade relationship with France, and its lack of self-sufficiency in food products is another source of concern. In years when the economy performs poorly, French aid accounts for around 35% of GDP.

Main Industries Agriculture accounts for 40% of GDP, industry contributes 14% and services make up the remainder. Agriculture employs over 80% of the workforce, with most people engaged in subsistence farming. Farm production consists mainly of vanilla, cloves, perfume essences, copra, coconuts, bananas and cassava (tapioca). The sector's exports are primarily vanilla, cloves, perfume oil and copra. The country is not self-sufficient in food production; rice, the main staple, accounts for the bulk of imports. The Comoros has a large natural forest that offers substantial scope for timber exporting but is not developed. The industrial sector is largely limited to the processing of essential oils, but there are also a few factories making soft drinks, plastics and timber products.

Energy All of the country's fuel requirements, apart from brushwood and similar fuels, are imported. A hydroelectric dam is under construction, and this should provide some degree of self-sufficiency in electricity.

	1999	2000	2001
Inflation (% change)	3.5	4.5	5.0
Exchange rate (per US$)	461.78	533.98	549.78
Interest rate			
GDP (% real growth)	1.9	-1.1	1.9
GDP (Billion units of national currency)	102.8	108.9	121.0
GDP (US$ million)	222.6	203.8	220.1
GDP per capita (US$)	327.2	293.7	299.4
Consumption (Billion units of national currency)	88.2	95.1	104.1
Consumption (US$ million)	191.0	178.2	189.4
Consumption per capita (US$)	280.9	256.7	257.7
Population, mid-year ('000)	680.2	694.0	735.0
Birth rate (per '000)	38.5	38.3	38.0
Death rate (per '000)	9.2	9.0	8.7
No. of households ('000)	114.1	117.3	125.3
Total exports (US$ million)			
Total imports (US$ million)			
Tourism receipts (US$ million)	19.0	20.3	14.7
Tourist spending (US$ million)			

Average household size 2001 (persons)	5.92				
Urban population 2001 (%)	33.8				
Age analysis (%) (2001)	0-14	43.4	15-64	54.0	65+ 2.6
Population by sex (%) (2001)	Male	50.0	Female	50.0	
Life expectancy (years) (2001)	Male	58.9	Female	61.7	
Infant mortality (deaths per '000 live births) (2001)	69.2				
Adult literacy (%) (1997)	55.4				

TRADING PARTNERS
Major export destinations 2001 (% share) — Major import sources 2001 (% share)

USA	26.2	FRANCE	29.1
FRANCE	20.0	SOUTH AFRICA	11.7
SINGAPORE	17.3	JAPAN	8.0
UNITED KINGDOM	12.8	UNITED ARAB EMIRATES	6.2

Congo, Democratic Republic

Area (km^2)   2,345,410

Currency   Congolese franc (F = 100 makuta)

Location   The Democratic Republic of the Congo, formerly known as Zaire, is the largest country in Central Africa. Its boundaries extend from the Central African Republic and Sudan in the north to Zambia and Angola in the south, with Tanzania, Uganda and the tiny states of Rwanda and Burundi to the east and Congo to the west. Despite its size, it has only one coastal access, a channel running to the Atlantic between Congo and Angola. The terrain ranges from the vast plains of the north and far south to the dry Zaire River valley in the west. The capital is Kinshasa.

Head of State   Joseph Kabila (2000)

Head of Government   Joseph Kabila (2000)

Ruling Party   A 4-party movement born in the eastern town of Lemera and known as the Alliance of Democratic Forces for the Liberation of the Congo (AFDL) now rules the country.

Political Structure   Until the AFDL's takeover in 1997, the then Zaire had a nominally executive president who was elected for a 7-year term by universal vote along with a 310-member Legislative Council (Parliament). The president was the de facto head of the ruling party. This system was scrapped when Mobutu Sese Seko seized power in 1972. When Mobutu's health failed, he lost influence and was replaced by Laurent Kabila, who was assassinated in 2000 and replaced by his son, Joseph. .

Last Elections   Legislative elections were last held in September 1987. Upon gaining power, the AFDL committed itself to new elections but there now appears to be little chance that the regime will allow a vote.

Political Risk   The country's instability is still great, but the risks have diminished significantly since Joseph Kabila assumed power. He allowed the UN to deploy peace monitors and won Western support by appointing a respectable government.

International Disputes   The Democratic Congo became the "fighting field" of Africa for several years. Most of these soldiers have now departed. The UN also has denounced both Uganda and Rwanda for the illegal exploitation of Congo's resources. In July 2002, Rwanda and the Congo signed a preliminary peace agreement that calls for the withdrawal of Rwandan troops. The presence of Angolan, Zimbabwean and Namibian troops in the country is seen as legitimate, since they were requested to intervene by the government. Belgium, the old colonial ruler, ended its decade-long break with the Congo in 2001 and immediately afterward announced new funding and aid.

Economy   The Congo saw its GDP decline by 4% in 2001 while prices soared, increasing by nearly 300%. Living standards were in a freefall in recent years but that has been reversed in 2002. The exchange rate has been floated and the budget brought back into surplus. Monetary growth is now strictly controlled and the central bank has been granted independence. Projects to help government services resume are now underway. All these moves have strong financial support from the international community.

Main Industries   The country's key industries - copper and cobalt mining and diamond extraction - were nearly destroyed during the war. Copper prices remain depressed but there is considerable optimism about a turnaround. A new, investor-friendly mining law has now been drafted. A number of small and medium-sized companies have reopened since the end of the war. The country's large informal economy is already thriving. Farming, which is carried out mainly on a subsistence basis, continues to be the dominant sector. Oil palms, coffee, rubber, cocoa and timber are grown for export, while cassava, cereals, fruit and tobacco are grown for the domestic market but production is below the pre-war levels.

Energy   The Democratic Congo has a limited amount of proven oil reserves located offshore, and some gas. There are expectations that more reserves could be located but the country's problems and its desperate economic situation deters investors.

	1999	2000	2001
Inflation (% change)	269.6	553.7	299.0
Exchange rate (per US$)	4.02	21.82	732.67
Interest rate (% per annum, lending rate)	124.6	165.0	
GDP (% real growth)	-10.4	-7.0	-4.0
GDP (Million units of national currency)	18,231.2	97,767.8	2,839,830.5
GDP (US$ million)	4,537.0	4,481.0	3,876.0
GDP per capita (US$)	89.6	86.8	71.6
Consumption			
Consumption (US$ million)			
Consumption per capita (US$)			
Population, mid-year ('000)	50,656.9	51,654.0	54,106.0
Birth rate (per '000)	47.5	47.4	47.3
Death rate (per '000)	14.5	14.2	13.9
No. of households ('000)	13,287.1	13,634.5	14,093.1
Total exports (US$ million)	490.0	450.0	359.1
Total imports (US$ million)	370.0	320.0	289.5
Tourism receipts (US$ million)			
Tourist spending (US$ million)			

Average household size 2001 (persons)		3.79				
Urban population 2001 (%)		30.8				
Age analysis (%) (2001)	*0-14*	47.8	*15-64*	49.4	*65+*	2.8
Population by sex (%) (2001)	*Male*	49.3	*Female*	50.7		
Life expectancy (years) (2001)	*Male*	50.6	*Female*	53.0		
Infant mortality (deaths per '000 live births) (2001)		80.4				
Adult literacy (%) (1997)		77.0				

TRADING PARTNERS

Major export destinations 2001 (% share)		Major import sources 2001 (% share)	
BELGIUM	59.7	SOUTH AFRICA	17.3
USA	12.8	BELGIUM	15.4
ZIMBABWE	7.4	NIGERIA	11.1
FINLAND	7.0	FRANCE	5.6

Congo-Brazzaville

Area (km²)   342,000

Currency   CFA franc (= 100 centimes)

Location   Congo is a long triangle of land, dominated by tropical forest, which follows the Congo River south from Cameroon and the Central African Republic, between Gabon and the Democratic Republic of the Congo (formerly Zaire), to meet the sea just north of Angola. The climate is hot and humid. The capital is Brazzaville.

Head of State   Denis Sassou-Nguesso (1997)

Head of Government   Denis Sassou-Nguesso (1997)

Ruling Party   Congolese Labour Party (PCT)

Political Structure   The constitution calls for the president to be elected for a 5-year term by the people. The National Assembly consists of 125 members, elected for a 5-year term in single-seat constituencies. The Senate had 60 members, elected partially every two years for a 6-year term by district, local and regional councils.

Last Elections   In presidential elections held in March 2002, Denis Sassou-Nguesso was re-elected with 58% of the vote. A body known as the National Transitional Council replaced parliament following a rebellion in 1998. The Council has 75 members. Elections to the National Assembly were last held in 1993.

Political Risk   The country has suffered three civil wars since 1992. The losers did not accept defeat, but armed their own ethnic militias. Brazzaville was blasted to rubble and around 800,000 people fled. A peace accord was signed in 1999 but several thousand guerrillas continue to fight on.

International Disputes   A long segment of the boundary with the Democratic Republic of the Congo along the Congo River is indefinite. No division of the river or its islands has been made.

Economy   GDP rose by 3.3% in 2001 and prices fell by 0.5%. Congo's business and administrative infrastructure was badly damaged during the 1997 and 1998-1999 civil wars, increasing the petroleum sector's dominance of the economy (since oil production was not directly harmed by the fighting). Economic activity was further hampered by the fact that nearly 30% of the population fled their homes during the 1998-1999 conflict. The cost of gasoline in Brazzaville climbed to three times the official level due to disruption of the rail line linking the capital with the port city and economic capital, Pointe-Noire, but this situation now has been remedied. In return for international loans, the government has committed itself to improve the management of its fiscal balance and external arrears (ie by reducing fraud in the customs area), and to reduce cost overruns for civil service salaries. In general, priorities for Congo in the next few years include structural reform (in the banking sector, for instance) and macroeconomic stabilisation. The country must operate under a heavy debt burden. In 1999, the total Congolese debt was approximately US$5 billion, amounting to a total debt-to-GDP ratio of more than 200%.

Main Industries   Congo's economy consists mainly of village agriculture, an urban informal sector (ie unregulated business, commerce and service activities), and an industrial sector dominated by oil and oil-related services. Since the 1980s, the oil industry has provided the major share of government revenues and exports, replacing timber production and exports as the main source of growth. Oil accounts for over 50% of Congo's real GDP, 60-80% of the government budget and about 90% of Congo's export earnings. Oil exports grew sharply, from approximately US$820 million in 1994 to around US$2.5 billion in 2001. Agriculture accounts for only about 20% of GDP and is poorly developed with less than 1% of the land area under cultivation. Most farming involves the cultivation of subsistence crops such as cassava, yams, groundnuts and manioc. Coffee, cocoa, sugar and tobacco are grown for export. The mineral sector has considerable scope for further development, but investors are hesitant in view of the shaky political situation in the country.

Energy   Congo is sub-Saharan Africa's fourth largest oil producer (after Nigeria, Angola and Gabon), with estimated proven reserves of 1.5 billion barrels. The majority of Congo's crude production is located offshore and is heavily reliant on foreign personnel and technology. Congo's crude production has nearly doubled, from 144,000 bbl/d in 1988 to an average of 262,000 bbl/d in 2001. This was down slightly from production in 2000, largely due to delays in bringing two fields online. About one third of this oil goes directly to the government and is sold on the state's behalf. New offshore oil fields are being developed at a cost of US$135 million. The new fields have reserves of 180 million barrels and are expected to be in production by 2004. The Congo also has at least 4.3 trillion cubic feet of natural gas reserves, making it the third largest oil and second largest natural gas source in sub-Saharan Africa. After completion of the 1-gigawatt capacity Sounda Gorge hydroelectric plant, the country should become a major regional exporter of electricity. In 1998, the government established a new national petroleum company which assumed all upstream functions of the former state-owned company. The process of privatising downstream operations has been underway since 1997.

	1999	2000	2001
Inflation (% change)	3.1	0.4	-0.5
Exchange rate (per US$)	615.70	711.98	733.04
Interest rate (% per annum, lending rate)	22.0	22.0	20.7
GDP (% real growth)	-3.0	7.9	3.3
GDP (Billion units of national currency)	1,365.3	2,288.9	2,108.9
GDP (US$ million)	2,217.5	3,214.9	2,876.9
GDP per capita (US$)	761.6	1,092.4	967.7
Consumption (Billion units of national currency)	597.5	437.3	517.3
Consumption (US$ million)	970.4	614.2	705.7
Consumption per capita (US$)	333.3	208.7	237.4
Population, mid-year ('000)	2,911.5	2,943.0	2,973.0
Birth rate (per '000)	44.4	44.3	44.3
Death rate (per '000)	14.5	14.3	14.2
No. of households ('000)	476.7	487.0	485.5
Total exports (US$ million)	1,560.0	1,997.0	1,853.5
Total imports (US$ million)	820.6	1,190.3	1,135.3
Tourism receipts (US$ million)	12.0	9.6	7.9
Tourist spending (US$ million)	60.0	63.7	44.6

Average household size 2001 (persons)	6.04					
Urban population 2001 (%)	63.1					
Age analysis (%) (2001)	*0-14*	46.1	*15-64*	50.6	*65+*	3.2
Population by sex (%) (2001)	*Male*	48.8	*Female*	51.2		
Life expectancy (years) (2001)	*Male*	49.4	*Female*	53.6		
Infant mortality (deaths per '000 live births) (2001)	67.4					
Adult literacy (%)						

TRADING PARTNERS

Major export destinations 2001 (% share)

USA	21.3
SOUTH KOREA	15.7
CHINA	7.3
GERMANY	6.9

Major import sources 2001 (% share)

FRANCE	20.3
ITALY	10.7
USA	9.4
BELGIUM	5.8

Costa Rica

Area (km^2)   50,900

Currency   Colón (= 100 céntimos)

Location   Costa Rica meets the Isthmus of Panama at its northern extreme. Nicaragua lies to the north. The country has coasts facing both the Caribbean and the Pacific. However, its coastal lowlands are too humid for intensive development while its upland plains have a pleasant climate. The capital is San José.

Head of State   Abel Pacheco de la Espriella (2002)

Head of Government   Abel Pacheco de la Espriella (2002)

Ruling Party   Christian Social Unity Party (PUSC)

Political Structure   Costa Rica has an executive president elected by universal suffrage for a term of four years. He is answerable to the 57-member Legislative Assembly, also elected for four years. The president is assisted by two vice presidents and appoints the Cabinet personally.

Last Elections   In parliamentary elections held in February 2002, the conservative PUSC became the largest party winning 19 seats. The social/democratic National Liberation Party received 17 seats and the Citizens' Action Party claimed 14 seats. Presidential elections held in February and April 2002 led to a victory for the conservative candidate Abel Pacheco de la Espriella.

Political Risk   The democratic system in Costa Rica is a mature and stable one but it is changing as the big political parties are divided over the issue of privatisation and reform. Many voters - and some politicians - fear that privatisation will quickly lead to corruption. Political scandals are already widespread, breeding disillusion about political parties. Yet the public sector is too large and high levels of indebtedness reduce the government's ability to introduce reforms. The inability to forge a coherent macroeconomic policy could eventually jeopardise the country's economic future.

International Disputes   In 2000, Costa Rica broke off bilateral border talks with Nicaragua. Costa Rica has no army and disputes the use of armed frontier patrols.

Economy   GDP grew by just 0.4% in 2001, while prices rose by 11%. Costa Rica faces the problem of how to sustain a European-style welfare state on a Latin American tax base. Tax revenues total just 12% of GDP, while public debt grew to almost US$9 billion, or 55% of GDP. Several small investments (mainly by foreigners) have stimulated clusters of high-tech local firms and helped to make Costa Rica a successful exporter but they are not enough to produce sustained growth. The economy has performed poorly due to a decline in the value of exports and a production lag in the high-technology electronics industry. The weak export performance has led to a current account deficit of over 5% of GDP. Reduced capital inflows, especially from FDI, are insufficient to finance this disequilibrium. Public finance also hinders stabilisation efforts. The consolidated public-sector deficit, including that of the central bank, amounts to 4%, and the central government deficit is close to 3% of GDP. Returns on FDI, which had been significant in the past, are lower owing to the drop in the profits of high-technology industries. Moreover, the benefits of growth are spread very unevenly across the economy. One result is that the number of families in extreme poverty continues to rise.

Main Industries   Costa Rica's economy relies largely on its agriculture, with coffee, bananas, sugar, cut flowers and cattle being exported. It is the world's second largest exporter of bananas. Cocoa, rice, maize, cassava, ginger, melons, pineapples and flowers are produced for domestic consumption. Many work in these traditional farming pursuits and all are struggling because the government has removed subsidies. Meanwhile, businessmen argue that the country's expensive state-run services such as electricity and telecoms undermine their competitiveness. Both business and agriculture are further burdened by the fact that the government's own substantial levels of debt keep interest rates high. Not surprisingly, output in both the agricultural sector and the manufacturing sector has been falling. The efforts of policy makers to rectify the country's problems have made little headway. Economic reforms face strong opposition in the country. The state employs over 10,000 and many could loose their jobs if the companies are privatised.

Energy   Although all hydrocarbon deposits belong to the state, private energy generators have appeared, although they are limited to about a quarter of the nation's total generating capacity. Costa Rica needs an estimated US$3 billion of investment in its power sector by 2011, and demand is forecast to grow by 10% annually. Approximately 80% of the population has access to electricity.

	1999	2000	2001
Inflation (% change)	10.1	11.5	11.0
Exchange rate (per US$)	285.69	308.19	328.87
Interest rate (% per annum, commercial lending rate)	25.7	24.9	23.8
GDP (% real growth)	8.4	1.7	0.4
GDP (Billion units of national currency)	4,431.4	5,024.3	5,599.5
GDP (US$ million)	15,511.5	16,302.7	17,026.4
GDP per capita (US$)	4,250.4	4,378.1	4,483.3
Consumption (Billion units of national currency)	9,757.1	1,000.8	1,015.5
Consumption (US$ million)	34,153.4	3,247.4	3,087.8
Consumption per capita (US$)	9,358.7	872.1	813.1
Population, mid-year ('000)	3,649.4	3,723.6	3,797.7
Birth rate (per '000)	22.8	22.5	22.2
Death rate (per '000)	3.9	3.9	4.0
No. of households ('000)	906.8	935.0	964.5
Total exports (US$ million)	6,577.2	5,864.6	5,009.8
Total imports (US$ million)	6,320.1	6,372.1	6,564.3
Tourism receipts (US$ million)	1,002.0	1,053.0	895.8
Tourist spending (US$ million)	428.0	449.1	403.4

Average household size 2001 (persons)	4.02				
Urban population 2001 (%)	48.1				
Age analysis (%) (2001)	*0-14* 32.9		*15-64* 62.0		*65+* 5.2
Population by sex (%) (2001)	*Male* 50.6		*Female* 49.4		
Life expectancy (years) (2001)	*Male* 74.8		*Female* 79.5		
Infant mortality (deaths per '000 live births) (2001)	11.2				
Adult literacy (%) (1997)	95.1				

TRADING PARTNERS

Major export destinations 2001 (% share)

USA	41.6
NETHERLANDS	12.0
GERMANY	3.6
GUATEMALA	3.4

Major import sources 2001 (% share)

USA	40.2
VENEZUELA	5.1
MEXICO	4.6
JAPAN	4.0

Côte d'Ivoire

Area (km^2) 322,465

Currency CFA franc (= 100 centimes)

Location Côte d'Ivoire is located on the Atlantic coast of West Africa, with a short coastal stretch facing southward into the Gulf of Guinea. Inland, the country broadens out considerably to meet Guinea, Burkina Faso and Mali in the north, Ghana in the east and Liberia in the west. The climate is tropical and humid, but a rich soil means that agriculture is strong. The seat of government is Abidjan.

Head of State Laurent Gbagbo (2000)

Head of Government Affi N'Guessan (2000)

Ruling Party The government is formed by a 3-party coalition led by the Ivorian People's Front (FPI).

Political Structure Côte d'Ivoire, the former Ivory Coast, became fully independent from France in 1960. The executive president exercises a large degree of power and is elected for five years by universal suffrage. Legislative authority is vested in the 225-member National Assembly, which is also elected for five years.

Last Elections Presidential elections were held in October 2000 when Gbagbo defeated General Robert Gueri with 59% of the vote. Gueri had, in 1999, seized power from Felix Houphouet-Boigny, who had led the country for three decades. Elections to the National Assembly were held in January 2001. The FPI took 96 seats, the Democratic Party of Ivory Coast won 94 seats and the remainder were divided among several parties.

Political Risk The country was a haven of political stability until the military coup in 1999. Muslims from the north, many of whom support one of the main opposition parties, complain of discrimination by the government. The tension led to violence during the latest elections. The issue of nationality lies at the heart of the dispute with many Muslims being labelled as foreigners. As much as 50% of the population may be "foreign", as defined by the law, and the issue of citizenship is highly contentious.

International Disputes In 2001, the EU declared that it would not resume aid to the government until all parties were included in a debate about the future. Relations with other West African states were strained during the civil war in neighbouring Liberia. An estimated 300,000-400,000 Liberian refugees entered Côte d'Ivoire, and periodic incursions by members of armed factions in the Liberian conflict occurred.

Economy GDP fell by 0.9% in 2001 but a recovery is underway. Growth should be 3% in 2002 and 4.5% in 2003. Inflation was 4.4% in 2001 and will be 3.6% in 2002. In 2003, prices are expected to rise by 3.4%. The government recently came close to defaulting on its gross external debt of US$13 billion but the situation improved in 2001. Fiscal resources dwindle when the price of commodities such as cocoa, coffee, rubber and palm-oil are weak and the government does not set aside funds when prices rise. Côte d'Ivoire has promised international lenders that it will reduce its budget deficit and liberalise the economy but there is little evidence of any progress. The country's programme of privatisation has faltered owing to mismanagement and a lack of investor interest.

Main Industries Côte d'Ivoire's economy is heavily reliant on agriculture Together, agriculture, forestry and fisheries account for over one third of GDP and two thirds of exports. Côte d'Ivoire produces 35-40% of the world's cocoa crop every year, and is a major exporter of bananas, coffee, cotton, palm oil, pineapples, rubber, tropical wood products and tuna. However, a fall in cocoa prices and the growing pressure of more people on the eland have caused serious problems in agriculture. Measures to diversify the economy, including the introduction of non-traditional cash crops and expansion of the industrial sector, have not met with much success. Manufacturing consists mainly of the processing of agricultural raw materials, with textiles, matting, carpets, footwear and leather goods being major activities. Private sector development continues to fall short of expectations and further liberalisation of the coffee sector is badly needed. The discovery of offshore natural gas could provide another boost to the economy.

Energy Côte d'Ivoire contains an estimated 100 million barrels of recoverable oil reserves, with offshore reserves first discovered in the 1970s. Natural gas reserves and excess electricity generating capacity could eventually provide a big boost to Côte d'Ivoire. Offshore discoveries in the Gulf of Guinea, including gas finds in its territorial waters, make the country a leading area for hydrocarbon exploration in sub-Saharan Africa. Côte d'Ivoire is self-sufficient in producing refined petroleum products and is a major supplier to the West African region.

	1999	2000	2001
Inflation (% change)	0.7	2.5	4.4
Exchange rate (per US$)	615.70	711.98	733.04
Interest rate			
GDP (% real growth)	1.6	-2.3	-0.9
GDP (Billion units of national currency)	7,731.0	7,541.9	7,631.4
GDP (US$ million)	12,556.5	10,592.9	10,410.6
GDP per capita (US$)	861.0	716.4	678.7
Consumption (Billion units of national currency)	4,515.2	4,620.7	4,717.6
Consumption (US$ million)	7,333.4	6,489.9	6,435.6
Consumption per capita (US$)	502.8	438.9	419.6
Population, mid-year ('000)	14,584.3	14,786.0	15,338.0
Birth rate (per '000)	35.8	35.6	35.5
Death rate (per '000)	15.4	15.3	15.3
No. of households ('000)	3,212.2	3,251.1	3,364.8
Total exports (US$ million)	4,661.5	3,888.1	4,054.3
Total imports (US$ million)	3,252.2	2,535.1	2,405.4
Tourism receipts (US$ million)	95.0	73.7	77.2
Tourist spending (US$ million)	306.4	238.3	227.5

Average household size 2001 (persons)	4.55				
Urban population 2001 (%)	46.9				
Age analysis (%) (2001)	*0-14*	44.2	*15-64*	53.0	*65+* 2.9
Population by sex (%) (2001)	*Male*	50.8	*Female*	49.2	
Life expectancy (years) (2001)	*Male*	47.6	*Female*	48.1	
Infant mortality (deaths per '000 live births) (2001)	82.9				
Adult literacy (%) (1997)	42.6				

TRADING PARTNERS

Major export destinations 2001 (% share)

NETHERLANDS	14.1
FRANCE	13.9
USA	7.5
MALI	5.6

Major import sources 2001 (% share)

FRANCE	21.1
NIGERIA	18.8
USA	5.2
ITALY	4.5

Croatia

Area (km^2)   56,538

Currency   Kuna (introduced May 1994)

Location   Croatia lies in the north of the old Yugoslavia, with its western edge straddling the Adriatic coast and sharing an eastern border with Hungary. To the north is Slovenia, with Bosnia and Serbia to the south. The coastal strip and islands soon give way to mountains but, in the east, a flat plain replaces the hills. The capital is Zagreb.

Head of State   President Stipe Mesic (2000)

Head of Government   Ivica Racan (2000)

Ruling Party   A multiparty coalition leads the government.

Political Structure   Before Franco Tudjman died, he created a political system which he dominated. As an executive president, Tudjman appointed both the Prime Minister and Cabinet. The new president, Mesic, has agreed that presidential powers will be reduced. Legislative authority is vested in a 136-seat Chamber of Deputies and a 63-seat Chamber of Districts.

Last Elections   In the general elections held in January 2000, Tudjman'a Croatian Democratic Union was soundly thrashed by liberal, westward-leaning opponents. Ivica Racan than became Prime Minister. In February 2000, Mesic, a moderate reformer who had long opposed Tudjman, won the presidency in the second round of voting. In January 2000, parliamentary elections were held. Together, the Social Democrats and Social Liberals took 71 seats in the Chamber of Deputies. The Croatian Democratic Union won only 46 seats.

Political Risk   The government's reform programme appears to have lost its way. More than half of all Croatians are thought to disapprove of Racan and his administration. The government is also under pressure to do more to counteract the legacy of the corruption which was rife among Tudjman's cronies during their days in power. This group is very rich, however, and will fight to keep their wealth and freedom. Despite their pro-Western views, most Croats want their government to go on resisting the demands of Western countries that alleged Croat war criminals be arrested and tried

International Disputes   The government is reluctant to speak out unequivocally in favour of prosecuting Croatian Army war criminal from the 1991-1995 war of independence. Many Westerners believe that nationalist elements are behind this stance. Outstanding issues with neighbouring countries include border disputes with Bosnia and Herzegovina, Slovenia and Montenegro. Relations with Western nations will depend upon progress in ethnic reconciliation, the return of refugees and democratisation.

Economy   Growth in Croatia was 4.2% in 2001 and should be 3.1% in 2002. Growth of 2.5% is forecast for 2003. Inflation was running at 4.9% in 2001 and will fall to 3.3% in 2002. In 2003, prices are forecast to rise by 3.1%. Unemployment remains persistently high - around 15.5% - and shows little sign of falling. Officials cite the number of jobless as the reason they are not pursuing reforms more aggressively. Proposals to trim the hugely expensive labour benefits face strong opposition from trade unions. Reform of the chaotic legal system and public administration has also been painfully slow. The government has managed to reduce the general deficit from 7.4% of GDFP in 1999 to 4.2% in 2002 and expects to cut it further to 2.5% in 2003. External demand took over as the main engine of growth. The growth of fixed investment declined somewhat due to the continuing cutbacks in the public investment programme. Rather than lifting barriers and introducing more deregulation, the government's tendency is to become more heavily involved in business activities. Exporters have received a boost after the EU removed import duties on 95% of Croatia's industrial goods.

Main Industries   Agriculture accounts for 9% of GDP and remains one of Croatia's most inefficient sectors, untouched by any reforms. Despite a mild climate and fertile land, the country is a net importer of food. In 2001, food imports rose by 23.7%. Industry makes up a third of GDP and survived the war relatively unscathed. Private industry is the main source of job creation, unlocking resources following the bank privatisation. Private industry has high investment, dynamic exports and employment growing by up to 9% a year. State-owned companies, however, have been stagnating and have recorded almost no investment. The government does plan to privatise the national oil and gas company in 2002 and an adviser has been appointed to sell of the state's biggest insurer. Tourism is one of the main sources of income, accounting for 40% of foreign exchange earnings and generating 15-17% of the country's GDP. The number of tourists grew since 2000 and is now about 10% below pre-war levels. The country has thousands of kilometres of coastline but poor infrastructure, a shortage of good hotels and high prices have limited growth. The industrial sector is hampered by a decline in electricity production. A great deal more investment will be required, however, before the industry can compete with other European producers.

Energy   Croatia's total proven reserves of oil amount to just 335 million barrels. The country, however, could assume more importance as a transit centre for energy supplies moving to the West. The majority of Croatia's oil fields are in the eastern region of Slavonia. Overall, Croatia's oil production is still lower than pre-1991 levels, with output estimated at 33,000 barrels per day (bbl/d) in 2001. Croatia's oil consumption in 2000 was estimated at 85,000 bbl/d. Much of the power-generating capacity was destroyed during the war but the power plants are slowly being rebuilt.

	1999	2000	2001
Inflation (% change)	4.1	6.2	4.9
Exchange rate (per US$)	7.11	8.28	8.34
Interest rate (% per annum, lending rate)	14.9	12.1	9.5
GDP (% real growth)	-0.4	3.7	4.2
GDP (Million units of national currency)	142,700.0	157,500.0	170,497.0
GDP (US$ million)	20,063.4	19,029.6	20,443.3
GDP per capita (US$)	4,457.4	4,200.8	4,510.6
Consumption (Million units of national currency)	82,304.0	88,366.5	94,393.2
Consumption (US$ million)	11,571.8	10,676.7	11,318.2
Consumption per capita (US$)	2,570.9	2,356.9	2,497.2
Population, mid-year ('000)	4,501.1	4,530.0	4,532.3
Birth rate (per '000)	11.6	11.6	11.5
Death rate (per '000)	11.0	11.1	11.2
No. of households ('000)	1,570.1	1,571.3	1,577.7
Total exports (US$ million)	4,302.5	4,431.6	4,659.3
Total imports (US$ million)	7,798.6	7,886.5	9,044.0
Tourism receipts (US$ million)	2,493.0	2,693.1	3,302.0
Tourist spending (US$ million)	751.0	806.5	907.6

Average household size 2001 (persons)	2.88				
Urban population 2001 (%)	57.9				
Age analysis (%) (2001)	*0-14*	19.9	*15-64* 67.8	*65+*	12.3
Population by sex (%) (2001)	*Male*	48.1	*Female* 51.9		
Life expectancy (years) (2001)	*Male*	70.1	*Female* 77.9		
Infant mortality (deaths per '000 live births) (2001)	8.5				
Adult literacy (%) (1997)	97.9				

TRADING PARTNERS
Major export destinations 2001 (% share)   **Major import sources 2001 (% share)**

Major export destinations 2001 (% share)		Major import sources 2001 (% share)	
ITALY	23.1	GERMANY	15.9
GERMANY	14.9	ITALY	15.4
BOSNIA-HERZEGOVINA	12.2	SLOVENIA	7.3
SLOVENIA	9.3	RUSSIA	6.8

Cuba

Area (km^2) 114,525

Currency Cuban peso (P = 100 centavos). A new, partially convertible peso was introduced in 1995.

Location The Republic of Cuba is an archipelago that includes Cuba, the largest island in the Caribbean. Extending more than 800km from east to west, the country lies just 145km south of the Florida coast. Its proximity has drawn the ire of successive US administrations - on account of both its communist ideology and the thousands of refugees who seek sanctuary in the US. The capital is Havana.

Head of State President Fidel Castro Ruz (1976)

Head of Government President Fidel Castro Ruz

Ruling Party Communist Party of Cuba

Political Structure The Council of Ministers is the highest executive body and power devolves largely from the Executive Committee of the Council. The president of the country is the chairman of the Executive Committee.

Last Elections In February 1998, Castro was re-elected by the National Assembly of Popular Power (Parliament) for another five years as president. In accordance with tradition, delegates to the National Assembly itself were appointed by the country's 14 provincial assemblies. The first direct elections to the Assembly took place in March 1993, when all 589 official candidates for the 589 seats were successful. The turnout was claimed to be 99.6%.

Political Risk Questions about the 75-year-old Castro's health continue to circulate. There is no guarantee that much will change after Castro. His brother lacks the charisma, although as head of the armed forces he carries some weight. Many predict that a team of top ministers could take control instead. In the meantime, 20,000 leave the island each year for the US to join the estimated two million already there.

International Disputes The current administration in the US is firmly enforcing the embargo of Cuba, although a growing number of Americans support the move to do away with it. In the meantime, the country is experiencing sharp increases in crime, prostitution and drug-trafficking. With Castro signalling that he will not allow any more changes in the economic system, rumours abound in Havana about another huge exodus.

Economy After a brief spurt of growth in the late 1990s, Cuba's economy is once again in a slump. Inflows of foreign capital continue but at lower rates than in the past. Foreign investors complain that the Cuban state partners take their money but ignore their advice. The EU has published a report on behalf of investors arguing that there are too many rules and regulations applied to foreign companies that are not always applied fairly. Havana continues to maintain its spending on health and education and the country retains its position as a leader in social fields with one of the lowest rates of poverty and illiteracy on the continent. Dollarisation, however, has created a massive gulf in Cuban society. Approximately 50% of the population have access to foreign currency - mainly through remittances or self-employment but also through tourism and hard currency incentive schemes for workers. The result is a growing inequality which undermines the social cohesion that has been a feature of Cuba since the Revolution. Venezuela, which is one of the island's main oil suppliers, with 53,000 barrels a day, has suggested that it is unlikely to resume exporting much-needed fuel to Cuba until it receives payment for previous deliveries.

Main Industries Tourism, the country's main foreign currency earner and the hope of so many government officials, was down by around 20% in the first six months of 2002. Cuba's biggest employer, the sugar industry, is also suffering as world prices stay low. According to recent estimates, the country's sugar exports, which average about US$550 million annually, fell to US$476 million in 2001. The government intends to close half its ageing and decrepit sugar mills and cut industrial capacity by 50%. Cuba is still the world's fourth largest sugar producer, but most analysts think the move is a correct one. The informal economy (which is made up of small-time private entrepreneurs, both legal and clandestine) is now so extensive that it threatens to undermine efforts to bolster efficiency in the formal state sector. The manufacturing sector is starved of cash with many state-owned firms operating at far less than full capacity (but fully staffed). Havana claims that the percentage of state companies that are not profitable fell sharply over the past several years but foreign analysts dismiss these claims.

Energy Cuban oil production more than doubled during the 1991-2000 period. In 2001, Cuba produced about 42,000 barrels per day and consumed 164,000 barrels per day. Production increases are due primarily to the application of new technologies, such as horizontal drilling. Most domestic production consists of heavy oil whose sulphur content is so high that it can only be used for converted power and cement plants. Refineries process imported crude oil, mainly from Venezuela and Mexico. These special financial arrangements, allowing for the sale of oil under preferential conditions, have recently collapsed between Venezuela and Cuba. This leaves the island about 53,000 barrels per day short, which constitutes approximately one third of Cuban demand. The US maintains an economic embargo against Cuba, and oil companies from other countries may be subject to US sanctions.

	1999	2000	2001
Inflation (% change)	3.2	3.0	
Exchange rate (per US$)	23.00	23.00	23.00
Interest rate			
GDP (% real growth)	1.7	2.1	
GDP (Million units of national currency)	430,721.7	452,959.8	474,933.8
GDP (US$ million)	18,727.0	19,693.9	20,649.3
GDP per capita (US$)	1,684.8	1,764.8	1,843.6
Consumption (Million units of national currency)	375,428.6	381,618.5	393,729.5
Consumption (US$ million)	16,323.0	16,592.1	17,118.7
Consumption per capita (US$)	1,468.5	1,486.9	1,528.4
Population, mid-year ('000)	11,115.5	11,159.0	11,200.5
Birth rate (per '000)	12.6	12.3	12.0
Death rate (per '000)	7.1	7.2	7.2
No. of households ('000)	2,792.1	2,817.7	2,845.0
Total exports (US$ million)	1,466.0	1,635.0	1,752.6
Total imports (US$ million)	4,301.0	4,900.0	4,958.6
Tourism receipts (US$ million)	1,714.0	1,794.7	1,462.8
Tourist spending (US$ million)			

Average household size 2001 (persons)	3.97				
Urban population 2001 (%)	75.5				
Age analysis (%) (2001)	*0-14*	21.0	*15-64*	69.3	*65+* 9.7
Population by sex (%) (2001)	*Male*	50.1	*Female*	49.9	
Life expectancy (years) (2001)	*Male*	74.7	*Female*	78.5	
Infant mortality (deaths per '000 live births) (2001)	16.6				
Adult literacy (%) (1997)	95.9				

TRADING PARTNERS

Major export destinations 2001 (% share)		Major import sources 2001 (% share)	
RUSSIA	25.4	SPAIN	20.0
CANADA	15.1	CHINA	10.2
NETHERLANDS	15.0	ITALY	9.0
SPAIN	7.0	CANADA	8.3

Cyprus

Area (km^2)   9,250

Currency   Cyprus pound (C£ = 100 cents)

Location   Cyprus is located in the eastern Mediterranean, barely 150km south of Turkey and much closer to Syria than to Greece, whose descendants represent by far the largest sector of the population. The climate is warm and dry. The capital is Nicosia.

Head of State   President Glafcos Clerides (1998) (Northern Cyprus: Rauf Denktash)

Head of Government   President Glafcos Clerides(1998) (Northern Cyprus: Dervis Eroglu, 1996)

Ruling Party   The Democratic Coalition (DISI) leads a coalition with the Democratic Party. In Northern Cyprus, the Democratic Party and the Republican Turkish Party form a coalition.

Political Structure   For international purposes, Cyprus is represented by the south of the island, where a Greek majority elects an executive President and a 56-seat House of Representatives. A further 24 unoccupied seats are reserved for Turkish Cypriots but have not been filled since 1963. The so-called "Turkish Republic of Northern Cyprus", which was declared after the Turkish invasion of 1974, has an executive president and 50-seat Parliament. The two sides have long discussed UN proposals for a federal union where each group would live in separate self-governing areas with separate parliaments.

Last Elections   In February 1998, Clerides narrowly defeated George Iakovou. Clerides won 50.2% of the vote to gain another five years as president of the Greek-Cypriot part of the divided island. Both the candidates were Greek nationalists, though Clerides is the more moderate. Elections to the House of Representatives took place in May 2001. The Progressive Party of the Working People took 20 seats, the DISI took 19 seats and the Democratic Party claimed 9 seats. The remaining seats were dispersed among several small parties. Parliamentary elections in northern Cyprus were held in December 1998. The Party of National Unity received 40% of the vote and captured 24 seats. The Democratic Party got 23% of the vote and 13 seats. Presidential elections were held in the Turkish sector in April 2000. Denktash was re-elected president of Northern Cyprus with 44% of the vote.

Political Risk   The prospect of EU accession is widening the division between the Greek and Turkish parts of the island. Greek Cypriots are aggressively pursuing this option but the Turkish Cypriots want to extract more concessions. If the two leaders can agree on some substantive hurdles such as methods of governing the island, security, territory and property, an accord with the EU could probably be reached by the end of 2002. In that case, Cyprus could look forward to eventual accession. If no accord is reached, the Greek-run part of the island might join anyway.

International Disputes   Cyprus has long been a focus for the historical conflict between Turkey and Greece. The issue came to a bloody head in 1974 when Turkish troops invaded. This followed a coup, planned in Athens, against the Cypriot government under its first president, Archbishop Makarious. The aim was to bring about union with Greece. About 80% of all Cypriots are of Greek descent, but the island was in Turkish control throughout most of its history. Both the US and the Europeans are pushing the Greek Cypriots to find a way to accommodate Denktash's demand for recognition of the north.

Economy   GDP grew by 4% in 2001 and will increase by another 3% in 2002. Growth in 2003 is expected to 4.2%. Inflation was 2% in 2001 and will fall to 1.8% in 2002 before rising to 2.2% in 2003. The drop in tourist revenues in 2001 and 2002 has led to an upward revision in the budget deficit for this year, from 2.2% to 2.6% of GDP. The VAT rate was raised to 13% in January 2002 and will go up further to 15% in 2003. This would be the lowest acceptable rate for an EU member. Per capita income in the Greek zone is around US$17,000 but it is only a fifth of that in the Turkish area. Many of the Turkish-Cypriots have left for a better life in Britain. In their place, Turks from the mainland have flooded in, mostly poor and uneducated. Unemployment is low and the demand for skilled workers (in the Greek sector) is strong. There is also substantial employment of foreign labour - estimated at 8% of the workforce. In the Turkish north, unemployment is high. Foreign remittances from the 200,000 Turkish Cypriots abroad help to keep the Turkish part of the economy afloat. In recent years, gains in productivity have lagged behind real wage increases, undermining the island's competitiveness in many of its manufacturing industries. Rising labour costs and strong unions (about 85% of the labour force is unionised) have forced many light-manufacturing firms to abandon Cyprus or to shut down altogether. The relatively large role of government in the economy of Cyprus is being reconsidered in many areas but no plans for privatisation have been formalised.

Main Industries   Agriculture (along with mining) accounts for only 5% of GDP and the manufacturing sector makes up another 21%, though its share is falling over time. Efforts to revive the manufacturing sector have not been successful. Officials hope that eventual membership in the EU will help to rejuvenate manufacturing on the island. Services account for almost 60% of GDP and the sector has been growing rapidly. Cyprus is rich in human capital with a large numbers of Greek Cypriots having advanced degrees from foreign universities. Within the services sector, the principal growth areas are tourism, finance, insurance and real estate. Tourism is especially important but has not performed well since 2000. Cyprus' thriving offshore sector is a valuable source of foreign exchange. The island has more than 32,000 registered offshore companies and approximately half of them are active. This sector's significance raises problems for the island in its efforts to attain EU accession. Though regulations are tight, Brussels fears that some banking units may be used for money laundering. Cyprus also has the fourth largest ship register in the world.

Energy   Crude oil, all of which has to be imported, is the primary source of energy in Cyprus. Thermal plants are used to meet the island's electricity requirements.

	1999	2000	2001
Inflation (% change)	1.6	4.1	2.0
Exchange rate (per US$)	0.54	0.62	0.64
Interest rate (% per annum, lending rate)	8.0	8.0	7.5
GDP (% real growth)	4.5	5.0	4.0
GDP (Million units of national currency)	5,009.1	5,457.7	5,811.0
GDP (US$ million)	9,225.7	8,768.7	9,035.8
GDP per capita (US$)	12,234.1	11,566.6	11,853.2
Consumption (Million units of national currency)	3,309.7	3,352.7	3,454.0
Consumption (US$ million)	6,095.8	5,386.7	5,370.8
Consumption per capita (US$)	8,083.5	7,105.5	7,045.4
Population, mid-year ('000)	754.1	758.1	762.3
Birth rate (per '000)	13.7	13.6	13.4
Death rate (per '000)	7.4	7.5	7.5
No. of households ('000)	263.0	264.2	264.5
Total exports (US$ million)	997.1	953.5	975.3
Total imports (US$ million)	3,618.0	3,846.3	3,937.9
Tourism receipts (US$ million)	1,878.0	2,033.8	1,841.5
Tourist spending (US$ million)	289.0	316.9	300.8

Average household size 2001 (persons)		2.86				
Urban population 2001 (%)		57.3				
Age analysis (%) (2001)	0-14	23.1	15-64	65.7	65+	11.3
Population by sex (%) (2001)	Male	49.8	Female	50.2		
Life expectancy (years) (2001)	Male	75.9	Female	80.4		
Infant mortality (deaths per '000 live births) (2001)		8.0				
Adult literacy (%) (1997)		95.9				

TRADING PARTNERS

Major export destinations 2001 (% share)		Major import sources 2001 (% share)	
UNITED KINGDOM	22.3	RUSSIA	17.0
FRANCE	14.6	FRANCE	6.0
GERMANY	8.7	UNITED KINGDOM	5.6
GREECE	5.7	SOUTH KOREA	5.2

▓ Czech Republic

Area (km²)   78,864

Currency   Koruna (CK = 100 heller)

Location   The Czech Republic formed part of a federation with Slovakia until January 1993, when the two parted. The country is located in central Europe, southeast of Germany, with Poland to the north, Austria to the south and Slovakia to the west. The climate is temperate with harsh winters. The capital is Prague.

Head of State   President Vaclav Havel (1993)

Head of Government   Milos Zeman (1998)

Ruling Party   The government is formed by the Czech Social Democratic Party (CSSD).

Political Structure   Until the end of 1992, Czechoslovakia was a federation of two ethnically distinct states, the Czech and Slovak republics, which had been forged in 1919. In 1993, the two states declared their independence. The Czech parliament has two chambers. The Chamber of Representatives has 200 members, elected for a 4-year term by proportional representation with a 4% barrier. The Senate has 81 members, elected for a 6-year term in single-seat constituencies, in which one third is renewed every two years. The president is elected for a 5-year term by the parliament.

Last Elections   Havel easily won re-election on the second ballot of presidential elections held in January 1998. Elections to the Senate were held in November 2000. A 4-party coalition won 39 seats, the Civic Democratic Party, took 22 seats and the Czech Social Democratic Party captured 15. Remaining seats were taken by minor parties. Elections to the Chamber of Representatives took place in June 2002. The social democratic Czech Social Democratic Party of Milos Zeman claimed victory, winning 70 seats. Other parties represented include the conservative Civic Democratic Party, the Communist Party of Bohemia and Moravia and the centrist Coalition.

Political Risk   The country's budget deficit poses a problem if the Czech Republic is to qualify as a member of the euro zone The issue is an especially important one, since the economy is small and already extensively integrated with the euro zone countries. By mid-2002, the deficit stood at 5% of GDP - and nearly 10% if the continuing costs of bank bailouts are included. The euro zone target, however, calls for a deficit of less than 3% of GDP. Any new programme of fiscal consolidation will have to focus on pension reform and improvements in tax collections, but such moves are sure to raise strong objections from many politicians and the public. Prague's official target is to meet the Maastricht criteria for adoption of the euro by 2006 or 2007 but in view of the problems to be addressed, these dates look to be optimistic. Meanwhile, government authorities acknowledge that the country should adopt the euro at the earliest possible date because of the growing dependence on Western markets.

International Disputes   In the late 1990s, the Czechs fell behind in their preparations for accession to the EU but the pace of progress has accelerated since 2000.

Economy   In 2001, GDP grew by 3.6% and should increase by 3.3% in 2002. In 2003, growth is forecast to be 3.7%. Inflation was 4.7% in 2001. In 2002, prices are set to rise by 4% and by another 3.7% in 2003. Consumer demand has increased moderately, while investment, reflecting very high levels of FDI, has expanded rapidly, approaching double-digit rates by the end of 2001. The rapid rise in demand was met by an increase in output, particularly in industry - reflecting both new capacity and much stronger productivity growth. For the economy as a whole productivity rose by about 4% in 2000 and 2001, well above the increase in real wages. Despite gains in output, the country's ongoing programmes of restructuring led to a decline in employment in 2000 and the early part of 2001. Only later have employment rolls begun to rise. The rate of unemployment nevertheless began to fall, reaching 8.2% in 2001. The drop was mainly the result of state-subsidised early-retirement programmes that shrank the labour force. Increasingly, unemployment is concentrated geographically and among the less well educated, while the incidence of long-term joblessness now exceeds 50%. Continued additions to capacity and moderate rises in labour costs should allow Czech exports to grow at double-digit rates over the near term. Exporters therefore expect to gain market share. Even so, the overall contribution of the external sector will remain negative because imports, in response to the high foreign content of exports and stronger domestic consumption, are also expected to grow quickly.

Main Industries   The Czech Republic's agricultural sector is not large but comparatively efficient. Agricultural productivity is high by Eastern European standards. The country has an ample exportable surplus of meat and is self-sufficient in wheat, barley, vegetables, potatoes and fruit. There are extensive forests offering substantial scope for timber development. In industry, traditional activities such as steel and engineering remain in crisis, creating unemployment in specific regions like northern Moravia, but new growth sectors such as information technology and electronics are helping to diversify the economy. The government plans to sell off its interests in telecoms, power, gas and petrochemicals which could yield revenues of more than 15% of GDP. The banking system is still in trouble and roughly half of the budget deficit in 2002 represents the cost of bailing out the insolvent banks before privatisation. Thanks to the boom in FDI, companies with foreign capital now make up 40% of industrial production (from 15% in 1997) and two thirds of industrial pre-tax profits. In the future, the government hopes to attract more FDI into services sector projects. Services and research are seen as vital because some manufacturing investors are bound to move further east when Czech wages rise as the country approaches EU membership.

Energy   The Czech Republic has limited oil reserves and relies almost exclusively on imported oil. Domestic oil production reached 6,400 barrels per day in 2001. In 2002, two small fields were discovered near Postorna. Czech oil consumption, which totalled 172,000 bbl/d in 2001, should be about the same in 2002. Oil imports are piped primarily from Russia, via the Druzhba pipeline, and Germany, via the Mero pipeline.

	1999	2000	2001
Inflation (% change)	2.1	3.9	4.7
Exchange rate (per US$)	34.57	38.60	38.04
Interest rate (% per annum, lending rate)	8.7	7.2	7.1
GDP (% real growth)	-0.4	2.9	3.6
GDP (Billion units of national currency)	1,887.3	1,959.5	2,146.1
GDP (US$ million)	54,595.6	50,765.8	56,423.9
GDP per capita (US$)	5,308.5	4,940.8	5,496.5
Consumption (Billion units of national currency)	934.4	983.3	1,070.4
Consumption (US$ million)	27,029.2	25,474.3	28,143.6
Consumption per capita (US$)	2,628.1	2,479.3	2,741.6
Population, mid-year ('000)	10,284.6	10,274.9	10,265.5
Birth rate (per '000)	8.8	8.8	8.8
Death rate (per '000)	10.9	10.8	10.8
No. of households ('000)	3,722.9	3,688.8	3,672.0
Total exports (US$ million)	26,242.0	28,996.0	33,369.0
Total imports (US$ million)	28,073.0	32,110.0	36,504.0
Tourism receipts (US$ million)	3,035.0	3,482.4	2,995.4
Tourist spending (US$ million)	1,474.0	1,985.6	2,223.7

Average household size 2001 (persons)	2.79					
Urban population 2001 (%)	67.7					
Age analysis (%) (2001)	*0-14*	16.2	*15-64*	69.9	*65+*	13.8
Population by sex (%) (2001)	*Male*	48.7	*Female*	51.3		
Life expectancy (years) (2001)	*Male*	71.8	*Female*	78.5		
Infant mortality (deaths per '000 live births) (2001)	5.2					
Adult literacy (%)						

TRADING PARTNERS

Major export destinations 2001 (% share)		Major import sources 2001 (% share)	
GERMANY	38.3	GERMANY	37.7
SLOVAKIA	8.0	SLOVAKIA	6.0
AUSTRIA	5.7	FRANCE	5.5
POLAND	5.6	ITALY	5.4

Denmark

Area (km^2)   43,075

Currency   Danish krone (DKr = 100 ore)

Location   Denmark is an archipelago of low-lying islands which control the straits between the Baltic Sea and the North Sea. The country borders on Germany to the south, but is close to Sweden (which is no more than 50km across the Oresund strait). Denmark controls the Faroe Islands in the North Sea and Greenland, which lies off the coast of Canada. The capital is Copenhagen.

Head of State   HM Queen Margrethe II

Head of Government   Anders Fogh Rasmussen (2001)

Ruling Party   The government is led by a coalition of the Liberal Party (V) and the Conservative People's Party (KF).

Political Structure   The Kingdom of Denmark is a constitutional monarchy in which executive authority lies with a Prime Minister who answers to a 179-member unicameral Parliament, the Folketing, with 175 members elected for a 4-year term (135 of them by proportional representation in 17 districts and 40 others allotted in proportion to their total vote). There are two representatives from both the Faroe Islands and Greenland.

Last Elections   In parliamentary elections held in November 2001, the Liberal Party gained 56 seats, the Party for Social Democracy in Denmark took 52 seats and the Danish People's Party won 22 seats. The remainder were divided among several parties.

Political Risk   Denmark opted out of the EU's single currency in September 2000 following a similar vote in a 1993 referendum. The rejection occurred despite strong support for the euro from the government, the opposition and industry. However, skilful manoeuvring by the country's central bank avoided serious consequences. There is some rising tension, however, over the issue of immigration. Foreigners - that is, immigrants plus their descendants - make up around 7% of the population. That figure is not particularly high but centre-right politicians have based much of the political appeal on a promise to curb immigration.

International Disputes   Denmark's overseas territories of Greenland and the Faroe Islands are pressing concerns. Greenland, which has been earmarked for a potential starring role in the US missile defence blueprint, requires particularly sensitive handling. In the Faroes, calls for complete independence continue.

Economy   Denmark's economy grew by just 0.9% in 2001 but a slightly better performance is anticipated with growth of 1.3% in 2002 and 2.4% in 2003. Inflation was 2.1% in 2001 and should rise to 2.3% in 2002. Prices are forecast to grow by 2.2% in 2003. Denmark's macroeconomic policies are generally very pro-growth and should offer a very favourable environment for a strong recovery during the first half of this decade. Monetary policy remains dedicated to maintaining the value of the Danish Krone against the euro. Growth in real public consumption has been relatively brisk and, if continued, would eventually have an impact on the tax structure. Public consumption rose by around 1.8% in 2001 and the local government budgets set for 2002 imply considerable expansion of spending on education, health and elderly care. Spending on public consumption in Denmark is already relatively high - 25% of GDP. This figure is five percentage points higher than the EU average and more than 10 percentage points higher than in most other OECD countries. The practice of channelling a relatively high proportion of resources through the public sector seems to enjoy strong public support in Denmark. However, as in other countries this comes at some cost, as the economic distortions of tax financing rise disproportionately. Some economists fear that higher-than-average wage rises may hurt the country's competitive position in international markets. There is general agreement that reforms in income support programmes, unemployment benefits and (most of all) pensions are needed.

Main Industries   The Danish economy was operating at close to its potential when the international downturn occurred. Growth of exports (in volume) fell to less than 4% and business investment shrank as sales prospects deteriorated. Nevertheless, increases in public and private consumption underpinned aggregate demand, total employment continued to rise, and unemployment fell further. With the labour market remaining tight, hourly earnings continued to rise, increasing by a surprising 4.3% in the third quarter of 2001. In 2002, private consumption should remain buoyant, supported by steady growth in real disposable incomes. The household saving ratio is projected to rise a little further in 2002, given uncertainties about job prospects as unemployment creeps upward. Danish industry has negotiated the downturn with relative ease. Engineering, food processing, pharmaceuticals and brewing are among Denmark's most successful industries. Biotechnology is also making strides but even more important is the country's elaborate infrastructure for information technology. Denmark's biotech firms account for 10% of all products in European pipelines, while per capita sales of computer hardware, software and related services are among the highest in Europe. The government zealously supports the development of all types of information technology. A spate of cross-border mergers and acquisitions (mainly with other Nordic companies) has strengthened the competitiveness of Danish manufacturers and similar trends are emerging in the financial sector. After passing through a long period of mergers and consolidation, the country's financial sector has begun to look abroad where growth prospects are better than at home. Agriculture consists of thousands of mainly small farms supplying pig meat products, dairy goods and cereals such as wheat and barley. In general, farming is so intensive that it has recurrently threatened serious environmental consequences in Denmark's low-lying and often marshy landscape. Farmers are bound by special legislation requiring safe storage and treatment of wastes.

Energy   Denmark has maintained an "open door" policy towards oil companies. Under this policy, oil companies are invited to bid for licences in specified acreage and are not required to commit to drilling wells before seismic work has been completed. There has been very little new activity in the Danish North Sea. Production of oil from the North Sea is around 240,000 bbl/d.

	1999	2000	2001
Inflation (% change)	2.5	2.9	2.1
Exchange rate (per US$)	6.98	8.08	8.32
Interest rate (% per annum, lending rate)	7.1	8.1	8.2
GDP (% real growth)	2.3	3.0	0.9
GDP (Billion units of national currency)	1,296.1	1,343.3	1,390.5
GDP (US$ million)	185,792.9	166,190.6	167,076.1
GDP per capita (US$)	34,904.6	31,113.7	31,172.1
Consumption (Billion units of national currency)	598.5	616.6	638.8
Consumption (US$ million)	85,787.2	76,283.4	76,749.9
Consumption per capita (US$)	16,116.7	14,281.5	14,319.6
Population, mid-year ('000)	5,322.9	5,341.4	5,359.8
Birth rate (per '000)	11.9	11.6	11.3
Death rate (per '000)	11.5	11.4	11.4
No. of households ('000)	2,472.0	2,485.0	2,496.9
Total exports (US$ million)	48,699.6	53,789.4	45,608.0
Total imports (US$ million)	44,067.6	43,704.8	45,047.8
Tourism receipts (US$ million)	3,682.0	4,520.3	3,558.2
Tourist spending (US$ million)	5,084.0	4,919.8	4,416.9

Average household size 2001 (persons)	2.15				
Urban population 2001 (%)	85.7				
Age analysis (%) (2001)	0-14	18.6	15-64	66.6	65+	14.8
Population by sex (%) (2001)	Male	49.4	Female	50.6	
Life expectancy (years) (2001)	Male	74.0	Female	78.9	
Infant mortality (deaths per '000 live births) (2001)	5.2				
Adult literacy (%) (1999)	99.0				

TRADING PARTNERS

Major export destinations 2001 (% share)

GERMANY	17.2
SWEDEN	14.3
USA	7.4
UNITED KINGDOM	7.2

Major import sources 2001 (% share)

GERMANY	21.8
SWEDEN	11.0
FRANCE	8.0
NETHERLANDS	7.7

■ Djibouti

Area (km²) 23,000

Currency Djibouti franc (= 100 centimes)

Location The Republic of Djibouti is a tiny country on the northeast African approach from the Indian Ocean to the Red Sea (the so-called Horn of Africa). It is bounded in the north, west and southwest by Eritrea and Ethiopia, and in the southeast by Somalia. Across the Gulf of Aden it faces the Republic of Yemen. The capital is Djibouti.

Head of State President Ismail Omasr Guelleh (1999)

Head of Government Dileita Mohamed Dileita (2001)

Ruling Party Rassemblement Populaire pour le Progress (RPP)

Political Structure Djibouti became independent from France in 1977. The president is elected by popular vote for a 6-year term. There is a National Assembly of 65 members, elected for 5-year terms in multi-seat constituencies.

Last Elections Elections to the National Assembly took place in December 1997. The RPP and the Front pour la Restauration de l'Unité et de la Démocratie (FRUD) won 78% of the vote and claimed all the seats in the Assembly. The RPP took 54 seats and the FRUD captured 11 seats. Presidential elections took place in April 1999 when Guelleh received 74% of the vote, defeating Moussa Ahmed Iddris.

Political Risk The repeated periods of fighting between Eritrea, Ethiopia and Somalia generated floods of refugees and disrupted Djibouti's tiny economy.

International Disputes Relations with Somalia are strained as a result of past differences.

Economy GDP grew by 2% in 2001 while inflation was 1.8%. Per capita consumption dropped an estimated 35% over the past several years because of recession, civil war and a high population growth rate (including immigrants and refugees). An unemployment rate of 40-50% is a major problem. Inflation is not a concern, however, because of the fixed tie of the franc to the US dollar. Faced with a multitude of economic difficulties, the government fell in arrears on long-term external debt and has been struggling to meet the stipulations of foreign aid donors. Officials are working to improve the tax and revenue administration and budget management. A privatisation programme has also been launched but progress has been slow. Foreign assistance is a major source of income and an important supplement to GDP. These funds help Djibouti support its balance of payments and to finance development projects.

Main Industries The economy is based on service activities connected with the country's strategic location and status as a free trade zone in northeast Africa. Much of Djibouti's income derives from its port facilities and its strategic position in the approaches to the Red Sea. The country provides services as both a transit port for the region and an international transhipment and refuelling centre. Agriculture accounts for a meagre 2% of GDP and services make up the remainder. Two thirds of the inhabitants live in the capital city, the remainder being mostly herders. Scanty rainfall limits crop production to fruits and vegetables. Owing mainly to the poor climate and the nomadic lifestyle of rural inhabitants, 95% of all food requirements are imported. Djibouti has few natural resources and industry represents no more than 20% of GDP. Djibouti has a substantial construction sector that feeds a large cement industry. Smaller industries that are being encouraged include water bottling, tanning, paint processing and meat processing. There are some mineral deposits, mainly copper, gypsum and sulphur, but these are not mined commercially. More important has been the discovery of an offshore gas field.

Energy There is currently no upstream (exploration or production) oil activity in Djibouti. The downstream oil sector is an important aspect of Djibouti's economy, given the role the capital city plays as a significant regional bunkering and refuelling facility. Total storage capacity at the port facility is 1.26 million barrels (200,000 cubic metres). There are plans to increase Djibouti's handling capacity from 125,000 metric tonnes to 300,000 metric tonnes per year, and to make it the leading transhipment point on the African continent. Planned port expansion and modernisation will also entail an upgrade to the petroleum receiving and storage facilities.

	1999	2000	2001
Inflation (% change)	2.0	2.4	1.8
Exchange rate (per US$)	177.72	177.72	177.72
Interest rate			
GDP (% real growth)	2.2	0.7	2.0
GDP (Million units of national currency)	95,273.0	98,267.0	102,046.0
GDP (US$ million)	536.1	552.9	574.2
GDP per capita (US$)	848.2	866.7	874.0
Consumption (Million units of national currency)	46,231.1	46,253.4	47,253.1
Consumption (US$ million)	260.1	260.3	265.9
Consumption per capita (US$)	411.6	407.9	404.7
Population, mid-year ('000)	632.0	638.0	657.0
Birth rate (per '000)	39.8	39.2	38.6
Death rate (per '000)	19.0	19.5	20.1
No. of households ('000)	127.5	127.9	130.5
Total exports (US$ million)	12.2	12.0	13.3
Total imports (US$ million)	270.0	288.7	308.6
Tourism receipts (US$ million)			
Tourist spending (US$ million)			

Average household size 2001 (persons)		4.99			
Urban population 2001 (%)		83.5			
Age analysis (%) (2001)	*0-14*	41.3	*15-64* 55.5	*65+*	3.2
Population by sex (%) (2001)	*Male*	49.0	*Female* 51.0		
Life expectancy (years) (2001)	*Male*	40.5	*Female* 42.5		
Infant mortality (deaths per '000 live births) (2001)		117.0			
Adult literacy (%) (1997)		48.3			

TRADING PARTNERS

Major export destinations 2001 (% share) **Major import sources 2001 (% share)**

SOMALIA	44.9	SAUDI ARABIA	18.4
FRANCE	23.5	FRANCE	16.0
YEMEN	19.2	ETHIOPIA	10.2
ETHIOPIA	3.5	CHINA	8.1

▨ Dominica

Area (km^2)   751

Currency   East Caribbean dollar (EC$ = 100 cents)

Location   Dominica forms part of the Lesser Antilles, in the Windward Islands group, lying between Guadeloupe and Martinique. Its volcanic soil is very fertile and its climate is generally equable, although subject to hurricanes. The capital is Roseau.

Head of State   President Vernon Shaw (1998)

Head of Government   Rosie Douglas (2000)

Ruling Party   The government is formed by the Dominica Labour Party (DLP) and the Dominica Freedom Party (DFP).

Political Structure   Dominica, an independent republic within the Commonwealth, is formally ruled by an executive president, who in practice hands most of his legislative authority to the prime minister and her cabinet. There is a unicameral House of Assembly with 32 members. They include 21 members elected for a 5-year term in single-seat constituencies, 9 appointed senators, the Speaker and 1 ex-officio member. The House then elects the president, for a maximum of two 5-year terms.

Last Elections   Elections were held in January 2000 to the House of Assembly. The United Workers' Party (UWP) took 43% of the vote and nine seats in the Assembly. The DLP won 43% of the vote and 10 seats while the DFP received 14% of the vote and two seats. The parliament elected Vernon Shaw as president in 1998.

Political Risk   Labour unrest is frequent in Dominica and government policies are hotly disputed. Another serious development is the emergence of Dominica as a transhipment point for illicit drugs bound for the US and Europe.

International Disputes   Despite the government's efforts, Dominica continues to be attacked for its banking practices which Western countries regard as inadequate to guard against money laundering. The country has abandoned its programme of "economic citizenship" which allowed non-nationals to receive passports for an "investment" of up to US$50,000.

Economy   The Dominican economy performed poorly in recent years. The government's widening deficits and the decreased earnings of its citizens became apparent in 1999 and have been made worse by 2001's global slowdown and the attacks of 11 September. In 2002, the government presented a budget that calls for higher taxes on fuel, sales and telephones, and raised fees for passports and stamps. In addition, it imposed more taxes on annual incomes of more than US$3,300. The proposals are highly unpopular and may have to be withdrawn. The economy's problems stem from low levels of public investment in infrastructure, structural impediments which prevent economic diversification and the adverse effects of a series of natural calamities such as hurricanes, droughts and windstorms. Unemployment rose in recent years and is estimated to exceed 25%.

Main Industries   The financial sector remains under pressure from Western nations because of suspected money laundering. The administration tightened regulations in 2001 but more elaborate regulations are sought by Western countries. Dominica's fertile volcanic soil provides ample opportunity for the development of an excellent agricultural industry. Agriculture accounts for 28% of GDP and employs 40% of the labour force. The main agricultural product is bananas although limes, oranges, grapefruit, copra and bay oil are also produced for export. Dominica exports 25-35 tonnes of bananas in a year and this is the main earner of foreign exchange. Banana growers are relatively inefficient, however. Dominica relies on the EU to pay grants equal to almost 2% of GDP a year until 2004 to help its banana farmers switch to other crops. Most industrial enterprises are geared to the processing of agricultural raw materials: rum manufacture is a major activity. There are also fruit canning plants, tobacco processing sheds and plants making soap and other light products. Tourism, although growing fast, is less developed than in other Caribbean states. The problem is due partly to the poor provision of roads, airports and other infrastructure facilities, and partly to the fact that nearly all beaches comprise black volcanic sand.

Energy   The government of Dominica has sold off a controlling interest in its power company. Dominica imports all of its fuel requirements, with oil and gas predominating. Just over half of its electricity derives from hydroelectric schemes, with thermal stations providing the rest.

	1999	**2000**	**2001**
Inflation (% change)	1.6	1.9	1.8
Exchange rate (per US$)	2.70	2.70	2.70
Interest rate (% per annum, lending rate)	10.5	10.5	10.5
GDP (% real growth)	0.9	0.5	
GDP (Million units of national currency)	714.0	729.0	747.0
GDP (US$ million)	264.4	270.0	276.7
GDP per capita (US$)	3,724.6	3,802.8	3,896.7
Consumption (Million units of national currency)	448.1	447.2	454.9
Consumption (US$ million)	166.0	165.6	168.5
Consumption per capita (US$)	2,337.5	2,332.7	2,372.9
Population, mid-year ('000)	71.0	71.0	71.0
Birth rate (per '000)	17.5	17.2	16.8
Death rate (per '000)	6.0	6.0	6.0
No. of households ('000)	16.6	16.5	16.4
Total exports (US$ million)	54.3	53.0	56.1
Total imports (US$ million)	140.8	146.8	153.0
Tourism receipts (US$ million)	49.0	45.5	35.2
Tourist spending (US$ million)	7.9	8.1	7.9

Average household size 2001 (persons)	4.30				
Urban population 2001 (%)	71.3				
Age analysis (%) (2001)	*0-14*	30.2	*15-64*	63.0	*65+* 6.7
Population by sex (%) (2001)	*Male*	49.5	*Female*	50.5	
Life expectancy (years) (2001)	*Male*	70.8	*Female*	76.6	
Infant mortality (deaths per '000 live births) (2001)	8.3				
Adult literacy (%) (1997)	94.0				

TRADING PARTNERS

Major export destinations 2001 (% share)

UNITED KINGDOM	24.6
JAMAICA	22.0
USA	8.1
ANTIGUA	6.8

Major import sources 2001 (% share)

CHINA	22.1
USA	16.1
TRINIDAD AND TOBAGO	12.6
UNITED KINGDOM	7.6

▓ Dominican Republic

Area (km^2) 48,440

Currency Dominican Republic peso (RD$ = 100 centavos)

Location The Dominican Republic lies in the Greater Antilles, north of Venezuela. It occupies the eastern half of the island of Hispaniola, with the state of Haiti in the west. The climate is equable, although often humid at sea level, and the soil is adequate for agriculture. The capital is Santo Domingo.

Head of State President Hipolito Mejia (2000)

Head of Government President Hipolito Mejia (2000)

Ruling Party Dominican Revolutionary Party (PRD)

Political Structure The Dominican Republic has an executive president who is elected for a 4-year term by parliament. Parliament has two chambers. The Chamber of Deputies has 150 members, elected for 4-year terms by proportional representation in each of the provinces. The Senate has 32 members, elected for a 4-year term in single-seat constituencies. The country consists of 26 provinces, each of which is run by an appointed governor, and the National District around the capital Santo Domingo.

Last Elections Presidential elections were held in May 2000 when Hipolito Mejia defeated two other candidates with 50% of the vote. Parliamentary elections were last held in May 2002. The PRD won 73 seats in the Chamber of Deputies and 29 in the Senate. The other parliamentary parties are the centrist Dominican Liberation Party (41 seats in the Chamber and 2 in the Senate) and the conservative Social Christian Reformist Party (36 seats in the Chamber and 1 in the Senate).

Political Risk The economy is expanding but the poor - especially those in the countryside - are not benefiting. Violent crime, and especially drug-related crime, is soaring with gang-slayings and armed robberies becoming commonplace.

International Disputes Colombian traffickers increasingly use the island as a smuggling route to the US and this has brought criticism from American politicians. Meanwhile, the government complains about the American policy of deporting criminals who hold Dominican citizenship but have lived for long periods in the US. Several thousand criminals have been deported from the US.

Economy GDP increased by 3% in 2001 and should expand by 3.5% in 2002. Inflation was 8.8% in 2001 but will fall to around 3.7% in 2002. The unemployment rate is estimated to be at least 14% and capital inflows are insufficient to offset the deficit on the current account. Government revenues have expanded, but expenditures continue to increase even faster. In the area of trade policy, export-reactivation and promotion regulations were adopted, and negotiations were concluded on the protocol relating to the establishment of the free-trade agreement between the Dominican Republic and the Caribbean Community. The growth in aggregate demand has been led by consumption. Investment declined because of a fall in public investment. Rural and urban poverty remains widespread and the benefits of economic growth are not enjoyed by many. The Dominican Republic's economy is closely tied with that of the US. The island is the US's seventh largest export market in the Western Hemisphere and a major destination for US foreign direct investments.

Main Industries The Dominican economy experienced dramatic growth over the last decade, even though the economy was hit hard by Hurricane Georges in 1998. Although the country has long been viewed primarily as an exporter of sugar, coffee and tobacco, in recent years the services sector overtook agriculture as the economy's largest employer, due to growth in tourism and free-trade zones. The country suffers from marked income inequality; the poorest half of the population receives less than 20% of GNP, while the richest 10% enjoy 40% of national income. The Dominican Republic receives more tourists each year than any other Caribbean holiday destination, but like other destinations, it suffered a sharp drop in arrivals after 11 September 2001. The island has made a determined start in its privatisation programme. Manufacturing is performing well thanks to the ready availability of raw materials, the efficiency of production processes and the expansion in production capacity. Industries that are relatively open to foreign investment and have close ties to international markets grow rapidly, while domestically-oriented industries have slower growth. The free-trade zones lived up to expectations generated by the entry into force in October of the expanded benefits granted under the Caribbean Basin Initiative. The construction sector is also enjoying a boom, driven by growth in private sector housing and commercial construction. Mining output picked up following the rise in nickel prices.

Energy The Dominican Republic has sought to alleviate chronic electricity shortages by buying power from private producers and also by privatising selected power plants. However, this privatisation so far has not resolved the Dominican Republic's fundamental problem of assuring a steady supply of electricity to its population. Power demand is growing at about 7% per year, yet demand already outstrips supply. Despite the need for further structural reform, foreign firms continue to invest in the Dominican Republic's power infrastructure. The Dominican Republic, along with Barbados, Haiti and Jamaica is party to the San Jose pact, under which Mexico and Venezuela supply crude oil and refined products on favourable terms. Small deposits of crude oil have been located at Chaco Largo, but the country remains dependent on oil imports for most of its energy needs and all of its electricity generating requirements.

	1999	2000	2001
Inflation (% change)	6.5	7.7	8.8
Exchange rate (per US$)	16.03	16.41	16.95
Interest rate (% per annum, lending rate)	25.0	26.8	24.3
GDP (% real growth)	8.0	7.8	3.0
GDP (Million units of national currency)	278,164.0	322,866.0	362,484.0
GDP (US$ million)	17,349.4	19,669.0	21,383.5
GDP per capita (US$)	2,107.6	2,351.5	2,517.1
Consumption (Million units of national currency)	209,068.0	250,209.0	277,447.8
Consumption (US$ million)	13,039.8	15,242.7	16,367.1
Consumption per capita (US$)	1,584.1	1,822.3	1,926.6
Population, mid-year ('000)	8,231.7	8,364.5	8,495.4
Birth rate (per '000)	24.2	23.9	23.6
Death rate (per '000)	6.5	6.6	6.8
No. of households ('000)	1,755.6	1,798.2	1,849.0
Total exports (US$ million)	805.2	966.2	1,075.0
Total imports (US$ million)	5,987.8	7,378.5	7,506.2
Tourism receipts (US$ million)	2,524.0	2,698.7	2,274.1
Tourist spending (US$ million)	267.0	302.3	334.4

Average household size 2001 (persons)	4.69				
Urban population 2001 (%)	65.6				
Age analysis (%) (2001)	*0-14*	32.8	*15-64*	62.6	*65+* 4.5
Population by sex (%) (2001)	*Male*	50.8	*Female*	49.2	
Life expectancy (years) (2001)	*Male*	64.6	*Female*	70.1	
Infant mortality (deaths per '000 live births) (2001)	37.2				
Adult literacy (%) (1997)	82.6				

TRADING PARTNERS

Major export destinations 2001 (% share)

USA	86.5
NETHERLANDS	1.8
BELGIUM	1.7
FRANCE	1.2

Major import sources 2001 (% share)

USA	60.6
VENEZUELA	10.2
MEXICO	4.7
SPAIN	3.6

■ Ecuador

Area (km^2)   263,950

Currency   US dollar (US$ = 100 cents)

Location   Ecuador lies on the western (Pacific) coast of South America, where it is bordered in the north and east by Colombia and in the south and east by Peru. The republic also includes the territory covered by the Galapagos Islands, about 1,000km off the coast. The country has some of the highest mountains in South America, peaking at over 6,000 metres, and is extensively forested - although the coastal regions are often damp and humid. The capital is Quito.

Head of State   Gustavo Noboa Bejarano (2000)

Head of Government   Gustavo Noboa Bejarano (2000)

Ruling Party   The Democracia Popular-Unión Demócrata Cristiana (DP-UDC) leads a coalition of smaller parties.

Political Structure   Ecuador has an executive president who is chosen by universal suffrage for a single, non-renewable 4-year term and appoints his own cabinet. The president is answerable to the National Congress which has 125 members elected for a 5-year term. Of these, 105 members elected in 2- or multi-seat constituencies and 20 members elected at large by proportional representation. There is also a Constitutional Assembly of 70 members elected in single- or multi-seat constituencies with the task to enact a new constitution.

Last Elections   In elections held in July 1998, Mahuad won 51.2% of the vote for president, defeating Alvaro Noboa in a run-off for the presidency. The loser claimed that there was vote rigging and fraud but international observers said the vote was fair. Noboa subsequently assumed power in a coup. Parliamentary elections were held in May 1998. The DP-UDC won 35 seats while the Partido Social Cristiano (PSC) took 26 and the Partido Roldosista Ecuatoriana (PRE) captured 25. The remaining seats were scattered among minor parties.

Political Risk   The risks faced by Ecuador are rapidly mounting. The country defaulted on part of its foreign debt in 1999 and is in danger of doing so again. Deep regional cleavages exist and there are frequent clashes between the legislature and the executive.

International Disputes   Ecuador reached an agreement with Peru in October 1998 ending its 56-year border dispute with Peru. The new agreement is expected to encourage greater trade between the neighbouring countries.

Economy   Ecuador's GDP increased by 5.2% in 2001 and should grow by 3.1% in 2002. In 2003, growth of 6% is forecast. Inflation was 37% in 2001 but will fall to around 15.5% in 2002. In 2003, prices are expected to rise by about 8%. In 2002, the government faces a shortfall in its funds for debt repayments of US$500 million on top of a budget deficit of US$500 million - in all an obligation equivalent to 6% of GDP. Since the government adopted the US dollar in 2000, it can no longer print money to pay these debts. Yet the economy is growing strongly thanks to oil. In line with IMF guidelines, Ecuador continues to stress structural reform, increased foreign investment and fiscal stabilisation. Revenues from the construction of a US$1.1 billion heavy oil pipeline are helping to finance the country's fiscal stabilisation fund and to pay off debt. Ecuador also is vulnerable to an economic downturn in the US, since remittances from Ecuadorian workers living there are Ecuador's second largest source of foreign exchange earnings (around US$1.4 billion in 2001). The economy's growth is reflected in a moderate decrease in unemployment which is presently around 14.5%. Seeking to make the labour market more flexible, the government introduced contracts based on the number of hours worked and began a process of wage consolidation. The VAT rate was raised from 10% to 12%, and income tax from 15% to 25%.

Main Industries   Agriculture employs almost half the workforce but farm productivity is low. Despite the favourable climate and good soil quality, farms are small, vulnerable to hurricanes and flooding and rather inefficient. Fishing is an important foreign exchange earner with tuna, sardines and shrimps dominating. New pipeline construction (expected to be completed in late 2003) also is expected to generate over 50,000 new jobs and to attract US$3 billion in foreign investment. Overall, Ecuador's oil sector accounts for around one fifth of the country's economy, and is the country's most important source of foreign exchange. Oil export revenues accounted for around 45% of Ecuador's total merchandise exports in 2001. This reliance on oil exports makes Ecuador's economy vulnerable to sharp fluctuations in oil prices, such as the sharp decline in prices since October 2001. Industry depends mainly on agro-processing activities such as fish canning, rum manufacture and palm oil milling. The financial system remains fragile with a high percentage of the portfolio in arrears. Around 95% of banking credit is extended to just 5% of depositors, many of them linked to the political contacts.

Energy   Since oil was discovered in Ecuador in the 1970s, it has become an increasingly important part of the Ecuadorian economy. The country has 2.1 billion barrels of proven oil reserves, with crude production of around 415,000 barrels per day during the first 10 months of 2001 (up from 395,000 bbl/d in 2000). Most of Ecuador's oil reserves are located in the eastern Amazon region, known as the Oriente. Ecuador consumes around 149,000 bbl/d domestically, with the remaining 276,000 bbl/d being exported. Petroecuador, the government-owned oil company, is attempting to attract foreign investment in the country's largest oil fields, and to boost its production from 230,000 bbl/d (about 56% of national production) today to 600,000 bbl/d by 2005. The company also is planning to step up its marketing efforts internationally, in anticipation of increased exports beginning in 2003. Ecuador's main export market currently is the US West Coast. Recurring problems between oil producers and the government on one side, and indigenous peoples on the other, continue to plague the development of oil supplies. Native tribes inhabit most of the highly productive southeastern area of Ecuador, and these tribes do not get any monetary compensation for the drilling that occurs in the territory.

	1999	2000	2001
Inflation (% change)	52.2	96.2	37.0
Exchange rate (per US$)	11,786.80	24,988.40	25,000.00
Interest rate (% per annum, lending rate)	16.5	16.3	15.5
GDP (% real growth)	-7.3	2.3	5.2
GDP (Billion units of national currency)	13.6	13.6	17.8
GDP (US$ million)	13,594.0	13,601.0	17,828.0
GDP per capita (US$)	1,085.0	1,065.7	1,371.8
Consumption (Billion units of national currency)	105,659.2	99,551.2	130,289.9
Consumption (US$ million)	8,964.2	3,983.9	5,211.6
Consumption per capita (US$)	715.5	312.1	401.0
Population, mid-year ('000)	12,528.7	12,762.8	12,995.7
Birth rate (per '000)	24.8	24.3	23.8
Death rate (per '000)	5.9	5.9	5.8
No. of households ('000)	2,525.4	2,574.9	2,616.1
Total exports (US$ million)	4,451.0	4,926.5	4,495.4
Total imports (US$ million)	3,017.3	3,721.1	5,299.2
Tourism receipts (US$ million)	343.0	370.2	294.3
Tourist spending (US$ million)	271.0	236.3	261.8

Average household size 2001 (persons)	4.96				
Urban population 2001 (%)	63.1				
Age analysis (%) (2001)	0-14	33.3	15-64	61.9	65+ 4.8
Population by sex (%) (2001)	Male	50.2	Female	49.8	
Life expectancy (years) (2001)	Male	68.1	Female	73.3	
Infant mortality (deaths per '000 live births) (2001)	42.2				
Adult literacy (%) (1997)	90.7				

TRADING PARTNERS

Major export destinations 2001 (% share)		Major import sources 2001 (% share)	
USA	39.3	USA	28.2
COLOMBIA	5.4	COLOMBIA	13.9
SOUTH KOREA	5.0	JAPAN	8.2
GERMANY	4.6	VENEZUELA	4.5

Egypt

Area (km^2)   997,739

Currency   Egyptian pound (E£ = 100 piastres)

Location   The Arab Republic of Egypt is situated at the extreme eastern end of North Africa's Mediterranean coast. Bordering on Israel to the north and east, with Sudan to the south and Libya to the west, it is in fact more closely linked with Saudi Arabia, with which it shares the strategically important Red Sea. Egypt is the keeper of the Suez Canal, one of its main sources of income. There is agriculture around the Nile delta, elsewhere the terrain is mostly desert. The capital is Cairo.

Head of State   President Muhammad Hosni Mubarak (1981)

Head of Government   Atif Muhammad Ubaid (1999)

Ruling Party   The government is led by the National Democratic Party (HDW).

Political Structure   Egypt's 1972 Constitution provides for an executive president who answers to a unicameral People's Assembly with 454 members, 10 of whom he appoints personally. The People's Assembly is elected by universal suffrage for a term of five years and then elects the president for a 6-year term. There is also a 210-member Consultative Council which consists of 140 elected members with 70 appointed by the president.

Last Elections   Elections to the People's Assembly took place in November 2000. The HDW won 353 seats while independents aligned with the HDW took another 35 seats. Other seats were scattered among several parties and independents.

Political Risk   The authoritarian regime of President Mubarak, underpinned by the military establishment, remains determined to monopolise the country's politics. Despite having decisively crushed an Islamist insurrection that killed 1,300 people in mid-1992, the government has extended emergency law until 2003. The law allows for unlimited detention of suspects, permits eavesdropping without a warrant and restricts the holding of meetings. Egypt is also under attack for other violations of human rights. The government's treatment not only of its Muslims but also the Coptic Christian minority is often criticised. Another dimension of the Egyptian problem is the distribution of wealth. Per capita incomes rose steadily but so, too, has the proportion of Egyptians living below the poverty line. The share of the poverty-ridden increased from 39% in 1980 to 43% at the end of the 1990s.

International Disputes   For more than a decade, Egypt's foreign policy has focused on promoting a comprehensive peace between Israel and its Arab neighbours and the collapse of those efforts is a harsh blow. Egypt's relations with Syria have improved but are still not warm. The country also has had strained relations with Sudan and Iran. In the past, Cairo has accused both countries of fomenting religious discontent. Egypt is working hard behind the scenes to persuade Washington to forgo its plans to topple Saddam in Iraq.

Economy   Egypt's GDP grew by 3.3% in 2001 and growth in 2002 will be 1.7%. In 2003, growth of 3.5% is forecast. Prices rose by 2.4% in 2001 and will increase by 3.2% in 2002. In 2003, inflation is forecast to be 4.4%. The Egyptian economy has stumbled owing to a combination of policy and external factors. On the policy side, credit growth remained rapid and structural reform slowed. Tourism experienced a downturn and global financing has tightened. These developments together resulted in sizeable official reserve losses, albeit from a high level and the reserve position remained comfortable. In terms of structural policy, several initiatives were taken in 2000 and 2001. In the fiscal area, the general sales tax was extended to the wholesale and retail levels by parliament and implemented in 2001. The authorities also signed an Association Agreement with the EU which, once ratified, will provide for a phased, multi-year reduction of tariffs on EU imports. Egypt's rapidly rising labour force remains a matter of some concern and will require significant new structural reforms to foster strong output and employment growth.

Main Industries   Egypt's economy is well diversified and it has a large, consumer-oriented domestic market. It also has several important sources of foreign exchange, each bringing in US$2-3 billion per year. These include remittances from expatriate Egyptians, dues from ships passing through the Suez Canal and oil exports. Important dollar-earning industries, such as tourism and oil, have held up and the public sector has expanded but other sectors such as construction and property are suffering badly. Tourism revenues account for about 5% of Egypt's GDP, and are among the country's five main sources of hard currency inflows. Tourism is critical since one in seven Egyptians depend on the industry for their livelihood. The average growth rate for tourism between 1993 and 2000 was 12.5%. Even after a 17% fall in 2001 (mainly due to the terrorist attacks on 11 September), revenues were still far above the levels recorded as recently as 1997. By March 2002, tourist revenues had recovered to 98.5% of their level in the previous year. Agriculture is the mainstay of the economy. Farming is still concentrated in the fertile Nile delta where cotton is the major cash crop and a big earner of foreign exchange. Cairo is trying to boost production of wheat since the country is one of the five largest importers in the world. Domestic production can meet only about half of the country's demand. The government, however, is pushing farmers away from the Nile into the desert. Lured by cheap land, tax holidays and government encouragement, desert farmers are producing olives, poultry and various other minor crops that do not require large amounts of water. Egypt intends to develop its agricultural sector further with the help of ambitious irrigation projects and other improvements in infrastructure.

Energy   Egypt produced an average of 639,000 barrels of crude oil per day in 2001, down from 710,000 bbl/d in 2000. Meanwhile, domestic consumption of petroleum products reached 585,000 bbl/d in 2001. Egypt is likely to become a net oil importer within the next decade. The government hopes that exploration activity, particularly in new areas, will discover sufficient oil in coming years to slow the decline in output. Egyptian oil production comes from four main areas: the Gulf of Suez (about 70%), the Western Desert, the Eastern Desert and the Sinai Peninsula. In 2000, the government estimated that crude oil reserves were 8.2 billion barrels.

	1999	2000	2001
Inflation (% change)	3.8	2.8	2.4
Exchange rate (per US$)	3.40	3.47	3.97
Interest rate (% per annum, lending rate)	13.0	13.2	13.3
GDP (% real growth)	6.1	5.1	3.3
GDP (Million units of national currency)	302,300.0	322,866.0	362,484.0
GDP (US$ million)	89,036.2	92,990.0	91,236.8
GDP per capita (US$)	1,451.4	1,493.1	1,441.5
Consumption (Million units of national currency)	227,243.7	244,894.5	259,893.7
Consumption (US$ million)	66,929.9	70,533.1	65,415.0
Consumption per capita (US$)	1,091.0	1,132.6	1,033.5
Population, mid-year ('000)	61,345.0	62,278.1	63,294.1
Birth rate (per '000)	25.2	24.6	24.0
Death rate (per '000)	6.6	6.4	6.3
No. of households ('000)	13,478.1	13,718.3	13,956.2
Total exports (US$ million)	3,559.4	4,689.1	4,127.6
Total imports (US$ million)	16,022.1	14,009.6	12,755.9
Tourism receipts (US$ million)	3,903.0	4,357.2	3,326.9
Tourist spending (US$ million)	1,078.0	1,592.1	1,237.5

Average household size 2001 (persons)	4.54				
Urban population 2001 (%)	46.0				
Age analysis (%) (2001)	0-14	37.2	15-64	59.3	65+	3.4
Population by sex (%) (2001)	Male	51.1	Female	48.9	
Life expectancy (years) (2001)	Male	66.2	Female	69.4	
Infant mortality (deaths per '000 live births) (2001)	42.6				
Adult literacy (%) (1997)	52.7				

TRADING PARTNERS

Major export destinations 2001 (% share)		Major import sources 2001 (% share)	
ITALY	15.0	USA	18.7
USA	14.4	ITALY	6.6
UNITED KINGDOM	9.3	GERMANY	6.5
FRANCE	4.7	FRANCE	4.9

El Salvador

Area (km^2) 21,395

Currency Salvadorean colón (C = 100 centavos)

Location El Salvador is a long coastal strip, never more than 80km in width, which extends for some 250km along the Pacific coast of Central America, with Guatemala to the north and west and Honduras to the east and northeast. Its favourable climate and important position have helped to make it one of the most densely populated areas of the developing world. The terrain is mainly mountainous, with several extinct volcanoes. The capital is San Salvador.

Head of State Francisco Flores (March 1999)

Head of Government Francisco Flores (March 1999)

Ruling Party Alianza Republicana Nacionalista (ARENA)

Political Structure The executive president is elected by universal suffrage for a term of five years, and answers to a unicameral Legislative Assembly whose membership was expanded from 60 to 84 seats in March 1991.

Last Elections The second presidential elections since the end of the civil war were held in March 1999, when Francisco Flores defeated six other candidates with 52% of the votes cast. Elections to the 84-seat Legislative Assembly were held in March 2000, when ARENA won 29 seats with 36% of the vote. The Marti National Liberation Front (a former guerrilla movement) won 31 seats with 35% of the vote.

Political Risk A US programme to return the thousands of illegal Salvadoran immigrants who work in that country is strongly opposed in El Salvador. Approximately 20% of the Salvador's economically active population live in the US. The money they send home each year exceeds US$1 billion and is the country's biggest foreign earner.

International Disputes The violent political disputes that wrecked the country during the civil war have subsided, leaving no outstanding international disagreements.

Economy GDP increased by 2% in 2001 while inflation was 3.8%. After a promising spurt in the mid-1990s, El Salvador's economy has slumped owing to the adoption of more restrictive monetary policies, the rise in fuel prices and a slowdown in key economic sectors. Remittances from overseas workers (mainly in the US) have been a crucial factor contributing to the stability of the economy. In foreign trade, the government focuses on trade negotiations, while maintaining the tariff reduction programme. The free-trade treaty between Mexico and the Northern Triangle (El Salvador, Guatemala and Honduras) was signed, and negotiations on the treaty on free trade and protocol with Chile were concluded. In addition, negotiations are continuing with the Andean Community and with Canada. The government has made considerable progress in restructuring the economy, although the country must boost its growth rate in order to reduce its widespread poverty. The fiscal deficit is high and remains a concern to policy makers.

Main Industries Agriculture accounts for almost 18% of GDP. Farming dominates the economy but plots are small, farms are relatively inefficient and productivity is low. Most farming is for subsistence but cash crops include sugar, cotton and especially coffee. Products grown for the domestic market include maize, rice, sesame and fruit. Manufacturing makes up about a quarter of GDP and has expanded briskly in the past few years. An exception is the many clothing factories set up in the country over the past decade. They now face stiff competition from factories in Mexico and elsewhere in Central America. The value of merchandise exports rose sharply since 2000. Leading industries include textiles, food processing, beverages, petroleum, chemicals, fertiliser and furniture manufacture. The country has made significant progress in its programme of privatisation.

Energy Power generated in El Salvador can be exported to Guatemala via an existing interconnection, and a connection to Honduras is planned. El Salvador relies on imports for its entire supply of petroleum and petroleum products and has little refining capacity.

	1999	2000	2001
Inflation (% change)	0.5	2.3	3.8
Exchange rate (per US$)	8.76	8.76	8.75
Interest rate (% per annum, lending rate)	15.5	14.0	
GDP (% real growth)	3.4	2.0	2.0
GDP (Million units of national currency)	109,066.0	115,600.0	122,200.0
GDP (US$ million)	12,457.6	13,203.9	13,965.7
GDP per capita (US$)	2,056.8	2,133.5	2,210.0
Consumption (Million units of national currency)	93,686.0	101,547.0	105,702.0
Consumption (US$ million)	10,700.9	11,598.7	12,080.2
Consumption per capita (US$)	1,766.8	1,874.1	1,911.6
Population, mid-year ('000)	6,056.7	6,188.8	6,319.4
Birth rate (per '000)	26.9	26.4	25.9
Death rate (per '000)	6.0	6.0	5.9
No. of households ('000)	1,405.5	1,428.3	1,477.3
Total exports (US$ million)	1,176.6	1,332.3	1,213.5
Total imports (US$ million)	3,140.0	3,794.7	3,865.8
Tourism receipts (US$ million)	211.0	238.7	199.0
Tourist spending (US$ million)	80.0	90.5	95.4

Average household size 2001 (persons)	4.38				
Urban population 2001 (%)	47.0				
Age analysis (%) (2001)	*0-14* 35.4	*15-64* 59.8	*65+* 4.8
Population by sex (%) (2001)	*Male* 49.1	*Female* 50.9	
Life expectancy (years) (2001)	*Male* 67.4	*Female* 73.4	
Infant mortality (deaths per '000 live births) (2001)	27.4				
Adult literacy (%) (1997)	77.0				

TRADING PARTNERS

Major export destinations 2001 (% share)

GUATEMALA	26.6
USA	18.8
HONDURAS	15.2
NICARAGUA	9.9

Major import sources 2001 (% share)

USA	32.7
GUATEMALA	10.8
MEXICO	7.7
COSTA RICA	4.0

Equatorial Guinea

Area (km^2)   28,050

Currency   CFA franc (= 100 centimes)

Location   Equatorial Guinea comprises the mainland territory of Rio Muni, located on the West African Atlantic coast between Cameroon and Gabon, and also the islands of Bioko, Pagalu and the Corisco group. The region has a warm, dry climate and has suffered from drought and environmental mismanagement in recent years. The capital is Malabo.

Head of State   President Teodoro Obiang Nguema Mbasogo

Head of Government   Cándido Muatetema Rivas (2001)

Ruling Party   Partido Democràtico de Guinea Ecuatorial (PDGE)

Political Structure   The president is elected for a 7-year term by the people. The Chamber of People's Representatives has 80 members, elected for a 5-year term by proportional representation in multi-member constituencies. Although officially a multiparty state, Equatorial Guinea's politics is completely dominated by the PDGE. Four other political parties exist, but no serious opposition to the president is tolerated.

Last Elections   Teodoro Obiang Nguema Mbasogo was elected unopposed in February 1996. Elections to the Chamber of People's Representatives took place in March 1999 when the PDGE took 75 of the 80 seats. Each recent poll has been criticised as unrepresentative by both domestic and foreign observers, and the percentage of those voting is very low.

Political Risk   A separatist group known as the Movimento de Autodeterminacion has occasionally launched violent attacks against government facilities.

International Disputes   Foreign aid historically has been an important part of the country's economy, but aid programmes have been suspended in recent years due to allegations of government mismanagement and corruption. The EU has stated that a gradual resumption of aid will resume in step with democratic reforms. With oil revenue increasing rapidly, the government may continue to resist donor pressure for economic reforms. The Nigerian government has questioned Equatorial Guinea's claim to sole ownership of the Zafiro oil field. Officials from the two countries have discussed ways to resolve the problem but no results have emerged.

Economy   The country's GDP increased by an impressive near 47% in 2001 while prices rose by 12%. The tremendous surge in growth was due predominately to the large increase in oil production once new fields came on stream. The external current account deficit (including official transfers) narrowed from more than 80% of GDP in 1998 to 25% of GDP in 2001, owing to the strong increase in oil output and prices. The government's cashflow situation improved considerably, reflecting growing oil revenue, but fiscal policy performance continued to weaken, as evidenced by the lack of control over government financial operations. The management of oil contracts lacks transparency, and there is no fiscal control over the payments due from, and paid by the oil companies. Government oil revenue is paid into treasury accounts held abroad. Moreover, large extra-budgetary expenditures have been financed since 1996 through advances on oil revenue, and the oil companies have been withholding government oil revenue at source to repay these advances. Opposition groups complain of escalating corruption and say the diversion of oil money will help perpetuate clan dictatorship and the abuse of human rights. Standards of living certainly remain low, even in urban areas. Running water and electricity are rare luxuries outside the capital. Education and healthcare are in abject decay. Malaria and a host of other diseases are some of the reasons why life expectancy is 48 years. An increase in oil revenues could dramatically improve the situation.

Main Industries   Recent economic developments in Equatorial Guinea have been dominated by rapid growth in the country's oil sector and subsequent sharp increases in government expenditure. Over 60% of GDP and over 90% of total exports originate in the oil sector. Expansion of the petroleum sector, mainly the result of exploration and foreign investment, has been the main impetus behind the country's high rates of growth in recent years. Annual oil investment now tops US$2 billion. While oil sector expansion has spurred new construction in the capital, Malabo, other sectors of the economy have stagnated, with the exception of the growing timber export industry. The government has largely liberalised the economy, with the exception of the commercialisation of major agricultural export commodities. Authorities first adopted a new forestry law aimed at improving supervision and monitoring and at scaling down timber production to a sustainable level. Later, two laws were passed to reduce export taxes on processed wood and reclassify one third of the wooded area as protected zones. The authorities also privatised and liberalised the distribution of petroleum. The country's sparse landscape offers little scope for intensive farming. Cocoa and coffee are the major exports but can be grown in only a small area of the country. Elsewhere, cassava, sweet potatoes, palm oil and bananas are produced as subsistence crops. Gradually, the country has become a large importer of food.

Energy   Oil production in Equatorial Guinea averaged 181,000 barrels per day (bbl/d) in 2001. This amounts to an increase of more than tenfold since 1996, when production averaged 17,000 bbl/d. Continuing exploration activities and field development could result in more substantial increases over the next few years. The government estimates that US$3.4 billion will be invested in offshore field development projects in Equatorial Guinea during the 2000-2004 period. Production currently comes from three offshore fields. Equatorial Guinea should soon replace Gabon as sub-Saharan Africa's third largest producer.

	1999	2000	2001
Inflation (% change)	6.5	6.0	12.0
Exchange rate (per US$)	615.70	711.98	733.04
Interest rate (% per annum, lending rate)	22.0	22.0	20.7
GDP (% real growth)	50.1	16.9	46.5
GDP (Million units of national currency)	536,883.0	954,221.0	1,250,685.0
GDP (US$ million)	872.0	1,340.2	1,706.2
GDP per capita (US$)	1,965.4	2,958.6	3,599.5
Consumption (Million units of national currency)	361,399.8	669,621.2	892,421.8
Consumption (US$ million)	587.0	940.5	1,217.4
Consumption per capita (US$)	1,323.0	2,076.2	2,568.4
Population, mid-year ('000)	443.7	453.0	474.0
Birth rate (per '000)	43.2	43.2	43.2
Death rate (per '000)	16.0	15.7	15.4
No. of households ('000)	107.1	108.3	111.3
Total exports (US$ million)	714.0	936.0	1,166.4
Total imports (US$ million)	66.2	181.0	240.0
Tourism receipts (US$ million)			
Tourist spending (US$ million)	443.7	453.0	474.0

Average household size 2001 (persons)	4.18				
Urban population 2001 (%)	49.3				
Age analysis (%) (2001)	0-14	43.2	15-64	52.8	65+ 4.0
Population by sex (%) (2001)	Male	49.2	Female	50.8	
Life expectancy (years) (2001)	Male	49.9	Female	53.1	
Infant mortality (deaths per '000 live births) (2001)	101.2				
Adult literacy (%) (1997)	79.9				

TRADING PARTNERS
Major export destinations 2001 (% share)   **Major import sources 2001 (% share)**

SPAIN	32.4	USA	28.2
CHINA	27.9	SPAIN	15.6
USA	26.2	UNITED KINGDOM	12.6
CANADA	4.3	FRANCE	8.8

Eritrea

Area (km^2) 93,679

Currency Birr (= 100 cents)

Location Eritrea, a large and predominantly mountainous area of the old Ethiopian republic, became independent in May 1993. The state lies in northeast Africa along the Red Sea coast, facing Saudi Arabia and the Republic of Yemen across the water. In the west it borders on Djibouti, in the south on Kenya, in the east on Sudan and in the southwest on Somalia. The country has a warm and desert climate and is prone to periodic drought. The capital is Asmara.

Head of State President Issaias Afewerki (May 1993)

Head of Government President Issaias Afewerki

Ruling Party People's Front for Democracy and Justice (PFDJ) is the only legal political party.

Political Structure Eritrea has an executive president and a unicameral 150-member National Assembly which consists of 75 Central Committee members of the ruling PFDJ, together with 75 others, of whom at least 11 must be women. The National Assembly elects the president directly. Executive power is vested in a 24-member State Council chaired by the president.

Last Elections In January-March 1997, voters elected 399 representatives in a lengthy process that led to the formation of a constituent assembly. Only representatives of the PFDJ were permitted to stand.

Political Risk International acceptance of the new Eritrean state was rapid, but the government's problems are immense. As much as 20% of the population was displaced during the independence war with Ethiopia and around 500,000 refugees were scattered throughout the region. The fighting which erupted anew in 2000 further damaged the economy.

International Disputes Eritrea's independence came at the end of a 10-year battle with Ethiopia. Tensions between the two countries subsided after the war but again escalated in 1998 when no agreement could be reached over a 150-mile stretch of the common border. Fighting erupted 1999, with many lost on each side. A ceasefire and peace agreement was signed with Ethiopia in December 2000. In 1996, Eritrea came close to war with Yemen over the Dahlak Islands in the Red Sea. The issue has now been submitted to arbitration under the auspices of the International Court of Justice.

Economy Eritrea's GDP increased 6.4% in 2001 and prices rose by 15%. The country's debt has soared during its war with Ethiopia. Government revenues come from custom duties and income and sales taxes. Eritrea has inherited the entire coastline of Ethiopia and has long-term prospects for revenues from the development of offshore oil, offshore fishing and tourism. The country's territory also contains much of the good arable land in the former Ethiopia, though like Ethiopia, it has faced recurrent droughts in recent years. Foreign investment remains very limited even though peace has been restored.

Main Industries Some experts believe that Eritrea could quickly attain food self-sufficiency now that the government can focus on the economy and not its disputes with Ethiopia. However, such a turnaround would require major improvements in irrigation systems to compensate for the lack of regular rainfall. Revival and expansion of traditional agricultural products such as beef, mutton, leather, citrus fruits and cotton are critical to a prosperous economy. At the time of writing, agriculture accounted for 9% of GDP. Construction, communications and energy are other key sectors that require immediate investment. Rehabilitation of the country's two major ports in the Red Sea, Massawa and Assab, is underway. Eritrea's coastline, stretching over 1,200km, is rich with commercially important marine life and the government hopes to revitalise the fishing industry, though efforts continue to be hampered by the limited number of storage and processing facilities. Tourism is another sector with great potential. Eritrea's close proximity to both Europe and the Middle East, the abundance of historical and archaeological sites, and rich supply of natural resources that can be enjoyed by all visitors are distinct advantages. Given the country's low labour costs and domestic availability of raw materials, light manufacturing of finished leather goods and cotton clothing has the potential to become a significant export earner. Eritrea also has some mineral reserves, mainly copper, potash, gold and platinum, but these have not yet been exploited seriously.

Energy Hydrocarbon exploration, primarily offshore in the Red Sea, began in the 1960s when Eritrea was still federated with Ethiopia. Little oil of commercial volumes has been discovered, however. Eritrea has crude refining capacity of 18,000 bbl/d, but the refinery located in the Red Sea port of Assab has been shutdown since 1997 due to the high operating and maintenance costs. Geothermal energy is a potential source of development in the eastern escarpment area of Eritrea and is being actively investigated by foreign investors. Eritrea also has substantial hydroelectric power generating capacity.

	1999	2000	2001
Inflation (% change)	8.4	19.9	15.1
Exchange rate (per US$)	7.71	9.17	9.55
Interest rate			
GDP (% real growth)	1.2	-8.6	6.4
GDP (Million units of national currency)	5,214.0	5,691.0	6,918.0
GDP (US$ million)	675.9	620.4	724.4
GDP per capita (US$)	180.5	161.1	177.0
Consumption			
Consumption (US$ million)			
Consumption per capita (US$)			
Population, mid-year ('000)	3,744.4	3,850.0	4,092.0
Birth rate (per '000)	40.1	39.6	39.1
Death rate (per '000)	13.8	13.6	13.5
No. of households ('000)			
Total exports (US$ million)			
Total imports (US$ million)			
Tourism receipts (US$ million)	28.0		
Tourist spending (US$ million)	3,744.4	3,850.0	4,092.0

Average household size 2001 (persons)					
Urban population 2001 (%)		19.1			
Age analysis (%) (2001)	*0-14* 44.3		*15-64* 52.9		*65+* 2.8
Population by sex (%) (2001)	*Male* 51.2		*Female* 48.8		
Life expectancy (years) (2001)	*Male* 50.9		*Female* 53.5		
Infant mortality (deaths per '000 live births) (2001)		83.7			
Adult literacy (%) (1997)		25.0			

Estonia

Area (km^2)   45,226

Currency   Kroon (linked to German Mark)

Location   Estonia, the smallest of the three Baltic republics, faces Finland across the Gulf of Finland, with Latvia to the south and Russia dominating its entire eastern frontier. Like Latvia, its land is mainly low-lying and marshy, and its territory includes some 800 islands in the Baltic. The capital is Tallin.

Head of State   President Lennart Meri (1992)

Head of Government   Mart Laar (1997)

Ruling Party   The Centre Party leads a coalition with the Isamaaliit Party and other minor parties.

Political Structure   Estonia was one of the first Soviet states to declare its formal secession from the USSR, in the summer of 1991. It was recognised in September 1991. The Riigikogu (Parliament, or Supreme Council) has 101 members and appoints the president directly. However, a referendum held in June 1992 endorsed a new constitution allowing for the first new president to be directly elected, with subsequent presidents being appointed by the parliament.

Last Elections   In parliamentary elections held in March 1999, the Centre Party won the most seats (28 out of 101). The Isamaaliit Party and the First Reform party each won 18 seats with the remainder being dispersed among minor parties.

Political Risk   Relations with Russia - the major power in the region - are critical. Estonia has a sizeable ethnic Russian population, particularly in the northeast part of the country and this population has become a focus of Russian policy towards Estonia. In addition, Russia is a major trading partner and Estonia depends upon Russia for its oil and gas supplies.

International Disputes   Estonia still has an ongoing disagreement with Russia involving 2,000 sq km of Russian territory in the Narva and Pechora regions. The argument revolves around the boundaries established under the 1921 Peace Treaty of Tartu. Estonia also has a dispute about the maritime border with Latvia, with the primary concern being fishing rights around Ruhne, the Island in the Gulf of Riga and various pieces of land that Russia had previously annexed from Estonia.

Economy   Estonia's GDP rose by 5% in 2001 and should grow by 3.7% in 2002. In 2003, growth of 5.5% is forecast. Prices increased by 5.8% in 2001 and will rise by 3.5% in 2002. In 2003, prices are forecast to rise by another 3.5%. Growth in 2001/2002 has been driven largely by a pickup in investment demand. Estonia continues to be an outstanding performer among the transition economies reflecting the authorities' continued commitment to market-based reforms, pursuit of sound macroeconomic policies, emphasis on institution-building and a commitment to transparency. The cornerstone of Estonia's success is based to a large degree on sound fiscal policies with an extremely low level of public debt, a credible foreign exchange regime in form of a currency board, broad ranging structural changes, which led to the near completion of the privatisation process, and a view toward integrating the country into west Europe. Furthermore, Estonia opted to eliminate restrictions on current and capital account transactions early in the transition process. Conditions in the labour market improved somewhat and the unemployment rate fell slightly to 12.6%. The government was successful in generating a small fiscal surplus. While local governments continued to generate a deficit, this was offset by a corresponding surplus in the central government. The improvement in the fiscal position reflected the authorities' commitment to reduce the overall size of the government.

Main Industries   Agriculture is based mainly on livestock rearing, although dairy farming is also important. There are well-established engineering, machine-building and textile industries, along with important consumer goods and food-processing industries. Estonia's close ties with Scandinavian countries provide ready-made markets for some of its products along with a source of capital and technological know-how. Export-oriented manufacturing investment is becoming increasingly important with Finnish companies using Estonia as a low-cost production base. Most exporters performed relatively well in 2001 and exports to Russia experienced a substantial boost albeit from a very low level. The adverse implications of a fallout in the telecommunications sector for the trade account was limited since most production in Estonia in this sector is largely based on low-value-added subcontracting for Scandinavian electronics companies which led to a simultaneous fall in both exports and imports. Measured in terms of output, over 80% of the economy is under private ownership including the banking system, services and trade, most of industry and some utilities. Growth in domestic demand has been strong as both private consumption and investment are increasing. Estonia has substantial deposits of minerals (including phosphate and oil shale) as well as extensive forest resources. The latter benefit greatly from Scandinavian investment and should soon provide a substantial resource base for development of competitive industries in the fields of timber, paper and paper products.

Energy   Estonia has no proven crude oil reserves, but oil shale is abundant in the northeastern part of the country. Oil shale provides over 75% of the country's total energy supply, making Estonia the only country in the world where it is the primary source of energy. Indigenous oil shale production, however, is not sufficient to meet domestic demand for oil, which was 28,000 bbl/d in 2001. The government expects the oil shale industry to continue operations for another 40 years, but no new mines are scheduled to be built, and Estonia is coming under heavy pressure from the EU to cut back significantly on oil shale production. Estonian politicians have announced they will ask the EU to accord special treatment to oil shale, approaching it the same way that the EU does coal, since the problems of the two natural resources are similar. Meanwhile, Estonia is positioning itself as a major transit centre for oil exports from Russia and the newly independent states to Europe. In more recent years, Estonia's ports at Tallinn and nearby Muuga have become major terminals for the export of petroleum products from the former Soviet Union.

	1999	2000	2001
Inflation (% change)	3.3	4.0	5.8
Exchange rate (per US$)	14.68	16.97	17.56
Interest rate (% per annum, lending rate)	8.7	7.6	9.4
GDP (% real growth)	-0.7	6.9	5.0
GDP (Million units of national currency)	76,327.1	85,436.3	94,283.0
GDP (US$ million)	5,200.2	5,035.0	5,367.9
GDP per capita (US$)	3,607.7	3,513.3	3,767.5
Consumption (Million units of national currency)	43,603.1	50,156.4	55,059.5
Consumption (US$ million)	2,970.7	2,955.8	3,134.8
Consumption per capita (US$)	2,061.0	2,062.5	2,200.2
Population, mid-year ('000)	1,441.4	1,433.1	1,424.8
Birth rate (per '000)	8.7	8.7	8.7
Death rate (per '000)	13.3	13.3	13.3
No. of households ('000)	591.5	585.2	584.3
Total exports (US$ million)	2,935.7	3,176.0	3,305.0
Total imports (US$ million)	4,093.7	4,241.5	4,279.8
Tourism receipts (US$ million)	560.0	656.0	551.1
Tourist spending (US$ million)	217.0	232.8	210.8

Average household size 2001 (persons)	2.45				
Urban population 2001 (%)	73.3				
Age analysis (%) (2001)	*0-14*	17.4	*15-64* 67.9	*65+*	14.7
Population by sex (%) (2001)	*Male*	46.5	*Female* 53.5		
Life expectancy (years) (2001)	*Male*	65.4	*Female* 76.2		
Infant mortality (deaths per '000 live births) (2001)	10.2				
Adult literacy (%) (1996)	99.8				

TRADING PARTNERS

Major export destinations 2001 (% share)

FINLAND	24.5
SWEDEN	17.0
UNITED KINGDOM	9.4
GERMANY	6.1

Major import sources 2001 (% share)

RUSSIA	17.1
FINLAND	13.6
GERMANY	6.5
SWEDEN	6.0

Ethiopia

Area (km^2) 1,023,050

Currency Birr (= 100 cents)

Location Ethiopia is a large, landlocked country with much mountainous terrain. It lies in northeast Africa and is bordered in the north by Eritrea. In the west it borders on Djibouti, in the south on Kenya, in the east on Sudan and in the southwest on Somalia. The country has a warm and desert climate and is prone to periodic drought. The capital is Addis Ababa.

Head of State President Negaso Gidada (1995)

Head of Government Meles Zenawi (1995)

Ruling Party Ethiopian People's Revolutionary Democratic Front (EPRF) leads a broad-based coalition.

Political Structure Ethiopia has an executive president who serves a 4-year term. The Federal Parliamentary Assembly has two chambers. The Council of People's Representatives has a maximum of 550 members, elected for 5-year terms. The Council of the Federation has 117 members, one each from the 22 minority nationalities and one from each professional sector. Members are designated by the regional councils, which may elect them directly or provide their direct elections. The constitution declared in December 1994 established a federal government and divided the country into nine states, each of which retains the right to secede if it wishes.

Last Elections Elections to the Council of People's Representatives were held in May and August 2000. The Oromo People's Democratic Organization won 178 seats, the Amhara National Democratic Movement took 134 seats, the Tigray Peoples Liberation Front claimed 38 seats and the remainder were scattered among a number of parties.

Political Risk Ethiopia is a country made up of 82 ethnic groups and many separatist movements. Extreme poverty, together with the difficulties of famine, continually plagues the country. There is constant famine somewhere in Ethiopia but the situation is slowly improving. Each year millions of Ethiopians depend fearfully on rain.

International Disputes A ceasefire and peace agreement was signed with Eritrea in December 2000. Donors have now returned to help the poverty-ridden country.

Economy Ethiopia's GDP grew by 7.9% in 2001 and prices fell by 7.1%. The country is still overwhelmingly reliant on subsistence agriculture and dependent on foreign aid. The process of liberalisation has gradually been resumed, now that peace is restored. Structural reforms include a reduction in the average import tariff and modifications to the investment code allowing foreign participation in the telecommunications and power sectors. The government's agenda also extends to reform of the financial sector, trade liberalisation and improvements in health and education standards. In the financial sector, the immediate focus is on building up the supervisory capacity of the central bank. In acknowledgement of this effort, the IMF has approved another US$112 million in aid for 2001-2004.

Main Industries Ethiopia's agricultural sector employs some 85% of the workforce, produces about half of the country's GDP and generates most its export earnings. The government encourages the provision of micro-loans for peasants to buy fertiliser and seed but the price of these inputs are high in the hinterland. Authorities also want to move some people from the driest areas but many object to this solution. Much of the harsh, arid landscape is suitable only for cattle herding, but herds have been depleted from droughts in previous years. In the river valleys, wheat, maize and barley are grown. Another difficulty is that the government insists on state ownership of farmland and a land tenure system, which results in progressively smaller plots for each successive generation. The manufacturing sector is heavily dependent on inputs from the agricultural sector. Most manufacturing is carried out only on a local scale and caters to the domestic market. There are mineral reserves, mainly copper, potash, gold and platinum, but these have not yet been exploited seriously.

Energy Ethiopia's current proven hydrocarbon reserves are minimal, but the potential to increase reserves to commercial viability is seen as promising. The country's geology is similar to that of its oil-producing neighbours to the east (on the Arabian peninsula) and the west (Sudan). In 2001, the Ministry of Mines and Energy reported that hydrocarbon seeps had been discovered in several regions. The government plans to conduct feasibility studies to establish the extent and viability of the deposits. Ethiopia's petroleum consumption was estimated to be 22,000 bbl/d in 2000. With the closure of the Assab refinery in 1997, Ethiopia is totally reliant on imports to meet its petroleum requirements. Petroleum imports are received at the port of Djibouti, and shipped via rail and tanker truck to Ethiopia.

	1999	2000	2001
Inflation (% change)	3.9	4.2	-7.1
Exchange rate (per US$)	7.94	8.22	8.46
Interest rate (% per annum, lending rate)	10.6	10.9	10.9
GDP (% real growth)	6.3	5.4	7.9
GDP (Million units of national currency)	48,688.0	52,074.0	53,011.0
GDP (US$ million)	6,130.3	6,337.1	6,267.9
GDP per capita (US$)	99.8	101.3	96.3
Consumption (Million units of national currency)	39,671.0	43,448.2	42,793.9
Consumption (US$ million)	4,994.9	5,287.4	5,059.9
Consumption per capita (US$)	81.3	84.5	77.8
Population, mid-year ('000)	61,411.4	62,565.0	65,063.0
Birth rate (per '000)	44.3	44.2	44.0
Death rate (per '000)	19.1	19.2	19.3
No. of households ('000)	13,072.8	13,229.8	13,623.4
Total exports (US$ million)	574.4	531.0	544.2
Total imports (US$ million)	1,317.3	1,343.0	1,400.5
Tourism receipts (US$ million)	16.0	32.6	26.0
Tourist spending (US$ million)	55.0	51.1	47.6

Average household size 2001 (persons)	4.73				
Urban population 2001 (%)	18.1				
Age analysis (%) (2001)	*0-14*	46.0	*15-64*	51.2	*65+* 2.9
Population by sex (%) (2001)	*Male*	50.1	*Female*	49.9	
Life expectancy (years) (2001)	*Male*	43.0	*Female*	44.2	
Infant mortality (deaths per '000 live births) (2001)	108.2				
Adult literacy (%) (1997)	35.4				

TRADING PARTNERS

Major export destinations 2001 (% share)		Major import sources 2001 (% share)	
DJIBOUTI	13.3	SAUDI ARABIA	28.4
ITALY	9.5	ITALY	6.9
JAPAN	9.2	INDIA	6.6
ASIA	9.0	CHINA	4.7

Fiji

Area (km^2) 18,330

Currency Fiji dollar (F$ = 100 cents)

Location Fiji lies in the South Pacific, about 1,600km north of New Zealand and northeast of Tonga. The country comprises 332 islands and some 500 atolls and reefs, of which about 100 are inhabited. The terrain is mainly low-lying, although there are large volcanic ranges on most of the larger islands. The climate is warm and tropical, with some risk of cyclones. The capital is Suva.

Head of State President Ratu Josefa Iloilo (2000)

Head of Government Laisenia Qarase (2000)

Ruling Party The government is formed by United Fiji Party (SDL) and the Conservative Alliance Party (MV).

Political Structure Fiji left the Commonwealth in 1987 after two successive coups in which ethnic Fijians asserted their precedence over the ethnic Chinese and Indians who were effectively running the country at the time. Eventually, international pressure led to changes in the constitution which ensure that all Fijians (including Indians) have equal rights of representation. That constitution was again scrapped in 2000, following a coup led by indigenous Fijians. The House of Representatives is now made up of 71 members elected for a 5-year term in single-seat constituencies, divided in 23 Fijian communal, 19 Indian communal, 3 general communal, 1 Rotuman and 25 open seats. The Senate has 32 members, elected for a 5-year term: 14 members elected by the Council of Chiefs, 9 members appointed by the prime minister, 8 nominated by the leader of the opposition and 1 Rotuma representative.

Last Elections Elections to the House of Representatives occurred in September 2001. The SDL received 32 seats, the Fiji Labour Party won 27 seats and the remaining seats were divided among several parties. Iloilo was subsequently appointed president.

Political Risk The economy suffered greatly as a result of the coup in 2000. Looting and the destruction of property led to the suspension of operations by many businesses, particularly in the main centres of Suva, Lautoka and Nadi. Government activities were also adversely affected, including basic services such as power and water, and the operation of government departments. Fiji is a racially divided country with just over half the population claiming ancestry back to antiquity while the rest are descended from Indians who came to the island in the 19th century.

International Disputes Fiji's relations with much of the international community were shaky prior to the latest coup, and have deteriorated further in the aftermath. The international community's responses included reduced aid flows, imposition of diplomatic and trade sanctions, and travel advisories to tourists. Fijian relations with Kiribati have been strained as a result of the protracted bid by the residents of Banaban Island in Kiribati to secede to have their island placed under the protection of Fiji.

Economy Fiji's economy slumped badly in the past two years but a modest recovery is expected. GDP should rise by around 3.5% in 2002 and 4.7% in 2003. Inflation should be between 3-4% in both years. Monetary policy continued to focus on maintaining low inflation and ensuring adequate foreign reserves, but it was eased in 2001 in order to stimulate aggregate demand. Money and credit growth in 2001 continued to reflect slow economic growth, and weak consumer and business confidence. Despite a substantial improvement in VAT collection, operating revenues declined due to a sharp drop in direct taxation revenues, reflecting the lagged effect of the 2000 recession. Revenue arrears were also substantial. The 2002 budget stated that the government was committed to a more interventionist role in rebuilding the economy. Priorities include a strong redistributive spending policy aimed at addressing people's basic needs; improving economic efficiency and international competitiveness; and reforming the civil service, public enterprises and public financial management. The budget proposed an expansionary fiscal policy along with a deficit of 6% of GDP. The government is making an effort to stimulate aggregate demand through an expansionary fiscal policy and an accommodative monetary policy. While emphasis on public investment in basic infrastructure and in health and education is appropriate, the crucial issue is ensuring that these efforts do not raise the already substantial public debt burden and threaten macroeconomic stability and growth.

Main Industries The trade, restaurant and hotel sector, and the transport and communications sector expanded by 4.2% and 7.3%, respectively in 2001. Mining and quarrying activity rose by 2% due to improved gold ore extraction, while the community, social and personal services sector also registered modest growth, of 2.2%, mainly because of increased civil service employment. Construction activity grew by 2.9%, primarily as a result of public investment projects completed during the year, while the electricity and water sector strengthened by 3.5%. The primary sector contracted by 0.5% in 2001, largely due to a 10.2% drop in sugarcane production, reflecting transport problems and underlying uncertainty over the renewal of land leases. Aggregate manufacturing output fell by 5.5%. The services sector (mainly finance, insurance, real estate and business services) declined by 3.1% in 2001, reflecting weaker business and consumer confidence. The labour market remained sluggish in 2001 as a result of the slow economic growth. In the period from May 2000 to the end of 2001, an estimated 9,000 workers at least were laid off, of whom 2,700, or 30%, were in the garment industry. Furthermore, skills shortages became more apparent in both the public and private sectors, as qualified and skilled citizens emigrated.

Energy Fiji relies on imported oil and gas for most of its energy needs which it cannot cover with indigenous resources such as brushwood or timber. There may be scope for geothermal power in the future. Meanwhile, three-quarters of the country's electricity is produced by hydroelectric plants.

	1999	2000	2001
Inflation (% change)	0.2	3.0	5.0
Exchange rate (per US$)	1.97	2.13	2.28
Interest rate (% per annum, commercial lending rate)	8.8	8.4	8.3
GDP (% real growth)	9.7	-2.8	
GDP (Million units of national currency)	3,665.0	3,505.0	3,724.0
GDP (US$ million)	1,860.8	1,646.6	1,635.7
GDP per capita (US$)	2,337.4	2,042.3	2,004.3
Consumption (Million units of national currency)	2,105.3	2,180.7	2,320.5
Consumption (US$ million)	1,068.9	1,024.5	1,019.3
Consumption per capita (US$)	1,342.7	1,270.7	1,249.0
Population, mid-year ('000)	796.1	806.2	816.1
Birth rate (per '000)	25.5	25.2	25.0
Death rate (per '000)	5.6	5.5	5.5
No. of households ('000)	152.5	153.6	153.8
Total exports (US$ million)	531.3	563.0	495.0
Total imports (US$ million)	841.0	648.0	584.0
Tourism receipts (US$ million)	275.0	261.7	254.6
Tourist spending (US$ million)	66.0	45.8	50.1

Average household size 2001 (persons)	5.28					
Urban population 2001 (%)	50.2					
Age analysis (%) (2001)	*0-14*	31.1	*15-64*	64.2	*65+*	4.7
Population by sex (%) (2001)	*Male*	50.8	*Female*	49.2		
Life expectancy (years) (2001)	*Male*	67.7	*Female*	71.2		
Infant mortality (deaths per '000 live births) (2001)	18.1					
Adult literacy (%) (1997)	91.8					

TRADING PARTNERS

Major export destinations 2001 (% share)   **Major import sources 2001 (% share)**

Export	%	Import	%
USA	28.9	AUSTRALIA	43.9
AUSTRALIA	19.8	NEW ZEALAND	14.7
UNITED KINGDOM	10.7	SINGAPORE	8.4
JAPAN	5.0	JAPAN	3.8

Finland

Area (km^2)   337,030

Currency   Euro (= 100 cents)

Location   Finland, lying on the Baltic coast with its western border bridging Sweden and Norway, and with its entire eastern flank meeting the countries of the former Soviet Union, was ideally placed to develop a role as an entrepôt for East-West trade in the 1970s and 1980s. Most of the territory is forested, with the main habitation centres to the south. The climate ranges from sub-Arctic in the north to temperate in the south. The capital is Helsinki.

Head of State   Tarja Halonen (2000)

Head of Government   Paavo Lipponen (April 1995)

Ruling Party   A multiparty coalition leads the country.

Political Structure   Finland has a semi-executive president who exercises extensive political powers even though the main executive functions are vested in the prime minister. Elected by universal suffrage for a 6-year term, the president may appoint any prime minister and cabinet which can secure the approval of the 200-member Eduskunta (Parliament). Members of parliament are also elected for 4-year terms. In January 1995, Finland became a full member of the EU.

Last Elections   In February 2000, Tarja Halonen narrowly defeated Esko Aho, the leader of the Centre Party, to become president. Parliamentary elections were held in March 1999. The Social Democrat's share of the vote fell from 28% to 23% and they won only 51 seats in the 200-member parliament (down from 63 in the previous election). Their main coalition partner, the NCP took 46 seats (up from 39 in 1995). The shift in power meant that the Social Democrats lost some influence within their coalition.

Political Risk   Finland is a country with few serious worries. Perhaps the most difficult decision that the government has had to face in recent years has been whether to go ahead with the construction of a fifth nuclear power plant. By mid-2002, the decision to proceed had been made despite strong objections from the Greens and related parties.

International Disputes   Finland's non-aligned status may come into question, particularly with the prospect of the Baltic States being admitted to NATO in the next few years. It is unclear whether their admission will contribute to stability in the Baltic region or not and what the implications of the move will be for Finland. Finland and Sweden disagree over the ownership of a group of islands in the Gulf of Bothnia, which Finland, the current owner, calls Ahvenanmaa and Sweden calls the Aaland Islands. The issue, which dates back to 1809, will not harm bilateral relations, however.

Economy   GDP grew by a paltry 0.7% in 2001 while growth in 2002 is expected to be 1.4% and rise to 3.1% in 2003. Inflation was 2.6% in 2001 and is expected to fall to 1.5% in 2002. In 2003, prices are expected to rise by 1.6%. A rise in unemployment and a further widening of the output gap is also expected. Private consumption growth will be supported by a substantial tax cut and real wage gains, but business investment will suffer from poor business sentiment. The authorities have set a central government surplus target of 1.5-2% of GDP for this decade. However, as a result of the economic slowdown and tax cuts, the central government balance will be far below this target in 2002 and may even move into deficit. Finland could soon encounter some problems owing to its rapidly ageing population. Economic growth could be sharply curtailed in the face of a shrinking labour force and there would be too few workers to support the growing number of pensioners. Finland is far from alone in this respect, however, and for the time being its prospects are relatively bright.

Main Industries   Though the country is small, the Finns boast several world-class industries. The most important is forestry, which accounts for almost 30% of exports and a sizeable portion of GDP. The Finns alone account for a third of West Europe's total capacity in the forestry industry. The country is also the world's second largest exporter of paper products behind Canada. The electronics industry - of which Nokia is the biggest part - accounts for more than a quarter of all exports and close to 7% of GDP. The electronics industry's short-term prospects are in doubt, however, following the recent slump in world spending in this area. Metal and engineering industries were other important agents of growth. Orders in the country's troubled shipbuilding industry have recovered somewhat but the industry's long-term outlook remains bleak. Agriculture accounts for just 4% of GDP in Finland. Farm production, however, is on the increase as many farms are being consolidated and reorganised. These changes are driven by greater investment in agriculture, and are being encouraged by public aid. However, the future of Finnish agriculture hinges upon further gains in competitiveness. Many of the EU's proposals for reform of its common agricultural policy will be very difficult for Finland to implement.

Energy   Finland relies totally on imports of oil and gas, which it once obtained from the Soviet Union. Plans for a substantial expansion of Finnish gas drilling projects in Russia have been considered but never implemented. Nuclear energy accounts for about a sixth of the country's total energy needs and the government is deeply split over the plans to build another nuclear plant. The Nordic area has a common power market, and any shortage in one country may push up prices throughout the region.

	1999	2000	2001
Inflation (% change)	0.9	1.1	1.1
Exchange rate (per US$)	0.94	1.09	1.12
Interest rate (% per annum, lending rate)	4.7	5.6	5.8
GDP (% real growth)	4.2	5.7	0.7
GDP (Million units of national currency)	120,491.0	131,670.0	133,935.0
GDP (US$ million)	128,474.7	114,371.2	119,850.9
GDP per capita (US$)	24,870.8	22,089.2	23,094.9
Consumption (Million units of national currency)	58,868.8	63,844.5	1.0
Consumption (US$ million)	62,769.4	55,456.6	59,069.0
Consumption per capita (US$)	12,151.2	10,710.7	11,382.4
Population, mid-year ('000)	5,165.7	5,177.7	5,189.5
Birth rate (per '000)	10.8	10.4	10.1
Death rate (per '000)	9.7	9.7	9.8
No. of households ('000)	2,272.9	2,295.4	2,307.7
Total exports (US$ million)	40,665.3	44,524.3	41,705.6
Total imports (US$ million)	30,726.0	32,603.6	30,443.8
Tourism receipts (US$ million)	1,517.0	1,609.5	1,253.0
Tourist spending (US$ million)	2,021.0	1,929.5	1,829.1

Average household size 2001 (persons)	2.26				
Urban population 2001 (%)	65.6				
Age analysis (%) (2001)	*0-14* 18.1		*15-64* 66.9		*65+* 15.0
Population by sex (%) (2001)	*Male* 48.8		*Female* 51.2		
Life expectancy (years) (2001)	*Male* 74.2		*Female* 81.3		
Infant mortality (deaths per '000 live births) (2001)	4.0				
Adult literacy (%) (1998)	99.0				

TRADING PARTNERS

Major export destinations 2001 (% share)

GERMANY	12.4
USA	9.8
UNITED KINGDOM	9.6
SWEDEN	8.4

Major import sources 2001 (% share)

GERMANY	14.4
SWEDEN	10.0
RUSSIA	9.6
UNITED KINGDOM	6.3

◼ France

Area (km^2) 543,965

Currency Euro (= 100 cents)

Location France, the largest country in Western Europe, also lies at the heart of the continent. It meets Spain and Andorra in the south, across the Pyrenees and Italy in the southeast. Switzerland and Germany lie to the east and Belgium and Luxembourg in the north. The terrain is extremely varied, and its climate ranges from temperate and wet in the north to Mediterranean in the south. The capital is Paris.

Head of State President Jacques Chirac (1995)

Head of Government Jean-Pierre Raffarin (2002) DL

Ruling Party The government is formed by the Rally for the Republic (RPR), Union for the French Democracy (UDF) and the Liberal Democracy (DL) parties.

Political Structure France has a semi-executive presidency in which the head of state, elected by universal suffrage for a 7-year term, appoints a prime minister in accordance with the bicameral Parliament. The 577-seat National Assembly is elected every five years, and one third of the Senate's 321 members come up for re-election every three years, for a 9-year term. France has an unusually centralised decision-making process for a country of its size - even those concerning the four overseas departments (Guadeloupe, Martinique, French Guiana and Reunion).

Last Elections Presidential elections were held in April and May 2002 when Chirac received 82% of the vote, defeating Jean-Marie le Pen of the National Front. Parliamentary elections, which were held in June 2002, produced a victory for the union of the RPR and the DL. Together, these parties took 357 seats in parliament while the Socialist Party won 140 seats. The National Front won 11% of the vote but no seats. Other parties in the new parliament include the communists (21 seats), the UDF (29 seats), the Diverse Right (9 seats) and the Greens (3 seats).

Political Risk The huge pockets of foreign, unassimilated minorities in France are creating a politically and socially volatile situation. The country is home to around five million Muslims, mostly of North African extraction, and about 600,000 Jews. Altogether, France has more Muslims and Jews than any other country in Western Europe. This situation, as much as conditions in the Middle East, is the reason for the year-long wave of anti-Jewish acts that have plagued the country. Anti-racist groups in the country claim they have documented over 400 anti-Jewish incidents since 2000.

International Disputes France has relinquished control over most of its former dependencies but most of those that remain under control from Paris are unhappy with the relationship. Ties with Algeria are complicated by the terrorist acts of the latter's Muslim extremists and the admission by French military leaders of atrocities committed during the war.

Economy GDP grew by 2% in 2001 and should increase by 1.4% in 2002. In 2003, growth is forecast at 3%. Inflation was 1.8% in 2001 and will fall to 1.5% in 2002 and 1.4% in 2003. Growth of private consumption began to slow by 2002, though it will continue to bolster activity via real wage growth and net job creation. Tax receipts are lower than forecast and unlikely to show much increase in the short term. The budget deficit will consequently be higher than the projections in the 2002-2004 multiyear programme of public finance. This deterioration is temporary and does not necessitate corrective measures. Control of public expenditure will be the cornerstone of macroeconomic policy for many years to come. Authorities have put mechanisms in place to control the growth of general government expenditure. Spending increase norms are set in the multiyear programmes of public finance and then written into the budget. However, the present norms are unlikely to be stringent enough to consolidate public finances in the future, especially if economic growth falls short of the authorities' hopes. More ambitious and more tightly enforced norms will have to be incorporated. Authorities must also strengthen their efforts to address long-standing structural problems so as to promote further growth and lower unemployment.

Main Industries Agriculture accounts for just 2% of GDP but plays an important role in French politics. Farms are small, and even though the soil quality is usually excellent, they remain inefficient and require massive financial support. France grows soft fruits, cereals, maize, root vegetables, sugar beet and sunflowers, and is famed for its wine production. The structure of the French economy is changing rapidly as a result of large capital inflows to industries such as information technology and related high-tech activities. More recently, these same industries have begun to suffer as a result of the recession in high-tech operations. Privatisation is another reason for the rapid structural change. Between 1997 and 2002, the government sold off nearly half of France Telecom, the remaining stakes in the steelmaker, Usinor, and its share of Pechiney, the aluminium group. It also sold controlling stakes in the fifth largest banking network and in a large insurer. In the case of several defence electronics firms, the state's stakes fell below 50%. The banking sector has enjoyed a period of respite after going through a wave of consolidations and mergers that almost halved the number of banks operating in the country. Insurance and financial services have also experienced major reforms in more recent years. Manufacturing accounts for 25% of all jobs while employment in services makes up nearly 70%. France's transportation sector is among the most advanced in the world, benefiting from new technologies and extraordinary investment by the government. The country has 12 major seaports, many of which are equipped for containerships. There are also extensive highway and river-transport systems and a state-owned rail network that is among the most comprehensive and technologically advanced in the world.

Energy French energy policy has been relatively consistent in recent decades, with the main objectives including: securing energy supply, achieving international competitiveness and protecting the environment. The focus on energy security has led France to become one of the world's top producers and consumers of nuclear power. France itself has reserves totalling only 140 million barrels. Despite France's limited domestic reserves and production, the French oil industry is an important player in world energy markets. Major oil assets of French oil companies are located in the North Sea, Africa and Latin America.

	1999	2000	2001
Inflation (% change)	0.9	1.1	1.1
Exchange rate (per US$)	0.94	1.09	1.12
Interest rate (% per annum, lending rate)	6.4	6.7	7.0
GDP (% real growth)	3.0	3.6	2.0
GDP (Million units of national currency)	1,349,481.0	1,408,417.0	1,459,638.0
GDP (US$ million)	1,438,897.7	1,223,379.2	1,306,155.4
GDP per capita (US$)	24,375.5	20,686.3	22,038.2
Consumption (Million units of national currency)	736,305.4	778,940.1	1.0
Consumption (US$ million)	785,093.1	676,603.0	718,914.4
Consumption per capita (US$)	13,299.8	11,440.8	12,130.0
Population, mid-year ('000)	59,030.4	59,139.7	59,267.7
Birth rate (per '000)	12.4	12.3	12.3
Death rate (per '000)	9.4	9.4	9.4
No. of households ('000)	23,810.0	24,085.0	24,232.6
Total exports (US$ million)	300,757.0	298,841.0	292,503.0
Total imports (US$ million)	289,906.0	300,954.0	292,533.0
Tourism receipts (US$ million)	31,507.0	33,400.7	29,283.2
Tourist spending (US$ million)	18,631.0	18,381.4	17,583.6

Average household size 2001 (persons)	2.45				
Urban population 2001 (%)	75.8				
Age analysis (%) (2001)	0-14	18.0	15-64	64.8	65+ 17.2
Population by sex (%) (2001)	Male	47.7	Female	52.3	
Life expectancy (years) (2001)	Male	75.0	Female	82.6	
Infant mortality (deaths per '000 live births) (2001)	5.2				
Adult literacy (%) (1998)	99.0				

TRADING PARTNERS
Major export destinations 2001 (% share)   **Major import sources 2001 (% share)**

Export	%	Import	%
GERMANY	14.4	GERMANY	17.8
UNITED KINGDOM	9.7	BELGIUM	9.5
SPAIN	9.1	ITALY	8.7
USA	8.6	UNITED KINGDOM	7.6

French Guiana

Area (km^2) 91,000

Currency Euro (= 100 cents)

Location Located on the northeastern Atlantic coast of South America, between Suriname in the west and Brazil in the east and south, French Guiana is a predominantly forested region with a number of large rivers flowing down from a high sierra in the south. The climate is humid and tropical. The capital is Cayenne.

Head of State President Jacques Chirac (France)

Head of Government Stephan Phinera-Horth (1994)

Ruling Party Parti Socialiste Guyanais (PSG)

Political Structure French Guiana is an external department of France and is therefore governed to a considerable degree from Paris. The country sends deputies to the French Assemblée Nationale, and is represented at the EU. Since being accorded regional status in 1974, however, it elects its own 31-member Regional Council for a term of six years, with responsibility for economic and social planning. Other executive power rests in a 19-member General Council.

Last Elections Elections to the Regional Council were held in March 1998 and the PSG took 11 seats. Elections to the General Council took place in 1994 with the PSG taking eight seats. The last full elections to the French Assemblée Nationale were in 1998, when the Rassemblement pour la République returned one delegate and the left wing returned one "dissident" member.

Political Risk French Guiana has one of the lowest per capita incomes in the Caribbean region. Unemployment is a persistent problem, particularly among younger workers. Sporadic unrest occurs, reflecting dissatisfaction with the state of rule from Paris.

International Disputes Part of French Guiana's southwestern corner is claimed by Suriname, which alleges that a poor interpretation of a bilateral French-British agreement in the 19th century wrongly awarded the land between the Itany and Marouini (subsidiaries of the Litany and Maroni rivers) to the French. The land is deeply impenetrable and has little mineral significance; however, there is some hydroelectric potential.

Economy The rate of growth was less than 2% in 2001 while inflation probably exceeded 5%. Unemployment is a serious problem for the country, particularly among younger workers. The economy is closely tied to that of France through subsidies and imports. The European Space Agency's launch site at Kourou is the single most important contributor to GDP. Dependence on Paris has not always proved to the country's advantage and it has been difficult to attract foreign investors. At present, France continues to be its principal economic mainstay.

Main Industries French Guiana relies almost exclusively on its agricultural sector to employ and feed the population, and yet only 0.1% of the land surface is actually cultivated - most of the remainder being jungle. Export crops are limited to sugar and fish products. Most of the population is engaged in subsistence farming of rice, maize and bananas. There are also, a small number of cattle farms. Timber, the most obvious natural asset, is only marginally exploited because of a lack of infrastructure facilities. The hardwoods that are harvested support an expanding sawmill industry that provides sawn logs for export. There is also a growing fishing fleet and shrimp processing is an important industry. Industry tends to be restricted to the small area around the European Space Agency's launch site at Kourou - which alone generates a fifth of GDP. The mining sector produces a modest quantity of gold.

Energy Much of the French Guiana's energy is hydroelectric. Otherwise, the country relies almost entirely on imports for all fuel supplies except natural resources such as brushwood and timber.

	1999	2000	2001
Inflation (% change)	0.9	1.1	1.1
Exchange rate (per US$)	0.94	1.09	1.12
Interest rate			
GDP (% real growth)	2.6	1.9	
GDP (Million units of national currency)	692.2	738.5	787.2
GDP (US$ million)	738.0	641.5	704.4
GDP per capita (US$)	4,241.6	3,543.9	3,612.4
Consumption (Million units of national currency)	459.2	510.7	1.0
Consumption (US$ million)	489.6	443.6	478.1
Consumption per capita (US$)	2,814.0	2,451.1	2,451.8
Population, mid-year ('000)	174.0	181.0	195.0
Birth rate (per '000)	29.8	29.4	28.9
Death rate (per '000)	4.3	4.3	4.2
No. of households ('000)	31.1	32.2	34.9
Total exports (US$ million)			
Total imports (US$ million)			
Tourism receipts (US$ million)			
Tourist spending (US$ million)	174.0	181.0	195.0

Average household size 2001 (persons)	5.62				
Urban population 2001 (%)	78.4				
Age analysis (%) (2001)	*0-14*	30.2	*15-64*	63.0	*65+* 6.7
Population by sex (%) (2001)	*Male*	49.4	*Female*	50.6	
Life expectancy (years)					
Infant mortality (deaths per '000 live births) (2001)	29.7				
Adult literacy (%)					

French Polynesia

Area (km^2) 3,940

Currency Franc CFP (= 100 centimes)

Location French Polynesia consists of five separate groups of islands in the South Pacific. Included are Tahiti and Moorea, the remaining Society Islands, the Leeward Islands, the Tuamotu Islands, the Gambier Islands and the Marquesa Islands. With most of the territory composed of coral reefs, the land seldom rises far above sea level. The capital is Papeete.

Head of State President Jacques Chirac (France)

Head of Government Gaston Flosse (1991)

Ruling Party People's Rally for the Republic

Political Structure French Polynesia is one of the four French Overseas Territories, which do not enjoy full department status but are regarded as an integral part of France. As such, most important decisions are taken in France rather than locally. The 49-member Territorial Assembly is elected by universal suffrage and elects its own representatives to the National Assembly in Paris. Executive power is wielded locally by the President of the Territorial Government, who approximates to a Prime Minister.

Last Elections The most recent election was held in May 2001 when the People's Rally for the Republic (Gaullist) captured 28 seats in the Territorial Assembly. The People's Servant Party won 13 seats with the remainder spread among several parties.

Political Risk So far, French Polynesia has seen little of the anti-French attitudes that are common in New Caledonia. However, the latter's recent success in extracting a more lucrative treaty with Paris may inspire nationalists in the islands. There have occasionally been violent protests over tax increases but these have had limited political significance.

International Disputes France's practice of using Mururoa and Fangataufa atolls for nuclear weapons testing is strongly opposed by the country.

Economy GDP has been growing by 5-6% in recent years but growth fell sharply in 2001 as a result of the worldwide slump in tourism. Since 1962, when France stationed military personnel in the region, French Polynesia has changed from a subsistence economy to one in which a high proportion of the workforce is either employed by the military or supports the tourist industry. It is possible that the French military presence will be reduced over the course of this decade and, if so, the islands' economy will suffer greatly. The tourist sector accounts for a fifth of GDP and is the primary source of foreign exchange, although it employs only a small proportion of the population. The local government also hopes to develop the infrastructure and make the country more self-sufficient.

Main Industries Farm land is of poor quality and agriculture remains underdeveloped, accounting for no more than 4% of GDP but the government is seeking to expand the sector. Industry contributes 20% of GDP and services make up the remainder. Tourism, alone, contributes about 20% to GDP and is a primary source of hard currency earnings, although it employs only a small proportion of the population. The country is particularly popular with French, German and American visitors but a sharp decline in the number of visitors occurred in the latter part of 2001 and 2002. Copra, vanilla and fruit are grown for the export market, and pineapples, bananas, mangoes, pawpaws and cereals for the home market. Timber is grown for export. The country's industries consist mainly of pearls, handicrafts, fruit canning, soap making with coconut oil, and brewing. The islands have cobalt and phosphate reserves, although there has been little mining since the 1930s.

Energy The country relies on imports for the greater part of its energy needs, except for timber and fuel wood.

	1999	2000	2001
Inflation (% change)	5.4	5.6	2.8
Exchange rate (per US$)	85.14	98.45	101.36
Interest rate			
GDP (% real growth)	1.7	2.0	1.6
GDP (Million units of national currency)	163,200.8	175,786.8	183,600.2
GDP (US$ million)	1,916.9	1,785.5	1,811.3
GDP per capita (US$)	8,439.2	7,725.3	7,703.7
Consumption (Million units of national currency)	72,957.3	77,470.2	84,386.7
Consumption (US$ million)	856.9	786.9	832.5
Consumption per capita (US$)	3,772.7	3,404.6	3,540.8
Population, mid-year ('000)	227.1	231.1	235.1
Birth rate (per '000)	21.2	21.0	20.8
Death rate (per '000)	4.9	4.8	4.8
No. of households ('000)	40.0	41.0	40.8
Total exports (US$ million)			
Total imports (US$ million)			
Tourism receipts (US$ million)	308.9	357.2	266.1
Tourist spending (US$ million)	227.1	231.1	235.1

Average household size 2001 (persons)	5.63				
Urban population 2001 (%)	53.3				
Age analysis (%) (2001)	*0-14*	32.9	*15-64*	62.8	*65+* 4.3
Population by sex (%) (2001)	*Male*	51.4	*Female*	48.6	
Life expectancy (years) (2001)	*Male*	70.3	*Female*	75.4	
Infant mortality (deaths per '000 live births) (2001)	9.4				
Adult literacy (%)					

TRADING PARTNERS

Major export destinations 2001 (% share)		Major import sources 2001 (% share)	
FRANCE	37.9	FRANCE	53.4
JAPAN	30.6	AUSTRALIA	12.1
USA	20.1	USA	9.3
GERMANY	3.0	NEW ZEALAND	8.0

Gabon

Area (km^2)   267,665

Currency   CFA franc (= 100 centimes)

Location   The Gabonese Republic straddles the equator on the Atlantic coast of Africa between Equatorial Guinea and Cameroon in the north and Congo in the south and southeast. It has a warm and occasionally humid equatorial climate. The capital is Libreville.

Head of State   President El Hadj Omar Bongo (1967)

Head of Government   Jean-François Ntoutoume (1999)

Ruling Party   Parti Democratique Gabonais (PDG)

Political Structure   Gabon, which achieved independence from France in 1960, was run as a single-party socialist system from 1968 until March 1991, when a new multiparty Constitution came into force. The country has an executive president who is elected by universal suffrage for a 5-year term. Parliament has two chambers. The National Assembly has 120 members, 111 members elected for a 5-year term in single-seat constituencies and 9 members appointed by the president. The Senate has 91 members, elected for a 6-year term in single-seat constituencies.

Last Elections   Omar Bongo was re-elected as president in December 1998 with 67% of the vote. Bongo has been in power since 1967. Elections to the National Assembly were held in December 2001. The PDG took 85 seats with the remainder scattered among several parties and non-partisans. Elections to the Senate were last held in February 1997 when the PDG took 54 seats and the National Woodcutters Rally won 20 seats. The remainder were divided among several parties.

Political Risk   Gabon's transition from a single-party to a multiparty state has been difficult. Political opposition is fierce and Bongo's relations with Paris are poor. This position will be precarious if oil reserves should be exhausted in the near future.

International Disputes   Gabon has a maritime boundary dispute with Equatorial Guinea with regard to sovereignty over several islands in Corisco Bay.

Economy   GDP grew by 1.5% in 2001 and inflation was 2.6%. Following a severe financial crisis in 1998, Gabon has made considerable progress in putting public finances on a sound footing, reducing government indebtedness, and regularising relations with external and domestic creditors. Fiscal and structural reform efforts continued during 2001. During 2000-2001, Gabon made significant progress in improving public finances, with the primary fiscal surplus averaging some 17% of GDP. However, fiscal performance in 2001 fell short of the government's objective, owing mainly to weaknesses in non-oil revenue collection, unbudgeted support for public enterprises and a relaxation of expenditure controls. Gabon's challenges in the medium term are the projected rapid decline in oil production and the continued high external debt service burden. Prospects for sustained growth and poverty reduction depend on the development of the non-oil sector. This objective will require significant efforts to mobilise domestic savings, enhanced access to foreign financing and further improvements in the environment for private sector activity.

Main Industries   Non-oil economic activity in Gabon rose by 4% in 2001, following a severe contraction in 1999 and a moderate recovery in 2000. Private investment picked up as confidence strengthened further, helped by substantial repayments of government domestic debt. Services, agriculture and wood processing were the main sectors contributing to growth. However, delays occurred in the privatisation of public enterprises in the agro-industry, telecommunications and air transport sectors. Agriculture accounts for no more than 5% of GDP and less than 1% of the total land area is under cultivation. Cocoa, coffee, rubber, sugar cane and coffee are the major exports while cassava, maize, groundnuts and vegetables are produced for the domestic market. Industrial development is very limited, consisting mainly of food and beverages, textiles, lumbering and plywood, cement, petroleum extraction and refining, chemicals and ship repairs. Gabon contains substantial natural resources and is currently the eighth largest supplier of uranium ore in the world, producing an average of 500-600 tonnes of uranium dioxide yearly.

Energy   Gabon is sub-Saharan Africa's third largest oil producer. The country's oil production was 325,000 barrels per day (bbl/d) in 2001 and has been declining in recent years. However, Gabon's proven oil reserves increased to 2.5 billion barrels in 2001 from 1.3 billion barrels in 1996. The Gabonese government is promoting increased petroleum exploration and investment in the oil and non-oil sectors. To help boost reserves and production, Gabon's oil ministry has revised its production-sharing contracts to attract new investors and has increased the number of exploration permits issued.

	1999	2000	2001
Inflation (% change)	-0.7	1.0	2.6
Exchange rate (per US$)	615.70	711.98	733.04
Interest rate (% per annum, lending rate)	22.0	22.0	20.7
GDP (% real growth)	-9.6	-1.9	1.5
GDP (Billion units of national currency)	2,839.6	3,576.9	3,387.4
GDP (US$ million)	4,612.0	5,023.9	4,621.0
GDP per capita (US$)	3,836.8	4,097.8	3,585.0
Consumption (Billion units of national currency)	1,420.0	1,833.2	1,757.2
Consumption (US$ million)	2,306.3	2,574.8	2,397.1
Consumption per capita (US$)	1,918.6	2,100.2	1,859.7
Population, mid-year ('000)	1,202.0	1,226.0	1,289.0
Birth rate (per '000)	37.7	37.7	37.6
Death rate (per '000)	15.6	15.5	15.3
No. of households ('000)	166.8	172.2	183.0
Total exports (US$ million)	2,666.8	2,790.0	2,595.9
Total imports (US$ million)	1,084.4	996.0	877.1
Tourism receipts (US$ million)	11.0	10.9	9.3
Tourist spending (US$ million)	183.0	175.3	154.4

Average household size 2001 (persons)		7.12				
Urban population 2001 (%)		81.8				
Age analysis (%) (2001)	*0-14*	39.4	*15-64*	54.7	*65+*	5.9
Population by sex (%) (2001)	*Male*	49.0	*Female*	51.0		
Life expectancy (years) (2001)	*Male*	51.7	*Female*	53.9		
Infant mortality (deaths per '000 live births) (2001)		81.9				
Adult literacy (%) (1997)		66.2				

TRADING PARTNERS

Major export destinations 2001 (% share)		Major import sources 2001 (% share)	
USA	44.3	FRANCE	62.0
FRANCE	21.6	USA	5.6
CHINA	6.6	UNITED KINGDOM	3.8
NETHERLANDS ANTILLES	5.2	BELGIUM	2.6

■ Gambia

Area (km^2) 10,690

Currency Dalasi (D = 100 butut)

Location The state of The Gambia takes the form of a narrow strip bordering the banks of the River Gambia on the Atlantic coast of West Africa, It has a short coastline but is otherwise surrounded by the republic of Senegal. The climate is generally hot and extremely dry, although there is rain in the spring. The capital is Banjul.

Head of State Captain Yahya Jameh (July 1994)

Head of Government Captain Yahya Jameh (July 1994)

Ruling Party The Provisional Revolutionary Council (PRC) is the dominant party.

Political Structure The Gambia has been independent since 1965 and became a republic in 1970. The constitution provides for an executive president who is elected for a 5-year term by universal suffrage, along with a 53-member unicameral legislative assembly, the House of Representatives. Among the representatives, 48 are elected for 5-year terms and 5 are appointed. In 1994, the constitution was suspended when President Alhaji Sir Dawda Kairaba Jawara was deposed in a bloodless coup led by Captain Yahya Jameh who continues to rule with an iron hand.

Last Elections In presidential elections held in October 2001, President Jameh received 53% of the vote, defeating Ousinou Darboe who received 33%. Elections to the House of Representatives were held in January 2002. The PRC secured 45 seats and the Peoples' Democratic Organisation won 3. The remainder were appointed. The centrist United Democratic Party boycotted the elections.

Political Risk In the past, the government has squandered much of its resources on exotic projects. But as international criticism and pressure has mounted, stronger efforts at reform and better governance are obvious. Risks remain high, but there are modest reasons for optimism.

International Disputes A short section of the boundary with Senegal is undetermined.

Economy GDP rose by 5.8% in Gambia in 2001 and inflation was 4%. Gambia has made substantial progress in implementing economic reforms but remains one of the poorest countries in the world. Important reforms, including a further reduction in external tariff, increase in petroleum product prices, privatisation of public enterprises, and improvements in budgetary reporting and control were implemented. However, there have been policy slippages in implementing the government budget. The government has implemented corrective budgetary measures that are expected to bring fiscal performance back on track to a sustainable level of the deficit and reduce government borrowing from the banking system. This outcome should also make it feasible to maintain a prudent monetary policy. The government has also approved a comprehensive reform programme that targets judicial reforms, government decentralisation and civic education.

Main Industries Agriculture accounts for 37% of GDP, industry makes up 15% and services account for the remainder. The main agricultural products include peanuts, millet, sorghum, rice, corn, cassava (tapioca) and palm kernels. Cattle, sheep and goats are also raised. Farm productivity is low and suffers from climatic problems. As a result, imports of both food and live animals rose. Peanuts and peanut products are the dominate crops and account for more than 70% of the country's exports. Gambia's forestry and fishing resources are modest but are not fully exploited. There are no important mineral or other natural resources and the country's agricultural sector suffers from deforestation and desertification. Small-scale manufacturing activity is limited to the processing of agricultural products, tanning and related activities dependent on agricultural inputs. Reform measures focus on strengthening structural reforms to improve the environment for private sector activity and to enhance the delivery and monitoring of public services. There are known deposits of kaolin, but little extraction at present.

Energy All energy requirements except for fuel wood are imported. The country's electricity is generated by thermal power stations, although hydroelectric resources are to be developed if investment funds or international aid can be obtained.

	1999	2000	2001
Inflation (% change)	3.8	0.9	4.0
Exchange rate (per US$)	11.40	12.79	15.76
Interest rate (% per annum, commercial lending rate)	24.0	24.0	
GDP (% real growth)	6.4	5.6	5.8
GDP (Million units of national currency)	4,922.0	5,382.0	6,060.0
GDP (US$ million)	431.9	420.9	384.6
GDP per capita (US$)	338.9	322.5	279.9
Consumption (Million units of national currency)	2,255.8	2,571.4	3,031.5
Consumption (US$ million)	198.0	201.1	192.4
Consumption per capita (US$)	155.3	154.1	140.0
Population, mid-year ('000)	1,274.6	1,305.0	1,374.0
Birth rate (per '000)	39.3	38.7	38.0
Death rate (per '000)	18.0	17.7	17.4
No. of households ('000)	236.5	244.5	253.8
Total exports (US$ million)	7.1	18.2	18.2
Total imports (US$ million)	191.9	219.6	207.4
Tourism receipts (US$ million)	32.2	37.2	42.2
Tourist spending (US$ million)	15.9	16.0	14.4

Average household size 2001 (persons)	5.34				
Urban population 2001 (%)	33.2				
Age analysis (%) (2001)	*0-14*	40.7	*15-64*	56.3	*65+* 3.0
Population by sex (%) (2001)	*Male*	49.6	*Female*	50.4	
Life expectancy (years) (2001)	*Male*	45.3	*Female*	48.1	
Infant mortality (deaths per '000 live births) (2001)	117.4				
Adult literacy (%) (1997)	33.1				

TRADING PARTNERS

Major export destinations 2001 (% share)

UNITED KINGDOM	36.8
BELGIUM	9.9
CANADA	7.6
BRAZIL	5.6

Major import sources 2001 (% share)

CHINA	17.7
SENEGAL	9.4
UNITED KINGDOM	7.7
BELGIUM	7.3

Georgia

Area (km^2) 70,000

Currency Lari (= 100 tetri)

Location Georgia is one of the smallest but most influential states to have emerged from the former USSR. Located on the Black Sea, it borders on Turkey in the south, Armenia in the east and the Russian Federation in the north. Its mainly mountainous terrain includes the Greater Caucasus in the north and the Lesser Caucasus in the south, with a plain in between, divided by a further ridge. The climate is temperate to warm. The capital is Tblisi.

Head of State President Eduard Shevardnadze (1993)

Head of Government Otar Patsatsia (August 1993)

Ruling Party Sakartvelos Mokalaketa Kavshiri (SMK)

Political Structure Georgia's independent stance is underlined by the fact that it was the last of the former Soviet states (apart from the Baltic states) to join the Confederation of Independent States; its decision was taken only in October 1993. Georgia has an executive president who is elected for a 5-year term by the people. Parliament has 235 members, elected for 4-year terms; 150 seats by proportional representation and 85 in single-seat constituencies.

Last Elections Full elections to the Supreme Soviet were held in November 1999 when the SMK received 42% of the vote, taking 130 of the 235 seats. Shevardnadze received 79% of the votes in the presidential election in April 2000.

Political Risk The autonomous republic of Abkhazia declared its independence from Georgia, although Tblisi does not recognise the move. Nor has the republic received international recognition. Abkhazia has its own executive and its own parliament. An uneasy peace is maintained with the Abkhaz rebels but the fighting has left much bitterness. Two of Georgia's main land connections to Russia pass through the separatist region. A third connection through the breakaway Russian region of Chechnya has also been problematic. The government seeks to develop a network of international agreements with its neighbours in order stabilise the region.

International Disputes Georgia's relations with Azerbaijan are uneasy even though the two countries agreed in 1999 to cooperate on the development of a pipeline stretching from Baku through the mountains of Georgia to the Black Sea. Russia's war in Chechnya has led to fighting along the Georgian-Chechen border in northeast Georgia. The conflicts have left Georgia with Russian troops stationed in this region and in Abkhazia.

Economy In 2001, GDP increased by 4.5%. In 2002, growth will be 3.5% and 4% in 2003. Inflation was 4.7% in 2001 and the rate of increase in 2002 will be 4.6%. In 2003, prices are forecast to rise by 5%. Georgia has struggled to address deep-rooted economic problems. GDP growth has been lacklustre since the Russian crisis in 1998, reflecting energy supply problems, two droughts and uneven progress in structural reform. Poverty has remained widespread and the state's financial position has been too weak to offer an effective social safety net. Since 2001, there has been some progress in addressing some of the macroeconomic imbalances. The rapid accumulation of budgetary expenditure arrears has been halted and the general government deficit was reduced from almost 7% of GDP in 1999 to below 2% in the first half of 2001, reflecting a sharp reduction in expenditure commitments and a modest improvement in tax revenues. Some initial steps have been taken to address corruption, including through the establishment of an anti-corruption council and two presidential decrees. Other structural reforms have been slow, including in the energy sector, which remains burdened by old debts and low collection ratios. Georgia has also been unable to service its external debts in full.

Main Industries Current growth is based solidly on higher exports and transit revenues. The port of Poti is booming, railway loadings were up more than 50% in 2000 and the Supsa oil pipeline brings in US$8 million a year in transit fees. As the Caspian oil and gas industry moves into the production phase, the volume of equipment and other imports into the region will grow. Many small and medium-sized enterprises have been privatised but domestic entrepreneurs badly need encouragement. Corruption has undermined both private sector development and fiscal stability. The country has one of the lowest tax-to-GDP ratios in the region and has accumulated a large stock of budgetary expenditure arrears, including on wages and pensions. Structural reforms in the fiscal area and in the financial sector have been emphasised since 2000. Faced with a fragile banking system, the central bank's supervisory capacity has been strengthened. Georgia has a fertile agricultural sector that makes an important contribution to the economy. Farming output has also been rising in recent years. A wide range of crops are produced, including tea, tobacco, citrus fruits and flowers. Georgia also has deposits of manganese and coal, and a number of oil refineries. Industry is very capital-intensive and based mainly on mineral resources. Metallurgy, construction materials and machine building represent the core of the industrial sector, though many of these enterprises are badly in need of modernisation and additional capital investment.

Energy Georgia's has limited oil reserves (approximately 35 million barrels) and the country's small oil industry does not produce enough to meet domestic needs. As the country continues its recovery from civil strife in the mid-1990s, oil consumption is on the rise, but so is investment in the country's oil sector. Approximately US$125 million was invested in Georgia's oil production sector in the 1996-2001 period and authorities have estimated that, between 2001 and 2005, an additional US$453 million will be invested in oil and natural gas exploration and production in the country by nine joint ventures. In addition, Georgia has approximately 300 billion cubic feet in natural gas reserves.

	1999	2000	2001
Inflation (% change)	19.1	4.0	4.7
Exchange rate (per US$)	2.02	1.98	2.07
Interest rate (% per annum, lending rate)	33.4	32.8	27.3
GDP (% real growth)	3.0	1.9	4.5
GDP (Million units of national currency)	5,666.0	5,971.0	6,506.0
GDP (US$ million)	2,798.7	3,021.5	3,138.4
GDP per capita (US$)	515.5	554.9	575.4
Consumption (Million units of national currency)	4,210.2	4,662.2	4,894.5
Consumption (US$ million)	2,079.6	2,359.2	2,361.1
Consumption per capita (US$)	383.1	433.3	432.9
Population, mid-year ('000)	5,428.9	5,445.2	5,454.4
Birth rate (per '000)	11.2	10.9	10.6
Death rate (per '000)	9.6	9.7	9.8
No. of households ('000)	1,224.7	1,252.3	1,289.7
Total exports (US$ million)	238.0	330.0	320.0
Total imports (US$ million)	602.0	651.0	684.0
Tourism receipts (US$ million)	400.0	317.6	338.6
Tourist spending (US$ million)	270.0	192.0	175.8

Average household size 2001 (persons)		4.35				
Urban population 2001 (%)		61.2				
Age analysis (%) (2001)	*0-14*	22.1	*15-64*	64.1	*65+*	13.8
Population by sex (%) (2001)	*Male*	47.3	*Female*	52.7		
Life expectancy (years) (2001)	*Male*	69.3	*Female*	77.4		
Infant mortality (deaths per '000 live births) (2001)		18.2				
Adult literacy (%) (1998)		99.0				

TRADING PARTNERS

Major export destinations 2001 (% share)		Major import sources 2001 (% share)	
TURKEY	19.9	TURKEY	13.9
SPAIN	17.4	USA	10.3
RUSSIA	12.9	GERMANY	7.1
ITALY	12.0	RUSSIA	5.6

■ Germany

Area (km^2)   356,840

Currency   Euro (= 100 cents)

Location   Germany occupies a central position in Western Europe bordering on no less than six other Western European countries. The country's terrain ranges from the marshes of the Danish border in the north to the Bavarian Alps in the south. The five eastern Länder, together with the eastern sector of Berlin, formed the German Democratic Republic until unification in 1990. The capital is Berlin.

Head of State   Johannes Rau (1999)

Head of Government   Gerhard Schröder (1998)

Ruling Party   The Social Democrats (SPD), in coalition with the Green Party.

Political Structure   The Federal Republic consists of 16 states (Länder), of which 11 are in western Germany and five in the east. Germany has an extensively devolved political structure. At federal level the non-executive president appoints a Chancellor as leader, in accordance with a 669-member Bundestag (Parliament) elected for four years. The Bundesrat (Upper House) is indirectly elected. A presidential election body made up of deputies and regional representatives convenes every five years. There is a Federal Council with 69 members representing the governments of the states. Each state has its own Parliament and Premier.

Last Elections   Bundestag elections were held in September 1998, in which the ruling centre-right coalition was defeated by the SPD/Greens. The SPD took 49% of the vote and won 298 seats while the Greens received 7% of the vote and won 47 seats. Presidential elections were held in May 1999 and Johannes Rau was easily chosen.

Political Risk   The German government is in the midst of a tax-evasion scandal which is only overshadowed by even bigger corporate scandals in the US. The German problem involves phantom companies and fake invoices. The latest round of problems is just one more piece of evidence in an ever-widening series of disclosures. As a result, Germany's reputation has been seriously tarnished. Independent monitors now regard the country as one of the most corrupt in Europe. While total recorded crime has been falling since 1994, business crime in Germany has climbed by more than 50%.

International Disputes   Germany has no outstanding territorial issues with any of its immediate neighbours, and has abandoned its former claims for the restoration of the East German lands lost to Poland and the Soviet Union after World War II. With the reunification of the two countries, all outstanding disputes came to an end.

Economy   GDP grew by just 0.6% in 2001 and will rise by 0.9% in 2002. In 2003, growth is expected to be 2.7%. Inflation was 2.4% in 2001 but should be 1.5% in 2002. Prices are forecast to rise by 1.2% in 2003. The abrupt economic slowdown in 2001-2002 was largely caused by the same set of external factors that affected other European economies. The result was a sharp fall in private consumption, a large drop in exports and stagnating imports. Today, the seriously weakened economy is posing real challenges to policy makers who are searching for ways to boost growth. In fact, Germany faced some serious fiscal and structural problems at the end of the 1990s but their significance was partially masked by the economy's strong performance at the end of the decade. Traditionally, the German economy has often relied heavily on exports and external demand as the major impetus for growth. However, during 2001 and 2002, foreign markets for German products were weak. Low levels of external demand have prompted a fall in German investment in machinery and equipment and a correspondingly sharp drop in imports. The growth of private consumption will also remain anemic at least through 2003. The country's general government balances were improving through 2001 but a sharp fall in expected income tax receipts in 2002 will reverse this trend.

Main Industries   Agriculture makes up only a tiny portion of GDP but the government has ambitious plans for transforming the sector. Tighter controls and a greater emphasis on organic farming are advocated. Farms are small (although larger in the east), and crops include wheat, barley, potatoes, apples and grapes for winemaking. Germany's manufacturing sector accounts for a quarter of GDP and is dominated by many large companies producing motor vehicles, precision engineering, brewing, chemicals, pharmaceuticals and heavy metal products. The main impetus for growth in manufacturing, however, comes from the country's many small and medium-sized companies. A shortage of skilled workers and a rapidly ageing population has highlighted the need to recruit from outside the country. The pace of consolidation continues in the banking sector. The country's 12 Landesbanks are hoping to find mergers to create large banks with greater economies of scale. Meanwhile, manufacturing has undergone a string of multibillion dollar takeovers. Analysts interpret these developments as indications that even the largest German companies need economies of scale to compete in global markets. Major companies appear determined to press ahead with their plans for reorganisation despite the recent slowdown.

Energy   German relies heavily on energy imports. Coal accounts for almost half of domestic energy production and nuclear power for 30%. Oil, however, accounts for 41% of consumption. Germany consumes about 2.8 million barrels per day of oil, making the country the third largest oil importer in the world. The EU requires privatisation and competition in member states, and Germany has been a leader in this field. With the aid of hefty federal taxes on gasoline consumption, oil consumption fell in more recent years. For instance, Germans pay about four times more for motor gasoline than do Americans, despite having the most competitive retail gasoline market in Europe.

	1999	2000	2001
Inflation (% change)	0.9	1.1	1.1
Exchange rate (per US$)	0.94	1.09	1.12
Interest rate (% per annum, deposit rate)	8.8	9.6	10.0
GDP (% real growth)	1.8	3.0	0.6
GDP (Million units of national currency)	1,974,200.0	2,025,534.0	2,063,000.0
GDP (US$ million)	2,103,281.1	1,759,419.4	1,846,090.5
GDP per capita (US$)	25,648.7	21,472.2	22,545.2
Consumption (Million units of national currency)	1,083,326.5	1,139,856.5	1.0
Consumption (US$ million)	1,154,158.7	990,102.2	1,040,916.2
Consumption per capita (US$)	14,074.5	12,083.3	12,712.1
Population, mid-year ('000)	82,003.3	81,939.4	81,884.0
Birth rate (per '000)	8.9	8.7	8.5
Death rate (per '000)	10.7	10.8	10.8
No. of households ('000)	37,795.0	38,124.0	38,124.3
Total exports (US$ million)	542,869.0	549,578.0	570,522.0
Total imports (US$ million)	473,539.0	497,803.0	486,294.0
Tourism receipts (US$ million)	16,730.0	16,309.1	14,358.5
Tourist spending (US$ million)	48,495.0	48,107.1	47,493.7

Average household size 2001 (persons)	2.15					
Urban population 2001 (%)	87.7					
Age analysis (%) (2001)	*0-14*	15.6	*15-64*	67.8	*65+*	16.6
Population by sex (%) (2001)	*Male*	48.8	*Female*	51.2		
Life expectancy (years) (2001)	*Male*	74.8	*Female*	80.9		
Infant mortality (deaths per '000 live births) (2001)	5.0					
Adult literacy (%)						

TRADING PARTNERS

Major export destinations 2001 (% share)

FRANCE	11.1
USA	10.6
UNITED KINGDOM	8.4
ITALY	7.5

Major import sources 2001 (% share)

FRANCE	9.4
NETHERLANDS	8.4
USA	8.3
UNITED KINGDOM	7.0

▪ Ghana

Area (km²)   238,305

Currency   Cedi (C = 100 pesawas)

Location   Ghana, the former Gold Coast, lies on the Atlantic coast of West Africa, facing southward in the Gulf of Guinea. Côte d'Ivoire lies to the east, Burkina Faso to the north and Togo to the east. The climate is warm and tropical and occasionally humid. The capital is Accra.

Head of State   John Agyekum Kufuor (2000)

Head of Government   Alhaji Aliu Mahama (2000)

Ruling Party   New Patriotic Party (NPP)

Political Structure   Ghana has an executive president who governs through an essentially benevolent military administration. The current administration seized power in a military coup in 1981. However, political dissent has been allowed for some time under the freedom of association laws. The Fourth Republic was pronounced in January 1993, following the 1992 elections. The president is elected for a 4-year term by the people. Parliament has 200 members, elected for 4-year terms in single-seat constituencies.

Last Elections   Presidential elections took place in January 2001, when Kufuor took 57% of the vote, defeating John Mills who garnered 43%. Parliamentary elections were also held In January 2001. The NPP won 45% of the vote and 100 seats while the National Democratic Congress received 41% of the vote and 92 seats.

Political Risk   Ghana has been a showcase for economic reform and enjoys warm relations with international lenders. However, its economy is still extremely vulnerable to shocks. One reason is that it depends very heavily on just two exports - gold and cocoa. Another is that Ghana has often enough refused to accept the advice of the reformers and international institutions that advise it.

International Disputes   Ghana and Togo dispute the sovereignty over the northern reaches of the Volta River in the east of the country and the southern coastal area around Lomé. The two areas, part of the former German Togoland, were awarded to Ghana in 1919 but the issue remains unresolved despite UN mediation.

Economy   Real GDP grew by just 0.6% in 2001 and growth in 2002 will be little better at only 0.9%. In 2003, GDP is forecast to increase by 2.7%. Inflation was 32.9% in 2001 and fell to 15.9% in 2002. Prices should rise by 10.2% in 2003. The government has pledged to push ahead with reforms. These include additional measures to help improve Ghana's economic situation, cutting government expenditures, overhauling revenue collection, instituting anti-corruption measures and continuing the privatisation of state enterprises. Several reforms enacted or planned will affect Ghana's energy sector. Despite these efforts - both present and past - the bulk of all formal employment is still in government jobs. And as many as half of these jobs are superfluous. The fiscal position is also dire, with very high domestic borrowing made worse by mounting arrears. The external financing gap for 2001 stands at US$1 billion, interest rates are more than 50% and foreign investment is falling. While non-traditional exports have more than doubled since 1996, gold and cocoa continue to account for the bulk of export receipts.

Main Industries   Ghana's economy is heavily reliant on agriculture and mining. Agriculture, forestry and fishing constitute over 40% of the country's GDP. Exports of gold and cocoa are the primary sources of government revenue and foreign exchange. In 2000, gold accounted for 31% and cocoa for 24% of export revenues, respectively. Depressed prices for its main commodities, coupled with a rise in world petroleum prices, government budgetary problems and a depreciation of Ghana's currency (cedi), led to a severe recession in 2000. While Ghana's most recent economic problems are due mainly to external forces, the government is taking a proactive stance in reducing poverty and corruption, accelerating agricultural development and encouraging higher value-added processing of agricultural and mineral commodities. The government is also promoting the expansion of several non-traditional exports including cotton, cashews, tuna, handicrafts and textiles. In 2001, the government removed the subsidies on petroleum products put in place by the previous administration. The action resulted in a 64% increase in fuel prices. The prices of utility services (electricity and water) also have been raised.

Energy   Ghana's estimated 16.5 million barrels of recoverable oil reserves are located in five sedimentary basins. Exploration offshore began in the 1970s but only modest discoveries have been made and levels of commercial production are very low. The government has reorganised the Ghana National Petroleum Company, the parastatal primarily responsible for the importation of crude and petroleum products, and intends for its activities to focus solely on the exploration of Ghana's hydrocarbon resources in the future.

	1999	2000	2001
Inflation (% change)	12.4	25.2	32.9
Exchange rate (per US$)	2,669.30	5,455.06	7,170.76
Interest rate			
GDP (% real growth)	4.4	3.7	4.0
GDP (Billion units of national currency)	20,579.8	27,152.5	38,013.9
GDP (US$ million)	7,709.8	4,977.5	5,301.2
GDP per capita (US$)	389.3	246.3	251.2
Consumption (Billion units of national currency)	15,535.8	21,041.2	28,973.7
Consumption (US$ million)	5,820.2	3,857.2	4,040.5
Consumption per capita (US$)	293.9	190.8	191.5
Population, mid-year ('000)	19,802.1	20,212.0	21,104.0
Birth rate (per '000)	33.5	33.2	32.9
Death rate (per '000)	10.7	10.6	10.5
No. of households ('000)	3,384.5	3,467.8	3,637.5
Total exports (US$ million)	1,851.5	1,326.0	1,431.6
Total imports (US$ million)	3,479.6	2,972.7	2,949.5
Tourism receipts (US$ million)	304.0	201.9	178.0
Tourist spending (US$ million)	25.9	18.0	16.6

Average household size 2001 (persons)		5.83				
Urban population 2001 (%)		39.0				
Age analysis (%) (2001)	*0-14*	44.0	*15-64*	53.0	*65+*	3.1
Population by sex (%) (2001)	*Male*	49.6	*Female*	50.4		
Life expectancy (years) (2001)	*Male*	55.8	*Female*	58.3		
Infant mortality (deaths per '000 live births) (2001)		63.7				
Adult literacy (%) (1997)		66.4				

TRADING PARTNERS

Major export destinations 2001 (% share)		Major import sources 2001 (% share)	
NETHERLANDS	13.8	NIGERIA	21.5
USA	12.0	UNITED KINGDOM	7.6
UNITED KINGDOM	11.2	USA	7.3
GERMANY	7.2	COTE D'IVOIRE	6.0

Gibraltar

Area (km^2) 5

Currency Gibraltar pound (G£ = 100 pence)

Location Located on the southern tip of Spain, Gibraltar faces the coast of North Africa across a narrow strip of water which controls the western access to the Mediterranean Sea. Hence the immense strategic importance attached over the centuries to its ownership, both as a defensive position and as a centre for the trans-shipment of sea cargoes. The capital is Gibraltar.

Head of State HM Queen Elizabeth II

Head of Government Peter Caruana (1996)

Ruling Party Gibraltar Social Democratic Party (GSD)

Political Structure Gibraltar, a British dependent territory, is technically ruled from London, although in practice most decisions are taken not by the UK-appointed Governor but by the locally elected chief minister and his cabinet. They are answerable to a House of Assembly (Parliament) comprising 15 elected members, an independent Speaker, the Attorney-General and the Financial & Development Secretary.

Last Elections Elections in February 2000 gave 8 of the 15 elected seats in the House of Assembly to Peter Caruana and his GSD. The Socialist Party won the remainder of the seats.

Political Risk Gibraltar remains the subject of a territorial dispute between Britain and Spain. The two EU countries resumed discussions on the issue in July 2002. The EU is pressing both countries to end Gibraltar's status as a tax haven in any deal they eventually conclude. The UK promises that any agreement will be subject to the approval of Gibraltar's people. The most likely outcome is thought to be an agreement that the UK and Spain would share sovereignty, but Gibraltar would be given a great deal of autonomy.

International Disputes Formally, Spain claims the entire territory of Gibraltar. The country wants to establish warmer relations with Spain but has yet to succeed in a dialogue with Madrid.

Economy The territory's considerable dependence on the UK has been one of the major characteristics of the last few decades; yet its attractive and strategic location has enabled it to develop its role as a tourist resort. The British military presence has been sharply reduced and now contributes only about 8% to the local economy. Tourism contributes up to half of all economic activity in one form or another. Local authorities have also had some success in developing a centre for financial services. Many businessmen now believe that some accommodation with Spain is essential if the economy is to show further progress. This goal would receive a big boost if Gibraltar's status could one day be renegotiated to resemble that of Andorra.

Main Industries In recent years, Gibraltar has seen major structural change from a public to a private sector economy, but changes in government spending still have a major impact on the level of employment. The tiny economy relies very heavily on tourism, which contributes up to half of all economic activity in one form or another. Spanish visitors often arrive for shopping or for short breaks though others may be motivated more by reasons to do with tax evasion than duty-free shopping. The annual number of visitors now exceeds six million. In more recent years, Gibraltar has built up a respectable finance centre that now accounts for a fifth of the economy. Gibraltar's port and transhipment activities continue to make an important contribution to the economy. The colony's proximity to the North African coast is only one reason for the 3,000-4,000 merchant vessels that dock every year. Local authorities hope to develop an offshore tax haven and centre for financial services but related policy matters involving both the UK and Spain will first have to be resolved.

Energy Gibraltar depends completely on imports for all its fuel needs - primarily from Spain. Thermal power stations provide all domestic electricity.

	1999	2000	2001
Inflation (% change)	2.8	3.3	
Exchange rate (per US$)	0.62	0.66	0.69
Interest rate			
GDP (% real growth)	2.8	2.4	
GDP (Million units of national currency)	179.8	190.2	198.9
GDP (US$ million)	291.4	288.9	287.2
GDP per capita (US$)	11,656.8	11,554.8	11,488.7
Consumption (Million units of national currency)	114.1	116.7	121.0
Consumption (US$ million)	184.9	177.2	174.8
Consumption per capita (US$)	7,398.0	7,088.2	6,992.6
Population, mid-year ('000)	25.0	25.0	25.0
Birth rate (per '000)	13.1	13.0	12.8
Death rate (per '000)	8.7	8.7	8.7
No. of households ('000)	6.6	6.7	6.7
Total exports (US$ million)			
Total imports (US$ million)			
Tourism receipts (US$ million)	241.9	232.4	192.5
Tourist spending (US$ million)	25.0	25.0	25.0

Average household size 2001 (persons)	3.76				
Urban population 2001 (%)	100.0				
Age analysis (%) (2001)	*0-14*	18.0	*15-64*	68.0	*65+* 14.1
Population by sex (%) (2001)	*Male*	49.1	*Female*	50.9	
Life expectancy (years)					
Infant mortality (deaths per '000 live births) (2001)	6.3				
Adult literacy (%)					

TRADING PARTNERS

Major export destinations 2001 (% share) **Major import sources 2001 (% share)**

SPAIN	19.1	SPAIN	18.5
SWITZERLAND	17.0	RUSSIA	17.3
FRANCE	15.4	GERMANY	11.4
ITALY	14.7	UNITED KINGDOM	10.2

Greece

Area (km^2) 131,985

Currency Euro (= 100 cents)

Location Greece comprises the mainland and the archipelago which lies in the Mediterranean between the Adriatic and the Aegean and also includes the larger islands of Corfu and Crete, some distance to the southeast. The country is mountainous but there are lowlands in the east along the Bulgarian and Turkish borders. The close proximity with Turkey and the large numbers of Greek islands (some within 20km of the Turkish coast) have caused occasional conflict between the two states. The capital is Athens.

Head of State President Kostas Stephanopoulos (March 1995)

Head of Government Costas Simitis (1996)

Ruling Party Pan-Hellenic Socialist Movement (PASOK)

Political Structure Greece's modern political system was installed in 1975 following a national referendum. The country has a non-executive president elected by parliament for a 5-year term. The president's main function is to guarantee its political system and supervise its proper functioning. The president appoints his own cabinet, and is answerable to a 300-member Assembly (Parliament) which is also elected for a 5-year term.

Last Elections The incumbent prime minister, Costas Simitis, narrowly won re-election in April 2000. His party, PASOK, received 43% of the votes and 158 seats in the parliament. The New Democracy Party took 42.7% of the ballots and 125 seats.

Political Risk A wave of illegal migration has increased Greece's population by 8% since the early 1990s. Greeks are used to a homogeneous society and resent is growing rapidly. Awkward decisions on privatisation and fundamental changes that are necessary - if Greece is ever to catch up with other EU members - are looming and must be dealt with speedily if the country is to close the income gap.

International Disputes Greece's disputes with Turkey over the Aegean and Cyprus's accession to the EU remain unresolved but the two countries have definitely made progress. Since 1998, about 60 Greek companies have invested in Turkey. The two governments recently agreed on a joint bid to hold the European Football Championship in 2008 and their government officials now meet much more frequently than in the past. Greece and Turkey signed an agreement in 2002 valued at US$300 million to build a pipeline to take gas from Iran and ex-Soviet Central Asia through Turkey to Greece and thence on to markets in Western Europe. In 2002, the countries diplomats also met, for the first time, to discuss their long-running disputes in the Aegean. Greek-Cypriots and Turkish-Cypriots have made little progress in their own talks, but at least these continue. The UN, in an effort to take advantage of the improved relations between Greece and Turkey, is now trying to reopen international talks on the status of Cyprus.

Economy GDP increased by 4.1% in 2001 and will grow by 3.4% in 2002 and 2.9% in 2003. Inflation was 3.7% in 2001 and should be about 3.3% in 2002. In 2003, prices will rise by 2.7%. Greece is one of the very few European economies where analysts believe there is a danger of overheating in the short term. Thus, many officials are pushing for a tight fiscal policy despite the slow growth in exports markets and in other parts of Europe. Further tax cuts are under consideration but will be implemented only if accompanied by spending cuts. The primary surplus of 6% of GDP is already very high. However, a move towards a larger primary surplus would allow a more rapid reduction of public debt, which is still above 100% of GDP. It would also provide greater scope for fiscal easing during cyclical downturns. Over the longer term, severe spending pressures will build and the goal of maintaining a sizeable primary surplus will be a challenge. In order to contain spending pressures, reforms in pension, health and public management would need to be implemented quickly. The 1992 and 1998 pension reforms ensured the viability of the pension system until 2005, but they did not tackle the system's long-term financial sustainability. Adverse demographics, a low effective retirement age and benefits that are generous compared to contributions mean that a substantial hike in the tax burden will be needed to cover future pension expenditure.

Main Industries Greece's preparations for the 2004 Athens Olympics are finally picking up speed after a long period in which preparations lagged behind. Agriculture employs a quarter of the population and accounts for nearly a third of GDP, producing tree fruits, vegetables, olives, tobacco, sugar, rice and some wheat. Nursery products, frozen fish, tree nuts and wood products are among the fastest growing fields in this sector. The country's main agricultural exports are fresh and processed fruits and vegetables, especially canned peaches and tomato products, olive oil, durum wheat and tobacco. The manufacturing sector is led by the food industry, which is expanding fast to support new markets in neighbouring countries. Other important industries include footwear and building materials. In 2002, the government tried to introduce reforms to make the industrial sector more competitive within the euro zone but failed after opposition from trade unions. Businessmen also complain that the government is reneging on its promise to simplify and reduce taxes. Services represent the largest and fastest growing sector of the Greek economy. Tourism, shipping, trade, banking, transportation, communications and construction dominate this sector. Consolidation in the banking sector has been followed by a spate of acquisitions and mergers in transport, construction and manufacturing as companies prepare for tougher competition in the euro zone.

Energy Greece has limited oil reserves of 10 million barrels. The country produces 8,750 barrels per day (bbl/d) and is highly reliant on imports to meet its consumption needs which amount to about 400,000 bbl/d. Oil is Greece's most important fuel source, accounting for 63% of total energy consumption, a percentage that has remained fairly stable since the mid-1980s. Greece's oil industry is dominated by state-owned Hellenic Petroleum (HP), which was formed in 1998. Domestic oil production comes from the Prinos area in the Aegean Sea, off the coast of Kavala. In February 2001, a new oilfield was found offshore the Aegean island of Thasos (also near Kavala).

	1999	2000	2001
Inflation (% change)	0.9	1.1	1.1
Exchange rate (per US$)	0.94	1.09	1.12
Interest rate (% per annum, commercial lending rate)	15.0	12.3	8.6
GDP (% real growth)	3.4	4.3	4.1
GDP (Million units of national currency)	112,661.0	121,516.0	130,546.0
GDP (US$ million)	125,599.9	113,318.8	116,818.1
GDP per capita (US$)	11,932.7	10,756.2	11,076.7
Consumption (Million units of national currency)	82,920.7	87,876.2	1.0
Consumption (US$ million)	92,444.0	81,948.3	84,259.9
Consumption per capita (US$)	8,782.7	7,778.5	7,989.5
Population, mid-year ('000)	10,525.7	10,535.2	10,546.3
Birth rate (per '000)	9.3	9.2	9.0
Death rate (per '000)	10.0	10.1	10.3
No. of households ('000)	3,437.1	3,472.3	3,503.9
Total exports (US$ million)	9,814.9	10,209.4	8,692.7
Total imports (US$ million)	25,432.6	27,759.8	28,547.0
Tourism receipts (US$ million)	8,783.0	8,474.4	7,510.7
Tourist spending (US$ million)	3,989.0	4,292.6	3,436.8

Average household size 2001 (persons)	3.03				
Urban population 2001 (%)	60.3				
Age analysis (%) (2001)	*0-14*	14.9	*15-64*	67.4	*65+* 17.7
Population by sex (%) (2001)	*Male*	49.3	*Female*	50.7	
Life expectancy (years) (2001)	*Male*	75.8	*Female*	81.1	
Infant mortality (deaths per '000 live births) (2001)	6.2				
Adult literacy (%) (1997)	96.6				

TRADING PARTNERS
Major export destinations 2001 (% share)   **Major import sources 2001 (% share)**

GERMANY	12.5	ITALY	13.1
ITALY	9.5	GERMANY	12.5
UNITED KINGDOM	8.3	FRANCE	6.6
USA	5.1	NETHERLANDS	5.9

■ Grenada

Area (km²)   345

Currency   East Caribbean dollar (EC$ = 100 cents)

Location   The island of Grenada lies at the southernmost tip of the archipelago known as the Windward Islands, in the Eastern Caribbean, about 140km north of Trinidad and Tobago and 170km northwest of Barbados. The territory includes some of the Grenadines islets. The climate is equable, although increasingly subject to hurricanes. The capital is St George's.

Head of State   HM Queen Elizabeth II

Head of Government   Keith Mitchell (May 1995)

Ruling Party   New National Party. (NNP)

Political Structure   As an independent member of the Commonwealth, Grenada is essentially self-governing, with the British Crown being represented by a governor-general. The prime minister is answerable to a 15-member Parliament elected by popular mandate for a term of five years. There is also a 13-member Senate, appointed by the governor-general.

Last Elections   New elections were required in January 1999 following the defection of several key members of the NNP. Despite charges of corruption, Mitchell easily won re-election and the NNP took all 15 seats in the Assembly. This is the first time any party has held all seats in the Assembly since the restoration of parliamentary government in 1984.

Political Risk   Periodic charges of corruption have been levelled against leading politicians. Grenada is actively seeking to build stronger ties with other parts of the Caribbean community and generally favours some form of integration with St Vincent, St Lucia and Dominica. In 1997, the island signed an agreement with Cuba involving cooperation in areas such as health, sports, education and construction. It was Grenada's ties with Cuba in the 1980s that originally prompted the US invasion.

International Disputes   Grenada is one of several Caribbean states where the banking system is regarded as providing inadequate safeguards against money laundering.

Economy   GDP increased by 3.5% in 2001 while inflation was 2.5%. There is considerable concern about the financial strength of the economy following policy shifts which included a net tax cut, generous wage increases for central government employees and adoption of a relatively ambitious investment programme. This fiscal stance has helped to boost economic activity but it has also led to deterioration in the fiscal and external accounts. The rapid growth of the island's financial sector has been stymied by the international community which objects to the lax regulations. Unemployment remains high - over 20% - and more efforts are needed to improve infrastructure and export performance. The tourist industry faces stiff competition over the next few years and foreign investment is needed if the sector is to thrive.

Main Industries   Agriculture and tourism are the dominant sectors of the economy. Farming accounts for over half of all merchandise exports, and a large portion of the population is employed, either directly or indirectly, in that sector. Agricultural revenues have been hurt by pests, hurricanes and drought which have periodically destroyed much of the cocoa harvest. Bananas, another major foreign exchange earner, also suffer due to falling prices, low production and poor quality. Tourism, the leading foreign exchange earner, has done well in most years but suffered following 11 September 2001. Officials are trying to develop the island's financial sector. In 2001, the government shut down eight banks as part of its effort to eliminate institutions that could be conduits for laundered money.

Energy   Grenada has no domestic energy sources, importing most its supplies from other Caribbean countries. Reluctantly, the government agreed to ratify a privatisation agreement initiated by the previous administration after international arbitration ruled against it.

	1999	2000	2001
Inflation (% change)	0.5	2.2	2.5
Exchange rate (per US$)	2.70	2.70	2.70
Interest rate (% per annum, lending rate)	10.5	10.5	10.5
GDP (% real growth)	7.5	6.4	3.5
GDP (Million units of national currency)	1,020.0	1,108.0	1,172.0
GDP (US$ million)	377.8	410.4	434.1
GDP per capita (US$)	4,062.1	4,365.6	4,617.8
Consumption (Million units of national currency)	544.0	758.6	779.7
Consumption (US$ million)	201.5	281.0	288.8
Consumption per capita (US$)	2,166.7	2,989.0	3,072.0
Population, mid-year ('000)	93.0	94.0	94.0
Birth rate (per '000)	28.1	27.8	27.4
Death rate (per '000)	5.6	5.6	5.5
No. of households ('000)	17.8	17.9	17.7
Total exports (US$ million)	26.1	28.0	32.0
Total imports (US$ million)	210.4	206.0	220.7
Tourism receipts (US$ million)	63.0	74.9	60.9
Tourist spending (US$ million)	5.3	5.9	6.1

Average household size 2001 (persons)	5.27					
Urban population 2001 (%)	38.4					
Age analysis (%) (2001)	*0-14*	30.2	*15-64*	63.0	*65+*	6.7
Population by sex (%) (2001)	*Male*	49.4	*Female*	50.6		
Life expectancy (years)						
Infant mortality (deaths per '000 live births) (2001)	11.1					
Adult literacy (%) (1997)	96.0					

TRADING PARTNERS

Major export destinations 2001 (% share) | **Major import sources 2001 (% share)**

USA	32.9	USA	34.1
FRANCE	20.5	TRINIDAD AND TOBAGO	26.5
GERMANY	11.0	UNITED KINGDOM	5.7
ST LUCIA	4.1	BARBADOS	4.2

Guadeloupe

Area (km^2)   1,780

Currency   Euro (= 100 cents)

Location   The French overseas department of Guadeloupe is the northernmost territory of the Windward Islands group of the Caribbean. It comprises the two islands of Grande-Terre and Basse-Terre, together with Marie-Galante, La Dísirade and Iles des Saintes, and the St Martin and St Barthélemy group, which lie within the Leeward group. The climate is tropical/Caribbean, with some tendency toward hurricanes in the autumn months. The capital is Basse-Terre.

Head of State   Jacques Chirac (France)

Head of Government   Marcellin Lubeth (President of the General Council, 1998)

Ruling Party   Federation Guadeloupíenne du Rassemblement pour la République (RPG)

Political Structure   As a part of the French Antilles, Guadeloupe is an external department of France and is governed to a considerable degree from Paris. The country sends deputies to the French Assemblée Nationale, and is represented at the EU. Since being accorded regional status in 1974, however, Guadeloupe elects its own 41-member Regional Council for a term of six years, with responsibility for economic and social planning. Other executive power rests in a 42-member General Council.

Last Elections   The last full elections were to the French Assemblée Nationale in 2002, when the Rassemblement pour la République returned one delegate, dissents gained two seats and the Progressive Democratic Party received one. Elections to the General and Regional Council were held in March 1998. The RPG and the Progressive Democratic Party both won eight seats in the General Council. The RPG won control of the Regional Council with 49% of the vote.

Political Risk   In St. Martin, much of the population resents the fact that the island is part of the overseas department of Guadeloupe but there is no organised opposition to this fact.

International Disputes   There are no international disputes.

Economy   Guadeloupe's agricultural sector, although the largest part of the economy, is far from self-sufficient. A large proportion of the country's food is imported from France. The island's perennial trade deficit is only partially covered by its tourism revenues, and for the most part the country is forced to rely on remittances from France. Unemployment exceeds 30% and is especially high among the young.

Main Industries   The economy consists mainly of agriculture, tourism, light industry, and services. It is heavily dependent on France for large subsidies and imports. Tourism is the most important activity, with most visitors coming from the US. In addition, an increasingly large number of cruise ships visit the islands. The traditionally important sugarcane crop is slowly being replaced by other crops, such as bananas (which now account for more than half of all export earnings), eggplant and flowers. Other vegetables and root crops are cultivated for local consumption, although Guadeloupe is still dependent on imported food, which comes mainly from France. The industrial sector employs 22% of the workforce and contributes 10% of GDP. The most important industries are sugar processing and rum production. Some processing of food and timber production is also carried out. There is an industrial free port at Jarry, and a fair-sized ship repair business. Most manufactured goods and fuel are imported.

Energy   The country's fuel needs are met exclusively with imports, the only viable local resource being fuel wood and brushwood. Thermal stations generate all electricity.

	1999	2000	2001
Inflation (% change)	0.9	1.1	1.1
Exchange rate (per US$)	0.94	1.09	1.12
Interest rate			
GDP (% real growth)	2.7	2.9	
GDP (Million units of national currency)	5,038.1	5,494.2	5,873.4
GDP (US$ million)	5,371.9	4,772.4	5,255.8
GDP per capita (US$)	11,927.1	10,465.8	11,064.8
Consumption (Million units of national currency)	3,197.4	3,370.4	1.0
Consumption (US$ million)	3,409.3	2,927.6	3,281.6
Consumption per capita (US$)	7,569.5	6,420.1	6,908.7
Population, mid-year ('000)	450.4	456.0	475.0
Birth rate (per '000)	16.8	16.6	16.3
Death rate (per '000)	6.0	6.1	6.1
No. of households ('000)	93.9	94.3	97.0
Total exports (US$ million)			
Total imports (US$ million)			
Tourism receipts (US$ million)	375.0	399.3	338.9
Tourist spending (US$ million)	450.4	456.0	475.0

Average household size 2001 (persons)	4.83					
Urban population 2001 (%)	99.7					
Age analysis (%) (2001)	*0-14*	30.2	*15-64*	63.0	*65+*	6.7
Population by sex (%) (2001)	*Male*	49.6	*Female*	50.4		
Life expectancy (years) (2001)	*Male*	74.5	*Female*	81.5		
Infant mortality (deaths per '000 live births) (2001)	7.2					
Adult literacy (%)						

Guam

Area (km^2)   450

Currency   US dollar (US$ = 100 cents)

Location   Guam is the largest island in the Mariana group, lying 5,300km west of Honolulu and 2,170km south of Japan. The climate is characterised by hot wet weather from June to November, but is cooler and drier in the winter months. The capital is Agaña.

Head of State   President George W. Bush (US)

Head of Government   Carl T.C. Gutierrez (Governor)

Ruling Party   Democratic Party.

Political Structure   Guam's status as a US unincorporated territory is currently under review in the light of the general US withdrawal from the Pacific region. A referendum in 1982 produced a majority in favour of commonwealth status, but since then opinion has shifted back toward the status quo. The Guam authorities are particularly anxious to acquire a right of veto over the extraterritorial application of US law. The Governor is elected every four years and the 21-member Legislature for two years. Guam also elects one non-voting delegate to the US Congress in Washington.

Last Elections   Elections to the Guam Legislature took place in October 2001. The Republicans won eight seats and the Democrats won seven. In 1998, Carl T.C. Gutierrez was elected governor, defeating the incumbent, Joseph Ada.

Political Risk   The potential for secessionist dissent exists only among the indigenous Chamorros, who make up 45% of the population, but the issue could assume more importance if the US reduces its military presence. A serious deterioration in the local economy would exacerbate the situation. The island is occasionally subject to severe earthquakes, with the last major one occurring in 1993.

International Disputes   There are no international disputes.

Economy   Guam's economy grew slowly in recent years and the rate of growth for GDP fell further to around 1.4% in 2001. Prospects for a recovery in the near future are not good and it is possible that GDP could decline in 2002. The local economy is heavily dependent on the US military presence, which provides a big boost to the island's income and once provided most of the employment. However, this source of growth is declining. Tourism is Guam's best hope for the future and already accounts for a substantial portion of GDP. The industry grew from 6,600 visitors in 1967 to more 1.5 million visitors today. The government hopes to encourage foreign investment with a range of incentives aimed at widening the economic base. More than 300 US foreign sales corporations have established offices in Guam and the interest of foreign and domestic companies continues to grow. Although Guam receives no foreign aid, it does receive large transfer payments from the general revenues of the US Federal Treasury into which Guamanians pay no income or excise taxes. Under the provisions of a special law of Congress, the Guamanian Treasury, rather than the US Treasury, receives federal income taxes paid by military and civilian Federal employees stationed in Guam.

Main Industries   Agriculture is only of modest significance, with most farms being run on a part-time basis. The country is a producer of cassava, bananas, coconuts, sugar cane, fruit, vegetables, sweet potatoes and breadfruit. Fishing is important, and animals are grown for local consumption. Guam's most prominent and profitable activities have traditionally centred on servicing the US troop presence, which once provided most of the employment on the island. These activities are gradually declining in importance as the number of troops is scaled back. Otherwise, tourism is the main activity, with substantial revenues especially from the Japanese who comprise 70% of all visitors. More than one million tourists visit Guam in a typical year but the number dropped sharply in 2002. The island has over 8,000 hotel rooms, and the number is expected to reach 12,000 by 2005. Industry is modest in scope, employing less than 4% of the workforce although it offers a wide range of activities: cement production, food processing, textiles and clothing, oil processing and even watch manufacture.

Energy   Guam imports all of its fuel needs, although it has an ample supply of petroleum products on tap as a result of its own oil processing activities.

	1999	2000	2001
Inflation (% change)	2.0	2.4	2.0
Exchange rate (per US$)	1.00	1.00	1.00
Interest rate			
GDP (% real growth)	3.5	4.1	1.4
GDP (Million units of national currency)	1,263.4	1,346.7	1,392.9
GDP (US$ million)	1,263.4	1,346.7	1,392.9
GDP per capita (US$)	7,836.4	8,189.9	8,305.0
Consumption (Million units of national currency)	837.9	914.6	931.2
Consumption (US$ million)	837.9	914.6	931.2
Consumption per capita (US$)	5,197.1	5,561.9	5,552.4
Population, mid-year ('000)	161.2	164.4	167.7
Birth rate (per '000)	27.8	27.5	27.2
Death rate (per '000)	4.8	4.8	4.9
No. of households ('000)	26.6	26.9	28.0
Total exports (US$ million)			
Total imports (US$ million)			
Tourism receipts (US$ million)	1,908.0		
Tourist spending (US$ million)			

Average household size 2001 (persons)	6.12				
Urban population 2001 (%)	39.5				
Age analysis (%) (2001)	*0-14*	32.9	*15-64*	61.6	*65+* 5.5
Population by sex (%) (2001)	*Male*	52.6	*Female*	47.4	
Life expectancy (years) (2001)	*Male*	72.1	*Female*	76.7	
Infant mortality (deaths per '000 live births) (2001)	10.4				
Adult literacy (%)					

TRADING PARTNERS

Major export destinations 2001 (% share)		Major import sources 2001 (% share)	
JAPAN	89.1	SOUTH KOREA	34.3
THAILAND	2.6	SINGAPORE	34.3
SINGAPORE	1.9	JAPAN	22.5
PHILIPPINES	1.7	PHILIPPINES	3.0

Guatemala

Area (km^2)　108,890

Currency　Quetzal (Q$ = 100 centavos)

Location　Guatemala lies directly across the Central American isthmus to the south of Mexico. It has a short coastline on the Caribbean Sea and a much longer one on the Pacific Ocean. The southern part of the country is mountainous, while the northern areas, bounded by Mexico and Belize, are relatively flat. The climate is generally humid and much of the country is forested. Earthquakes are frequent, as a result of the volcanic activity in the country. The capital is Guatemala City.

Head of State　President Alfonso Antonio Portillo Cabrera (2000)

Head of Government　Alfonso Antonio Portillo Cabrera

Ruling Party　Republic Guatemalan Front (FRG)

Political Structure　Guatemala is a republic with an executive president who is elected by popular mandate for a 4-year term. The congress has 80 members elected for 4-year terms; 64 members represent departmental constituencies and 16 are determined by proportional representation.

Last Elections　In general elections held in December 1999, Cabrera defeated Oscar Berger Perdomo, receiving 68% of the vote. Elections to Congress were last held in November 1999. The FRG captured 63 seats while the National Progress Party received 37. In May 1999, voters rejected amendments to the constitution that would recognise Guatemala's multi-ethnic society. The amendments had the support of all the main political parties in Congress.

Political Risk　Guatemala's bloody 36-year civil war ended in December 1996 and there were hopes that the rule of law might return. Now, those who defend human rights are once again becoming targets of violence in what looks like a campaign by former army officers to avoid being brought to book for past abuses.. Tax evasion is another problem, running as high as 50% with richest 10% paying just 2% of their income to the state.

International Disputes　Guatemala's relations with Mexico are occasionally strained owing to its assumed contacts with the Chaiapas rebels in the southern part of that country. Relations with Belize worsened in 2000 when a member of the administration demanded the return of half the land area of the country. The claim dates back to the Spanish era when Guatemala ruled Belize.

Economy　GDP rose by 1.8% in 2001. In 2002, growth should be 2.3% and rise to 3.5% in 2003. Prices rose by 8.7% in 2001 and the rate of price increase in 2002 will be 5%. In 2003, inflation should be about 3.9%. Guatemala made progress towards restoration of domestic and external equilibria, which had been threatened by the expansionary fiscal policy applied and by the worsening terms of trade. Monetary policy seeks to place the country on a low-inflation path; to that end, an attempt is being made to control liquidity through intense participation by the Bank of Guatemala in open-market operations. Persistent problems of non-performing loans continue to restrict credit to the private sector. In 2000, after four years of negotiations, the three "northern triangle" Central American countries — El Salvador, Guatemala, and Honduras - signed a free-trade agreement with Mexico. The agreement was to have taken effect in 2001, but has been delayed by political opposition and other problems. If and when the deal actually takes effect, it will facilitate trade in raw materials and process exportable products under standardised rules of origin. The agreement also is to establish an 11-year schedule for complete elimination of tariffs on manufactured goods. Besides this agreement, Guatemala is reportedly negotiating a trade agreement with the Andean Community.

Main Industries　Agriculture accounts for around a quarter of GDP and provides jobs for almost 60% of all workers. Industry makes up another 20% of GDP and services account for the remainder. Coffee, sugar cane, bananas and cotton are the main cash crops. The country's main exports are coffee, sugar, bananas, cardamom and beef but coffee is by far the most important. However, coffee prices on world markets fell significantly, owing mainly to the emergence of new producers such as Vietnam. In the future, Guatemala's coffee production is expected to be halved, leaving only the high-quality coffee that can fetch a premium on the international market. Sugar exports also fell in both value and volume. On the other hand, non-traditional exports have grown briskly since 1999. The industrial sector is dominated by small-scale manufacturing geared mainly to serve the domestic economy.

Energy　Guatemala is the only oil-producing country in Central America. Current production stands at about 30,000 barrels per day (bbl/d), and is expected to rise in the future. There is interest in exploring for oil in Guatemala's northern Peten jungle region, where about 23,000 barrels per day (bbl/d) of heavy oil already is being produced (at the Xan field). Recent estimates of oil reserves in the adjacent Mexican state of Chiapas indicate larger reserves than previously thought, and these deposits seem to extend into Guatemala. Since the end of the country's civil war in 1996, the government has been opening areas for bidding and granting concessions for oil exploration. Just over half of all households have access to electricity and demand is growing rapidly. The availability of electricity is virtually non-existent in many rural areas. Even those who do have electricity experience inadequate supplies and brownouts.

	1999	2000	2001
Inflation (% change)	4.9	5.1	8.7
Exchange rate (per US$)	7.39	7.76	7.86
Interest rate (% per annum, commercial lending rate)	19.5	20.9	19.0
GDP (% real growth)	3.8	3.6	1.8
GDP (Million units of national currency)	135,287.0	148,447.0	162,241.0
GDP (US$ million)	18,317.6	19,122.0	20,645.1
GDP per capita (US$)	1,695.8	1,724.2	1,813.3
Consumption (Million units of national currency)	114,554.0	124,568.0	136,867.0
Consumption (US$ million)	15,510.4	16,046.0	17,416.2
Consumption per capita (US$)	1,435.9	1,446.8	1,529.7
Population, mid-year ('000)	10,801.5	11,090.5	11,385.3
Birth rate (per '000)	35.8	35.3	34.8
Death rate (per '000)	7.2	7.1	6.9
No. of households ('000)	2,322.1	2,356.9	2,377.6
Total exports (US$ million)	2,397.5	2,695.6	2,466.0
Total imports (US$ million)	4,381.7	4,790.9	5,606.8
Tourism receipts (US$ million)	570.0	654.5	556.9
Tourist spending (US$ million)	183.0	187.2	225.0

Average household size 2001 (persons)	4.77				
Urban population 2001 (%)	40.0				
Age analysis (%) (2001)	*0-14*	43.5	*15-64*	53.0	*65+* 3.6
Population by sex (%) (2001)	*Male*	50.4	*Female*	49.6	
Life expectancy (years) (2001)	*Male*	62.6	*Female*	68.5	
Infant mortality (deaths per '000 live births) (2001)	42.2				
Adult literacy (%) (1997)	66.6				

TRADING PARTNERS

Major export destinations 2001 (% share)   **Major import sources 2001 (% share)**

Major export destinations 2001 (% share)		Major import sources 2001 (% share)	
USA	57.2	USA	33.1
EL SALVADOR	9.1	MEXICO	9.4
COSTA RICA	4.0	SOUTH KOREA	8.3
NICARAGUA	3.2	EL SALVADOR	5.7

■ Guinea

Area (km^2)　245,855

Currency　Franc guinéen (= 100 centimes)

Location　Guinea lies on the Atlantic coast of West Africa with Senegal and Guinea-Bissau to the north, Mali and Côte d'Ivoire to the east, and Liberia and Sierra Leone to the south. The climate is dry, despite the presence of the sources of major African rivers such as the Senegal, the Niger and the Gambia. The capital is Conakry.

Head of State　President Maj.-Gen. Lansana Conté (1984)

Head of Government　Laimine Sidime (1999)

Ruling Party　Party for Unity and Progress (PUP)

Political Structure　Guinea's 1982 Constitution was suspended after the military takeover of 1984 that brought the present administration to power. A new draft was approved by a national referendum in December 1990. The current version of the constitution provides for the president to be elected for a 5-year term by the people. The National Assembly has 114 members, elected for 4-year terms, 38 members in single-seat constituencies and 76 members by proportional representation.

Last Elections　Presidential elections were last held in December 1998 when Conté retained his office with 54% of the vote. Elections to the National Assembly took place in June 1995, with the PUP gaining 71 seats.

Political Risk　Poverty at home and instability in the region creates substantial risks for Guinea.

International Disputes　Liberia is supporting Guinean dissidents who have crossed the border on occasions to launch raids in Guinea.

Economy　One of the poorest countries in the world, Guinea has struggled to implement a reform programme. GDP grew by 2.9% in 2001 and inflation was 6.8%. The economy has been adversely affected by conflict in neighbouring countries that has had severe humanitarian costs. Officials are emphasising the promotion of private sector activity by strengthening economic infrastructure, improving governance and enhancing the legal and regulatory frameworks. Improving revenue mobilisation is the main fiscal policy challenge over the medium term, and the authorities intend to intensify their efforts to reduce excessive exemptions and to complete administrative reforms, especially at customs. Monetary policy aims to keep inflation in check and to improve bank liquidity management. The dangerous security situation in neighbouring countries has required increasing financial commitments to peacekeeping forces and continued expenditure to defend the country's borders and host a refugee community between 5-10% of its population. There has also been some improvement in mining sector efficiency, thanks to greater private sector involvement. Mining, however, is the only part of the economy that is attracting foreign investment.

Main Industries　Over 80% of Guinea's population depend on subsistence farming for their livelihood. Nevertheless, agriculture accounts for less than a quarter of GDP. Only 3% of the land is cultivated with the main products being bananas, groundnuts, oil palm, cotton and pineapples. Coffee is grown for export. Cassava, rice and maize are the staples for the domestic market. Industry accounts for almost a third of GDP but production is geared to serve the domestic market. The only large-scale manufacturing installation is a bauxite smelting plant though many small-scale plants are engaged in light manufacturing and food processing. Mining generates a quarter of GDP and accounts for practically all the country's export revenues. Authorities have begun to reform the civil service and the social security system. The fight against corruption, coupled with judicial reform, will strengthen private sector confidence Guinea possesses over 25% of the world's bauxite reserves and is the world's second largest bauxite producer. It also has significant diamond stocks and some gold. Foreign investment is minimal, however, except in the bauxite industry.

Energy　Although the country is actively searching for offshore petroleum resources, its only indigenous energy source is its considerable hydroelectric potential.

	1999	2000	2001
Inflation (% change)	4.6	6.8	6.8
Exchange rate (per US$)	1,387.40	1,746.87	1,950.56
Interest rate (% per annum, deposit rate)	19.9	19.4	
GDP (% real growth)	3.6	2.0	2.9
GDP (Billion units of national currency)	4,759.9	5,261.1	5,620.6
GDP (US$ million)	3,430.8	3,011.7	2,881.6
GDP per capita (US$)	464.5	405.3	380.1
Consumption (Billion units of national currency)	2,759.1	3,179.2	3,356.0
Consumption (US$ million)	1,988.7	1,819.9	1,720.5
Consumption per capita (US$)	269.2	244.9	227.0
Population, mid-year ('000)	7,386.3	7,430.0	7,581.0
Birth rate (per '000)	44.9	44.5	44.0
Death rate (per '000)	17.7	17.4	17.1
No. of households ('000)	1,372.2	1,367.2	1,376.2
Total exports (US$ million)	963.3	868.0	876.8
Total imports (US$ million)	772.6	707.0	701.0
Tourism receipts (US$ million)	7.0	4.2	3.3
Tourist spending (US$ million)	31.0	27.9	30.8

Average household size 2001 (persons)	5.43					
Urban population 2001 (%)	33.5					
Age analysis (%) (2001)	0-14	44.7	15-64	52.6	65+	2.7
Population by sex (%) (2001)	Male	50.1	Female	49.9		
Life expectancy (years) (2001)	Male	47.5	Female	48.5		
Infant mortality (deaths per '000 live births) (2001)	116.4					
Adult literacy (%) (1997)	37.9					

TRADING PARTNERS

Major export destinations 2001 (% share)		Major import sources 2001 (% share)	
BELGIUM	14.6	FRANCE	15.8
USA	11.7	USA	11.4
SPAIN	11.3	COTE D'IVOIRE	8.1
IRELAND	10.6	BELGIUM	8.0

Guinea-Bissau

Area (km^2)   36,125

Currency   Guinea peso (= 100 centavos)

Location   Guinea-Bissau, the former Portuguese Guinea, is a small triangle of land lying on the Atlantic coast of West Africa, between Senegal to the north and Guinea to the south and east. Until the 19th century, it shared a political union with Cape Verde. Attempts to revive that union were hurriedly dropped in the mid-1980s after a coup attempt. The country is low-lying, yet suffers from recurrent drought. The capital is Bissau.

Head of State   Kumba Ialá (2000)

Head of Government   Caetano N'Tchama (2000)

Ruling Party   The government is formed by the Party for Social Renewal, progressive (PRS) and the Resistance of Guinea-Bissau-Bafatá Movement (RGB).

Political Structure   The democratic system was restored in 1994. The president is elected for a 5-year term by the people. The People's National Assembly has 100 members, elected for 4-year terms in multi-member constituencies.

Last Elections   In presidential elections held in January 2000, Ialá received 72% of the vote, defeating Malam Bacai Sanhá who received 28% of the vote. Elections to the National Assembly were held in November 1999. The PRS won 38 seats while the RGB took 28 seats. The African Independence Party of Guinea and Cape Verde (PAIGC) took 24 seats.

Political Risk   The president has become increasingly erratic in 2001/2002. He has threatened to sack 60% of the civil service and to suspend parliament for 10 years. Senior judges are in detention, newspapers have been closed and radio stations shut down. The army remains determined to preserve its autonomy and new disputes can erupt at any time.

International Disputes   Western donors say they will return to the country only if political and military stability is regained.

Economy   Guinea-Bissau is one of the poorest countries in the world. Its situation was only worsened by the military conflict that took place in Guinea-Bissau from June 1998 to early 1999. War broke out again in 2000. The conflicts have caused severe damage to the infrastructure and disrupted economic activity. Today, the country's fortunes fluctuate mainly with the price of groundnuts. The economy grew by 4% in 2001 and prices rose by 5%. The government is desperate to woo back investors and drew up a list of industries to privatise. Few investors, however, are interested. Programmes for military demobilisation and civil service reform are key features of the fiscal policy framework.

Main Industries   Agriculture and fishing employ over 80% of the population and account for the bulk of the country's meagre income. Only about 8% of the land area is under cultivation, and subsistence farming predominates — with intermittent and frequent serious droughts. Cashews and groundnuts are grown for export, together with tobacco, sugar and palm kernels. Agricultural production has been significantly reduced as a result of the war. Cashew nut output, the main export crop, fell sharply and commercial imports were stopped for several months. The domestic population relies on cassava, millet, sorghum and maize. The industrial sector contributes only about a fifth of GDP. The country's main industrial belt is a wasteland of derelict factories and broken machinery. Apart from a small car assembly plant, most activity centres on the processing of agricultural produce and the production of simple items such as beer and soft drinks. Structural reform is a major component of the authorities' programme, especially in the important banking and energy sectors and in the area of privatisation. Guinea-Bissau has bauxite resources, but it is uneconomic at present to exploit them.

Energy   Guinea-Bissau depends entirely on imported oil at present, but there are moves to develop the country's hydroelectric potential.

	1999	2000	2001
Inflation (% change)	-2.1	8.6	5.0
Exchange rate (per US$)	615.70	711.98	733.04
Interest rate			
GDP (% real growth)	7.8	7.5	4.0
GDP (Million units of national currency)	134,432.0	159,877.0	179,613.0
GDP (US$ million)	218.3	224.6	245.0
GDP per capita (US$)	183.1	185.1	194.0
Consumption (Million units of national currency)	107,565.3	130,995.3	142,391.9
Consumption (US$ million)	174.7	184.0	194.2
Consumption per capita (US$)	146.5	151.7	153.8
Population, mid-year ('000)	1,192.7	1,213.0	1,263.0
Birth rate (per '000)	44.7	44.7	44.6
Death rate (per '000)	20.0	19.8	19.6
No. of households ('000)	221.6	228.9	241.9
Total exports (US$ million)	51.2	62.1	72.0
Total imports (US$ million)	68.7	62.2	71.7
Tourism receipts (US$ million)			
Tourist spending (US$ million)	1,192.7	1,213.0	1,263.0

Average household size 2001 (persons)	5.30					
Urban population 2001 (%)	24.2					
Age analysis (%) (2001)	*0-14*	42.6	*15-64*	53.3	*65+*	4.1
Population by sex (%) (2001)	*Male*	49.2	*Female*	50.8		
Life expectancy (years) (2001)	*Male*	43.7	*Female*	46.6		
Infant mortality (deaths per '000 live births) (2001)	123.4					
Adult literacy (%) (1997)	53.6					

TRADING PARTNERS

Major export destinations 2001 (% share)		Major import sources 2001 (% share)	
URUGUAY	40.9	PORTUGAL	24.5
THAILAND	27.9	SENEGAL	15.9
INDIA	25.7	CHINA	11.0
PORTUGAL	1.6	THAILAND	4.8

Guyana

Area (km^2) 214,970

Currency Guyana dollar (G$ = 100 cents)

Location Guyana, the former British Guiana, lies on the north-eastern coast of South America, its coast facing north-east into the Atlantic. It is bordered in the west by Venezuela, in the east by Suriname (the former Dutch Guiana), and in the far south by Brazil. The terrain is heavily forested, and the climate is humid and sub-tropical. The capital is Georgetown.

Head of State Bharrat Jagdeo (1999)

Head of Government Sam Hinds (December 1997)

Ruling Party The People's Progressive Party-Civic (PPP)

Political Structure Guyana, an independent member of the Commonwealth, has a semi-executive president who exercises considerable powers. The president also leads a 65-member National Assembly, which includes 53 members elected for a 5-year term and 12 regional deputies. The country was for many years so firmly identified with the policies of the former ruling People's National Congress (PNC) that it amounted to a single-party state.

Last Elections Elections to the National Assembly were held in March 2001. The PPP-Civic 35 seats, the Peoples' National Congress took 27 seats with the other seats divided among several parties.

Political Risk Supporters of the PPP are predominantly Indo-Guyanese, whereas the opposition PNC is predominately Guyanese of African origin. There are deep racial divisions between the two parties. Tensions are high and are exacerbated as a result of Guyana's economic problems.

International Disputes Guyana claims an offshore area believed to contain commercial deposits of oil but Suriname disputes this claim. Venezuela has reopened a century-old claim to Essequibo province, which makes up two- thirds of Guyana and is the country's economic heartland. Like French Guiana, Guyana faces a claim from Suriname for the return of a triangle of jungle land deep in the interior of the country. The so-called New River Triangle dispute arose because of an erroneous assumption as to which of two tributaries of the Corantijn River was the longer. The area in question has little economic significance, although some strategic importance.

Economy Guyana's economy has deteriorated badly in recent years. GDP rose by just 0.8% in 2001 while inflation was 2.4%. Authorities have adopted a programme designed to return the economy to a sustainable growth path but they will be hard pressed to stimulate an economy that is so dependent on agriculture and has few natural resources to develop. Most major industries are controlled by the government and there are no plans for privatisation. Net foreign investment fell to US$56 million in 2001, or 8% of GDP compared with 9.4% in 2000. Major new investments such as the oil exploration project in the Guyana Basin failed to materialise.

Main Industries Guyana's economy depends heavily on sugar and rice production, gold and bauxite mining, and logging. Reduced output of sugar and rice, caused by lower acreage and adverse weather, has hurt growth. The sugar industry will be modernised but not privatised, while the indebted rice industry will be restructured. Officials are anxious to diversify the economy, but foreign investors remain aloof. Farming accounts for over a quarter of GDP and is mainly for subsistence purposes. Most cash crops are grown near the coast since the inland terrain is too elevated and hostile. Domestic markets consume mainly cereals, fruit and vegetables. Export performance reflects a decade of terms of trade deterioration, for which adjustment was made more difficult by the sustained appreciation of the exchange rate. In 2001, while output increased in all sectors except for bauxite, timber and government services, the value of exports declined by 3% on average, with bauxite and timber exports each declining by 20%, sugar by 8% and rice by 3%.

Energy Efforts to exploit offshore oil fields were foiled in 2000 when the navy from Suriname chased a Canadian rig from a concession granted by Guyana, but which Suriname claims. Guyana had hoped to bolster its domestic production of energy with a massive hydro-electricity project but investors remain wary. Meanwhile, Guyana remains heavily dependent on imported oil supplies, despite some promising oil finds on its own territory.

	1999	2000	2001
Inflation (% change)	7.5	6.1	2.4
Exchange rate (per US$)	178.00	182.43	187.32
Interest rate (% per annum, lending rate)	17.1	17.3	17.0
GDP (% real growth)	3.0	-0.7	0.8
GDP (Million units of national currency)	123,665.0	125,990.0	122,605.0
GDP (US$ million)	694.8	690.6	654.5
GDP per capita (US$)	811.2	802.1	749.7
Consumption (Million units of national currency)	52,935.6	57,395.9	56,216.2
Consumption (US$ million)	297.4	314.6	300.1
Consumption per capita (US$)	347.2	365.4	343.8
Population, mid-year ('000)	856.4	861.0	873.0
Birth rate (per '000)	23.1	22.7	22.3
Death rate (per '000)	8.7	8.9	9.2
No. of households ('000)	185.6	184.4	183.0
Total exports (US$ million)	522.7	497.8	477.9
Total imports (US$ million)	520.3	587.0	583.9
Tourism receipts (US$ million)	50.0	52.9	46.7
Tourist spending (US$ million)			

Average household size 2001 (persons)	4.67				
Urban population 2001 (%)	38.8				
Age analysis (%) (2001)	*0-14*	31.0	*15-64*	64.8	*65+* 4.1
Population by sex (%) (2001)	*Male*	49.3	*Female*	50.7	
Life expectancy (years) (2001)	*Male*	58.4	*Female*	67.1	
Infant mortality (deaths per '000 live births) (2001)	53.0				
Adult literacy (%) (1997)	98.1				

TRADING PARTNERS

Major export destinations 2001 (% share)

USA	22.0
CANADA	20.4
NETHERLANDS ANTILLES	12.2
UNITED KINGDOM	12.0

Major import sources 2001 (% share)

USA	28.3
NETHERLANDS ANTILLES	20.2
TRINIDAD AND TOBAGO	15.3
UNITED KINGDOM	6.5

▨ Haiti

Area (km^2) 27,750

Currency   Gourde (G = 100 centimes)

Location   Haiti shares the large Caribbean island of Hispaniola with the Dominican Republic, occupying the western half. At its western extreme the country is no more than 80km from Cuba and 160km from Jamaica. The terrain is largely mountainous with fertile valleys. The climate is tropical and generally constant in character. The capital is Port-au-Prince.

Head of State   Jean Bertrand Aristide (2001)

Head of Government   Jean-Marie Chérestal (2001)

Ruling Party   The Lavalas Party

Political Structure   The constitution calls for the president to be elected by popular vote for a 5-year term. The National Assembly has two chambers. The Chamber of Deputies has 82 members, elected for four years in single-seat constituencies. The Senate has 27 members, elected for six years, one third renewed every two years, in single-seat constituencies.

Last Elections   Presidential elections were held in November 2000 when Aristide received 92% of the vote. Elections to the Chamber of Deputies took place at the same time. The Lavalas Party received 72 out of 82 seats with the remainder dispersed among several parties. In elections to the Senate (also in November 2000), the Lavalas Party won 26 of the 27 seats.

Political Risk   Serious signs of instability have re-emerged. After almost a decade without a coup, there were two attempts in 2001. Drug-running flourishes and violence, associated both with drugs and political infighting, is growing.

International Disputes   In June 2001, Aristide agreed to hold new parliamentary elections. In return, the Organisation of American States said it would help Haiti obtain US$500 million of suspended aid. A year later, the aid has still not arrived. The government's spendthrift practices (the government has purchased four presidential mansions in the past year) and its links with drug runners has convinced donors to withhold aid.

Economy   Haiti's economy contracted in 2001 by 1.7% but prices rose by 16.7%. Two-thirds of Haiti's inhabitants live in poverty, half of all adults are illiterate, and less than a quarter of rural children attend primary school. Haiti also produces more cases of HIV-AIDS each year than the entire US. The government has failed to pass a budget in six years. Instead, diplomats suspect, the country's depleted coffers are being filled with pay-offs from drug-dealers who use the country to trans-ship an estimated 10-15% of the cocaine that enters the US. Some of Haiti's richest families are selling out and moving abroad. International economists estimate that as much as 70% of the workforce is unemployed or working only part-time.

Main Industries   Drug-running continues to be the main money-earner in Haiti. American officials believe that exports of cocaine are steadily rising. Legally, the economy relies overwhelmingly on the agricultural sector, which employs 70% of the workforce. Farm productivity, however, is very low. Drought and erosion have destroyed much of the arable land. Today, agriculture accounts for only about 30% of GDP. Coffee is grown for export, but foreign exchange earnings have shrunk as world prices fell. Other exports include sugar and mangoes; yet most people rely on the subsistence farming of maize, sorghum, rice, beans and fruit. The most dynamic sectors are construction and manufacturing, but growth in these fields is not strong enough to offset the contraction in agriculture and other parts of the economy. The restructuring of public enterprises has made almost no progress. In fact, the privatisation of telephone services, as well as ports, airports and electricity has been suspended owing to the deadlock in the legislature. Efforts to expand Haiti's tourism sector are impeded by poor infrastructure and inadequate capacity. The only significant investment is a US$40 million Hilton hotel being built near the airport. Industry contributes about 15% of GDP in a typical year but its share, too, is declining. Food processing and related activities involving raw materials dominate, and there is some manufacturing of other low-cost goods. Haiti has deposits of copper, silver, bauxite, gold, marble, lignite and asphalt, but only bauxite has ever been mined, and there is virtually no foreign investment in the country at present.

Energy   With no natural fuels except for lignite, Haiti must rely almost completely on imports to meet its energy needs. The country, along with Barbados, the Dominican Republic and Jamaica, is party to the San Jose pact, under which Mexico and Venezuela supply crude oil and refined products on favourable terms.

	1999	2000	2001
Inflation (% change)	8.1	11.5	16.7
Exchange rate (per US$)	16.94	21.17	24.43
Interest rate (% per annum, lending rate)	22.9	25.1	28.6
GDP (% real growth)	2.7	0.9	-1.7
GDP (Million units of national currency)	69,254.0	77,580.0	88,997.0
GDP (US$ million)	4,088.7	3,664.5	3,643.1
GDP per capita (US$)	535.4	470.0	457.7
Consumption (Million units of national currency)	62,157.0	72,446.0	82,353.0
Consumption (US$ million)	3,669.7	3,422.0	3,371.1
Consumption per capita (US$)	480.5	438.9	423.6
Population, mid-year ('000)	7,637.4	7,796.5	7,959.0
Birth rate (per '000)	31.5	31.2	30.9
Death rate (per '000)	13.1	13.0	12.8
No. of households ('000)	1,537.8	1,555.4	1,569.1
Total exports (US$ million)	196.4	163.6	140.7
Total imports (US$ million)	1,025.3	1,036.2	1,013.0
Tourism receipts (US$ million)	74.0	68.6	55.8
Tourist spending (US$ million)	33.1	45.8	37.0

Average household size 2001 (persons)	5.06					
Urban population 2001 (%)	36.3					
Age analysis (%) (2001)	*0-14*	39.8	*15-64*	56.4	*65+*	3.8
Population by sex (%) (2001)	*Male*	49.2	*Female*	50.8		
Life expectancy (years) (2001)	*Male*	49.9	*Female*	56.1		
Infant mortality (deaths per '000 live births) (2001)	62.7					
Adult literacy (%) (1997)	45.8					

TRADING PARTNERS

Major export destinations 2001 (% share)

USA	84.5
DOMINICAN REPUBLIC	5.9
EUROPEAN UNION	5.0
CANADA	2.4

Major import sources 2001 (% share)

USA	52.1
DOMINICAN REPUBLIC	11.9
COLOMBIA	2.7
TRINIDAD AND TOBAGO	2.5

Honduras

Area (km^2)　112,085

Currency　Lempira (L = 100 centavos)

Location　Honduras occupies a central position in the Central American isthmus, located between Guatemala in the west and Nicaragua in the east, with El Salvador on its southern border. Consequently, its Caribbean coastline is significantly longer than its Pacific frontage, which is less than 80km in total. The country has a largely mountainous character, and three- quarters of the land is covered by forest. The climate is tropical and generally humid. The capital is Tegucigalpa.

Head of State　Ricardo Maduro (2002)

Head of Government　Ricardo Maduro

Ruling Party　National Party of Honduras (PNH)

Political Structure　Honduras has an executive president who is directly elected by popular mandate for a 4-year term. He and his cabinet are answerable to a 128-member National Assembly.

Last Elections　Presidential elections were held in November 2001. Ricardo Maduro received 52% of the vote, defeating Pineda Ponce of the Liberal Party. Elections to the National Congress were held at the same time. The PNH gained 61 seats, followed by the Liberal party which won 55 seats. The remainder were spread among several smaller parties.

Political Risk　Honduras has been used as a staging post to ship drugs to the US from South America. Honduran authorities also fear that Zapatista guerrillas from Mexico are working with Honduran Indians and advising them in their demands for land. Human rights groups claim that many leaders of the Honduran Indian minority have been assassinated in disputes over land tenure. The present administration has vowed to crack down on corruption.

International Disputes　In 1999, a border dispute broke out between Honduras and Nicaragua. This followed the ratification by Honduras of a treaty with Colombia dividing a portion of the Caribbean Sea and islands claimed by Nicaragua between them. In 2000, the two countries' navies clashed in the Gulf of Fonseca. Subsequently, both sides agreed to submit the issue to the International Court of Justice.

Economy　GDP grew by 2.5% in 2001 and prices rose by 9.7%. Macroeconomic policies have remained sound in the period since presidential elections in November 2001. The central government recorded a deficit of 1.2% of GDP and monetary policy remained tight. However, fiscal consolidation will require the maintenance of a cautious wage policy and the pressure to raise wages is mounting. An adjustment in exchange rate policy is designed to prevent any further real appreciation of the currency. Tax revenues are growing at a slightly slower rate than inflation and this puts pressure on government spending. In 2001, the government adopted a strategy to reduce the overall rate of poverty from 66% of the population to 42% by 2015. It has also announced an ambitious, but rather vague plan for reform.

Main Industries　Agriculture is the largest sector of the economy. In a typical year farming accounts for about a quarter of GDP and up to 60-70% of export revenues. Agriculture is also the fastest- growing sector, a fact which is largely attributable to an upturn in export crops (bananas, coffee and African palm). Authorities have faced a number of difficult economic conditions associated with the economic slowdown in the US, the collapse in world coffee prices and the drought affecting most of Central America. Aside from farming, Honduras has a relative abundance of natural resources. These include timber, gold, silver, copper, lead, zinc, iron ore, antimony and coal. There are no funds to develop these industries, however, and for the present the country must concentrate on feeding itself. Progress on structural reform has slowed as the privatisation of the telecommunications company was delayed, the reform of the social security system stalled, while the law for civil service reform, which will strengthen public sector wage policy, was not submitted to congress. The country's tiny tourism sector has potential but is underdeveloped. Industry consists mainly of small-scale establishments that process agricultural products including sugar, coffee, textiles, timber and food.

Energy　In addition to the extensive damage sustained from Hurricane Mitch, a fire at a large dam knocked out 60% of the country's electrical supply. Electricity is frequently rationed, highlighting Honduras' over-dependence on hydro power.

	1999	2000	2001
Inflation (% change)	11.7	11.1	9.7
Exchange rate (per US$)	14.21	14.84	15.47
Interest rate (% per annum, lending rate)	30.2	26.8	23.8
GDP (% real growth)	-1.9	5.0	2.5
GDP (Million units of national currency)	69,254.0	77,580.0	88,997.0
GDP (US$ million)	4,872.5	5,228.0	5,751.5
GDP per capita (US$)	792.6	827.7	886.8
Consumption (Million units of national currency)	53,240.0	62,909.0	71,684.0
Consumption (US$ million)	3,745.8	4,239.4	4,632.6
Consumption per capita (US$)	609.3	671.2	714.3
Population, mid-year ('000)	6,147.9	6,316.3	6,485.5
Birth rate (per '000)	32.3	31.7	30.9
Death rate (per '000)	6.6	6.5	6.5
No. of households ('000)	1,303.7	1,351.6	1,404.0
Total exports (US$ million)	1,248.7	1,322.2	1,318.0
Total imports (US$ million)	2,727.8	2,884.7	2,917.6
Tourism receipts (US$ million)	195.0	216.4	187.6
Tourist spending (US$ million)	94.0	77.1	84.9

Average household size 2001 (persons)	4.74					
Urban population 2001 (%)	53.5					
Age analysis (%) (2001)	*0-14*	41.4	*15-64*	55.1	*65+*	3.5
Population by sex (%) (2001)	*Male*	50.4	*Female*	49.6		
Life expectancy (years) (2001)	*Male*	63.2	*Female*	69.0		
Infant mortality (deaths per '000 live births) (2001)	34.0					
Adult literacy (%) (1997)	70.7					

TRADING PARTNERS

Major export destinations 2001 (% share)		Major import sources 2001 (% share)	
USA	70.2	USA	53.0
EL SALVADOR	2.9	NICARAGUA	5.3
NICARAGUA	2.2	MEXICO	4.4
GUATEMALA	2.0	EL SALVADOR	4.0

Hong Kong, China

Area (km^2) 1,062

Currency Hong Kong dollar (HK$ = 100 cents)

Location Hong Kong occupies an important strategic position at the mouth of the Pearl River where it conducts an active trading business on behalf of the People's Republic of China. Hong Kong, which is now part of China, includes the Kowloon island area and the so-called New Territories. It has a mild climate, but summers and early autumns are very wet.

Head of State Jiang Zemin

Head of Government Tung-Chee-hwa (1997)

Ruling Party Chinese Communist party.

Political Structure Hong Kong was a Crown Colony until it was returned to China in July 1997. At that time, Hong Kong's democratically elected Legislative Council (Legco) was replaced with a curious "provisional" legislature of 60 seats. Half the legislators are chosen by "functional" constituencies made up of narrowly defined professional groups including even corporations. Another 10 are selected by a pro-China group of supporters. The remaining 20 seats are filled by universal franchise.

Last Elections Tung won re-election in February 2002 when no rival candidates were nominated to challenge him.

Political Risk Five years after Beijing's takeover, civil liberties have been eroded and the promises to protect Hong Kong's autonomy look doubtful. Democracy at the grassroots level has been scaled back significantly. Members of the local District Council have been replaced by government appointees and an entire system of councils has been abolished. The mainland's control over the city is slowly but steadily growing.

International Disputes Hong Kong, itself, has no international disputes.

Economy Real GDP is expected to increase by just 1.5% in 2002 but the economy should begin to recover in 2003 with growth of 3.6%. The economy is still experiencing deflation with prices falling by around 2.5% in 2002 and with a zero rate of inflation in 2003. Growth in domestic demand slumped to just 0.2% in 2001 from 10% in 2000. Expansion in private consumption fell to 2% from 5.4% over this period, reflecting consumer sentiment that was undermined by a drop in asset prices and rising uncertainty over employment. Labour market conditions also deteriorated during the year. The seasonally adjusted unemployment rate, having fallen from a peak of 6.4% at the beginning of 1999 to 4.4% in the fourth quarter of 2000, edged up to 6.1% by the fourth quarter of 2001. The rise was attributed to increased corporate downsizing and layoffs in the context of slowing aggregate demand and the skills mismatch caused by ongoing economic restructuring. Over the longer term, the economy will continue to suffer the restructuring pains of intensifying integration with lower-cost production centres in mainland China. Structural unemployment will likely remain high as displacement of employees in traditional manufacturing and low-end services continues. Unemployment, coupled with subdued consumer sentiment and ongoing supply and demand integration with the Pearl River Delta, will continue to exert a downward pressure on prices for several more years. Thus, deflation could continue to be problem for several more years.

Main Industries Hong Kong's industrial sector covers a range of activities from heavy chemicals and steel manufacturing to electronic goods. The share of manufacturing in GDP has been falling steadily as companies shift production facilities to lower cost locations in China and elsewhere. Major activities include textile and clothing/apparel, electronics, watches and clocks, and chemical and industrial machinery. Services dominate Hong Kong's economy, accounting for 85% of GDP and employing more than 80% of the workforce. Major sectors include the trade and travel related sector (wholesale trade, retail trade, import-export operations, restaurants and hotels), which, together, account for a quarter of GDP. The profitability of the retail banks (locally incorporated banks plus a number of the larger foreign banks which operate a branch network and which are active in retail banking) held up well, recording only a moderate decline. The government plans the development of other types of services in the next few years. These include merger of its stock and future exchanges, a new high-tech industrial park and the development of a Disney theme park. Tourism is Hong Kong's largest earner of foreign exchange after the textile and apparel industries. Although the number of visitors fell after the events of 11 September 2001, the government has announced several moves to reinforce the city's comparative advantage.

Energy Hong Kong is entirely dependent on imports for all its fuel needs. Electricity and coal are imported from China, and oil from Southeast Asia. Hong Kong has benefited from the opening of a Chinese nuclear power station in Shenzhen, but the development has aroused environmental fears in the ex-colony.

	1999	2000	2001
Inflation (% change)	-4.0	-3.7	-1.6
Exchange rate (per US$)	7.76	7.79	7.80
Interest rate (% per annum, lending rate)	8.5	9.5	5.1
GDP (% real growth)	3.1	10.5	0.1
GDP (Billion units of national currency)	1,227.0	1,270.6	1,262.4
GDP (US$ million)	158,167.0	163,078.0	161,870.0
GDP per capita (US$)	23,652.2	23,831.4	23,063.9
Consumption (Billion units of national currency)	713.5	716.0	709.7
Consumption (US$ million)	91,970.1	91,900.8	91,007.5
Consumption per capita (US$)	13,753.2	13,429.9	12,967.1
Population, mid-year ('000)	6,687.2	6,843.0	7,018.3
Birth rate (per '000)	10.1	9.9	9.8
Death rate (per '000)	5.7	5.7	5.8
No. of households ('000)	2,050.8	2,092.5	2,130.3
Total exports (US$ million)	173,885.0	201,860.0	189,894.0
Total imports (US$ million)	180,711.0	214,042.0	202,252.0
Tourism receipts (US$ million)	7,210.0	6,463.7	6,463.7
Tourist spending (US$ million)	6,687.2	6,843.0	7,018.3

Average household size 2001 (persons)	3.27				
Urban population 2001 (%)	100.0				
Age analysis (%) (2001)	*0-14*	16.2	*15-64*	72.9	*65+*	10.9
Population by sex (%) (2001)	*Male*	50.3	*Female*	49.7	
Life expectancy (years) (2001)	*Male*	77.1	*Female*	82.6	
Infant mortality (deaths per '000 live births) (2001)	4.0				
Adult literacy (%) (1997)	92.4				

TRADING PARTNERS

Major export destinations 2001 (% share)

CHINA	37.6
USA	20.9
JAPAN	5.5
UNITED KINGDOM	4.1

Major import sources 2001 (% share)

CHINA	42.5
JAPAN	11.5
USA	6.8
SINGAPORE	4.9

Hungary

Area (km^2) 93,030

Currency Forint (= 100 fillér)

Location Hungary has long-standing historical ties with Austria to the west, which have been renewed in recent years. Bordering on Serbia, Croatia and Slovenia to the south, Romania and Ukraine to the east and the Slovak Republic to the north, it is an important gateway between Western Europe and the developing East. Its terrain is mixed, with large agricultural areas but with mountains along the border with Romania. The capital is Budapest.

Head of State Ferenc Madl (2000)

Head of Government Viktor Orban (1998)

Ruling Party The Hungarian Citizens' Party (Fidesz) leads a coalition.

Political Structure Hungary has a non-executive president and a prime minister who is accountable to a unicameral National Assembly elected by popular mandate for a term of five years. The 386-seat National Assembly elects the president. Since April 1995, the country's Romany element has had its own 53-seat parliament.

Last Elections Parliamentary elections to the unicameral National Assembly were held in April 2002. Orban's right wing Fidesz Party took 164 seats while its coalition partner, the Hungarian Democratic Forum captured 24 seats. The largest party in the Assembly, however, is the Hungarian Socialist Party which won 178 seats. In June 2000, parliament elected Madl president.

Political Risk The domestic political climate is much more acrimonious than might be expected, given Hungary's successes in economics and foreign policy. The country is sharply divided along economic lines. These divisions jeopardise the reform process but it is unlikely that the Hungarians will let differences of opinion derail their plans to join the EU.

International Disputes Budapest's relations with the three million ethnic Hungarians living in neighbouring countries, particularly Romania and Slovakia, can pose problems. Of particular concern is how these groups will be affected by Hungary's membership in the EU and that organisation's policy of open internal borders. EU membership could mean opening Hungary's border with the EU while turning the rest of its borders into the EU's external frontier. Budapest continues to insist that the borders of the Hungarian state and the Hungarian nation are not the same. This argument makes Western diplomats uneasy but Hungary is unlikely to let relations with neighbouring states deteriorate simply because it could greatly complicate negotiations with Brussels.

Economy GDP grew by 3.8% in 2001 and is expected to increase another 3.5% in 2002. Growth in 2003 should be about 4%. Inflation was 9.2% in 2001 and should be about 5.4% in 2002. Prices are forecast to rise by 4% in 2003. After 10 years of transition, Hungary has a booming economy and has emerged as a frontrunner for EU accession. By any measure, performance over the past several years has been excellent. Since 1997, growth of GDP has been strong and exports have expanded at double-digit rates. Meanwhile, unemployment is the lowest in all of East Europe and inflation continues to fall. On the micro-economic level, the privatisation of industry and the banking sector to strategic investors and the implementation of a strict bankruptcy law helped create solid corporate governance structure, which reinforced Hungary's position as a favourite destination for FDI. The availability of credit is improving and for the first time since the transition began, credits extended to households and smaller businesses are growing faster than those to larger enterprises. The ratio of individuals over 65 to those of working age is projected to more than double through to 2050. Even assuming a moderate rise in immigration and significant improvements in both fertility and life expectancy, the working population is expected to decline by as much as 20%. Therefore, the need to make better use of the country's potential workforce will only grow.

Main Industries The agricultural sector accounts for 6% of GDP and is performing well but needs better infrastructure. The subject of agricultural reform is dominated by the question of accession to the EU and is one of the most contentious issues in these negotiations. The government subsidies low-quality food products but has devoted little to modernisation. Given the country's traditional strengths in this field, an infusion of new technology could offer bright prospects. The wine industry, with the help of foreign investors, has nevertheless made real progress and gained market share in West Europe. Industrial output grew by 9.3% in 2001 and is expected to rise by 6.5% in 2002. The sector accounts for 25% of GDP. Over 80% of the country's industries have been privatised in an aggressive programme begun several years ago. More than 70% of the country's manufactured exports come from foreign-owned plants set up by IBM, Philips and others. In the automotive industry, major companies including Ford, General Motors, Audi, and Suzuki have established multi-million dollar plants for auto assembly and/or component manufacture. Electronics is the second largest industry within manufacturing and plans to invest an additional US$200 million by 2005. Government officials are trying to convert Hungary into a regional hub for transportation, informatics and finance. Services, including financial services, advertising and retailing, are all becoming more competitive and customer friendly. Banking, in particular, is undergoing rapid consolidation.

Energy Hungary is one the largest producers of crude oil in Central Europe, though still a small producer by international standards. Crude oil production rose very slightly in 2001 to about 27,000 bbl/d, but production of natural gas liquids fell by about 5,000 bbl/d. Hungary's oil production had been declining steadily since its peak in the mid-to-late 1980s. Nearly half of Hungary's crude oil comes from the Algyo field in the south central part of the country, and the remainder is produced from numerous fields in amounts less than 2,000 bbl/d. Oil reserves are approximately 110 million barrels. Hungary's oil and natural gas company undertook increased domestic exploration, and the company estimates that only 60% of the country has been thoroughly explored.

	1999	2000	2001
Inflation (% change)	10.0	9.8	9.2
Exchange rate (per US$)	237.15	282.18	286.49
Interest rate (% per annum, lending rate)	16.3	12.6	12.1
GDP (% real growth)	4.5	5.2	3.8
GDP (Billion units of national currency)	11,486.5	12,957.1	13,449.5
GDP (US$ million)	48,436.3	45,918.0	46,945.7
GDP per capita (US$)	4,804.1	4,562.8	4,673.3
Consumption (Billion units of national currency)	5,350.1	6,070.3	6,795.8
Consumption (US$ million)	22,560.3	21,512.3	23,721.0
Consumption per capita (US$)	2,237.6	2,137.6	2,361.4
Population, mid-year ('000)	10,082.3	10,063.5	10,045.5
Birth rate (per '000)	9.5	9.3	9.0
Death rate (per '000)	13.8	13.7	13.6
No. of households ('000)	3,766.1	3,753.5	3,747.8
Total exports (US$ million)	25,012.0	28,092.0	30,498.0
Total imports (US$ million)	28,008.0	32,080.0	33,682.0
Tourism receipts (US$ million)	3,394.0	3,893.7	3,136.9
Tourist spending (US$ million)	1,191.0	1,083.2	1,228.6

Average household size 2001 (persons)	2.68				
Urban population 2001 (%)	66.5				
Age analysis (%) (2001)	*0-14*	16.9	*15-64*	68.0	*65+* 15.2
Population by sex (%) (2001)	*Male*	47.6	*Female*	52.4	
Life expectancy (years) (2001)	*Male*	67.4	*Female*	75.9	
Infant mortality (deaths per '000 live births) (2001)	9.2				
Adult literacy (%) (1996)	99.2				

TRADING PARTNERS

Major export destinations 2001 (% share)

GERMANY	35.5
AUSTRIA	8.9
ITALY	6.0
USA	5.7

Major import sources 2001 (% share)

GERMANY	26.2
ITALY	8.2
AUSTRIA	7.9
RUSSIA	6.8

Iceland

Area (km^2) 102,820

Currency Icelandic krona (= 100 aurar)

Location Located in the North Atlantic, Iceland is a large volcanic island and enjoys generally clear summers. Recurrent volcanic eruptions in the 13-17th centuries almost depopulated the island, but they have not been serious in recent times. Rich fishing grounds and the harnessing of geothermal energy are important to the economy. The capital is Reykjavik.

Head of State Olafur Ragnar Grimsson (June 1996)

Head of Government David Oddsson

Ruling Party Independence Party (SSF) leads a coalition with the Progressive Party (FSF).

Political Structure Iceland's president exercises somewhat more than merely a ceremonial role, being deeply involved in both domestic and international affairs. However, the day-to-day running of the country is left to the prime minister and the cabinet, who are appointed by the 63-member parliament (Althing). The parliament is a unicameral assembly. Although elected in one body by universal mandate, it designates one-third of its members after the election as an Upper House. The parliament sits for a term of four years, as does the president.

Last Elections Iceland's centre-right coalition easily retained its parliamentary majority in the general election held in May 1999. The IP received 41% of the votes and won 26 seats in the parliament. Its coalition partner, the Progressive Party, took 18% of the vote and received 12 parliamentary seats.

Political Risk Iceland sees its destiny firmly in Europe and is worried about being marginalised by the ongoing enlargement process. The issue of NATO membership and the presence of US troops in the country are a source of political division among the major political parties. Most Icelanders would approve of talks on EU membership but politicians refrain because it would be very difficult to gain the special status for the country's fisheries that would be a prerequisite for joining.

International Disputes Recurrent disputes break out between Iceland and its neighbours over fishery rights, and especially over its alleged infringement of EU fisheries. Although Iceland has managed to negotiate more generous fishing concessions in recent years, politicians still argue that existing constraints hold back the development of many isolated areas in the country.

Economy Iceland's GDP increased by 2.1% in 2001 but will fall by 0.9% in 2002. In 2003, growth is expected to be 1.9%. Prices rose by 6.7% in 2001 and will grow by another 6.4% in 2002. Inflation is forecast to be 3.5% in 2003. The balance of demand switched swiftly from consumption and other domestic expenditure to net exports and, as a result, the current account deficit fell to about 4.5% of GDP in 2001. The steep depreciation of the krona in 2001 and the attendant inflationary spike hindered the management of monetary policy and consolidation of the new inflation-targeting regime. The general government deficit in 2002 is projected at 0.5% of GDP, slightly higher than the deficit outturn in 2001. The redirection of demand and activity towards the external sector is expected to continue as households and businesses, which have both accumulated high levels of indebtedness, consolidate their balance sheets. As a consequence, the current account deficit is projected to contract to 2% of GDP in 2002. In the longer term, the government will face pressure to consider some form of linkage with the euro. This is particularly important for the tourist industry which has suffered from the relative high level of the krona in recent years.

Main Industries Rapid growth has changed the structure of the economy. Before the latest boom, the fishing industry accounted for 16.8% of GDP but that share shrank to less than 13% in 2001. There has also been strong growth in sectors such as tourism, as well as the emergence of significant initiatives in bio-technology and information technology. In recent years, tourism has accounted for 13-14% of the country's foreign currency earnings but that share dropped sharply in 2001 following 11 September. Diversification has been driven by power-intensive industries such as aluminium, which rely on the country's abundant supplies of cheap energy and by a surge in the performance of the computer software industry. Manufacturing is fragmented and suffers from poor transport connections, including an almost total lack of road or rail links in many areas. Light manufacturers, including most consumer goods, are imported. In the banking sector, the rapid expansion of bank lending - financed mainly by external borrowing for domestic on-lending - has led to increased risk exposures and weakened banking sector prudential indicators. The government plans to reform the tax system to foster saving and minimise economic distortions while bringing corporate taxation closer to international practices. The privatisation process will be resumed and the proceeds devoted mainly to redeeming public debt. Sheep are reared in large numbers, but otherwise agricultural activity tends to be restrained by the poor weather conditions.

Energy Iceland has vast geothermal potential in its volcanic rock structure, of which only a small part is currently exploited. With sufficient capital investment, it could easily become a major exporter of electricity.

	1999	2000	2001
Inflation (% change)	3.4	5.0	6.7
Exchange rate (per US$)	72.34	78.62	97.42
Interest rate (% per annum, lending rate)	13.3	16.8	18.0
GDP (% real growth)	3.9	5.0	2.1
GDP (Million units of national currency)	622,651.0	671,927.0	733,486.0
GDP (US$ million)	8,607.8	8,547.0	7,528.8
GDP per capita (US$)	31,020.8	30,416.4	26,467.0
Consumption (Million units of national currency)	365,909.0	398,740.0	417,717.0
Consumption (US$ million)	5,058.5	5,072.0	4,287.6
Consumption per capita (US$)	18,229.8	18,049.9	15,072.8
Population, mid-year ('000)	277.5	281.0	284.5
Birth rate (per '000)	14.8	14.5	14.1
Death rate (per '000)	6.9	7.0	7.0
No. of households ('000)	118.4	120.3	121.6
Total exports (US$ million)	2,004.6	1,891.3	1,773.2
Total imports (US$ million)	2,503.1	2,591.1	2,256.3
Tourism receipts (US$ million)	227.0	251.7	192.5
Tourist spending (US$ million)	430.0	405.6	339.1

Average household size 2001 (persons)	2.34				
Urban population 2001 (%)	93.2				
Age analysis (%) (2001)	*0-14*	22.9	*15-64*	65.3	*65+* 11.8
Population by sex (%) (2001)	*Male*	50.0	*Female*	50.0	
Life expectancy (years) (2001)	*Male*	77.0	*Female*	81.7	
Infant mortality (deaths per '000 live births) (2001)	5.0				
Adult literacy (%) (1997)	99.0				

TRADING PARTNERS

Major export destinations 2001 (% share)		Major import sources 2001 (% share)	
UNITED KINGDOM	18.2	GERMANY	11.7
GERMANY	15.0	USA	11.0
NETHERLANDS	11.0	DENMARK	8.3
USA	10.5	NORWAY	7.5

India

Area (km^2) 3,166,830

Currency Indian rupee (Rs = 100 paise)

Location India occupies the central northern coast of the Indian Ocean, where it is bounded in the west by Pakistan, in the north by Tibet (a region of China), Bhutan and Nepal, and in the east by Myanmar and Bangladesh. Spanning the equator, its climate is tropical and occasionally prone to violent storms. The capital is New Delhi.

Head of State President A. P. J. Abdul Kalam (July 2002)

Head of Government Atal Behari Vajpayee (1999)

Ruling Party The Hindu-nationalist Bharatiya Janata (BJP) leads a coalition.

Political Structure India is essentially a federation of 25 states and seven union territories, encompassing a large number of ethnic groups. The President holds all executive power, and appoints the Prime Minister and his cabinet on the basis of election results to the Lok Sabha (Parliament). The Parliament has 545 seats while the Council of States has 245 members.

Last Elections In parliamentary elections in October 1999, the BJP won only 182 seats in the Lok Sabha and 41 in the Council of States. The Indian National Congress took 112 seats in the Lok Sabha and 81 in the Council. Kalam was elected president by parliament in 2002.

Political Risk The Indian government's willingness to exploit tensions between the country's Hindus and Muslims is generating increased concerns about the stability of some states in the country. The BJP has adopted a strongly pro-Hindu slant to education and religion and appointed a number of Hindu hardliners to key positions in 2002. Many of India's 25 states are big enough and different enough to be large countries in their own right. Regional bids for autonomy have been accommodated, bought off or suppressed. Analysts get no comfort from the fact that India sometimes behaves as if it were several different nations.

International Disputes India disputes Pakistan's claims to Kashmir, and the two countries have come close to war. Both countries went on wartime footing in 2002 before US diplomats intervened. Eventually, Pakistan promised to end infiltration by terrorists into Indian-administrated Kashmir, and India pulled back its navy from the Pakistani coast. The armies of the two nuclear powers are still mobilised, however. India's entire approach to foreign policy is in a period of transition in the aftermath of the Cold War. Relations with Nepal, Bhutan and China are marred by the latter's two claims in Arunachal Pradesh and in the far north.

Economy GDP should grow by around 5.5% in 2002 and accelerate to 5.8% in 2003. The annual inflation rate in 2002 and 2003 is likely to be about 4%. An exceptionally strong export performance and a stable capital account helped the economy in recent years. In contrast, export growth collapsed in 2001 because of the protracted global economic slowdown. FDI increased by over 61% compared with the same period in 2000, to US$2.4 billion from US$1.5 billion. India's external debt position is expected to remain manageable over the near term. As of September 2001, external debt rose marginally to US$100.4 billion, a 2.1% increase from the previous quarter's figure of US$98.3 billion. In 2001, the government announced a comprehensive programme of second-generation reforms aimed at fiscal consolidation. The 2002 budget seeks to build on this platform through a two-pronged approach comprising both revenue-generating measures and reducing subsidies. At the same time, the budget made significant provisions for investment in infrastructure. Proposed finance sector reforms include implementation of measures to strengthen creditor rights, establishment of a pilot asset reconstruction company, allowance of foreign banks to establish subsidiaries in India and reform of pensions. India's economic prospects depend largely on the extent to which the government will succeed in implementing these reforms, and particularly on its ability to achieve fiscal adjustment. They will also depend on the enactment of reforms to eliminate existing distortions in the factor market, including the reform of labour laws.

Main Industries Due to relatively favourable weather conditions, the performance of agriculture improved significantly with growth of 5.7% in 2001. This raises expectations of a possible demand-led pickup in economic performance, fuelled by higher rural incomes. However, prospects for continued sustainable agricultural improvement over the medium term depend on investment to ease infrastructure bottlenecks and to modernise the sector. As export demand shrank in 2001, industrial growth slowed significantly. In the first nine months of the year, the index of industrial production rose by 2.3% compared with 5.1% in the comparable period in 2000. Manufacturing expanded by a mere 2.3% in both the first and second quarters of 2001 However, moderate signs of improvement in growth momentum were evident from the second quarter of 2001 in some subsectors, such as electricity, gas, water supply and construction. Industrial growth for the whole of 2001 was around 3.3%, the lowest rate in five years. The performance of the services sector improved moderately in 2001, but fell short of the outstanding growth rates recorded in the 1990s. The sector recorded year-on-year increases of 6.7% and 7.4% in the first two quarters of 2001, respectively, with the figure for the whole year estimated at 6.5%. This is due to a robust performance in the financial and business services segment, particularly the key information technology and software services sector, which expanded by 25% during the third quarter of 2001 compared with the same quarter in 2000. Telecommunications is also expanding rapidly but the country will need 64 million phone lines in order to meet demand in 2006 (up from 21 million lines today).

Energy India, the world's sixth largest energy consumer, plans major energy infrastructure investments to keep up with increasing demand. India also is the world's third largest producer of coal, and relies on coal for more than half of its total energy needs. The majority of India's roughly 4.8 billion barrels in oil reserves are located in several different offshore basins. India's average crude oil production level in 2001 was estimated at 640,000 bbl/d. India had net oil imports of over 1.1 million bbl/d in 2001. Future oil consumption in India is expected to grow rapidly, to 3.4 million bbl/d by 2010, from 1.9 million bbl/d in 2001. The country's consumption of natural gas is also expected to increase rapidly. By 2005, gas consumption should be double the level recorded for 1996. India is attempting to limit its dependence on oil imports somewhat by expanding domestic exploration and production.

	1999	2000	2001
Inflation (% change)	4.7	4.0	3.8
Exchange rate (per US$)	43.06	44.94	47.19
Interest rate (% per annum, commercial lending rate)	12.5	12.3	12.1
GDP (% real growth)	6.7	5.4	4.3
GDP (Billion units of national currency)	18,751.7	20,561.7	22,337.5
GDP (US$ million)	435,524.7	457,520.4	473,388.0
GDP per capita (US$)	434.3	451.8	461.0
Consumption (Billion units of national currency)	11,213.4	12,546.6	12,514.8
Consumption (US$ million)	260,441.2	279,176.5	265,220.6
Consumption per capita (US$)	259.7	275.7	258.3
Population, mid-year ('000)	1,002,874.0	1,012,611.0	1,026,877.6
Birth rate (per '000)	25.5	25.1	24.8
Death rate (per '000)	8.8	8.6	8.5
No. of households ('000)	168,212.0	169,857.0	171,310.7
Total exports (US$ million)	35,666.7	42,379.3	43,611.0
Total imports (US$ million)	46,979.2	51,294.5	50,533.0
Tourism receipts (US$ million)	3,036.0	3,511.0	2,790.8
Tourist spending (US$ million)	2,010.0	1,406.7	1,639.5

Average household size 2001 (persons)	5.96				
Urban population 2001 (%)	28.8				
Age analysis (%) (2001)	*0-14*	33.6	*15-64*	61.7	*65+* 4.7
Population by sex (%) (2001)	*Male*	52.0	*Female*	48.0	
Life expectancy (years) (2001)	*Male*	63.1	*Female*	64.3	
Infant mortality (deaths per '000 live births) (2001)	67.9				
Adult literacy (%) (1997)	53.5				

TRADING PARTNERS

Major export destinations 2001 (% share)

USA	21.0
UNITED KINGDOM	5.5
HONG KONG, CHINA	4.8
JAPAN	4.7

Major import sources 2001 (% share)

USA	8.4
BELGIUM	6.3
SINGAPORE	6.1
UNITED KINGDOM	5.7

◼ Indonesia

Area (km^2)   1,919,445

Currency   Rupiah (Rp = 100 sen)

Location   Indonesia, the largest Muslim state in the world, is also one of the most geographically dispersed nations. It consists of a group of archipelagos which range from the large islands of Sumatra and Java (in the west), through Sulawesi (in the centre) to the territory of Irian Jaya (Western New Guinea). To this is added the territory of Kalimtan and the Molucca Islands. The capital is Jakarta.

Head of State   Megawati Sukarno-putri (2001)

Head of Government   Megawati Sukarno-putri (2001)

Ruling Party   The government is formed by the Indonesian Democratic Party (PDIP), the Sekretariat Bersana Golongan (Golkar) and others.

Political Structure   The 1,000-member People's Consultative Assembly elects the president for a 5-year term. Half the assembly is elected by universal franchise with the remainder appointed by the president, often from the armed forces.

Last Elections   The first elections in the post-Suharto era were held in June 1999. The PDIP received 37% of the vote and 154 seats in the Assembly. Golkar got 21% of the vote and 120 seats. Abdurrahman Wahid then became president. In July 2001, Wahid was impeached and Sukarno-putri, the vice president and daughter of Indonesia' first president, assumed office.

Political Risk   Analysts fear that the process of devolution in Indonesia is occurring too rapidly. Their concerns are only heightened by East Timor's emergence as a new nation after years of struggle with Jakarta. Many believe that Timorese independence will set an example for other, restive parts of the country - particularly the oil- and gas-rich province of Aceh. New laws which came into effect in 2001 are already changing the way Indonesia is run. Regions will take charge of public services and handle more than 40% of state revenues. The army's brutal repression of separatists has continued for years, creating an atmosphere of total distrust of Jakarta. The government can partially defuse the situation if it keeps the army under control in its dealing with independence activists.

International Disputes   The independence of East Timor calls into question the Timor Gap Treaty under which Indonesia and Australia had agreed to split revenues from oil and gas development in the Timor Gap. Relations with Papua New Guinea are strained and Indonesia faces claims from Malaysia for the return of two islands, Sipadan and Ligitan, where Jakarta wants to develop tourist facilities. Finally, Indonesia is one of the many claimants of the Spratly Islands in the South China Sea, where oil deposits are thought to have been located.

Economy   GDP should grow by about 3.5% in 2002 and accelerate to 4% in 2003. Inflation will be over 12% in 2002 but fall to around 8.2% in 2003. Private consumption rose by about 6% in 2001-the sharpest rise since 1997 - with consumers responding to income increases in 2000 and early 2001. Although consumer spending remained strong throughout 2001, it is unlikely that this trend can continue as spending increased faster than overall income during the second half of the year. Likewise, the 8.2% growth in general government expenditures seen in 2001 is probably unsustainable, given the size and recent expansion of the public debt burden. Deficit spending in 2001 partly reflected efforts by the central government to ensure a smooth transition under the decentralisation process initiated at the beginning of the year. The external debt ballooned during the financial crisis, rising from less than half of GDP in 1996 to 88% of GDP at the end of 2001. Domestic debt increased likewise, rising from 21% of GDP in 1998 to 80% in 2001. The outlook for the Indonesian economy is highly promising but subject to considerable risks. Much depends on the capability and imagination of the country's leadership and government. Implementation of any significant reform programme is likely to be delayed until the political situation can be stabilised and the issue of devolution resolved.

Main Industries   Manufacturing output grew by 4.3% in 2001, and utilities and some services sectors also showed strong growth. Manufacturing benefited from a high level of investment early in the year as well as sustained consumer spending. Business spending was muted in response to recurrent political difficulties, although the relatively peaceful change in the presidency in July provided for a moment of calm before the events of 11 September 2001 in the US and the subsequent rise in tension that again unnerved businesses. Investment in plant and equipment in the first two quarters of 2001 grew at an average rate of almost 18% (on a 4-quarter basis). Though spending declined thereafter, the year as a whole showed only 4% increase. In contrast, agriculture continued to reflect weak productivity growth and other problems in the rural sector, and managed less than 1% growth in 2001. Employment edged up by 1.1% in 2001, but this rise was insufficient to offset the population increase and the labour force participation rate. Increased employment was reported mainly in the formal sector, which accounts for about one third of the economy, while little jobs growth was reported in the informal sector, which depends heavily on employment in the poorly performing agriculture sector.

Energy   Indonesia currently holds proven oil reserves of five billion barrels. This represents a 14% decline since 1994. Much of Indonesia's proven oil reserve base is located onshore. Central Sumatra is the country's largest oil producing province. Other significant oil field development and production is located in accessible areas such as offshore northwestern Java, East Kalimantan and the Natuna Sea. Indonesia's current OPEC crude oil production quota is 1.125 million bbl/d. Oil production has stagnated as output from new fields offsets the decline of mature oil fields. To meet its goal of increasing production, Indonesia has stepped up efforts to sign new oil exploration contracts. Nine new contracts were signed during 2001, and there are plans to offer 17 new blocks during 2002.

	1999	2000	2001
Inflation (% change)	20.5	3.7	11.5
Exchange rate (per US$)	7,855.15	8,421.77	10,260.80
Interest rate (% per annum, lending rate)	27.7	18.5	18.5
GDP (% real growth)	0.9	4.8	3.2
GDP (Trillion units of national currency)	1,110.0	1,282.0	1,491.0
GDP (US$ million)	141,306.0	152,226.6	145,307.8
GDP per capita (US$)	676.3	720.1	678.3
Consumption (Trillion units of national currency)	832.5	888.6	1,002.6
Consumption (US$ million)	105,983.2	105,516.0	97,716.1
Consumption per capita (US$)	507.2	499.2	456.1
Population, mid-year ('000)	208,939.4	211,388.1	214,236.8
Birth rate (per '000)	21.8	21.4	21.0
Death rate (per '000)	7.3	7.3	7.2
No. of households ('000)	51,203.7	52,348.5	53,207.6
Total exports (US$ million)	48,665.4	62,124.0	56,716.0
Total imports (US$ million)	24,004.3	33,514.8	31,170.0
Tourism receipts (US$ million)	4,710.0	3,880.5	3,473.9
Tourist spending (US$ million)	2,353.0	1,995.2	1,640.7

Average household size 2001 (persons)	4.04				
Urban population 2001 (%)	41.9				
Age analysis (%) (2001)	*0-14*	30.4	*15-64*	65.0	*65+* 4.6
Population by sex (%) (2001)	*Male*	49.9	*Female*	50.1	
Life expectancy (years) (2001)	*Male*	64.7	*Female*	68.7	
Infant mortality (deaths per '000 live births) (2001)	42.9				
Adult literacy (%) (1997)	85.0				

TRADING PARTNERS
Major export destinations 2001 (% share)   **Major import sources 2001 (% share)**

JAPAN	21.9	JAPAN	18.8
USA	15.0	SINGAPORE	10.2
SINGAPORE	10.7	SOUTH KOREA	9.8
SOUTH KOREA	6.2	USA	7.4

▪ Iran

Area (km^2) 1,648,000

Currency Iranian rial (R = 100 dinars)

Location Iran, the largest non-Arab country in the Middle East, occupies the land mass between the Caucasus in the north (Turkey, Azerbaijan and Turkmenistan), the Afghan and Pakistani borders to the east and southeast, and Iraq to the west. It lies on the coast of the Persian (Arabian) Gulf, facing Saudi Arabia, Bahrain and the United Arab Emirates. The capital is Tehran.

Head of State President Mohammad Khatami (1997)

Head of Government President Mohammad Khatami (1997)

Ruling Party The Islamic Iran Participation Front leads a coalition of reformers.

Political Structure Modern Iran has its foundations in the Islamic revolution supporters of Ayatollah Ruhollah Khomeini. Political power rests loosely in the clerical and religious hierarchy, which exercises authority through the 76-member Assembly of Experts. The country's Majlis consists of 290 members which are popularly elected. There is also a 12-member Council of Guardians, which includes six clerical members appointed by Ayatollah Sayed Ali Khamenei. The council has to pass all legislation coming from parliament and vets all would-be candidates.

Last Elections In presidential elections in June 2001, Khatami was re-elected with 77% of the vote. In parliamentary elections held in May 2000, the Reformist Party won 189 seats, the Radical Islamists won 54 seats and independents took 42 seats. The remainder went to religious minorities.

Political Risk Iran's economy faces some serious problems in the future. Exporters have little chance of gaining access to world markets unless the US lifts its veto of Iran's membership of the World Trade Organisation. Inflows of foreign investment are also meagre (again due to the US embargo) and the population is growing by more than 3% a year. By 2005, when Khatami steps down, unemployment could have risen to at least 15 million.

International Disputes Iran officially denies US allegations that that it is developing weapons of mass destruction. Yet the government points out that many of its own enemies have such weapons and states that Iran should too. The country is certainly encircled by hostility. Of all its neighbours, Iran enjoys normal relations only with Armenia. Iran has still not signed a peace pact with Iraq, long after the war between the two countries. Israel accuses Iran of supporting the Hamas in an attempt to undermine the Palestinian peace process. The US imposes mandatory and discretionary sanctions on non-US companies investing in Iran. Negotiations with the UAE over Abu Musa and Tunb Islands remained stalled. Iran seized the islands in 1971 and has rejected proposals by the Gulf Cooperation Council to resolve the dispute.

Economy Iran's economy, which relies heavily on oil export revenues, was hit hard by record-low oil prices during 1998 and early 1999, but improved once oil prices strengthened. GDP rose by 5.1% in 2001 and should increase by another 5.3% in 2002. Growth of 5.1% is forecast in 2003. Inflation was 11.7% in 2001 and will be 15% in 2002. In 2003, prices are forecast to rise by 12%. The economy, however, faces a number of problems. About one million Iranians enter the labour market each year, but there are jobs for less than half of them. Unemployment is unofficially estimated to be 18% and rising. Since 2000, about 285,000 qualified Iranians have emigrated. Meanwhile, the country's reform-minded government is unable to dismantle the socialist-style economy. It continues to dole out US$1.1 billion each year in the form of soft loans to employers who hire extra workers. The government has managed to cut corporate tax and income tax for the poor, and has removed many import barriers. In 2002, however, spending has gone up by 54%.

Main Industries Oil export revenues account for around 80% of total export earnings, 40-50% of the government budget and 10-20% of GDP. Relatively high oil export revenues in 2001 allowed Iran to set up an oil stabilisation fund. Despite the high returns on oil, Iran continues to face budgetary pressures. The pressures are due to expensive state subsidies (billions of dollars per year) on many basic goods; a large, inefficient public sector and state monopolies which control at least a quarter of the economy and constitutionally are answerable only to supreme leader Ayatollah Ali Khamenei. To cope with its economic (and social) problems, Iran's government has proposed a variety of privatisation and other restructuring and diversification measures, although these remain politically contentious. President Khatami announced an ambitious programme to privatise several major industries, including communications, post, rail, petrochemicals, and even upstream oil and natural gas. The present 5-year plan (which began in 2000) calls for the creation of 750,000 new jobs per year and a reduction in subsidies for basic commodities (bread, rice, sugar, vegetable oil, wheat, fuels), plus a wide range of fiscal and structural reforms. Implementation of these plans, however, has been delayed by lack of domestic political consensus (as well as the Iranian constitution). Agriculture generates 20% of GDP and is concentrated in the fertile valleys of the north and west. Iran's budget shortfall, which is a chronic problem, is due in part to large-scale state subsidies - totalling some US$11 billion per year - which are mainly for foodstuffs. Wheat, barley, rice, cotton and sugar beet are grown for domestic consumption; there are also timber resources in the north and west.

Energy Iran holds 90 billion barrels of proven oil reserves, or roughly 9% of the world's total. The vast majority of crude oil reserves are located in giant onshore fields in south-western Khuzestan near the Iraqi border and the Persian Gulf. During 2001, Iran produced about 3.8 million bbl/d of oil. Current sustainable crude oil production capacity is estimated to be 3.85 million bbl/d, which is more than 650,000 bbl/d above Iran's latest OPEC production quota of 3.19 million bbl/d. In 2001, Iran consumed an estimated 1.1 million bbl/d of oil and had net exports of 2.7 million bbl/d. Domestic oil consumption is increasing rapidly (about 7% per year) as the economy and population grow. In addition, Iran subsidises the price of oil products, resulting in a large amount of waste and inefficiency in oil consumption. Currently, Iran is forced to spend around US$1 billion per year to import oil products (mainly gasoline) which it cannot produce locally.

	1999	2000	2001
Inflation (% change)	20.4	12.6	11.7
Exchange rate (per US$)	1,752.93	1,764.43	1,753.56
Interest rate			
GDP (% real growth)	2.6	4.9	5.1
GDP (Billion units of national currency)	420,935.1	603,169.3	664,132.5
GDP (US$ million)	240,132.3	341,849.4	378,733.8
GDP per capita (US$)	3,651.7	5,117.8	5,578.1
Consumption (Billion units of national currency)	241,647.0	263,936.0	302,632.4
Consumption (US$ million)	137,853.2	149,587.1	172,581.7
Consumption per capita (US$)	2,096.4	2,239.5	2,541.9
Population, mid-year ('000)	65,758.2	66,796.3	67,896.0
Birth rate (per '000)	21.7	21.6	21.8
Death rate (per '000)	5.2	5.1	5.1
No. of households ('000)	12,673.9	12,693.0	12,609.4
Total exports (US$ million)	21,030.0	28,345.0	33,175.8
Total imports (US$ million)	12,683.0	14,296.0	18,543.0
Tourism receipts (US$ million)	662.0	968.0	891.4
Tourist spending (US$ million)	918.0	1,421.3	1,998.9

Average household size 2001 (persons)	5.31				
Urban population 2001 (%)	62.1				
Age analysis (%) (2001)	*0-14*	35.8	*15-64*	59.8	*65+* 4.4
Population by sex (%) (2001)	*Male*	50.7	*Female*	49.3	
Life expectancy (years) (2001)	*Male*	68.4	*Female*	70.3	
Infant mortality (deaths per '000 live births) (2001)	37.9				
Adult literacy (%) (1997)	73.3				

TRADING PARTNERS

Major export destinations 2001 (% share)   **Major import sources 2001 (% share)**

Major export destinations	%	Major import sources	%
JAPAN	18.0	GERMANY	9.9
CHINA	8.7	FRANCE	6.2
UNITED ARAB EMIRATES	7.9	ITALY	6.0
ITALY	7.6	RUSSIA	5.2

▪ **Iraq**

Area (km^2)　438,445

Currency　Iraqi dinar (ID = 100 fils)

Location　Iraq, situated across the Persian (Arabian) Gulf from Iran, is much less of a desert state, being watered by the Tigris and Euphrates rivers. The country borders on Saudi Arabia and Kuwait in the south, on Syria and Jordan in the west, and on Turkey in the north. It has substantial oil resources. The capital is Baghdad.

Head of State　President Saddam Hussein (1979)

Head of Government　None

Ruling Party　Arab Ba'ath Socialist Party

Political Structure　The overthrow of the monarchy in 1958 led to the creation of a republic which has been dominated since the late 1970s by Saddam Hussein. Hussein, who has been chief of the armed forces for most of this time, was also prime minister from 1979 to March 1991. The president is elected by the Revolutionary Command Council (RCC) from among its members, and appoints the cabinet. The RCC shares legislative powers with the 250-member National Assembly, which is elected by universal suffrage for a term of four years. The Kurdish parliament has 115 members, elected by proportional representation, 100 seats reserved for Kurds, 5 for Assyrians and 10 for Turkmens.

Last Elections　A national referendum to affirm Hussein as president for seven more years took place in October 1995. In August 2002, Iraq's parliament unanimously voted to nominate him to stand for another 7-year term in a referendum set for mid-October. The Kurdish minority held their own (officially unrecognised) elections to the (equally unrecognised) Iraqi Kurdistan parliament in May 1992, when the Kurdistan Democratic Party and the Patriotic Union of Kurdistan each obtained 50 seats.

Political Risk　The international embargo on trade with Iraq has devastated the domestic economy. Under the new rules Iraq will still have to place all its oil earning under UN control. Food and drugs no longer have to be vetted by a sanctions committee but the onus for blocking "dual use" items is now placed on UN agencies. Political opposition among the population remains muted, while Iraq's efforts to divide the Kurdish opposition have meant that many of Saddam's enemies remain disorganised and ineffective. Nevertheless, there have been several unofficial reports of coup attempts against Saddam.

International Disputes　The US-UK imposition of a "no-fly" zone continues and warplanes occasionally attack radar sites in the country, and the US is believed to have plans for a full-scale invasion to topple Saddam. Iraq still has a border dispute with Saudi Arabia over an ill-defined treaty, which has been shelved by the creation of a 300-km diamond-shaped neutral zone where neither is allowed to be active. The Kurdish regions of northern Iraq have been another source of turmoil. The land border had been closed since the Iraqi invasion of Kuwait in 1990. In January 2001, Iraq signed free-trade deals with Egypt and Syria. Despite the acrimonious history of Iraq and its neighbours, the Arab world (including even Kuwait) began to show much more support for the country in 2002 in response to the US threat of invasion. The support is not for Saddam but for the Iraqi people and to demonstrate Arab anger at the US reluctance to rein in Israel.

Economy　Iraq's GDP fell sharply since the Iraqi invasion of Kuwait, with per -capita income and living standards far below pre-war levels. For 2001, with net oil exports flat and oil prices down, Iraq's real GDP growth was estimated to have fallen by 6%. For 2002, with higher oil prices, Iraq's real GDP growth is expected to rebound, possibly to 15%, but this is dependent largely on political developments. Iraqi inflation is estimated at around 60% in 2001 (down from 100% in 2000), with unemployment (and underemployment) high as well. Iraq's merchandise trade surplus is about US$4.8 billion, although much of this is under United Nations (UN) control. Iraq has a heavy debt burden, possibly as high as US$140 billion if debts to Gulf States and Russia are included. Iraq also has no meaningful taxation system, plus erratic fiscal and monetary policies. The long squeeze on investment in Iraqi oil fields keeps its production capacity far below the potential of a country with the world's second largest oil reserves. Iraq used to import almost three -quarters of its food, but prices now put imports out of the reach of most. Nearly three- quarters of all Iraqis are forced to survive on government handouts. Health standards inside Iraq are thought to have been set back 50 years. Nearly 30% of children under five are severely malnourished and the infant mortality rate in this once prosperous country rose to match that of impoverished Sudan.

Main Industries　Before the embargo, the oil industry contributed 98% of all export revenues in a typical year. Prior to the war and the resultant embargo, agriculture in Iraq was diversified and well developed. However, limited rainfall meant that there were only two harvests a year. Farming is on the decline now, owing to a lack of investment, access to the necessary inputs and the deterioration in the quality of the soil. Industry was once moderately well developed but with the embargo Iraqi's industrial capability has declined markedly.

Energy　Iraq contains 112 billion barrels of proven oil reserves, the second largest in the world (behind Saudi Arabia) along with roughly 220 billion barrels of probable and possible resources. Iraq's true resource potential may be far greater than this, however, as the country is relatively unexplored due to years of war and sanctions. Deep oil-bearing formations located mainly in the vast Western Desert region, for instance, could yield large additional oil resources, but have not been explored. For 2001, Iraqi crude oil production averaged 245,000 barrels per day down from about 259,000 in 2000, with large weekly and monthly fluctuations. Iraqi officials had hoped to increase the country's oil production capacity to 350,000 barrels per day by the end of 2001, but did not accomplish this given technical problems with Iraqi oil fields, pipelines and other oil infrastructure. Industry experts generally assess Iraq's sustainable production capacity at no higher than 280,000 bbl/d. Iraq's oil ministry recently introduced amendments to existing development and production contracts (DPCs). Among other things, the duration of DPCs has been reduced from 23 to 12 years. In addition, Iraq has added a clause referring to "an explicit commitment to achieve target production within a set period".

	1999	2000	2001
Inflation (% change)	100.0	60.0	
Exchange rate (per US$)	0.31	0.31	0.31
Interest rate			
GDP (% real growth)	18.0	4.0	-6.0
GDP (Million units of national currency)	102,422.4		
GDP (US$ million)	329,482.9		
GDP per capita (US$)	14,558.3		
Consumption			
Consumption (US$ million)			
Consumption per capita (US$)			
Population, mid-year ('000)	22,632.0	23,115.0	24,339.0
Birth rate (per '000)	35.6	35.1	34.5
Death rate (per '000)	8.9	8.3	7.7
No. of households ('000)	4,264.3	4,313.5	4,471.4
Total exports (US$ million)		20,200.0	
Total imports (US$ million)		12,900.0	
Tourism receipts (US$ million)			
Tourist spending (US$ million)	22,632.0	23,115.0	24,339.0

Average household size 2001 (persons)	5.36				
Urban population 2001 (%)	77.2				
Age analysis (%) (2001)	*0-14* 42.0		*15-64* 54.9		*65+* 3.1
Population by sex (%) (2001)	*Male* 50.9		*Female* 49.1		
Life expectancy (years) (2001)	*Male* 62.0		*Female* 69.0		
Infant mortality (deaths per '000 live births) (2001)	70.7				
Adult literacy (%) (1997)	52.6				

TRADING PARTNERS

Major export destinations 2001 (% share)		Major import sources 2001 (% share)	
USA	52.5	FRANCE	19.0
JORDAN	7.9	AUSTRALIA	14.1
FRANCE	7.4	ITALY	10.5
NETHERLANDS	6.4	GERMANY	9.7

▪ Ireland

Area (km^2) 68,895

Currency Euro (= 100 cents)

Location The Republic of Ireland (Eire) comprises the greater part of an island off the west coast of Great Britain, the remaining northern part of the island forming part of the UK. With little mountainous terrain but considerable areas of hills and down, Ireland's wet though pleasantly mild climate contributes to good agricultural conditions. The capital is Dublin.

Head of State President Mary Patricia McAleese (1997)

Head of Government Bertie Ahern (June 1997)

Ruling Party The government is formed by the Fianna Fáil (FF) and the Progressive Democrats (PD).

Political Structure Ireland's president is elected for a 7-year term by universal suffrage, but most executive powers are exercised by a prime minister and cabinet appointed from among the National Parliament (Oireachtas). The House of Representatives (Dail Eireann), or Lower House, has 166 members elected by universal suffrage for five years, and the Senate (Seanad Eireann), or Upper House, has 60.

Last Elections Presidential elections were held in November 1997 when Mary McAleese easily won. Elections to the House of Representatives took place in June 2002. They were won by the conservative Fianna Fáil Party of prime minister Bertie Ahern, which took 80 seats. The main other parties are the Christian-Democratic Fine Gael (31 seats) and the Social-Democratic Labour Party (21 seats). Elections to the Senate were held in August 1997 when the Fianna Fáil won 29 seats and the Fine Gael won 17 seats. The remainder were spread among three small parties.

Political Risk Ireland faces a crisis in its pension system which will begin to become evident during the course of the next 10 years. The country will still enjoy a "demographic dividend" until around 2006 when the proportion of pensioners to numbers in work starts to rise. Without drastic changes in the system, the state's pension contribution will rise from 1.7% at the end of the 1990s to almost 7% over the next three decades. Politicians had originally hoped to avert this crisis by setting aside US$600-700 million per year to pre-fund part of the future liability. Recently, however, this option has become less appealing as other, more immediate financial needs emerged.

International Disputes Ireland maintains a constitutional claim to the territory of Northern Ireland — an issue which gave rise to three decades of violent terrorist activity. However, in May 1998, 94% of voters approved an Anglo-Irish peace plan for Northern Ireland and the chances for peace on the island are now greatly improved.

Economy Ireland's GDP grew by 6% in 2001 and will increase by another 3.2% in 2002. Growth in 2003 is expected to be 6.2%. Prices rose by 4% in 2001 and will increase by another 4.4% in 2002. In 2003, inflation is forecast to be 3%. Neither exports nor imports are forecast to regain their pre-recession momentum in the next couple of years and, in fact, it may be a number of years before double-digit rates of growth in exports are once again realised. While the strength of the expected recovery is somewhat disappointing, more serious concerns focus on the fiscal consequences of the recession and recovery. For an economy experiencing a temporary downturn, the shift in fiscal stance from sizeable structural surplus to small deficit appears to be inappropriately large and suggests weakness in the budgetary system. Current public expenditures need to be better managed to avoid the choice of either allowing further fiscal slippage or cutting infrastructure investment. Policy makers have made several adjustments in order to boost rates of growth. They have continued the process of lowering corporate taxes on activities which are not internationally traded to the unified target rate of 12.5%. Further progress has been made in restructuring the household tax system to favour labour force participation, especially by women, and to reduce high marginal tax rates for single workers at higher levels of income. This means tax rates now compare well with those in the UK with which the Irish labour market is closely linked via immigration. The authorities also took steps to strengthen the pension system by prepaying pension liabilities to privatised enterprises and have now established a pension fund which will receive at least 1% of GNP each year up to 2025. The fund already amounts to 6% of GDP. In the near term, another important element of the growth strategy has been to augment the provision of skills demanded by the economy. The move involves a skills-oriented immigration policy and training for the unemployed.

Main Industries Originally an agrarian economy, Ireland's industrial base has fundamentally transformed in the 10 years through 2002. The cornerstone of this industrial success has been an economic strategy focused on inward foreign investment in dynamic, export-oriented industries such as semiconductors, development of computer software and pharmaceuticals. Investors' interests in these high-tech fields reflects the country's success in establishing a stable macroeconomic environment, favourable costs, a youthful, fast-growing and increasingly well-educated labour force, a business-friendly tax regime and the country's position in the EU. Attracted by the low tax regime and the skilled labour pool, all leading US information technology companies have a presence in the country. With a population of less than four million, Ireland today accounts for a third of all US electronics investment in Europe. While these efforts have certainly been of great benefit, Ireland's economy has suffered significantly during the recent downturn in high-tech markets. An offsetting factor is that the country has also become a key location for pharmaceuticals, with nine of the top 10 companies operating here. Rapid growth has produced many bottlenecks in infrastructure but the government has recently launched an expensive, 7-year programme to improve facilities. The buoyant economy has led to a flourishing financial services sector.

Energy Ireland has large reserves of coal and peat, but its oil and gas requirements are met through imports. Some oil reserves have been located in the Irish Sea.

	1999	2000	2001
Inflation (% change)	0.9	1.1	1.1
Exchange rate (per US$)	0.94	1.09	1.12
Interest rate (% per annum, lending rate)	3.3	4.8	4.8
GDP (% real growth)	10.9	11.5	6.0
GDP (Million units of national currency)	89,029.0	103,470.0	113,479.0
GDP (US$ million)	94,928.1	95,593.9	101,546.3
GDP per capita (US$)	25,278.3	25,177.6	26,449.7
Consumption (Million units of national currency)	41,673.5	44,208.6	1.0
Consumption (US$ million)	44,434.8	40,843.5	44,319.9
Consumption per capita (US$)	11,832.5	10,757.4	11,544.0
Population, mid-year ('000)	3,755.3	3,796.8	3,839.2
Birth rate (per '000)	14.6	14.8	15.0
Death rate (per '000)	8.5	8.4	8.3
No. of households ('000)	1,135.9	1,157.6	1,175.7
Total exports (US$ million)	70,537.0	76,840.4	83,335.4
Total imports (US$ million)	46,520.7	50,541.2	50,622.4
Tourism receipts (US$ million)	3,392.0	3,667.4	3,836.0
Tourist spending (US$ million)	2,620.0	2,528.2	2,479.9

Average household size 2001 (persons)	3.28				
Urban population 2001 (%)	58.8				
Age analysis (%) (2001)	0-14	21.6	15-64	67.2	65+ 11.2
Population by sex (%) (2001)	Male	49.7	Female	50.3	
Life expectancy (years) (2001)	Male	74.2	Female	79.4	
Infant mortality (deaths per '000 live births) (2001)	6.2				
Adult literacy (%) (1998)	99.0				

TRADING PARTNERS

Major export destinations 2001 (% share)		Major import sources 2001 (% share)	
UNITED KINGDOM	21.9	UNITED KINGDOM	37.2
USA	16.9	USA	15.0
GERMANY	12.8	GERMANY	6.3
FRANCE	6.1	FRANCE	4.8

Israel

Area (km^2) 20,770

Currency New shekel (NIS = 100 agorot)

Location Israel, which occupies the lower third of the eastern Mediterranean coastline, was formed in 1948 as a thin strip of mainly Jordanian and Palestinian-owned land. But its territory was extended in the Six-Day War of 1967 to include territories seized from Jordan on the West Bank of the Jordan River, as well as some Syrian and Egyptian land. The country has a typically Middle Eastern climate, with warm summers. The capital is Jerusalem.

Head of State President Moshe Katzav (2000)

Head of Government Ariel Sharon (2001)

Ruling Party The government is formed by a multi-party coalition led by the Likud Party.

Political Structure The territory of Israel was created in 1948 to provide a homeland for displaced Jews. Carved out of mainly Palestinian-owned land, it was effectively extended after the 1967 war to the West Bank territory, including East Jerusalem (formerly in Jordan). A 7-year campaign of Palestinian disruption and non-co-operation was partially resolved in 1994 with Israeli recognition of Palestinian autonomy in the West Bank and the creation of a Palestinian parliament. Israel also withdrew from the Gaza Strip in 1994, after occupying it since 1967. Israel has a non-executive president and a parliament (Knesset) of 120 members. In 1996, a change was introduced which allows voters to cast two ballots, one for the prime minister and the other for a party. Until now, people only voted for one of 30-odd parties which then haggled over the prime minister. The change is meant to reduce the negotiating power of the small parties.

Last Elections Presidential elections took place in February 2001 when Sharon defeated Ehud Barak with 62% of the vote. In July 2000, parliament elected Moshe Katzav as president following the resignation of Ezer Weizmann, who had been involved in a political scandal. Elections to the 120-member Lower House of Parliament took place in May 1999. Barak's One Israel coalition took the largest share of seats (25) while Likud won 19 seats. The remainder were widely distributed among several parties.

Political Risk The Palestinian problem has worsened as the level of violence has escalated. At present, the international community cannot even agree on the best way to restore peace.

International Disputes Sharon's aggressive policies towards the Palestinians have done nothing to restore calm but have increased tensions with the EU and even the US. Israel's comparatively warm relations with Jordan have soured as a result of the growing Palestinian problem as well as a dispute over water rights. Internationally, the country is more isolated than it has been in many years.

Economy GDP contracted by 0.6% in 2001 and will grow by just 1.3% in 2002. In 2003, growth of 3.8% is forecast. Prices rose by 1.1% in 2001 and should increase by another 3.1% in 2002. In 2003, inflation should be 2.1%. The Israeli economy has continued to stagnate as a result of the global slowdown, especially the high-tech slump, and the increasingly worsening security situation. Macroeconomic policies cannot fully offset these negative shocks. In fact, too vigorous policy reactions to these shocks could cause adverse consequences elsewhere, such as high inflation, a loss of fiscal discipline and financial market instability. Rather, their main task is to attenuate the impact of these shocks by providing a stable, transparent and supportive environment to economic activity, until the economy begins a solid recovery. In a sudden departure from its gradualist approach, the Bank of Israel was forced to cut interest rates by two percentage points in the first half of 2002. The move clearly had a major impact on the view and behaviour of market participants, as evidenced by a sharp depreciation of the shekel. Part of this depreciation was intended by policy makers, and will have the desired effect of stimulating net exports. By mid-year in 2002, unemployment was approaching 11%. With significant additional (unplanned) expenditures relating to the security situation, the Israeli government is under growing pressure to tighten its budget for 2003. The government took steps to cut expenditures and has frozen most social benefits and the minimum wage. Authorities are trying to minimise the impact of all these expenditure cuts on infrastructure, a seed of sustainable growth in the future. The budget continues to deviate from the government's medium-term objective of reducing expenditure and debt as a share of GDP. Analysts expect that the deficit overrun could reach 3% of GDP or more due to a likely revenue shortfall.

Main Industries The country's agricultural sector is highly productive due to the mild climate and fertile soil. Wheat, avocados, millet, sorghum and a wide variety of fruits are produced. The area under cultivation includes a substantial part of the occupied West Bank. Besides a booming high-technology sector, Israel undertook important structural reforms such as privatisation and reduced controls on foreign currency exchanges and profit remittances by foreign companies. The tourist industry was also booming until the latest round of clashes with the Palestinians but has collapsed in 2002. Several government-owned companies, including the Ports and Railways Authority, the Oil Refineries Company and others have been privatised. Infrastructure investments are likely to remain high in the near term, in response to increasing affluence and a 2.5% annual population growth. Israel is also a major clothing and textiles manufacturer. Major exports include machinery and mechanical equipment, cut diamonds, chemicals, textiles and apparel, and agricultural products.

Energy Until recently, with a significant offshore natural gas discovery, Israel had no commercial fossil fuel resources and has been forced to depend on energy imports. Israel has attempted to diversify its supply sources and to utilise alternatives like solar and wind energy. Traditionally, Israel has relied on expensive, long-term contracts with nations like Mexico (oil), Norway (oil), the UK (oil), Australia (coal), South Africa (coal) and Colombia (coal) for its energy supplies. Although the government favours privatisation of state-owned companies, the energy sector remains largely nationalised and state-regulated, ostensibly for national security reasons. In 2000, Israel and the US signed an energy cooperation agreement. The agreement includes cooperation in the fields of gas, coal, solar power technology and electric power generation.

	1999	2000	2001
Inflation (% change)	5.2	1.1	1.1
Exchange rate (per US$)	4.14	4.08	4.21
Interest rate (% per annum, lending rate)	16.4	12.9	
GDP (% real growth)	2.6	6.4	-0.6
GDP (Million units of national currency)	423,127.0	458,808.0	464,608.0
GDP (US$ million)	102,211.5	112,526.6	110,472.3
GDP per capita (US$)	17,149.0	18,452.3	17,717.8
Consumption (Million units of national currency)	245,854.0	265,199.3	274,830.3
Consumption (US$ million)	59,389.0	65,042.4	65,347.9
Consumption per capita (US$)	9,964.3	10,665.7	10,480.6
Population, mid-year ('000)	5,960.2	6,098.3	6,235.1
Birth rate (per '000)	20.9	20.5	20.2
Death rate (per '000)	6.2	6.1	6.1
No. of households ('000)	1,699.0	1,746.0	1,773.3
Total exports (US$ million)	25,794.3	31,404.2	29,409.5
Total imports (US$ million)	33,165.5	31,404.2	31,434.9
Tourism receipts (US$ million)	2,974.0	2,479.1	1,652.6
Tourist spending (US$ million)	2,566.0	3,492.7	3,127.5

Average household size 2001 (persons)	3.49				
Urban population 2001 (%)	91.3				
Age analysis (%) (2001)	0-14	28.6	15-64	61.5	65+	9.9
Population by sex (%) (2001)	Male	49.5	Female	50.5	
Life expectancy (years) (2001)	Male	76.9	Female	69.8	
Infant mortality (deaths per '000 live births) (2001)	6.0				
Adult literacy (%) (1997)	95.4				

TRADING PARTNERS

Major export destinations 2001 (% share)		Major import sources 2001 (% share)	
USA	36.9	USA	20.9
BELGIUM	6.4	BELGIUM	9.0
GERMANY	5.2	GERMANY	7.1
UNITED KINGDOM	4.2	UNITED KINGDOM	6.0

◼ Italy

Area (km²) 301,245

Currency Euro (= 100 cents)

Location Located in the centre of southern Europe, Italy is a long strip of land, seldom exceeding 200km in width, which extends south-eastward for some 1,000km into the Mediterranean. In the north, where it meets with France, Switzerland, Austria and Slovenia, the territory broadens out to include the industrial cities of Milan, Turin and Genoa; in the south it divides into two peninsulas, the lower of which almost connects with the island of Sicily. The capital is Rome.

Head of State President Carlo Ciampi (1999)

Head of Government Silvio Berlusconi (2001)

Ruling Party The House of Freedoms coalition leads the government.

Political Structure Italy has been a republic since 1946, when it abolished the monarchy. Its president, elected by parliament for a 7-year term, exercises only semi-executive functions. In practice, however, the country's repeated political crises demand almost constant involvement by the president. The 630-member Chamber of Deputies (Lower House) is elected for five years by universal suffrage, as are all but seven of the 315-member Senate.

Last Elections Presidential elections were held in May 1999 when Ciampi took 770 votes of the 990 in the ballot. In May 2001, Berlusconi was finally elected prime minister. At the same time, his House of Freedoms coalition took 367 seats in the lower house and 177 in the Senate. The Olive Tree Party won 248 seats in the lower house, with the remainder scattered among smaller parties.

Political Risk Italy's jobless rate is 9% and in the poor south, one person in five is looking for work. Most workers can retire on pensions in their 50s. Spending on pensions swallows up 14% of Italy's GDP. More generally, Italy is thought to have Europe's most rigid labour market. It is urgent that Berlusconi finds some way to modernise labour markets but so far he has shown little taste for battle. Meanwhile, in the streets the fight goes on. In March 2002, the technocrat who had helped draft the controversial legislation on employment rules, was murdered.

International Disputes Italy has no active and outstanding territorial disputes, having never accepted the claims made by some Austrian groups in respect of the German-speaking South Tyrolean regions in Trentino. However, it does demand compensation from Slovenia for the dispossession of Italian citizens during the post-war era. Italy's neighbours - notably Germany and France - are uncomfortable with the Berlusconi government. His relations with right-wing movements in other countries make his critics very uneasy.

Economy Growth was just 1.8% in 2001. Economists expect growth of 1.4% in 2002 and 2.9% in 2003. Inflation was 2.7% in 2001 and will fall to 2.2% in 2002. In 2003, prices are expected to rise by 1.6%. Although productivity growth in Italy had typically been significantly higher than the EU average in earlier decades, it dropped to the modest rates of the other large EU countries in the 1990s. The effort to raise growth potential is being supported by an ambitious medium-term growth strategy, which encompasses initiatives across a wide range of areas, aimed at creating a more business-friendly environment. The programme includes tax measures designed to encourage business investment, together with labour-, product- and financial-market initiatives and steps to improve human capital acquisition and innovation potential. It is too early to assess the impact of the programme but many analysts are calling for even more aggressive action to improve the way labour markets operate. For example, unemployment insurance needs to be expanded and new initiatives such as more generous provisions for child care and old-age care are necessary to boost the low rate of female participation in the workforce. Modernisation of the pension system could help finance these reforms, while also encouraging the continued employment of older workers. Another area where Italy lags behind is the low level of worker training. Faster growth also requires competitive and efficient product markets. But innovation, as well as competitiveness, remained blocked by barriers to entry and high service prices.

Main Industries The 2001/2002 economic slowdown has complicated the government's promises for radical economic reforms and tax cuts. Nevertheless, the country's populous prime minister has raised the minimum public pension to at least L1 million and given tax breaks to companies in the south that hire young people. But these moves have not helped the backbone of Italy's industrial sector which is the many small and medium-sized companies producing everything from speciality steels to leather and footwear. About 95% of the workforce is employed in companies with fewer than 10 employees. These firms have encountered difficulties obtaining the technologies that would allow them to compete effectively. All businesses - large and small - are urging the new government to accelerate the process of privatisation. Italy's energy sector has undergone a partial privatisation but there have been few sales in other industries. Italy's widely criticised banking sector is slowly being restructured, although much of it is still in public hands. Agriculture is well diversified, producing soft fruits and vegetables, as well as wheat, olives and citrus products for export. The most fertile areas are in the north; but in the south, agriculture is mainly for subsistence purposes.

Energy Italy holds 622 million barrels in proven oil reserves. In 2000, the country produced an estimated 145,000 barrels per day (bbl/d) of oil and consumed about 1.9 million bbl/d, making it one of Europe's largest oil importers. Former Italian colony Libya is Italy's main source of oil imports. It is estimated that oil's share of Italy's energy consumption fell to just under 50% for the first time in over 20 years in 2000. Italy is in the process of decreasing its reliance on oil, especially for heating and electricity generation. Heating oil consumption in 2000 was about one- third of that of 1981 and fuel oil consumption fell 38% since 1995. Natural gas consumption is expected to rise as oil consumption falls in coming years. To ensure access to foreign oil, the Italian government has promoted Italy as an export refining centre. There are large facilities along the Mediterranean coast and on Mediterranean islands, capable of processing a wide range of crude oils from North Africa and the Persian Gulf. As a result, Italy now has Europe's largest surplus of refining capacity.

	1999	2000	2001
Inflation (% change)	0.9	1.1	1.1
Exchange rate (per US$)	0.94	1.09	1.12
Interest rate (% per annum, lending rate)	5.6	6.3	6.5
GDP (% real growth)	1.6	2.9	1.8
GDP (Million units of national currency)	1,108,497.0	1,164,766.0	1,216,583.0
GDP (US$ million)	1,181,946.0	1,011,739.1	1,088,652.3
GDP per capita (US$)	20,543.4	17,593.2	18,884.5
Consumption (Million units of national currency)	660,295.3	699,639.8	1.0
Consumption (US$ million)	704,046.5	607,721.1	653,389.5
Consumption per capita (US$)	12,237.0	10,567.7	11,334.2
Population, mid-year ('000)	57,534.2	57,507.4	57,647.8
Birth rate (per '000)	8.9	8.8	8.7
Death rate (per '000)	10.6	10.7	10.8
No. of households ('000)	21,529.0	22,004.0	22,319.9
Total exports (US$ million)	235,175.0	238,262.0	243,375.9
Total imports (US$ million)	220,322.0	236,624.0	234,382.0
Tourism receipts (US$ million)	28,359.0	30,571.7	24,439.2
Tourist spending (US$ million)	16,913.0	17,712.4	15,177.1

Average household size 2001 (persons)	2.61				
Urban population 2001 (%)	67.1				
Age analysis (%) (2001)	*0-14*	14.3	*15-64*	67.3	*65+* 18.0
Population by sex (%) (2001)	*Male*	48.4	*Female*	51.2	
Life expectancy (years) (2001)	*Male*	75.4	*Female*	81.8	
Infant mortality (deaths per '000 live births) (2001)	5.2				
Adult literacy (%) (1997)	98.3				

TRADING PARTNERS

Major export destinations 2001 (% share)		Major import sources 2001 (% share)	
GERMANY	14.6	GERMANY	17.8
FRANCE	12.3	FRANCE	11.2
USA	9.8	NETHERLANDS	6.2
UNITED KINGDOM	6.7	UNITED KINGDOM	5.1

Jamaica

Area (km^2)   11,425

Currency   Jamaican dollar (J$ = 100 cents)

Location   Jamaica is centrally located in the western Caribbean, lying some 145km south of Cuba and 160km south-west of Haiti. The country has a pleasant climate, although subject to hurricanes and heavy rains in the October-November period. The capital is Kingston.

Head of State   HM Queen Elizabeth II

Head of Government   Percival Patterson (March 1989)

Ruling Party   People's National Party (PNP)

Political Structure   Jamaica, an independent member of the Commonwealth, is ruled by a prime minister and cabinet who are drawn from a 60-member House of Representatives (Lower House), elected by universal suffrage for a 5-year term. The governor-general, who represents the Crown, has only formal functions. There is a 21-member Senate (Upper House), whose functions are mainly advisory. The constituency character of the electoral system means that parliamentary representation is often out of proportion to the levels of actual electoral support.

Last Elections   General elections were held in December 1997, when Patterson and his People's National Party were returned to power with a majority of 50 parliamentary seats.

Political Risk   Jamaica has become an extremely violent society. On a per capita basis, only Colombia and Central America have more murders each year. As many as half the murders are the work of the island's politically-linked drug gangs. The police sometimes react just as violently and have been criticised by Amnesty International. The rise in crime and violence is hurting the economy and especially the tourist industry.

International Disputes   There are no international disputes.

Economy   Jamaica's GDP rose by 3% in 2001, while inflation was 5%. In 2001, the unemployment rate stood at 16%, where it has held steady in recent years. However, it is likely that unemployment rose since then because of the labour-intensive nature of some of the weaker performing industries and sectors, including tourism. Balance of payments figures for 2001 indicate a sharp deterioration in the current account. Underlying this decline is a 138% increase in the merchandise trade deficit. The ratio of total debt to GDP stood at 140% at the end of 2001, having declined from 144% at the end of 2000. This figured is projected to decline further to 131% by the end of fiscal year 2002. As a result of the high debt, interest payments are currently absorbing 50% of total revenue and grants of the central government. Jamaica's economy continues to be characterised by a combination of protectionism, extravagant public spending and excessive dependence on a few commodities which are subject to wide swings in world prices. Despite progress, the structure of the island's economy is still a barrier to development. The Jamaican economy faces serious competitive problems. It also suffers from an excess of crime and violence which has been a problem for the island's tourist industry.

Main Industries   Jamaica's most important industry is tourism but there are fears that some parts of the sector are growing to quickly. By 2003, Jamaica plans to have added 2,650 rooms to its complement of 15,500. American and Canadian visitors are the main source of revenues but the industry has also been targeting the European market. However, the sector suffered substantially after 11 September 2001 and is still trying to recover. Jamaica also faces increasing competition from other Caribbean destinations. A sizeable portion of the tourist sector is state-owned. Performance improved in construction and installation, manufacturing, transport, storage and communications, and financial services. In 2001, agriculture output benefited from favourable weather conditions and expanded by 10%. Agriculture contributes only 5-10% of GDP, though it employs a quarter of the workforce. Sugar cane, coffee, pineapples and bananas are grown for export, while rice, maize and vegetables are produced for domestic consumption. The tropical climate makes for rapid growth, but vulnerability to hurricanes is a problem. Mining and quarrying output has been subject to much volatility since 1999 when most of the country's bauxite processing facilities sustained damage. These facilities are now back in operation and bauxite production and exports rebounded by 17% in 2001, rising significantly above the 1999 levels. Manufacturing expanded by 3%, continuing a growth trend that had been observed in recent years. The industrial base is fairly well diversified with food processing, textiles, clothing and timber and wood products being especially important. Jamaica also has a major petrochemicals plant, and export-free zones have been established to encourage further diversification.

Energy   Imports provide for almost all of Jamaica's energy needs. In 2001, a US-based utility completed an 80% acquisition of the island nation's main power provider. The new investor has stated that it will make progress in reducing the number of blackouts currently affecting Jamaica due to lack of capacity. The island, along with Barbados, the Dominican Republic and Haiti, is party to the San Jose pact, under which Mexico and Venezuela supply crude oil and refined products on favourable terms.

	1999	2000	2001
Inflation (% change)	8.4	6.4	5.0
Exchange rate (per US$)	39.04	42.70	46.00
Interest rate (% per annum, lending rate)	27.0	23.3	20.6
GDP (% real growth)	-0.1	1.1	3.0
GDP (Million units of national currency)	296,136.0	327,726.0	359,362.0
GDP (US$ million)	7,584.8	7,674.9	7,812.9
GDP per capita (US$)	2,956.9	2,971.3	2,958.3
Consumption (Million units of national currency)	196,641.0	223,341.0	245,990.0
Consumption (US$ million)	5,036.5	5,230.3	5,348.1
Consumption per capita (US$)	1,963.5	2,024.9	2,025.0
Population, mid-year ('000)	2,565.1	2,583.0	2,641.0
Birth rate (per '000)	21.1	20.8	20.5
Death rate (per '000)	5.8	5.8	5.7
No. of households ('000)	533.4	531.4	534.9
Total exports (US$ million)	1,240.4	1,296.1	1,225.3
Total imports (US$ million)	2,899.5	3,216.4	3,330.8
Tourism receipts (US$ million)	1,279.0	1,432.1	1,106.2
Tourist spending (US$ million)	227.0	197.9	156.0

Average household size 2001 (persons)	4.86					
Urban population 2001 (%)	56.6					
Age analysis (%) (2001)	*0-14*	32.0	*15-64*	60.9	*65+*	7.1
Population by sex (%) (2001)	*Male*	49.6	*Female*	50.4		
Life expectancy (years) (2001)	*Male*	73.5	*Female*	77.6		
Infant mortality (deaths per '000 live births) (2001)	20.5					
Adult literacy (%) (1997)	85.5					

TRADING PARTNERS

Major export destinations 2001 (% share)		Major import sources 2001 (% share)	
USA	31.0	USA	44.9
CANADA	14.4	TRINIDAD AND TOBAGO	10.2
UNITED KINGDOM	10.6	MEXICO	4.8
NORWAY	7.6	VENEZUELA	3.9

▧ Japan

Area (km²) 369,700

Currency Yen (∅ = 100 sen)

Location Located (at its nearest point) 150km east of the Korean peninsula and about 1,500 km northeast of the Chinese mainland, Japan is situated in the northern Pacific Ocean with the Sea of Japan to its east. The country mainly comprises four volcanic islands - Hokkaido, Honshu, Shikoku and Kyushu, of which Honshu is the largest. There are also a considerable number of smaller islands. The climate is temperate, with mild winters. The capital is Tokyo.

Head of State HM Emperor Akihito (1989)

Head of Government Junichiro Koizumi (2001)

Ruling Party The Liberal Democratic Party (LDP) leads a coalition.

Political Structure Japan is a constitutional monarchy in which the Emperor Akihito plays only a ceremonial role. All political power is vested in a Diet (Parliament). Parliament includes a 480-member House of Representatives elected by universal suffrage for a term of four years, and a 247-member House of Councillors that serves a 6-year term of office with half of its members coming up for election every three years.

Last Elections In elections to the House of Representatives held in June 2000, the LDP lost support, winning 233 seats (down from 271 in the previous parliament). Elections to the House of Councillors were held in July 2001. The LDP won 110 seats, the Social-Democratic Party won 59 seats, the Communist Party of Japan won 20 seats and the remainder were scattered among various other parties.

Political Risk The country has too many banks, which are chronically weak and heavily burdened by bad loans. These loans stand at around ∅37 trillion (roughly 7% of GDP) but the true figure is more than twice that sum. Disaster has been predicted for Japan's banks for years and has not happened. However, there is clearly a big risk. Japan's fortunes are closely tied not just with Asia's but also those of the US. At a minimum, 30 to 50 heavily indebted companies would be casualties but the number could be much larger. The country's deflation greatly complicates the banking problem. Many companies - over 2,000 of Japan's 3,700 listed businesses - are not investing but merely paying down their debts. The reason they must do this (even when interest rates are low) is to clean up their balance sheets, which have been thrown into disarray by the fall in asset prices.

International Disputes Japan had a territorial dispute with the former Soviet Union, concerning the ownership of the four southern Kurile islands which were seized by the USSR after World War II and now administered by Russia. The Senkaku Islands are administered by Japan but are claimed by China and Taiwan. The country still struggles to address its record of barbarism in Korea, Malaysia and mainland China during the 1930s and 1940s. Tensions with North Korea rose in 2001 after a Korean warship violated Japan's waters.

Economy GDP is expected to contract by about 1% in 2002 and grow by less than 1% in 2003. Meanwhile, prices will fall by more than 1% in 2002 and decline another 0.5% in 2003. The cyclical downturn, however, should gradually come to an end as exports recover and inventories reach low levels. With a favourable exchange rate, profitability should improve, leading to a stabilisation of business investment. Challenges in the future, however, remain significant. Intensified corporate restructuring is likely to lower employment and household incomes, keeping consumption growth weak. Major downside risks arise from financial sector weakness and rapidly rising public debt, both of which could lift longer-term interest rates, intensify deflation and reduce activity. Monetary policy should continue to provide ample liquidity, through the use of a broader range of instruments. Fiscal consolidation needs a clear medium-term strategy to contain the increase in public debt and raise household confidence, while short-term fiscal stimulus should be avoided. Planned structural reforms should be implemented without delay.

Main Industries Japanese agriculture is steadily contracting. Efficiency is hampered by the small and scattered nature of farmlands and by inordinately high input costs. Most industries are performing poorly. Key to these developments has been the information technology sector, which not only contributed to the rapid growth of exports in 1999 and 2000 but also underpinned investment as capacity rapidly expanded. The sector accounted for over a half of the decline in industrial production in the first half of 2001 and, through reduced investment demand, weakness has been transmitted to the capital goods sector. As the need to cut costs has become increasingly severe, manufacturers have begun to look for ways to bring in high-quality, low-cost components and materials from foreign suppliers. Should this trend continue, overseas suppliers would see new opportunities in some areas of the Japanese market, although they will be challenged to supply products at competitive prices. By the year 2025, more than one of every four Japanese will be 65 or older (up from about one in every six in 2002). As a result, manufacturers are designing production to minimise labour inputs and ensure increased demand for capital-intensive, high value-added manufacturing.

Energy Japan contains almost no oil reserves of its own but is the world's second largest oil consumer. In 2001, Japan consumed an estimated 5.44 million barrels per day (bbl/d) of oil, down from 5.53 million bbl/d in 2000. Most (75-80%) of this oil came from OPEC exporters in the Middle East. Japan has worked - with relatively little success - to diversify its oil import sources away from the Middle East. Since 1997, the country's oil consumption has declined as its economic slump caused demand by industrial and other users to fall. In 2002, Japan had 4.8 million bbl/d of oil refining capacity at 33 refineries, down from five million bbl/d on 2001. As Japan's petroleum product consumption has stagnated, the country's refining industry has suffered from overcapacity. Japan also began to allow imports of petroleum products in the mid-1990s, putting additional pressure on Japanese refiners to cut costs and become internationally competitive.

	1999	2000	2001
Inflation (% change)	-0.3	-0.7	-0.7
Exchange rate (per US$)	113.91	107.77	121.53
Interest rate (% per annum, lending rate)	2.2	2.1	2.0
GDP (% real growth)	0.7	2.2	-0.4
GDP (Billion units of national currency)	512,434.8	513,822.2	504,181.0
GDP (US$ million)	4,498,712.3	4,767,987.3	4,148,647.4
GDP per capita (US$)	35,473.4	37,552.6	32,663.0
Consumption (Billion units of national currency)	299,113.9	303,547.5	303,710.3
Consumption (US$ million)	2,625,948.3	2,816,754.4	2,499,076.6
Consumption per capita (US$)	20,706.2	22,184.7	19,675.7
Population, mid-year ('000)	126,819.2	126,968.4	127,013.6
Birth rate (per '000)	9.6	9.5	9.4
Death rate (per '000)	7.9	8.0	8.2
No. of households ('000)	46,207.0	47,031.0	47,689.8
Total exports (US$ million)	419,367.0	479,249.0	403,496.0
Total imports (US$ million)	311,262.0	379,511.0	350,095.0
Tourism receipts (US$ million)	3,428.0	3,962.8	2,736.4
Tourist spending (US$ million)	32,808.0	35,629.2	28,763.6

Average household size 2001 (persons)	2.70				
Urban population 2001 (%)	79.0				
Age analysis (%) (2001)	*0-14*	14.6	*15-64*	68.1	*65+*	17.3
Population by sex (%) (2001)	*Male*	48.9	*Female*	51.1	
Life expectancy (years) (2001)	*Male*	77.6	*Female*	84.7	
Infant mortality (deaths per '000 live births) (2001)	3.4				
Adult literacy (%) (1997)	99.0				

TRADING PARTNERS

Major export destinations 2001 (% share) **Major import sources 2001 (% share)**

Export destination	%	Import source	%
USA	30.3	USA	17.8
CHINA	7.8	CHINA	16.2
SOUTH KOREA	6.2	SOUTH KOREA	4.9
HONG KONG, CHINA	5.7	INDONESIA	4.5

Jordan

Area (km^2)   90,650

Currency   Jordanian dinar (JD = 1,000 fils)

Location   The Hashemite Kingdom of Jordan lies just to the east of Israel, at the eastern end of the Mediterranean, and would have been landlocked by the creation of Israel in 1948 if it did not have access to a narrow channel running into the Red Sea. Jordan is bounded in the north by Syria, in the south by Saudi Arabia and in the east by Iraq. It lost much of its West Bank territory to Israel after the 1967 war. The capital is Amman.

Head of State   King Abdullah ibn Hussein as-Hashemi (1999)

Head of Government   Ali Abu Ragheb (1999)

Ruling Party   The Parliamentary Arab-Islamic Coalition Front, a coalition of Islamic groups and nationalists.

Political Structure   Jordan is a constitutional monarchy in which the King plays an especially active role. In February 1999, King Hussein ibn Talal died after ruling the country for more than 40 years. Just before his death, he appointed his son, Abdullah, to succeed him. Jordan has a bicameral national Assembly. A Chamber of Deputies, made up of 80 members, is directly elected while the king appoints a Senate of 40 members. Political parties were legalised in July 1992.

Last Elections   Parliamentary elections were held in November 1997. Most of the 524 candidates for Jordan's 80-member parliament were independents or tribal leaders, running on local issues rather the grander questions of peace with Israel. Non-partisans won 76 of the 80 seats. Nine opposition parties, led by the Islamic Action Front (IAF), boycotted the election. The IAF called the boycott in protest at the peace treaty with Israel and a new restrictive press law. The IAF's real grievance, however, was the government's refusal to change Jordan's electoral laws which favour rural communities where its support is strong.

Political Risk   Jordan has long been one of the more stable countries in a highly unstable region. King Abdullah enjoys warm support, both in Jordan and in the West and is dedicated to economic reform. There are worries that social unrest will increase, driven in part by the growing conflict between the Palestinians and Israelis.

International Disputes   In the past, Jordan enjoyed moderately good relations with Israel. However, the government has had to shift its policies in order to maintain its relations with other Arab countries. The King appears determined to build on that base to develop even closer relationships in the future. The country is strongly opposed to a possible US attack on Iraq.

Economy   GDP rose by 4.2% in 2001 and will increase by another 5.1% in 2002. Growth in 2003 is expected to be 6%. Prices increased by 1.8% in 2001 and should rise by 3.5% in 2002. Inflation in 2003 will be 2.4%. After a decade of declining living standards, a somewhat stronger economic performance will be a welcome relief for Jordan's young king who faces a stifling bureaucracy and a web of vested interests and other obstacles to liberalisation. However, Jordan needs even faster growth to absorb the unemployed, which are estimated to exceed 20%. The country's budget deficit is another serious concern. Excluding grants, in mid-2002 it stood at a high 7.5% of GDP. The government hopes to bring the budget deficit under control by 2005 but policymakers have limited room for manoeuvre. About 70% of the budget is tied up in military spending, interest payments on Jordan's US$7.2 billion of foreign debt, wages and pensions. Revenues, meanwhile, will come under increased pressure as Jordan brings down trade barriers and implements free-trade accords, including one signed with the EU to create a Mediterranean free-trade zone by 2010. To compensate, a value-added tax has been introduced, following on the reform of the general sales tax. Ultimately, Jordan's economy remains a hostage to wider developments in the Middle East. Events in Iraq, Israel and Palestinian territories have significant effects on the country.

Main Industries   Jordan's economy relies mainly on farming, with smallholders producing wheat, barley, olives, lentils, tobacco, fruit and vegetables. A persistent shortage of water and a lack of irrigation facilities keep farm productivity low and prevent any large-scale operations. The country is seeking to increase its fresh water supplies, as its underground aquifers are being depleted as the country's water consumption rises along with the rapidly growing population. One proposal is for a US$5 billion canal linking the Red Sea with the Dead Sea, where desalination plants would produce water for consumption in Israel and Jordan. Typically, the country is able to meet only a quarter of its food needs. A privatisation programme has been undertaken to reduce the government's stake in sectors of the economy previously dominated by state-controlled firms. The government sold a 40% stake in the Jordan Telecommunications Company in 2000, in the most significant privatisation to date. Oil and electric power generation, as well as the country's large phosphate and potash industries, also are targeted for privatisation. As part of its preparations for admission to the WTO, Jordan lifted in 2000 most limits on foreign ownership of formerly state-owned companies. The country's large phosphate and potash industries are also slated for privatisation. The manufacturing sector is well diversified with production of cement, steel, glass, paints, plastics, fertilisers, food products and pharmaceuticals being prominent. Almost all manufacturing firms are small and few are capable of exporting. Amman is also working hard to develop its tourism sector but the number of visitors is falling drastically in 2002.

Energy   Jordan has no significant oil resources of its own, and relies on Iraqi oil for nearly all of its needs (currently around 100,000 barrels per day - bbl/d). Jordan's oil imports from Iraq are permitted by the United Nations under a special dispensation from the general UN embargo. Jordan has one refinery, at Zarqa, with a capacity of 90,400 bbl/d. An expansion of the facility to a capacity of 150,000 bbl/d is under consideration, but has not yet been implemented. Jordan does possess a significant quantity of oil shale resources, possibly as much as 40 billion tonnes. Foreign investors have conducted limited exploration digging in the Lajjun area, southwest of Amman, and are currently negotiating with the Jordanian government on the possible development of an oil shale extraction facility. If the project is implemented, it could be in production by 2006 at a rate of 17,000 bbl/d.

	1999	2000	2001
Inflation (% change)	0.6	0.7	1.8
Exchange rate (per US$)	0.71	0.71	0.71
Interest rate (% per annum, lending rate)	12.3	11.8	10.9
GDP (% real growth)	3.1	4.0	4.2
GDP (Million units of national currency)	5,767.0	5,992.0	6,260.0
GDP (US$ million)	8,134.0	8,451.3	8,829.5
GDP per capita (US$)	1,631.1	1,643.1	1,670.9
Consumption (Million units of national currency)	4,718.2	5,287.8	5,506.7
Consumption (US$ million)	6,654.7	7,458.2	7,767.0
Consumption per capita (US$)	1,334.5	1,450.0	1,469.8
Population, mid-year ('000)	4,986.7	5,143.5	5,284.3
Birth rate (per '000)	33.8	33.5	33.2
Death rate (per '000)	4.5	4.4	4.4
No. of households ('000)	808.8	835.2	855.0
Total exports (US$ million)	1,831.9	1,897.5	2,179.7
Total imports (US$ million)	3,716.8	4,538.9	4,423.0
Tourism receipts (US$ million)	795.0	857.2	518.7
Tourist spending (US$ million)	355.0	470.5	367.8

Average household size 2001 (persons)	6.16				
Urban population 2001 (%)	74.2				
Age analysis (%) (2001)	*0-14*	38.6	*15-64*	58.9	*65+* 2.5
Population by sex (%) (2001)	*Male*	52.3	*Female*	47.7	
Life expectancy (years) (2001)	*Male*	69.4	*Female*	72.1	
Infant mortality (deaths per '000 live births) (2001)	24.0				
Adult literacy (%) (1997)	87.2				

TRADING PARTNERS

Major export destinations 2001 (% share)		Major import sources 2001 (% share)	
INDIA	18.4	GERMANY	9.5
USA	15.1	USA	8.4
SAUDI ARABIA	8.9	ITALY	6.0
ISRAEL	5.8	FRANCE	6.0

Kazakhstan

Area (km^2) 2,717,300

Currency Tenge

Location Until it achieved independence in 1991, Kazakhstan was one of the largest states in the old USSR. Lying directly to the south of Russia, it extends some 2,500km from the Caspian Sea in the west to the Chinese/Mongolian border in the east, and borders on the almost dried out Aral Sea and Lake Balkash. The land is mainly of steppe type, or of desert, and is richly endowed with minerals. The capital is Astana.

Head of State President Nursultan Nazarbayev (1991)

Head of Government Kasymzhomart Tokayev (1999)

Ruling Party Republican Party Otan (OTAN)

Political Structure Kazakhstan declared its independence only in October 1990, having tried in vain to campaign for the vanishing Soviet Union. The president is elected for a 5-year term by the people. Parliament has two chambers. The Assembly has 67 seats, elected for a 4-year term in single-seat constituencies. The Senate has 47 members, 40 members elected for a 4-year term in double-seat constituencies by the local assemblies, half renewed every two years, and seven presidential appointees.

Last Elections Presidential elections took place in January 1999 when Nazarbayev received 80% of the vote. In October 1999, elections to the Assembly gave 23 seats to the OTAN, 13 seats to the Civil Party of Kazakhstan, with the remainder distributed among small parties and non-aligned candidates. Elections to the Senate were held in January 1996. The Peoples' Party of Kazakhstan took 6 seats, the Democratic Party gained 5 seats and the remainder went to non-aligned candidates.

Political Risk Concerns about the role of radical Muslim groups, guns and drugs have diminished but are still a worry. In the past, experts estimated that 85% of Central Asia's drugs passed through the country. This flow could resume if drug producers in Afghanistan should once again begin large-scale operations. The government has eliminated much inefficiency but economists are worried about the country's vulnerability to large swings in the price of oil on world markets.

International Disputes Ethnic Kazakhs believe that the 1997 decision to move the country's capital from Almaty in the southeast to Astana in the north is a security measure to discourage Russian nationalists on both sides of the Russian-Kazakh border who want to redraw the northern border so that Kazakh Russians live in Russia. China and Kazakhstan have settled a long-running border dispute but have yet to agree on water rights concerning rivers that pass through both countries. The country has similar disputes with other neighbours.

Economy Kazakhstan's recovery seems set to continue with growth of 7% in 2002 and 5.1% in 2003. Inflation should fall to 6.4% in 2002 and decline further to 5.1% in 2003. The government continued its efforts in 2001 toward fiscal sustainability. A new tax code designed to broaden the tax base was approved by Parliament in 2001 and became effective in 2002. A number of tax exemptions were abolished and fiscal stimulus was provided through a lowering of the social insurance tax and VAT rates. In 2001, the government revised the state budget and increased revenues and expenditures: revenues mainly as a result of improved tax collection and buoyant prices for the country's major exports. As budget revenues remain sensitive to oil and other mineral prices, the government needs to restore fiscal balance in the coming years by expanding the tax base through diversifying the economy and accelerating privatisation. The government maintained its liberal trade policy, as accession to WTO remains a priority. Selected customs tariffs were abolished, and further simplification of the tariff system is expected.

Main Industries Manufacturing performed well in 2001 while production and exports of oil and other minerals were buoyed by high prices in the first three quarters of the year. However, the economy, dependent on a narrow range of exports, remains vulnerable to external factors. Agricultural output grew by 16.9%, compared with a contraction of 3.3% in 2000. Aided by good weather and an extension of the sown area, grain production increased by 37% in 2001 to 15.9 million tonnes from 11.6 million tonnes in 2000. Cotton production rose by 45% in 2001, also partly because of an extension of the sown area. The services sector accelerated to 13.6% growth in 2001 from 9.3% in the previous year as private sector activities in wholesale and retail trade, hotels, restaurants and housing continued to expand

Energy Kazakhstan has significant petroleum reserves, with estimates of proven reserves ranging from 5.4 billion to 17.6 billion barrels of oil. The country's possible reserves, both onshore and offshore, dwarf proven reserves. As a result, foreign investment has poured into the oil and gas sector, helping the country boost its oil production from 530,000 barrels per day (bbl/d) in 1992 to 803,000 bbl/d in 2001. In order to reach its oil production potential, Kazakhstan has opened up its oil sector to privatisation and development by foreign energy companies. International oil projects took the form of joint ventures, as well as production-sharing agreements, and exploration/field concessions. With a number of major oil fields coming on-stream recently, including North Buzachi, Sazankurak, Saztobe, Chinarevskoye and Airankol, and with others such as Alibekmola, Urikhtau and Kozhasai set to begin producing shortly, Kazakhstan is set to ramp up its oil production over the next decade. Kazakh oil production is expected to reach 925,000 bbl/d in 2002, 1.2 million bbl/d in 2005 and potentially 3 million bbl/d by 2010.

	1999	2000	2001
Inflation (% change)	8.4	13.3	8.4
Exchange rate (per US$)	119.52	142.13	146.74
Interest rate (% per annum, lending rate)	23.7	19.4	
GDP (% real growth)	2.8	9.4	9.0
GDP (Billion units of national currency)	2,016.5	2,599.9	3,285.4
GDP (US$ million)	16,870.9	18,292.0	22,390.0
GDP per capita (US$)	1,039.0	1,130.0	1,388.0
Consumption (Billion units of national currency)	1,416.1	1,679.0	1,921.1
Consumption (US$ million)	11,848.3	11,813.1	13,092.5
Consumption per capita (US$)	729.7	729.8	811.6
Population, mid-year ('000)	16,237.3	16,187.2	16,131.5
Birth rate (per '000)	16.7	16.6	16.5
Death rate (per '000)	10.0	10.1	10.1
No. of households ('000)	4,152.7	4,011.0	3,930.6
Total exports (US$ million)	5,598.0	9,125.5	8,750.0
Total imports (US$ million)	3,686.5	5,050.7	6,445.0
Tourism receipts (US$ million)	363.0	370.4	411.7
Tourist spending (US$ million)	394.0	362.9	362.9

Average household size 2001 (persons)	4.04				
Urban population 2001 (%)	56.6				
Age analysis (%) (2001)	*0-14*	27.2	*15-64*	65.5	*65+* 7.3
Population by sex (%) (2001)	*Male*	48.7	*Female*	51.3	
Life expectancy (years) (2001)	*Male*	59.3	*Female*	70.5	
Infant mortality (deaths per '000 live births) (2001)	43.1				
Adult literacy (%)					

TRADING PARTNERS

Major export destinations 2001 (% share)		Major import sources 2001 (% share)	
RUSSIA	16.6	RUSSIA	30.6
BERMUDA	14.9	GERMANY	5.9
GERMANY	9.5	CHINA	3.3
CHINA	8.7	ITALY	2.8

Kenya

Area (km²) 582,645

Currency Kenya shilling (Ksh = 100 cents)

Location Kenya lies on the Indian Ocean coast of central East Africa, where it is bounded in the north by Eritrea, Ethiopia, Sudan and Somalia, in the west by Uganda and in the south by Tanzania. Although subject to occasional drought, the country has an equable climate and numerous major watercourses. The capital is Nairobi.

Head of State President Daniel arap Moi

Head of Government President Daniel arap Moi

Ruling Party Kenya African National Union (KANU)

Political Structure Kenya has an executive presidency; however, the current president (Moi) exerts an almost unchallenged level of influence over the country's affairs. There is a multi-party system but the president has used his extensive personal powers to frustrate — and even imprison — many opponents. In late 1997, parliament approved several constitutional amendments, including changes that would allow a coalition government and permit an electoral commission. The president is elected for a 5-year term by the people. The National Assembly has 224 members, 210 members elected for 5-year terms in single-seat constituencies, 12 members appointed and 2 ex officio members.

Last Elections Presidential elections took place in a chaotic atmosphere in December 1997 when President Moi was returned to office with 40% of the total vote. Legislative elections at the same time gave Moi's KANU party a much-reduced majority with 114 seats in parliament.

Political Risk A fifth of all Kenyans are poorer today than when Moi assumed power in 1978. The government is almost totally corrupt. Roads and sewers have been allowed to crumble and rust. Corruption and illegal paybacks supplement the salary of members of the National Assembly by 700% (a generous US$120,000 a year) and the money keeps them in office. The level of political violence remains high, with much of it being orchestrated by KANU. Both KANU and the president are uninterested in economic reform, contemptuous of political pluralism and unconcerned about corruption. According to the government, 8% of the adult population is HIV-positive but foreign experts believe the number is more than twice as high.

International Disputes Kenya's border with Somalia is disputed but the issue has been dormant for more than a decade. The government of Sudan accuses Kenya of supporting the rebels fighting in the south of that country. In 2002, the Kenyan military made several excursions into Sudan.

Economy GDP grew by 1.1% in 2001 and should increase by 1.4% in 2002. Growth in 2003 is expected to be 2.4%. Inflation was 0.8% in 2001 and will be 3.2% in 2002. Prices are expected to rise by 3.9% in 2003. Kenya's economic performance during the past decade has been well below its potential. This reflects the failure to sustain prudent macroeconomic policies and the slow pace of structural reform. Consequently, Kenya's real per capita GDP is now lower than it was in 1990 and poverty is much more prevalent. In recent years, the HIV/AIDS pandemic has been incapacitating and killing an increasing number of the population and imposing a rising social and economic burden. Structural reforms are crucial, but Kenya has made little or no progress since 2000. The country's lax fiscal policy has led to a rapid buildup of short-term government debt. These problems, together with other high costs of doing business in Kenya - because of corruption, a deteriorating infrastructure and an inefficient parastatal sector (eg, utilities, and transportation services) - have significantly reduced investment.

Main Industries The agricultural sector remains the cornerstone of the economy, accounting for over a quarter of GDP and more than 70% of the workforce. Coffee, tea, cotton, sugar, tobacco and pyrethrum are produced for export. Domestic crops include maize, sorghum, cassava and beans, and there are substantial livestock herds. Kenyan agriculture has been hit by four years of drought and the effects were still being felt in 2002. It wiped out many herds and left four million dependent on international food aid. Kenya's infrastructure is also crumbling. Roads and railways are not always useable while electricity, telephones and postal services are erratic. Meanwhile, the government has bungled its privatisation programme and scandal haunts the private sector. Tourism, traditionally Kenya's biggest foreign-exchange earner (along with tea) now earns much less than in years past. Political uncertainties, together with the poor management of the country's game reserves and the growth of crime, have handicapped the sector. Manufacturing provides 15-20% of GDP but attracts very little foreign investment. Beside the normal food processing activities, Kenya has a significant engineering industry along with textiles, glass and construction materials.

Energy Kenya has no oil of its own, and must import all of its 50,000 bbl/d consumption. The government recently stepped up efforts aimed at attracting partners to assist with oil exploration in the country. Recent oil surveys have indicated that more than half of the country has oil potential. Limited oil exploration has been going on for the last 40 years, but only 30 wells have been drilled so far with little success.

	1999	2000	2001
Inflation (% change)	3.5	6.2	0.8
Exchange rate (per US$)	70.33	76.18	78.56
Interest rate (% per annum, commercial lending rate)	22.4	22.3	19.7
GDP (% real growth)	1.3	-0.2	1.1
GDP (Million units of national currency)	740,330.0	788,917.0	824,951.0
GDP (US$ million)	10,527.1	10,356.6	10,500.5
GDP per capita (US$)	355.4	344.3	3,296.9
Consumption (Million units of national currency)	536,389.0	553,304.6	575,961.2
Consumption (US$ million)	7,627.2	7,263.6	7,331.2
Consumption per capita (US$)	257.5	241.5	2,301.8
Population, mid-year ('000)	29,622.5	30,080.0	3,185.0
Birth rate (per '000)	35.0	34.7	34.4
Death rate (per '000)	12.6	13.0	13.3
No. of households ('000)	6,630.9	6,687.2	6,988.0
Total exports (US$ million)	1,747.2	1,733.9	1,797.3
Total imports (US$ million)	2,832.3	3,105.5	3,214.8
Tourism receipts (US$ million)	304.0	433.0	320.9
Tourist spending (US$ million)	115.0	95.4	93.6

Average household size 2001 (persons)	4.50				
Urban population 2001 (%)	34.0				
Age analysis (%) (2001)	0-14	44.4	15-64	52.6	65+ 3.0
Population by sex (%) (2001)	Male	50.2	Female	49.8	
Life expectancy (years) (2001)	Male	49.3	Female	50.7	
Infant mortality (deaths per '000 live births) (2001)	60.4				
Adult literacy (%) (1997)	79.3				

TRADING PARTNERS

Major export destinations 2001 (% share)

UGANDA	17.6
UNITED KINGDOM	12.6
NETHERLANDS	6.6
PAKISTAN	5.7

Major import sources 2001 (% share)

USA	16.4
UNITED ARAB EMIRATES	10.7
SAUDI ARABIA	7.8
SOUTH AFRICA	7.1

▦ Kiribati

Area (km^2)   684

Currency   Australian dollar (A$ = 100 cents)

Location   Kiribati, the former Gilbert Islands, is a group of 33 islands and atolls in the southwest central Pacific, of which the largest is Banaban, the former Ocean Island. The climate is warm and equable, but the terrain is extremely flat, seldom rising more than 4m above sea level. The capital is Bairiki.

Head of State   President Teburoro Tito (October 1994)

Head of Government   President Teburoro Tito (October 1994)

Ruling Party   Maneaban Te Mauri (MTM) Party

Political Structure   Kiribati (pronounced Kiribass) is an independent republic within the Commonwealth. The people elect the executive president for a 4-year term. The House of Assembly has 41 members, 39 elected for 4-year terms in single-seat and multi-seat constituencies, 1 delegate from Banaba Island and 1 ex offico member.

Last Elections   Presidential elections were held in December 1998 when Tito regained his office with 52% of the vote. Elections to the House of Assembly were held in September 1998. The MTM took 14 seats in the Assembly, the Boutokanto Koaua Party won 11 seats and the remainder were spread among minor parties.

Political Risk   A major source of conflict has been the protracted bid by the residents of Banaban Island to secede to have their island placed under the protection of Fiji. The government's attempts to placate the Banabans include specific provisions in the constitution, such as giving them a seat in the house of assembly and returning to them land on Banaban acquired by the government for phosphate mining. Kiribati's legislative system has been under scrutiny following allegations of electoral fraud.

International Disputes   Kiribati's relations with Fiji are problematic, given the Banabans' desire to secede and place themselves under Fijian protection.

Economy   Kiribati's economy has been growing rather slowly in recent years and the pace decelerated in 2001. Prospects are for growth of only 1-1.5% in 2002. Meanwhile, inflation jumped to more than 7% in 2001 (owing largely to an increase in energy prices). The rate of price increase in the next couple of years is expected to be about 2.7%. The economy strengthened during 2001 as government expenditures grew and copra production recovered. The economy is dominated by the public sector and is likely to remain reasonably stable over the medium term given the anticipated continued high level of government expenditures. Key emerging issues are the shift to an expansionary fiscal stance and an apparent change in attitude to the use of earnings of the country's trust fund. The Revenue Equalization Reserve Fund (RERF) has almost tripled in value over the past 10 years and, by the end of 2001, stood at US$329 million. All funds are currently invested in offshore markets, and so declined in value a little during 2001 due to the downturn in world equity markets. The RERF is designed to maintain its real per capita value over time, but good returns over recent years allowed a US$7 million drawdown of income - the first since 1997 - to fund government expenditures during the year. Fiscal management has tended to be conservative in Kiribati but has now shifted to an expansionary stance. The deficit, very small in 2000, grew substantially in 2001 to 37.5% of GDP. A large part of the additional expenditure in 2001 was attributed to a higher wages and salaries bill, higher subsidies to government-owned businesses and the copra industry, payments for landing craft and a large contribution to development projects.

Main Industries   Kiribati's small-scale economy relies heavily on its agricultural sector, which produces copra and fish for world markets. The 2001 fishing season turned out much better than initially expected, and licence fees reached a record level of US$22 million, representing more than half the revenues raised locally over the year. Nearly 20% of the formally employed labour force work on foreign merchant or fishing vessels and generate a substantial amount of factor income. This is an important source of income, particularly for people from the outer islands where poverty levels are higher and opportunities for formal employment are very limited. The copra industry too provides an important source of income on the outer islands. For many years, funds from Stabex - an EU scheme to stabilise export earnings - have been used to subsidize the copra price but these funds were largely exhausted in 2000. The government has since pledged to fund the subsidy itself, which amounted to US$2 million in 2001. In addition, it has committed US$2 million to build a copra mill. The mill, to be operated by a private firm, is intended to increase value added from Kiribati's copra and reduce the subsidy required.

Energy   Kiribati's limited energy needs are met in part by domestic resources such as fuel wood and brushwood. Otherwise, all requirements have to be imported.

	1999	2000	2001
Inflation (% change)	2.0	3.0	7.1
Exchange rate (per US$)	1.55	1.72	1.93
Interest rate			
GDP (% real growth)	2.5	2.0	1.5
GDP (Million units of national currency)	74.4	74.2	83.1
GDP (US$ million)	48.0	43.0	43.0
GDP per capita (US$)	585.4	518.1	505.9
Consumption (Million units of national currency)	41.6	47.0	51.0
Consumption (US$ million)	26.9	27.2	26.4
Consumption per capita (US$)	327.5	328.2	310.3
Population, mid-year ('000)	82.0	83.0	85.0
Birth rate (per '000)	27.5	27.2	26.9
Death rate (per '000)	7.6	7.5	7.4
No. of households ('000)	14.2	14.3	14.3
Total exports (US$ million)	6.0	165.0	24.0
Total imports (US$ million)	35.0	41.0	36.0
Tourism receipts (US$ million)	1.5	1.9	
Tourist spending (US$ million)			

Average household size 2001 (persons)	5.82				
Urban population 2001 (%)	39.7				
Age analysis (%) (2001)	*0-14*	34.5	*15-64*	52.5	*65+* 13.0
Population by sex (%) (2001)	*Male*	51.3	*Female*	48.7	
Life expectancy (years) (2001)	*Male*	57.2	*Female*	63.1	
Infant mortality (deaths per '000 live births) (2001)	50.1				
Adult literacy (%)					

TRADING PARTNERS

Major export destinations 2001 (% share)		Major import sources 2001 (% share)	
JAPAN	45.9	AUSTRALIA	28.0
THAILAND	24.2	POLAND	16.6
SOUTH KOREA	10.4	FIJI	15.7
BANGLADESH	5.3	USA	10.0

Kuwait

Area (km^2)   24,280

Currency   Kuwaiti dinar (= 10 dirhams)

Location   The tiny state of Kuwait includes a mainland area and several small islands. It lies at a strategically important point on the northern extreme of the Persian (Arabian) Gulf, which allows it to serve as a transhipment point for oil supplies from Saudi Arabia (and formerly Iraq). Lacking any fresh river water or other natural water supplies, it is obliged to manufacture its own through massive desalination plants. The greater part of the population lives in the capital, Kuwait City.

Head of State   HH Shaikh Jaber al-Ahmed al-Sabah

Head of Government   HH Sheikh Saad Abdullah al-Salem al-Sabah

Ruling Party   There are no political parties in Kuwait.

Political Structure   Kuwait became an independent state in 1961, having been a British protectorate since 1899. The Emir exercises almost complete political control. In 1986, he dissolved the National Assembly (Parliament), and ruled by decree for some years thereafter. In April 1991, following the Gulf War, the Emir appointed an interim government and the democratic process was later resumed. The National Assembly has 50 members elected for 4-year terms in double-seat constituencies and the ministers who sit as ex-officio members. The Emir again dissolved the National Assembly in 1999 in an effort to end a long paralysis between parliament and government. In May 1999, he decreed that women could vote and stand in elections, with the same rights as men.

Last Elections   Elections to the National Assembly took place in July 1999. Only non-partisans were allowed to stand. The country is the only one in the Gulf to have an elected legislature — a source of great pride for Kuwaitis.

Political Risk   The emir has suffered a stroke while both the crown prince, Sheikh Saad al-Abdullan and the prime minister have cancer. For now, Kuwait's foreign minister has been named acting price minister and is effectively running the country. The issue of who will take over the country when its present generation dies is a delicate one with important ramifications.

International Disputes   Iraq has renounced its territorial claims on Kuwait, but many remain uneasy about Iraq's long-term motives. Kuwait's mutual boundary with Saudi Arabia has never been adequately defined to the two countries' mutual satisfaction, although there is no serious hostility over the issue. Kuwait maintains close ties with Saudi Arabia as well as with several powerful Western nations. This gives it a high measure of security. There are persistent allegations of human rights abuses, especially against the large immigrant population, which performs most of the manual labour in the country.

Economy   GDP grew by 2.7% in 2001 but is expected to contract by 1.8% in 2002. In 2003, growth of 3.3% is forecast. Inflation was 2.5% in 2001 and should be the same in both 2002 and 2003. As one of the world's leading oil producing states, Kuwait's economy is heavily dependent on oil revenues. With the rebound in oil prices since late 1999, Kuwait has reaped a revenue windfall. Kuwait recorded a record trade surplus and a large budget surplus (of around US$5-6 billion) in 2001. Every year, the government siphons off 10% of its revenues to the Fund for Future Generations. The country's savings abroad amounts to US$200,000 for every citizen. But with population growing by 3.5% a year, the state is always hard pressed to keep its people in the style they expect. This includes free health and education, generous housing, cheap petrol, power and water, subsidised food and a job for the asking. Kuwait's other investments abroad - which contribute substantial income to the government - have been falling sharply as world markets slide. The government's own desire for reform appears to fluctuate with the price of oil. When prices fall, there is talk of reducing the burden on the state. An estimated 93% of all Kuwaitis work in the public sector. Their incomes are unlikely to change in the medium-term whatever the level of international oil prices or returns on foreign investments. Kuwait, today, looks much like it did before Iraqi troops sacked its towns and put its oilfields to the torch.

Main Industries   The period of low oil prices in 1998 and early 1999 spurred the Kuwaiti government to move towards reducing government subsidies, which provide many services to Kuwaiti citizens at little or no cost. Even with the recent rise in oil prices, these efforts have continued. Kuwait hopes to attract additional foreign investment, and as part of this effort is considering a reduction in the income tax cap on non-Kuwaiti companies from 55% to 25%. Kuwait has started a programme to privatise state-owned businesses (outside the oil sector) as a way of reducing subsidies. As part of this programme, the Kuwaiti government has begun privatising healthcare, electricity and telecommunications assets. Privatisation is complicated by the need to protect the jobs of Kuwaiti citizens, who are employed in state-owned enterprises and the government. In 2001, the government introduced an economic reform package which, among other things, eases restrictions on foreign banks, provides long-term protection to foreign investors against nationalisation or confiscation, and eliminates the requirement for foreign companies to have a Kuwaiti sponsor or partner. In the oil sector, the constitution forbids foreign ownership of mineral resources, but the government may allow foreign investment in upstream oil development under terms which provide for per-barrel fees rather than traditional production sharing agreements.

Energy   Kuwait contains 96.5 billion barrels of proven oil reserves (including its share of the Neutral Zone), or roughly 9% of the world's total oil reserves. Along with Saudi Arabia and the United Arab Emirates, Kuwait remains one of the few oil-producing countries with significant excess oil production capacity. Most of Kuwait's oil reserves are located in the 70-billion barrel Greater Burgan area, which comprises the Burgan, Magwa and Ahmadi structures. Greater Burgan is widely considered the world's second largest oil field, surpassed only by Saudi Arabia's Ghawar field, and has been producing oil since 1938. Kuwait's Raudhatain, Sabriya and Minagish fields have large proven reserves as well, with 6 billion, 3.8 billion, and 2 billion barrels of oil, respectively.

	1999	2000	2001
Inflation (% change)	3.0	1.7	2.5
Exchange rate (per US$)	0.30	0.31	0.31
Interest rate (% per annum, lending rate)	8.6	8.9	7.9
GDP (% real growth)	-1.7	1.7	2.7
GDP (Million units of national currency)	9,075.0	11,590.0	10,903.0
GDP (US$ million)	29,811.3	37,783.0	35,565.3
GDP per capita (US$)	13,875.8	17,055.9	15,517.3
Consumption (Million units of national currency)	3,900.5	4,064.1	3,887.8
Consumption (US$ million)	12,813.1	13,248.9	12,682.0
Consumption per capita (US$)	5,963.9	5,980.8	5,533.2
Population, mid-year ('000)	2,148.4	2,215.2	2,292.0
Birth rate (per '000)	17.0	17.7	18.4
Death rate (per '000)	2.4	2.5	2.6
No. of households ('000)	257.6	263.8	269.5
Total exports (US$ million)	12,217.9	42,962.8	16,178.8
Total imports (US$ million)	7,616.8	7,156.9	7,324.4
Tourism receipts (US$ million)	243.0	213.2	178.4
Tourist spending (US$ million)	2,510.0	3,140.1	2,975.4

Average household size 2001 (persons)	8.40				
Urban population 2001 (%)	97.6				
Age analysis (%) (2001)	*0-14* 24.2		*15-64* 74.3		*65+* 1.5
Population by sex (%) (2001)	*Male* 59.1		*Female* 40.9		
Life expectancy (years) (2001)	*Male* 74.7		*Female* 78.8		
Infant mortality (deaths per '000 live births) (2001)	11.2				
Adult literacy (%) (1997)	80.4				

TRADING PARTNERS

Major export destinations 2001 (% share)

JAPAN	28.4
SOUTH KOREA	14.4
USA	14.2
SINGAPORE	8.7

Major import sources 2001 (% share)

USA	18.2
GERMANY	13.4
JAPAN	13.2
UNITED KINGDOM	10.3

▦ **Kyrgyzstan**

Area (km^2)　198,500

Currency　Som (= 200 roubles)

Location　Kyrgyzstan is a mountainous region lying in the northern part of Soviet Central Asia, and borders on China, from which it is separated by the Pamir-Altai mountain range. The capital is Bishkek.

Head of State　President Askar Akayev (1990)

Head of Government　Amangeldi Muraliev (1999)

Ruling Party　The government is formed by non-partisans, loyal to the president.

Political Structure　Kyrgyzstan declared independence in December 1990. The country has an executive president who is elected by universal suffrage for a maximum of two 5-year terms, and who leads a Cabinet of Ministers. The Supreme Council has two chambers. The Legislative Assembly has 45 members, elected for 5-year terms in single-seat constituencies. The Assembly of People's Representatives has 70 members, elected for 5-year terms in single-seat constituencies.

Last Elections　In presidential elections held in October 2000, Askar Akayev was returned to power with 74% of the vote. Elections to the Assembly of People's Representatives were held in February 2000. The Communist Party received 28% of the vote and 15 seats, the Union of Democratic Forces received 19% of the vote and 4 seats and the Women's' Democratic Party of Kyrgyzstan took 13% and 2 seats. The remaining votes were distributed among several parties. Voting for the Legislative Assembly took place at the same time, when all 45 elected officials were non-partisan.

Political Risk　The influence of Islamic insurgents has been diminished following the defeat of the Taliban in neighbouring Afghanistan. However, relations between the country's ethnic Uzbek and Kyrgyz populations remain tense. The country's per capita annual income is only about US$290. Such a low standard of living creates even more tension. Many investors nevertheless believe that these dangers are outweighed by the enormous potential of the country's mineral resources, but the risks are high. In 1996, the country joined a customs union with Russia, Kazakhstan and Belarus and signed a political-military treaty with Russia, China, Tajikistan and Kazakhstan intended to enhance mutual trust in the region.

International Disputes　Kyrgyzstan has uneasy relations with its neighbours as a result of disagreements over water rights, border incursions and political issues.

Economy　Growth of GDP is expected to be about 4.5% in both 2002 and 2003. Meanwhile, inflation should come down to 6.1% in 2002 and reach 5.5% in 2003. The macroeconomic situation stabilised in 2001 as the government pursued prudent fiscal and monetary policies and implemented key structural reforms. The recently concluded Paris Club meeting has addressed the short-term problems of debt burden and bunching of debt service payments. Long-term prospects depend on further debt rescheduling by bilateral creditors in 2004. The unemployment rate increased from 5.9% of the labour force in 1998, to 7.5% in 2000. The level of unemployment is not officially available, but on the basis of estimates of the registered unemployed, it seems that there has been very little reduction in unemployment in spite of robust growth in 2000-2001. However, poverty incidence has dropped, from 52% at the end of 2000 to 47.4% in September 2001, as a result of higher agricultural growth and stable food prices. This suggests that the insensitivity of the unemployment rate to significant growth may be the result of an increase in labour force participation rates. The high burden of public debt prevented the government from devoting more resources to consumption and investment expenditures. Total external debt was estimated to be about US$1.7 billion (112% of GDP) at the end of 2001, of which 55% was multilateral and 29% bilateral (owed mainly to Japan, the Russian Federation and Turkey), and the rest commercial debt. The debt service burden is high at around 30% of exports of goods and services.

Main Industries　In agriculture, which expanded by a healthy 6.8%, productivity growth and an expansion in the area under cultivation generated a large food grain harvest of 1.8 million tonnes. This was 16.3% higher than 2001's output and 12% more than the previous peak. However, the output of animal husbandry, important for the poorer mountainous regions, rose by only 2.2%. Though the industry sector grew by 5.4%, growth was uneven and masks the decline in the output of several subsectors. Excluding the metallurgical sector, whose gross production increased by 13.8%, industrial output fell by 1.6% in 2001 due to a significant decline in the output of power generation, agro-processing, oil refining and pharmaceuticals. A sharp drop in transport services restricted growth in the services sector to a modest 2.4%, reflecting the decline in both industrial and foreign trade activity. Gross domestic investment fell from 18% of GDP in 1999 to about 16% in 2000 due to a fall in the Public Investment Program, from 9% of GDP to 7% over this period. In 2001, the rate of investment declined further, by about 35%. The country is one of the largest producers of mercury and antimony, for which there is high demand in world markets. The mining sector is already the major source of foreign exchange.

Energy　With estimated petroleum reserves of only 40 million barrels, Kyrgyzstan is reliant on imports to meet its domestic supply needs. Kyrgyzstan has seven developed oil fields and two oil/gas fields, but due to the country's mountainous topography, extraction is difficult, and water encroachment means that recovery rates are low. In 2000, Kyrgyzstan produced an estimated 2,100 barrels per day (bbl/d) of oil. Although the country's oil consumption has declined sharply since 1992, when it consumed 32,500 bbl/d, Kyrgyzstan's estimated oil consumption in 2000 of 12,000 bbl/d still required imported supplies to meet domestic demand. Kyrgyzstan is looking to increase its oil production, and the government is undertaking a programme of intensive oil extraction in order to meet the country's domestic petroleum needs. As part of the programme, Kyrgyzstan is planning to produce 3,000 bbl/d by 2005.

	1999	2000	2001
Inflation (% change)	35.9	18.7	6.9
Exchange rate (per US$)	39.01	47.70	48.38
Interest rate (% per annum, lending rate)	60.9	51.9	37.3
GDP (% real growth)	3.7	5.0	5.0
GDP (Million units of national currency)	48,744.0	62,202.0	70,907.0
GDP (US$ million)	1,249.6	1,303.9	1,465.7
GDP per capita (US$)	269.1	279.3	312.3
Consumption (Million units of national currency)	37,848.2	49,952.2	55,766.2
Consumption (US$ million)	970.3	1,047.1	1,152.7
Consumption per capita (US$)	209.0	224.3	245.6
Population, mid-year ('000)	4,642.9	4,669.2	4,693.8
Birth rate (per '000)	22.1	21.5	21.0
Death rate (per '000)	7.4	7.3	7.2
No. of households ('000)	902.7	915.3	927.8
Total exports (US$ million)	455.0	505.0	560.0
Total imports (US$ million)	600.0	555.0	475.0
Tourism receipts (US$ million)	4.3	4.2	5.1
Tourist spending (US$ million)	3.3	4.4	4.8

Average household size 2001 (persons)	5.11				
Urban population 2001 (%)	33.3				
Age analysis (%) (2001)	*0-14*	34.8	*15-64*	59.2	*65+* 6.0
Population by sex (%) (2001)	*Male*	49.0	*Female*	51.0	
Life expectancy (years) (2001)	*Male*	64.2	*Female*	72.0	
Infant mortality (deaths per '000 live births) (2001)	39.2				
Adult literacy (%) (1997)	97.0				

TRADING PARTNERS

Major export destinations 2001 (% share)

GERMANY	23.8
UZBEKISTAN	18.6
RUSSIA	15.3
KAZAKHSTAN	9.7

Major import sources 2001 (% share)

RUSSIA	11.8
UZBEKISTAN	11.4
KAZAKHSTAN	8.7
CHINA	6.3

Laos

Area (km^2)   236,725

Currency   Kip (= 100 at)

Location   Laos runs from northeast to southwest through the northernmost part of the central Indochina peninsula. The country borders on China and Myanmar in the north, on Thailand in the west and on Cambodia in the south. In the east, Vietnam follows its entire length in such a way as to shut it off from the South China Sea. The country has a tropical and generally humid climate. The capital is Vientiane.

Head of State   President Khamtai Siphandone (1998)

Head of Government   Boungnang Vorachith (2001)

Ruling Party   Revolutionary People's Party of Laos (dictatorial communist)

Political Structure   The Lao Constitution, approved in August 1991, provides in principle for the creation of a National Assembly to be elected by universal suffrage and to serve for five years. The Assembly consists of 99 members and elects the executive President, who also serves for five years.

Last Elections   In parliamentary elections held in February 2002, the Revolutionary People's Party of Laos (PPPL) won 98 seats. Only one (approved) non-partisan candidate won a seat.

Political Risk   Evidence suggests that economic growth has had a positive effect on poverty reduction, not equitably though: between 1993 and 1998, per capita income grew by 25% but the proportion of poor people dropped only by seven percentage points. The gains that the poor might have expected to realise from economic growth have been reduced due to increased inequality. The government needs to address this problem in order to relieve social tensions. It must also undertake the structural reforms necessary to restore investor confidence and strengthen the economy's ability to withstand external shocks. Perhaps the most pressing problem is the weakness of the banking system.

International Disputes   Relations with neighbouring Thailand have been repeatedly strained by the high level of border activity involving Thai and Cambodian militias and the movement of drugs from Laos to Thailand.

Economy   GDP grew by 5.2% in 2001 and improvements are anticipated in 2002 and 2003 with growth rates of 5.8% and 6.1% respectively. Inflation, which peaked at 134% in 1999, dropped to 8% in 2001 and is expected to fall to 6.5% in 2002 and 6% in 2003. Laos is officially classified as a heavily indebted poor country, though official statistics overstate the seriousness of the country's foreign debt problem. Approximately half the debt is owed to the Russian Federation. This debt is carried on the books at an unrealistic exchange rate and is not currently being serviced. The governments of Laos and the Russian Federation are renegotiating the terms of the debt, which will lead to a significant reduction in its book value. Finance sector reform remains a priority for the economy. Currently, the system is dominated by three state-owned commercial banks and the Agriculture Promotion Bank, although foreign banks and joint ventures also operate, primarily in Vientiane. The percentage of non-performing loans is quite high. Exports are expected to increase by around 9% in both 2002 and 2003. Expenditures are forecast to rise to 22.8% of GDP by 2003. Further reforms in public expenditures should improve their quality, with a greater share going to recurrent expenses and human resources development.

Main Industries   Agriculture, which employs around 85% of the population and accounts for about half the economy, grew at an estimated rate of 3.9% in 2001. This represents a slowdown after several years of strong expansion, led by extensive investment in irrigation and increased (albeit informal) cross-border trade in agricultural commodities with neighbouring Thailand. Leading exports included timber and wood products, electricity (from hydropower plants) and garments. Industry remained the fastest-growing sector, with construction and garments playing a key role. The services sector, which accounts for about a quarter of the economy, also saw steady growth of around 6% in 2001. Tourism continued to play an important role, contributing both to GDP growth and the balance of payments. Tourism has strengthened steadily every year since the mid-1990s.

Energy   Laos manages to meet only a small proportion of its own oil needs, relying mainly on domestically mined coal. The country has a number of agreements to develop hydroelectric plants but work has been halted and the interest of foreign investors has diminished.

	1999	2000	2001
Inflation (% change)	134.0	27.1	7.8
Exchange rate (per US$)	7,102.02	7,887.64	8,954.58
Interest rate (% per annum, lending rate)	32.0	32.0	26.2
GDP (% real growth)	5.0	5.8	5.2
GDP (Billion units of national currency)	20,908.3	30,414.7	39,230.0
GDP (US$ million)	2,944.0	3,856.0	4,381.0
GDP per capita (US$)	570.2	728.0	807.0
Consumption (Billion units of national currency)	37.8	50.0	55.8
Consumption (US$ million)	5.3	6.3	6.2
Consumption per capita (US$)	1.0	1.2	1.1
Population, mid-year ('000)	5,163.1	5,296.7	5,428.8
Birth rate (per '000)	37.5	37.1	36.7
Death rate (per '000)	13.5	13.2	12.9
No. of households ('000)	983.8	999.1	1,003.7
Total exports (US$ million)	310.8	330.3	335.9
Total imports (US$ million)	524.8	500.0	437.0
Tourism receipts (US$ million)	97.0	148.6	125.6
Tourist spending (US$ million)	12.0	21.8	26.7

Average household size 2001 (persons)	5.37				
Urban population 2001 (%)	24.1				
Age analysis (%) (2001)	*0-14*	43.8	*15-64*	52.9	*65+* 3.3
Population by sex (%) (2001)	*Male*	50.4	*Female*	49.6	
Life expectancy (years) (2001)	*Male*	52.7	*Female*	55.2	
Infant mortality (deaths per '000 live births) (2001)	86.5				
Adult literacy (%) (1997)	58.6				

TRADING PARTNERS

Major export destinations 2001 (% share)

VIETNAM	41.8
THAILAND	14.9
FRANCE	6.2
GERMANY	4.7

Major import sources 2001 (% share)

THAILAND	52.0
VIETNAM	26.5
CHINA	5.7
SINGAPORE	3.3

▪ Latvia

Area (km^2) 64,589

Currency Lat

Location Latvia, the second smallest of the three Baltic republics, lies between Lithuania in the south and Estonia in the north, with Russia dominating its eastern border, and with the Baltic Sea and the Gulf of Finland extending to the west. The land is mainly flat and low-lying, although chains of hills run through it. The capital is Riga.

Head of State President Vaira Vike-Freiberga (1999)

Head of Government Andris Berzins (May 2000)

Ruling Party A centre-right wing coalition of three parties governs the country.

Political Structure Latvia's independence was officially recognised in September 1991, some six months after its original declaration. The country has a semi-executive president, who is the de facto Chairman of the Supreme Council (or Parliament). He is elected for a 3-year term by the parliament. The Diet has 100 members, elected for a 3-year term by proportional representation.

Last Elections Parliamentary elections were last held in October 1998. The Peoples Party received 21% of the vote and obtained 24 seats, the Latvian Way received 18% of the vote and 21 seats. Other representation was scattered among smaller parties. Vike-Freiberga was also elected president by a narrow margin in parliament in July 1999. In May 2000, Vike-Freiberga nominated Berzins as prime minister following the resignation of Andris Skele. Berzins is a member of Latvia's Way, the second largest party in the ruling coalition.

Political Risk Corruption remains a problem in Latvia, with foreign businesses, in particular, complaining of local and state bureaucracies demanding bribes for the myriad permits needed to carry on business. In addition, Russia's strategy of divide-and-rule prevents many companies from taking full advantage or Latvia's natural and acquired resources. Private and business interests have too strong a grip on Latvian politics and their rivalries cause the instability.

International Disputes Latvia has almost 700,000 Russians living in the country and their status has been a constant source of tension with Moscow. Citizenship laws have been made more liberal, with many of the previous obstacles removed. Language, however, remains a sensitive issue and many Russian-speakers complain of exclusion from Latvian society. Latvia has applied to join the North Atlantic Treaty Organization (NATO), and has made membership in the EU a stated foreign policy goal.

Economy Real GDP grew by 7% in 2001 and should further increase by 4.5% in 2002. In 2003, growth of 3.9% is forecast. Inflation was 2.5% in 2001 and will be 3% in both 2002 and 2003. Growth has been led primarily by investment. The current account deficit fell to 7% of GDP in 2000, after reaching almost 10% of GDP in 1998-1999, during the Russian crisis. However, further reduction of the current account deficit in 2001 was halted, due to the combination of continued strong growth in Latvia and a slowdown among Latvia's main trading partners. Nevertheless, robust export growth (9% in 2000) appears to have been sustained in 2001, as exporters have quickly reoriented toward other markets. Nearly two- thirds of Latvia's exports now go to the EU, and accession negotiations have advanced steadily under the tutelage of Sweden. Strong inflows of foreign direct investment have financed about -60% of the current account deficit, helping to keep external debt levels moderate. Productivity gains continue to outstrip the rise in wages.

Main Industries Russian oil, shipped by rail and pipeline to the Baltic Sea and the export of timber have long been the engines of the Latvian economy. Transit trade in oil contributes 14-17% of GDP, while timber and wood products account for more than 37% of exports. Privatisation has proceeded slowly and continues to face considerable opposition. Significant structural changes are taking place nonetheless. Latvia has a good resource base and transport system but investors are still hesitating between many rival projects in Estonia, Lithuania, Poland and Germany. In the longer term, the government believes that banking, information technology, tourism and other services will provide plenty of opportunities for growth. The country has a relatively efficient manufacturing base which presently accounts for almost two- thirds of GDP. The bulk of industrial activity is in heavy industries such as chemicals and petrochemicals, metalworking and machine building. Agriculture contributes around one- fifth of GNP and is centred on the cultivation of crops such as potatoes, cereals and fodder crops, along with dairy farming.

Energy Latvia has no domestic oil production or refineries, so it is entirely dependent on imports of petroleum products to meet its consumption needs. In 2000, Latvia imported 38,000 bbl/d of oil-related products from Russia, Belarus and Lithuania, with only a small amount coming from the EU. Analysts have estimated the country's possible offshore oil reserves at 300 million barrels of crude oil. For the time being, Latvia is heavily dependent on Russia for its energy requirements. This gives Moscow considerable leverage in disputes between the two countries. The government is set to sell 75% of the state-owned firm in charge of the country's oil products distribution.

	1999	2000	2001
Inflation (% change)	2.4	2.7	2.5
Exchange rate (per US$)	0.59	0.61	0.63
Interest rate (% per annum, lending rate)	14.2	11.9	11.2
GDP (% real growth)	0.7	4.4	7.0
GDP (Million units of national currency)	3,897.0	4,336.1	4,753.0
GDP (US$ million)	6,659.6	7,149.4	7,569.5
GDP per capita (US$)	2,740.7	2,965.6	3,165.0
Consumption (Million units of national currency)	3,104.4	3,439.6	3,749.4
Consumption (US$ million)	5,305.2	5,671.3	5,971.2
Consumption per capita (US$)	2,183.3	2,352.5	2,496.7
Population, mid-year ('000)	2,429.9	2,410.8	2,391.6
Birth rate (per '000)	7.7	7.8	7.8
Death rate (per '000)	13.4	13.4	13.4
No. of households ('000)	984.8	985.0	986.8
Total exports (US$ million)	1,723.1	1,865.3	2,000.7
Total imports (US$ million)	2,945.3	3,183.8	3,504.5
Tourism receipts (US$ million)	118.0	248.9	246.8
Tourist spending (US$ million)	268.0	344.1	379.3

Average household size 2001 (persons)	2.45				
Urban population 2001 (%)	73.4				
Age analysis (%) (2001)	*0-14*	17.0	*15-64*	68.1	*65+*	14.9
Population by sex (%) (2001)	*Male*	46.3	*Female*	53.7	
Life expectancy (years) (2001)	*Male*	65.2	*Female*	76.0	
Infant mortality (deaths per '000 live births) (2001)	14.5				
Adult literacy (%) (1996)	99.7				

TRADING PARTNERS
Major export destinations 2001 (% share)   **Major import sources 2001 (% share)**

Major export destinations 2001 (% share)		Major import sources 2001 (% share)	
GERMANY	16.7	GERMANY	13.1
UNITED KINGDOM	15.7	RUSSIA	7.1
SWEDEN	9.6	LITHUANIA	6.5
LITHUANIA	8.1	FINLAND	6.2

■ **Lebanon**

Area (km^2) 10,400

Currency Lebanese pound (£L = 100 piastres)

Location Lebanon is a narrow (100km wide) strip of land running from north to south for about 220km along the eastern coastline of the Mediterranean. In the south it is bordered by Israel and in the north and east by Syria. The country has a temperate Mediterranean climate with warm summers but occasionally cool winters, especially in the hills. The capital is Beirut.

Head of State President Émile Lahoud (1998)

Head of Government Rafiq al-Hariri (2000)

Ruling Party Parti Socialiste Progressiste leads a coalition.

Political Structure The electoral system has been only recently restored, having been effectively shelved since 1979. In May 2000, the government announced its plans for a complicated new electoral system. Each sectarian group will receive a fixed number of the 128 seats in parliament. Voters must cast ballots not only for candidates from their own sect, but also vote for candidates from other sects. The president is elected for a 6-year term. The prime minister is chosen by the president after consultation with parliamentary deputies. The Assembly of Representatives has 128 members, elected for a term of four years by the religious communities.

Last Elections In August-September 2000, elections to the Assembly of Representatives were held. The Resistance and Development Party won 23 seats, the Dignity Party took 18 seats and the Baalbeck-Hermel Coalition captured 9 seats. Other seats were distributed among a number of parties.

Political Risk The government's inability to alter its long-standing system of patronage has proved to be a serious obstacle to modernisation. Tension between several of the country's 18 recognised religious groups is still high. There are multiple factions in the country, though only one, Hizbullah, has been allowed to keep its arms.

International Disputes The US listing of terrorist groups includes several based in Lebanon. This is making it very difficult for Lebanon to refinance its massive debts. To appease the Americans, Lebanon has cracked down on recognised terrorists, including the arrest of one group associated with al-Qaeda. With a weak central government, the country also remains extremely vulnerable to outside influences.

Economy GDP rose by 1.3% in 2001 while inflation was nil. Gross public debt reached 160% of GDP in 2001. Interest obligations on this debt exceed 90% of government revenue. The bulk of the debt is held by Lebanese banks and is denominated in Lebanese pounds, although the share of foreign currency loans is growing. Banks have been able to finance the deficits because of robust growth in the deposit base. The government is preparing for a major fiscal effort starting to halt the growth in public debt. The objective is to turn the primary deficit of 1.5% of GDP in 2001 into a surplus of 4% in 2003, and reduce the overall deficit to 15% of GDP by 2003. The main measures to achieve this are the introduction of a VAT and expenditure cuts. To restore competitiveness and spur economic growth, the authorities rely on structural reforms, and key priorities are privatisation, tariff reductions and improvements in the business environment. Ending patronage is proving very difficult for a government whose members are appointed on political lines. Discussion regarding the possibility of privatising some public services and companies continues but there is very little progress. Such a move could help to relieve the debt burden, but there is no indication that the government is prepared to move in this direction in the short- or even medium- term. Meanwhile, the reconstruction programme to rebuild Lebanon after the civil war is far behind schedule. The costs were to be paid off by 1999, but it now appears that this will not be done before the year 2005.

Main Industries Lebanon's development programme has made only limited progress. There is some gains in the areas around Beirut, though the country's poorest regions are in the south where more than a third of all families live in poverty. The government has cut its spending brutally in order to rein in public debt. Lebanon has much fertile farmland, producing wheat, barley, maize, fruit, potatoes, tobacco and olives. Farms are small but relatively efficient and there is little need to import foodstuffs. Manufacturing is concentrated around the coastal urban areas. The more important industries include textiles, cement, chemicals, refining and light industries making goods for the domestic consumer market. All these types of industries have flourished since 2000, but reconstruction has proven to be a much bigger problem for the more capital-intensive industries and country's infrastructure. The banking sector contributes 8% to GDP and most of the sector is profitable despite considerable fragmentation. Petroleum refining and financial services were two of the mainstays of the Lebanese economy prior to the war but the country will probably never regain its position in these two industries.

Energy Lebanon is self-sufficient in hydrocarbons and has a number of electricity generating stations, 90% of which are thermal with the remainder hydroelectric. The country's energy companies are very inefficient, however. Several oil refineries have been out of operation since the early 1990s.

	1999	2000	2001
Inflation (% change)	0.2	-0.4	
Exchange rate (per US$)	1,507.84	1,507.50	1,507.50
Interest rate (% per annum, lending rate)	19.5	18.2	17.2
GDP (% real growth)	1.0	0.0	1.3
GDP (Billion units of national currency)	24,944.7	24,855.7	25,188.9
GDP (US$ million)	16,543.3	16,488.1	16,709.0
GDP per capita (US$)	5,108.5	5,023.8	4,921.7
Consumption (Billion units of national currency)	19,946.6	20,556.1	20,612.0
Consumption (US$ million)	13,228.6	13,635.9	13,673.0
Consumption per capita (US$)	4,084.9	4,154.8	4,027.4
Population, mid-year ('000)	3,238.4	3,282.0	3,395.0
Birth rate (per '000)	19.9	19.6	19.3
Death rate (per '000)	5.4	5.4	5.4
No. of households ('000)	720.3	735.5	767.3
Total exports (US$ million)	676.8	714.6	870.1
Total imports (US$ million)	6,207.2	6,230.0	7,293.5
Tourism receipts (US$ million)	673.0	849.2	748.0
Tourist spending (US$ million)	3,238.4	3,282.0	3,395.0

Average household size 2001 (persons)	4.46				
Urban population 2001 (%)	90.0				
Age analysis (%) (2001)	*0-14*	33.3	*15-64*	61.0	*65+* 5.7
Population by sex (%) (2001)	*Male*	49.7	*Female*	50.3	
Life expectancy (years) (2001)	*Male*	71.7	*Female*	74.9	
Infant mortality (deaths per '000 live births) (2001)	17.7				
Adult literacy (%) (1997)	84.4				

TRADING PARTNERS
Major export destinations 2001 (% share) **Major import sources 2001 (% share)**

FRANCE	11.8	ITALY	10.1
USA	10.2	FRANCE	8.7
SAUDI ARABIA	9.4	GERMANY	7.6
UNITED ARAB EMIRATES	9.1	SWITZERLAND	6.6

■ Lesotho

Area (km²) 30,345

Currency Loti (= 100 lisente)

Location Lesotho is a small mountainous territory situated in southern Africa. It is surrounded on all sides by the Republic of South Africa. Although a third of its land is classified as lowland, the remainder is all above 2,000 metres and rises to more than 3,500 metres. The capital is Maseru.

Head of State HM King Letsie III (1996)

Head of Government Pakalitha Mosisili (1998)

Ruling Party Lesotho Congress for Democracy (LCD)

Political Structure The country's parliament has two chambers. The National Assembly has 120 members, elected for a 5-year term, 80 in single-seat constituencies and 40 by proportional representation. The Senate has 33 nominated members.

Last Elections In parliamentary elections held in May 2002, the ruling LCD won 77 seats. The conservative Basotho National Party took 21 seats and the remainder were spread among several parties.

Political Risk The degree of political risk has diminished significantly in recent years as a result of policy changes in South Africa and King Letsie's withdrawal from the local political scene. Political corruption remains a problem, but Mosisili has cracked down on those taking bribes. At least 40% of the population lives in poverty, aggravated by the serious HIV/AIDS problem. An estimated quarter of the adult population is HIV positive and life expectancy is declining.

International Disputes The entire validity of Lesotho's borders with South Africa remains in dispute, with Lesotho claiming that a tribal agreement signed in 1869 was unjust.

Economy GDP increased by 2.9% in 2001, while prices rose by 7.8%. The Lesotho loti is pegged to the South African rand and depreciated by 37% against the US dollar during 2001. This decline is expected to raise inflation. The nominal and effective exchange rates, however, have been largely unaffected because most of Lesotho's trade is with South Africa and because their inflation rates have moved in tandem. The current account deficit for 2001 is estimated to be 17% of GDP, underscoring Lesotho's long-standing trade imbalance. However, strong export growth of textiles under the US Africa Growth and Opportunity Act and lower imports helped reduce this deficit to 7.5% of GDP in 2001. Unemployment is estimated at over 40%, and poverty is widespread. The fiscal and balance of payments situations have also deteriorated. Declining public revenue and one-off expenditures associated with the restructuring of a public enterprise and state banks have caused the budget deficit to rise to 16% of GDP. Unexpected expenditures such as the settlement of a tax dispute with South Africa mean that fiscal pressures will continue. Additional investment in the manufacturing sector is desperately needed to reduce the country's high rate of unemployment and to provide employment for miners released from jobs in South Africa.

Main Industries Agriculture accounts for most of the employment in Lesotho but productivity is low and the sector contributes no more than 12% to GDP. Most farming is for subsistence purposes. Maize, sorghum and beans dominate, though livestock herding is also important. Droughts and persistent mismanagement have reduced yields in recent years. The industrial sector makes up 44% of GDP and produces textiles, clothing, food products and pharmaceuticals. Many of these manufactured items are exported. In 2001, the country reported exports of US$215 million to the US. That figure was double the amount in 2000. Lesotho's diamond mining activities have been closed down after many years of decline, although there is still some freelancing. The country has deposits of peat, iron ore, uranium and lead. There are concerns about the delays in making the Lesotho Revenue Authority operational (originally scheduled to take place by end-September 2001), and the consequent postponement in replacing sales tax with a value-added tax. The government has continued to make progress with its privatisation programme with the sale of the telecommunications company in 2001. Restructuring of the electricity company is underway with plans for privatisation in 2002. Following the successful introduction of treasury bills for monetary policy, the central bank will develop a strategy to boost financial intermediation.

Energy Apart from firewood, Lesotho depends on imports for all its fuel resources. Completion of the US$4 billion Highlands Water Scheme should provide enough hydroelectricity for the whole country and allow it to become a substantial exporter of electricity. The construction phase of this project accounts for as much as 15% of Lesotho's GDP and scheduled for completion in 2003. The country's building boom will probably be over then and growth is likely to suffer.

	1999	2000	2001
Inflation (% change)	8.7	6.1	7.8
Exchange rate (per US$)	6.11	6.94	8.61
Interest rate (% per annum, lending rate)	19.1	17.1	16.6
GDP (% real growth)	2.4	3.2	2.9
GDP (Million units of national currency)	5,733.0	6,377.0	6,975.0
GDP (US$ million)	938.4	918.9	810.2
GDP per capita (US$)	443.5	426.8	360.4
Consumption (Million units of national currency)	5,723.1	6,351.9	6,442.3
Consumption (US$ million)	936.8	915.3	748.3
Consumption per capita (US$)	442.7	425.1	332.9
Population, mid-year ('000)	2,116.0	2,153.0	2,248.0
Birth rate (per '000)	34.1	33.6	33.1
Death rate (per '000)	17.1	18.5	20.1
No. of households ('000)	376.8	383.7	399.8
Total exports (US$ million)	175.4	173.0	154.0
Total imports (US$ million)	781.3	727.6	680.6
Tourism receipts (US$ million)	19.0	22.1	25.3
Tourist spending (US$ million)	12.0	9.5	9.1

Average household size 2001 (persons)	5.61				
Urban population 2001 (%)	28.8				
Age analysis (%) (2001)	*0-14*	40.1	*15-64*	55.8	*65+* 4.1
Population by sex (%) (2001)	*Male*	49.0	*Female*	51.0	
Life expectancy (years) (2001)	*Male*	43.3	*Female*	42.5	
Infant mortality (deaths per '000 live births) (2001)	110.3				
Adult literacy (%) (1997)	72.3				

Liberia

Area (km²) 111,370

Currency Liberian dollar (L$ = 100 cents)

Location Located on the Atlantic coast of West Africa, Liberia lies between Sierra Leone in the north-west, Guinea in the north-east, and Côte d'Ivoire in the south-east. The country has a mixed landscape, rising from the coastal plains to the upper plateau further inland. The climate is tropical, and is often humid. The capital is Monrovia.

Head of State Charles Taylor (1997)

Head of Government Charles Taylor (1997)

Ruling Party National Patriotic Front (NPP)

Political Structure Liberia's political system disappeared during the first half of the 1990s. Two peace treaties signed in 1993 and 1995 respectively failed to hold. West African (mainly Nigerian) peacekeepers eventually managed to restore order. The constitution calls for the president to be elected for a 6-year term by the people. Parliament has two chambers. The House of Representatives has 64 members, elected for a 6-year term in single-seat constituencies. The Senate has 26 members, elected for a 9-year term in 2-seat constituencies.

Last Elections Elections for president were held in July 1997 with 13 candidates running for the office. The ex-war lord, Charles Taylor, took 75% of the vote in a poll that was described as reasonably free by international observers. Parliamentary elections took place at the same time. The NPP received 75% of the vote, taking 49 seats in the House and 21 seats in the Senate.

Political Risk Rebels who call themselves Liberians United for Reconciliation control parts of the north and have attacked several refugee camps.

International Disputes Liberia claims that rebels within the country are backed by Sierra Leone and Guinea. In May 2001, the UN Security Council imposed sanctions on Liberia and these are still in place (although they are up for review). For some time, the Liberians are believed to have supplied arms to rebels in Sierra Leone in exchange for diamonds. Presumably, that exchange ended with the war. The country has also been supporting rebels in neighbouring Guinea.

Economy During Liberia's devastating 7-year civil war, economic activity was severely disrupted. The war took a heavy toll on the population and the country's infrastructure was largely destroyed. However, domestic production has rebounded strongly, although it still remains far below the pre-war level. The country's economic policy objectives are to achieve economic growth of some 15-20%, largely reflecting continued recovery in the forestry and agriculture sectors, with inflation in the range of 5% and the exchange rate stable, despite the recent decline in donor financing. Achievement of these ambitious goals is highly unlikely in view of the muddled macroeconomic policies currently in place.

Main Industries Richly endowed with water, mineral resources, forests, and a climate favourable for agriculture, Liberia had been a producer and exporter of basic products before the civil war. For most people, farming is still the most important activity. Employing nearly 80% of the workforce, the sector produces rubber, coffee, cocoa and timber for export. A combination of the war and reckless farming has brought deforestation to the country's tropical rain forest, while soil erosion is an increasing problem for farmers. Liberia's main industrial activity is the mining of iron ore, and to a lesser extent, diamonds and gold. These three minerals contribute two-thirds of export revenues although they account for only 5% of all employment. There has been an environmental cost with these activities, however. Pollution of rivers from the dumping of iron ore tailings and of coastal waters from oil residue is a growing problem. A majority of the population lives on a subsistence basis, growing cassava, rice and various root vegetables. Manufacturing is at a very rudimentary stage, with mainly small companies producing textiles, food products, timber goods, chemicals and cement. A plan to restructure and liberalise petroleum imports was also not completed and the liberalisation of rice imports has not been implemented. Both steps were agreed between the government and international authorities.

Energy Liberia relies on imports for all its petroleum needs, although exploration is under way for domestic resources. The general lack of hydroelectric capacity means that oil is still the most popular means of generating electricity.

	1999	2000	2001
Inflation (% change)	3.0	5.0	
Exchange rate (per US$)	41.90	40.95	48.58
Interest rate (% per annum, lending rate)	16.7	20.5	22.1
GDP (% real growth)			
GDP (Million units of national currency)	128,526.7	142,912.7	
GDP (US$ million)	3,067.3	3,489.7	
GDP per capita (US$)	1,028.0	1,106.4	
Consumption (Million units of national currency)	90,459.1	105,008.9	
Consumption (US$ million)	2,158.8	2,564.2	
Consumption per capita (US$)	723.5	813.0	
Population, mid-year ('000)	2,983.6	3,154.0	3,592.0
Birth rate (per '000)	51.9	53.0	54.2
Death rate (per '000)	15.1	14.2	13.3
No. of households ('000)	599.1	626.5	701.2
Total exports (US$ million)	500.0	500.0	478.6
Total imports (US$ million)			
Tourism receipts (US$ million)			
Tourist spending (US$ million)	2,983.6	3,154.0	3,592.0

Average household size 2001 (persons)	5.03				
Urban population 2001 (%)	45.6				
Age analysis (%) (2001)	0-14	48.2	15-64	48.9	65+ 2.9
Population by sex (%) (2001)	Male	50.4	Female	49.6	
Life expectancy (years) (2001)	Male	52.8	Female	54.9	
Infant mortality (deaths per '000 live births) (2001)	86.7				
Adult literacy (%) (1997)	46.9				

TRADING PARTNERS
Major export destinations 2001 (% share)   **Major import sources 2001 (% share)**

GERMANY	50.0	FRANCE	26.2
GREECE	11.9	SOUTH KOREA	24.4
ITALY	6.9	JAPAN	15.1
USA	5.2	SINGAPORE	8.2

Libya

Area (km^2) 1,759,540

Currency Libyan dinar (LD = 100 dirhams)

Location The Arab Jamahiriya of Libya occupies the centre of the North African Mediterranean coast, lying between Algeria and Tunisia in the west, Egypt and Sudan in the east and Niger and Chad in the south. The interior of the country consists almost entirely of rocky and sandy deserts. The south forms part of the Sahara desert, peopled mainly by nomads. On the coast, however, the terrain becomes much milder and greener. Temperatures are generally Saharan. The capital is Tripoli.

Head of State President Col Muammar al-Qaddafi

Head of Government Muhammad Ahmad al-Mangoush (Secretary of the General People's Congress)

Ruling Party There are no parties, with the Arab Socialist Union the sole authorised political group.

Political Structure Strictly speaking, Qaddafi has no formal post and no title except "Leader of the Revolution and Supreme Commander of the Armed Forces". In practice, he is effectively the country's president. Power is nominally vested in the Libyan people, acting through some 1,500 "basic people's congresses" at local level, and influencing the activities of the national General People's Congress (GPC) and its Secretariat. The GPC meets for about one week every year. In 1994, the country took a step toward Islamic rule, when Sharia law was introduced throughout the country and the clergy were empowered to issue decrees for the first time.

Last Elections There have been no multi-party elections in recent years.

Political Risk Libya continues to be a high-risk country with an arbitrary leader and a bewildering bureaucracy. But there is no doubt that its oil and gas will continue to excite interest.

International Disputes The transformation of Qaddafi from international pariah to statesman continues. US officials now accept that Libya has not been directly involved in terrorist activities in the past few years. An agreement on the Lockerbie air explosion now seems close. Libya is reported to have offered a total compensation of US$2.7 billion, though it has denied making the offer. US trade sanctions still remain in place, however. Libya's policies have sometimes brought it into conflict with its neighbours. The country has had to return to Chad a piece of land known as the Aozou Strip — a mineral-rich border area some 300km wide across the whole 1,200km border. Although Libya was originally awarded the land after World War II, Chad maintained its protests and in 1994 the International Court of Justice found in Chad's favour.

Economy GDP grew by 0.6% in 2001 while prices fell by 8.5%. Stronger economic growth is badly needed to help reduce Libya's 30% unemployment rate and make it easier for the country to maintain a budget surplus. Libya's relatively poor infrastructure (ie roads and logistics), unclear legal structure, often-arbitrary government decision-making process, bloated public sector (as much as 60% of government spending goes towards paying public sector employees' salaries) and various structural rigidities all have been impediments to foreign investment and economic growth. Libya's need for increased foreign investment may help push the country towards economic liberalisation. Libya has eased foreign exchange controls and has established a free-trade zone. The country's development plan calls for US$35 billion in investments in 2000-2005, 30-40% of which would come from private investors, mainly foreigners. Much of this would be for the oil and gas industry but the Libyans also want foreign capital to improve their infrastructure. With the country's youthful population set to double by 2025, job-creation has much to do with the new plan. Life is not as easy as might be expected in an oil-rich state that subsidises food, health and education. The state undertakes to find jobs for 30,000 new workers each year.

Main Industries Oil export revenues, which account for about 95% of Libya's hard currency earnings (and 75% of government receipts), were hurt severely by the dramatic decline in oil prices during 1998, as well as by reduced oil exports and production - in part as a result of US and UN sanctions. With sharply higher oil prices since 1999, however, Libyan oil export revenues have more than doubled (to US$12.9 billion in 2000, and forecast at around US$12.5 billion in 2001. Despite this oil revenues windfall, Libya is hoping to reduce its dependency on oil as the country's sole source of income, and to increase investment in agriculture, tourism, fisheries, mining and natural gas. The country's oil and gas industries have been starved for capital but now that sanctions have been lifted European investors are rushing back. The government is also looking for foreign investment for vast projects in transport, power generation and telecoms and is welcoming businessmen who offer capital or want to start up their own ventures. The tourist sector is another target for development. With its long Mediterranean coast and Roman antiquities, Libya has much to attract tourists. Libya's agricultural sector is a top governmental priority. Hopes are that the Great Man Made River (GMR), a 5-phase, US$30-billion project to bring water from underground aquifers beneath the Sahara to the Mediterranean coast, will reduce the country's water shortage and its dependence on food imports. At present, agriculture accounts for a meagre 2% of GDP, though it employs 15-20% of the workforce. Cultivated land is limited to the coastal areas and a few oases. Barley, wheat, oats, dates, potatoes, tomatoes and fruit are grown. Industry includes a wide range of activities providing a high degree of self-sufficiency, though almost all these enterprises are owned by the state.

Energy Libya's oil industry is run by the state-owned National Oil Corporation (NOC), along with smaller subsidiary companies. In 2001, NOC had an estimated total oil production capacity of around 810,000 bbl/d, accounting for over half the country's total. Several international oil companies are engaged in exploration/production agreements with NOC. Libya would like foreign companies' help to increase the country's oil production capacity from 1.5-1.6 million bbl/d at present to two million bbl/d by 2003. This would restore oil production capacity to the level of the early 1970s. Currently, Libya has 12 oil fields with reserves of one billion barrels or more and two others with reserves of 500 million to -one billion barrels. The major component of Libya's expansion plans is the development of the el-Bouri offshore oil field off the western coast, the largest producing oil field in the Mediterranean Sea (at around 60,000 bbl/d).

	1999	2000	2001
Inflation (% change)	2.6	-2.9	-8.5
Exchange rate (per US$)	0.50	0.51	0.60
Interest rate (% per annum, lending rate)	7.0	7.0	7.0
GDP (% real growth)	0.7	4.4	0.6
GDP (Million units of national currency)	14,138.0	17,790.0	17,278.0
GDP (US$ million)	28,312.1	34,911.7	28,950.4
GDP per capita (US$)	5,145.1	6,228.7	4,961.5
Consumption (Million units of national currency)	8,514.0	7,962.0	7,770.5
Consumption (US$ million)	17,049.8	15,624.9	13,019.9
Consumption per capita (US$)	3,098.4	2,787.7	2,231.4
Population, mid-year ('000)	5,502.8	5,605.0	5,835.0
Birth rate (per '000)	26.5	26.6	26.7
Death rate (per '000)	4.7	4.8	4.8
No. of households ('000)	1,120.9	1,179.2	1,211.2
Total exports (US$ million)	5,969.8	9,100.0	7,812.3
Total imports (US$ million)	5,032.7	6,166.0	5,440.9
Tourism receipts (US$ million)	28.0	34.5	16.6
Tourist spending (US$ million)	150.0	172.0	149.0

Average household size 2001 (persons)	4.75				
Urban population 2001 (%)	87.9				
Age analysis (%) (2001)	0-14	39.4	15-64	57.6	65+	3.0
Population by sex (%) (2001)	Male	51.8	Female	48.2	
Life expectancy (years) (2001)	Male	69.0	Female	73.0	
Infant mortality (deaths per '000 live births) (2001)	25.7				
Adult literacy (%) (1997)	77.0				

TRADING PARTNERS

Major export destinations 2001 (% share)		Major import sources 2001 (% share)	
ITALY	39.5	ITALY	28.7
GERMANY	15.5	GERMANY	12.2
SPAIN	14.0	UNITED KINGDOM	6.6
TURKEY	6.8	TUNISIA	6.0

▦ Liechtenstein

Area (km^2)   160

Currency   Swiss franc (SFr = 100 rappen)

Location   Liechtenstein lies in Alpine territory to the east of Switzerland, bordering on the Austrian province of Vorarlberg. Thanks in part to excellent communications, the country's prominence is mainly to due to its activities as a tax haven and banking centre. Swiss authorities represent the country abroad. The capital is Vaduz.

Head of State   Prince Hans-Adam II

Head of Government   Otmar Hasler (2001)

Ruling Party   The government is formed by the Progressive Citizens' Party (FBP).

Political Structure   Liechtenstein is a constitutional monarchy in which executive power is exercised by the prime minister, although the constitution gives the monarchy considerable powers. The Landtag (Parliament) is elected by popular mandate for a 5-year term and has 25 members. Only a few of the residents are eligible to vote, since the great majority of the population comprises foreign nationals. Prince Hans-Adam persuaded the conservative legislators to join the European Economic Area in 1995, taking the country one step ahead of Switzerland, with which it is linked in an economic union.

Last Elections   Elections to the 25-seat Landtag was held in February 2001, when the FBP won 49% of the vote and 13 seats. The Patriotic Union (VU) captured 11 seats. The Free Voters' List took the remaining seat. Women were allowed to vote for the first time in 1989 but moves to lower the voting age from 20 to 18 were rejected in a national referendum in 1992.

Political Risk   Liechtenstein is regarded as one of the most stable and affluent societies in Europe. Its ability to attract foreign capital is founded on strong banking secrecy laws, but these have been relaxed somewhat and some investors have gone elsewhere. The situation is made worse by the financial scandal in May 2000 when several leading asset managers were accused of money laundering. In addition, there is a constitutional dispute between the Prince and local politicians.

International Disputes   Liechtenstein has been taken off the OECD's list of money laundering countries and has strengthened banking regulations. Some other governments want more concessions but Vaduz is unwilling to concede.

Economy   Growth has not been impressive in recent years but it is more than 20 years since there was a recession in Liechtenstein. In fact, this tiny Alpine principality is one of the world's richest spots. Despite its small size and limited natural resources, Liechtenstein has developed into a prosperous, highly industrialised, free-enterprise economy with a vital financial service sector and living standards on a par with the urban areas of its large European neighbours. Low business taxes - the maximum tax rate is 18% - and easy incorporation rules have induced about 74,000 holding or so-called "letter box companies" to establish nominal offices in Liechtenstein, providing 30% of state revenues. Unemployment is consistently below 2% and per capita exports are roughly four times more than Switzerland's. The country participates in a customs union with Switzerland and is a member of the European Economic Area. Liechtenstein's main challenge is to balance the need for integration in a European framework with the implementation of steps to safeguard its independence.

Main Industries   Liechtenstein's principal activity is the provision of financial services. The financial sector accounts for more than half of the tiny country's GDP. Industry is limited in scale but of a specialist nature and the largest source of employment in the country. A small but sophisticated light engineering industry has expertise in machine tools, heating system, artificial limbs and semiconductor technology. Also included in the industrial sector are textile manufacturers and companies making domestic water heating equipment. Liechtenstein is also one of the world's biggest producers of false teeth. Farming is important despite the relative lack of available land, with cattle, fruit and vegetables being grown mainly on small plots of land.

Energy   Liechtenstein imports more than 90% of its energy requirements.

	1999	2000	2001
Inflation (% change)	0.4	0.7	
Exchange rate (per US$)	1.50	1.69	1.69
Interest rate			
GDP (% real growth)	2.4	2.7	
GDP (Million units of national currency)	1,667.3	1,724.3	1,771.1
GDP (US$ million)	1,111.6	1,021.0	1,049.3
GDP per capita (US$)	34,343.5	30,889.0	31,087.0
Consumption (Million units of national currency)	930.5	949.5	991.9
Consumption (US$ million)	620.4	562.2	587.6
Consumption per capita (US$)	19,167.0	17,009.0	17,409.6
Population, mid-year ('000)	32.4	33.1	33.8
Birth rate (per '000)	12.6	12.4	12.2
Death rate (per '000)	7.3	7.2	7.2
No. of households ('000)	12.5	12.9	13.1
Total exports (US$ million)			
Total imports (US$ million)			
Tourism receipts (US$ million)			
Tourist spending (US$ million)			

Average household size 2001 (persons)	2.57				
Urban population 2001 (%)	23.0				
Age analysis (%) (2001)	0-14	18.8	15-64	71.2	65+ 10.0
Population by sex (%) (2001)	Male	49.3	Female	50.7	
Life expectancy (years) (2001)	Male	75.3	Female	82.6	
Infant mortality (deaths per '000 live births) (2001)	5.3				
Adult literacy (%)					

Lithuania

Area (km^2) 65,300

Currency Litas

Location Lithuania, the most southerly of the three Baltic republics, lies on the Baltic coast with Latvia to its north, Poland to the south, and Belarus to the east. There is also a small Russian enclave on the Baltic coast, around Zelenogradsk. The region is largely swampland and lakes, with forestry being the most important natural resource. The capital is Vilnius.

Head of State President Valdas Adamkus (1998)

Head of Government Algirdas Brazauskas (2001)

Ruling Party A Social Liberal/Social Democratic coalition leads the government.

Political Structure The country has an executive president who chairs the 141-seat Seimas (formerly known as the Supreme Council). The Council, for its part, is elected by popular mandate for a term of four years.

Last Elections In presidential election in January 1998, Valdas Adamkus narrowly won the office. At the parliamentary elections held in November 1996, the conservative Homeland Union, a party led by the ex-president Vytautas Landsbergis, won a near-majority (70) of seats. The Christian-Democratic Party took another 16 seats and the Democratic Labour Party (formerly the Communist Party) gained 12 seats. In June 2001, the country had three prime ministers in less than a week. The turmoil was caused by differences about energy sector privatisations. Brazauskas was himself president of Lithuania in 1993-1998.

Political Risk Lithuania has moved rapidly towards integration with Europe. It considers itself to be the best positioned Baltic state to offer an economic, diplomatic and political bridge between the EU and Russia. But difficult negotiations still lie ahead. These negotiations are complicated by the Russian enclave of Kalingrad on its western border and a long border with maverick Belarus to the east. Lithuania has applied to join the North Atlantic Treaty Organization (NATO), and has made membership in the EU a stated foreign policy goal. However, as much as Lithuania moves towards the West, relations with Russia - the major power in the region - remains of great importance. Lithuania depends upon Russia for almost all of its oil and gas supply.

International Disputes Lithuania has a boundary dispute with Latvia which has delayed offshore oil exploration in the Baltic Sea. However, Lithuania is particularly vulnerable to Russian pressure because it provides the only land link to the Russian enclave of Kalingrad, which would be the first line of defence against an expanded NATO.

Economy GDP rose by 4.5% in 2001 and should increase by 4% in 2002. In 2003, growth of 4.8% is forecast. Prices rose by 1.3% in 2001 and are expected to increase another 2.8% in 2002. Inflation is 2003 should be 3%. Weaker external demand, mainly in the EU area, has been largely offset by stronger domestic demand. Rapid growth in private investment and private consumption has led to a widening of the external current account deficit to 5.9% of GDP at the end of 2001. This deficit, however, will be financed by sizeable capital inflows, including a pick-up in greenfield foreign direct investment and privatisation receipts. The external economic position has improved, with the current account deficit narrowing to 4.8% at the end of 2001, as exports of goods and services grew by 21%. The litas was successfully re-pegged to the euro in February 2002. Meanwhile, the unemployment rate dropped to 11.8% at end-April 2002. Over the medium term, macroeconomic policies continue to aim at achieving real growth rates of 5-6% per year, with low inflation and faster productivity growth than in trading partners, to maintain competitiveness. An appropriately cautious fiscal position remains essential, in light of remaining fiscal weaknesses and the need to provide for substantial financing of EU- and NATO-accession-related projects. Those supporting EU membership may still be in the minority, although the political elite clearly recognise that economic reforms and membership in the EU and NATO are the country's only chance of escaping Russian domination. The present government is committed to privatisation and is slicing away at Lithuania's bloated bureaucracy. More transparent government and tax regimes are planned. Government officials claim that the country will be ready for EU accession by 2004.

Main Industries Lithuania inherited the disproportionate weight of several enormous Soviet-era industrial projects. These included the Ignalina nuclear power complex and the Mazeikiu Nafta oil refinery, both geared to the needs of the integrated Soviet economy. The collapse of the Russian consumer market in the aftermath of the 1998 crisis forced Lithuanian exporters to seek new markets in Europe and beyond. As a result, exports to Russian and other parts of the former Soviet Union have plummeted since 1999. Traditional Lithuanian exporters of textiles, furniture and foodstuffs, have made a successful transition to Western markets and remain wary of selling to Russia. Structural reforms have advanced, particularly in the energy sector and banking privatisation. The pace of structural reform is expected to accelerate with continuing negotiations for EU entry. Other important manufacturing industries are machine-building and metal-working which concentrate on the production of agricultural machinery, food processing equipment, shipbuilding and maintenance equipment. Before independence, the bulk of this machinery was sold within the former Soviet Union but now many of these firms have shrunk as they struggle to find Western markets and buyers. The agricultural sector accounts for 11% of GDP with meat, dairy and fish products being major exports. Significant reforms in the farming sector promise higher levels of productivity in the future.

Energy Lithuania has 12 million barrels of proven reserves, but the country's estimated total onshore oil resources amount to 337 million barrels, with reserves in the Lithuanian shelf of the Baltic Sea estimated between 220 million and 440 million barrels. Several companies have begun onshore drilling projects in western Lithuania. Oil production is expected to be 4,500 bbl/d in 2002, but with an average rate of 66,000 bbl/d of consumption, the country remains a net oil importer. Russia is Lithuania's main supplier of crude oil. Meanwhile, the country is positioning itself as a major transit centre for oil and gas exports from Russia and the newly independent states to Europe. It also has a large nuclear reactor with the same design as the Chernobyl nuclear plant. The power station must be shut down as a condition of EU membership, but the Russians and some Lithuanians want it to keep producing cheap electricity to avoid a power vacuum.

	1999	2000	2001
Inflation (% change)	0.8	1.0	1.3
Exchange rate (per US$)	4.00	4.00	4.00
Interest rate (% per annum, lending rate)	13.1	12.1	9.6
GDP (% real growth)	-3.9	3.9	4.5
GDP (Million units of national currency)	42,654.6	45,254.2	48,087.0
GDP (US$ million)	10,663.7	11,313.6	12,021.8
GDP per capita (US$)	2,881.8	3,058.0	3,249.8
Consumption (Million units of national currency)	28,544.9	29,702.8	31,168.5
Consumption (US$ million)	7,136.2	7,425.7	7,792.1
Consumption per capita (US$)	1,928.5	2,007.1	2,106.4
Population, mid-year ('000)	3,700.3	3,699.7	3,699.3
Birth rate (per '000)	9.7	9.4	9.1
Death rate (per '000)	11.2	11.2	11.2
No. of households ('000)	1,400.0	1,411.6	1,421.7
Total exports (US$ million)	3,003.8	3,809.5	4,583.0
Total imports (US$ million)	4,834.5	5,456.5	6,281.0
Tourism receipts (US$ million)	550.0	593.9	461.8
Tourist spending (US$ million)	341.0	371.1	412.3

Average household size 2001 (persons)	2.62					
Urban population 2001 (%)	73.8					
Age analysis (%) (2001)	*0-14*	19.4	*15-64*	66.9	*65+*	13.7
Population by sex (%) (2001)	*Male*	47.1	*Female*	52.9		
Life expectancy (years) (2001)	*Male*	67.2	*Female*	77.5		
Infant mortality (deaths per '000 live births) (2001)	9.5					
Adult literacy (%) (1996)	99.5					

TRADING PARTNERS

Major export destinations 2001 (% share)

UNITED KINGDOM	13.8
LATVIA	12.6
GERMANY	12.6
RUSSIA	11.0

Major import sources 2001 (% share)

RUSSIA	19.3
GERMANY	13.1
POLAND	3.7
ITALY	3.2

Luxembourg

Area (km^2) 2,585

Currency Euro (= 100 cents)

Location The Duchy of Luxembourg is situated in north-western Europe, on the coalfields which extend from Lille in northern France through Belgium and into the Ruhr valley. With Germany to its east, Belgium to the north-west and France to the south, its excellent communications have helped to make it one of the most important trade and transport centres in the EU. Its climate is temperate, with generally mild winters. The capital is Luxembourg-Ville.

Head of State Grand Duke Jean (1964)

Head of Government Jean-Claude Juncker (January 1995)

Ruling Party Liberal Democratic Party leads a coalition.

Political Structure As a constitutional monarchy, Luxembourg vests all legislative authority in the unicameral Chamber of Deputies and in the cabinet. In the 10 years to 2002, the country has been ruled by a broad coalition of right and left, allowing a substantial degree of continuity and stability. In 1989, the Chamber of Deputies was reduced in size from 64 seats to 60 in order to accommodate a smaller electorate. The Chamber is elected by popular mandate for a term of five years.

Last Elections Elections to the Chamber of Deputies were held in June 1999. The Liberal Democratic Party received the largest share of votes and replaced the Socialist Party in the governing coalition with the Christian Democrats. Minor parties, including the Socialist Workers' Party and the Green Alternative received a scattering of seats. Juncker was re-elected as prime minister.

Political Risk The imminent expansion of the EU is, perhaps, the greatest threat to the tiny country. Up to six new members could be added by 2005 and will generate calls to curtail the powers of small states like Luxembourg and prevent them from clubbing together. Luxembourg has the highest standard of living in the EU and has used its sovereign status and outward-looking perspective to make itself a world centre of finance and administration. One consequence of this success is that workers are scarce and jobs can only be filled by bringing in foreigners. The country's job training schemes are poorly designed while the influx of foreigners creates resentment. The country's all-important banking sector is under pressure to relax its standards of banking secrecy but, so far, has managed to deflect most of these moves.

International Disputes There are no international disputes.

Economy With annual income per head of more than US$45,000, Luxembourg's inhabitants are among the world's richest and their prospects are high. GDP increased by 5.1% in 2001 and will grow by 3% in 2002. In 2003, growth of 6% is forecast. Inflation was 2.7% in 2001 and will be 1.9% in 2002. In 2003, prices are forecast to rise by 1.8%. Unemployment is a barely noticeable 2.5% and employment rates continued to rise in 2001 by more than 5%. Public finances remain in surplus and are forecast to be that way for the foreseeable future. The government has reduced both the corporate tax and private income tax. There is an automatic link between inflation and salaries, a high minimum wage and a lavish state pension scheme. Luxembourg is in the unique position of being able to draw on a reservoir of well-educated labour from neighbouring regions in Germany, France and Belgium. As a consequence, the pace of growth in Luxembourg can change for prolonged periods of time without triggering wage and price pressures. The country's long-term prospects are very good although there is a danger that greater integration of the EU will stiffen competitive pressures for its financial sector and erode some of the country's locational advantages.

Main Industries The agricultural sector is small but allows for self-sufficiency in food products, mainly wheat, potatoes and other vegetables. The country's grape growers are beginning to establish themselves as major suppliers of wine. The tourist sector attracted almost a million visitors in 2000 and the estimated number for 2001 is even higher. The country refrains from encouraging mass tourism but earns substantial income off the visitors it receives. Luxembourg's largest businesses have successfully crossed borders to forge global concerns. During the past year, three companies have expanded and acquired their way to become genuinely global groups - the world's largest steelmaker, the world's largest satellite operator and Europe's largest commercial broadcaster. The service sector is the largest part of the economy, accounting for 65% of GDP. Services are led by the country's thriving financial institutions, reflecting Luxembourg's success in diversifying its economy. Luxembourg has 185 banks and which, in 2001, earned a profit of over US$3 billion despite the global slowdown. The country is one of Europe's leading centres for the investment fund industry which reported a record value for net assets of more than US$900 billion in 2001. The finance sector has ambitious plans to develop a pan-European market in securitised assets and to make the Grand Duchy a centre for electronic commerce and banking. Bankers remain confident that they will not have to relinquish bank secrecy despite growing international and EU pressure.

Energy Luxembourg has large coal stocks, but it relies on oil and gas imports from abroad for much proportion of its energy needs.

	1999	2000	2001
Inflation (% change)	0.9	1.1	1.1
Exchange rate (per US$)	0.94	1.09	1.12
Interest rate			
GDP (% real growth)	6.0	7.5	5.1
GDP (Million units of national currency)	18,449.0	20,564.0	21,810.0
GDP (US$ million)	19,671.5	17,862.3	19,516.5
GDP per capita (US$)	45,562.5	40,877.7	44,123.6
Consumption (Million units of national currency)	7,916.8	8,813.2	1.0
Consumption (US$ million)	8,441.4	7,655.3	8,710.2
Consumption per capita (US$)	19,551.7	17,519.1	19,692.4
Population, mid-year ('000)	431.7	437.0	442.3
Birth rate (per '000)	12.6	12.5	12.3
Death rate (per '000)	9.3	9.2	9.2
No. of households ('000)	147.9	147.4	150.1
Total exports (US$ million)	7,849.1	7,823.7	8,157.2
Total imports (US$ million)	10,786.4	10,613.5	11,022.9
Tourism receipts (US$ million)			
Tourist spending (US$ million)	431.7	437.0	442.3

Average household size 2001 (persons)	2.96					
Urban population 2001 (%)	91.9					
Age analysis (%) (2001)	*0-14*	19.0	*15-64*	66.7	*65+*	14.2
Population by sex (%) (2001)	*Male*	49.4	*Female*	50.6		
Life expectancy (years) (2001)	*Male*	74.4	*Female*	80.7		
Infant mortality (deaths per '000 live births) (2001)	6.2					
Adult literacy (%) (1997)	99.0					

TRADING PARTNERS

Major export destinations 2001 (% share)		Major import sources 2001 (% share)	
GERMANY	23.1	BELGIUM	30.0
FRANCE	18.6	GERMANY	22.2
BELGIUM	10.1	FRANCE	12.4
UNITED KINGDOM	7.6	NETHERLANDS	4.8

■ Macau

Area (km^2)   16

Currency   Pataca (Pt = 100 avos)

Location   Macao (Macau) is a tiny territory at the mouth of the Pearl River in southern China. It is adjacent to Hong Kong, with which it has a ferry link. Consisting almost entirely of a port and two small islands, Taipa and Coloane, the entire country is only 16 sq km in size. Like Hong Kong, it was built to service Portugal's trade with China in the 19th century. The capital is Macao.

Head of State   President Jiang Zemin

Head of Government   Edmund Ho (1999)

Ruling Party   Chinese Communist Party

Political Structure   Macao was a Special Territory of Portugal but returned to Chinese rule on 19 December 1999 when it became the Chinese Special Administrative Region (SAR) of Macao.

Last Elections   In May 1999, elections were held to determine Macao's leader once it returned to Chinese rule. Edmund Ho, a local banker, easily won the contest, which was dominated by Beijing-appointed voters.

Political Risk   Incidents of corruption and gang-related violence have posed problems in the past. In response, the current administration is strengthening laws against organised crime and stepping up police operations.

International Disputes   There are no international disputes.

Economy   GDP grew by just 2% in 2001 and the outlook is not for any substantial improvement in the short term. Macao's economy is becoming extensively dominated by Beijing. Mainland interests have a half ownership in the new airport while the state-owned Bank of China and its affiliates account for over 40% of Macao's banking deposits. Easy money policies in China during the early 1990s led to a wave of real estate investments in Macao. By 1996 there were some 30% more homes than there were households in the city and roughly half of all households were owned by mainland Chinese. Competition for jobs is intense. The neighbouring economic zone of Zhuhai has a workforce six times that of Macao's and the average pay is only a sixth of the rate in the city-state. Chinese officials hope to turn Macao into a service hub for the southern part of the Pearl River Delta.

Main Industries   Agriculture accounts for just 1% of GDP, industry contributes 40% and services make up the remainder. Macao's principal industry is tourism, which attracts visitors from all over the world to its gambling centres. Gambling taxes account for almost two thirds of all government revenues. There are a number of manufacturing companies making textiles and high-technology goods. Efforts to diversify have spawned other small industries such as toys and artificial flowers. The city earns considerable revenues from foreign trade, especially with Hong Kong and China. A huge land reclamation project, funded with mainland money, will double the amount of acreage available to Macao.

Energy   Macao depends entirely on imports for all forms of energy.

	1999	2000	2001
Inflation (% change)	0.7	1.0	1.1
Exchange rate (per US$)	7.99	8.01	8.03
Interest rate			
GDP (% real growth)	4.7	2.3	2.0
GDP (Million units of national currency)	48,500.4	50,112.1	51,676.6
GDP (US$ million)	6,070.0	6,255.8	6,432.8
GDP per capita (US$)	13,223.7	13,396.9	13,522.7
Consumption (Million units of national currency)	21,750.7	23,854.9	24,855.0
Consumption (US$ million)	2,722.2	2,978.0	3,094.0
Consumption per capita (US$)	5,930.4	6,377.3	6,504.0
Population, mid-year ('000)	459.0	467.0	475.7
Birth rate (per '000)	10.2	9.9	9.6
Death rate (per '000)	4.4	4.5	4.5
No. of households ('000)	144.9	145.4	145.1
Total exports (US$ million)	2,199.6	2,539.0	2,299.5
Total imports (US$ million)	2,039.5	2,254.7	2,386.3
Tourism receipts (US$ million)	2,466.0	2,401.7	1,769.5
Tourist spending (US$ million)	131.0	161.2	169.1

Average household size 2001 (persons)	3.24				
Urban population 2001 (%)	98.8				
Age analysis (%) (2001)	*0-14*	22.6	*15-64*	70.5	*65+* 6.9
Population by sex (%) (2001)	*Male*	49.0	*Female*	51.0	
Life expectancy (years) (2001)	*Male*	76.7	*Female*	81.4	
Infant mortality (deaths per '000 live births) (2001)	8.4				
Adult literacy (%)					

TRADING PARTNERS

Major export destinations 2001 (% share)

USA	48.2
CHINA	11.7
GERMANY	7.7
HONG KONG	6.4

Major import sources 2001 (% share)

CHINA	42.7
HONG KONG, CHINA	13.9
SOUTH KOREA	5.5
JAPAN	5.4

Macedonia

Area (km^2)　25,713

Currency　Denar

Location　Macedonia covers 25,713 sq km in the far south of the old Yugoslavia and borders Bulgaria in the east, Albania in the west and Greece to the south. The geography is mainly mountainous with a river valley running north to south through the centre of the country. The capital is Skopje.

Head of State　President Boris Trajkovski (1999)

Head of Government　Ljupco Georgievski (1998)

Ruling Party　The Party for Macedonian National Unity (VMRO) leads a coalition.

Political Structure　The country has a non-executive president and an elected cabinet that answers to a unicameral parliament. The president is elected for a 5-year term by popular vote. Parliament has 120 members; each elected for 4-year terms, 85 members in single-seat constituencies and 35 members by proportional representation.

Last Elections　In presidential elections held in December 1999, Boris Trajkovski received 53% of the vote, defeating Tito Petkovski. Parliamentary elections were last held in October and November 1998. Together, the VMRO and the Democratic Alternative (DA) captured 59 seats while the Social Democratic League of Macedonia won 29. Albanian minority parties took most of the remainder.

Political Risk　In 2001, ethnic Albanian guerillas in Macedonia started a rebellion in Tetovo, the country's second largest city. After several months, the Macedonian government agreed to a NATO-brokered cease-fire with the ethnic Albanians. The fighting, however, partially disrupted the country's economy. Tensions remain high and fighting could break out once again if Western governments should relax their pressure.

International Disputes　Both the EU and NATO have assured the Macedonian government of their support in return for which the government must refrain from declaring war on its Albanian minority. Both the government and the Albanian minority have signed separate, open-ended cease-fires which could lead to peace negotiations. Relations with neighbouring countries such as Greece have improved now that Slobodan Milosevic has been jailed. The main threats to Macedonia are instability in Kosovo, more unrest in southern Serbia and internal conflicts within Serbia.

Economy　Macedonia's GDP grew by 4.7% in 2001 while prices rose by just 5.3%. The country's total foreign debt has declined to about 46% of GDP. The government has reduced interest rates and is trying to impose a tighter rein on public spending. Officials are anxious to attract more foreign investment but have had little success. They have managed to boost the growth of credit to small and medium businesses. The country's ambitious privatisation programme should free up funds for private investment, which, together with internationally-funded projects to improve roads, power water and other infrastructure, would lay the basis for sustainable future growth. A major stumbling block to all these sell-offs is that 3.500 government jobs will have to be cut at the same time.

Main Industries　Most of the country is agrarian. Macedonia's 180,000 private farmers produce about three quarters of agricultural output on fragmented holdings with an average size of only 2.8 hectares. Export crops include tobacco, strawberries and table grapes. Farming accounts for about 25% of all economic activity and is expected to become more important as the transition to a market economy gains momentum. Industries in Macedonia include brewing, flour milling, tobacco, textiles, carpets and cement. The government has sold off the state-owned telecommunications company but otherwise there has been little privatisation. The banking industry is the subject of a modest round of reforms, including the entry of foreign investors in three commercial banks. This development is expected to lead to consolidation, halving the number of banks to around 10. The government has also pledged to privatise the 40 biggest loss-makers, the state-controlled mines, engineering and other companies which account for the bulk of bad loans, non-payment of taxes and inter-enterprise debts.

Energy　Macedonia experiences perennial shortages of fuel. Electricity supply problems have sometimes led to a declaration of a state of emergency.

	1999	2000	2001
Inflation (% change)	-0.7	5.8	5.3
Exchange rate (per US$)	56.90	65.90	68.04
Interest rate (% per annum, lending rate)	20.4	18.9	19.4
GDP (% real growth)	2.7	6.0	-4.6
GDP (Million units of national currency)	209,010.0	236,211.0	234,718.0
GDP (US$ million)	3,673.2	3,584.2	3,449.9
GDP per capita (US$)	1,821.0	1,769.6	1,696.6
Consumption (Million units of national currency)	143,605.0	167,852.5	159,622.3
Consumption (US$ million)	2,523.7	2,546.9	2,346.1
Consumption per capita (US$)	1,251.1	1,257.5	1,153.8
Population, mid-year ('000)	2,017.1	2,025.4	2,033.4
Birth rate (per '000)	13.6	12.9	12.2
Death rate (per '000)	8.3	8.3	8.4
No. of households ('000)			
Total exports (US$ million)	1,192.0	1,319.0	1,155.0
Total imports (US$ million)	1,773.0	2,085.0	1,688.0
Tourism receipts (US$ million)	37.0	19.0	16.4
Tourist spending (US$ million)	32.0	31.2	29.5

Average household size 2001 (persons)					
Urban population 2001 (%)		62.4			
Age analysis (%) (2001)	0-14	22.2	15-64	67.8	65+ 10.1
Population by sex (%) (2001)	Male	50.0	Female	50.0	
Life expectancy (years) (2001)	Male	71.2	Female	75.6	
Infant mortality (deaths per '000 live births) (2001)		16.5			
Adult literacy (%) (1997)		94.0			

TRADING PARTNERS

Major export destinations 2001 (% share)		Major import sources 2001 (% share)	
SERBIA AND MONTENEGRO	29.3	GREECE	14.4
GERMANY	18.1	GERMANY	9.7
USA	8.4	UKRAINE	8.9
ITALY	7.5	ITALY	6.7

▨ Madagascar

Area (km^2)   594,180

Currency   Franc malgache (franc MG = 100 centimes)

Location   The island of Madagascar lies in the Indian Ocean, about 500km off the coast of Mozambique. It is the fourth largest island in the world, measuring some 2,000km from north to south. The country has a mountainous elevation, with substantial lowland areas, and enjoys a warm and moderate climate. The capital is Antananarivo.

Head of State   President Marc Ravalomanana (2002)

Head of Government   vacant

Ruling Party   A coalition of socialist parties leads the government.

Political Structure   Madagascar, which was known until 1975 as the Malagasy Republic, became independent from France in 1960. The president is elected by universal suffrage for a 5-year term. The National Assembly has 150 members, elected for a 4-year term in 82 single-member and 34 two-member constituencies. In 1995, a referendum was approved which gives the president - and not parliament - the right to appoint the prime minister. A new constitution was approved in 1998.

Last Elections   Presidential elections held in December 2001 produced much confusion. Marc Ravalomanana competed in the election against the standing president, Didier Ratsiraka. Ravalomanana claimed to have won the election outright though official results gave him only a plurality. Ratsiraka and Ravalomanana later agreed to a recount. The result confirmed the absolute majority of Ravalomanana. Ratsiraka continued to fight on until July 2002 when he fled the country. In the final vote count, Ravalomanana apparently received 67% of the vote and has assumed office as president. Elections to the National People's Assembly were last held in May 1998. AREMA, a socialist party, took the largest share of seats - 63. The remainder of seats was widely dispersed among several parties.

Political Risk   The country came close to a civil war after the most recent elections. As many as 150,000 people lost their jobs and malnutrition, especially among children, is getting worse. The economy's prospects are also hostage to any wide swings in world commodity prices and the erratic commitment of the government to economic reform.

International Disputes   Madagascar has a claim against France for the return of various largely uninhabited islands, which are currently administered as part of Réunion's territory. The UN has endorsed Madagascar's claim for the islands.

Economy   Real GDP grew by 6.7% in 2001, while prices rose by 5%. Because of the strength of the export performance, in 2001 the external current account deficit is expected to be lower than targeted by 1.5 percentage points of GDP. Exports are estimated to have grown by 14% in 2001. Efforts are underway to strengthen customs administration, while cross-checks of tax returns have been intensified between customs and the domestic tax directorate. Madagascar made further progress in structural reforms in 2001, with the emphasis on strengthening budgetary management, treasury accounting and public finance auditing, and on widening the privatisation process. Private capital inflows have contributed to a significant increase in the official reserves of the central bank. The government's efforts to attract private savings and investment, both domestic and foreign, also met with some success but this support disappeared following the post-election dispute.

Main Industries   Agriculture, including fishing and forestry, is the mainstay of the economy, accounting for almost a third of GDP and contributing more than 70% to export earnings. Farming is mainly in a subsistence capacity and most is in the drier, western half of the island where rice, maize, bananas and sweet potatoes are grown for the domestic market. Forestry is important, though conservationists are pressing for restraint. Industry is limited and dominated by small-scale activities such as food processing, soap making, textile manufacture and brewing. The sector's share of GDP has been declining in recent years to around 13%. The largest manufacturing operations are plants making cement and fertilisers. In 2001, there was a 25% increase in manufactured exports from the export-processing zone, which mainly consisted of clothing. Economists were encouraged by the strong performance of the external sector and the ability of the country to attract foreign investment - particularly in the export-processing zone. These gains were not sustained during the first half of 2002, however, due to the disruptions experienced in the aftermath of the elections. Money growth, at an annual rate of 14%, was higher than projected in 2001, reflecting an increase in money demand from the business sector. The privatisation of the last components of the state petroleum company was finalised in September, 2001 while the tenders for the sale of the state telecommunication company was launched. The preparation of the sale of the state cotton and sugar companies is well advanced. There are a number of companies mining precious and semi-precious stones.

Energy   Madagascar has offshore oil deposits of up to 200 million barrels, but these are unlikely to be enough for self-sufficiency. At the time of writing, all supplies were imported. There are hydroelectric resources, which generate some 60% of the country's electricity requirements.

	1999	2000	2001
Inflation (% change)	9.9	11.9	5.0
Exchange rate (per US$)	6,283.77	6,767.48	6,588.49
Interest rate (% per annum, lending rate)	28.0	26.5	
GDP (% real growth)	4.7	4.8	6.7
GDP (Billion units of national currency)	23,379.0	26,242.0	30,084.0
GDP (US$ million)	3,720.5	3,877.7	4,566.1
GDP per capita (US$)	238.7	243.2	271.5
Consumption (Billion units of national currency)	20,589.6	23,437.6	26,129.1
Consumption (US$ million)	3,276.6	3,463.3	3,965.9
Consumption per capita (US$)	210.2	217.2	235.8
Population, mid-year ('000)	15,589.9	15,942.0	16,820.0
Birth rate (per '000)	43.2	42.7	42.1
Death rate (per '000)	14.2	13.9	13.6
No. of households ('000)	3,003.5	3,048.7	3,179.2
Total exports (US$ million)	220.0	298.0	372.7
Total imports (US$ million)	378.0	551.0	670.4
Tourism receipts (US$ million)	100.0	104.1	96.6
Tourist spending (US$ million)	111.0	93.2	118.9

Average household size 2001 (persons)	5.23				
Urban population 2001 (%)	30.3				
Age analysis (%) (2001)	*0-14*	44.2	*15-64*	52.8	*65+* 2.9
Population by sex (%) (2001)	*Male*	49.4	*Female*	50.6	
Life expectancy (years) (2001)	*Male*	52.0	*Female*	54.3	
Infant mortality (deaths per '000 live births) (2001)	93.2				
Adult literacy (%) (1997)	47.0				

TRADING PARTNERS

Major export destinations 2001 (% share)		Major import sources 2001 (% share)	
FRANCE	29.5	FRANCE	24.0
USA	27.3	IRAN	9.7
SINGAPORE	7.5	BAHRAIN	8.1
GERMANY	6.3	HONG KONG, CHINA	6.9

Malawi

Area (km^2)　94,080

Currency　Kwacha (K = 100 tambala)

Location　Malawi is a long, landlocked triangular strip of country in central southeast Africa. It is bounded in the south by Mozambique, in the north by Tanzania and in the west by Zambia. The territory is fertile and permeated with large rivers, and has a pleasant subtropical climate. The capital is Lilongwe.

Head of State　President Baktili Muluzu (May 1994)

Head of Government　Baktili Muluzu

Ruling Party　The United Democratic Party (UDP) dominates a coalition.

Political Structure　Malawi has an executive president who is elected for a 5-year term and appoints his own cabinet. Theoretically, all legislative power is vested in the National Assembly with 177 officials elected for 5-year terms. The constitution of 1995 also provides for a Senate of 80 seats to be installed in the near future.

Last Elections　Presidential elections were held in June 1999 when Muluzu retained his position with 52% of the vote. Elections to the National Assembly were held at the same time. The UDP received 47% of the vote and gained 93 seats. The Malawi Congress Party took 34% of the vote and 66 seats. Other parties received smaller proportions.

Political Risk　Food is so scarce in Malawi that prices rose sixfold during the first half of 2002. Aid workers fear that thousands will be dying of starvation by 2003. Not surprisingly, unrest is growing. Muluzu banned political marches beginning in May 2002. Meanwhile, his party and its allies are pushing for a constitutional amendment to eliminate presidential term limits and allow Muluzu to prolong his rule. Dissatisfaction has spread and demonstrations are now frequent. AIDS has cut life expectancy drastically and the country is horribly poor.

International Disputes　Malawi has a dispute with Tanzania, however, over the ownership of territorial water rights in Lake Malawi (called Lake Nyasa by Tanzania) where their borders meet.

Economy　Malawi is one of the world's poorest countries, income is unequally distributed and about half of the population lives below the poverty line. GDP rose by 2.8% in 2001, while prices increased by more than 27%. The country's problems have been compounded by occasional inconsistencies in the application of its macroeconomic policies. Slippages involving excess public spending, the accumulation of domestic spending arrears and an increase in the fiscal deficit have all complicated the economic environment. More headway has been made in the field of structural reform. Important steps included a decision by the authorities to refrain from further intervention in the maize market and the establishment of an independent revenue authority. The country's privatisation programme has faltered, despite assistance from the IMF and other international institutions. Malawi is a member of the Southern African Development Community and the Common Market for Eastern and Southern Africa, both of which launched free-trade agreements in 2000.

Main Industries　Agriculture contributes around 45% of GDP and employs almost 90% of the country's workforce. Most of the country's population is engaged in subsistence farming. Export crops such as tobacco, tea or sugar account for over 75% of export revenues and have traditionally been produced by the larger farms. The harvest in 2001 left a shortfall of at least 800,000 tonnes of maize, the main stable, out of a total requirement of about two million tonnes. The present harvest would have been better, except for the fact that many starving people have been eating the maize before it is fully grown. Meanwhile, the country's currency has plunged, leaving two thirds of small farmers unable to afford imported fertiliser and high-yielding hybrid seed. To make matters worse, maize reserves are completely exhausted. Industry accounts for up 30% of GDP and consists mainly of sugar processing, sawmill products, cement and the production of consumer goods (for example, processed foods, pharmaceuticals, cement and tobacco products). Tourism has considerable potential but facilities remain rudimentary. Malawi has an abundance of natural resources with large reserves of coal, some of which is extracted. There are also known deposits of uranium, phosphates, bauxite, graphite and asbestos.

Energy　Half of the country's fuel requirements are met with domestic coal mining. Otherwise, the country depends on imports of oil. Most of Malawi's electricity is supplied by hydroelectric power stations.

	1999	2000	2001
Inflation (% change)	44.8	29.6	27.2
Exchange rate (per US$)	44.09	59.54	72.20
Interest rate (% per annum, lending rate)	53.6	53.1	56.2
GDP (% real growth)	4.0	1.7	2.8
GDP (Million units of national currency)	79,804.0	101,634.0	131,844.0
GDP (US$ million)	1,810.1	1,706.9	1,826.2
GDP per capita (US$)	168.8	156.2	157.7
Consumption (Million units of national currency)	69,784.2	80,064.2	101,504.2
Consumption (US$ million)	1,582.8	1,344.6	1,405.9
Consumption per capita (US$)	147.6	123.1	121.4
Population, mid-year ('000)	10,724.1	10,925.0	11,580.0
Birth rate (per '000)	46.4	46.0	45.5
Death rate (per '000)	22.3	22.4	22.5
No. of households ('000)	1,827.1	1,837.6	1,973.0
Total exports (US$ million)	441.7	354.5	399.3
Total imports (US$ million)	697.8	568.8	661.9
Tourism receipts (US$ million)	20.0	21.9	18.4
Tourist spending (US$ million)			

Average household size 2001 (persons)	5.95					
Urban population 2001 (%)	25.8					
Age analysis (%) (2001)	*0-14*	47.2	*15-64*	50.1	*65+*	2.7
Population by sex (%) (2001)	*Male*	49.6	*Female*	50.4		
Life expectancy (years) (2001)	*Male*	39.9	*Female*	39.4		
Infant mortality (deaths per '000 live births) (2001)	132.4					
Adult literacy (%) (1997)	57.7					

TRADING PARTNERS

Major export destinations 2001 (% share)		Major import sources 2001 (% share)	
SOUTH AFRICA	19.9	SOUTH AFRICA	39.5
USA	16.1	ZIMBABWE	15.9
GERMANY	11.7	ZAMBIA	10.9
JAPAN	6.9	INDIA	3.1

▦ Malaysia

Area (km^2) 332,965

Currency Malaysian dollar (also called the ringgit; RM = 100 cents)

Location Malaysia, one of the largest countries in the Asia-Pacific group, comprises the 11 states of Peninsular Malaysia, where the bulk of the population live, as well as the predominantly forested areas of Sabah and Sarawak, across the South China Sea on the northern coast of Borneo. Its climate is tropical and often humid. The capital is Kuala Lumpur.

Head of State Syed Sirajuddin ibni al-Marhum Syed Putra Jamalullail (2001)

Head of Government Datuk Seri Dr Mahathir Mohamed

Ruling Party The government is formed by the member-parties of the Barisan Nasional.

Political Structure Malaysia is a constitutional monarchy in which the monarch is elected every five years from among the tribal elders of peninsular Malaysia. The influence of the monarchy is limited, however. All effective power is actually exercised by the Prime Minister, who reports to a bicameral legislature. The House of Representatives (or Lower House) is composed of 193 members elected for five years, while the 69-member Senate consists of 26 representatives of the States, elected for a 6-year term, and 43 appointed members. Constitutional amendments in 1993 reduced the legal immunity of the nine Malay rulers. A new federal capital, to be called Putrajaya, is now being built near Kuala Lumpur, and is due for completion in 2008.

Last Elections The sultans elected Putra as king in 2001. In November 1999, elections to the House of Representatives were held. UMNO, the leading party of the Barisan Nasional, won 71 seats, the Malaysian/Chinese Front took 29 seats and the United Traditional Bumiputera Party won 10 seats.

Political Risk Mahathir's desire to depart from the political scene appears to be genuine. After such a long and autocratic reign, the uncertainty about future leadership is great. Ethnic tensions could become a serious problem following his departure. The country's Indians and Chinese minorities have uneasy relations with the Malay majority. Because of the country's labour shortage, illegal immigration is widespread. Immigrants account for an eighth of the workforce and more than 500,000 are illegal. A more insidious threat to the country's long-run stability is the inequitable distribution of income and wealth.

International Disputes Malaysia resolutely rejects a claim by the Philippines for the sovereignty of the entire territory of Sabah, its easternmost province. Negotiations on the issue have continued without agreement since 1969. Malaysia is pressing Indonesia for the return of two islands, Sipadan and Ligitan, and is one of many claimants for the sovereignty of the Spratly Islands in the South China Sea.

Economy Malaysia's GDP should rise by around 2.5% in 2002 and increase by more than 3% in 2003. Inflation will be only 1.8% in 2002, rising to 2.5% in 2003. Compared with some other regional economies, Malaysia is better able to deal with weakness of activity in the industrial economies. Important contributory factors are the resilience of private consumption and the beneficial effects of the government's policy actions. Given that total consumption accounts for about 60% of GDP, its resilience helps to absorb some of the contractionary forces resulting from the collapse in external demand. Fiscal pump priming is expected to continue over the next few years to act as a very important driver of growth, especially so long as export growth remains. The 2002 budget announced plans to cut the individual tax rate in the top bracket marginally from 29% to 28%, and increased government salaries by 10%. On the corporate front, the government has extended the reinvestment allowance from five to 15 years and implemented tariff concessions for a wide range of intermediate products. These measures are designed to boost domestic demand directly, rather than letting it rely on the traditional multiplier effects emanating from public infrastructure projects.

Main Industries Manufacturing suffered a sharp contraction of 4.8% in 2001, from 21% growth in 2000. Within manufacturing, while domestic-oriented industries recorded growth of 8% in 2001, this did not fully offset the contraction in export-oriented industries. The agriculture sector was the only area, apart from construction, where growth actually picked up - to 2.3% from 0.6% in 2000. This was mainly due to the bumper harvest of palm oil. The services sector grew by 3.9%, primarily due to the resilience of finance, insurance, real estate and business-related activities. A low interest rate environment was a catalyst for these activities. Among major expenditure categories, consumption spending grew, propped up by a surge in public spending. Given that total consumption accounts for about 60% of GDP, its resilience helped absorb some of the contractionary forces resulting from the collapse in external demand. While a fall in disposable income and a sluggish labour market exerted downward pressure on consumption spending, this was cushioned by retail discounts, tax deductions, a turnaround in palm-oil prices in the middle of the year, low interest rates and a sharp increase in public spending. Private consumer spending growth, accounting for about 80% of total consumption, fell to 2.4% in 2001 from 12.2% in the previous year. Public consumption spending accelerated to 14.1% from 1.7% in 2000, as the government adopted stimulus measures.

Energy Malaysia's domestic oil production occurs offshore and primarily near Peninsular Malaysia. The country has proven oil reserves of 3.9 billion barrels, down from 4.3 billion barrels in 1996. Crude oil production has been stable in recent years, with monthly production numbers fluctuating between 660,000 barrels per day (bbl/d) and 730,000 bbl/d between 1996 and early 2001. To offset the effects of declining oil reserves, Petronas, the state oil and gas company, has embarked on an international exploration and production strategy. The government estimated that investments of up to US$16 billion would be pumped into Malaysia's oil and gas industry over the next five years. Of this amount, approximately a third will be in the form of foreign direct investment.

	1999	2000	2001
Inflation (% change)	2.7	1.5	1.4
Exchange rate (per US$)	3.80	3.80	3.80
Interest rate (% per annum, lending rate)	7.3	6.8	6.7
GDP (% real growth)	5.8	8.5	0.3
GDP (Million units of national currency)	300,340.6	340,704.2	332,652.0
GDP (US$ million)	79,037.0	89,659.0	87,540.0
GDP per capita (US$)	3,581.5	3,993.7	3,825.9
Consumption (Million units of national currency)	126,797.0	146,564.8	146,696.6
Consumption (US$ million)	33,367.6	38,569.7	38,604.4
Consumption per capita (US$)	1,512.0	1,718.0	1,687.2
Population, mid-year ('000)	22,068.3	22,450.3	22,880.8
Birth rate (per '000)	24.3	23.9	23.5
Death rate (per '000)	4.8	4.7	4.7
No. of households ('000)	4,732.6	4,911.0	4,964.9
Total exports (US$ million)	84,455.0	98,135.0	88,521.0
Total imports (US$ million)	64,965.8	82,198.7	74,384.0
Tourism receipts (US$ million)	3,540.0	2,931.5	2,515.0
Tourist spending (US$ million)	1,973.0	2,724.6	2,825.9

Average household size 2001 (persons)	4.57				
Urban population 2001 (%)	57.3				
Age analysis (%) (2001)	*0-14*	33.8	*15-64*	61.9	*65+* 4.2
Population by sex (%) (2001)	*Male*	50.7	*Female*	49.3	
Life expectancy (years) (2001)	*Male*	70.3	*Female*	75.2	
Infant mortality (deaths per '000 live births) (2001)	10.7				
Adult literacy (%) (1998)	87.5				

TRADING PARTNERS

Major export destinations 2001 (% share)		Major import sources 2001 (% share)	
USA	20.3	JAPAN	19.3
SINGAPORE	17.0	USA	15.9
JAPAN	13.6	SINGAPORE	13.6
HONG KONG, CHINA	4.6	CHINA	4.9

Maldives

Area (km^2)   298

Currency   Rufiyaa (Rf = 100 laris)

Location   The Maldives are a group of 1,190 coral islands lying in the central Indian Ocean, some 675km southwest of Sri Lanka and extending for almost 1,000km from one extreme to the other. Only about 200 of the islands are inhabited and none extends more than 2.5 metres above sea level. The capital is Male.

Head of State   President Maumoon Abdul Gayoom (1978)

Head of Government   President Maumoon Abdul Gayoom

Ruling Party   There are no political parties in the Maldives.

Political Structure   The Republic of Maldives is an independent member of the Commonwealth in which all executive functions are vested in the president and his cabinet. The president is elected for a 5-year term by parliament and confirmed in a referendum by the people. He reports to a 48-member Citizens' Assembly (Majlis) and appoints eight members of that group. The remainder are elected by universal adult suffrage for a term of five years.

Last Elections   The latest referendum on the presidency took place in October 1998 when 91% voted in favour of Gayoom. Elections to the Citizens' Assembly were held in November 1999, when all candidates were obliged to campaign on independent tickets in the absence of political parties.

Political Risk   The country's population of around 260,000 is increasing at an extremely rapid 3% annual rate — one of the highest population growth rates in the world. Allegations of corruption and nepotism have continually plagued the president and his family. A full-scale coup attempt was launched in 1988, although it was foiled by a contingent of paratroopers called in from India. More recently, there have been calls for a fully elected Assembly, but these have been energetically suppressed by the government.

International Disputes   The Maldives is an outspoken supporter of international moves to curb global warming. Fears of a rise in global sea levels gave rise to the very real possibility that a sizeable proportion of the landmass could become submerged in the next 30 years.

Economy   The Maldives' economy has been slowing. GDP grew by 4.9% in 2001 but growth is expected to be just 2% in 2002 and nil in 2003. Inflation should fall to around 1% in 2002. The downturn in tourism has had spillover effects for the entire economy. The fiscal deficit widened from 4.9% in 2000 to 5.3% in 2001, largely due to a rise in government expenditures to 41.3% of GDP from 40.8% in 2000. Monetary policy was more expansionary than in 2000, with money supply growth rising to 9% in 2001 from 4.1%. The current account deficit worsened to US$62 million, or 10.9% of GDP, in 2001 from US$53 million, or 9.5% of GDP, in the previous year. Net non-monetary capital inflows in 2001 amounted to US$36 million, a 20% decline from the 2000 level. In aggregate, the balance-of-payments deficit surged to US$26 million in 2001 from US$7.9 million in 2000. Foreign exchange reserves declined to US$94.3 million at the end of 2001, sufficient to cover 2.9 months of imports. The government made some important economic policy changes in 2001. First, the rufiyaa, pegged to the US dollar under a de facto fixed exchange rate policy, was devalued in July 2001 by 8% to Rf12.80 to the US dollar from Rf11.77. A major reason for the devaluation was to respond to accumulated stresses in the foreign exchange market. Second, the Maldives Monetary Authority further liberalised financial markets. The health of the tourism sector will depend on recovery in the EU and Japanese economies, which are the major markets for Maldives' tourism, and on an improvement in the security situation in South Asia. The tourism sector is unlikely to fully recover in 2002, though it has made some headway. A significant increase in the disbursement of official assistance is expected, which will help offset the weakening current account.

Main Industries   Tourism - which accounts for more than one third of GDP and is the largest source of foreign exchange earnings - stagnated in 2001, due primarily to concerns over travel safety, as well as to declines in global consumer spending and confidence. In October and November 2001, tourist arrivals dropped off by 20.1% and 22.2%, respectively, compared with the corresponding months in the previous year. Overall, the tourism sector, which had shown annual growth of about 6% in recent years, declined by 0.5% in 2001. Wholesale and retail trade contracted by 0.4% during 2001. Transport and communications, the second largest sector, grew fairly strongly at 6.3%, but even this was significantly lower than the double-digit annual growth rates in 1996-1999. Other sectors, including fisheries, financial and business services, real estate and retail trade, were weak, growing at 1% or less in 2001.

Energy   The Maldives produces no oil, and consumes only about 2,000 barrels per day (bbl/d), all of which is imported. Around 77% of the Maldives' oil product consumption is accounted for by distillate, with the remainder consisting of jet fuel (18%) and gasoline (5%). The Maldives has searched for oil without success.

	1999	2000	2001
Inflation (% change)	3.0	-1.1	3.7
Exchange rate (per US$)	11.77	11.77	12.24
Interest rate			
GDP (% real growth)	8.5	5.6	4.9
GDP (Million units of national currency)	6,583.0	6,547.0	7,116.0
GDP (US$ million)	559.3	556.2	581.3
GDP per capita (US$)	2,065.0	1,997.6	2,032.8
Consumption (Million units of national currency)	2,680.6	3,097.1	
Consumption (US$ million)	227.8	263.1	
Consumption per capita (US$)	840.9	945.0	
Population, mid-year ('000)	270.8	278.5	285.9
Birth rate (per '000)	34.4	34.1	
Death rate (per '000)	6.9	6.7	
No. of households ('000)	48.6	50.7	53.3
Total exports (US$ million)	63.7	75.9	76.2
Total imports (US$ million)	402.2	388.6	396.0
Tourism receipts (US$ million)	308.6	358.1	
Tourist spending (US$ million)	41.0	45.9	

Average household size 2001 (persons)		5.50				
Urban population 2000 (%)		27.0				
Age analysis (%) (2001)	0-14	42.7	15-64	53.8	65+	3.5
Population by sex (%) (2001)	Male	51.4	Female	48.6		
Life expectancy (years) (2000)	Male	66.8	Female	64.6		
Infant mortality (deaths per '000 live births) (2001)		43.4				
Adult literacy (%) (1997)		95.7				

TRADING PARTNERS

Major export destinations 2001 (% share)		Major import sources 2001 (% share)	
BRAZIL	37.6	SINGAPORE	23.7
USA	34.1	SRI LANKA	22.6
SRI LANKA	11.4	UNITED ARAB EMIRATES	11.2
CANADA	3.4	INDIA	10.3

Mali

Area (km²)   1,240,140

Currency   CFA franc (= 100 centimes)

Location   Mali, the former French colony of Soudan, lies in the geographic centre of northwest Africa, an area of almost unbroken desert except for the marshlands of the upper Niger and the slightly more hospitable Niger valley further down towards the capital Bamako. With Algeria to the north, Mauritania and Senegal to the west, Burkina Faso and Niger to the east and Côte d'Ivoire and Guinea to the south, its only access to the sea is through Senegal, Guinea or The Gambia. The capital is Bamako.

Head of State   President Amadou Toumani Touré (2002)

Head of Government   Modibo Keita (2002)

Ruling Party   Alliance for Democracy in Mali (ADEMA) leads a coalition.

Political Structure   Mali was ruled by military-backed autocrats from 1968 until 1991 when the regime was overthrown by Alpha Oumar Konaré. In 1992, Konaré was voted in as president and his party, ADEMA, has come to dominate the political landscape with no opposition party having a nationwide organisation. The people elect the president for a 5-year term. The National Assembly has 160 members, elected for 5-year terms, with 147 members elected in single-seat constituencies and 13 members elected by the Malinese abroad.

Last Elections   Touré was elected president in May 2002 with 64% of the vote. He defeated Soumaïla Cissé of the Alliance for Democracy in Mali and Ibrahim Boubacar Keita of the Rally for Mali. In parliamentary elections in August 1997, ADEMA swept to power, taking 128 of 147 seats. Minor parties claimed the remainder of the seats.

Political Risk   Recurrent droughts and frequent disturbances in Mali have created problems in recent years. Religion has also become a more sensitive issue in Mali. Although 95% of Malians are Muslim, the state is firmly secular. Periodic rebellions by the nomadic Tuareg tribesmen have eased since 1992, when a cease-fire was agreed.

International Disputes   A dispute regarding the international boundary between Burkina Faso and Mali was submitted to the International Court of Justice which issued a final ruling that both sides agreed to accept. Burkina Faso and Mali are proceeding with boundary demarcation, including the tri-point with Niger.

Economy   Mali has managed to maintain its pace of economic growth in recent years despite severe difficulties in the cotton and energy sectors. GDP grew by a meagre 0.1% in 2001, while prices rose by 5%. Fiscal revenue has been lower than envisaged mainly owing to the downturn. The current account deficit, excluding grants, widened to 12% of GDP in 2001, largely reflecting the drop in export volume. Monetary policy, conducted at the regional level by the Central Bank for West African States, has remained prudent. While credit to the economy declined in 2000, it picked up in 2001 with the satisfactory implementation of a financial rescue plan in the cotton sector. Mali remains extremely vulnerable to exogenous shocks and needs to diversify the economic base, especially through the development of downstream activities in the cotton sector. Important fiscal reforms to be introduced include implementation of the Common External Tariff of the West African Economic and Monetary Union, the move to a single-rate value-added tax at 18% and preparations for the modernisation of the domestic income taxation.

Main Industries   About 10% of the population are nomadic and some 80% of the labour force are employed in agriculture and fishing. Most farmers are engaged in a subsistence capacity. Altogether, agriculture accounts for 47% of GDP. Cotton, groundnuts, wheat, sorghum and fruit and vegetables are grown for export, while rice, millet, sorghum, maize and groundnuts are the staples for the domestic population. There is a substantial amount of cattle herding in the dry zones. The agricultural sector has been buffeted by a number of exogenous shocks, including a severe drought, which depressed cereal production, the hike in oil prices, and adverse developments in the sub-region, which raised transport costs. In addition, cotton production was halved owing to a producers' boycott in protest of the low producer price paid by the state-owned cotton company. The cotton sector crisis was triggered by weaknesses in the management of the cotton monopsonist, and was compounded by the depressed world price for cotton fibre. With a view to tackling the weaknesses in the management of the cotton sector, the government, has launched a reform programme for the sector. Minerals are an important source of foreign currency, with uranium, salt, gold and phosphates being mined. There are known deposits of bauxite, iron, manganese and tin, but these are only marginally exploited. Industry remains limited to the fulfilment of local needs, and centres on the processing of agricultural raw materials.

Energy   Mali relies on imports for the greater part of its modest energy requirements. It does, however, have enough electricity to meet its own needs. The electricity sector, however, has encountered serious problems in recent years. Officials have also raised the retail price of petroleum in order to reduce losses.

	1999	2000	2001
Inflation (% change)	-1.2	-0.7	5.0
Exchange rate (per US$)	615.70	711.98	733.04
Interest rate			
GDP (% real growth)	6.7	4.6	0.1
GDP (Billion units of national currency)	1,670.7	1,811.2	1,895.9
GDP (US$ million)	2,713.5	2,543.9	2,586.3
GDP per capita (US$)	246.1	226.4	220.6
Consumption (Billion units of national currency)	1,203.0	1,384.8	1,448.4
Consumption (US$ million)	1,953.9	1,945.0	1,975.9
Consumption per capita (US$)	177.2	173.1	168.5
Population, mid-year ('000)	11,027.5	11,234.0	11,725.0
Birth rate (per '000)	49.8	49.7	49.7
Death rate (per '000)	18.1	17.9	17.6
No. of households ('000)	3,433.9	3,535.7	3,736.4
Total exports (US$ million)	571.0	545.1	739.8
Total imports (US$ million)	819.7	592.1	656.7
Tourism receipts (US$ million)	50.0	51.3	32.7
Tourist spending (US$ million)	29.0	34.7	42.3

Average household size 2001 (persons)	5.10				
Urban population 2001 (%)	30.7				
Age analysis (%) (2001)	*0-14*	48.0	*15-64*	51.1	*65+* 3.7
Population by sex (%) (2001)	*Male*	49.4	*Female*	50.6	
Life expectancy (years) (2001)	*Male*	50.8	*Female*	52.7	
Infant mortality (deaths per '000 live births) (2001)	122.4				
Adult literacy (%) (1997)	35.5				

TRADING PARTNERS

Major export destinations 2001 (% share)		Major import sources 2001 (% share)	
THAILAND	17.5	COTE D'IVOIRE	16.0
BRAZIL	12.9	FRANCE	14.2
ITALY	6.2	GERMANY	4.6
MAURITIUS	5.6	SENEGAL	3.9

Malta

Area (km^2) 316

Currency Maltese lira (LM = 100 cents)

Location Malta lies in the southern half of the central Mediterranean, some 100km south of Sicily. Its close proximity to North Africa (Algeria, Tunisia and Libya) has left its mark on the country's character, as has its traditional activity in the world of shipping. The climate is warm and generally dry. The capital is Valletta.

Head of State President Guido de Marco (1999)

Head of Government Eddie Fenech (1998)

Ruling Party Nationalist Party

Political Structure Malta, an independent member of the Commonwealth, has a House of Representatives whose 65 members are elected for a 5-year term by universal suffrage. It in turn appoints the president for five years, and he then appoints the prime minister and his cabinet.

Last Elections In September 1998, the Nationalist Party gained a majority in the House of Representatives, defeating the ruling Labour Party with 53% of the vote. The Nationalist Party took 35 seats. The Labour Party got 47% of the vote and 30 seats.

Political Risk Malta has long maintained its independent existence, but the population is becoming increasingly convinced that their future lies with Europe. The decision to apply for EU membership will require a significant overhaul of the economy.

International Disputes There are no international disputes.

Economy Malta's GDP rose by only 0.4% in 2001 but should increase by 4.4% in 2002 and 4.9% in 2003. Inflation was 2.9% in 2001 and is expected to be 2% in both 2002 and 2003. A major challenge for the government is to gain control over the budget deficit, which stood at 5% at the end of 2001. Similarly, the national debt has ballooned to 53% of GDP. The public sector, which employs more than 30,000 people, is overstaffed and in many ways, inefficient. Funds to update infrastructure are also lacking. The government is focusing on these problems and pledges to have the country's finances back in sound shape by 2004. It plans to reduce tax evasion by 30% by 2004 and hopes to push through the sale of more publicly-owned companies. Both moves will help to alleviate the financial situation. By the end of 2001, unemployment fell to 4.5% and the number of those gainfully employed rose to 141,000. Malta has also emerged as the most popular destination for FDI among all the countries currently vying for membership in the EU. Malta's main hopes for a healthier economy are a continued recovery in West Europe (which could boost tourism) and realisation of its goal of converting the island into a centre for transhipment throughout the Mediterranean.

Main Industries The country's main earner of foreign exchange is tourism. In most years the sector accounts for 25-30% of GDP. About one million people visit the island each year and an estimated 35,000 people - one tenth of the island's total population - are directly or indirectly employed in tourism. Malta is regarded as a safe holiday destination but experienced its share of cancellations after 11 September 2001. The island specialises in four- and five-star leisure holidays which are of the "long stay and low spend" type. It has also proved to be an attractive venue for conferences for a wide range of European multinational companies. Agriculture is the second most important foreign exchange earner with exports of fruit, vegetables, wheat, grapes and horticultural products (especially cut flowers). In its negotiations with the EU, the government demands a 25-mile conservation zone around the island to protect it from EU fishing. Manufacturing accounts for almost a quarter of GDP and has performed poorly in the years since 1999. In services, the most important activities are banking, insurance and real estate which, together, grew by more than 60% since 1993 and now account for over 10% of GDP. There are plans to privatise Malta International Airport, the Freeport, a container duty-free facility and part of the Bank of Valletta. Most remaining public enterprises are neither profitable nor efficient, and the government must finance recurrent operational deficits.

Energy Malta has no domestic energy sources and relies entirely on imports for its fuel requirements.

	1999	2000	2001
Inflation (% change)	2.1	2.4	2.9
Exchange rate (per US$)	0.40	0.44	0.45
Interest rate (% per annum, lending rate)	7.7	7.3	6.9
GDP (% real growth)	4.1	5.4	0.4
GDP (Million units of national currency)	1,456.1	1,561.0	1,606.0
GDP (US$ million)	3,650.3	3,562.0	3,568.3
GDP per capita (US$)	9,592.0	9,313.3	9,288.5
Consumption (Million units of national currency)	915.0	998.3	1,039.3
Consumption (US$ million)	2,293.8	2,278.0	2,309.2
Consumption per capita (US$)	6,027.5	5,956.1	6,010.9
Population, mid-year ('000)	380.6	382.5	384.2
Birth rate (per '000)	12.3	12.2	12.0
Death rate (per '000)	7.7	7.8	7.8
No. of households ('000)	120.7	120.4	119.3
Total exports (US$ million)	1,785.6	2,336.5	1,916.7
Total imports (US$ million)	2,845.8	3,415.9	2,592.3
Tourism receipts (US$ million)	675.0	790.5	608.1
Tourist spending (US$ million)	201.0	214.9	190.8

Average household size 2001 (persons)	3.18				
Urban population 2001 (%)	90.7				
Age analysis (%) (2001)	*0-14*	21.5	*15-64*	66.2	*65+* 12.4
Population by sex (%) (2001)	*Male*	49.6	*Female*	50.4	
Life expectancy (years) (2001)	*Male*	75.7	*Female*	81.5	
Infant mortality (deaths per '000 live births) (2001)	7.2				
Adult literacy (%) (1997)	91.1				

TRADING PARTNERS
Major export destinations 2001 (% share)   **Major import sources 2001 (% share)**

USA	14.7	ITALY	17.1
GERMANY	13.0	FRANCE	10.2
SINGAPORE	11.2	SINGAPORE	8.2
FRANCE	8.7	JAPAN	7.5

■ Martinique

Area (km^2)　1,079

Currency　Euro (= 100 cents)

Location　The French overseas department of Martinique is a single island in the Windward Islands group, situated between Dominica in the north and St Lucia in the south. With a benign climate and relatively little hurricane risk, it is a popular tourist resort. The capital is Fort de France.

Head of State　President Jacques Chirac (France)

Head of Government　Claude Lise (President of General Council, 1992)

Ruling Party　Union pour la Démocratie Francaise (RPR-UDF)

Political Structure　As an external department of France, Martinique is governed to a considerable degree from Paris. The country sends four deputies to the French National Assembly and is represented at the EU. Since being accorded regional status in 1974, Martinique elects its own 41-member Regional Council for a term of six years, with responsibility for economic and social planning. Other executive power rests in a 42-member General Council.

Last Elections　The Regional Council elections of 1998 produced a victory for the RPR-UDF, which won 14 of the 41 seats. The Martinique Independence Movement captured 13 seats and the Martinique Progressive Party took 7 seats. Other seats were divided among various parties. In elections to the General Council, the Martinique Progressive Party won a plurality. The last full elections to the French Assemblée Nationale returned two delegates for the RPR, one for the Socialists and one for other left-wing groupings.

Political Risk　Secessionist sentiment in Martinique, although not sufficient to arouse severe concern, grew in more recent years. The island's finely balanced political system has meant that even quite small groupings exert disproportionate influence on the political scene. Martinique is a transhipment point for cocaine and marijuana bound for the US and Europe.

International Disputes　There are no international disputes.

Economy　Martinique, like many other French overseas territories, has occasionally felt left out of the mainstream of the decision-making process with regard to its own economy, although it has achieved a better development than most. Unemployment remains very high (well over 30%) and is the major cause of concern among public officials. The bulk of the island's exports consist of refined petroleum products, bananas, rum and pineapples. The tourism sector is the fastest growing area of the economy, with French tourists providing the great majority of the country's annual total of 500,000 visitors.

Main Industries　The economy is based on sugar cane, bananas, tourism and light industry. Agriculture accounts for about 6% of GDP, the industrial sector contributes another 11% and services make up the remainder. The majority of the workforce is employed in the services sector and in administration. Sugar production has experienced a secular decline, with most of the sugar cane now being used for the production of rum. Just over a quarter of the total land area is cultivated. Banana exports are increasing, going mostly to France. The bulk of meat, vegetable and grain requirements must be imported - contributing to a chronic trade deficit that requires large annual transfers of aid from France. Fishing is important, with lobsters, crabs and octopus among the major export activities. Tourism has great potential and has become more important than agricultural exports as a source of foreign exchange. Major industries consist of construction, rum, cement, oil refining and sugar. Industry is only moderately developed, although it employs 15% of the workforce. There is also a major ship repair yard and an industrial free port at Jarry.

Energy　Martinique relies on imports for all its energy requirements. There is no hydroelectric capacity, with all electricity being supplied by oil-fired generators.

	1999	2000	2001
Inflation (% change)	0.9	1.1	1.1
Exchange rate (per US$)	0.94	1.09	1.12
Interest rate			
GDP (% real growth)	3.4	2.8	
GDP (Million units of national currency)	2,673.9	2,908.2	3,120.7
GDP (US$ million)	2,851.1	2,526.1	2,792.6
GDP per capita (US$)	7,256.6	6,395.2	6,912.3
Consumption (Million units of national currency)	2,101.9	2,209.6	1.0
Consumption (US$ million)	2,241.1	1,919.3	2,085.6
Consumption per capita (US$)	5,704.1	4,859.1	5,162.5
Population, mid-year ('000)	392.9	395.0	404.0
Birth rate (per '000)	14.3	14.0	13.7
Death rate (per '000)	6.4	6.5	6.6
No. of households ('000)	85.9	86.5	88.4
Total exports (US$ million)	303.8	282.0	306.6
Total imports (US$ million)			
Tourism receipts (US$ million)	404.0	394.8	341.1
Tourist spending (US$ million)	392.9	395.0	404.0

Average household size 2001 (persons)		4.56				
Urban population 2001 (%)		95.1				
Age analysis (%) (2001)	0-14	23.0	15-64	66.1	65+	10.8
Population by sex (%) (2001)	Male	48.6	Female	51.4		
Life expectancy (years) (2001)	Male	75.7	Female	82.2		
Infant mortality (deaths per '000 live births) (2001)		7.0				
Adult literacy (%)						

Mauritania

Area (km^2)   1,030,700

Currency   Ouguiya (UM = 5 khous)

Location   Mauritania occupies a substantial part of central West Africa, meeting the Atlantic Ocean between Senegal and the disputed territory known as Western Sahara, but extending eastward as far as Mali. It shares a border with Algeria in the northeast. The country is mainly of Saharan type with most of its major settlements located on or near the coast. The capital is Nouakchott.

Head of State   President Maaouiya Ould Sidi Mohamed Taya (1984)

Head of Government   Cheikh El Afia Ould Mohamed Khouna (1996)

Ruling Party   Democratic and Social Republican Party (PRDS)

Political Structure   Faced with growing pressure from abroad, Mauritania has been gradually liberalising its political institutions. Political parties were legalised for the first time in July 1991 and the first free elections were held the following spring. The president is elected for a 6-year term by the people. Parliament has two chambers. The National Assembly has 81 members, elected for 5-year terms in single-seat constituencies. The Senate has 56 members, 53 members elected for 6-year terms by municipal councillors with one third renewed every two years and 3 members elected by Mauritanians abroad.

Last Elections   In presidential elections held in December 1997, Taya was returned to office with 90% of the vote. Parliamentary elections were held in October 2001. The ruling PRDS won 64 seats in the National Assembly. The remainder were scattered among six parties. Elections to the Senate took place in April 2000 and the PRDS won 52 seats.

Political Risk   Mauritania's Western Sahara war with Morocco is over and tensions with neighbouring Senegal appear to have abated but Islamic opposition to the elected government continues to raise problems.

International Disputes   Mauritania fought a long war with the Algerian-sponsored Polisario rebels who opposed its move to co-occupy the Western Sahara after Spain had abandoned it in 1976. The country formally relinquished its claim to the southern sector of the Western Sahara, leaving Algeria and Morocco to fight out the dispute thereafter. Mauritania still has a boundary dispute with Senegal.

Economy   Mauritania's GDP increased by 6.7% in 2001, while inflation was 4.7%. Authorities have earned praise from international analysts for their good record of economic performance. Among the most noteworthy achievements are a comfortable level of international reserves, an effective programme of tax reform and the preparation of a credible poverty reduction strategy. However, the poverty situation remains very difficult, with half of the population living in poverty, and one third in extreme poverty. Fiscal policy is being eased in order for the government to address the needs of the poorest segment of the population. The economy's narrow export base leaves it vulnerable to external shocks. In the future, policy makers hope to introduce policies to foster private sector development, liberalise markets and promote competition, all with the goal of stimulating employment and promoting growth.

Main Industries   Mauritania's agricultural sector employs well over 80% of the workforce. Farm productivity, however, is very low and the sector accounts for just a fifth of GDP. Arable or fruit crops can be grown only around the Senegal River. Cattle are raised in some parts of the country. Fishing is particularly important, with a large fleet producing a substantial proportion of foreign exchange revenues. However, over-exploitation by foreigners threatens this key source of revenue. Mining is the single most important area of the economy, with extensive deposits of iron ore accounting for almost 50% of the country's total exports. The decline in world demand for this ore has led to cutbacks in production. There is also some copper mining, as well as gold and uranium. Industry (including mining) accounts for 30% of GDP. Most manufacturers are geared mainly to serve the local market and are engaged in the processing of agricultural products, raw fish processing, iron smelting, the production of footwear and sugar.

Energy   Mauritania has not been an important energy producer but this may now be changing as exploration has yielded some positive signs. In 2001, a significant oil discovery was made in deep waters off the country's southwest coast and more discoveries are anticipated. For the present, the overwhelming majority (99%) of Mauritania's commercial energy consumption consists of imported oil. Mauritania also consumes a significant percentage of "non-commercial" (ie wood, biomass) energy.

	1999	2000	2001
Inflation (% change)	4.1	3.3	4.7
Exchange rate (per US$)	209.51	238.92	255.25
Interest rate			
GDP (% real growth)	5.9	3.6	6.7
GDP (Million units of national currency)	106,042.0	112,290.0	124,665.0
GDP (US$ million)	506.1	470.0	488.4
GDP per capita (US$)	193.6	176.0	173.5
Consumption (Million units of national currency)	133,590.4	150,433.7	157,937.4
Consumption (US$ million)	637.6	629.6	618.8
Consumption per capita (US$)	243.8	235.8	219.8
Population, mid-year ('000)	2,614.9	2,670.0	2,815.0
Birth rate (per '000)	43.6	43.6	43.7
Death rate (per '000)	15.0	14.8	14.5
No. of households ('000)	639.9	649.1	675.9
Total exports (US$ million)	373.0	300.0	300.1
Total imports (US$ million)	305.0	340.0	376.8
Tourism receipts (US$ million)	28.0	25.2	27.4
Tourist spending (US$ million)	55.0	26.1	24.1

Average household size 2001 (persons)	4.11					
Urban population 2001 (%)	58.7					
Age analysis (%) (2001)	*0-14*	43.9	*15-64*	52.9	*65+*	3.2
Population by sex (%) (2001)	*Male*	49.8	*Female*	50.2		
Life expectancy (years) (2001)	*Male*	50.4	*Female*	53.6		
Infant mortality (deaths per '000 live births) (2001)	99.2					
Adult literacy (%) (1997)	38.4					

TRADING PARTNERS

Major export destinations 2001 (% share)

ITALY	15.0
FRANCE	15.0
SPAIN	12.4
BELGIUM	8.5

Major import sources 2001 (% share)

FRANCE	22.8
BELGIUM	8.0
ITALY	5.6
SPAIN	5.5

■ Mauritius

Area (km^2)   1,865

Currency   Mauritian rupee (Rs = 100 cents)

Location   Mauritius comprises a group of islands lying in the Indian Ocean, some 800km off the eastern coast of Madagascar. It has a mixed population of Asian, European and some African origin. The country has a subtropical climate with high humidity throughout the year. The capital is Port Louis.

Head of State   Acting President Ariranga Govindasamy Pillay (2002)

Head of Government   Anerood Jugnauth (2000)

Ruling Party   The government is formed by the Militant Socialist Movement (MSM) and the Mauritian Militant Movement (MMM).

Political Structure   Mauritius became an independent republic in March 1992. Shortly thereafter, it left the Commonwealth. The president is elected for a 5-year term by the parliament. The National Assembly has 66 members, 62 elected for a 4-year term in single-seat constituencies and four additional members appointed by the Supreme Court. Operation of the political system is sometimes hampered by serious differences between the minority Creoles and the dominant Hindus.

Last Elections   Elections to the Assembly took place in September 2000, when the MSM and the MMM together received 52% of the vote and 55 seats. The former prime minister, Anerood Jugnauth, was then returned to the office.

Political Risk   A series of riots in the island's capital occurred in 1999. These events marked a drastic change after years of political stability and economic success. The underlying reason for the protests is that a large minority of the population was excluded from the benefits of the island's economic growth over the 10 years to 2001. Creoles, who make up almost a third of the population, resent the political power of Hindus and the economic dominance of the Mauritians of French origin. The fear is that violence will become communal, as it did at independence in 1968.

International Disputes   Mauritius seeks the return of Diego Garcia, an island 1,900km northeast of Mauritius. The tiny island forms part of the British Indian Ocean Territory and is home to a large US naval installation. The island is of strategic importance and the claim is not treated seriously.

Economy   One of the richest countries in Africa, Mauritius largely avoided the disastrous problems existing in other parts of the continent. GDP grew by 6.7% in 2001 and prices rose by 4.4%. However, the long-term rise in unemployment, evident since the early 1990s, has continued with the unemployment rate climbing to 7.2% in 2000, and close to 8% in 2001. Real wage growth in excess of increases in productivity accounted in part for this development. Despite a 4.4% decline in the terms of trade (resulting mainly from higher oil prices) and a real effective appreciation of the Mauritian rupee, the external current account balance has shifted to a surplus. Significant reductions in external tariffs have been put into effect, mainly on raw materials and intermediates, along with certain income tax and indirect tax reductions. The economy's main weakness is that a sizeable proportion of the population is excluded from the island's increasing wealth. With buoyant tax receipts and non-tax revenues, the overall fiscal deficit is expected to remain around 4% of GDP, despite higher-than-expected off-budget outlays. Mauritius continues to have a low external debt-service ratio of slightly more than 8% of exports of goods and services.

Main Industries   The farming sector is enjoying a strong recovery, spurred by a rebound in agricultural production following the drought in 2000. Agriculture is the country's main employer, with sugar cane, tea and tobacco grown for export. Staples produced for the indigenous population include cereals, fruit and coconut products. The farming sector is enjoying a strong recovery, spurred by a rebound in agricultural production following the drought in 1999/2000. Growth is broad based, with significant contributions recorded in manufacturing (especially in the export processing zone), financial and business services (including offshore activities), and other services (particularly transport and communications). A strong productivity performance in the manufacturing sector has contributed to a rise in exports. The tourist industry is very important and was performing well until after 11 September 2001. The sector caters mainly for French, South African and British visitors. Tourism was already approaching a saturation point prior to the latest downturn, with local operators admitting the islands may not be able to handle more than 500,000 visitors without suffering serious environmental damage. The island's tax treaty with India has spurred the development of a thriving financial services sector.

Energy   Mauritius relies on imports for all its energy needs, except for a small amount of fuel wood. All but one sixth of its electricity derives from thermal power stations.

	1999	2000	2001
Inflation (% change)	7.9	5.3	4.4
Exchange rate (per US$)	25.19	26.25	29.13
Interest rate (% per annum, lending rate)	21.6	20.8	21.1
GDP (% real growth)	5.9	3.6	6.7
GDP (Million units of national currency)	106,042.0	112,290.0	124,665.0
GDP (US$ million)	4,210.4	4,277.8	4,279.7
GDP per capita (US$)	3,656.9	3,694.1	3,620.7
Consumption (Million units of national currency)	68,711.0	73,938.0	80,942.0
Consumption (US$ million)	2,728.2	2,816.7	2,778.7
Consumption per capita (US$)	2,369.5	2,432.4	2,350.9
Population, mid-year ('000)	1,151.4	1,158.0	1,182.0
Birth rate (per '000)	16.6	16.3	16.0
Death rate (per '000)	6.7	6.7	6.7
No. of households ('000)	227.7	226.6	226.1
Total exports (US$ million)	1,553.9	1,804.1	1,745.4
Total imports (US$ million)	2,247.4	2,389.4	2,327.8
Tourism receipts (US$ million)	545.0	649.5	493.3
Tourist spending (US$ million)	187.0	193.6	156.3

Average household size 2001 (persons)	5.11				
Urban population 2001 (%)	41.6				
Age analysis (%) (2001)	*0-14*	26.3	*15-64*	67.6	*65+* 6.1
Population by sex (%) (2001)	*Male*	49.7	*Female*	50.3	
Life expectancy (years) (2001)	*Male*	68.0	*Female*	75.6	
Infant mortality (deaths per '000 live births) (2001)	16.7				
Adult literacy (%) (1997)	83.0				

TRADING PARTNERS

Major export destinations 2001 (% share)

UNITED KINGDOM	28.5
FRANCE	23.7
USA	17.3
MADAGASCAR	5.4

Major import sources 2001 (% share)

FRANCE	18.9
SOUTH AFRICA	14.2
INDIA	8.4
CHINA	5.9

Mexico

Area (km^2)   1,972,545

Currency   Mexican new peso (NP = 100 centavos)

Location   Mexico, perhaps the most affluent state in Latin America, extends for well over 2,000km from its northern border with the US down to the boundaries with Guatemala and Belize in the south. It has coastlines on both the Atlantic and the Pacific and embraces a wide range of territorial types. The landscape is partly volcanic and is subject to earthquakes, although in the south it becomes jungle. The capital is Mexico City.

Head of State   President Vincente Fox (December 2000)

Head of Government   Vincente Fox (December 2000))

Ruling Party   National Action Party (PAN)

Political Structure   Mexico, a parliamentary democracy with an executive president, has one of the longest democratic traditions in Latin America. Yet its politics - until the latest elections - have been dominated completely by the Partido Revolucionario Institucional (PRI) since 1917. The president is elected for a 6-year term by universal suffrage. Parliament has two chambers. The Chamber of Deputies has 500 members, elected for 3-year terms, 300 members elected in single-seat constituencies and 200 members elected by proportional representation, 300 members in single-seat constituencies and 200 members by proportional representation. The Chamber of Senators has 128 members, elected for 3-year terms in 4-seat constituencies.

Last Elections   Presidential elections were held in July 2000. For the first time in many decades, the candidate of PAN, Vincente Fox, defeated the PRI candidate, Francisco Labastida. Fox received 43% of the vote, Labastida got 36% and Cardenas of the Revolutionary Democratic Party (PRD) won 16%. Mid-term elections were held in July 2000. In the Chamber of Deputies, PAN took 218 seats, the PRI won 209 seats and the remainder were divided among several parties.

Political Risk   Mexico's government has been unable to make any headway with its agenda of reforms. Problems start with the Mexican Congress. In 2001, there were almost no legislative gains for the government. The government's tax reform bill, for example, was entirely revised by Congress in late 2001. Those who expected that the transformation of Mexico would begin with the election of Vicente Fox in late 2000 are extremely disappointed. If a Mexican president is to attain real power democratically, he will have to be much more effective than Fox in making a forceful case for change and economic reform.

International Disputes   Mexico's relations with Guatemala are occasionally strained owing to its assumed contacts with the Chaiapas rebels in the southern part of that country. The country's relations with the US have improved since it became a member of the North American Free Trade Association (NAFTA) and it continues to enjoy warm relations with Cuba, despite objections from its northern neighbour. Mexican policies on oil production and pricing have sometimes tracked those of OPEC, although it is not a member.

Economy   GDP contracted slightly by 0.3% in 2001 and will grow by just 1.7% in 2002. In 2003, growth should be much stronger at 4.9%. Inflation was 6.4% in 2001 and will be about 4.3% in 2002. Prices will rise by 3.8% in 2003. Investment plans were quick to respond to the recent weakening of foreign demand. Employment growth fell in the course of 2001; and, with a lag, consumer confidence wavered. Rising uncertainties following the terrorist attacks in the US exacerbated these trends. Even so, it is important to recognise that the present downturn, unlike previous ones, has not been associated with macroeconomic instability or a crisis of confidence, but rather reflects the increasing integration of Mexico into the North American Free Trade Agreement and the resulting synchronisation between Mexico and the US economic cycles. A number of structural weaknesses persist, however. A large informal sector co-exists with formal employment. Poverty is widespread and acute poverty remains significant. The productive sector continues to be characterised by a dual structure, with a dynamic export sector made of large firms with easy access to financing including from abroad, and a less efficient domestic market-oriented sector.

Main Industries   The share of agriculture has declined to just 5% of GDP, but the sector still employs around 20% of the workforce. Major exports are citrus crops, tomatoes, peppers, cotton, coffee and sugar cane. In 2001, agricultural output shrank slightly and a drought in large parts of the country in 2002 may lead to another decline. Oil accounts for about 7% of Mexico's total export earnings, and about 33% of government revenues. The government has been trying to restructure and part-privatise the oil industry since dwindling oil reserves, increasing fuel deficits and poor provision of electricity have exposed inefficiencies in the petrochemicals and energy sectors. Manufacturing accounts for around 90% of all export earnings. Mexico has a sophisticated industrial base, but output shrank in 2001. Industries producing clothing and household goods have benefited greatly from Mexico's membership in NAFTA and have gained market share in the US at the expense of their Caribbean competitors. Altogether, industry contributes 25% to GDP while services accounts for 70%. After extended debate, changes to Mexico's tax codes were passed in January 2002. New taxes on a range of "luxury goods" are expected to generate about US$6.5 billion. Fox's proposed tax increases were intended to move the country away from oil dependence; the modest increase that was passed is not expected to reduce significantly the vulnerability to oil price fluctuations. There are reserves of uranium, iron ore, gold, silver, copper, zinc and lead.

Energy   Mexico has the second largest proven crude oil reserves in the Western Hemisphere (28.3 billion barrels) after Venezuela. In 2001, Mexico produced about 3.6 million barrels per day (bbl/d) of oil, with net oil exports of roughly 1.6 million bbl/d. Mexico ranked as the world's fifth largest oil producer, behind the US, Saudi Arabia, Russia and Iran. Pemex, Mexico's state-owned oil company, is the world's sixth largest oil company, the single most important entity in the Mexican economy, and a symbol of Mexican sovereignty and independence. It has exclusive rights to oil exploration and production in Mexico. While Pemex is criticised widely as being bloated and inefficient, privatisation is not on the agenda. The state-run organisation enjoys enthusiastic public support, and President Fox retracted early campaign promises to privatise it. He has vowed instead to modernise and streamline the oil giant. With the Mexican economy predicted to grow at an average rate of just over 5% per year for the next two decades, energy demand is expected to rise significantly. Oil and natural gas will likely remain the dominant energy sources through 2020, accounting for well over 80% of total energy consumed.

	1999	2000	2001
Inflation (% change)	16.6	9.5	6.4
Exchange rate (per US$)	9.56	9.46	9.34
Interest rate (% per annum, lending rate)	25.9	18.2	13.9
GDP (% real growth)	3.6	6.6	-0.3
GDP (Billion units of national currency)	4,599.4	5,491.0	5,771.9
GDP (US$ million)	481,093.8	580,718.4	617,817.1
GDP per capita (US$)	4,902.9	5,828.9	6,110.4
Consumption (Billion units of national currency)	3,181.3	3,816.6	3,990.1
Consumption (US$ million)	332,756.2	403,630.6	427,102.2
Consumption per capita (US$)	3,391.2	4,051.4	4,224.1
Population, mid-year ('000)	98,124.2	99,627.1	101,109.8
Birth rate (per '000)	23.8	23.3	22.8
Death rate (per '000)	5.1	5.1	5.1
No. of households ('000)	22,407.4	22,640.4	22,830.5
Total exports (US$ million)	136,391.0	166,367.0	158,547.0
Total imports (US$ million)	148,648.0	182,702.0	147,742.4
Tourism receipts (US$ million)	7,223.0	8,945.1	8,203.7
Tourist spending (US$ million)	4,541.0	5,718.5	4,825.2

Average household size 2001 (persons)	4.40				
Urban population 2001 (%)	74.6				
Age analysis (%) (2001)	*0-14*	32.7	*15-64*	62.5	*65+* 4.8
Population by sex (%) (2001)	*Male*	49.5	*Female*	50.5	
Life expectancy (years) (2001)	*Male*	70.2	*Female*	76.2	
Infant mortality (deaths per '000 live births) (2001)	28.7				
Adult literacy (%) (1997)	90.1				

TRADING PARTNERS

Major export destinations 2001 (% share)

USA	82.8
CANADA	4.9
JAPAN	1.2
SPAIN	0.9

Major import sources 2001 (% share)

USA	72.2
GERMANY	3.4
JAPAN	3.0
CHINA	1.6

Moldova

Area (km^2)   33,700

Currency   Leu

Location   Located in the western part of the former Soviet Union, Moldova is sandwiched between Romania and Ukraine. It includes a substantial part of the territory to the east of the Pruth river, once known as Bessarabia, and also a predominantly Russian area to the east. The climate is warm and pleasant, and agriculture flourishes. The capital is Kishinev.

Head of State   President Vladimir Voronin (2001)

Head of Government   Vasile Tarlev (2001)

Ruling Party   The government is Party of the Communists of the Republic of Moldova (PCRM).

Political Structure   Moldova comprises the bulk of the former Moldavian SSR within the former Soviet Union. It has an executive president elected for a 4-year term by the people. Parliament) has 101 members, elected for 4-year terms by proportional representation.

Last Elections   Parliamentary elections in February 2001 gave the Communist Party 49% of the vote and 71 seats. The Electoral Bloc Braghis Alliance (BEAB) received 13% of the vote and 19 seats. The remaining seats were divided among several parties. The parliament then elected Voronin as president.

Political Risk   The period since independence in August 1991 has been marked by a long-running dispute between the ethnic Russians who make up over half the population of the Transdniestria province, which borders on Ukraine and their Romanian-speaking counterparts in the rest of the country. Supported by Moscow, rebels in the province started a secessionist war in 1992. Russia agreed to withdraw all its troops from Transdniestria in 1995 but the semi-criminal statelet survives on contraband. More recently, it may have begun to assassinate political opponents in other parts of the country.

International Disputes   Much of Moldova's rocky relations with its neighbours date back to the 1940s, when the fascist government of Romania was forced to hand over a large part of its most productive land (Bessarabia) to the Soviets. That territory was then attached to a section of land carved out of Ukraine and renamed the Soviet Republic of Moldova. The Romanian language was downgraded, but remained dominant in daily use. Romania has protested ever since at its loss. In 2001, the president proposed to join Moldova with the Russia-Belarus union and is trying to Russify the school curriculum.

Economy   Moldova has become the poorest country in Europe (replacing Albania for that dubious distinction). Fortunately, the economy has finally begun to grow. Moldova's GDP rose by 4% in 2001 and is forecast to grow by another 4.8% in 2002. In 2003, growth is expected to be 5%. Meanwhile, inflation was 9.8% in 2001 and will fall to 6.6% in 2002 and 6% in 2003. Moldova is badly in need of the stronger growth that has been forecast. At the moment, the economy is pitiful. Half the country survives on what it grows. The average wage, for those with jobs, is US$60 per month. Moldavians are emigrating at a record pace. Moldova's dismal economic performance since independence can also be explained by the extended delays in structural reform and the partial nature of those undertaken. In addition, the country's institutional framework is still far removed from what is required for a well-functioning market economy. This has contributed to very low levels of foreign investment and private sector activity. Public and publicly guaranteed external debt now amounts to more than US$1 billion, equivalent to nearly 70% of GDP. Adding arrears on energy imports puts the debt stock at over 100% of GDP. Meeting debt service obligations places a large burden on the government budget.

Main Industries   Moldova enjoys a favourable climate and good farmland but has no major mineral deposits. As a result, the economy depends heavily on agriculture, featuring fruits, vegetables, wine and tobacco. However, the privatisation of this key sector - including agro-processing - has only just started. Light industry consists mainly of textiles and consumer goods. In addition, there is a modest chemical industry. The Moldovan parliament has approved a programme that would allow the privatisation of five wineries and the tobacco companies and has moved forward to establish a legal framework for defining property rights and contractual obligations. As part of its reform efforts, Moldova has introduced a stable convertible currency, freed all prices, stopped issuing preferential credits to state enterprises and backed land privatisation, removed export controls and freed interest rates.

Energy   Moldova has minimal proven oil reserves, and the country currently does not produce any oil, although a plan to develop a field in the southern region of the country could yield up to 2,000 bbl/d. Since Moldova does not have any refineries, the country must rely on imported petroleum products to meet domestic demand. Following the break-up of the Soviet Union, Moldova's oil consumption plummeted by 71%, from 56,900 bbl/d in 1992 to just 16,700 bbl/d in 1996. In 2001, consumption is projected to reach 21,000 bbl/d. As recently as 1997, Moldova imported the majority of its oil products from Russia, but currently Romania and Ukraine supply Moldova with nearly 99% of its oil demand. Oil products account for over 40% of Moldova's energy imports, which make up nearly one third of the country's total imports.

	1999	2000	2001
Inflation (% change)	39.3	31.3	9.8
Exchange rate (per US$)	10.52	12.43	12.87
Interest rate (% per annum, lending rate)	35.5	33.8	28.7
GDP (% real growth)	-3.4	2.1	4.0
GDP (Million units of national currency)	13,804.0	17,815.0	20,343.0
GDP (US$ million)	1,312.7	1,432.7	1,581.3
GDP per capita (US$)	299.7	327.1	361.0
Consumption (Million units of national currency)	9,136.8	14,030.9	17,037.1
Consumption (US$ million)	868.9	1,128.4	1,324.3
Consumption per capita (US$)	198.4	257.6	302.3
Population, mid-year ('000)	4,380.0	4,380.0	4,380.0
Birth rate (per '000)	12.0	11.9	11.7
Death rate (per '000)	12.0	12.1	12.2
No. of households ('000)	1,115.4	1,083.2	1,046.3
Total exports (US$ million)	464.0	472.0	570.0
Total imports (US$ million)	587.0	776.0	897.0
Tourism receipts (US$ million)	38.0	42.6	33.1
Tourist spending (US$ million)	58.0	40.7	37.7

Average household size 2001 (persons)		3.97			
Urban population 2001 (%)		55.1			
Age analysis (%) (2001)	0-14	25.2	15-64	66.9	65+ 7.9
Population by sex (%) (2001)	Male	48.7	Female	51.3	
Life expectancy (years) (2001)	Male	62.8	Female	70.3	
Infant mortality (deaths per '000 live births) (2001)		20.0			
Adult literacy (%) (1997)		98.3			

TRADING PARTNERS

Major export destinations 2001 (% share)

RUSSIA	43.6
UKRAINE	10.0
ITALY	8.1
GERMANY	7.2

Major import sources 2001 (% share)

UKRAINE	12.2
RUSSIA	11.5
ROMANIA	7.5
GERMANY	6.8

Monaco

Area (km^2)   2

Currency   Euro (= 100 cents)

Location   Monaco, one of the smallest states in Europe, is a Mediterranean principality that is surrounded on all its land borders by France, although the Italian coastline is within easy reach. The country is entirely urban, having no undeveloped land whatever, apart from parks and gardens. The capital is Monte Carlo.

Head of State   HSH Prince Rainier III

Head of Government   Patrick Leclercq (2000)

Ruling Party   National and Democratic Union (UND)

Political Structure   The Principality of Monaco is a hereditary monarchy, which has enjoyed French protection since 1861. Legislative power is vested jointly in the Prince and in the 18-member unicameral National Council, which is elected for a 5-year term by universal suffrage. Executive power is exercised by the Prince in collaboration with a 4-member Council of Government. The judicial code of France applies.

Last Elections   National Council elections took place in February 1998 when the UND won all 18 seats. Although the principality has 30,000 residents, only the 5,000 Monégasques are eligible to vote.

Political Risk   The Principality's legendary stability, combined with its considerable tourist industry and its favourable climate, help to make Monaco one of the most attractive investment destinations in Western Europe. Unlike Liechtenstein, Monaco does not rely significantly on offshore banking services for its income, and is not vulnerable to changes in EU banking laws. It has, however, been drawn into the EU's system of value-added taxes.

International Disputes   The EU, the US and other countries charge that Monaco's financial institutions are reluctant to enforce laws on money laundering.

Economy   In an area of less than 200 hectares and with a total resident population of 32,000, Monaco manages to generate over FF50 billion of business. The state carries no debts and possess unpublished liquid reserves of at least FF10 billion. Though Monaco is not a member of the EU, it adopted the euro in 2002 and received permission to issue its own coins. Monaco has no equal along the Mediterranean coast for per capita wealth, provision of public services and sheer scale of development in such a confined space. The principality's special protected status, under the control of France, gives it a high degree of security. Authorities are reluctant to admit it, but one of the reasons for the principality's success is its privileged fiscal status. Residents pay no personal income tax. Nor are they subject to a capital gains tax when they sell assets such as shares or property. In theory, corporate profits are taxed at the same rate as in France but professional firms pay no taxes. Nor do local firms that conduct 75% of their operations within the principality. Some Monaco-based companies conduct business between themselves in order to raise the proportion of activity in their country and therefore obtain eligibility for tax exemption.

Main Industries   The government has presided over a successful transformation of Monaco's economy into services and small, non-polluting industries producing high value products. The state has no income tax and low business taxes and thrives as a tax haven both for individuals who have established residence and for foreign companies that have set up businesses and offices. About 55% of Monaco's annual revenue is generated from VAT levied on hotels, banks and the industrial sector. Another 25% of revenue is derived from tourism. Most of the wealthy visitors to Monaco come from Italy, the US and France. Approximately 40% of all tourism is business related. Monaco is also a popular location for international companies that employ close to 20% of the workforce. The principality is investing heavily in telecommunications and intends to carve out a role as a carrier of transit traffic. Monaco also plays host to over 40 financial institutions and has a number of manufacturing companies making plastics, electrical goods and electronics, textiles and clothing.

Energy   The country depends on imports for all its energy needs.

	1999	2000	2001
Inflation (% change)	0.9	1.1	1.1
Exchange rate (per US$)	0.94	1.09	1.12
Interest rate			
GDP (% real growth)			
GDP			
GDP (US$ million)			
GDP per capita (US$)			
Consumption			
Consumption (US$ million)			
Consumption per capita (US$)			
Population, mid-year ('000)	33.0	34.0	34.0
Birth rate (per '000)	10.5	10.3	10.1
Death rate (per '000)	11.8	11.8	11.8
No. of households ('000)	15.0	15.3	14.6
Total exports (US$ million)			
Total imports (US$ million)			
Tourism receipts (US$ million)			
Tourist spending (US$ million)			

Average household size 2001 (persons)	2.23					
Urban population 2001 (%)	100.0					
Age analysis (%) (2001)	0-14	18.0	15-64	67.9	65+	14.1
Population by sex (%) (2001)	Male	49.1	Female	50.9		
Life expectancy (years) (2001)	Male	75.1	Female	83.2		
Infant mortality (deaths per '000 live births) (2001)	6.2					
Adult literacy (%)						

Mongolia

Area (km²)   1,565,000

Currency   Tugruk (= 100 möng)

Location   The Mongolian Republic extends some 1,800km across the eastern centre of the Asian landmass, running from the Kazakh/Russian border in the west to the start of the Yablonovy mountain range in the east, with Russia always to the north and with China always to the south. The terrain is mountainous, with the south giving way to the Gobi desert. The capital is Ulan Bator.

Head of State   President N. Bagabandi (1997)

Head of Government   Nambarlin Enkhbayar (2000)

Ruling Party   The Mongolian People's Revolutionary Party (MPRP)

Political Structure   Mongolia's semi-executive President is elected for a 4-year term by the people. The State Assembly has 76 members, elected for 4-year terms in single-seat constituencies.

Last Elections   Elections to the State Assembly in June 2000 returned the former communist party, the MPRP, to power. The Party won 72 of the 76 seats in the Assembly. Presidential elections in May 2001 produced another victory for the former communists led by Bagabandi. He received 58% of the vote compared to 37% for Radnaasumbereliyn Gonchigdorj.

Political Risk   Abject poverty, which was unknown in Soviet days, is now widespread in rural areas. The extreme severity of the winters in 2000/1 and 2001/2 revealed the vulnerability of the rural economy and accelerated the migration of people seeking better access to social services and employment opportunities from remote to urban areas, particularly to Ulaanbaatar. National unemployment, as measured by international standards, stood at 17% in 2000; 60% of the unemployed were under 35 years of age. The most vulnerable layers of Mongolian society - small livestock herders, the urban poor and street children - are subject to even minor external shocks, adverse weather patterns and the ongoing reform process. Hence, a social safety net for the very poor needs to be built as a matter of urgency. Since 1995, the proportion of people living below the official poverty line has remained high at about 36%, while both the depth and severity of poverty have increased. The country receives almost as much Western aid today as it did from the Soviets but the standard of living is much lower now. To avoid social unrest, the government continues to subsidise the cost of fuel and utilities. In a country where the average temperature is below freezing seven months each year, big rises in heating costs are unacceptable.

International Disputes   Mongolia has accused its neighbour, China, of ill-treating the Mongol population of Inner Mongolia, a Chinese Autonomous Region. Relations between the two states have stabilised but the Mongolians remain wary. Like Inner Mongolia, many Chinese officials consider what they call "Outer Mongolia" to be part of China.

Economy   Mongolia's economy should begin a recovery with GDP rising by 3% in 2002 and 5% in 2003. Inflation is expected to be around 6% in 2002 and 5% in 2003. Domestic investment reached 28% of GDP in 2001, but savings have remained low at 18%. This gap contributed to the current account deficit and the external debt. Growing unemployment, with only a poor social safety net, remains the government's main concern and a primary cause of poverty. Mongolia achieved some progress in restoring macroeconomic stability by reducing the budget deficit from 6.8% of GDP in 2000 to 5.1% in 2001. The enhanced revenue collections generated from an introduction of temporary excise taxes and an increase in VAT from 13% to 15% (both measures were budget amendments) permitted a slight expansion in the provision for selected social programmes without putting greater pressure on the overall deficit. A privatisation scheme scheduled for 2001 was postponed to 2002-2003, removing from the budget the potential benefits of the sales of the major state-owned enterprises. The global economic slowdown made it difficult for the trade targets to be met. With exports declining faster than imports, the current account deficit widened beyond target and increased the stock of foreign debt. Further efforts to keep the exchange rate stable through central bank intervention, and preliminary steps to bolster domestic savings, helped slow the rate of growth of foreign debt by the end of the year.

Main Industries   In 2001, the economy continued to be affected by exogenous factors, mainly severe natural shocks and declining exports, which kept its performance below potential. The modest growth that was recorded was due primarily to the expansion of the industry sector that helped cushion a sharp drop in agricultural output. The losses in the livestock sector in 2001, still reeling from the ill effects of two successive harsh winters and the outbreak of foot-and-mouth disease, were estimated at 10% of the country's total herd, or about four million animals. As a result, agricultural output, which still accounts for about 30% of GDP, posted an alarming 16% decline. The industry sector grew by 11.8%, driven by its main components, namely mining and manufacturing, which grew by 10% and 23%, respectively. The services sector, accounting for about half of GDP, registered 9.2% growth due to the buoyant outcome of the wholesale and retail trade, financial services, and transport and communications.

Energy   Mongolia has substantial coal resources, which are being developed to encourage industrial expansion; otherwise the country depends on imports for its energy needs. Exploration continues for indigenous hydrocarbon resources.

	1999	2000	2001
Inflation (% change)	7.6	11.6	8.2
Exchange rate (per US$)	1,021.87	1,076.67	1,097.70
Interest rate (% per annum, lending rate)	37.7	30.3	31.8
GDP (% real growth)	3.2	1.1	1.1
GDP (Million units of national currency)	925,346.0	1,044,578.0	1,130,502.0
GDP (US$ million)	905.5	970.2	1,029.9
GDP per capita (US$)	351.1	370.2	386.8
Consumption (Million units of national currency)	701,284.1	757,677.4	839,517.9
Consumption (US$ million)	686.3	703.7	764.8
Consumption per capita (US$)	266.1	268.5	287.2
Population, mid-year ('000)	2,579.1	2,620.7	2,662.6
Birth rate (per '000)	23.5	23.1	22.7
Death rate (per '000)	7.8	7.5	7.4
No. of households ('000)	525.3	526.0	522.1
Total exports (US$ million)	233.3	336.1	250.0
Total imports (US$ million)	425.8	510.0	461.0
Tourism receipts (US$ million)	36.0	36.9	19.5
Tourist spending (US$ million)	41.0	45.6	50.0

Average household size 2001 (persons)	5.02				
Urban population 2001 (%)	64.0				
Age analysis (%) (2001)	*0-14* 34.2		*15-64* 61.8		*65+* 4.0
Population by sex (%) (2001)	*Male* 50.2		*Female* 49.8		
Life expectancy (years) (2001)	*Male* 61.3		*Female* 65.3		
Infant mortality (deaths per '000 live births) (2001)	60.9				
Adult literacy (%) (1997)	84.0				

TRADING PARTNERS

Major export destinations 2001 (% share)		Major import sources 2001 (% share)	
CHINA	47.9	RUSSIA	25.3
USA	30.5	CHINA	14.2
RUSSIA	7.0	SOUTH KOREA	9.2
ITALY	3.3	JAPAN	4.5

▪ Morocco

Area (km^2) 458,730

Currency Moroccan dirham (DH = 100 centimes)

Location Although one of the smaller countries in northwest Africa, Morocco is probably the most affluent. Its rocky terrain almost meets with Europe across the Strait of Gibraltar, and most of the settlements of any size are located along the Atlantic coast just southwest of Gibraltar. The capital is Rabat.

Head of State HM King Mohammed (1999)

Head of Government Ali Abu al-Ragheb (2000)

Ruling Party The government is formed by a multiparty coalition.

Political Structure Morocco is a constitutional monarchy with legislative authority vested in a unicameral Chamber of Representatives. At present, two thirds of the Chamber's 333 members are elected by universal suffrage for a 6-year term, while the remainder are chosen by an electoral college. The prime minister is appointed by the monarch. A significant reshaping of the country's regional administrative network took place in 1994 when four new governorates were created. King Hassan subsequently pushed through a new constitution and coaxed the country's 17 political parties into three main blocks. In July 1999, Hassan died after ruling the country for 38 years. He was replaced by his son, Mohammed. In June 2000, the new king appointed a liberal prime minister, al-Ragheb.

Last Elections Elections were held in March 1998. The centrist and right-wing blocks took 197 seats compared to 102 for the left-wing opposition.

Political Risk Morocco is doing rather well and its policies are offered as an example to other Arab countries. But it is saddled with disturbing legacies and enormous social problems. More than 50% of the population is illiterate and there are huge disparities between urban and rural areas. Another threat could come from emboldened fundamentalists who may challenge the government.

International Disputes Morocco's dispute with the Polisario National Liberation Front over the future of the Western Sahara, which was originally a Spanish colony, drags on. A referendum on the area was first scheduled in 1992 but never held. Early hopes of a resolution by Mohammed VI, the young Morrocan king, have proved to be premature. Negotiations have frustrated the UN, proved debilitating for Sahrawi refugees and a danger to Morocco's traditional strained relations with Algeria. Morocco has released many Sahrawi prisoners but thousands more remain in desolate refugee camps where resentment against the country builds. Generations have lived in squalor in the camps since 1974. Morocco still has a claim against Spain for the Spanish enclaves of Ceuta and Melilla and three small islands off the coast which form part of Spain. Spain has rejected talks on the issue.

Economy Morocco's GDP grew by 6.3% in 2001 and is expected to increase by 4.4% in 2002 and another 2.8% in 2003. Inflation was just 0.5% in 2001 and should rise to 1.4% in 2002 and 1.8% in 2003. Morocco's policy makers are proceeding with structural reforms on several fronts. These include liberalisation of the telecommunications sector, the removal of price subsidies on key agricultural products, the implementation of rural infrastructure programmes and trade liberalisation in the context of the free-trade agreement with the EU. Relying on the proceeds from privatisation, the country's fiscal policy has been adjusted to foster stronger economic growth. Monetary policy took an accommodating stance and provides ample liquidity to maintain low interest rates and encourage private investment. The devaluation of the dirham in 2001, the country's currency, is regarded as a very important step considering the losses in competitiveness that Morocco has suffered over the past 10 years to 2001. This move is expected to represent the first step in a wider-ranging programme to move towards a more flexible exchange rate policy for Morocco. Such a policy will better fit the country's needs to respond to exogenous shocks, the challenges posed by trade liberalisation and the need to strengthen competitiveness.

Main Industries Agriculture makes up a large share (around 17-20%) of Morocco's economy and accounts for a substantial portion of the country's workforce (around 40-50%). Farming, however, is heavily dependent on rainfall patterns. In 2000, the agricultural sector contracted by around 18% as the result of a severe drought and has yet to recover. The vulnerability that this implies for Morocco's economy has encouraged the government in its attempts at economic diversification, particularly towards manufacturing and services (including tourism). Tourism is the second largest earner of foreign exchange (after mining), though it is underdeveloped and has suffered after the terrorist attacks in September 2001. The opportunities for tourism are substantial, however. For example, the country has 3,800km of coastline but not one seaside resort. Tourism generates about 5% of GDP and employs one out of every 10 workers. Morocco also has a strong manufacturing base and the sector accounts for around 17% of GDP. Morocco's mineral sector is the mainstay of the economy, producing phosphates, fluorite, manganese, cobalt, lead, zinc, copper and antimony. The country is estimated to hold three quarters of the world's phosphate reserves. Morocco has very little oil but good prospects after the discovery of oil at Talsint, near the border with Algeria. Initial reports indicate that the new find contains as much as 20 billion barrels equivalent of oil and natural gas.

Energy Morocco has only 1.8 million barrels of proven oil reserves, although most sedimentary basins (especially offshore on the Atlantic continental shelf) in the country have not been explored. In the meantime, the government is actively pursuing expansion of its upstream oil and natural gas sector. At present, the country relies on imports (mainly from Saudi Arabia, Iran, Iraq and Nigeria) for nearly all of its oil needs. Morocco contains only small natural gas reserves - around 100 billion cu ft but it is a major transit centre for Algerian gas exports across the Strait of Gibraltar to Spain.

	1999	2000	2001
Inflation (% change)	0.7	1.9	0.5
Exchange rate (per US$)	9.80	10.63	11.30
Interest rate (% per annum, commercial lending rate)	13.5	13.3	13.3
GDP (% real growth)	-0.7	2.4	6.3
GDP (Million units of national currency)	343,132.0	354,316.0	378,565.0
GDP (US$ million)	34,997.7	33,345.5	33,492.4
GDP per capita (US$)	1,260.0	1,180.9	1,166.9
Consumption (Million units of national currency)	224,408.9	232,553.0	252,380.8
Consumption (US$ million)	22,888.5	21,886.1	22,328.7
Consumption per capita (US$)	824.1	775.1	777.9
Population, mid-year ('000)	27,775.0	28,238.0	28,702.9
Birth rate (per '000)	26.1	25.7	25.3
Death rate (per '000)	6.4	6.3	6.1
No. of households ('000)	5,193.0	5,322.0	5,428.7
Total exports (US$ million)	7,366.9	6,961.0	7,115.9
Total imports (US$ million)	9,924.8	11,533.6	11,387.2
Tourism receipts (US$ million)	1,880.0	1,988.2	1,757.3
Tourist spending (US$ million)	440.0	434.4	343.9

Average household size 2001 (persons)	5.31					
Urban population 2001 (%)	55.8					
Age analysis (%) (2001)	*0-14*	32.1	*15-64*	62.8	*65+*	5.1
Population by sex (%) (2001)	*Male*	49.8	*Female*	50.2		
Life expectancy (years) (2001)	*Male*	66.3	*Female*	70.0		
Infant mortality (deaths per '000 live births) (2001)	44.4					
Adult literacy (%) (1997)	45.9					

TRADING PARTNERS

Major export destinations 2001 (% share)		Major import sources 2001 (% share)	
FRANCE	24.5	FRANCE	22.3
SPAIN	11.5	SPAIN	11.6
UNITED KINGDOM	7.1	ITALY	6.5
ITALY	5.6	GERMANY	5.4

Mozambique

Area (km²)   784,755

Currency   Metical (MT = 100 centavos)

Location   Mozambique extends for as much as 2,500km along the Indian Ocean coast of East Africa, running from the borders with South Africa and Swaziland in the south to Tanzania in the north. Inland, it borders on Malawi, Zimbabwe and Zambia. Less elevated than other countries in the region, the most fertile areas are in the west, where the Zambezi River is dammed at Cabora Bassa, and on the coast. The climate is tropical but prone to devastating drought. The capital is Maputo.

Head of State   President Joaquim Alberto Chissano (1986)

Head of Government   Pascoal Mocumbi (December 1994)

Ruling Party   Frelimo (Mozambique Liberation Front)

Political Structure   Mozambique's 1990 constitution marked a significant departure from the single-party collectivist state, which had dominated the country since 1975. The executive president is elected by universal suffrage for a maximum of two 5-year terms. The Assembly of the Republic has 250 members, elected for 5-year terms by proportional representation.

Last Elections   Presidential elections were held in December 1999. Chissano was re-elected president with 52% of the vote. He defeated Afonso Marceta Macacho Dhlakama. In parliamentary elections occurring at the same time, Frelimo took 49% of the vote and 133 seats. Renamo (National Resistance of Mozambique) received 39% of the vote and won 117 seats.

Political Risk   Anti-government demonstrations are common among the opposition Renamo Party. Renamo has accused the government of fraud in connection with the privatisation of a state-owned bank. The economy was severely damaged by the floods in early 2000. The rural economy remains weak as many farmers lost an entire year's harvest.

International Disputes   Mozambique's relations with neighbouring countries have improved significantly as the effects of its civil war recede into the past.

Economy   GDP rose by 12.9% in 2001, while inflation was 9%. The sharp increase in inflation in 2000-2001 has been a cause for concern. However, the subsequent tightening of monetary policy initiated in mid-2001 has reinforced the normal easing in prices in the first half of 2002. The government aims to bring inflation down to single digits during 2002. At the same time, fiscal policy is geared to meeting priority needs, while lowering the primary fiscal deficit and avoiding recourse to domestic borrowing. In line with these objectives, the government's plans for structural reform in 2002 focus on the implementation of a new income tax law and a new public financial management law, which is intended to improve public expenditure management. Despite adverse developments in the world economy, there has been no deterioration in debt indicators. The government is also pursuing a programme of trade liberalisation (despite strong opposition). Although the economy is growing rapidly at the moment, it remains very fragile and the country is still heavily dependent on foreign aid.

Main Industries   Agriculture is the backbone of the economy but the sector is still recovering from severe flooding in 2000. Farmers are also struggling to recover from the legacy of collectivisation in the 1970s and 1980s. Farming is mainly on a subsistence basis but small farmers are being encouraged to develop their own operations. Sugar, cashews, cotton, tea and sisal are grown for export, and there is an important fishing industry. The sugar industry is appealing for protectionist measures to halt imports but reform-minded officials are reluctant to help. Foreign investors have poured billions of dollars into a wide range of projects involving mining, transportation, energy, manufacturing, farming and tourism. Aluminium smelting, tourism and financial services are driving growth. Other manufacturing operations are still geared to replace imports and all are concentrated around Beira and Maputo. The authorities have faced difficult challenges in the banking system, including capital shortfalls in two of Mozambique's largest banks. Steps taken to resolve these difficulties, including the sale of one of these banks, have been complex and costly. The government is committed to a rigorous and transparent process to recover non-performing loans and improve accountability. There are also plans to tighten banking regulations and strengthen banking supervision.

Energy   Mozambique has coal deposits but no oil has been discovered. It does have vast and still only partially developed hydroelectric potential. International aid that was originally intended to develop hydroelectric power has been diverted to emergency road-building projects following the floods.

	1999	2000	2001
Inflation (% change)	2.9	12.7	9.0
Exchange rate (per US$)	13,028.60	15,447.10	20,703.60
Interest rate (% per annum, lending rate)	19.6	19.0	22.6
GDP (% real growth)	7.5	1.6	12.9
GDP (Billion units of national currency)	51,915.0	58,896.0	73,561.0
GDP (US$ million)	3,984.7	3,812.8	3,553.1
GDP per capita (US$)	206.3	193.7	172.4
Consumption (Billion units of national currency)	41,117.0	46,023.6	51,469.6
Consumption (US$ million)	3,155.9	2,979.4	2,486.0
Consumption per capita (US$)	163.4	151.4	120.6
Population, mid-year ('000)	19,313.8	19,680.0	20,615.0
Birth rate (per '000)	43.7	43.1	42.4
Death rate (per '000)	22.9	23.2	23.5
No. of households ('000)	3,445.1	3,489.8	3,700.0
Total exports (US$ million)	262.9	364.0	360.5
Total imports (US$ million)	1,138.6	1,158.0	1,047.9
Tourism receipts (US$ million)			
Tourist spending (US$ million)	19,313.8	19,680.0	20,615.0

Average household size 2001 (persons)	5.64				
Urban population 2001 (%)	41.2				
Age analysis (%) (2001)	*0-14* 44.8	*15-64* 51.9	*65+* 3.3
Population by sex (%) (2001)	*Male* 49.2	*Female* 50.8	
Life expectancy (years) (2001)	*Male* 37.8	*Female* 39.4	
Infant mortality (deaths per '000 live births) (2001)	130.2		
Adult literacy (%) (1997)	40.5		

TRADING PARTNERS

Major export destinations 2001 (% share)		Major import sources 2001 (% share)	
BELGIUM	34.2	SOUTH AFRICA	41.1
ZIMBABWE	9.8	AUSTRALIA	7.7
SOUTH AFRICA	7.1	PORTUGAL	4.4
GERMANY	6.3	USA	2.2

■ Myanmar

Area (km^2) 678,030

Currency Kyat (= 100 pyas)

Location Myanmar (Burma) occupies most of the westward-facing coastline of the Indochinese peninsula, extending from the northern Chinese/Laotian border, with Assam (India) and Bangladesh to the west, down to the 600-km-long finger of coastal territory which effectively seals off most of Thailand from the Indian Ocean. The climate is tropical and mainly humid. The capital is Rangoon.

Head of State President Gen. Than Shwe

Head of Government President Gen. Than Shwe

Ruling Party National Unity Party is in power. No other parties are allowed.

Political Structure Myanmar, or Burma as it was known until 1988, was run as a 1-party socialist state until September 1988, when a military coup overthrew the administration and declared martial law. A 485-member Constituent Assembly was formed in May 1990, but never met. In 1996, a military-run constitutional convention decreed that a newly elected assembly would choose its president from among three vice-presidents that it elects. All three are to serve 5-year terms.

Last Elections Multi-party elections to the newly created Constituent Assembly were held in 1990 and contested by some 93 different parties, as well as 87 independents. The election produced a crushing defeat for the ruling junta, the State Law and Order Restoration Council, whose own favoured party, the National Unity Party, collected less than 20% of the vote. Meanwhile, the opposition National League for Democracy (NLD) led by Aung San Suu Kyi received more than 50% of the ballots. Shortly afterwards, the junta banned the new Assembly and refused to allow Aung San to assume office.

Political Risk In May 2002, the government released Aung San Suu Kyi from house arrest. However, there is little evidence that Myanmar's dictators are relaxing their grip. After decades in power, the junta has done little, except to repress democratic parties. Many of the ethnically-based rebel groups that signed ceasefires in the 1990s now seem to regret it. Meanwhile, the government is busily undermining the autonomy it granted them. The country also faces a huge range of development problems. Its physical and social infrastructure is extremely inadequate and an increasing incidence of HIV/AIDS and drug-related problems are adding to social stress.

International Disputes The release of Aung San has reduced international pressure but Western governments have no faith in the present regime. The US has banned firms from investing in Myanmar, while the EU refuses to grant visas to senior government officials. Myanmar's disregard for human rights and its reputation as a big producer of illicit drugs continues to plague its relations with the international community. Much of the world's heroin originates in the "golden triangle", a region bordering Myanmar, Laos and Thailand. Outsiders believe that the government itself benefits from this activity.

Economy GDP grew by 4.8% in 2001 but the rate of growth is expected to fall over the next few years. Meanwhile, inflation remains high, running at 15% in 2001. Over the long term, prospects for growth and for lasting poverty reduction remain uncertain in a context where macroeconomic and structural distortions are acute. In addition to depressed external demand conditions, economic sanctions are likely to have held economic expansion in check. To cover the losses of state-owned enterprises, direct financial transfers are made by the government. Expenditures on state-owned enterprises account for about 75% of all public expenditures and, historically, these firms have been responsible for the bulk of public sector deficits. In 1999, the consolidated budget deficit was estimated at about 5% of GDP. However, significant off-budget spending and the subsidies implicit in the application of the official exchange rate mean that the true public sector resource gap could be much larger. Poor prospects for improved revenue mobilisation and a large increase in public sector pay imply that the public sector deficit persisted through 2000 and 2001. Despite an increase in approvals, there was a sharp fall in disbursed FDI in 2001. In the first half of the year, inflows were down by about 50% over the same period in 2000. International sanctions and consumer boycotts are deterring investors. Other than limited flows for humanitarian needs, official development assistance to Myanmar has also largely ceased.

Main Industries Agricultural output, which contributes substantially to aggregate activity, was adversely affected by rains that hindered dry-season rice cropping. Exports of garments grew strongly, as did exports of gas and metals, reflecting earlier investments in these sectors. Commodity exports also performed well. Exports of pulses surged, due both to an expansion of the area under cultivation that boosted supply and to rising international prices. While trade data are incomplete and may be subject to measurement error, it seems that the trade deficit narrowed in 2001. However, on the services account, reduced receipts from tourism and a decline in remittances from overseas workers may have resulted in a deficit. Productivity in several sectors, particularly agriculture, is low and opportunities are impaired by a variety of policies and procedures that unnecessarily regulate and impede commerce. In sectors where state enterprises benefit from large exchange rate subsidies, it is impossible for the private sector to compete. The reform process that was started over a decade ago has effectively stalled.

Energy Much of the foreign investment going to Myanmar is associated with the oil and gas sector (about US$1.6 billion since 1994). The country's reserves are dwindling, however, and there have been no promising new finds in recent years. Half of all electricity is generated by hydroelectric systems.

	1999	2000	2001
Inflation (% change)	11.4	10.3	15.0
Exchange rate (per US$)	6.29	6.52	6.75
Interest rate (% per annum, lending rate)	16.1	15.3	15.0
GDP (% real growth)	10.9	5.5	4.8
GDP (Billion units of national currency)	2,190.3	2,551.8	2,870.3
GDP (US$ million)	348,452.6	391,575.6	425,305.4
GDP per capita (US$)	7,830.9	8,690.2	9,322.7
Consumption (Billion units of national currency)	1,906.1	39.2	40.7
Consumption (US$ million)	303,245.9	6,022.3	6,038.0
Consumption per capita (US$)	6,815.0	133.7	132.4
Population, mid-year ('000)	44,497.0	45,059.2	45,620.5
Birth rate (per '000)	25.5	25.0	24.5
Death rate (per '000)	11.7	11.7	11.6
No. of households ('000)	14,535.0	14,468.5	14,225.0
Total exports (US$ million)	1,124.6	1,620.2	1,760.0
Total imports (US$ million)	2,300.1	2,370.9	2,461.0
Tourism receipts (US$ million)	35.0	42.6	36.5
Tourist spending (US$ million)	18.0	35.8	39.1

Average household size 2001 (persons)	3.13				
Urban population 2001 (%)	28.2				
Age analysis (%) (2001)	0-14	27.7	15-64	67.4	65+	4.9
Population by sex (%) (2001)	Male	49.8	Female	50.2	
Life expectancy (years) (2001)	Male	53.7	Female	58.7	
Infant mortality (deaths per '000 live births) (2001)	88.8				
Adult literacy (%) (1997)	83.6				

TRADING PARTNERS

Major export destinations 2001 (% share)		Major import sources 2001 (% share)	
THAILAND	26.4	CHINA	21.6
USA	16.4	SINGAPORE	16.4
INDIA	10.4	THAILAND	13.8
CHINA	4.4	SOUTH KOREA	9.0

▥ Namibia

Area (km^2)   824,295

Currency   Namibian dollar (= 100 cents)

Location   Namibia, the former South West Africa, lies on the southern Atlantic coast of the continent, where it is bounded in the south by its former occupying power, South Africa, in the north by Angola and in the east by Botswana. The country's climate is generally dry, although drought is rare. The capital is Windhoek.

Head of State   President Sam Nujoma (1990)

Head of Government   Hage Geingob (1990)

Ruling Party   South West Africa People's Organisation (SWAPO)

Political Structure   The Republic of Namibia became fully independent in March 1990, having been effectively annexed by South Africa in 1966 after the UN ended that country's right to act as administrator to the territory. Namibia has an executive president who is elected by the people for a maximum of two 5-year terms. Parliament has two chambers. The National Assembly has 78 members, elected for 5-year terms, 72 members elected by proportional representation and 68 members appointed by the president. The National Council has 26 members, elected for 6-year terms in double-seat constituencies (regions).

Last Elections   Sam Nujoma was re-elected as president in December 1999 with 77% of the vote. Elections to the National Assembly were held at the same time. SWAPO delegates won 76% of the vote and 55 seats. The Congress of Democrats received 10% of the vote and 7 seats, while the right-wing Democratic Turnhalle Alliance also obtained 10% of the vote and 7 seats.

Political Risk   Occasional violence has occurred in the north of the country as fighting in Angola has spilled over the border. The country's tourism industry has been hurt by the attacks.

International Disputes   Until recently, Namibia had soldiers fighting in the Democratic Congo in support of the government. There have been some tensions with Botswana over the construction of a new military base near Gaborone, the sovereignty of the tiny island of Kasikili on the Lobe River and a short section of the boundary between the two countries. The quadri point with Botswana, Zambia and Zimbabwe is also in disagreement. The country's long-standing dispute with South Africa over the ownership of Walvis Bay (434 sq m) has been resolved in favour of Namibia.

Economy   Growth in Namibia's economy has slowed as a result of the slump in neighbouring South Africa. Namibia's economic ties with its larger neighbour have been very close since South Africa granted Namibia independence in 1990. GDP grew by 2.7% in 2001 and prices rose by 9.2%. A major problem is unemployment which has remained high, at about 35% of the labour force. Nor has economic growth in recent years been sufficient to achieve gains in per capita income or a reduction in poverty. In 2001, the budget deficit fell to 1.5% of GDP, a fall which reflected buoyant diamond receipts and under spending on capital outlays. The external current account recorded a surplus of 5% of GDP. For the first time since independence in 1990, the 2001/2002 budget was presented in the context of a rolling 3-year expenditure framework. The medium-term approach to budget preparation was intended to strengthen fiscal management, especially expenditure control. The main guiding principle for the budget is to limit the ratio of government debt to GDP to no more than 25%. The original 2002 budget envisaged a deficit of about 3.75% of GDP, and the budgets for 2003 and 2004 (expressed in constant prices for 2001) targeted deficits of 3% of GDP. The government's main goals are to strengthen the agricultural and industrial sectors, upgrade education and improve the rural infrastructure. Although per capita GDP is three to six times the level in Africa's poorest countries, the majority of Namibia's people live in pronounced poverty because of the great inequality of income distribution and the large amounts of income controlled by foreigners.

Main Industries   Agriculture accounts for 15% of GDP, industry and mining each contribute 20% and services make up the remainder. Half of the population depends on agriculture (largely subsistence agriculture) for its livelihood. Namibia must import some of its food. The main agricultural crops are millet, sorghum and peanuts. The economy's performance has been hurt by slower agricultural growth and a fall in fishing output, despite buoyant diamond receipts. The major source of income and foreign exchange is the extraction of its vast wealth in minerals, particularly diamonds, uranium and tin and lithium. Other natural resources are copper, gold, lead, cadmium, zinc, salt, vanadium, natural gas and fish. Deposits of oil, natural gas, coal and iron ore are also thought to exist, while the country has the world's largest open cast uranium mine at Rossing. The extraction and processing of minerals for export is a significant activity. Industry is still on a small scale but is growing fast. The main industries include meatpacking, fish processing and dairy products. Public expenditures are expected to increase sharply on account of a larger wage bill than budgeted, a substantial transfer to Air Namibia and one-time allowances for military personnel withdrawn from overseas. The prospects for stronger growth beyond 2002 depend on the expansion of offshore mining activity, the operation of a new zinc mine expected in 2003 and foreign direct investment inflows. Namibia also has strong tourism potential, but this has yet to be fully developed.

Energy   Namibia is at present entirely dependent on imports of energy supplies, although prospecting is under way for petroleum. In 2000, Namibia renewed a stalled agreement with Russia granting Moscow the right to explore for oil and natural gas along Namibia's northern coastline. Namibia's government also awarded an oil and gas exploration licence in 2000 to a consortium led by US companies. The country has natural gas reserves of 3,000 billion cu ft. Although natural gas is still in early stages of use in the region, some projects have been identified.

	1999	2000	2001
Inflation (% change)	8.6	9.3	9.2
Exchange rate (per US$)	6.11	6.94	8.61
Interest rate (% per annum, lending rate)	18.5	15.3	14.5
GDP (% real growth)	3.4	3.3	2.7
GDP (Million units of national currency)	20,693.0	23,787.0	26,689.0
GDP (US$ million)	3,387.0	3,427.6	3,100.1
GDP per capita (US$)	1,996.8	1,985.9	1,738.7
Consumption (Million units of national currency)	12,235.0	13,636.0	15,634.6
Consumption (US$ million)	2,002.6	1,964.9	1,816.0
Consumption per capita (US$)	1,180.6	1,138.4	1,018.5
Population, mid-year ('000)	1,696.3	1,726.0	1,783.0
Birth rate (per '000)	36.5	35.9	35.2
Death rate (per '000)	17.7	17.7	17.8
No. of households ('000)	353.2	362.4	377.7
Total exports (US$ million)	1,141.1	1,037.0	948.7
Total imports (US$ million)	1,161.0	1,036.0	1,028.7
Tourism receipts (US$ million)	294.9	260.6	202.6
Tourist spending (US$ million)	86.3	79.8	66.8

Average household size 2001 (persons)	4.76				
Urban population 2001 (%)	31.3				
Age analysis (%) (2001)	*0-14* 41.9		*15-64* 54.3		*65+* 3.8
Population by sex (%) (2001)	*Male* 49.8		*Female* 50.2		
Life expectancy (years) (2001)	*Male* 44.4		*Female* 44.4		
Infant mortality (deaths per '000 live births) (2001)	68.1				
Adult literacy (%) (1997)	79.8				

Nauru

Area (km^2)   21

Currency   Australian dollar (A$ = 100 cents)

Location   Nauru is a single island, located between Kiribati, the Marshall Islands and the Solomon Islands. Almost circular in shape, it is remarkable for its low-lying terrain and for the virtual exhaustion of viable agricultural land. The climate is warm and dry. The capital is Yaren District.

Head of State   President Bernard Dowiyogo (2000)

Head of Government   Bernard Dowiyogo (2000)

Ruling Party   The Democratic Party of Nauru is the only legal political party.

Political Structure   The Republic of Nauru is an associate member of the Commonwealth, in which the executive president governs with the aid of a cabinet whose number may not exceed six people. The president is elected for a period of three years from the 18-member unicameral parliament, which is also elected, by universal suffrage, for a period of three years. Voting is compulsory in all elections.

Last Elections   A parliamentary election was held in April 2000. Only non-partisans were elected. Bernard Dowiyogo was subsequently elected president.

Political Risk   Like the Maldives, Nauru has expressed concern at the possibility of being swamped by rising seas in the event that global warming continues to worsen.

International Disputes   Nauru has settled its claim against the Australian government for the latter's over-exploitation of its only mineral resource, the phosphate (guano) deposits.

Economy   GDP grew very slowly in recent years and rose by only about 1% in 2001. Inflation on the island fell to 4% in 2001. Nauru's recent pattern of minimal growth is expected to persist. While the economy was boosted toward the end of 2001 by external financial support, the medium-term outlook is weak, given the adverse effect of declining phosphate reserves and many years of poor fiscal management. The provision of basic public services is regularly disrupted and is at serious risk over the medium term. The government faced serious cash constraints in 2001. This was due mainly to the suspension of phosphate exports in the second half of the year caused by the blockade of a processing plant as landowners sought additional compensation for the land occupied by the plant. By early 2002, government payrolls and payments to several creditors were delayed. The government continued to rely heavily on the practically insolvent Bank of Nauru to help fund its budget deficits and royalty payments. In the second half of 2001, the government of Nauru agreed with the government of Australia to house and process over 1,000 asylum seekers transferred from Australian waters. In return, Australia has agreed to fund a range of Nauru's equipment, material and services needs, as well as all costs of caring for the asylum seekers. These payments will both enhance government service delivery and provide an injection of demand into the economy that will help support economic activity in 2002 and, potentially, beyond. In total, Australia's net contribution to Nauru's economy is expected to be substantial. A pressing problem for the economy is the frequent disruptions of supplies of food, fuel, equipment and materials. Air Nauru, the only airline servicing the country, faced repeated interruptions in 2001 due to a shortage of funds for lease payments, fuel, maintenance and other running costs. Prior to Australian support, fuel supplies on the island had frequently been exhausted before the next shipment arrived. Public services, notably power, telecommunications, water and healthcare also faced increasing problems over the year.

Main Industries   Power, water, telephone, post, banking and air transport services are all provided by state-owned enterprises. The government also owns the country's main on-island income-earning activity, a phosphate mining operation. The private sector is very small and consists largely of trade stores, an offshore banking sector and some fishing operations. Phosphate output dropped off sharply in the early 1990s and is now at around a quarter of the levels seen in the late 1980s. This decline has led to economic activity becoming increasingly dependent on the government wages bill, compensation and royalty payments to landowners, and other initiatives as the main stimulus to demand, and this trend continued through 2001. It is expected that government revenues from phosphate mining will continue to weaken over the medium term: primary phosphate resources are largely exhausted and difficult to access; much of the mining operation's equipment is in a poor state; there is gross overstaffing; and plans to mine secondary deposits are not well developed. This decline in revenues will place considerable pressure on the budget.

Energy   All energy requirements are imported at present. There is no scope for hydroelectric development.

	1999	2000	2001
Inflation (% change)	6.7	7.5	4.0
Exchange rate (per US$)	1.55	1.72	1.94
Interest rate			
GDP (% real growth)	1.3	0.5	1.1
GDP (Million units of national currency)	304.1	328.6	345.5
GDP (US$ million)	196.2	190.5	178.0
GDP per capita (US$)	17,837.4	15,874.1	13,690.7
Consumption (Million units of national currency)	189.3	212.8	235.8
Consumption (US$ million)	122.1	123.4	121.5
Consumption per capita (US$)	11,102.0	10,281.7	9,343.6
Population, mid-year ('000)	11.0	12.0	13.0
Birth rate (per '000)	19.0	18.7	18.4
Death rate (per '000)	4.9	4.8	4.7
No. of households ('000)	1.7	1.9	2.1
Total exports (US$ million)		2.0	
Total imports (US$ million)			
Tourism receipts (US$ million)			
Tourist spending (US$ million)	11.0	12.0	13.0

Average household size 2001 (persons)	6.30		
Urban population 2001 (%)	100.0		
Age analysis (%)			
Population by sex (%) ()	*Male* 57.7		
Life expectancy (years) (2001)	*Male* 57.7	*Female* 65.8	
Infant mortality (deaths per '000 live births) (2001)	41.2		
Adult literacy (%)			

TRADING PARTNERS

Major export destinations 2001 (% share)		Major import sources 2001 (% share)	
NEW ZEALAND	29.2	AUSTRALIA	49.3
AUSTRALIA	24.0	USA	16.9
THAILAND	15.0	INDONESIA	7.9
SOUTH KOREA	11.7	INDIA	4.8

■ Nepal

Area (km^2)   141,415

Currency   Nepalese rupee (N Rp = 100 paisa)

Location   Nepal is a 700-km strip of land lying along the summit of the Himalayan mountain range between India and the Tibet Autonomous Region of China. Only a small proportion of the country is less than 2,000 metres above sea level, and the highest peaks approach 9,000 metres. Half the population lives in the lowlands, however, with three major rivers feeding into the Ganges river basin. The capital is Kathmandu.

Head of State   HM King Gyanendra (2001)

Head of Government   Sher Bahadur Deuba (2001)

Ruling Party   The National Congress Party of Nepal leads the government.

Political Structure   The Kingdom of Nepal is a constitutional monarchy in which the King, as the "symbol of Nepalese nationality and the unity of the people of Nepal", has extensive powers. He appoints 10 of the 60 members in the National Council (Rashtriya Sabha) - 15 of the remainder being chosen by an electoral college and 35 being elected by the House of Representatives (Pratinidhi Sabha). The 205 members of the latter are elected by universal adult suffrage for a 5-year term. Political parties were banned from 1960 to 1990. Electoral opinion is subject to deep schisms and to factional feuding.

Last Elections   Parliamentary elections were held in May 1999. The Congress Party secured a comfortable majority, winning 110 seats. The Communist Party took 67 seats and the right-wing National Party captured 11. Deuba was appointed as Prime Minister in July 2001 following the assassination of the king.

Political Risk   Tensions in Nepal reached fever pitch on some occasions in 2002. There is frequent talk of a military coup and the Prime Minister is under constant attack from his opponents in parliament. Meanwhile, guerrillas, with increasingly violent tendencies, want to replace Nepal's constitutional monarchy with a communist republic. All this unrest has made a serious economic dent in the country which depends heavily on tourism.

International Disputes   Nepal's relations with India, where a large proportion of the workforce is engaged, have been occasionally strained. The country also accuses Bhutan of maltreatment of its Nepalese minorities. Nepal and Bangladesh have also recently expanded their cooperation in an effort to improve trade and transit arrangements, including facilitating the use of Bangladeshi ports by Nepalese businesses. India and Nepal renewed a treaty that gives landlocked Nepal access to Indian seaports for another seven years. Most Nepalese cargo is carried by truck, or a combination of train and truck, to and from Calcutta.

Economy   Nepal's economy turned in another reasonably good performance in 2001 with growth of 5.3%. A slowdown is expected in the short term, however, in view of the country's domestic problems and the slump in tourism. Inflation was 2.9% in 2001 but is forecast to rise to 5% in both 2002 and 2003. Labour market conditions, characterised in 1999/2000 by a 47% underemployment rate and a 7% urban unemployment rate, likely deteriorated somewhat in 2001, given the slowing pace of urban expansion and the rapid enlargement of the labour force. The budget deficit widened to 4.2% of GDP in 2001 from 3.3% in 2000. At the end of 2001, foreign exchange reserves amounted to US$1 billion, or sufficient to cover more than seven months of imports of goods and services. Dependence on foreign assistance became more pronounced in 2001, with foreign grants and loans financing 58% of development expenditures, a sharp increase from the 47% level of the previous five years. Although the 2002 budget is not as ambitious as 2001's, it is still expansionary, with a total outlay of NPR90.1 billion, representing an increase of 22% over the previous year. Historically, high population growth rates and low economic growth rates have limited progress in poverty reduction. To achieve the level of growth necessary to reduce poverty in the country, Nepal needs to restore law and order. It must also accelerate the reforms that began in the early 1990s.

Main Industries   Agricultural output slowed to 4% growth in 2001 from 5% in 2000, while industry sector growth fell to 2.5% from over 8% during the same period. Tourism-related services were hit by the escalating insurgency and the shocking circumstances surrounding the deaths of members of the royal family. These factors contributed to a 21% drop in tourist arrivals by air during the year. Growth in merchandise exports fell sharply to 3.7% in 2001 from the substantial rate of 42% in 2000. Most of the decline was due to the sharp drop in the growth rate of exports of ready-made garments and woollen carpets. While net services receipts continued to fall that year, this was offset by an increase in net transfers, mainly due to rising remittances from overseas workers. While the Middle Marshyangi hydropower project and the Melamchi water supply project entail a high level of investment and resource transfers, development spending is likely to be severely curtailed due to increasing expenditures on security operations and the adverse impact of the insurgency on development projects and programmes. The government has recently indicated that about 25% of the 2002 development budget will be reallocated to additional security expenditures.

Energy   Nepal has no reserves of oil or gas, and only small (about two million short tons) coal reserves. Commercial energy consumption is made up of hydroelectricity, coal and small amounts of oil products. Non-commercial energy sources, such as wood, animal wastes and crop residues, account for a significant share of the country's total energy consumption. Nepal produces a small amount of coal and also imports coal, mainly from China, Bhutan and India.

	1999	2000	2001
Inflation (% change)	8.0	1.5	2.9
Exchange rate (per US$)	68.24	71.09	74.95
Interest rate (% per annum, commercial lending rate)	11.3	9.5	7.7
GDP (% real growth)	4.4	6.5	5.3
GDP (Million units of national currency)	341,197.0	392,508.9	448,720.9
GDP (US$ million)	5,000.0	5,521.0	5,987.0
GDP per capita (US$)	218.8	236.1	250.3
Consumption (Million units of national currency)	264,944.0	287,947.0	309,107.0
Consumption (US$ million)	3,882.6	4,050.2	4,124.2
Consumption per capita (US$)	169.9	173.2	172.4
Population, mid-year ('000)	22,847.3	23,385.2	23,918.5
Birth rate (per '000)	35.6	35.2	34.9
Death rate (per '000)	10.7	10.4	10.2
No. of households ('000)	5,363.4	5,423.7	5,430.9
Total exports (US$ million)	601.9	804.4	646.0
Total imports (US$ million)	1,422.2	1,573.3	1,235.0
Tourism receipts (US$ million)	168.0	136.3	112.4
Tourist spending (US$ million)	71.0	135.8	134.2

Average household size 2001 (persons)	4.36					
Urban population 2001 (%)	12.3					
Age analysis (%) (2001)	*0-14*	40.8	*15-64*	55.6	*65+*	3.6
Population by sex (%) (2001)	*Male*	50.7	*Female*	49.3		
Life expectancy (years) (2001)	*Male*	59.4	*Female*	58.9		
Infant mortality (deaths per '000 live births) (2001)	75.3					
Adult literacy (%) (1997)	38.1					

TRADING PARTNERS

Major export destinations 2001 (% share)		Major import sources 2001 (% share)	
USA	31.6	INDIA	36.5
INDIA	31.2	ARGENTINA	15.4
GERMANY	10.4	CHINA	13.2
ARGENTINA	7.7	UNITED ARAB EMIRATES	5.8

▨ Netherlands

Area (km^2)   41,160

Currency   Euro (= 100 cents)

Location   The Netherlands occupies some 250km of the North Sea coast between Belgium in the south and Germany in the north and east. In reality, its sea frontage is considerably more extensive than this would suggest because of the numerous inlets and tidal internal seas such as the Ijsselmeer and the Wadden Sea. About a third of the country is below water level, having been reclaimed from the sea by an extensive reclamation programme. The capital is Amsterdam.

Head of State   HM Queen Beatrix

Head of Government   Jan Peter Balkenende (2002)

Ruling Party   A 3-party coalition leads the government.

Political Structure   The Kingdom of the Netherlands is a constitutional monarchy in which the monarch rules through a Council of Ministers. The bicameral parliament comprises a 150-member Lower House (the Second Chamber), whose members are elected by universal suffrage for 4-year terms, and a 75-seat First Chamber which is appointed by the various provincial legislatures for a term of four years. The Netherlands formally rules over the Netherlands Antilles and Aruba, but in practice wide autonomy prevails.

Last Elections   In parliamentary elections held in May 2002, the Christian-Democratic Appeal Party of Jan-Peter van Balkenende took 43 of 150 seats and he was subsequently appointed as prime minister. The new populist party, List, whose leader Pim Fortuyn was assassinated a week before the elections, won 26 seats and is part of the ruling coalition. The conservative-liberal People's Party for Freedom and Democracy claimed 24 seats in the new parliament.

Political Risk   The Dutch political establishment has received a series of shocks in 2002 in an already turbulent period. In April, the entire cabinet was forced to resign after widespread disclosure of the failures of the Dutch military at Srebrenica during the Balkan peacekeeping mission. Elections were already scheduled to be held shortly but the debacle only added to the public's scepticism about their political leaders. The assassination of politician Pim Fortuyn in May 2002 just preceded elections and was more than just another vicious act of violence. It also reflected some deep-seated imperfections in the Dutch political process. The country's political process is consensus-driven, meaning that decisions come only very slowly and are often unevenly enforced.

International Disputes   Dutch politicians are sometimes frustrated by their apparent inability to influence decisions in Brussels but there are no serious differences with the EU.

Economy   GDP grew by 1.1% in 2001 and should rise by 1.4% in 2002. In 2003, growth is forecast to be 2.7%. Inflation was 5.1% in 2001 and will fall to 3.4% in 2002 and 2.3% in 2003. While at the moment the focus is on external risks and uncertainties, on the domestic side the recent departure from wage moderation is worrisome. Up to now, the increase in wages and labour costs were similar to those in other parts of the euro zone and with other trading partners. The pattern was thought to represent part of a normal adjustment process, entailing the reversal of earlier trends and a decrease in the Dutch competitive position to more sustainable levels. However, a reduced degree of wage restraint could result in an over-adjustment, entailing an excessive loss of competitiveness and additional increases in unemployment. Given the rigidities in the Dutch labour market and social security system, this outcome could prove very difficult to reverse. Structural reform, which has been one of the success stories of the Netherlands and an integral part of the Dutch model, is another area of concern to analysts because it seems to have lost momentum. Barriers to entry urgently need to be dismantled, for instance, by reforming the bankruptcy law and by reducing impediments for innovative entrepreneurs - such as the lack of support during the start-up phase, lack of access to research facilities and the limited availability of venture capital. Liberalisation is required in both the utility and energy sectors in order to boost efficiency to levels already existing in other EU countries. The liberalisation process in the public transport sector has been especially slow and the current and prospective levels of congestion in rail and road traffic may increasingly become a threat to productivity and economic growth.

Main Industries   More than most countries, the Netherlands is extensively integrated into the global system of trade and investment. Virtually all the country's industries are open to competition and foreign investment. As a result, foreign capital employed in Dutch businesses represents over a quarter of GDP, or more than twice the EU average. Trade, especially in petroleum products, is of the utmost importance. Industry makes up a third of GDP and is reasonably well developed with engineering, vehicle manufacture, electrical and electronic products, chemicals, aerospace and petrochemicals all of international importance. The country's agricultural sector accounts for a only a tiny portion of GDP. Farms, however, are efficient and farmers benefit from the low-lying and well-irrigated character of the landscape. Netherlands has an unrivalled distribution network with the world's busiest port at Rotterdam and one of Europe's leading airports at Schiphol. There are also a large number of coastal and international vessels providing cargo services, and an important ship servicing and repair industry exists around Rotterdam. The cuts in income taxes and social security contributions that occurred during 2001 as part of the tax reform have significantly boosted household disposable income. The economic slowdown in recent years has eased concerns that wage and price pressures might intensify. Rising labour costs and the consequent deterioration in international competitiveness would make it especially difficult for industries to regain some of the market share they have lost in recent years.

Energy   Dutch offshore oil production reached its peak in the mid-1980s. Since then, production has declined to about 60,000 bbl/d. Many of Netherlands' oil fields are nearing the decommissioning stage. Despite the decline, new field developments over the next few years using low-cost minimum facilities and sub-sea systems should at least maintain oil output for the Netherlands. The Dutch gas sector is much larger than its oil sector. The Netherlands is the second largest producer of natural gas among North Sea countries, behind the UK (although not all of this production comes from the North Sea; the Netherlands has considerable onshore gas reserves).

	1999	2000	2001
Inflation (% change)	0.9	1.1	1.1
Exchange rate (per US$)	0.94	1.09	1.12
Interest rate (% per annum, lending rate)	3.5	4.8	5.0
GDP (% real growth)	3.7	3.5	1.1
GDP (Million units of national currency)	373,664.0	401,089.0	424,714.0
GDP (US$ million)	398,423.0	348,393.9	380,062.6
GDP per capita (US$)	25,194.7	21,882.1	23,709.3
Consumption (Million units of national currency)	182,001.6	194,356.1	1.0
Consumption (US$ million)	194,061.1	168,821.6	183,884.8
Consumption per capita (US$)	12,271.6	10,603.4	11,471.2
Population, mid-year ('000)	15,813.8	15,921.4	16,030.1
Birth rate (per '000)	11.5	11.2	10.9
Death rate (per '000)	8.9	8.9	9.0
No. of households ('000)	6,785.0	6,819.0	6,851.5
Total exports (US$ million)	200,191.0	208,343.0	216,099.0
Total imports (US$ million)	190,281.0	196,736.0	194,461.0
Tourism receipts (US$ million)	7,092.0	7,536.0	6,217.1
Tourist spending (US$ million)	11,366.0	10,746.7	9,193.0

Average household size 2001 (persons)	2.33				
Urban population 2001 (%)	89.4				
Age analysis (%) (2001)	*0-14*	18.6	*15-64*	67.8	*65+* 13.6
Population by sex (%) (2001)	*Male*	49.5	*Female*	50.5	
Life expectancy (years) (2001)	*Male*	75.5	*Female*	80.9	
Infant mortality (deaths per '000 live births) (2001)	5.0				
Adult literacy (%) (1998)	99.0				

TRADING PARTNERS

Major export destinations 2001 (% share)		Major import sources 2001 (% share)	
GERMANY	26.7	GERMANY	17.5
BELGIUM	11.7	USA	9.8
UNITED KINGDOM	10.9	BELGIUM	8.8
FRANCE	10.6	UNITED KINGDOM	7.3

▪ Netherlands Antilles

Area (km^2)   993

Currency   Netherlands Antilles guilder (N Fl = 100 cents)

Location   The Netherlands Antilles consists of two groups of islands lying in the Caribbean Sea about 800km apart. The principal group, which includes the capital Curacao, lies just 150km off the coast of Venezuela. Being some 600km from the nearest other island states (Grenada, to the west), the group has acquired its own character under Dutch domination. Aruba, which once belonged to the group under Dutch sovereignty, negotiated its independence in 1986. The capital is Willemstad.

Head of State   HM Queen Beatrix (Netherlands)

Head of Government   Miguel Arcangel Pourier (1999)

Ruling Party   The People's National Party (PNP) leads a 6-party coalition.

Political Structure   The Netherlands Antilles is a Dutch overseas dependency ruled by the Dutch monarch through an appointed governor. In practice, the country enjoys a high degree of political autonomy and is edging toward independence. The country has a unicameral Parliament (Staten) of 22 members elected by universal suffrage for a 4-year term. Aruba, which was part of the group until 1986, became fully independent in 1996. In June 2000, the island of St Maarten voted to become independent. This move would eventually give it the same status as Aruba. Much attention now focuses on the question of secession by Curacao, the most affluent island. But like, St Eustatius and Saba, Curacao has voted to remain within the Netherlands Antilles in previous ballots.

Last Elections   General elections were held in January 2002. The Party Workers' Liberation Front 30th of May won 5 seats, the Party for the Restructured Antilles claimed 4 seats, the (PNP) took 3 seats with the remaining seats divided among 5 monitor parties.

Political Risk   The possible session of Curacao would have a significant impact on the country's political structure. Because the economy depends heavily on earnings from a few commodity exports it is vulnerable to movements in the world prices of these products. Illegal immigration (mainly from the Dominican Republic and from Haiti) is another source of concern. The islands are suspected of being a money-laundering centre and serve as a transhipment point for South American cocaine and marijuana bound for the US and Europe. Drug trafficking, especially in Curacao, has been widely blamed for an upsurge in criminal violence.

International Disputes   Aruba's departure from the Netherlands Antilles was initially resisted because of that island's important contribution to tourism. Eventually, opposition lessened as the sentiment in favour of independence grew in the other islands. The departure of St. Maarten will generate more controversy.

Economy   Growth was nil in 2001, while prices rose by 3.9%. Tourism and oil refining account for the bulk of income. Tourism is the most dynamic sector but experienced a fall in visitors after 11 September 2001. Nevertheless, the sector probably holds the most potential for the future, with most facilities being located on Curacao and St. Maarten. Visitors from the Netherlands, the US and other parts of the Caribbean make up the bulk of visitors. The Netherlands Antilles' offshore financial sector currently handles over US$65 billion of assets and a significant portion of total income is derived from these activities. The islands enjoy a reasonably high per capita income and a well-developed infrastructure compared with other countries in the region. Economic conditions are volatile, being influenced by erratic movements in world commodity prices (especially oil) and conditions in international financial markets.

Main Industries   The agricultural sector is tiny. Poor soil and inadequate water supplies hamper the development of farming. Industry accounts for 15% and services contribute the remainder. Tourism, petroleum transhipment and offshore finance are the mainstays of the economy, which is closely tied to the outside world. The islands enjoy a high per capita income and a well-developed infrastructure as compared with other countries in the region. The main industries are petroleum refining (Curacao), petroleum, transhipment facilities (Curacao and Bonaire) and light manufacturing (Curacao). Almost all consumer and capital goods are imported.

Energy   The country has no indigenous energy resources and depends on imports for all its fuel needs.

	1999	2000	2001
Inflation (% change)	0.8	4.7	3.9
Exchange rate (per US$)	1.79	1.79	1.79
Interest rate (% per annum, lending rate)	13.6	10.0	10.4
GDP (% real growth)	-1.9	-2.3	
GDP (Million units of national currency)	4,345.0	4,458.0	4,557.0
GDP (US$ million)	2,427.4	2,490.5	2,545.8
GDP per capita (US$)	11,304.0	11,477.0	11,467.6
Consumption (Million units of national currency)	2,309.1	2,454.8	2,509.3
Consumption (US$ million)	1,290.0	1,371.4	1,401.8
Consumption per capita (US$)	6,007.3	6,319.7	6,314.6
Population, mid-year ('000)	214.7	217.0	222.0
Birth rate (per '000)	15.8	15.7	15.5
Death rate (per '000)	6.2	6.2	6.2
No. of households ('000)	42.4	43.6	45.3
Total exports (US$ million)			
Total imports (US$ million)	1,360.0	1,290.0	1,361.6
Tourism receipts (US$ million)			
Tourist spending (US$ million)	214.7	217.0	222.0

Average household size 2001 (persons)	4.98				
Urban population 2001 (%)	70.7				
Age analysis (%) (2001)	*0-14*	25.4	*15-64*	67.1	*65+*	7.5
Population by sex (%) (2001)	*Male*	48.6	*Female*	51.4	
Life expectancy (years) (2001)	*Male*	73.1	*Female*	79.0	
Infant mortality (deaths per '000 live births) (2001)	13.2				
Adult literacy (%)					

TRADING PARTNERS

Major export destinations 2001 (% share)

USA	25.0
VENEZUELA	16.6
GUATEMALA	9.8
SINGAPORE	5.8

Major import sources 2001 (% share)

VENEZUELA	56.1
MEXICO	11.5
USA	10.8
BRAZIL	3.4

New Caledonia

Area (km^2) 19,105

Currency Franc CFP (= 100 centimes)

Location New Caledonia, situated in the Western Pacific about 1,500km east of Australia, is basically a single large island which controls numerous smaller coral reefs and islets. Vanuatu lies directly to the northeast. The capital is Noumea.

Head of State President Jacques Chirac (France)

Head of Government Pierre Frogier (2001)

Ruling Party The government is led by the Rassemblement pour la Caledonie dans la Republique (RPCR) in coalition with two smaller parties.

Political Structure New Caledonia is an external department of France and is governed, in part, from Paris. The country sends deputies to the French national Assembly and is represented at the EU. Since being accorded regional status in 1974, the country elects its own regional council. There are 56 members who serve for a term of six years. A referendum on independence from France was held in 1987, but the vote was boycotted by the Kanak majority, which opposed the move. Another referendum was scheduled for 1998 but a last-minute compromise by Paris postponed the vote for at least 15 years. Under the new agreement, New Caledonia will have control over employment rights, trade, natural resources and primary education while Paris retains responsibility for foreign policy, justice, public order and defence.

Last Elections Elections to the regional council were held in May 1999. The RPCR won 24 seats and the Front de Liberation Nationale Kanake Socialiste captured 18 seats. The remaining seats were divided among anti-independence and pro-independence parties.

Political Risk Ethnic tensions in New Caledonia are constantly just beneath the surface. The 1987 referendum on independence failed only because of the Kanak boycott. Surprisingly, however, Paris persuaded the Kanaks to defer the 1998 referendum on the same question for at least 15 years.

International Disputes The Matthew and Hunter Islands are claimed by France and Vanuatu. Ethnic tensions in the country are fuelled by resentment at the allegedly excessive control being exercised from Paris.

Economy The island's economy continues to struggle with growth of just 1.8% in 2001. Inflation has been below 3% for a number of years and is expected to remain below this level over the short term. Many decisions regarding New Caledonia's economy are made in Paris rather than Noumea. Export earnings rose in recent years as world prices strengthened. The local government, however, remains terribly short of cash and demands more aid from France. The island's mining operations represent the most important sector of the economy, with nickel and chrome extraction accounting for the bulk of national income. New Caledonia's reserves of nickel account for over 40% of known world deposits.

Main Industries New Caledonia's mining operations represent the most important sector of the economy, with nickel and chrome extraction earning well over US$8 million a year. New Caledonia is the world's third largest nickel producer, with over 40% of known world deposits. There are also reserves of iron ore, manganese, cobalt, zinc and lead. Agriculture performs poorly and productivity in the sector is low owing to a lack of investment which is related to the continuing political uncertainty in the country. Only a negligible amount of the land is suitable for cultivation, and food accounts for about 25% of imports. Farmers nevertheless have some export crops including copra and coffee, while sweet potatoes, bananas, pawpaws and vegetables are grown for the domestic market. Cattle are raised in various parts of the country and there are extensive timber removal programmes under way. Industry is varied, ranging from heavy activities like nickel smelting to light industries, textiles and electronics. The tourist industry is also extremely important, but is performing poorly. Travel fears following the events of 11 September 2001 coupled with more competition from other destinations in the region has led to a slump in the number of arrivals.

Energy The country relies on imports for all its basic requirements. Demand for electricity has been generally falling since the mid-1980s.

	1999	2000	2001
Inflation (% change)	2.4	2.8	2.5
Exchange rate (per US$)	85.14	98.45	101.36
Interest rate			
GDP (% real growth)	2.4	2.0	1.8
GDP (Million units of national currency)	292,751.6	306,967.6	320,305.3
GDP (US$ million)	3,438.5	3,117.9	3,159.9
GDP per capita (US$)	16,667.3	14,831.3	14,746.7
Consumption (Million units of national currency)	188,753.8	195,730.7	212,078.9
Consumption (US$ million)	2,217.0	1,988.1	2,092.2
Consumption per capita (US$)	10,746.4	9,456.9	9,764.0
Population, mid-year ('000)	206.3	210.2	214.3
Birth rate (per '000)	20.8	20.5	20.3
Death rate (per '000)	4.9	4.9	4.9
No. of households ('000)	41.0	41.2	41.4
Total exports (US$ million)	395.0	635.0	554.0
Total imports (US$ million)	1,008.0	1,017.0	983.0
Tourism receipts (US$ million)			
Tourist spending (US$ million)	206.3	210.2	214.3

Average household size 2001 (persons)	5.10				
Urban population 2001 (%)	77.8				
Age analysis (%) (2001)	*0-14*	29.8	*15-64*	64.9	*65+* 5.3
Population by sex (%) (2001)	*Male*	51.1	*Female*	48.9	
Life expectancy (years) (2001)	*Male*	72.2	*Female*	77.4	
Infant mortality (deaths per '000 live births) (2001)	7.0				
Adult literacy (%)					

TRADING PARTNERS

Major export destinations 2001 (% share)

FRANCE	26.9
JAPAN	23.8
SPAIN	8.3
AUSTRALIA	6.0

Major import sources 2001 (% share)

FRANCE	48.4
AUSTRALIA	13.1
SINGAPORE	10.2
NEW ZEALAND	4.2

■ New Zealand

Area (km^2)   265,150

Currency   New Zealand dollar (NZ$ = 100 cents)

Location   The two large islands which make up the greater part of New Zealand are located between the southern Tasmanian Sea and the South Pacific. They have a total length of almost 1,500km and extend to a maximum altitude of just over 4,000 metres along the volcanic ridges. The climate is pleasant, though cool in winter. The capital is Wellington.

Head of State   HM Queen Elizabeth II

Head of Government   Helen Clark (1999)

Ruling Party   The Labour Party leads a coalition.

Political Structure   New Zealand, an independent member of the Commonwealth, is ruled by the Crown acting through a Governor-General. Executive power is exercised by the prime minister, who is appointed by the unicameral House of Representatives (Parliament). The 120 members of the House are elected by universal suffrage for a term of three years. A proportional representation system was introduced in 1995. The present government has raised the possibility of abolishing its link to the Queen.

Last Elections   Elections to the House of Representatives were held in July 2002. The Labour Party won 52 seats while its coalition partner, the Alliance Party, took only 2 seats. The National Party took 27 seats, the anti-immigration New Zealand First Party received 13 seats and the remainder were divided among several smaller parties. Helen Clark retained her position as prime minister.

Political Risk   The rewards from New Zealand's zealous, decade-long experiment with economic reform have proven to be disappointing. The government's recent decision to undo many of these reforms has led business confidence to plummet and earned officials a reputation (perhaps undeserved) of being anti-business. Businesses generally support the idea of forming a common currency with Australia but many New Zealanders suspect that their larger neighbour is not interested. Australia, itself, may soon open talks with the US on a free-trade agreement between the two countries. This prospect creates considerable uncertainty in the country. Both Australia and New Zealand rely heavily on exports of commodities and New Zealand's exporters would suffer considerably if their larger neighbour gained preferential access to the huge US market. New Zealand has resolved an argument with its Maori indigenous peoples over compensation for expropriations of land and property in the past.

International Disputes   Immigration, mainly from South Korea, Taiwan and Hong Kong, has created some tension with those countries. New Zealand's first racially-based political party, the Ethnic Minority Party, was launched in 1996. The move has heightened Asians' growing uneasiness about anti-immigration campaigns that are mainly associated with the party. New Zealand also differs with Australia on points of defence policy.

Economy   New Zealand's GDP grew by 2.4% in 2001 and will increase by 2.6% in 2002. In 2003, growth is expected to be 3%. Inflation was 2.7% in 2001 and should fall to about 1.8% in 2002. The rate of price increase is forecast to drop further to 1.5% in 2003. The New Zealand economy is proving to be remarkably resilient, particularly given the background of a world economy in mild recession. The impact of slowing external demand and subdued investment was more than offset by the vigorous expansion of consumer spending, supported by robust employment growth and rising export incomes. In this, New Zealand benefited from the favourable effects of high world prices for its export commodities (particularly dairy and meat products), together with a weak real exchange rate. The unemployment rate reached its lowest level in more than a decade, and there was a temporary pick-up in wage increases, especially in the public sector. As the headline rate of consumer price inflation trended down over the course of 2001, real wage gains supported the expansion of disposable income and consumer spending.

Main Industries   Agriculture accounts for 11% of GDP but is an especially important contributor to the country's exports. Half the country's land area consists of pasture land for sheep and cattle, with much of the remainder being woodlands and forests which are used for the extraction of hardwoods. There are nearly 70 million sheep in the country. New Zealand's economy strengthened in 2001 owing to a strong export-led recovery. Industry accounts for about a third of GDP. Activities range from heavy smelting to light industry, with the production of light engineering and consumer goods being the most prominent. New Zealand is reasonably well endowed with mineral resources, which include sulphur, iron ore and iron sand, titanium, gold, silver, limestone and dolomite. It also has ample energy reserves which mainly consist of coal and lignite along with a massive offshore gas field. As this field is developed, New Zealand should have an exportable surplus of energy supplies.

Energy   With ample reserves of coal and lignite and a massive offshore gas field, New Zealand should have an exportable surplus of energy supplies. However, it relies on imports for its oil supplies while exporting both gas and coal. At least 80% of all electricity comes from hydroelectric installations.

	1999	2000	2001
Inflation (% change)	1.1	2.7	2.7
Exchange rate (per US$)	1.89	2.20	2.38
Interest rate (% per annum, lending rate)	8.5	10.2	9.9
GDP (% real growth)	3.9	3.9	2.4
GDP (Million units of national currency)	103,933.0	110,433.0	117,716.0
GDP (US$ million)	55,002.4	50,170.6	49,486.5
GDP per capita (US$)	14,334.1	13,005.8	12,739.9
Consumption (Million units of national currency)	64,357.7	69,839.7	73,757.8
Consumption (US$ million)	34,058.7	31,728.7	31,007.0
Consumption per capita (US$)	8,876.0	8,225.1	7,982.5
Population, mid-year ('000)	3,837.2	3,857.6	3,884.4
Birth rate (per '000)	14.5	14.3	14.0
Death rate (per '000)	7.6	7.7	7.7
No. of households ('000)	1,321.0	1,338.0	1,353.7
Total exports (US$ million)	12,454.9	13,266.3	13,726.0
Total imports (US$ million)	14,298.5	13,906.0	13,346.9
Tourism receipts (US$ million)	2,083.0	1,735.8	1,592.1
Tourist spending (US$ million)	1,493.0	1,346.4	1,258.3

Average household size 2001 (persons)	2.88				
Urban population 2001 (%)	86.8				
Age analysis (%) (2001)	*0-14* 22.7		*15-64* 65.4		*65+* 11.8
Population by sex (%) (2001)	*Male* 49.3		*Female* 50.7		
Life expectancy (years) (2001)	*Male* 75.1		*Female* 80.5		
Infant mortality (deaths per '000 live births) (2001)	6.2				
Adult literacy (%) (1997)	99.0				

TRADING PARTNERS

Major export destinations 2001 (% share)		Major import sources 2001 (% share)	
AUSTRALIA	18.8	AUSTRALIA	21.9
USA	15.1	USA	16.1
JAPAN	12.5	JAPAN	11.0
UNITED KINGDOM	4.9	CHINA	7.0

Nicaragua

Area (km^2) 148,000

Currency Cordoba oro (gold cordoba) (C = 100 centavos)

Location Nicaragua is the second largest state in Central America, after Mexico. It bridges the section of the Panamanian isthmus that lies between Costa Rica and Honduras and has coastlines on both the Pacific and the Caribbean. The terrain is mountainous to the west, but descends to lowlands in the coastal east. There are two huge inland lakes situated to the northwest and southeast of the capital Managua. The capital is Managua.

Head of State Enrique Bolaños Geyer (2001)

Head of Government Enrique Bolaños Geyer (2001)

Ruling Party The government is supported by the Constitutional Liberal Party (PLC).

Political Structure The 1987 Constitution provides for an executive president, directly elected for a 5-year term and a unicameral National Assembly (Parliament) of 93 members, elected by universal suffrage every six years.

Last Elections Presidential elections in November 2001 produced a victory for Geyer, leader of the PLC. He received 56% of the vote. José Daniel Ortega, leader of the Sandinista Front, was second with 42% of the vote. In parliamentary elections held at the same time, the PLC won 47 seats while the Sandinistas took 43. The remainder went to the Conservative Party.

Political Risk Bolaños wants to investigate the charges of corruption that surround the previous president, Arnolodo Aleman. Aleman's declared wealth rose ninefold between 19992 and 1997 but he remains protected because his cronies dominate the Liberal Party.

International Disputes In 1999, a border dispute broke out between Nicaragua and Honduras. This followed the ratification by Honduras of a treaty with Colombia dividing a portion of the Caribbean Sea and islands claimed by Nicaragua between them. In 2000, the two countries' navies clashed in the Gulf of Fonseca. Subsequently, both sides agreed to submit the issue to the International Court of Justice.

Economy In 2001, GDP grew by 3% while inflation was 8.3%. The deficit of the public sector rose in 2001 owing to substantial spending overruns. The fiscal stance remained weak during the first half of 2001 owing to the cost of bank resolutions, continued high spending and payments of domestic arrears. While difficulties in the banking system intensified, the authorities took decisive actions to strengthen banking supervision. In addition, since August 2000 four banks, found to be weak, were sold to other private banks. The increase in central bank debt associated with these bank resolutions is estimated at about 10% of GDP. The real effective exchange rate appreciated by about 11% during the 18-month period ending in June 2001, largely as a result of the appreciation of the US dollar, while the terms of trade deteriorated owing to a significant drop in coffee prices and an increase in oil-import prices. Structural reforms advanced during 2001. The national assembly approved legislation to reform the social security system and improve government procurement. Nicaragua joined with El Salvador and Guatemala in signing a tri-national declaration calling for the establishment of a regional system for ensuring economic and social justice and wellbeing, the formation of a customs union and the consolidation of the financial system.

Main Industries Nicaragua's agricultural sector accounts for 31% of GDP. Food processing, coffee roasting, textiles, timber and handicrafts are all important. Farming specialists estimate that it will take at least five years for Nicaragua's agricultural sector to recover from the hurricane which struck in 1998. The government took steps to deepen trade liberalisation, including the removal of the temporary protection tariff. A punitive 35% tariff charged on imports from two countries in the region has been eliminated. The long-term decline in coffee prices is a trend that greatly concerns both farmers and public officials. On the demand side, the main contributors to growth are public expenditures (on consumption and, to a lesser degree, investment) and a recovery of exports. Although the construction industry has remained buoyant, its pace of activity has gradually been declining because government allocations for the special reconstruction programme launched in the wake of Hurricane Mitch in 1998 are being scaled back and because private investment in non-residential construction is decreasing as a number of major hotel projects have reached their final stages. The country has only limited mineral resources, notably salt, gold, silver, tungsten and lead and zinc.

Energy With electricity demand expected to continue growing rapidly (a projected 6.1% annually over the next 20 years), Nicaragua will require large amounts of investment in new power plants. For the present, its main domestic source of energy is geothermal. Nicaragua hopes to boost generation capacity by 1,200 mega-watts over the next 20 years.

	1999	2000	2001
Inflation (% change)	11.2	11.6	8.3
Exchange rate (per US$)	11.81	12.68	13.37
Interest rate (% per annum, lending rate)	22.1	21.4	22.8
GDP (% real growth)	7.4	4.3	3.0
GDP (Million units of national currency)	26,126.0	30,409.0	33,904.0
GDP (US$ million)	2,212.3	2,397.4	2,535.5
GDP per capita (US$)	495.7	523.7	540.1
Consumption (Million units of national currency)	24,877.6	27,710.9	30,144.1
Consumption (US$ million)	2,106.6	2,184.6	2,254.3
Consumption per capita (US$)	472.0	477.2	480.2
Population, mid-year ('000)	4,463.2	4,578.1	4,694.4
Birth rate (per '000)	34.2	33.6	32.9
Death rate (per '000)	5.5	5.4	5.3
No. of households ('000)	1,301.9	1,321.1	1,337.0
Total exports (US$ million)	545.3	631.1	605.6
Total imports (US$ million)	1,861.9	1,758.6	1,776.4
Tourism receipts (US$ million)	107.0	79.3	72.1
Tourist spending (US$ million)	74.0	72.4	84.8

Average household size 2001 (persons)	3.51					
Urban population 2001 (%)	56.4					
Age analysis (%) (2001)	*0-14*	40.6	*15-64*	56.2	*65+*	3.2
Population by sex (%) (2001)	*Male*	49.9	*Female*	50.1		
Life expectancy (years) (2001)	*Male*	66.8	*Female*	71.5		
Infant mortality (deaths per '000 live births) (2001)	36.7					
Adult literacy (%) (1997)	63.4					

TRADING PARTNERS

Major export destinations 2001 (% share)		Major import sources 2001 (% share)	
USA	52.9	USA	24.1
EL SALVADOR	7.4	COSTA RICA	10.8
RUSSIA	3.2	VENEZUELA	8.5
GERMANY	3.2	GUATEMALA	7.5

▪ Niger

Area (km^2)   1,186,410

Currency   CFA franc (= 100 centimes)

Location   Niger, occupying much of the centre of northwest Africa, is a large and landlocked state which borders on Algeria in the northwest, Libya in the far north, Chad in the east, Nigeria in the south and Benin, Burkina Faso and Mali in the west and southwest. The only cultivable soil in the country lies along the Niger River; elsewhere it is mainly desert or savanna. The capital is Niamey.

Head of State   President Mamadou Tandja (1999)

Head of Government   Hama Amadou (2000)

Ruling Party   The government is formed by the National Movement for the Development Society (MNSD) and the Democratic and Social Convention (CDS).

Political Structure   From 1974 until the return of parliamentary democracy in 1993, Niger was run by a military administration. Ibrahim Bare Mainassara assumed the presidency in 1996 and was assassinated in 1999. Under the present constitution, the people elect the president for a 5-year term. The National Assembly has 83 members, elected for 5-year terms, 75 members elected in multi-seat constituencies and 8 members elected in single-seat national minority constituencies.

Last Elections   Presidential elections were held in November 1999 Mamadou Tandja received 60% of the vote, defeating Mahamane Ousmane. In parliamentary elections occurring in November 1999, the MNSD took 38 seats while the CDS won 17 seats. The remainder were scattered among several parties.

Political Risk   Niger has suffered a series of social and political upheavals in the 10 years to 2001, which has hindered economic growth. In 1999, President Mainassara was assassinated. The killing came amid opposition calls for his resignation after the annulment of regional elections. Unrest and occasional rebellion among the Tuaregs in the north of the country complicate a shaky political situation. For now, the present government seems to have re-established economic, social, and political stability in the country.

International Disputes   Libya claims about 19,400 sq km in northern Niger. The demarcation of international boundaries in Lake Chad, which has led to border incidents in the past, is completed and awaiting ratification by Cameroon, Chad, Niger and Nigeria. Burkina Faso and Mali are proceeding with boundary demarcation, including the tri-point with Niger.

Economy   GDP rose by 5.1% in 2001 and prices increased by 4%. The external current account deficit (excluding official transfers) is estimated to have widened slightly in 2001 to around 8.5% of GDP. This development was due mainly to a deterioration in the terms of trade. The authorities are working to strengthen external debt management and to maintain the momentum of the privatisation programme, in particular, through divestiture from the energy and petroleum companies. Niger's balance of payments should remain sustainable over the medium term if adequate international support is provided. To achieve this, authorities must implement a prudent external debt management policy. Monetary policy, which is conducted at the regional level by the West African Economic and Monetary Union central bank, continues to be tight in order to contain the inflationary pressures fuelled by an overall credit expansion.

Main Industries   With a per capita income of about US$200, Niger is one of the poorest countries in Africa and is ranked very low on all social indicators. The country is highly vulnerable to external and weather-related shocks. Its main economic activities are agriculture and livestock. These account approximately for 40% of output, while the export base is largely limited to a few minerals. Niger also has coal, iron ore, gold, molybdenum, tin and phosphates but produces very little of these minerals. Minerals account for no more than 8% of GDP. Uranium revenues have dropped sharply since the mid-1980s with the end of the uranium boom. The main exports are uranium ore (67%), livestock products (20%) and a few agricultural products. Employing over 90% of the workforce, the agricultural sector produces cotton, hides, leather goods, sorghum, millet, rice and vegetables. Industry generates about 2% of GDP, mainly producing goods destined for the domestic market. These operations include processed foods, plastics and construction materials and chemicals. The privatisation programme started during the 1990s was revived in 2000, with the adoption of privatisation strategies for the four largest public enterprises still in the government's portfolio.

Energy   Despite recent oil finds, Niger relies on imports for nearly all its petroleum needs. The only alternatives, apart from coal, are the country's considerable timber resources for fuel wood.

	1999	2000	2001
Inflation (% change)	-2.3	2.9	4.0
Exchange rate (per US$)	615.70	711.98	733.04
Interest rate (% per annum, lending rate)	5.0	5.0	
GDP (% real growth)	-0.6	-1.4	5.1
GDP (Billion units of national currency)	1,242.6	1,280.4	1,399.1
GDP (US$ million)	2,018.1	1,798.3	1,908.6
GDP per capita (US$)	192.6	167.6	167.3
Consumption (Billion units of national currency)	717.9	765.1	801.4
Consumption (US$ million)	1,166.0	1,074.5	1,093.3
Consumption per capita (US$)	111.3	100.1	95.9
Population, mid-year ('000)	10,477.1	10,730.0	11,405.0
Birth rate (per '000)	55.3	55.3	55.2
Death rate (per '000)	20.2	19.8	19.5
No. of households ('000)	1,778.6	1,789.5	1,912.4
Total exports (US$ million)	286.8	283.0	304.5
Total imports (US$ million)	404.3	372.1	439.5
Tourism receipts (US$ million)	24.0	17.1	18.4
Tourist spending (US$ million)	25.2	25.0	21.3

Average household size 2001 (persons)	6.00				
Urban population 2001 (%)	21.1				
Age analysis (%) (2001)	*0-14*	48.3	*15-64*	49.3	*65+* 2.5
Population by sex (%) (2001)	*Male*	49.4	*Female*	50.6	
Life expectancy (years) (2001)	*Male*	45.4	*Female*	46.0	
Infant mortality (deaths per '000 live births) (2001)	128.4				
Adult literacy (%) (1997)	14.3				

TRADING PARTNERS

Major export destinations 2001 (% share)

NIGERIA	37.1
FRANCE	36.5
JAPAN	16.5
SPAIN	3.8

Major import sources 2001 (% share)

FRANCE	19.2
COTE D'IVOIRE	14.6
NIGERIA	10.2
CHINA	6.4

■ Nigeria

Area (km^2) 923,850

Currency Naira (N = 100 kobo)

Location Nigeria is located on the Atlantic coast of West Africa, where it is bounded in the north by Niger, in the west by Benin, in the east by Chad and on the southeast by Cameroon. It has a generally warm and pleasant tropical climate, although conditions along the 100-km-wide mangrove swamps of the coast are less favourable. The capital is Abuja.

Head of State Olusegun Obasanjo (1999)

Head of Government Olusegun Obasanjo (1999)

Ruling Party People's Democratic Party (PDP)

Political Structure Nigeria, an independent member of the Commonwealth, has been ruled by civilian administrations for only nine of its 36 years of independence. General Abacha, who seized power in 1993, jailed most leading politicians including Obasanjo. In June 1998, Abacha died in office and was replaced by Gen. Abbdulsalami Abubakaar, who oversaw the return to civilian rule that brought Obasanjo to office.

Last Elections Elections were held in February 1999. Obasanjo was elected head of state with 60% of the vote. His party, the PDP, won 208 of the 360 seats in the House of Representatives and 59 out of 109 in the Senate. The two main opposition parties, the All People's Party (APP) and the Alliance for Democracy (AD), together won 145 seats in the House and 44 in the Senate.

Political Risk Three years after democracy was restored, Nigeria can look back on several successes. Even so, many Nigerians are disappointed. One reason for this is that ethnic and religious violence has actually worsened since the country returned to democracy. More than 6,000 people have been killed in communal clashes. Muslims fight Christians and dozens of Nigeria's 250 tribes fight over land. Several states are trying to introduce Muslim law but the central government opposes their right to do this. There is also a danger of military action by one part of the army or another. Some even fear that the army could even split along ethnic lines.

International Disputes Under Obasanjo's leadership, Nigeria has regained some of its international reputation and is once again able to influence African policies. Closer to home, both Cameroon and Nigeria have claimed the Bakassi peninsula, a 1,000-sq-km (400 sq m) area located in the Gulf of Guinea believed to contain significant reserves of oil. Several oil discoveries have been made on the peninsula and its adjoining waters, but at present operations in the disputed area have been suspended. The Nigerian government has questioned Equatorial Guinea's sole ownership of another oil field. At issue is whether the field is a separate one, or part of an oil structure that straddles the territorial waters of both countries.

Economy GDP increased by 4% in 2001 and is expected to contract by 1.1% in 2002. Growth should resume in 2003 with GDP rising by about 3.4%. Inflation was 18.9% in 2001 and is expected to be 14.7% in 2002 and 11.2% in 2003. The Obasanjo administration is working on a number of economic reforms, including the privatisation of parastatals, exchange rate management and the phasing out of subsidies. However, there have been several delays in the 3-part privatisation programme. In July 2002, the government had privatised just 14 of the 107 companies it says that it wants to sell and most of those sold were among the smallest. In the present environment the chances of any genuine reforms are minimal. None of the three registered political parties have any ideology. All are the vehicles for rich, influential men. Members of parliament spend most of their time fighting for a larger share of Nigeria's oil wealth, and refuse to reveal, even to the president, how much they pay themselves. Donors are openly critical of the pattern of government spending, claiming that it is skewed in favour of personnel costs and new projects. The structure of investment is equally disconcerting. Since 1995, when investment averaged 21% of GDP, the private sector share has been less than 8%. In turn, such low levels of private sector investment help to explain why productivity has been so low.

Main Industries Nominally the wealthiest state in sub-Saharan Africa, Nigeria owes most of its riches to its oil deposits. Over two million barrels are produced each day, accounting for a fifth of GDP and the great majority of all export revenues. Oil accounts for nearly 80% of government revenues, 90-95% of export revenues and over 90% of foreign exchange earnings. At one time, 50% of all oil revenues were retained locally but the official figure is now less than 5%. The present government has now introduced a new law for revenue sharing with the nine oil-producing states by which the latter receive 13% of oil revenues versus the previously allotted 3%. Nigeria also has four refineries with a combined capacity one third greater than domestic requirements. Yet these refineries still produce at only 30% of capacity. Not surprisingly, there are frequent shortages of electricity with some parts of the country having no power for weeks at a time. Medium-sized enterprises are thought to spend up to 30% of their operating costs on private power-generation. The agricultural sector depends on exports of cocoa, coffee, cotton, palm oil and rubber. Both the industrial and agricultural sectors have stagnated in recent years, with a few bright exceptions such as the mobile telephone business. The state's involvement in industry remains widespread but the government has little idea of how to get firms back on track. The country has deposits of coal, tin, iron ore, uranium, lead, zinc and gold, not all of which are being exploited.

Energy Nigeria contains estimated proven oil reserves of 22.5 billion barrels and production is currently 2.3 million barrels per day. Almost all reserves are found in relatively simple geological structures along the country's coastal Niger River Delta. The majority of this oil lies in about 250 small fields, most of which hold reserves of less than 50 million barrels each. Nigerian crude oil production averaged 2.14 million barrels per day (bbl/d) in 2000, and for the first six months of 2001, crude oil production was 2.23 million bbl/d. Nigeria's OPEC quota is 1.5 million b/d, effective 1 January 2002. Production from joint ventures accounts for nearly all (about 95%) of Nigeria's crude oil production. The largest joint venture, operated by Shell, produces nearly 50% of Nigeria's crude oil. A major problem facing Nigeria's upstream oil sector has been insufficient government funding of its joint venture commitments. In the 2001 budget, the government allocated US$3.5 billion for joint venture operations. The allocation, US$1 billion higher than the 2000 appropriation, contains nearly US$500 million towards the settlement of outstanding arrears. The total budget for Nigerian joint venture oil operations in 2001, including oil company contributions, is just over US$5 billion.

	1999	2000	2001
Inflation (% change)	6.6	6.9	18.9
Exchange rate (per US$)	92.34	101.70	111.23
Interest rate (% per annum, lending rate)	20.3	21.3	
GDP (% real growth)	1.1	3.8	4.0
GDP (Billion units of national currency)	3,211.2	4,178.2	4,601.9
GDP (US$ million)	34,776.0	41,084.6	41,372.4
GDP per capita (US$)	301.0	345.0	337.2
Consumption (Billion units of national currency)	2,698.8	2,536.8	2,840.5
Consumption (US$ million)	29,226.9	24,945.0	25,537.3
Consumption per capita (US$)	253.0	209.4	208.1
Population, mid-year ('000)	115,533.5	119,101.0	122,696.6
Birth rate (per '000)	41.0	40.5	40.0
Death rate (per '000)	13.8	13.7	13.5
No. of households ('000)	21,934.0	22,580.0	23,196.6
Total exports (US$ million)	13,855.6	20,975.0	20,222.8
Total imports (US$ million)	8,587.8	8,721.3	10,748.4
Tourism receipts (US$ million)	133.1	117.6	95.0
Tourist spending (US$ million)	620.0	765.0	921.0

Average household size 2001 (persons)	5.27					
Urban population 2001 (%)	44.2					
Age analysis (%) (2001)	*0-14*	43.2	*15-64*	53.7	*65+*	3.1
Population by sex (%) (2001)	*Male*	50.2	*Female*	49.8		
Life expectancy (years) (2001)	*Male*	51.8	*Female*	52.0		
Infant mortality (deaths per '000 live births) (2001)	81.2					
Adult literacy (%) (1997)	59.5					

TRADING PARTNERS

Major export destinations 2001 (% share)		Major import sources 2001 (% share)	
USA	41.3	UNITED KINGDOM	9.7
SPAIN	8.6	USA	9.5
INDIA	6.7	GERMANY	8.7
FRANCE	5.3	FRANCE	7.5

North Korea

Area (km^2) 122,310

Currency Won (= 100 chon)

Location North Korea occupies slightly more than half of the Korean peninsula, which lies to the south of the Chinese city of Shenyang. Like South Korea, it has a mixed and often mountainous landscape with extensive tree cover. The climate is temperate and often wet. The capital is Pyongyang.

Head of State President Kim Jong Il

Head of Government Hong Song-nam

Ruling Party The Korean Workers' Party is the only legal political party.

Political Structure The Democratic People's Republic of Korea has been a communist one-party state since 1948. The 1972 Constitution provides for an executive president who is elected by the Supreme People's Assembly, or Parliament. The Assembly's members are elected every four years by universal suffrage, from a single list, but they meet only occasionally. In effect, power is exercised by the Central People's Committee, in which the Korean Workers' Party dominates.

Last Elections Parliamentary elections were held in July 1998 when over 600 deputies were selected. Among them was Kim Jong Il. Kim was elected general secretary of the ruling Workers' Party in October 1997. The decision secured the first dynastic succession in the communist world. The Workers' Party invariably wins all seats in the Supreme People's Assembly at each successive election and the reported turnout is always high.

Political Risk Relations with South Korea deteriorated significantly during 2001 and 2002. In June 2002, the two countries engaged in a naval gun battle which left several sailors dead. The clash is likely to prevent any improvement between the two Koreas as well as with the US, for some time. The immediate reason for the clash was a dispute over an extension of a land boundary between North and South. The increasingly negative attitude of the present US government has created more problems for the North.

International Disputes Relations with South Korea deteriorated significantly during 2001 and 2002. In July 2002, the two countries engaged in a naval gun battle which left several sailors dead. The clash is likely to prevent any improvement in between the two Koreas as well as with the US, for some time. The immediate reason for the clash was a dispute over an extension of a land boundary between North and South. Meanwhile, the North's relations with the US as well as Japan have worsened. The US continues to charge the North with drug-running and the development of terrorist weapons of mass destruction while Japan suspects the country of naval forays into its waters with heavily-armed ships. Tensions with China have disrupted the country's socialist-style barter trade and its access to technology and aid from traditional allies.

Economy North Korea's economy continues to be disorganised and weak with little hope for any improvement under the present regime. North Korea's communist ideology has been based on the concept of "juche," or self-reliance. Severe economic problems have, however, forced the country to accept international food aid and embark on a series of limited market reforms. Widespread famine in North Korea has reportedly killed hundreds of thousands of people - possibly up to two million. The government has permitted a small amount of foreign investment in recent years and established a free trade zone in Rajin-Sonbong, near the northern borders with China and Russia. Plans also have been under consideration for other such "bonded processing" zones, including one at Kaesong near the Demilitarized Zone (DMZ), but these have been held up by questions about the availability of electricity, among other issues.

Main Industries North Korea's economy remains under tight state control. Collectivised agriculture and state-owned companies account for about 90% of all economic activity. The economy relies very significantly on the agricultural sector, which employs 45% of the workforce although its contribution to GDP is somewhat smaller. Rice, maize, potatoes, millet, sorghum, vegetables, fruit and tobacco are grown for the domestic market. Silk is the only export. There was a drop in agricultural production in 2001 following a steady economic contraction from 1990 through 1998. North Korea's heavy industry has been affected by a severe energy shortage, which has forced production cutbacks at some plants. Few consumer durables are manufactured in North Korea. The country's generous mineral resources include coal, lignite, clays, phosphates, iron ore, magnesium and tungsten but extraction techniques are very rudimentary.

Energy North Korea relies on two domestic sources of commercial energy - coal and hydropower - for most of its energy needs. In 1999, coal accounted for almost 77% of primary energy consumption and hydropower for more than 13%. North Korea's electric generating capacity is split nearly evenly between coal-fired thermal plants and hydroelectric plants. In 1999, hydroelectric power plants generated about 65% of North Korea's electricity and thermal plants about 35%. The country's thermal generating capacity is underutilised due to a lack of fuels. The country's total electricity consumption in 1999 was only 55% of what it had been in 1991. As a result of an electricity shortage, North Korea has resorted to a rationing system. The country often experiences blackouts for extended periods of time, and power losses due to an antiquated transmission grid are high. Over the last few years, a lack of adequate rainfall and snowfall has presented problems for the country's hydroelectric generation, and many hydroelectric facilities are believed to be out of operation do to flood damage.

	1999	2000	2001
Inflation (% change)			
Exchange rate (per US$)	2.20	2.20	2.20
Interest rate			
GDP (% real growth)			
GDP			
GDP (US$ million)			
GDP per capita (US$)			
Consumption			
Consumption (US$ million)			
Consumption per capita (US$)			
Population, mid-year ('000)	23,347.6	23,702.1	24,064.6
Birth rate (per '000)	18.0	17.7	17.5
Death rate (per '000)	10.2	10.1	10.0
No. of households ('000)	3,913.1	3,947.9	3,969.1
Total exports (US$ million)			
Total imports (US$ million)			
Tourism receipts (US$ million)			
Tourist spending (US$ million)	23,347.6	23,702.1	24,064.6

Average household size 2001 (persons)	6.05				
Urban population 2001 (%)	60.5				
Age analysis (%) (2001)	0-14	27.6	15-64	67.0	65+ 5.4
Population by sex (%) (2001)	Male	50.1	Female	49.9	
Life expectancy (years) (2001)	Male	61.9	Female	67.4	
Infant mortality (deaths per '000 live births) (2001)	41.2				
Adult literacy (%)					

TRADING PARTNERS

Major export destinations 2001 (% share)

JAPAN	21.9
CHINA	16.6
BRAZIL	16.0
INDIA	4.7

Major import sources 2001 (% share)

JAPAN	40.3
CHINA	22.0
BRAZIL	4.3
SINGAPORE	4.3

Norway

Area (km²) 323,895

Currency Norwegian krone (NKr = 100 ore)

Location Norway occupies almost the entire western half of the peninsula which it shares with Sweden, running southwest from the Arctic Circle to meet up with Denmark across the Skagerrak straits which form the entry from the North Sea to the Baltic Sea. With an almost entirely mountainous geography, and with most of its western coastline characterised by deep-sea inlets (fjords), most of its population live in the southern coastal lowlands. The capital is Oslo.

Head of State HM King Harald V (1991)

Head of Government Kjell Magne Bondevik (2001)

Ruling Party A multiparty coalition controls the government.

Political Structure The Kingdom of Norway is a constitutional monarchy with executive power in a prime minister and cabinet, and legislative authority in a unicameral parliament (the Storting). Parliament's 165 members are elected by universal suffrage for a 4-year term. For legislative purposes they divide themselves into an Upper and Lower Chamber.

Last Elections Parliamentary elections were held in September 2001. The Norwegian Labour Party won 43 seats, the Conservative party took 38 seats, the Progress Party received 26 seats, the Christian People's Party won 22 seats and the Socialist Left Party claimed 23 seats. Remaining seats were divided among minor parties. Bondevik of the Christian People's Party then was nominated as prime minister.

Political Risk Norway's stable and trouble-free economy poses few risks. However, the state's involvement in the economy is extensive and it will be some time before authorities can expect to scale back these responsibilities. At present, one worker in three is employed in the public domain. Roughly 80% of all healthcare and education is state-provided. So are pensions, water, electricity, roads, railways and fixed-line telecommunications. In addition, most of the country's larger corporations are partially owned by the state.

International Disputes Norway has a recurrent dispute with Iceland regarding the territorial waters around the Svalbard Islands, where Norway claims a 200km fishing limit, and has similar, though less heated, disagreements with other countries.

Economy GDP increased by 1.4% in 2001. It is expected to rise by 2.3% in 2002 and 2.2% in 2003. Inflation was 3% in 2001. Prices are expected to rise by 1.5% in 2002 and 2.5% in 2003. Labour market conditions remain tight in service sectors, but weakened in technology and traditional export industries. Employment grew by 0.5%, keeping the average unemployment rate broadly unchanged at 3.5% in 2001. A decline in competitiveness and slowing external demand impaired non-oil exports, but peak oil production and high oil prices through most of 2001 contributed to an expected current account surplus in excess of 12% of GDP. High oil revenues also contributed to a general government surplus of around 16% of GDP. An inflation targeting regime was formally adopted in 2001. The operational target is defined as an annual increase in consumer prices of 2.5%. In general, inflation is expected to be within a one percentage point deviation from either side of the target. A policy to accelerate the use of oil revenues was also adopted in 2001, implying a cumulative fiscal stimulus in excess of 3% of GDP through to 2010. Weak overseas demand and recent losses of competitiveness are expected to hold back non-oil exports. Sustained high real interest rates, weak business profitability and the continued decline of oil-related investment could also dampen demand.

Main Industries Oil has transformed the Norwegian economy, moving ahead of fishing, timber and agriculture as the country's leading industry. Output of natural gas should double by 2005. At present, the oil business contributes just over a fifth of GDP and employs a similar proportion of the workforce, either directly or indirectly. Industry accounts for another quarter of GDP and about a third of all exports in a typical year. The industrial sector is strongest in engineering, chemicals and timber products as well as oil products. Fishing provides 10% of total exports and is an integral part of the country's political and social culture. Norway brings in around 2.5 million tonnes of fish each year and is the largest supplier in Europe. Farming has shrunk in the face of the oil boom and nowadays contributes only about 2% of GDP. Farms tend to be small in size, and have required consistent government aid to survive. Many markets are still characterised by substantial state ownership and by high government support, especially in the agricultural sector. Deregulation has been carried out to improve competition, but so far not much emphasis has been put on privatisation of public enterprises. The country's Petroleum Fund is intended to help fill government coffers when oil is exhausted. The fund reached NKr600 billion in 2001 and should steadily grow in the years thereafter.

Energy Norway has proven oil reserves of 9.4 billion barrels. In 2000, Norway was the world's third largest oil exporter. However, the country consumes very little of the oil it produces, and its oil exports are its greatest source of revenue. Oil reserves are located exclusively offshore and mostly in the North Sea, with smaller deposits in the Norwegian Sea. The Barents Sea is being explored. Norwegian oil investment in 2001 was about US$5.3 billion in 2001, a drop from the US$6.2 billion invested in 2000. Oil investment peaked in 1998. This reflects expectations that Norway's oil production will remain at current levels until 2004, and then begin a gradual decline. As Norwegian fields mature, the Norwegian government has become involved in finding new resources for its companies to develop outside the North Sea region. In 1999, a government-business partnership launched for that purpose.

	1999	2000	2001
Inflation (% change)	2.3	3.1	3.0
Exchange rate (per US$)	7.80	8.80	8.99
Interest rate (% per annum, lending rate)	8.2	8.2	8.9
GDP (% real growth)	1.1	2.3	1.4
GDP (Billion units of national currency)	1,197.5	1,423.9	1,472.0
GDP (US$ million)	153,536.5	161,768.9	163,711.7
GDP per capita (US$)	34,431.9	36,055.5	36,266.9
Consumption (Billion units of national currency)	542.3	572.8	597.4
Consumption (US$ million)	69,531.9	65,073.2	66,440.8
Consumption per capita (US$)	15,593.2	14,503.7	14,718.6
Population, mid-year ('000)	4,459.1	4,486.7	4,514.1
Birth rate (per '000)	12.5	12.2	11.8
Death rate (per '000)	10.1	10.0	10.0
No. of households ('000)	2,057.0	2,065.0	2,082.0
Total exports (US$ million)	44,883.6	57,514.5	57,638.5
Total imports (US$ million)	34,041.3	32,655.3	32,955.1
Tourism receipts (US$ million)	2,229.0	2,122.8	1,954.0
Tourist spending (US$ million)	4,751.0	4,937.8	4,407.6

Average household size 2001 (persons)	2.17				
Urban population 2001 (%)	74.7				
Age analysis (%) (2001)	*0-14*	20.0	*15-64*	64.9	*65+* 15.1
Population by sex (%) (2001)	*Male*	49.5	*Female*	50.5	
Life expectancy (years) (2001)	*Male*	75.8	*Female*	81.7	
Infant mortality (deaths per '000 live births) (2001)	5.0				
Adult literacy (%) (1998)	99.0				

TRADING PARTNERS

Major export destinations 2001 (% share)		Major import sources 2001 (% share)	
UNITED KINGDOM	19.8	SWEDEN	15.7
FRANCE	11.9	GERMANY	13.0
GERMANY	11.7	UNITED KINGDOM	7.9
NETHERLANDS	10.1	DENMARK	7.3

Oman

Area (km^2)   271,950

Currency   Omani rial (OR = 1000 baiza)

Location   Oman, which lies in the southeastern extremity of the Arabian peninsula, actually consists of two separate pieces of land. The larger lies on the Arabian Sea, controlling the southern access to the Gulf through the Gulf of Oman; the smaller, but more significant territory, is on the headland which demarcates the boundary between the two related waterways on the tip of the United Arab Emirates territory in the Gulf. The capital is Muscat.

Head of State   Sultan Qaboos Bin-Said (1970)

Head of Government   Sultan Qaboos Bin-Said

Ruling Party   There are no legal political parties in Oman.

Political Structure   The Sultanate of Oman is ruled by decree by the Sultan who deposed his father in the coup of 1970. The Sultan is also prime minister and is advised by a cabinet that he appoints. Oman has a bicameral parliament. The Consultative Assembly has 82 elected members with only consultative tasks. The Council of State has 40 appointed members. Although the Council has no powers whatever, its introduction was seen as a move toward greater democratisation. Oman favours closer cooperation within the Gulf region.

Last Elections   The last elections were 14 September 2000.

Political Risk   The absolute character of Oman's political leadership and the tight media censorship prevents dissent. The country's efforts to integrate its policies with its Gulf Co-operation Council partners reflect its dependence on the all-important business of oil transhipments. Oman has only a modest amount of oil reserves and these will be exhausted within two decades.

International Disputes   There is no defined boundary with most of the United Arab Emirates, only an administrative line in the far north.

Economy   GDP increased by 6.5% in 2001 and prices fell by 2.6%. Within a framework of open trade and exchange system, Oman continues to use its relatively limited oil resources prudently for rapid social development and economic diversification. Oman also has put forth great efforts to attract foreign investments, particularly in light industry, tourism and power generation. Foreign investment incentives include a 5-year tax holiday for companies in certain industries, an income tax reduction for publicly held companies with at least 51% Omani ownership, and soft loans to finance new and existing projects. The country's total external debt remains manageable at less than 45% of GDP. The overall fiscal balance reached an estimated surplus of about 12% of GDP in 2000 despite larger-than-budgeted increases in government spending. Oman became a member of the World Trade Organization in 2000.

Main Industries   Oil contributes around 40% of GDP and 70% of fiscal and export receipts. Agriculture accounts for a mere 3% of GDP while industry (including oil) makes up 69%. The country's non-oil exports, including many agricultural products and textiles, have increased sharply, although they still account for less than 10% of total exports. The main products are alfalfa, dates, bananas, wheat, mangoes and limes together with tomatoes and other water-dependent crops. Fishing is a traditional activity with a long history in Oman. Manufacturing is limited, accounting for just 1% of GDP. There are factories producing cement, steel sections, cattle feed plants and a variety of consumer goods. There is also an important mining industry, producing chromate, copper and manganese, and deposits of many more metals have been located. Oman has made privatisation and diversification of its economy one of its highest policy priorities. Expanded utilisation of natural gas is central to Omani diversification plans, both for export as well as for domestic use.

Energy   In many ways, Oman is atypical of Middle Eastern oil producers. Oman's oil fields are generally smaller, more widely scattered, less productive and more costly per barrel than in other countries. This means that the average well in Oman produces about one tenth the volume per well compared to neighbouring countries. Oman continues to use a variety of enhanced oil recovery techniques in order to minimise the costs of exploration and further development at new and existing oil fields. Using these technologies, Oman has succeeded in bringing down the cost of oil production to US$3 per barrel in some fields and US$4 per barrel in others - but these figures, while still low by world standards, are substantially above most other Persian Gulf oil fields. At current production rates, Oman is projected to exhaust its oil reserves by around 2020. It is for this reason that government officials put together a plan to spend US$4 billion in oil exploration and development. Roughly 18% of this amount has been targeted for exploration, 44% for the development and installation of production facilities and the remaining 38% for operating expenses. Oman is not a member of OPEC but has agreed in recent years to cooperate with OPEC countries by reducing its oil production in an effort to restore stability to world oil prices.

	1999	2000	2001
Inflation (% change)	0.5	-1.0	-2.6
Exchange rate (per US$)	0.38	0.38	0.38
Interest rate (% per annum, lending rate)	10.3	10.1	9.2
GDP (% real growth)	-1.0	4.9	6.5
GDP (Million units of national currency)	6,000.0	7,635.0	7,434.0
GDP (US$ million)	15,606.4	19,857.0	19,334.2
GDP per capita (US$)	6,293.6	7,811.5	7,174.1
Consumption (Million units of national currency)	3,030.8	3,011.6	3,086.9
Consumption (US$ million)	7,883.3	7,832.5	8,028.3
Consumption per capita (US$)	3,179.1	3,081.2	2,979.0
Population, mid-year ('000)	2,479.7	2,542.0	2,695.0
Birth rate (per '000)	35.5	35.7	35.8
Death rate (per '000)	4.2	4.2	4.1
No. of households ('000)	655.5	683.3	739.9
Total exports (US$ million)	4,970.8	8,363.0	7,439.1
Total imports (US$ million)	4,674.4	5,039.5	5,291.2
Tourism receipts (US$ million)	105.4	137.6	95.4
Tourist spending (US$ million)	47.0	64.0	56.8

Average household size 2001 (persons)		3.72				
Urban population 2001 (%)		85.0				
Age analysis (%) (2001)	*0-14*	44.9	*15-64*	52.6	*65+*	2.5
Population by sex (%) (2001)	*Male*	53.4	*Female*	46.6		
Life expectancy (years) (2001)	*Male*	70.0	*Female*	72.9		
Infant mortality (deaths per '000 live births) (2001)		24.0				
Adult literacy (%) (1997)		67.1				

TRADING PARTNERS

Major export destinations 2001 (% share)

JAPAN	21.0
SOUTH KOREA	20.6
CHINA	14.3
THAILAND	11.3

Major import sources 2001 (% share)

UNITED ARAB EMIRATES	28.4
JAPAN	14.9
UNITED KINGDOM	8.2
USA	5.8

Pakistan

Area (km²) 803,940

Currency Pakistani rupee (R = 100 paisa)

Location Pakistan lies in the northwest corner of the Indian Ocean, where it is bounded in the south and east by India and in the north and west by Afghanistan and Iran. The country is partially low-lying, although its northwestern border with Afghanistan is extremely mountainous. The climate is subtropical, with heavy rains. The capital is Islamabad.

Head of State General Pervez Musharraf (1999)

Head of Government Shaukat Aziz (2001)

Ruling Party The military rules the country.

Political Structure Pakistan, an independent member of the Commonwealth, has an executive president who is elected by universal suffrage and reports to an elected parliament. The constitution also allows the president to dismiss any prime minister without notice. Musharraf restored a number of presidential powers after taking office and appointing Aziz as prime minister in 2001. The National Assembly has 217 members, elected for a 5-year term, 207 members elected in single-seat constituencies and 10 members elected by non-Muslim minorities. The Senate had 87 members, elected for a 6-year term.

Last Elections Musharraf was confirmed as president in a referendum in 2002. In the last elections held prior to the military coup (in 1997), the Muslim League won a landslide victory, taking almost two-thirds of the seats in the National Assembly. These results were rendered moot when Musharraf took power in 1999.

Political Risk Internally, Musharraf still lacks control over large parts of his country and even some portions of the bureaucracy. He faces threats from ex-Taliban and other Muslim radicals who have entered Pakistan from Afghanistan and from other hardline Muslims who disagree with his new pro-US, anti-terrorist policies. Other long-standing political tensions within the country are ethnic in origin, but have been exacerbated by the recent problems with terrorists. Pakistan's three ethnically divided provinces, Sindh, Baluchistan and the North West Frontier, have long harboured secessionist movements.

International Disputes Pakistan's dispute with India came close to nuclear war in 2002 before US diplomats intervened. Musharraf eventually agreed to end infiltration by terrorists into Indian-administered Kashmir from the part of the state controlled by Pakistan. So far, he has largely kept his promise and India has pulled back its navy from Pakistani shores. The dangers remain great, however. Pakistan and India have fought three wars. In the most recent, Pakistan lost its eastern territory, now Bangladesh.

Economy GDP is expected to rise by 4.2% in 2002 and increase by 5.1% in 2003. Inflation should be around 3.7% in 2002 and rise to 4% in 2003. Despite a moderate rise in public investment, total investment fell to 14.7% of GDP in 2001 from 15.6% in 2000, because of a fall in private investment. This can be attributed to a range of factors, including the short-term impact of an anticorruption campaign and changes in the foreign exchange regime that eliminated subsidies, and the persistence of excess capacity in key industries, such as cement, sugar and power, which served to retard private investment in the industry sector. National savings slipped from 13.5% of GDP in 2000, to 12.8% in 2001. Corporate savings also moved lower in 2001, partly due to high cotton prices, which reduced profit margins in the textile sector. The annual population growth rate in Pakistan is estimated to be 2.2%, while the labour force is estimated to be growing at 2.4% a year. The unemployment rate was 7.8% in 2000 but the number of unemployed is likely to be pervasive. The fiscal deficit fell from 6.5% of GDP in 2000 to 5.3% in 2001, the lowest level in 23 years. This decrease is entirely due to the government's reduction in public expenditures to meet its fiscal target under an IMF standby arrangement. The government's attempts to rectify macroeconomic imbalances and stabilise the economy in 2001 were fairly successful, and the country's macroeconomic indicators showed significant improvement. Prudent fiscal and monetary policies succeeded in reducing the budget deficit significantly and in containing inflation. However, the reduction in the deficit was achieved at the expense of development spending, which in 2001 was at its lowest level ever recorded.

Main Industries A severe drought caused the agriculture sector to contract in 2001, though the rest of the economy registered strong expansion. The drought is estimated to have caused a loss of about 2% in national income. The drought also had adverse impacts on hydropower generation, while value added in the power and gas distribution sector declined by 3.1%. The large-scale manufacturing sector grew by an impressive 7.8% in 2001, as against a 0.2% decline in 2000, because of strong external demand, in part arising from exchange rate depreciation. This was the highest rate of expansion since the 1980s. The outlook for the medium term is for continued low growth, because of drought-induced weak agricultural performance and because industry will remain affected by weak external demand in a context of a slow improvement in the world economy and continued economic and political uncertainty. The performance of all major industry groups was good in 2001, but some of the better growth rates were recorded in paper and board (24.9%), automobiles (23.3%) and petroleum (16.6%). Growth in the services sector declined marginally in 2001, to 4.4% from 4.8% in 2000. The decrease was due mainly to a slowdown in the finance and insurance subsector, as well as to a reduction in the growth rate of the public administration and defence subsector from 7% to 3% over the period.

Energy Pakistan produced 57,000 barrels per day (bbl/d) of oil in 2001 and consumed 359,000 bbl/d of petroleum products. Net oil imports were 302,000 bbl/d. While there is no prospect for Pakistan to reach self sufficiency in oil, the government has encouraged private (including foreign) firms to develop domestic production capacity. Pakistan's net oil imports are projected to rise substantially as demand growth outpaces increases in production. Demand for refined petroleum products also greatly exceeds domestic oil refining capacity, so nearly half of Pakistani imports are refined products.

	1999	2000	2001
Inflation (% change)	4.1	4.4	3.8
Exchange rate (per US$)	49.12	53.65	61.93
Interest rate			
GDP (% real growth)	4.1	3.9	3.4
GDP (Billion units of national currency)	3,060.6	3,327.5	3,592.2
GDP (US$ million)	62,310.8	62,024.2	58,006.9
GDP per capita (US$)	405.3	396.4	362.0
Consumption (Billion units of national currency)	2,339.5	2,535.2	2,757.3
Consumption (US$ million)	47,629.4	47,256.8	44,525.6
Consumption per capita (US$)	309.8	302.1	277.8
Population, mid-year ('000)	153,757.7	156,451.3	160,250.9
Birth rate (per '000)	37.4	37.2	36.9
Death rate (per '000)	10.4	10.1	9.9
No. of households ('000)	20,189.5	20,564.9	20,842.3
Total exports (US$ million)	8,491.3	9,028.0	9,209.0
Total imports (US$ million)	10,296.7	11,292.7	10,206.0
Tourism receipts (US$ million)	76.0	89.8	70.3
Tourist spending (US$ million)	180.0	523.1	426.3

Average household size 2001 (persons)	7.61				
Urban population 2001 (%)	37.6				
Age analysis (%) (2001)	*0-14*	41.5	*15-64*	55.3	*65+*	3.2
Population by sex (%) (2001)	*Male*	51.6	*Female*	48.4	
Life expectancy (years) (2001)	*Male*	60.6	*Female*	60.3	
Infant mortality (deaths per '000 live births) (2001)	89.9				
Adult literacy (%) (1997)	40.9				

TRADING PARTNERS

Major export destinations 2001 (% share)

USA	24.3
UNITED ARAB EMIRATES	7.6
UNITED KINGDOM	6.8
GERMANY	5.2

Major import sources 2001 (% share)

UNITED ARAB EMIRATES	12.7
SAUDI ARABIA	11.0
KUWAIT	7.0
USA	5.6

■ Panama

Area (km^2) 78,515

Currency US dollar (US$ = 100 cents)

Location Panama forms the longest and most slender section of the isthmus which divides Central America from South America, and extends in an S-shape, some 700km from east to west, between Costa Rica and Colombia. The land is traversed by the Panama Canal, the all-important marine link that connects the Caribbean Sea (and thus the Atlantic Ocean) with the Pacific Ocean. The capital is Panama City.

Head of State President Mireya Moscoso (1999)

Head of Government President Mireya Moscoso (1999)

Ruling Party The government is formed by a multiparty coalition.

Political Structure The 1983 Constitution provides for an executive president who is elected by universal suffrage for a term of five years and a unicameral National Assembly with 71 members who are also elected for five years. Panamanian politics have changed considerably since the US invasion in 1989 and the removal of Gen. Manuel Noriega as president. In December 1991 the Assembly approved a constitutional amendment which abolished the national army.

Last Elections Presidential elections were held in May 1999 and were won by Mireya Moscoso, the widow of a former president. She took 45% of the vote, easily defeating other candidates. Voting for the National Assembly was held at the same time with the ruling coalition receiving 57% of the vote and 42 seats.

Political Risk Fears that the US handover of the Panama Canal would create a power vacuum in Central America have proved unfounded, but Panama's growing ties with China are creating unease in Washington and Taipei. China has also become the third largest user of the canal, behind the US and Japan.

International Disputes Relations with Colombia worsened in 1999, following an incursion by Colombian guerrillas into Panama's remote Darien border region. Panama is also pressing for a free-trade agreement with the Central American Common Market plus El Salvador. Officials hope that the move will bolster intra-regional trade and improve relations with other countries in the region.

Economy GDP grew by 2% in 2001, while prices rose by 1.8%. The sluggish pace of growth and low rates of inflation that have characterised Panama's economy in recent years are expected to continue in the near term. The contraction in capital formation that followed the completion of large-scale infrastructure works and slackening consumption has reduced domestic demand. External demand is stronger, mainly due to sales in the Colón Free Zone in the Panama Canal. Cutbacks in public investment expenditure have reduced the fiscal deficit, and measures were taken to curb the country's large deficit on the balance-of-payments current account. The unemployment rate for the metropolitan region continues to be more than 15%. Panamanians have the eighth highest average income in the continent but the wealth distribution is one of the most unequal. Two fifths of the population live in poverty.

Main Industries Panama stands apart from the rest of Central America by virtue of its services-based economy and its control over the Panama Canal. Ambitious plans to modernise and expand the canal are underway. In 1996, the government began expansion and modernisation of the ports at each end of the canal. More than US$120 million has been spent so far with another US$200 million on related projects. Additional projects include the procurement of new towing locomotives; rehabilitation of the tow track system; a locks modernisation programme; installation of the latest marine traffic control technology; and design of additional canal watershed plans. With the completion of these modernisation programmes in 2005, canal transit capacity is expected to increase by approximately 20%. Although there was an upturn in activity within the Colón Free Zone, the momentum of international services has waned, particularly in banking. Agriculture accounts for about 10% of GDP and employs a quarter of the workforce. However, the country's exports of farm products are of critical importance, generating up to two thirds of all foreign exchange. Panama's banana exports have been one of the country's major exports but have declined sharply. Exports of domestically-produced goods have increased, thanks to higher sales of products such as flour and fish oil, shrimp larvae, coffee and sugar. Domestic crops include rice, maize, potatoes, beans and beef. The fishing industry is another major source of foreign exchange revenues as Panama is the world's third biggest shrimp exporter. Manufacturing establishments are mostly small-scale and consist mainly of producers of clothing, footwear, textiles, paper, plastics and electronics products. There has been no progress in the sale of the main projects scheduled fro privatisation. These include the international airport, the Atlapa Convention Centre or the water and sewerage utility. Mineral deposits are also arousing interest from international investors, although local objections on environmental grounds are strong. The country has copper reserves of some six million tonnes, which rank it ninth in the world in this category. Optimists predict that mining could account for 15% of GDP within the next 10-15 years.

Energy Panama has negligible hydrocarbon energy reserves and imports over 70% of its energy. Virtually all oil is imported, and the country neither produces nor consumes natural gas. In 2000, neighbouring Colombia approved a bill allowing natural gas exports, which previously had been banned. This paves the way for the possible construction of a gas pipeline leading from offshore Colombian gas sources directly to Panama. The country has ambitious plans to develop its hydroelectric potential but little progress has been made in recent years.

	1999	2000	2001
Inflation (% change)	1.3	1.4	1.8
Exchange rate (per US$)	1.00	1.00	1.00
Interest rate (% per annum, commercial lending rate)	10.1	10.2	11.0
GDP (% real growth)	4.1	2.3	2.0
GDP (Million units of national currency)	9,545.0	9,889.0	10,238.0
GDP (US$ million)	9,545.0	9,889.0	10,238.0
GDP per capita (US$)	3,449.4	3,517.1	3,585.1
Consumption (Million units of national currency)	5,331.8	5,672.8	5,968.3
Consumption (US$ million)	5,331.8	5,672.8	5,968.3
Consumption per capita (US$)	1,926.8	2,017.5	2,089.9
Population, mid-year ('000)	2,767.2	2,811.7	2,855.7
Birth rate (per '000)	21.8	21.3	20.8
Death rate (per '000)	5.1	5.1	5.1
No. of households ('000)	565.4	570.7	587.7
Total exports (US$ million)	822.1	859.5	910.5
Total imports (US$ million)	3,515.8	3,378.7	2,963.5
Tourism receipts (US$ million)	538.0	628.4	689.8
Tourist spending (US$ million)	184.0	173.4	177.8

Average household size 2001 (persons)	4.97				
Urban population 2001 (%)	56.6				
Age analysis (%) (2001)	*0-14*	31.1	*15-64*	63.4	*65+* 5.6
Population by sex (%) (2001)	*Male*	50.4	*Female*	49.6	
Life expectancy (years) (2001)	*Male*	72.4	*Female*	77.1	
Infant mortality (deaths per '000 live births) (2001)	19.5				
Adult literacy (%) (1997)	91.1				

TRADING PARTNERS

Major export destinations 2001 (% share)		Major import sources 2001 (% share)	
USA	49.7	USA	32.9
NICARAGUA	5.1	ECUADOR	8.0
COSTA RICA	4.8	COLOMBIA	5.7
SWEDEN	3.7	VENEZUELA	5.2

Papua New Guinea

Area (km^2)   462,840

Currency   Kina (K = 100 toea)

Location   Papua New Guinea, one of the more important island states in the Asia-Pacific region, occupies the eastern half of the old island of New Guinea. It also includes territories in the Solomon Islands group, in the Trobriands and in the Louisiade Archipelago. The capital is Port Moresby.

Head of State   HM Queen Elizabeth II

Head of Government   Mekere Morauta (1999)

Ruling Party   The People's Progress Party (PPP) leads a multi-party coalition.

Political Structure   Papua New Guinea, a member of the British Commonwealth, has a Governor-General who represents the Queen. However, executive power is exercised by a prime minister and a national executive council. The council is appointed by the Governor on the advice of the unicameral national parliament. The 109 members of parliament are elected by universal suffrage for a period of not more than five years. Since 1993, members have been barred from forcing any vote of confidence in the prime minister until he is at least 18 months into a term of office.

Last Elections   Parliamentary elections occurred in June 1997 when the PPP took 16 seats and the PNC won 6 seats. Another 40 seats went to non-partisans with the remainder divided among minor parties. Morauta subsequently became prime minister.

Political Risk   The country's political system is chaotic. In July 1999, the head of government, William Skate, was forced to resign following his decision to recognise Taiwan in exchange for US$2.35 billion in financial aid. The previous prime minister was also forced to resign as a result of his decision to bring in mercenaries to help fight the guerrillas in the long-running secessionist battle on Bougainville island. The recent decline in GDP and per capita income has increased social tensions and unrest. This was reflected in a series of events during 2001, including student protests against privatisation and temporary halts in production at important mining and oil projects caused by landowners' actions. Increased political activities in 2002 have made the situation more volatile. These problems are adversely affecting business and investment activities, as businesses adopt an extremely cautious attitude to expansion.

International Disputes   Unrest in several parts of the country threatens stability. Bougainville's repeated efforts to withdraw from Papua New Guinea have been a long-standing source of animosity. Both the government of Papua New Guinea and the Bougainville Revolutionary Army have been criticised about their record on human rights. The gold mines in Bougainville, which are worked mainly by Australian interests, have raised local standards of living but resulted in periodic poisoning scares. In 2000, Papua New Guinea agreed to grant Bougainville autonomy in an attempt to settle the South Pacific's longest-running conflict.

Economy   The economy experienced a serious recession in 2001 when GDP fell by 3.4%. The government expects the economy to rebound moderately in the medium term, with GDP growth of 1.2% in 2002 and 1.8% in 2003, respectively. Inflation was uncomfortably high at 10% but should fall to about 8.3% in 2002 and 5% in 2003. The government faced major difficulties in managing its finances in the first half of 2001. This was due to repeated problems in accessing all the external extraordinary financing from various donors due to a delay in meeting a major milestone for readying the country's largest bank - the Papua New Guinea Banking Corporation - for privatisation. At the same time, tax revenues were lower than expected due to continuing problems with the implementation of VAT, falling oil prices and a weak domestic economy. The government had to cut back expenditure and put tight controls in place in the middle of the year. Overall, the budget recorded a deficit equal to 1.8% of GDP in 2001. Exports and imports declined by 6.3% and 2.2%, respectively, in 2001, reflecting weak global and domestic activities. As a result, both the trade and current account surpluses declined. The capital account deficit also fell from US$234.7 million to US$115.5 million in 2001, reflecting the large inflow of external extraordinary financing. A feature of the government's medium-term projections is an increase in the budget deficit to 2% of GDP in 2002, before a turnaround begins in 2003. While revenues and grants are projected to remain fairly stable, a cut in government expenditures is assumed after 2002. Privatisation is expected to provide the main source of financing in 2002. However, the government's domestic debt will have to rise thereafter, as increased domestic financing is required to offset rising external obligations.

Main Industries   The combination of a sharp decline in mining, weak domestic demand and poor industrial profitability kept the economy in recession in 2001. There may, however, be some improvement in economic growth in 2002 as agriculture expands, though it may take longer for economic fundamentals to improve and for growth to be sustained. A general decline in world commodity prices constrained most sectors over 2001, notably the mining and oil sector. World prices of coffee and copra fell by about 30% and of copper and oil by about 10%. As a result, the export sector failed to realise the full potential benefit of a weaker kina. The largest contractions by sector were seen in construction (9.3%); mining (9%); and transport, storage and communications (7.4%). Sectors estimated to have expanded over the year are electricity, gas and water (7.9%); finance, real estate and business services (3.8%); and agriculture, forestry and fisheries (0.9%).

Energy   The country has four huge and potentially oil-filled basins offshore, although their exact content remains uncertain. Meanwhile, it is dependent on thermal energy for three-quarters of its electricity.

	1999	2000	2001
Inflation (% change)	14.9	15.6	9.3
Exchange rate (per US$)	2.57	2.78	3.39
Interest rate (% per annum, commercial lending rate)	18.9	17.5	16.2
GDP (% real growth)	7.6	-0.8	-3.4
GDP (Million units of national currency)	8,781.0	9,414.0	9,879.0
GDP (US$ million)	3,415.7	3,383.7	2,915.3
GDP per capita (US$)	742.6	719.6	606.9
Consumption (Million units of national currency)	6,122.8	5,431.4	5,791.1
Consumption (US$ million)	2,381.7	1,952.2	1,708.9
Consumption per capita (US$)	517.8	415.2	355.7
Population, mid-year ('000)	4,599.7	4,702.3	4,803.9
Birth rate (per '000)	33.4	33.1	32.8
Death rate (per '000)	10.2	10.0	9.8
No. of households ('000)	806.3	815.2	818.8
Total exports (US$ million)	1,924.3	2,095.6	1,812.8
Total imports (US$ million)	1,232.8	1,151.0	1,072.8
Tourism receipts (US$ million)	76.0	64.1	33.6
Tourist spending (US$ million)	53.0	45.3	40.4

Average household size 2001 (persons)	5.83					
Urban population 2001 (%)	17.7					
Age analysis (%) (2001)	0-14	38.6	15-64	58.4	65+	3.0
Population by sex (%) (2001)	Male	51.5	Female	48.5		
Life expectancy (years) (2001)	Male	56.2	Female	58.1		
Infant mortality (deaths per '000 live births) (2001)	64.5					
Adult literacy (%) (1997)	73.7					

TRADING PARTNERS

Major export destinations 2001 (% share)		Major import sources 2001 (% share)	
AUSTRALIA	24.9	AUSTRALIA	50.5
ASIA	17.5	SINGAPORE	18.7
JAPAN	10.8	JAPAN	4.5
CHINA	4.3	NEW ZEALAND	4.0

Paraguay

Area (km^2)   406,750

Currency   Guaraní (G = 100 céntimos)

Location   Paraguay, the geographic centre of South America, is a landlocked state bordered in the north by Bolivia, in the east by Brazil, and in the south and southwest by Argentina. Its terrain is, however, less mountainous than any of these countries. Most of it consists of a marshy plain through which the Paraguay and Pilcomayo rivers flow, interspersed with vast tracts of forest and jungle. The capital is Asuncion.

Head of State   Luis González Macchi (1999)

Head of Government   Luis González Macchi (1999)

Ruling Party   The government is formed by the Partido Colorado and the Democratic Alliance.

Political Structure   The Republic of Paraguay has an executive president who is directly elected by universal suffrage for a 5-year term of office. The president answers to a bicameral national Congress comprising a 45-member Senate and an 80-member Chamber of Deputies - both similarly elected for five years. In elections to the Chamber of Deputies, the party receiving the most votes is automatically granted two thirds of the seats in both Houses.

Last Elections   In the congressional elections held in May 1998, the Partido Colorado received 54% of the vote for its candidates in the Chamber of Deputies and 52% for candidates running for the Senate. The Partido won 45 and 24 seats, respectively. In the same elections Raul Cubas, the Colorado candidate, took 54% of the vote compared with 42.5% for the Democratic Alliance candidate, Domingo Laino. Cubas resigned from office under threat of impeachment in March 1999.

Political Risk   Violent protests against the government have been frequent in 2002. Paraguay is prone to frequent coups and assassinations of political figures. Its political system remains immature and unstable, even by Latin American standards.

International Disputes   Paraguay's dispute with Bolivia concerning the area to the northeast of the Paraguay River has been resolved. Paraguay's occasional political tensions sometimes threaten to disrupt Mercosur, the customs union linking the country with Argentina, Brazil and Uruguay. Both Argentina and Brazil have repeatedly intervened in Paraguayan politics to shore up its frail democracy.

Economy   GDP rose by just 0.8% in 2001, while prices increased by 7.7%. The Paraguayan economy has been hit by the problems of its two big neighbours, Argentina and Brazil. The currency, the guarani, has lost 26% of its valued in the first half of 2002. Thanks to ineffective policies, combined with endemic corruption, income per capita has been sinking since the mid-1990s. Urban unemployment remains high - more than 10%. Monetary policy continues to be expansionary, with interest rates falling. The value of total exports decreased in 2001 in response to lower demand for exports linked to the informal border trade with Brazil and Argentina. These transactions, referred to as "unregistered and re-export trade", represent around three quarters of total exports and are facing increasingly stringent customs restrictions in Paraguay's neighbouring countries. The country's best hope may be its membership in Mercosur. Paraguay's taxes, as well as its labour and energy costs, are the lowest in the organisation. These advantages should attract investment in labour-intensive industries such as shoes, textiles and food processing if the country can ever bring its rampant corruption under control.

Main Industries   Paraguay's economy is dominated by the agricultural sector, which accounts for 25% of GDP and 90% of exports. These consist mainly of soya, cotton, vegetable oils and increasingly timber. In 2000, agriculture performed strongly due to an increase in the cotton harvest, which was more than enough to compensate for a decrease in soya production. Other agricultural products (maize, wheat and sugar cane) recorded increases in output of between 10% and 30%. Farming is subject to recurrent drought and only 5% of the land area is under cultivation. The country's varied and often-inaccessible landscape discourages large-scale exploitation of the mineral sector, which is currently limited to limestone and salt - although ample deposits of copper, iron ore and manganese are known to exist. Industry contributes 26% to GDP and depends mainly on the processing of raw materials, including textiles and timber products. Cement, steel and oil refining are other prominent industries. The government's plans for privatisation had to be scrapped in 2002 following violent protests. The sale of the country's telecoms monopoly was stopped, and the new law for privatisation was repealed. The case for privatisation has been undermined by corruption allegations involving the president's relatives.

Energy   Paraguay has no oil of its own and imports crude and refined petroleum in roughly equal quantities. Exploration by both local and North American companies continues, encouraged by the discovery in 1984 of substantial deposits in the Argentine province of Formosa, close to the Paraguayan border, and by exploration in the Bolivian Chaco. Paraguay has one of the highest hydroelectric power potentials per person in the world, and its major hydroelectric power plants more than satisfy the country's demand for electricity. With Paraguay's large hydroelectric capacity, it is seen as the main electric power supplier for the Southern Cone region.

	1999	2000	2001
Inflation (% change)	6.8	9.0	7.7
Exchange rate (per US$)	3,119.07	3,486.35	4,105.92
Interest rate (% per annum, lending rate)	30.2	26.8	28.3
GDP (% real growth)	0.5	-0.4	0.8
GDP (Billion units of national currency)	24,144.3	26,202.8	28,800.7
GDP (US$ million)	7,740.9	7,515.8	7,014.4
GDP per capita (US$)	1,482.1	1,402.6	1,276.2
Consumption (Billion units of national currency)	19,762.5	22,406.8	25,912.0
Consumption (US$ million)	6,336.0	6,427.0	6,310.9
Consumption per capita (US$)	1,213.2	1,199.4	1,148.2
Population, mid-year ('000)	5,222.8	5,358.6	5,496.5
Birth rate (per '000)	30.7	30.4	30.0
Death rate (per '000)	5.3	5.2	5.2
No. of households ('000)	1,146.1	1,170.2	1,192.9
Total exports (US$ million)	740.9	804.8	775.7
Total imports (US$ million)	1,725.1	2,153.2	2,175.2
Tourism receipts (US$ million)	81.0	195.7	182.6
Tourist spending (US$ million)	109.0	154.4	177.4

Average household size 2001 (persons)	4.64				
Urban population 2001 (%)	56.7				
Age analysis (%) (2001)	*0-14*	39.3	*15-64*	57.2	*65+* 3.5
Population by sex (%) (2001)	*Male*	50.4	*Female*	49.6	
Life expectancy (years) (2001)	*Male*	68.3	*Female*	72.8	
Infant mortality (deaths per '000 live births) (2001)	37.5				
Adult literacy (%) (1997)	92.4				

TRADING PARTNERS

Major export destinations 2001 (% share)

BRAZIL	27.6
ARGENTINA	27.1
CHILE	5.9
NETHERLANDS	5.2

Major import sources 2001 (% share)

BRAZIL	32.2
ARGENTINA	24.9
USA	14.2
HONG KONG, CHINA	4.8

Peru

Area (km²)   1,285,215

Currency   New sol (n/s = 100 céntimos)

Location   Peru's 2,000-km Pacific coastline extends from the Ecuadorian border in the north to Chile in the south. Its northeastern border abuts with Colombia and its eastern frontiers with Brazil and Bolivia. The country includes the northern part of the Andes, although there are also deep jungles in the northwest. The capital is Lima.

Head of State   President Alejandro Toledo (2001)

Head of Government   Luis Solari (2002)

Ruling Party   The Peru Posible Party leads a diverse coalition.

Political Structure   Under the 1993 Constitution, the president is elected by universal suffrage for a term of five years and reports to the 240-member Congress (120 in the Lower House and 120 in the Upper House) - also elected by universal suffrage for a 5-year term.

Last Elections   Alejandro Toledo of the Peru Posible Party won a narrow victory in a run-off ballot for the presidency in June 2001, defeating Alan Garcia, a former president. Toledo received 45.7% of the vote to Garcia's 40.6%. The vote was said by observers to be possibly the cleanest in Peru's history. In the congressional elections in April 2000, the Nuevo Majoridad-Cambio 90 party received 42% of the vote and 52 seats, the Peru Posible Party got 23% of the vote and 26 seats, the Independent Front took 7% of the vote and 8 seats. Minor parties accounted for the remainder. In an effort to revive his sagging popularity, Toledo appointed Solari as prime minister in July 2002.

Political Risk   Faced with dwindling popularity and an anti-free market backlash, the government is under growing pressure to tackle a "crisis of confidence". In July 2002, riots brought about the resignation of the interior minister. Accusations of weak leadership, indecision and a failure to fulfil campaign promises plague the president. His image has suffered further embarrassment as a result of a paternity suit.

International Disputes   Peru and neighbouring Ecuador have fought over a disputed 50-mile stretch of highland jungle in the Cordillera del Condor region along Peru's northeastern border three times in the last 47 years, most recently in 1995. The two nations almost went to war a fourth time in 1998, but pulled back and negotiated a border settlement and peace treaty - brokered by the US, Brazil, Argentina and Chile. As part of the peace settlement, the two sides pledged to forgo weapons purchases for their respective armed forces for the next four years. In August 1999, the countries signed bilateral agreements to build bridges and roads between the neighbours. In 1997, Peru joined the Asia Pacific Economic Cooperation (APEC) forum. Peru also hopes to join Mercosur, the South American common market group now consisting of Brazil, Argentina, Uruguay and Paraguay. Being a member of both APEC and Mercosur could encourage Peru's hope of becoming an economic link between Asia and Latin America.

Economy   GDP increased by only 0.2% in 2001. Growth of 3.7% is expected in 2002 and an increase of 2.9% is forecast for 2003. Inflation was 2% in 2001 and will be 1.8% in 2002. In 2003, prices are expected to rise by 2.3%. The government's political frailty risks causing problems for an economy which has been reviving since Toledo took office. One of the most tangible bits of evidence that some things are improving is that in 2002 Peruvians are selling US dollars and buying sols for the first time in two decades. In February 2002, investors snapped up US$500 million of Peruvian sovereign bonds - the first issue since 1928. Yet despite lower interest rates, investment is expanding only modestly. In part, that is because the banks are still weighed down by bad loans after the collapse of a credit bubble. The administration is also committed to market reforms and privatisation but there is strong opposition. Only around 40% of the workforce has a proper job and 54% of Peruvians are classified as poor. During his campaign, Toledo promised to create 2.5 million jobs over the next five years, partly through an emergency employment programme costing US$170 million a year. So far, he has been unable to find the money to fund job creation and meet all his other obligations. The government has said it will cut the sales tax and a special payroll tax but that will promote investment only if it is seen as part of a credible overall plan. Real changes in the Peruvian economy will probably take decades.

Main Industries   Peru's agricultural sector accounts for 7% of GDP. The sector employs 40% of the workforce who survive on subsistence farming but farming is also an important earner of foreign exchange. Fishmeal and fish oil exports have finally recovered after being depressed by El Niño in 1999. Coca farming, once endemic throughout the region, has been reduced but even now is thought to account for 30% of total exports. Cotton, sugar cane, coffee and soya are grown for export while rice, maize, sorghum, potatoes and vegetables are produced for the domestic market. Manufacturing accounts about 37% of GDP and construction accounts for another 10%. The sector is widely diversified, including rubber, vehicle assembly, engineering, food processing and chemicals. Peru's privatisation earnings during the first half of 2001 totalled only US$40 million but revenues could increase through the sale of some large state assets, including the Talara oil refinery and the Mantaro hydroelectric complex, possibly in 2003. One successful privatisation last year was that of a power generating company for US$227 million. The country has vast mineral potential, including copper, silver, zinc, gold, iron ore, phosphorus and manganese. Output of the mining sector has slowed as sectoral investment projects mature. Much of the economy's future hinges on increased copper and zinc exports from the new Antamina mine, officially inaugurated in November 2001.

Energy   In 2001, oil production was about 96,000 barrels per day (bbl/d), down from 100,000 bbl/d in 2000. With oil consumption at 180,000 bbl/d, the country has become a significant net oil importer. The main areas of current and potential oil activity are in the northern jungle as well as some offshore areas located from the northern city of Tumbes to Pisco, south of Lima. Peru's 37 million acres of offshore basins are largely unexplored. Peru has proven natural gas reserves of about 8.7 trillion cu ft, and production of around 14.8 billion cu ft (Bcf) per year. This production is likely to increase sharply in coming years with development of the giant Camisea natural gas field, the largest in South America, which contains an estimated 9-13 trillion cu ft of gas.

	1999	2000	2001
Inflation (% change)	3.5	3.8	2.0
Exchange rate (per US$)	3.38	3.49	3.51
Interest rate (% per annum, lending rate)	30.8	27.9	20.4
GDP (% real growth)	1.4	3.6	0.2
GDP (Million units of national currency)	174,719.0	186,756.0	189,532.0
GDP (US$ million)	51,641.1	53,511.7	54,046.5
GDP per capita (US$)	2,029.4	2,068.0	2,054.6
Consumption (Million units of national currency)	122,102.0	131,781.2	132,834.3
Consumption (US$ million)	36,089.3	37,759.7	37,878.8
Consumption per capita (US$)	1,418.2	1,459.3	1,440.0
Population, mid-year ('000)	25,447.0	25,876.0	26,305.5
Birth rate (per '000)	24.1	23.7	23.2
Death rate (per '000)	6.3	6.3	6.2
No. of households ('000)	5,325.9	5,436.0	5,522.8
Total exports (US$ million)	6,112.6	7,027.7	7,091.7
Total imports (US$ million)	8,074.8	8,796.8	7,646.9
Tourism receipts (US$ million)	890.0	996.9	683.5
Tourist spending (US$ million)	443.0	391.7	315.3

Average household size 2001 (persons)	4.76					
Urban population 2001 (%)	72.9					
Age analysis (%) (2001)	*0-14*	32.9	*15-64*	62.2	*65+*	4.9
Population by sex (%) (2001)	*Male*	49.6	*Female*	50.4		
Life expectancy (years) (2001)	*Male*	67.0	*Female*	72.0		
Infant mortality (deaths per '000 live births) (2001)	38.9					
Adult literacy (%) (1997)	88.7					

TRADING PARTNERS

Major export destinations 2001 (% share)		Major import sources 2001 (% share)	
USA	27.7	IMPORTS FROM UNITED STATES	25.7
SWITZERLAND	8.8	IMPORTS FROM CHILE	8.8
CHINA	7.0	IMPORTS FROM VENEZUELA	6.2
JAPAN	6.0	IMPORTS FROM BRAZIL	5.5

Philippines

Area (km^2)   300,000

Currency   Philippine peso (Ps = 100 centavos)

Location   Composed of 11 large islands and some 7,000 smaller islands and atolls, the Philippines lies some 800km off the coast of Indo-China, north-east of Papua New Guinea and north of Indonesia. The group of islands is some 900km in length from north to south. The capital is Manila.

Head of State   President Gloria Macapagal-Arroyo (2001)

Head of Government   Gloria Macapagal-Arroyo (2001)

Ruling Party   The government is formed by the Struggle of the Philippine Masses (LMP).

Political Structure   The Republic of the Philippines has an executive president who is elected by universal mandate and then appoints a cabinet. The Congress has two chambers. The House of Representatives has at most 260 seats elected for a 3-year term, 208 seats in single-seat constituencies and at most 52 seats allotted to party-lists according to proportional representation. The Senate has 24 members, elected for a 6-year term by proportional representation, half of them renewed every three years.

Last Elections   Joseph Estrada easily won the presidential elections held in 1998. In Congressional elections held at the same time, the LMP took 110 seats in the House and 10 in the Senate. The alliance of the National Union of Christian Democrats and the United Muslim Democratic Party won 50 seats in the House and 5 in the Senate. The remaining seats were spread among several parties. In 2001, Estrada was convicted of embezzlement and replaced by the vice president, Macapagal-Arroyo.

Political Risk   The government has had to cope with three different groups of Muslim separatists. The southern Philippines has been terrorised for several years by a brutal Islamic group known as the Abu Sayyaf. With the help of US forces acting as advisors, this group is now on the defensive. However, the Muslim problem in the southern Philippines is unlikely to be stamped out because the jungles are too deep and the local population very sympathetic. The effort might succeed with massive US assistance but that is not politically acceptable. Manila is having more success in dealing with other separatist movements. It is engaged in negotiations with the Moro Islamic Liberation Front, the largest of the three groups, with the help of the Libyan government. Another group, the Moro National Liberation Front, reached an agreement with Manila in 1996. The leader of this group now controls four Muslim-dominated provinces that voted to become a government-sponsored autonomous region.

International Disputes   The Philippines lays claim to the Malaysian territory of Sabah which it argues was illegally ceded to the new Malaysian state by Brunei. The dispute has been dormant since the late 1970s, however. The Philippines is one of the many claimants to the territory of the Spratly Islands in the South China Sea, where oil prospecting has been in progress. Following the US departure from Subic Bay, the discovery of Chinese "rogue" naval incursions into Philippine waters have occasionally created unease and heightened tensions between the two countries.

Economy   GDP is expected to grow by 4% in 2002 and 4.2% in 2003. Inflation is expected to be about 5% in both 2002 and 2003. One of the major policy initiatives is to reduce the fiscal deficit and government debt by cutting expenditures, strengthening the tax collection system and improving revenues, so as to allow greater expenditures for infrastructure investments and social development. The tax system is also being simplified. Other major policy initiatives of the government include efforts to curb money laundering, sell state-owned assets in power and construction enterprises, increase foreign and domestic investment in the economy, foster greater competition in domestic markets (eg shipping), and modernise the country's agriculture sector. In 2001, the unemployment rate held steady at around 11%, but remained among the highest in the region. This was partly the result of slow job creation as well as a large increase in new labour force entrants associated with the continued high population growth rate. High unemployment and population growth, combined with low economic growth, suggest that the incidence and severity of poverty in the country remains severe. The latest estimates of poverty incidence refer to the year 2000 and show that over 39% of the total population have incomes below the national poverty line.

Main Industries   The services sector displayed the strongest expansion during 2001, rising by 4.3% relative to the previous year. Expansion was also fuelled by the favourable performance of the agriculture sector (up by 3.9%), which benefited from good weather and some improvements in infrastructure. Agriculture remains important to the economy both because of its contribution to production and employment, and because agricultural products are important inputs to many manufacturing and services sector activities. An increase in both the harvested and irrigated areas as a result of investment to rehabilitate irrigation systems in some regions also helped in agriculture's improved performance. The industrial sector expanded by only 1.9% year-on-year in 2001, largely as a result of a sluggish performance in manufacturing. This subsector accounts for 71.1% of industry's output, but grew by only 2.2%, or roughly a third of the increase registered in 2000. The electronics subsector was particularly hard hit by low global demand; electronics exports declined by 17% in 2001 compared with 3.9% growth in 2000. Garment exports, which represent about 8% of total exports, also fell in 2001. The construction sector stagnated, growing at an estimated rate of only 0.7%. On the demand side, buoyant private consumption helped sustain economic growth. Government consumption expenditures bounced back from a 1.1% reduction in 2000 to a 0.1% increase in 2001. A large level of remittances, (over 8% of GNP) is one reason why consumption spending in the country held up so well, even though domestic income growth was weak.

Energy   The Philippines' energy sector is relatively dynamic. Major reforms include projects to electrify isolated villages and to reduce the Philippines' dependence on imported oil. The country began 2001 producing an average of only 1,000 barrels per day (bbl/d) of oil but by October production was 22,000 bbl/d. This increase was due primarily to the discovery of new deep-sea oil deposits beneath the natural gas-bearing structures. However, the country is still a highly dependent net oil importer, consuming on average 356,000 bbl/d in 2001. Oil consumption is expected to grow, but demand for power generation will diminish as a result of the government's drive to retire ageing oil-fired electric power plants and switch to alternative power sources.

	1999	2000	2001
Inflation (% change)	6.7	4.3	6.1
Exchange rate (per US$)	39.09	44.19	50.99
Interest rate (% per annum, commercial lending rate)	11.8	10.9	12.4
GDP (% real growth)	3.3	4.0	3.4
GDP (Billion units of national currency)	2,976.9	3,302.6	3,642.8
GDP (US$ million)	76,157.0	74,732.0	71,438.0
GDP per capita (US$)	1,008.4	972.8	912.0
Consumption (Billion units of national currency)	2,180.1	2,355.4	2,568.2
Consumption (US$ million)	55,772.0	53,300.0	50,364.3
Consumption per capita (US$)	738.5	693.8	643.0
Population, mid-year ('000)	75,521.8	76,822.7	78,330.3
Birth rate (per '000)	27.7	27.3	27.0
Death rate (per '000)	5.4	5.3	5.3
No. of households ('000)	14,912.3	15,271.5	15,690.0
Total exports (US$ million)	36,576.3	39,783.0	32,664.3
Total imports (US$ million)	32,568.0	33,808.0	31,358.1
Tourism receipts (US$ million)	2,534.0	2,513.5	1,648.8
Tourist spending (US$ million)	1,308.0	954.2	1,000.6

Average household size 2001 (persons)	5.03				
Urban population 2001 (%)	59.4				
Age analysis (%) (2001)	*0-14*	35.8	*15-64*	60.2	*65+* 4.0
Population by sex (%) (2001)	*Male*	50.4	*Female*	49.6	
Life expectancy (years) (2001)	*Male*	67.6	*Female*	71.6	
Infant mortality (deaths per '000 live births) (2001)	30.8				
Adult literacy (%) (1997)	94.6				

TRADING PARTNERS

Major export destinations 2001 (% share)

USA	28.2
JAPAN	16.5
SINGAPORE	6.7
NETHERLANDS	6.6

Major import sources 2001 (% share)

JAPAN	20.3
USA	18.5
SINGAPORE	6.6
SOUTH KOREA	6.3

Poland

Area (km^2)   312,685

Currency   New zloty

Location   Poland, one of the largest states in eastern central Europe, extends from the 400-km Baltic coast in the north to the Czech and Slovak borders, some 1,200km to the south, and from Germany in the west to Russia, Lithuania, Belarus and Ukraine in the east. The country's terrain is of mixed and mainly agricultural quality but is seldom elevated. The capital is Warsaw.

Head of State   President Alexander Kwasniewski (1996)

Head of Government   Leszek Miller (2001)

Ruling Party   The government is formed by the Coalition of the Alliance of Democratic Left (SLD), the Union of Labour (UP) and the Polish People's Party (PSL).

Political Structure   The 1997 constitution provides for executive powers to be shared between the prime minister and the president. The president is elected by popular vote for a 5-year term. The National Assembly has two chambers. The Diet (or Sejm) has 460 members, elected for a 4-year term. Of these, 391 members are elected by proportional representation in multi-seat constituencies and 69 are selected in a national constituency by proportional representation among parties obtaining more than 7% of the popular vote. The Senate has 100 members elected for a 4-year term in 47 2-seat constituencies and two 3-seat constituencies.

Last Elections   Parliamentary elections were last held in September 2001. The SLD/UP took 216 seats, Citizens' Platform won 65 seats, the Self Defence of the Polish Republic claimed 53 seats and the PSL received 42 seats. The remainder were split among several parties. Elections for president were held in October 2000. Kwasniewski received 54% of the vote, defeating his main rival, Andrzej Olechowski, who got 18% of the vote.

Political Risk   Led by Solidarity trade unionists, Polish workers are becoming increasingly unhappy with their plight. The frequency of strikes and the number of participants is steadily growing. More ominous for the country's leaders, Solidarity now says that it no longer wants to be part of the government but will devote itself to getting better deals for its workers. The move weakens government authority at a time when unpopular reforms need to be implemented. Another part of the same problem is the country's rising unemployment rolls. In 2002, about 18% are without a job but the rate of unemployment rises to 40% among those between 15 and 24 years.

International Disputes   Poland's negotiations on accession to the EU are proving more difficult than those involving Hungary or the Czech Republic. Warsaw is proving less amenable on sensitive issues such as land ownership and labour mobility. These countries have now banned together to negotiate on accession issues with the EU as a group. Poland has never sought to redress the loss of eastern territory in what is now Russia and Ukraine, during and after World War II. These issues will be suppressed in order not to complicate negotiations with Brussels.

Economy   GDP rose by 1.1% in 2001 and will increase by 1.4% in 2002. In 2003, growth is expected to be 3.2%. Prices increased by 5.5% in 2001 and should rise by 5.1% in 2002. In 2003, inflation is forecast to be 4.5%. The ongoing efforts to preserve macroeconomic stability and undertake structural reforms bode well for future output growth. Prospects for net job creation are unfortunately much less promising. The social model that has been promoted by successive governments has many features that are not employment friendly. Job protection is widespread, resulting in a rigid labour market. Wage indexation mechanisms lead to high labour costs that crowd out the low-skilled. Generous early-retirement and disability pensions have led to huge increases in social security contributions. Policies to cut labour supply have failed to achieve their intended goal because many recipients have remained active. More effective labour market policies will, however, take time to work, and many persons are likely to remain unemployed in the near future. This will increase poverty which, although not widespread, is not negligible in selected areas.

Main Industries   Poland's economic performance was impressive during the period 1995-2000 and average living standards improved considerably. This achievement reflected the persistent efforts of both the government and the private sector to lay the foundations for lasting growth. Many firms were privatised, restructured and modernised. Inflows of FDI reached the equivalent of 20% of GDP cumulatively during 1996-1999, bringing much needed capital and know-how to large companies. Two million small and medium-sized enterprises made a remarkable contribution to economic growth. Even the traditionally bloated state enterprises appeared to be stepping up their adjustment efforts. The agriculture sector has largely remained outside the vast efforts of restructuring and modernisation. Agricultural policy has attempted to protect farmers' incomes through price support and by limiting their exposure to international competition. This has not prevented the gradual decline in farm earnings over the past decade. High unemployment in rural areas also slowed down productivity enhancing restructuring and modernisation in farms. Agricultural policies should aim at promoting competitive activities and employment.

Energy   With proven oil reserves of only 115 million barrels, Poland relied on imports for 97% of its 2001 oil consumption. Poland's oil demand is expected to increase by as much as 50% by 2020. Polish oil production increased from 10,000 barrels per day (bbl/d) in 2000 to 14,000 bbl/d in 2001, but this is still a small fraction of oil demand (434,000 bbl/d). Polish oil production comes primarily from fields in southern and western Poland, with the southern reserves nearly exhausted. However, the Barnówko - Mostno - Buszewo field discovered in 1996 in the Polish part of the Permian Basin (near the German border directly east of Berlin) has potential reserves of about 73 million barrels and the Miedzychod field is estimated to have even more, so Poland should be able to increase its production as these fields come on line. Coal exports, which go primarily to customers in Europe and the former Soviet Union, have historically been a major source of foreign exchange. The country's guidelines for energy policy through 2010 emphasise greater use of oil and natural gas, but coal is expected to remain the dominant fuel, particularly in the electric power sector.

	1999	2000	2001
Inflation (% change)	7.3	10.1	5.5
Exchange rate (per US$)	3.97	4.35	4.09
Interest rate (% per annum, lending rate)	17.0	20.0	18.4
GDP (% real growth)	4.1	4.1	1.1
GDP (Million units of national currency)	615,115.0	686,166.0	721,809.0
GDP (US$ million)	155,053.7	157,881.9	176,313.3
GDP per capita (US$)	4,009.8	4,081.9	4,556.4
Consumption (Million units of national currency)	394,255.7	443,270.1	474,559.4
Consumption (US$ million)	99,381.1	101,993.3	115,918.7
Consumption per capita (US$)	2,570.1	2,637.0	2,995.6
Population, mid-year ('000)	38,668.2	38,678.1	38,695.7
Birth rate (per '000)	10.2	10.0	9.7
Death rate (per '000)	9.9	9.9	9.9
No. of households ('000)	13,219.6	13,431.7	13,621.4
Total exports (US$ million)	27,404.0	31,651.0	36,092.0
Total imports (US$ million)	45,903.1	48,940.2	50,275.1
Tourism receipts (US$ million)	6,100.0	8,708.5	8,050.8
Tourist spending (US$ million)	3,600.0	5,982.5	6,040.2

Average household size 2001 (persons)	2.88				
Urban population 2001 (%)	65.7				
Age analysis (%) (2001)	*0-14*	19.6	*15-64*	68.0	*65+* 12.4
Population by sex (%) (2001)	*Male*	48.6	*Female*	51.4	
Life expectancy (years) (2001)	*Male*	69.5	*Female*	77.8	
Infant mortality (deaths per '000 live births) (2001)	9.2				
Adult literacy (%) (1998)	99.0				

TRADING PARTNERS

Major export destinations 2001 (% share)		Major import sources 2001 (% share)	
GERMANY	34.3	GERMANY	28.7
ITALY	5.6	RUSSIA	8.4
FRANCE	5.0	ITALY	8.1
UNITED KINGDOM	4.9	FRANCE	6.7

Portugal

Area (km²) 91,630

Currency Euro (= 100 cents)

Location Portugal occupies about half of the Atlantic coast on the Iberian peninsula, and more than three quarters of the west-facing section, with Spain, its only immediate neighbour, accounting for the rest. The country is broadly rectangular in shape, extending only a maximum of 200km inland but about 600km from north to south. The Atlantic archipelagos of the Azores and Madeira also belong to Portugal. The terrain of the mainland country is largely mountainous inland, but there are innumerable fertile valleys lower down. The climate is Mediterranean. The capital is Lisbon.

Head of State Jorge Sampaio (1996)

Head of Government José Manuel Durao Barroso (2002)

Ruling Party The government is led by the Social Democrat Party (PSD) and the Peoples' Party (PP).

Political Structure The Republic of Portugal has an executive president who is elected by universal suffrage for a renewable term of five years and appoints the prime minister. Legislative authority is vested in the unicameral Assembly of the Republic, whose 230 members are elected by universal suffrage for up to four years at a time.

Last Elections Presidential elections took place in January 2001 when Sampaio received 56% of the vote, defeating Joaquim Martins Ferreira do Amaral. Elections to the Assembly of the Republic were held in March 2002. The PSD took 102 seats, the Socialist Party received 95 seats and the PP claimed 14 seats. The remaining seats were divided among several smaller parties.

Political Risk The government took emergency measures to curb the deficit which was created - it claims - by the calamitous state in which the Socialists left the country's public finances. The political debate rages but the new measures are already beginning to hurt. The EU came close to issuing Portugal with an unprecedented formal warning over the deficit in 2002 and remains concerned about the problem.

International Disputes Reform of the EU's fisheries policy will be one area of debate in the near future. Portugal, along with Spain, Greece and one or two other EU member states, has built up substantial excess capacity in this industry and local fish supplies are now seriously depleted. European authorities want to reduce quotas and scale back financial support. Lisbon and other major fishing nations will strongly oppose any reforms and should probably be able to retain most of its financial support for the industry. .

Economy GDP grew by 1.6% in 2001 and is expected to rise by only 0.8% in 2002. In 2003, growth will be about 2%. Inflation was 4.4% in 2001 and prices are expected to rise by 2.9% in 2002 and 2.2% in 2003. After an extended period when living standards in Portugal were gradually converging toward the euro zone average, the economy has slowed significantly. This setback was partially due to the waning effect of euro-entry-related declines in interest rates and private sector responses to rising indebtedness levels. With external demand also weakening, exports had stalled by the third quarter of 2001. The external current deficit narrowed moderately. Inflation has continued to exceed the euro zone average, due largely to the relatively strong cost pressures in Portugal. With low unemployment, wage increases (including in the public sector) have remained well above increases in the euro zone, and the differential has not been compensated by higher productivity growth. In the financial sector, credit growth has moderated, but continues to exceed nominal income growth by a wide margin. As a result, levels of private sector indebtedness have continued to rise, and bank credit (in relation to GDP) is well above the euro zone average. The credit boom has outstripped the growth in deposits, and banks have financed themselves extensively on international capital markets.

Main Industries Despite rapid growth in other sectors, agriculture remains the backbone of the economy with citrus fruits, olives, wines and vegetables being the dominant products. Cork is grown for export, and the country has an important fishery industry. Yet Portugal's farmers are the poorest in the EU. They benefit least from the Common Agricultural Policy because these funds are channelled mainly to meat, dairy and cereal production, which are not prominent in the country. On average, EU farmers are six times better off than their Portuguese counterparts. Portugal's traditional industries - clothing, textiles and footwear - account for about 18% of all exports. For decades, however, they have relied on a single competitive edge: low wages. But this advantage is fast disappearing. European markets, which account for more than 80% of Portuguese exports, are being opened to imports from developing countries, where wages are far lower. At the same time, unit labour costs in Portugal, although low in European terms, are growing significantly faster than the EU average. In 2001, real wage increases were higher than productivity gains for the fifth consecutive year. Improving productivity will require more investment in education, professional training and new technology. In the financial sector, credit growth has moderated, but continues to exceed nominal income growth by a wide margin. As a result, private sector indebtedness levels rose further, and bank credit (in relation to GDP) is well above the euro zone average. The credit boom has outstripped the growth in core deposits, and banks have financed themselves extensively on international capital markets. In the financial sector, there is concern that credit growth has far outstripped the growth in core bank deposits, with banks securing additional financing needs on international capital markets, which could expose the financial sector to potential liquidity risks.

Energy Portugal consumed 339,000 barrels per day (bbl/d) in 2001. Over 25% is used for electricity generation, as coal and natural gas use is lower than in most EU countries. In 2000, oil made up 64% of total Portuguese primary energy consumption. Portugal has almost no domestic petroleum resources, as exploration on the continental shelf in the 1970s discovered no commercially viable reserves. Privatisation in the Portuguese oil sector (nationalised in 1975) began in 1992, but the state retains its controlling share in Petroleos de Portugal (Petrogal), the country's state oil company. The Portuguese natural gas sector is young and growing rapidly. Annual consumption was nearly non-existent prior to 1997, but reached 80 billion cu ft (Bcf) in 1999, levelling off to 83 Bcf in 2000.

	1999	2000	2001
Inflation (% change)	0.9	1.1	1.1
Exchange rate (per US$)	0.94	1.09	1.12
Interest rate (% per annum, lending rate)	5.2	5.5	
GDP (% real growth)	3.4	3.2	1.6
GDP (Million units of national currency)	108,666.0	115,282.0	122,263.0
GDP (US$ million)	115,866.2	100,136.2	109,406.1
GDP per capita (US$)	11,598.6	10,002.8	10,904.8
Consumption (Million units of national currency)	71,581.1	74,963.5	1.0
Consumption (US$ million)	76,324.1	65,114.8	71,059.4
Consumption per capita (US$)	7,640.3	6,504.5	7,082.7
Population, mid-year ('000)	9,989.7	10,010.8	10,032.8
Birth rate (per '000)	11.2	11.1	11.1
Death rate (per '000)	10.7	10.7	10.8
No. of households ('000)	3,586.4	3,653.1	3,705.0
Total exports (US$ million)	25,227.1	23,309.9	23,933.4
Total imports (US$ million)	39,825.4	38,249.5	37,965.5
Tourism receipts (US$ million)	5,131.0	5,594.5	4,587.1
Tourist spending (US$ million)	2,266.0	2,339.5	2,408.0

Average household size 2001 (persons)		2.74					
Urban population 2001 (%)		43.5					
Age analysis (%) (2001)	0-14	16.4	15-64	68.0	65+	15.6	
Population by sex (%) (2001)	Male	48.2	Female	51.8			
Life expectancy (years) (2001)	Male	72.4	Female	79.4			
Infant mortality (deaths per '000 live births) (2001)		6.2					
Adult literacy (%) (1998)		90.8					

TRADING PARTNERS

Major export destinations 2001 (% share)		Major import sources 2001 (% share)	
GERMANY	19.2	SPAIN	26.5
SPAIN	18.6	GERMANY	13.9
FRANCE	12.6	FRANCE	10.3
UNITED KINGDOM	10.3	ITALY	6.7

Puerto Rico

Area (km^2)　8,960

Currency　US dollar (US$ = 100 cents)

Location　Puerto Rico is one of the larger islands in the Antilles group, located about 80km east of Haiti and about 800km off the coast of Venezuela. With a pleasant Caribbean climate, but with some vulnerability to hurricanes, it has a large population for its size. The capital is San Juan.

Head of State　Governor Sila Maria Calderon (2001)

Head of Government　Governor Sila Maria Calderon (2001)

Ruling Party　Popular Democratic Party (PDP)

Political Structure　The Commonwealth of Puerto Rico, an external territory of the US, has a Resident Commissioner who is elected by universal suffrage for a 4-year term, and who has a non-voting seat in the US House of Representatives. Executive authority is vested in an elected Governor and his cabinet, while legislative power rests with the bicameral Legislative Assembly - which consists of a 28-member Senate and a 54-member House of Representatives, both popularly elected for a 4-year term. In December 1998, voters rejected plans for full US statehood for the third time in the last decade. Thus Puerto Rico's "commonwealth" status, which provides people with US citizenship but limited control over the island's affairs, remains intact.

Last Elections　Elections to the office of governor took place in November 2000. Calderon narrowly defeated Carlos Pesquera. Elections to the House and Senate took place at the same time. In the House, the PDP received 49% of the vote and garnered 27 seats. The New Progressive Party won 46% of the vote and 23 seats. In the Senate, the PDP got 49% of the vote and 19 seats while the New Progressive Party won 46% of the vote and 7 seats. The Puertorican Independentists Party holds one seat in each chamber.

Political Risk　The island's efforts to get the US Navy to leave the islet of Vieques have partially succeeded but have cost it supporters in the US Congress. In the longer term, the proposed Free Trade Area of the Americas, to be created in 2005, poses both a challenge and an opportunity. The island will face competition for markets in the US from other nations in the free-trade area, many of which could be more competitive because of lower production costs. Puerto Rico is heavily dependent on the US, with more than 80% of its exports destined for the American market. Federal transfers and grants form a significant part of the island's revenues but are declining and there is little likelihood that the downward trend will be reversed.

International Disputes　If the US leaves Vieques, some of the tension between Washington and nationalists on the island will be removed. Other sources, however, remain. Puerto Rico's participation in regional organisations involved in tourism, trade and development finance has to be approved by Washington. With Cuba increasingly being involved in these regional organisations, Washington prevents Puerto Rico's participation.

Economy　Puerto Rico's economy is expected to grow by 2.4% in 2001 with inflation of 2.7%. The US government has phased out a programme of tax and wage credits which had attracted American companies to Puerto Rico and stimulated rapid expansion of its manufacturing sector. With this phase-out, local officials want to broaden the economy and reduce its dependence on manufacturing and tourism. The Free Trade Area of the Americas, proposed for creation in 2005, is regarded by Puerto Rico as both a challenge and an opportunity. The island would face competition for markets in the mainland US from other nations in the free-trade area, many of which could be more competitive because of lower production costs. Officials hope to expand the amount of high technology manufacturing on the island. The unemployment rate has finally begun to come down somewhat (from 13.5% in 1998 to 10% in 2002).

Main Industries　Manufacturing makes up 40% of GDP and is dominated by industries such as pharmaceuticals, electronics, textiles, petrochemicals, metal products and machinery, motor vehicles, glass, cement and processed foods. There are also many assembly operations that are allowed to import components and materials from the US and, after assembly, can re-export to the mainland duty-free. Much of the manufacturing investment in Puerto Rico was stimulated by tax breaks provided by the US Congress. Unfortunately, these breaks were discontinued in 1996. Farming remains the dominant economic activity in much of the country although it accounts for only 1% of GDP. The government plans to develop a huge new port on the western side of the island and has begun to restore the colonial district in the capital city. Puerto Rico already has a good basis for shipping as it handles 1.8 million containers a year. The new mega-port will include a transhipment facility which is a free-trade zone for manufacturing and distributive services. Experts forecast that within 10 years between 21 and 26 million containers will pass close to Puerto Rico and the new facility should capture most of this traffic.

Energy　Puerto Rico lacks domestic hydrocarbon reserves and relies on imports for nearly all of its energy requirements, except for a small hydropower generating potential. In 2000, the island's primary electric power producer announced a US$2.4-billion programme to increase the island's electric generation capacity. The move was spurred by concerns that electricity demands associated with economic growth would soon exceed generation capacity. A new, US$670-million power plant has also been connected to the Puerto Rican grid. Two more projects are planned, one to re-power ageing power stations in San Juan and another for a new power station, built by American firms.

	1999	2000	2001
Inflation (% change)	2.6	3.0	
Exchange rate (per US$)	1.00	1.00	1.00
Interest rate			
GDP (% real growth)	4.2	3.6	
GDP (Million units of national currency)	36,456.0	38,901.5	40,910.7
GDP (US$ million)	36,456.0	38,901.5	40,910.7
GDP per capita (US$)	9,484.1	10,054.7	10,378.2
Consumption (Million units of national currency)	24,178.3	25,482.0	27,319.7
Consumption (US$ million)	24,178.3	25,482.0	27,319.7
Consumption per capita (US$)	6,290.0	6,586.2	6,930.4
Population, mid-year ('000)	3,843.9	3,869.0	3,942.0
Birth rate (per '000)	15.8	15.6	15.3
Death rate (per '000)	7.7	7.8	7.8
No. of households ('000)	779.5	788.6	808.4
Total exports (US$ million)	30,152.8	31,532.0	32,698.7
Total imports (US$ million)	23,363.9	28,029.0	28,143.2
Tourism receipts (US$ million)	2,138.0	2,547.4	2,399.2
Tourist spending (US$ million)	815.0	883.3	810.9

Average household size 2001 (persons)	4.91					
Urban population 2001 (%)	75.6					
Age analysis (%) (2001)	*0-14*	24.8	*15-64*	65.1	*65+*	10.2
Population by sex (%) (2001)	*Male*	48.3	*Female*	51.7		
Life expectancy (years) (2001)	*Male*	71.0	*Female*	80.0		
Infant mortality (deaths per '000 live births) (2001)	10.2					
Adult literacy (%)						

◼ Qatar

Area (km^2)   11,435

Currency   Qatar riyal (QR = 100 dirhams)

Location   Qatar is a small peninsula protruding northward into the Persian (Arabian) Gulf from the northwestern extreme of the United Arab Emirates. It also has a very short border with Saudi Arabia. Most of the terrain is sandy and inhospitable and, except for a dwindling number of nomadic tribesmen, virtually all of the population now lives in the capital, Doha.

Head of State   HH Shaikh Hamad bin Khalifa al Thani (June 1995)

Head of Government   Sheikh Abdullah ibn Khalifah ath-Thani (1996)

Ruling Party   There are no political parties in Qatar.

Political Structure   HH Shaikh Hamad Khalifa al Thani assumed power in June 1995, following a palace coup against his father, HH Shaikh Khalifa bin Hamad al Thani, who had ruled since 1972. The coup was prompted by a prolonged period of disagreement between the two men, although it was not clear whether it also related to the growing calls for a democratisation of the country. As before, Qatar is ruled exclusively by the Emir and his immediate family. There is a Consultative Assembly of 35 appointed members.

Last Elections   There are no elections in Qatar, although the Emir has promised municipal elections and is considering a direct poll to determine the membership of his consultative council.

Political Risk   Despite the occasional dispute between members of the royal family, the country is generally very stable and offers little political risk. To prevent arguments over succession, the Emir has named his third son as heir. Indeed, the only major threats to the current situation would come from external claims on the country's territory or resources.

International Disputes   In a ruling issued in March 2001, the International Court of Justice resolved the dispute between Qatar and Bahrain over the Hawar Islands and neighbouring islands. Sovereignty over the Hawar Islands was awarded to Bahrain, while Qatar retained the neighbouring islands of Zubarah and Janan. The issue of gas and oil exploration rights is of some importance, having prompted an armed conflict in 1986 after Bahrain built an artificial island off one of the shoals. Peace was restored following Saudi Arabia's intervention. Qatar's relations with some of its neighbours (including Saudi Arabia) are shaky as a result of the Emir's policy of broadcasting uncensored news via satellite.

Economy   GDP grew by 7.2% in 2001, while prices fell by 0.7%. Qatar suffers from many of the same problems as other oil-dependent Persian Gulf states, especially the need to diversify economic development beyond crude oil exports and scale back the generous state subsidies for consumers, which date from the oil boom of the 1970s and early 1980s. The most pressing economic problem for Qatar is to service its debt, which rose from under US$5 billion to over US$10 billion between 1994 and 1996, and surged to nearly US$13 billion in 2000. Qatar accumulated this debt largely for infrastructure investment in oil and gas projects, which sharply increased Qatar's oil production capacity, construction of facilities for the export of LNG and petrochemical plants. Total debt fell to under US$8 billion in 2001, still more than 80% of the country's GDP. Lenders remain confident of the country's ability to make good on these debts and claims. Much will depend on future trends in the price of oil since the price of Qatar's natural gas is tied to oil prices. Despite these difficulties, the income of the average Qatari (excluding expatriates) is more than US$60,000. This level is twice as high as that for any other country in the Middle East apart from Kuwait and the UAE.

Main Industries   Qatar's policy of economic diversification has led to a surge in investment in projects for the export of liquefied natural gas and petrochemicals. The government expects that it will be able to earn more per barrel of crude oil produced if it can export refined products and petrochemicals, as well as create private sector jobs - in a country which has been overly dependent on government ministries to provide employment for the population. Qatar has twice the natural gas reserves of either Saudi Arabia or Abu Dhabi and, unlike these countries, all its gas is clean and easy to exploit. Altogether, the country's oil and gas industries employ the greater part of the active workforce and provide well over 90% of export revenues. Qatar also has a limited industrial sector, concentrating on basic materials such as cement, steel, ammonia, fertiliser and petrochemicals. Farming is generally restricted by a shortage of suitable land, but the government has ploughed vast resources into irrigation projects aimed at expanding the scope for vegetable cultivation. Fishing is a major industry.

Energy   Qatar contains the third largest natural gas reserves and the largest non-associated gas field in the world. Qatar is also emerging as a major exporter of liquefied natural gas. An OPEC member, Qatar exports over 800,000 barrels of oil per day. Qatar has proven, recoverable oil reserves of 13.2 billion barrels. Despite the country's significant oil production and reserves, oil accounts for less than 15% of domestic energy consumption. Qatar exports almost all of its oil production to Asia, with Japan by far its largest customer. In 2000, net oil exports totalled 796,000 barrels per day (bbl/d). With proven reserves of 394 trillion cu ft (Tcf), Qatar's natural gas resources are just behind those of Russia and Iran. Most of Qatar's gas is located in the North Field, which contains 380 Tcf of gas in-place and 239 Tcf of recoverable reserves, making it the largest known non-associated gas field in the world.

	1999	2000	2001
Inflation (% change)	2.2	1.7	-0.7
Exchange rate (per US$)	3.64	3.64	3.64
Interest rate			
GDP (% real growth)	5.3	11.6	7.2
GDP (Million units of national currency)	44,397.0	61,018.0	60,254.0
GDP (US$ million)	12,197.0	16,763.2	16,553.3
GDP per capita (US$)	20,641.2	27,985.3	26,698.9
Consumption (Million units of national currency)	11,074.2	13,964.6	14,595.0
Consumption (US$ million)	3,042.4	3,836.4	4,009.6
Consumption per capita (US$)	5,148.6	6,404.7	6,467.1
Population, mid-year ('000)	590.9	599.0	620.0
Birth rate (per '000)	19.1	18.6	18.0
Death rate (per '000)	4.0	4.0	4.1
No. of households ('000)	124.0	127.3	133.7
Total exports (US$ million)	7,061.4	8,669.0	8,426.7
Total imports (US$ million)	2,499.6	4,531.0	4,671.6
Tourism receipts (US$ million)			
Tourist spending (US$ million)	590.9	599.0	620.0

Average household size 2001 (persons)	4.71				
Urban population 2001 (%)	92.7				
Age analysis (%) (2001)	0-14	26.6	15-64	71.6	65+ 1.8
Population by sex (%) (2001)	Male	65.7	Female	34.3	
Life expectancy (years) (2001)	Male	69.1	Female	71.7	
Infant mortality (deaths per '000 live births) (2001)	11.7				
Adult literacy (%) (1997)	80.0				

TRADING PARTNERS

Major export destinations 2001 (% share)		Major import sources 2001 (% share)	
JAPAN	42.7	FRANCE	17.9
SOUTH KOREA	18.2	USA	9.2
SINGAPORE	5.0	ITALY	8.6
USA	4.1	JAPAN	8.3

■ Réunion

Area (km^2)   2,510

Currency   Euro (= 100 cents)

Location   Réunion, an overseas département of France, is located in the Indian Ocean about 800km east of the island of Madagascar. The local government also administers a number of other, largely uninhabited islands on behalf of the French authorities. With a warm and pleasant climate, Réunion has a thriving tourist industry. The capital is St Denis.

Head of State   President Jacques Chirac (France)

Head of Government   Christophe Payet (President of General Council, 1994)

Ruling Party   At the national level, the Gaullist Rassemblement pour la République leads a coalition with the Union pour la Démocratie Francaise. At the regional level, the Parti Socialiste dominates.

Political Structure   Réunion is an external department of France and is governed to a considerable degree from Paris. The country sends deputies to the French Assemblée Nationale and is represented at the EU. Since being accorded regional status in 1974, Réunion elects its own 45-member Regional Council for a term of six years, with responsibility for economic and social planning. Other executive powers rest in a 47-member General Council.

Last Elections   Elections to the Regional Council were held in March 1998. The Communist Party of Reunion captured 7 seats, the Union for French Democracy won 8 and the Socialist Party took 6. The remaining seats were dispersed among several parties. General Council elections were held in March 1994, when the Socialist Party won control and Christophe Payet became president of the General Council.

Political Risk   The white and Indian communities are substantially better off than other segments of the population, often approaching European standards. Indigenous groups suffer from poverty and the unemployment typical of the poorer nations of the African continent. The occasional outbreak of severe rioting illustrates the seriousness of socioeconomic tensions. The country's relationship with France is sometimes a source of concern, with pro-separatist demonstrations occurring in recent years. Economic problems have prompted demands for more direct action from Paris to deal with unemployment and poverty.

International Disputes   Réunion's administration of several largely uninhabited islands on behalf of France has been challenged by Madagascar.

Economy   Réunion's economy is heavily dependent on aid from France, which accounts for as much as half of the country's GDP. Government officials have long tried to develop a tourist industry in order to relieve the high rate of unemployment which exceeds 40%. The gap in Réunion between the well-off and the poor is extraordinary and accounts for the persistent social tensions.

Main Industries   Over 85% of the country's exports and 80% of its income derive from sugar cane, which is the only significant crop apart from vegetables grown for domestic consumption. There is also an important fishing industry. Industry is limited to the processing of agricultural raw materials. The major manufacturing activities include production of rum, cigarettes, handicraft items and flower oil. A small but dynamic tourist industry exists which caters mainly to visitors from France and Germany. Over 70% of the workforce is employed in the services sector, another 8% in agriculture and the remainder in industry.

Energy   Réunion has only a limited amount of domestic energy resources, although there are some natural gas deposits. It produces more than two thirds of its electricity from hydroelectric sources.

	1999	2000	2001
Inflation (% change)			
Exchange rate (per US$)	6.15	7.55	7.33
Interest rate			
GDP (% real growth)			
GDP			
GDP (US$ million)			
GDP per capita (US$)			
Consumption			
Consumption (US$ million)			
Consumption per capita (US$)			
Population, mid-year ('000)	692.4	699.0	715.0
Birth rate (per '000)	19.2	18.7	18.2
Death rate (per '000)	5.7	5.8	5.8
No. of households ('000)	119.0	119.2	120.6
Total exports (US$ million)			
Total imports (US$ million)			
Tourism receipts (US$ million)	270.0		
Tourist spending (US$ million)	692.4	699.0	715.0

Average household size 2001 (persons)	5.87				
Urban population 2001 (%)	71.4				
Age analysis (%) (2001)	*0-14*	28.3	*15-64*	65.2	*65+* 6.4
Population by sex (%) (2001)	*Male*	48.8	*Female*	51.2	
Life expectancy (years) (2001)	*Male*	70.3	*Female*	78.9	
Infant mortality (deaths per '000 live births) (2001)	8.2				
Adult literacy (%)					

■ Romania

Area (km^2)   237,500

Currency   Leu (= 100 bani)

Location   Romania borders on the Black Sea in the east and Ukraine and Moldova in the north, with Bulgaria in the south and Hungary and Serbia in the west. The country has hilly and, to some extent, mountainous areas in the west and the south, and is richly endowed with agricultural land. The capital is Bucharest.

Head of State   Ion Iliescu (2000)

Head of Government   Adrian Nastase (2000)

Ruling Party   The government is formed by a 5-party coalition.

Political Structure   The country's president is non-executive and answerable to a parliament. Nevertheless, he exercises considerable influence. The president is elected for a 4-year term by the people. The parliament has two chambers. The Chamber of Deputies has 343 members, elected for 4-year terms, 328 members by proportional representation and 15 members representing ethnic minorities. The Senate has 143 members, elected for 4-year terms by proportional representation.

Last Elections   Presidential elections were held in December 2000 when Ion Iliescu took 67% of the vote in the second round. Elections to the Chamber of Deputies took place in November 2000. A coalition known as the Democratic Social Pole of Romania won 153 seats, the Party of Great Romania received 84 seats and the Democratic Party took 31 seats. The remainder were divided among several parties. Elections to the Senate were held at the same time. The Democratic Social Pole of Romania took 65 seats while the Party of Great Romania was awarded 37 seats.

Political Risk   In terms of building a market-driven economy, Romania is still far behind its neighbours. Because the country's earlier communist governments took the goal of self-sufficiency to extremes, Romania's industry remains much more disjointed than elsewhere in the region. Previous democratic governments have failed to restructure the most important parts of the country's state-owned industry. To the surprise of many, the present government has made real headway but it is by no means clear that this zeal will be sustained over the longer term. At the very best, the next few years are likely to be marked by a number of false starts and turnarounds can be expected, coupled with heated battles between the liberal wing and the ex-communist powers in the country.

International Disputes   Romania's relationship with Hungary has traditionally been poor, as a result of its historical mistreatment of ethnic Hungarians in the north of its territory. Tensions have abated, however, as a result of pressure from the EU.

Economy   GDP grew by 5.3% in 2001 and should increase by 4.5% in 2002 and 5% in 2003. Inflation was 34.5% in 2001 but will be lower in 2002, at around 25%. Prices are forecast to rise by 17.5% in 2003. Romania has made important progress in structural reforms since the turn of the century as privatisation efforts were accelerated significantly. However, delays and procedural problems in bank restructuring slowed subsequent privatisation activities, and supporting loans from international lenders have been postponed. There has also been only limited progress in controlling inflation and strengthening the external position. A better performance will require fiscal consolidation combined with the pursuit of a prudent monetary policy as well as wage and financial discipline in the state-owned enterprises. Although the budget deficit has narrowed in recent years, there is concern that Romania's fiscal position remains precarious and will need to be strengthened to achieve stabilisation. Government officials are being urged to treat their medium-term fiscal deficit target of 3% of GDP as an upper limit.

Main Industries   Agriculture is the dominant sector but is in a parlous state because the restitution of farmland has divided the government. Subsistence farming is common, much of it on land returned to peasants after the fall of communism in 1989. The sector accounts for about 16% of GDP and provides employment for a third of the workforce. Most farms operate on a subsistence basis although fruit and vegetables, wines, wheat and flax are all produced for export. Private ownership of farmland makes up almost three quarters of the total but the government has failed to provide any supporting market-driven reforms. The mining sector is of special concern because it is the source of most resistance to economic reform. Mines producing copper, lead, zinc, gold, silver and coal are all losing money and require substantial subsidies. Industry (including manufacturing) accounts for 40% of GDP. The country has much heavy industry, including refineries, one of Europe's largest steel complexes, a big car manufacturer (Dacia) and several large chemical producers. Foreign investment, which is modest, amounts to about US$1.3 billion a year. It is concentrated in western Romania, notably in the export-oriented production of garments, shoes, furniture, electrical and auto equipment. Many large companies still remain under state control and suffer from weak corporate governance. Thus it is very important that policy makers control wage costs in these companies. Improvements in bank supervision and external audits of major state-owned banks will be key steps toward restructuring and privatisation. Government officials would like to reduce some of the many subsidies offered but this could cause serious political problems given the peoples' already low standard of living.

Energy   Romania has proven oil reserves of 1.4 billion barrels, and despite a steady decline in its crude oil production since the mid-1970s, the country remains the largest oil producer in Central and Eastern Europe. From 294,000 bbl/d in 1976, Romania's oil production has decreased more than 57% to 125,000 bbl/d in 2001, Romania's oil demand now outstrips domestic production by a ratio of more than two to one. Romania's oil consumption, which dropped from 345,000 bbl/d in 1989 to just 220,800 bbl/d in 1994, has been on the increase ever since, reaching 310,000 bbl/d for 2001. The Romanian government has committed itself to increasing domestic production of oil and gas in order to reduce the country's reliance on imports. The removal of state price ceilings, plus relatively high world prices, allowed the industry to restart some of its idle wells, and the introduction of Western technology and production methods is expected to boost Romania's reserves and production in the next few years.

	1999	2000	2001
Inflation (% change)	45.8	45.7	34.5
Exchange rate (per US$)	15,332.80	21,708.70	29,060.80
Interest rate (% per annum, lending rate)	65.5	53.8	
GDP (% real growth)	-1.2	1.8	5.3
GDP (Billion units of national currency)	545,730.2	800,308.1	1,154,126.4
GDP (US$ million)	35,592.3	36,865.8	39,714.2
GDP per capita (US$)	1,585.0	1,647.1	1,780.9
Consumption (Billion units of national currency)	361,123.3	528,932.6	734,979.5
Consumption (US$ million)	23,552.3	24,365.0	25,291.1
Consumption per capita (US$)	1,048.8	1,088.6	1,134.1
Population, mid-year ('000)	22,455.5	22,381.7	22,300.3
Birth rate (per '000)	10.3	10.4	10.4
Death rate (per '000)	12.3	12.4	12.6
No. of households ('000)	7,646.5	7,658.1	7,637.1
Total exports (US$ million)	8,504.7	10,366.5	11,385.0
Total imports (US$ million)	10,392.1	13,054.5	15,560.9
Tourism receipts (US$ million)	254.0	508.0	531.3
Tourist spending (US$ million)	395.0	419.1	494.9

Average household size 2001 (persons)	2.92				
Urban population 2001 (%)	57.9				
Age analysis (%) (2001)	*0-14*	18.1	*15-64*	68.7	*65+* 13.2
Population by sex (%) (2001)	*Male*	48.9	*Female*	51.1	
Life expectancy (years) (2001)	*Male*	66.5	*Female*	73.3	
Infant mortality (deaths per '000 live births) (2001)	22.0				
Adult literacy (%) (1996)	97.9				

TRADING PARTNERS

Major export destinations 2001 (% share)		Major import sources 2001 (% share)	
ITALY	23.2	ITALY	20.4
GERMANY	15.8	GERMANY	18.8
FRANCE	7.2	FRANCE	6.5
TURKEY	5.9	RUSSIA	5.1

▪ Russia

Area (km^2)   17,075,400

Currency   Rouble (Rb)

Location   Russia, the largest state in Asia, extends nearly 9,000km from the Finnish border in the west to the Bering Straits in the east, at which point it faces across to the US state of Alaska. The vast terrain ranges from the Arctic wastes of the north to the Caspian Sea in the south, and includes innumerable mountain ranges with vast mineral resources in the Siberian ranges to the east. The capital is Moscow.

Head of State   President Vladimir Putin (2000)

Head of Government   Mikhail Kasyanov (2000)

Ruling Party   The government is formed by the Inter-Regional Movement Unity (Medved) and non-partisan technocrats.

Political Structure   The Russian Republic represents the greater part of the former Soviet Union. The executive president is directly elected by universal suffrage, and answers to a 450-member Supreme Soviet (Parliament) comprising two chambers. There is also a prime minister, who is appointed by the president on the Soviet's recommendations, and an extensive network of local councils.

Last Elections   In presidential elections held in March 2000, Vladimir Putin defeated several other candidates in the first round with 53% of the vote. Elections to the lower chamber of the Supreme Soviet took place in December 1999. The Communist Party of the Russian Federation garnered 24% of the vote and took 113 seats. Medved took 23% of the vote and 72 seats while the Fatherland All Russia received 13% of the vote and 66 seats. The remaining seats were scattered among several parties.

Political Risk   Putin is pushing Russia's economy westward and reshaping the country's foreign policy accordingly. Perhaps the biggest risk to the country and its neighbours is that this pro-Western economic and policy strategy will be derailed. In the long term, the evolution of Russia's pro-Western policy depends on whether the government is able to stop the country's decline. High oil prices and new-found stability have masked some serious problems. These include a demographic collapse with the population shrinking by about 750,000 a year, an AIDS explosion, crumbling infrastructure and ethnic and regional tensions. Continued decline would eventually lead to another economic and political crisis. Russia appears to have won the war in Chechnya but the conflict is likely to continue as a partisan war, triggering fresh terrorist attacks in Chechnya and beyond.

International Disputes   Moscow has garnered much goodwill with its support of the war in Afghanistan and its agreement to scrap the treaty banning development of anti-ballistic missiles with the US. To some extent, Russia's future depends on what is decided in Washington. There is a battle in the American capital between those who regard Russia as too weak to matter and those who think that there are big benefits to be won from cooperation. The country remains at odds with Japan over four Southern Kurile Islands, which were seized at the end of World War II.

Economy   GDP rose by 5% in 2001. It is expected to increase by another 4.4% in 2002 and 4.9% in 2003. Inflation was 21.5% in 2001 but will fall to 14% in 2002 and to 11.6% in 2003. Other important positive trends can also be observed in macroeconomic stabilisation, commercial banking, relations with foreign creditors and political cooperation between the Russian government and the legislature. Fortuitous external conditions supported these developments, most particularly relatively strong prices for oil and other commodities on world markets, and an exceptionally weak rouble in the aftermath of the financial crisis of 1998. Economic policies and institutional change, however, have also played an important role. The commercial banking sector has shown significant signs of recovery and the Russian government has normalised relations with foreign creditors and boosted the international credit rating. Although household incomes have recovered, they were lower in 2001 than before the 1998 crisis, and poverty continues to be a serious problem. At least 20% of all Russians face the prospect of living on less than half the government's official minimum subsistence income, which currently amounts to only US$34 per month.

Main Industries   Agriculture contributes only 7% to GDP and is nominally privatised. Agricultural output is still about 60% lower than it was a decade ago. Farmers have suffered greatly because of the debt write-offs provided to state farms. Further damage has come from foreign food aid, which, a recently as 1999, was still depressing prices. Russia's huge industrial sector accounts for 35% of GDP and benefited substantially from the depreciation of the rouble in 1998. By 2002, however, industrial firms had lost almost three quarters of the cost advantage it gained from the rouble crash. Capital investment remains stubbornly low. The very difficult environment for business and investment is reflected in large net capital outflows from the country, rather low domestic investment outside of oil and gas, and relatively few small private businesses. The government is pushing up domestic energy prices close to world levels, in part to help the country's gas and electricity monopolies cover their capital needs. The move raises costs for all types of enterprises, however. Russia is presently the fourth largest supplier of military equipment but it has the technology, the workforce and the capacity to reclaim its position as the second largest exporter after the US. The country's information technology and computer software firms have access to a large pool of skilled labour but the slowdown has hurt this industry. Large chunks of the economy are vulnerable to swings in commodity prices. There are massive mineral and forest resources with iron ore, copper, aluminium, manganese, salt and precious metals all being produced, though facilities are in need of modernisation. The financial sector was hard hit by the financial crisis, the subsequent devaluation and the default on domestic debts. Now, the sector is recovering but regulations need to be strengthened.

Energy   Russia's oil industry has bounced back, posting strong profits and healthy increases in production. Russia is one of the world's biggest oil producers, but from 1992 to 1998, the country's oil production plummeted 23% due to decreased domestic industrial demand and a decline in drilling and capital investment. Since 1998, when production bottomed out, Russia's oil production has increased 20%, with overall production of 7.3 million bbl/d in 2001. Production is forecast to post a 1.9% year-on-year increase in 2002. Russia has proven oil reserves of 48.6 billion barrels, but ageing equipment and poorly developed fields are making it difficult to develop these reserves. In addition, the rate of oil production exceeds the rate of discovery of new reserves by a significant margin.

	1999	2000	2001
Inflation (% change)	85.7	20.8	21.5
Exchange rate (per US$)	24.62	28.13	29.17
Interest rate (% per annum, lending rate)	39.7	24.4	17.9
GDP (% real growth)	5.4	9.0	5.0
GDP (Billion units of national currency)	4,757.2	7,302.2	9,040.1
GDP (US$ million)	193,225.8	259,595.0	309,926.8
GDP per capita (US$)	1,324.0	1,787.2	2,147.3
Consumption (Billion units of national currency)	3,898.8	5,386.6	6,889.3
Consumption (US$ million)	158,360.6	191,495.3	236,190.5
Consumption per capita (US$)	1,085.1	1,318.4	1,636.4
Population, mid-year ('000)	145,943.1	145,252.7	144,336.1
Birth rate (per '000)	8.7	8.7	8.6
Death rate (per '000)	14.6	14.8	15.1
No. of households ('000)	51,752.0	51,683.0	51,806.6
Total exports (US$ million)	73,700.0	102,796.0	100,653.0
Total imports (US$ million)	31,000.0	33,769.0	41,237.0
Tourism receipts (US$ million)	7,510.0	7,166.7	6,297.3
Tourist spending (US$ million)	7,434.0	6,318.3	7,644.5

Average household size 2001 (persons)	2.81					
Urban population 2001 (%)	77.8					
Age analysis (%) (2001)	0-14	17.9	15-64	69.3	65+	12.8
Population by sex (%) (2001)	Male	46.7	Female	53.3		
Life expectancy (years) (2001)	Male	60.0	Female	72.5		
Infant mortality (deaths per '000 live births) (2001)	17.0					
Adult literacy (%) (1996)	99.5					

TRADING PARTNERS

Major export destinations 2001 (% share)		Major import sources 2001 (% share)	
GERMANY	9.9	GERMANY	15.5
ITALY	8.3	UKRAINE	10.2
USA	7.2	USA	8.7
UKRAINE	6.0	KAZAKHSTAN	5.0

Rwanda

Area (km^2)   26,330

Currency   Rwanda franc (RF = 100 centimes)

Location   Rwanda, a small state to the west of Tanzania, lies just north of Burundi and is bounded in the west by the Democratic Republic of the Congo (formerly Zaire) and in the north by Uganda. Its position on Lake Kivu has helped to ensure an adequate water supply for irrigation. The capital is Kigali.

Head of State   Paul Kagame (April 2000)

Head of Government   Bernard Makuza (2000)

Ruling Party   The Republican Democratic Movement (Hutu) leads a multiparty coalition.

Political Structure   Under normal circumstances, the country has a non-executive president who appoints the prime minister. In practice, the murdered president, Habyarimana, had banned opposition parties in 1991 and ruled by decree until his death. Neither Kagame nor the Tutsi government he succeeded has any democratic mandate. Kagame was "elected" by parliament after the resignation of his predecessor. There is a 70-member parliament, which is meant to be transitional but is under the control of Kagame. An election schedule and structure for the government was set up by the Arusha pact but few expect current officials to abide by this agreement.

Last Elections   No true multiparty elections have been held since 1994. In June 1999, the government extended its mandate to rule for another four years but Kagame assumed power in 2000.

Political Risk   More than 800,000 people, mostly Tutsis, lost their lives in the genocide that occurred between 1994 and 1998. Today, the country's prison population numbers 115,000, all suspects from the civil war.

International Disputes   Rwanda backed Congolese rebels fighting to overthrow that country's president, Laurent Kabila. Following Kabila's assassination, the UN condemned Rwanda for the invasion and called for sanctions against the country. In July 2002, Rwanda signed a preliminary peace agreement with the Congo and is expected to withdraw its soldiers from that country.

Economy   GDP grew 6.2% in 2001 and inflation was 3.5%. The external current account deficit is widening and amounted to 18% in 2001. The deterioration reflected weaker coffee export receipts, higher fuel and food import prices, an increase in international transport costs and a relaxation of monetary policy. The government is still trying to eliminate debts incurred before or during the 1994 war. Some of Rwanda's massive foreign debt has been written off by donors but it remains a problem. External security remains a serious problem and foreign donors still have serious concerns about defence spending when debt services are so high.

Main Industries   The agricultural sector dominates the economy, accounting for half of GDP. Coffee and tea are the most important farm products but coffee prices have been falling on world markets. Food production is still depressed in what would otherwise be a highly fertile country and a breadbasket for East Africa. In normal times, other cash crops were sugar cane, vegetables and fruit. Industry makes up 21% of GDP and was traditionally specialised in the processing of agricultural raw materials, such as timber, textiles, beverages and soap. The economy continues to suffer massively from the failure to maintain the infrastructure and the lack of healthcare facilities. Government spending is under control, and revenue collection is improving. Food, however, is in short supply and few industries operate at anything near full capacity.

Energy   The country has limited indigenous fuel resources and relies heavily on imports. It derives the greater part of its electricity needs from the hydroelectric sector.

	1999	2000	2001
Inflation (% change)	-2.4	3.9	3.5
Exchange rate (per US$)	333.94	389.70	442.99
Interest rate			
GDP (% real growth)	7.4	6.0	6.2
GDP (Million units of national currency)	643,992.0	696,659.0	763,694.0
GDP (US$ million)	1,928.5	1,787.7	1,723.9
GDP per capita (US$)	262.8	231.2	198.8
Consumption (Million units of national currency)	572,280.0	601,240.0	625,952.9
Consumption (US$ million)	1,713.7	1,542.8	1,413.0
Consumption per capita (US$)	233.6	199.5	163.0
Population, mid-year ('000)	7,337.6	7,733.0	8,670.0
Birth rate (per '000)	42.3	42.2	42.2
Death rate (per '000)	21.3	21.1	20.9
No. of households ('000)	1,190.6	1,261.9	1,423.9
Total exports (US$ million)	60.5	52.9	84.9
Total imports (US$ million)	252.8	213.2	249.7
Tourism receipts (US$ million)			
Tourist spending (US$ million)			

Average household size 2001 (persons)	6.13				
Urban population 2001 (%)	6.3				
Age analysis (%) (2001)	0-14	46.2	15-64	51.5	65+	2.4
Population by sex (%) (2001)	Male	49.2	Female	50.8	
Life expectancy (years) (2001)	Male	39.8	Female	41.3	
Infant mortality (deaths per '000 live births) (2001)	119.7				
Adult literacy (%) (1997)	63.0				

TRADING PARTNERS

Major export destinations 2001 (% share)		Major import sources 2001 (% share)	
GERMANY	27.1	KENYA	22.7
CHINA	10.1	BELGIUM	8.0
USA	5.7	USA	6.8
NETHERLANDS	5.1	GERMANY	3.2

▨ Sao Tomé e Príncipe

Area (km^2)   964

Currency   Dobra (D = 100 centimes)

Location   Sao Tomé e Príncipe is a federation of two eponymous islands and several islets in the Gulf of Guinea, some 300km off the Atlantic coast of West Africa. The nearest land point is Libreville in Gabon. The capital is Sao Tomé.

Head of State   President Fradique de Menzes (2001)

Head of Government   Manuel Pinto da Costa (2002)

Ruling Party   The government is formed by the Movimento de Libera ao de Sao Tomé e Príncipe (MLSTP) and the Democratic Convergence Party-Reflection Group (PCD).

Political Structure   The Democratic Republic of Sao Tomé e Príncipe was an overseas territory of Portugal until 1975, and quickly became a single-party state run by the socialist Movimento de Libera ao de Sao Tomé e Príncipe. In 1990, a new Constitution was introduced which provided for a semi-executive president who appoints the prime minister on the advice of the 55-member legislature. Legislators are elected for 4-year terms in 12 multi-member constituencies by proportional representation. There are plans to award Príncipe a substantial degree of regional autonomy, including the creation of a regional assembly.

Last Elections   Elections to the 55-member National People's Assembly were held in March 2002, when the MLSTP won 24 of the 55 seats. The Force for Change Democratic Movement gained 23 seats with the remainder scattered among smaller parties. Presidential elections were held in July 2001 when de Menzes received 56% of the vote, defeating Manuel Pinto da Costa of the Movimiento de Libertaçao de Sao Tomé e Príncipe who received 34% of the vote.

Political Risk   The country's prospects are vulnerable to swings in the world price of cocoa on which it depends heavily, while several political coups have occurred in the past.

International Disputes   There are no international disputes.

Economy   GDP increased by 4% in 2001 and prices rose by 9.3%. During the fourth quarter of 2000 and the first three quarters of 2001, fiscal slippages, delays in structural reforms and governance problems put Sao Tomé and Príncipe's spending programme off track. Despite strong revenue mobilisation, spending overruns, partly financed out of an unprogrammed signing bonus related to an oil exploration option contract, resulted in a primary budget deficit of 3% of GDP in 2001, compared with a targeted surplus of 2.7% of GDP. In the fiscal area, the government hopes to turn the primary budget balance from a deficit in 2001 to a small surplus in 2002, while safeguarding spending on health and education. Monetary policy will remain tight, with broad money projected to increase by 12% in 2002. At the moment, Sao Tomé is one of the most heavily indebted of the world's poorer countries, but will receive about US$200 million in debt relief over the next few years.

Main Industries   Agriculture is the mainstay of the economy, with cocoa providing 75% of GDP. However, production has been gradually declining as a result of drought and mismanagement. Output of minor crops such as coffee, copra and palm kernels has also been falling. There are some moves toward encouraging alternative crops but these have made little headway. Industry is limited in scale and is restricted to the coverage of domestic needs: soap, beverages and timber products. Most other products have to be imported. Considerable potential exists for the development of a tourist industry, and the government took a few steps to expand facilities in recent years.

Energy   The country has little domestic energy resources, and derives the bulk of its needs from imports of oil, gas and coal. It does, however, obtain half of its electricity from hydroelectric sources.

	1999	2000	2001
Inflation (% change)	16.3	11.0	9.3
Exchange rate (per US$)	7,118.96	7,978.17	8,842.11
Interest rate (% per annum, lending rate)	40.3	37.0	37.0
GDP (% real growth)	2.5	3.0	4.0
GDP (Million units of national currency)	334,109.0	369,533.0	421,990.0
GDP (US$ million)	46.9	46.3	47.7
GDP per capita (US$)	325.9	315.1	311.9
Consumption (Million units of national currency)	133,975.8	154,615.3	182,291.5
Consumption (US$ million)	18.8	19.4	20.6
Consumption per capita (US$)	130.7	131.8	134.7
Population, mid-year ('000)	144.0	147.0	153.0
Birth rate (per '000)	42.1	41.8	41.5
Death rate (per '000)	8.3	8.2	8.1
No. of households ('000)	26.0	27.0	28.4
Total exports (US$ million)	9.5	7.0	7.5
Total imports (US$ million)	32.2	27.0	28.5
Tourism receipts (US$ million)			
Tourist spending (US$ million)			

Average household size 2001 (persons)		5.44			
Urban population 2001 (%)		46.9			
Age analysis (%) (2001)	*0-14*	34.5	*15-64* 52.5	*65+*	13.0
Population by sex (%) (2001)	*Male*	51.2	*Female* 48.8		
Life expectancy (years) (2001)	*Male*	64.3	*Female* 67.1		
Infant mortality (deaths per '000 live births) (2001)		55.2			
Adult literacy (%) (1997)		75.0			

TRADING PARTNERS

Major export destinations 2001 (% share)		Major import sources 2001 (% share)	
NETHERLANDS	28.4	PORTUGAL	38.2
PORTUGAL	19.8	USA	21.5
TURKEY	12.8	UNITED KINGDOM	9.7
CANADA	7.7	BELGIUM	4.7

Saudi Arabia

Area (km²)   2,400,900

Currency   Saudi riyal (SR = 20 qursh = 100 halalas)

Location   Saudi Arabia, the largest country in the Middle East, occupies the greater part of the Arabian peninsula and borders on both the Persian (Arabian) Gulf and the Red Sea. It faces Iran across the Gulf to the east, and Egypt, Sudan and Ethiopia across the Red Sea to the west. In the south, it borders on Yemen and Oman. Its most crucial borders are in the north, where it meets Iraq, Jordan and Kuwait. The capital is Riyadh.

Head of State   HM King Fahd ibn Abdul Aziz (1982)

Head of Government   HM King Fahd ibn Abdul Aziz

Ruling Party   There are no political parties in Saudi Arabia.

Political Structure   Saudi Arabia is an absolute monarchy with most senior government posts filled by members of the royal family. Technically, there is no constitution except for the Koran, reflecting the country's role as keeper of the shrines of Makkah and Medina. Saudi Arabia is a Sunni state. Representation takes place through personal petitions to royal figures, but royal audiences are common. A new constitution with a 60-member Consultative Council is contemplated.

Last Elections   There are no general elections in Saudi Arabia.

Political Risk   Economic problems at home are making life even harder for the royal family. On the one hand, the government must find new and more effective ways to reduce the country's dependence on oil and its downstream industries. Oil revenues will certainly rise during the decade but the increase will not be adequate to meet the country's burgeoning financial requirements. Achievement of such a difficult goal will be expensive and require active government involvement. However, the government has also officially acknowledged - and accepted - the need to reduce state involvement and increase private sector (including foreign) participation in the economy. In reality, the country's policy makers are probably not capable of achieving both goals. Meanwhile, the country intends to move towards a policy of "Saudiisation", which is intended to increase employment of its own citizens by replacing 60% of the estimated 5-6 million foreign workers that presently work in Saudi Arabia. Looming behind these policy initiatives is the threat of increased "Islamisation" of the country.

International Disputes   The American-Saudi relationship, which dates back to the 1920s, came close to foundering during 2002. Throughout the cold war, the Americans used Saudi Arabia's fierce and evangelical brand of Islam to hit back at the Soviet Union in Afghanistan, the Balkans, the Muslim Central Asian republics and Nasser's Egypt. But problems have arisen now that the same brand of Islam has been turned on the US. It appears that many Saudis, including some powerful members of the ruling family, would like to see the departure of the 4,500 American troops and 1,000 British that are presently based in the country. Saudi Arabia has worked out a rapprochement with Iran and would like to do the same with Iraq. It is anxious to see other regional problems resolved and is urging the EU to become more involved in the Palestinian problem. The country has technical border disputes with most of its neighbours. In most cases, negotiations have created neutral zones where no oil development occurs. In the case of Kuwait, Saudi Arabia shares the output of one field. In return, Kuwait exports Saudi oil through its port. The dispute with Iraq is more complicated. A diamond-shaped neutral zone of some 300km in width was established where no oil activity is permitted.

Economy   GDP grew by 2.2% in 2001 and is expected to fall by 0.5% in 2002. In 2003, growth is expected to be about 3.2%. Prices fell by 1.4% in 2001 and will remain unchanged in 2002. Inflation is forecast to be 1.1% in 2003. In 2001, the country's external current account shifted to a surplus equivalent to about 9% of GDP. The improvement was due to a surge in both oil and non-oil exports (especially petrochemicals). As a result, net foreign assets rose to cover about 10 months of prospective imports. The country's fiscal balance is expected to remain strong because of continued expenditure restraint and tangible signs of increase in FDI. The economy, however, remains vulnerable to the downside oil price risks, and any weakening of global oil prices in the near term will put additional strains on fiscal and external balances with potentially negative effects on growth. A tight fiscal policy and structural strengthening of the budget will be required to put public debt on a permanently declining path and reduce the budget's vulnerability to oil price fluctuations in the medium term. It is urgent that officials move ahead with steps to mobilise non-oil revenues through improvements in tax administration and quickly introduce some form of indirect taxes.

Main Industries   The government is searching for ways to enhance the role of the private sector in its economy. The private sector currently accounts for about 40% of Saudi Arabia's GDP and almost 90% of all employment. However, only 5-10% of those working in the private sector are Saudi nationals. State subsidies and losses by unprofitable state-owned enterprises are large contributors to Saudi Arabia's budget deficit. Prior to the sharp downturn in oil prices and the resulting financial pressures on the Saudi budget during 1998 and early 1999, Saudi Arabia had been investing in refinery upgrades and expansions. The projects have now resumed but are far behind schedule. Diversification into oil-related industries such as bulk and fine chemicals, plastics and other heavy industries is being encouraged. Saudi Arabia has one of the world's harshest climates, but maintains a large and heavily subsidised agricultural sector.

Energy   Saudi Arabia contains 264.2 billion barrels of proven oil reserves (more than 25% of the world total) and up to one trillion barrels of ultimately recoverable oil. Saudi Arabia is the world's leading oil producer and exporter, and its location in the politically volatile Gulf region adds an element of concern for its major customers. Although Saudi Arabia has around 80 oil and gas fields (and over 1,000 wells), more than half of its oil reserves are contained in only eight fields, including Ghawar (the world's largest onshore oil field, with estimated remaining reserves of 70 billion barrels) and Safaniya (the world's largest offshore oilfield, with estimated reserves of 19 billion barrels). Given the turbulent situation in world oil markets, plans for expansion appear to have been postponed for the time being. Despite this, Saudi Aramco reported that it intends to spend as much as US$1.5 billion on its development drilling budget in 2002, including plans to drill 324 wells. This plan now appears somewhat unlikely, however.

	1999	2000	2001
Inflation (% change)	-1.3	-0.6	-1.4
Exchange rate (per US$)	3.75	3.75	3.75
Interest rate			
GDP (% real growth)	-0.8	4.5	2.2
GDP (Million units of national currency)	535,025.0	648,959.0	624,264.0
GDP (US$ million)	142,863.8	173,286.8	166,692.7
GDP per capita (US$)	7,010.5	8,111.0	7,457.1
Consumption (Million units of national currency)	200,823.0	207,653.9	203,792.7
Consumption (US$ million)	53,624.3	55,448.3	54,417.3
Consumption per capita (US$)	2,631.4	2,595.4	2,434.4
Population, mid-year ('000)	20,378.5	21,364.3	22,353.6
Birth rate (per '000)	34.5	34.3	34.1
Death rate (per '000)	4.3	4.2	4.2
No. of households ('000)	2,639.9	2,719.8	2,756.1
Total exports (US$ million)	50,761.0	77,583.4	74,622.0
Total imports (US$ million)	28,010.7	30,237.7	31,223.0
Tourism receipts (US$ million)			
Tourist spending (US$ million)	20,378.5	21,364.3	22,353.6

Average household size 2001 (persons)	7.86					
Urban population 2001 (%)	85.7					
Age analysis (%) (2001)	0-14	40.2	15-64	56.7	65+	3.2
Population by sex (%) (2001)	Male	55.2	Female	44.8		
Life expectancy (years) (2001)	Male	70.8	Female	73.3		
Infant mortality (deaths per '000 live births) (2001)	22.0					
Adult literacy (%) (1997)	73.4					

TRADING PARTNERS

Major export destinations 2001 (% share) | **Major import sources 2001 (% share)**

Export	%	Import	%
USA	18.2	USA	17.2
JAPAN	17.3	JAPAN	10.4
SOUTH KOREA	10.2	GERMANY	7.7
SINGAPORE	5.3	UNITED KINGDOM	6.3

▪ Senegal

Area (km^2)　196,720

Currency　CFA franc (= 100 centimes)

Location　Located on the Atlantic coast of West Africa, Senegal is the continent's westernmost point. With Mauritania to the north, Mali to the southeast, and Guinea and Guinea-Bissau to the south, it lies in a deeply depressed and drought-ridden belt with poor soil. Indeed, virtually all the cultivable ground lies along the banks of the River Gambia, which is enclosed for most of its useful length by the political enclave of The Gambia. The capital is Dakar.

Head of State　President Abdoulaye Wade (2000)

Head of Government　Mame Madior Boye (2000)

Ruling Party　The Senegalese Democratic Party (PDS) leads a multiparty coalition.

Political Structure　The Republic of Senegal was proclaimed in September 1960, having seceded from the Federation of Mali, which in turn had left French domination in June 1960. The executive president is elected by direct popular vote for a 7-year term. There is a 120-member National Assembly, which is elected by universal suffrage for a term of five years. The Senate has 60 members, 45 elected by legislators and local, municipal and regional councillors, 12 appointed by the president and 3 members elected by Senegalese living abroad.

Last Elections　Abdoulaye Wade won the presidency in March 2000, defeating Abdou Diouf. Wade received 60% of the popular vote. Elections to the National Assembly were held in April 2001. The coalition led by the PDS won 89 seats, the Alliance of Progress Forces took 11 seats and Socialist Party of Senegal (PSS) won 10 seats. The few remaining seats are divided among several parties. The Senate was elected in January 1999. The 45 elected members are all member of the PSS.

Political Risk　There is an off-and-on rebellion in the southern region of Casamance, where a fragmented separatist movement occasionally attacks the army and fought an 18-year war. There are also worries about Islamic religious extremists. One such group, the Moustarchidine Oua Moustarchidate, was banned after violent incidents in which dozens of people were killed.

International Disputes　A short section of the boundary with The Gambia is not defined and the boundary with Mauritania is in dispute. Relations between all three countries are improving, however, and the danger of a serious dispute is remote for the time being. Relations with Burkina Faso remain troubled.

Economy　GDP rose by 5.7% in 2001, while prices increased by 3%. The external current account deficit has widened slightly to 8.1% of GDP, following deterioration in the terms of trade. Money supply grew at a rate of 10.4%, significantly faster than nominal GDP growth. Credit to the economy expanded by more than 28%, linked to the financial difficulties of the groundnut and energy sectors. The basic budget surplus, which measures the underlying fiscal policy stance, declined from 1.7% of GDP to 1.2% of GDP in 2001. Outside the framework of the budget, long-standing structural problems led to a substantial build-up of debt by two public enterprises to local banks and suppliers. The government, which is very much in favour of a free market, has two overriding objectives. One is to transform Senegal's essentially peasant economy into a private sector-driven centre of agro-industry and services. The other is to capitalise on its relative proximity to Europe and the US to build a regional trading crossroads. One of the key steps in this plan has been to create an agency to speed through start-up approvals for new investment. The longer-term challenge is to build on the country's macroeconomic performance by boosting productivity and diversifying an economy which still relies on a limited number of commodities. Unemployment, even among well-qualified school-leavers, remains unacceptably high. The country is vulnerable to external shocks and poverty is still widespread. Resistance from various interest groups has also caused delays in implementing the programme of privatisation.

Main Industries　Senegal's agricultural sector accounts for 20% of GDP and employs 60% of the workforce. The country's savannah grasslands make it most suitable for cattle herding, mainly by nomadic farmers. Agricultural exports include fish, ground nuts (peanuts), petroleum products, phosphates and cotton. In the past, the country has been subject to several devastating droughts. Senegal's economy grew at a solid pace in recent years, driven by strong growth in agricultural output and a buoyant telecommunications sector. Tourism is the country's second largest foreign exchange earner and contributes about 3% to GDP. The manufacturing sector accounts for 16% to GDP. Most enterprises are small and activities are mainly limited to processing operations that serve domestic needs. The groundnut company (SONACOS) could not reimburse the 1999/2000 crop credit and borrowed an additional 2.7% of GDP from local and foreign banks in early 2001. The additional borrowing was in part supported by guarantee deposits, which the government placed in local banks. As a result, the public treasury faced a tight liquidity situation. The financial situation of the national power company worsened after the government decided to repurchase the shares from a private strategic investor in 2000 and its credit lines were reduced. The company has accumulated a substantial amount of arrears in 2001 with adverse financial repercussions for petroleum suppliers and the local refinery. The government is committed to taking actions to resolve the debt problems of the two public enterprises, notably through privatisation.

Energy　Although it produces some domestic natural gas, Senegal is a net energy importer. By itself, and in conjunction with neighbouring countries, Senegal is promoting increased offshore petroleum exploration. The country depends heavily on imports for all requirements that brushwood cannot fulfil. It has no hydroelectric capacity.

	1999	2000	2001
Inflation (% change)	0.8	0.7	3.0
Exchange rate (per US$)	615.70	711.98	733.04
Interest rate			
GDP (% real growth)	5.1	5.6	5.7
GDP (Billion units of national currency)	2,925.9	3,112.1	3,396.4
GDP (US$ million)	4,752.1	4,371.1	4,633.2
GDP per capita (US$)	511.2	461.0	466.1
Consumption (Billion units of national currency)	2,316.5	2,406.4	2,504.8
Consumption (US$ million)	3,762.3	3,379.9	3,417.0
Consumption per capita (US$)	404.7	356.5	343.8
Population, mid-year ('000)	9,296.9	9,481.0	9,940.0
Birth rate (per '000)	38.9	38.5	38.1
Death rate (per '000)	12.5	12.2	11.9
No. of households ('000)	1,591.9	1,643.8	1,747.4
Total exports (US$ million)	1,027.1	919.8	998.9
Total imports (US$ million)	1,470.9	1,521.3	1,577.6
Tourism receipts (US$ million)	166.0	180.9	164.3
Tourist spending (US$ million)			

Average household size 2001 (persons)	5.77				
Urban population 2001 (%)	48.0				
Age analysis (%) (2001)	*0-14* 45.0		*15-64* 52.5		*65+* 2.5
Population by sex (%) (2001)	*Male* 50.0		*Female* 50.0		
Life expectancy (years) (2001)	*Male* 52.0		*Female* 55.7		
Infant mortality (deaths per '000 live births) (2001)	58.2				
Adult literacy (%) (1997)	34.6				

TRADING PARTNERS

Major export destinations 2001 (% share)

FRANCE	19.4
INDIA	11.4
USA	11.1
ITALY	8.6

Major import sources 2001 (% share)

FRANCE	24.2
NIGERIA	15.1
THAILAND	7.1
USA	4.4

▪ Serbia and Montenegro

Area (km^2)   88,361

Currency   Serbia: Dinar; Montenegro: Euro (= 100 cents)

Location   Serbia, the largest region in the former Yugoslavia, is the dominant part of what remains of the country. Its northern border is with Hungary and on its eastern side are Romania and Bulgaria. In the centre of the region is Belgrade, the capital and largest town. The region is characterised in geographical terms by mountains and deep river valleys. The capital of Serbia is Belgrade. In addition to its shared border with Serbia, Montenegro borders on Bosnia-Herzegovina to the north and Albania to the south. Podgorica is the capital of Montenegro.

Head of State   Federal Prime Minister Dragisa Pesic; Federal President of Serbia Vojislav Kostunica; President of Montenegro Milo Djukanovic

Head of Government   Zoran Djindjic Serbian prime minister, (2000)

Ruling Party   The government is led by a 3-party coalition.

Political Structure   In the new system, Yugoslavia is made up only of Serbia and Montenegro. In 2002, the presidents of the two remaining parts of Yugoslavia signed an agreement that outlined a loose federal arrangement. The prime minister is elected for a term of four years. Parliament has two chambers. The Council of Citizens has 138 members, 60 members elected for a 4-year term in single-seat constituencies and 78 members by proportional representation. Of this total, 108 members are elected from the Serbs and 30 members elected from Montenegro. The Council of the Republics has 40 members elected by the people for a 4-year term, 20 members from Serbia and 20 members from Montenegro.

Last Elections   Elections for the president of Serbia took place in September 2000. Kostunica received 52% of the vote, defeating Milosevic. Elections to the Council of Citizens and the Council of the Republics also took place in September. The Democratic Opposition of Serbia won 58 seats, the Serb Socialist Party obtained 44 seats and the Socialist People's Party of Montenegro won 28 seats. In the Council of the Republics, the Socialist People's Party of Montenegro took 28 seats and the Serb Radical Party won 5 seats. Minor parties won the remaining seats.

Political Risk   The agreement on a loose federal arrangement was meant to send a message to the Kosovar and Macedonian Albanians that they, too, should end their separatist dreams. Montenegrins are the most dubious of the new agreement. Support for links with Serbia come mainly from rural areas but the young and urban population opposed the decision which was taken only under pressure from the EU. Djukanovic claims his country can walk away from the agreement at any time if it wishes. The new constitution, with the main details still to be worked out, is also a major issue dividing the Serbian president and his prime minister.

International Disputes   The country's international relations have improved drastically following the removal of Milosevic and the finalisation of the agreement between Serbia and Montenegro. The two countries have received several billion dollars in aid from Western donors. Relations with Albania remain tense in the aftermath of the war in Kosovo. Albanians account for 90% of Kosovo's ethnic population and their rebel army, the Kosovo Liberation Army, has not been completely disarmed.

Economy   The government that came to power in 2000 inherited exceptionally difficult starting conditions. Output stood at less than half its 1989 level; inflation exceeded 100%; confidence in the financial system had been decimated; the country's infrastructure was in disrepair; the enterprise and banking sectors were both deeply insolvent and isolated from the outside world; and external debt, mostly in arrears, rose to the equivalent of 140% of GDP. However, authorities have been able to take major steps toward stabilising and reforming the economy. 12-month inflation has come down sharply from 113% at end-2000 to 23% in April 2002. Real GDP rose further by an estimated 5.5% in 2001, but remained about one half of its 1989 level. The situation is not as good in Montenegro as in Serbia, however. The little country's conversion from the German Deutschmark to the euro has been accompanied by a big surge in prices. Ironically, the Serbian dinar, with inflation kept under control by the Serbian central bank, is proving to be a better inflation hedge than the euro. The rise in prices has prompted strikes in Montenegro which have hurt several key industries (including tourism) and cut into the government's meagre tax revenues. Official foreign exchange reserves reached US$1.6 billion at end-April 2002 (two and a half months of imports), up from US$0.5 billion at end-2000. The macroeconomic policies underlying these improvements have emphasised strict limits on bank credit and wage restraint in the public sector. The fiscal deficit was 1.3% of GDP in 2001, against a target of 6.1%, with borrowing from the banking system limited to 0.7% of GDP. The fiscal over-performance is explained by higher-than-budgeted revenue (1.8% of GDP). Revenue collections benefited from a major simplification of the tax system and curtailment of tax evasion by fighting corruption and smuggling.

Main Industries   Agriculture is traditionally the largest sector of both economies, with fruit, vegetables and tobacco of particular importance. Recent growth is attributed to a rebound in agricultural output after the drought in 2001, and increasing activity in services. Industrial production has been stagnant, reflecting capacity constraints after years of disinvestment and the ongoing economic restructuring. The banking systems of both countries are very shaky but that of Serbia has more credibility and enjoys more confidence from the public. The lack of credit, however, has stifled domestic investment everywhere. Montenegro places a great deal of hope in the development of its tourist industry. The aim is to achieve revenues of US$500 million by 2015 and US$1.1 billion by 2020. Large tourist-related construction projects have already been started.

Energy   Serbia produces small amounts of crude oil in the north. A number of small oil and gas fields were also discovered during the 1990s. The Serbian region near Pozarevac is believed to contain hydrocarbons. However, the bulk of Serbian and Montenegrin oil must be imported. Crude oil has been brought in primarily by the Adria pipeline. These facilities were all damaged during the war.

	1999	2000	2001
Inflation (% change)	10.9	11.6	62.1
Exchange rate (per US$)	10.92	11.61	62.12
Interest rate (% per annum, lending rate)	20.4	18.9	
GDP (% real growth)			
GDP			
GDP (US$ million)			
GDP per capita (US$)			
Consumption			
Consumption (US$ million)			
Consumption per capita (US$)			
Population, mid-year ('000)	10,641.9	10,662.7	10,689.5
Birth rate (per '000)	12.0	11.7	11.4
Death rate (per '000)	10.5	10.6	10.6
No. of households ('000)			
Total exports (US$ million)			
Total imports (US$ million)			
Tourism receipts (US$ million)			
Tourist spending (US$ million)	10,641.9	10,662.7	10,689.5

Average household size 2001 (persons)					
Urban population (%)					
Age analysis (%) (2001)	*0-14* 19.9		*15-64* 66.2		*65+* 13.9
Population by sex (%) (2001)	*Male* 49.6		*Female* 50.4		
Life expectancy (years) (2001)	*Male* 70.7		*Female* 75.4		
Infant mortality (deaths per '000 live births) (2001)	17.4				
Adult literacy (%) (1996)	97.9				

TRADING PARTNERS

Major export destinations 2001 (% share)

ITALY	28.4
GERMANY	20.5
GREECE	6.8
ROMANIA	5.4

Major import sources 2001 (% share)

ITALY	19.0
GERMANY	17.1
AUSTRIA	6.8
BULGARIA	6.1

Seychelles

Area (km²) 455

Currency Seychelles rupee (SR = 100 cents)

Location The Seychelles are a group of 115 islands located in the Indian Ocean, to the east of Tanzania and Kenya. Most of the population inhabit the Mah group of islands, which are of granite and contrast with the low-lying terrain of the other, mainly coral islands. The climate is tropical with the cooler season occurring during the southeast monsoons (late May to September). The capital is Victoria.

Head of State President France Albert Ren (1977)

Head of Government President France Albert Ren

Ruling Party Seychelles People's Progressive Front (FPPS)

Political Structure The rule of Sir James Mancham was overthrown in 1977 by a coup led by France Albert Ren, who thereupon suspended all political parties except for his own Seychelles People's Progressive Front and declared himself president. After fighting off a coup attempt by South African-backed mercenaries in 1981, Ren went on to institute an executive presidency in which the president, like all but 11 of the 34-member unicameral National Assembly, is elected for a 5-year term, renewable three times. Multiparty politics were readmitted in 1992 and a new constitution was approved by referendum in 1993.

Last Elections Ren and his Seychelles People's Progressive Front have dominated local politics since the coup in 1977. He easily won another election in September 2001 with 54 % of the vote. Elections to the National Assembly were last held in March 1998 when the FPPS won 30 seats in the National Assembly. The remaining seats were divided among two small centrist parties.

Political Risk The islands have changed greatly since the days of a Soviet-backed, 1-party state. However, the president and his political party dominate the economy, just as they do the government. Monopolies controlled by the leader and his friends abound. Some officials are thought to have made huge fortunes, and rumours of corruption are widespread.

International Disputes The Seychelles claims Chagos Archipelago in British Indian Ocean Territory. Meanwhile, its hopes of joining the World Trade Organisation are bleak owing to the many monopolies that the government operates.

Economy Seychelles has achieved one of the highest standards of living in Africa. In recent years, however, the sustainability of these achievements has been threatened by growing macroeconomic imbalances and structural problems that have made the economy less efficient and competitive. The economy contracted by 1% in 2001 while inflation was 6.2%. Growth is stagnating while the upward pressure on prices persists. Some serious balance of payments problems have emerged, causing a near depletion of net international reserves to less than two weeks of imports and the accumulation of some US$50-60 million in external payments arrears. The main difficulty is the large fiscal deficit incurred in recent years which has led to a huge increase in government debt. Steps have been taken to correct the problem but they have been offset by growth in capital spending. The government encourages private investment to upgrade its tourist industry and make it more competitive in international markets. However, public officials also want to reduce the country's dependence on this sector. Tax breaks and other benefits have been used to induce some 4,000 companies to register in the islands. The state continues to dominate the economy, with nearly 70% of all economic activity found in government-run businesses. This lack of competition is hurting efficiency and making the islands far too expensive.

Main Industries With over 1.3 million sq km of sea area and easy access for cruise liners, tourism is the country's largest money earner and employs about 30% of the workforce. The sector attracts over 140,000 international visitors a year and generates more than 70% of hard-currency earnings. The agricultural sector is small, since only 4% of the Seychelles can be farmed. Copra, cinnamon and fish products are the traditional products, but greater emphasis is now being placed on fruit and vegetable crops destined for domestic consumption. Tuna fishing accounts for more than half of GDP. Most industrial establishments are geared to meeting domestic needs for basic products such as timber, cement, tobacco and food processing. Seychelles faces serious structural impediments to economic growth, many of which arise from the extensive intervention of the government. These include controlled prices, a cumbersome system of foreign exchange allocation, a restrictive import licensing system and a practice of frequently intervening in manufacturing activities. The country's parastatals often enjoy a degree of monopoly power and privileges not granted to the private sector.

Energy The country has only limited fuel resources, apart from brushwood, and relies on imports to meet its energy needs. There is no hydroelectric capacity.

	1999	2000	2001
Inflation (% change)	6.2	7.6	6.2
Exchange rate (per US$)	5.34	5.71	5.86
Interest rate (% per annum, lending rate)	12.0	11.4	
GDP (% real growth)	-3.0	1.2	-1.0
GDP (Billion units of national currency)	3.3	3.5	3.6
GDP (US$ million)	610.2	604.1	617.7
GDP per capita (US$)	7,924.6	7,846.1	8,021.6
Consumption (Billion units of national currency)	1.8	1.9	2.0
Consumption (US$ million)	332.3	336.7	341.5
Consumption per capita (US$)	4,315.7	4,373.0	4,434.6
Population, mid-year ('000)	77.0	77.0	77.0
Birth rate (per '000)	19.7	19.4	19.0
Death rate (per '000)	6.5	6.4	6.3
No. of households ('000)	13.0	13.0	13.1
Total exports (US$ million)	145.1	125.5	134.4
Total imports (US$ million)	433.9	387.4	381.9
Tourism receipts (US$ million)	112.0	129.7	90.1
Tourist spending (US$ million)	21.0	35.8	36.4

Average household size 2001 (persons)	5.91					
Urban population 2001 (%)	64.5					
Age analysis (%) (2001)	0-14	34.5	15-64	52.5	65+	13.0
Population by sex (%) (2001)	Male	51.2	Female	48.8		
Life expectancy (years) (2001)	Male	65.3	Female	76.5		
Infant mortality (deaths per '000 live births) (2001)	15.4					
Adult literacy (%) (1997)	84.0					

TRADING PARTNERS

Major export destinations 2001 (% share)		Major import sources 2001 (% share)	
UNITED KINGDOM	29.4	USA	36.2
FRANCE	17.1	SAUDI ARABIA	9.9
ITALY	10.5	FRANCE	7.8
USA	10.4	SOUTH AFRICA	7.2

Sierra Leone

Area (km^2) 72,325

Currency Leone (Le = 100 cents)

Location Sierra Leone is located on the Atlantic coast of West Africa, where it is bounded in the north and east by Guinea and in the south by Liberia. The climate is tropical and humid, but affords significant agricultural possibilities. The capital is Freetown.

Head of State Ahmad Tejan Kabbah (1997)

Head of Government Solomon Berewa (2002)

Ruling Party The government is formed by Sierra Leone Peoples' Party (SLPP).

Political Structure The president is elected for a 4-year term by the people. The House of Representatives has 112 members elected for a 4-year term through proportional representation in 14 multi-seat constituencies with a constituency threshold of 12.5%.

Last Elections Both presidential and parliamentary elections were held in May 2002. Ahmad Tejan Kabbah was re-elected president with 70% of the vote. His party, the SLPP, took 83 seats in the House. The socialist All Peoples Party gained 22 seats and the remainder went to a minor party.

Political Risk Sierra Leone has enjoyed peace only since the beginning of 2002. The civil war was so barbaric that a quick return to normalcy is out of the question. The war left 45,000 dead and forced about one million to flee their homes. Now, the 65,000 rebels and pro-government militiamen who have surrendered must somehow be reintegrated into society.

International Disputes Liberia's president, Charles Taylor, supported the rebel forces of the Revolutionary United Front (RUF) and relations between the two countries are now strained.

Economy GDP grew by 5.4% in 2001 and prices rose by 6%. Returnees from the war had no time to plant in 2002 before the rainy season began. Few will be able to produce much food until 2003. Rates of growth are expected to relatively high over the next few years (7-8% a year) but from a dismally low base. An improvement in fiscal performance is expected and will be a help to the government. The state's revenues also rose, thanks to the pick-up in imports and improvement in tax administration. The overall budget deficit (excluding grants) is nevertheless estimated to be more than a quarter of GDP. Per capita incomes peaked in 1970 and were falling for the two decades before the war. Poverty is now severe and there are large resource requirements for rehabilitation and reconstruction.

Main Industries In peaceful times the farming sector produces cocoa, coffee, ginger and palm kernels. Agriculture is still the biggest contributors to exports but production fell to less than a quarter of its pre-war levels. Rice, cassava, maize and vegetables are grown for domestic consumption, and there was once a sizeable fishing industry. At present, most farming is for subsistence. Normal business life has only now begun to resume. Aid agencies are providing funding for training of the thousands of ex-soldiers and rebels but it will be some time before these people become workers again. Manufacturing activities in Sierra Leone are primarily concerned with the processing of raw materials. The country's mining sector has suffered during the war but still manages to export various minerals such as gold, bauxite and diamonds.

Energy The country is entirely dependent on imports for most of its requirements, although there is some coal. There are no hydroelectric facilities.

	1999	2000	2001
Inflation (% change)	34.1	-0.9	6.0
Exchange rate (per US$)	1,804.19	2,092.12	1,986.15
Interest rate (% per annum, commercial lending rate)	26.8	26.3	
GDP (% real growth)	-8.1	3.8	5.4
GDP (Billion units of national currency)	1,207.7	1,330.3	1,487.7
GDP (US$ million)	669.4	635.9	749.0
GDP per capita (US$)	141.0	131.0	149.5
Consumption (Billion units of national currency)	1,040.9	1,142.7	1,221.9
Consumption (US$ million)	576.9	546.2	615.2
Consumption per capita (US$)	121.5	112.5	122.8
Population, mid-year ('000)	4,747.7	4,854.0	5,010.0
Birth rate (per '000)	49.4	49.3	49.2
Death rate (per '000)	25.3	24.7	24.0
No. of households ('000)	820.6	828.7	856.6
Total exports (US$ million)	6.3	13.0	15.6
Total imports (US$ million)	80.8	149.4	194.8
Tourism receipts (US$ million)	8.0	6.1	5.1
Tourist spending (US$ million)	4.0	2.3	2.7

Average household size 2001 (persons)		5.86				
Urban population 2001 (%)		37.3				
Age analysis (%) (2001)	0-14	44.1	15-64	53.0	65+	2.9
Population by sex (%) (2001)	Male	49.2	Female	50.8		
Life expectancy (years) (2001)	Male	38.4	Female	41.0		
Infant mortality (deaths per '000 live births) (2001)		150.6				
Adult literacy (%) (1997)		33.3				

TRADING PARTNERS

Major export destinations 2001 (% share)		Major import sources 2001 (% share)	
BELGIUM	41.7	UNITED KINGDOM	24.4
USA	8.4	NETHERLANDS	9.7
UNITED KINGDOM	7.8	USA	7.6
GERMANY	7.2	GERMANY	6.1

Singapore

Area (km^2) 616

Currency Singapore dollar (S$ = 100 cents)

Location Singapore, although only a tiny and highly urbanised city state on the southeastern corner of Peninsular Malaysia, owes its extraordinary wealth entirely to its position. Its harbour facilities, oil processing and - most recently - its highly developed telecommunications systems gave it a central role in the development of the region.

Head of State President S. R. Nathan (1999)

Head of Government Goh Chok Tong (1991)

Ruling Party People's Action Party (PAP)

Political Structure The Republic of Singapore, an independent member of the Commonwealth, achieved independence in 1965. The president is elected for a 6-year term by the people. The prime minister and the cabinet are appointed by the president and are responsible to parliament. Parliament has 90 members, 84 members elected for a 5-year term in single-seat and multi-seat constituencies and 6 members appointed by the president.

Last Elections Parliamentary elections were held in November 2001. The PAP won 82 seats, the Workers' Party of Singapore gained 1 seat and the National Solidarity Party took the other with the remainder being appointed.

Political Risk 2001/2002 brought more political uncertainties in Indonesia, the Philippines, Thailand and Malaysia. These developments have served to widen the gap between stable Singapore and its neighbours and frustrated the city-state's efforts to strengthen the Association of South-East Asian Nations (ASEAN). Singapore is heavily dependent on regional markets and must maintain good relations with its trading partners. As a predominately Chinese society, Singapore also fears that it could eventually be isolated from its Muslim neighbours.

International Disputes Within the region, Singapore is in a precarious position. Its three million people are predominately Chinese but are encircled by the hostile Malay-dominated countries of Indonesia and Malaysia, with combined populations of around 230 million. Singaporeans argue that Indonesia and Malaysia are accustomed to governing the Chinese minorities in their own countries and have trouble accepting Singapore's own economic successes. At home, Singapore has a long tradition of keeping tight control over all political opponents and minority groups. This has made it a frequent target of international criticism. Tensions have escalated since the arrest of 13 Malays in December 2001 on suspicion of planning an anti-American bombing campaign.

Economy GDP is expected to rise by 3.2% in 2002 and 5.1% in 2003. Inflation remains dormant, growing at just 1.1% in 2002 and edging up to 1.6% in 2003. With worsening economic conditions both worldwide and domestically, the government enacted a series of off-budget measures to support the economy and help households and local companies over the severe slowdown. The first off-budget package, unveiled in July 2001, amounted to S$2.2 billion. It included measures to accelerate expenditures on economic and social infrastructure projects, and to cut business costs through property tax and rental rebates. A further S$11.3 billion-worth of stimulus measures were announced in October. These were to include a range of corporate and personal income tax rebates; cuts in utilities, education and hospital costs; the distribution of "New Singapore Shares" to citizens (providing a guaranteed investment return and a bonus tied to the economy's GDP growth; and expansion of the social safety net programme. Taken together, the two packages added up to 8.4% of GDP. The government continued restructuring and revitalising the economy to retain its competitiveness globally. Key economic sectors, particularly financial services, telecommunications, energy and the media were liberalised to enhance efficiency and competitiveness. In particular, as part of the comprehensive reform of domestic banking announced in 1998, the retail and wholesale banking markets were further liberalised in 2001, to allow foreign banks to engage in broader business in these markets. Reforms of the regulatory and supervisory environment to enhance the safety and soundness of the financial system were also implemented in 2001, and included setting guidelines on the issuance of new capital instruments for Singapore banks.

Main Industries The deterioration of economic conditions worldwide and a severe downturn in global electronics demand exerted a strong drag on the Singapore economy in 2001. The manufacturing sector bore the brunt of the slowdown, contracting by 11.5% in 2001, compared with 15.3% growth in the previous year. The contraction was mainly due to a double-digit decline in electronics, pulled down by a plunge in output of semiconductors, telecommunications equipment and computer peripherals. This also reflected a drop in the segments supporting electronics production, particularly fabricated metals and machinery, as well as printing and publishing. With a substantial drop in private construction activity and cutbacks in public sector residential projects, the construction sector further declined by 2.1% in 2001, following a 1.7% fall a year earlier. The services sector recorded slower expansion, given reduced international trade flows. Growth in transport and communications moderated to 2.7% in 2001 from 8.5% in the previous year, on account of falls in tourist arrivals and the volume of air and sea cargo handled. The retail and wholesale sector fell by 2.8% compared with 15.2% growth in 2000, dragged down by weak consumer sentiment and a deteriorated economic situation. The financial services sector decelerated to 2.2% growth in 2001 from 4.6% in 2000, as a result of weak equity markets and reduced regional demand for insurance and investment advice.

Energy Singapore is one of the major petroleum refining centres of Asia, with total crude oil refining capacity of 1.3 million barrels per day (bbl/d). The refinery business in Singapore comprised over 12% of its manufacturing sector in 2000. The Asian economic crisis of 1997-1998 had a negative impact on the industry, and Singapore's refining companies lost significant business due to declining demand for oil products in the region. Recent refinery expansions in several of its traditional markets also are hurting Singapore's exports.

	1999	2000	2001
Inflation (% change)	0.0	1.4	1.0
Exchange rate (per US$)	1.69	1.72	1.79
Interest rate (% per annum, lending rate)	5.8	5.8	5.7
GDP (% real growth)	6.9	10.3	-2.1
GDP (Million units of national currency)	140,071.5	159,888.7	158,079.9
GDP (US$ million)	82,640.0	92,745.0	88,228.0
GDP per capita (US$)	26,123.0	28,825.2	26,944.0
Consumption (Million units of national currency)	60,792.0	66,886.4	66,298.5
Consumption (US$ million)	35,866.3	38,798.1	37,002.7
Consumption per capita (US$)	11,337.5	12,058.5	11,300.3
Population, mid-year ('000)	3,163.5	3,217.5	3,274.5
Birth rate (per '000)	13.2	12.6	12.2
Death rate (per '000)	5.1	5.1	5.2
No. of households ('000)	888.4	923.3	952.2
Total exports (US$ million)	114,680.0	137,804.0	121,751.0
Total imports (US$ million)	111,060.0	134,545.0	116,000.0
Tourism receipts (US$ million)	5,974.0	7,798.7	6,162.3
Tourist spending (US$ million)	3,772.4	4,780.1	4,111.7

Average household size 2001 (persons)	3.48				
Urban population 2001 (%)	100.0				
Age analysis (%) (2001)	*0-14* 22.0		*15-64* 70.5		*65+* 7.4
Population by sex (%) (2001)	*Male* 50.1		*Female* 49.9		
Life expectancy (years) (2001)	*Male* 75.6		*Female* 80.0		
Infant mortality (deaths per '000 live births) (2001)	5.0				
Adult literacy (%) (1997)	91.4				

TRADING PARTNERS

Major export destinations 2001 (% share)   **Major import sources 2001 (% share)**

MALAYSIA	17.4	MALAYSIA	17.3
USA	15.4	USA	16.5
HONG KONG, CHINA	8.9	JAPAN	13.9
JAPAN	7.7	CHINA	6.2

Slovakia

Area (km^2)　49,035

Currency　Koruna (SKK = 100 heller)

Location　Slovakia, which was linked until January 1993 in a federation with the Czech Republic, is located in central Europe, southeast of Germany and south of Poland, but to the north of Austria and Hungary. The Czech Republic lies to the east. The climate is temperate, with occasionally harsh winters. The capital is Bratislava.

Head of State　Rudolf Schuster (1999)

Head of Government　Mikulás Dzurinda (1998)

Ruling Party　The Slovak Democratic Coalition (SDK) leads a 4-party coalition.

Political Structure　From 1919 until the end of 1992 Slovakia was part of a federation with the Czech Republic. At the start of 1993 the two countries began an independent existence. The president is elected for a 5-year term by the people. The National Council of the Slovak Republic has 150 members, elected for 4-year terms by proportional representation.

Last Elections　In presidential elections held in April-May 1999, Schuster defeated the ex-prime minister, Vladimir Meciar, garnering 57% of the vote. Parliamentary elections were held in December 1998. The SDK received 27% of the vote and won 43 seats. The Slovak Democratic Coalition obtained 26% of the vote and 42 seats. The remaining seats were divided among four other parties. Parliament then elected Dzurinda as prime minister.

Political Risk　The risks facing Slovakia are primarily related to the country's erratic record in macroeconomic policy. Political uncertainty threatens to delay or discourage FDI and any problems in this field would have a lasting impact on the economy. Continued weak external demand will adversely affect the manufacturing sector, further widen the external current account deficit, and, potentially, put off investment. These risks interact with policy slippages and policy-related uncertainties, foremost in the fiscal area, and could affect business confidence. Over the longer run, there is a danger that such events will increase Slovakia's vulnerability in international financial markets.

International Disputes　Slovakia is regularly embarrassed by waves of Roma (gypsies) seeking asylum in west Europe, a problem that could worsen once the country enters the single market. The government has a number of initiatives to improve the minority's lot, but much of it remains unimplemented.

Economy　GDP rose by 3.3% in 2001 and should increase by 3.7% in 2002. In 2003, growth of 3.9% is expected. Inflation was 7.3% in 2001 and fell to 4.1% in 2002. In 2003, prices are forecast to rise by 3.2%. Although the economy is recovering from setback in the late 1990s, macroeconomic imbalances have become increasingly evident since 2001. Growth of domestic demand has continued to outstrip production growth, and on current trends the 2002 fiscal deficit is projected to exceed significantly the target which has been agreed to with the IMF. The country's external current account deficit widened to over 9% of GDP in 2001 - more than doubling with respect to the previous year - and is projected to remain large in 2002. Although the country should be able to finance its fiscal and external deficits in 2002 even without recourse to the large expected privatisation receipts, these deficits are not sustainable. The authorities will be hard pressed to adhere to their commitment not to use privatisation receipts for current spending, and to implement policies that would bring the deficits to levels consistent with declining debt to GDP ratios. An important goal of government policy makers is to ensure that their actions do not add to current pressures on the balance of payments. This would require that they adhere to a general government deficit of 3.5% of GDP. Yet with current policies, the deficit could soon exceed 5% of GDP, reflecting expenditure overruns in the social area, shortfalls in non-tax revenue and the reclassification of some revenue items. Analysts are also concerned about the government's plans for spending on public wages and infrastructure. The planned increase in the public sector wage bill by about 15% could have a negative effect on the budget and, more generally, the country's competitive standing in world markets.

Main Industries　The country's agricultural sector is comparatively small. Major crops are grains (wheat, barley and corn), oilseeds, potatoes, sugar beets, fruits and vegetables. Declining livestock production is represented mainly by pork, beef, poultry, milk and egg production. The fastest-growing sectors in Slovakia are infrastructure, information technology, pharmaceuticals, industrial equipment, audiovisual equipment and services, medical equipment, chemicals and business services. The country's main exports are manufactures. Volkswagen, alone, accounts for 16% of Slovakia's exports. The firm is also building an industrial park near its Bratislava plant for its suppliers. However, there are few other large investors in Slovakian industry. The country is handicapped in these large deals by its small domestic market and its poor infrastructure. The government is working hard to attract more investors with a new package (assembled with advice from the EU) which allows tax holidays of up to 10 years and grants subsidies for job creation and training. New industrial parks are planned and the business and political environment will be improved. Tourism presently contributes only 2% to GDP and lacks the necessary infrastructure. There is no tourism ministry and poor transportation links.

Energy　Slovakia's oil production is tiny, only 1,000 bbl/d in 2001. This is an increase over the previous year, with most of the gain coming from reserves in western Slovakia. The country is a small oil consumer at about 72,000 bbl/d in 2001, and is nearly completely dependent on imports. The country still depends heavily on nuclear power stations for its electricity. Unfortunately, most these power stations are the accident-prone Soviet type as used at Chernobyl. Slovakia is self-sufficient in coal and lignite. These two fuels account for two thirds of the country's total energy requirements, but it depends on imports for all its oil and gas supplies.

	1999	2000	2001
Inflation (% change)	10.6	12.0	7.3
Exchange rate (per US$)	41.36	46.04	48.35
Interest rate (% per annum, lending rate)	21.1	14.9	11.2
GDP (% real growth)	1.9	2.2	3.3
GDP (Million units of national currency)	815,300.0	887,200.0	964,600.0
GDP (US$ million)	19,710.9	19,272.2	19,948.4
GDP per capita (US$)	3,652.5	3,567.1	3,688.1
Consumption (Million units of national currency)	443,491.2	478,186.7	523,070.0
Consumption (US$ million)	10,722.0	10,387.4	10,817.3
Consumption per capita (US$)	1,986.8	1,922.6	1,999.9
Population, mid-year ('000)	5,396.5	5,402.7	5,408.9
Birth rate (per '000)	10.6	10.5	10.3
Death rate (per '000)	9.9	9.8	9.8
No. of households ('000)	1,969.7	2,009.4	2,026.1
Total exports (US$ million)	10,277.0	11,908.0	12,691.0
Total imports (US$ million)	11,265.0	12,660.0	14,686.0
Tourism receipts (US$ million)	461.0	603.1	553.0
Tourist spending (US$ million)	339.0	423.3	465.4

Average household size 2001 (persons)		2.69				
Urban population 2001 (%)		61.3				
Age analysis (%) (2001)	0-14	19.3	15-64	69.2	65+	11.5
Population by sex (%) (2001)	Male	48.6	Female	51.4		
Life expectancy (years) (2001)	Male	69.6	Female	77.4		
Infant mortality (deaths per '000 live births) (2001)		8.2				
Adult literacy (%)						

TRADING PARTNERS

Major export destinations 2001 (% share)

GERMANY	28.1
CZECH REPUBLIC	18.9
ITALY	8.3
AUSTRIA	7.7

Major import sources 2001 (% share)

GERMANY	26.2
CZECH REPUBLIC	15.5
RUSSIA	15.1
AUSTRIA	6.4

■ Slovenia

Area (km²) 20,254

Currency Tolar (= 100 stotins)

Location Slovenia lies in the far north of the former Yugoslav Federation. It comprises mountains in the west and gentler, flatter land in the east. Three countries border the region - Austria in the north, Italy to the west and Hungary to the east. The capital is Ljubljana.

Head of State Milan Kucan (1992)

Head of Government Janes Drnovsek (2000)

Ruling Party Liberal Democratic Party (LDP) leads a centre-left coalition.

Political Structure Slovenia declared its independence in June 1991. The president, who has a mainly ceremonial function, is elected by universal suffrage for a 5-year once-renewable period. The bicameral legislature has 130 members - 90 in the National Assembly and 40 in the National Council which is mainly an advisory body. In August 1995, Slovenia gained membership to the Central European Trade Agreement which includes Bulgaria, the Czech Republic, Hungary, Poland and Romania and signed an association agreement with the EU in 1996.

Last Elections Elections to the National Assembly were held in October 2000. The Liberal Democrats took 34 seats, the Social Democrats won 14 and the United List of Social-Democrats received 11. Milan Kucan was re-elected as president in November 1997.

Political Risk There is continuing tension between the families of those who supported the partisans in World War II and those who did not. Opponents of the government also claim that too many of the top posts are filled by people who held high rank under communism.

International Disputes Slovenia relations with the Federal Republic of Yugoslavia (Serbia and Montenegro) have been difficult but have improved significantly now that Milosevic is gone. Relations with Croatia are cordial but the border between the two counties is still not delineated.

Economy Slovenia's GDP rose by 3% in 2001 and will increase by 2.6% in 2002. In 2003, growth is forecast to be 3.6%. Inflation was 8.4% in 2001. Prices should rise by 6.5% in 2002 and 5.5% in 2003. Benefiting from strict macroeconomic discipline, Slovenia is currently among the most successful transition economies. Tight fiscal discipline and a monetary policy based on monetary targeting and a managed float for the tolar brought inflation to the single digits since 1996; kept government debt to about 25% of GDP; maintained strong competitiveness and a balanced current account for most of the 1990s; and earned it the highest investment rating and per capita income among transition countries. Although domestic demand fell sharply in 2001 and external demand weakened, competitiveness remained strong. The current account deficit narrowed to about 0.5 percentage point of GDP. The planned reduction in the budget deficit in 2001 did not materialise because of expenditure overruns. The 2001 budget aimed at a general government deficit of 1% of GDP, down from 1.4% of GDP in 2000. In the event, higher-than-budgeted wage, consumption and pension outlays resulted in a general government deficit of 1.3% of GDP in 2001. The tightening of monetary conditions helped curb inflation in late 2001. However, capital account liberalisation and foreign direct investment inflows boosted broad liquidity. Slovenia is very open to trade and increasingly integrated with west Europe. There is strong demand from the EU for various high value-added manufacturing products from Slovenia. As early as 1997 the country had reached a standard of living that was comparable with that of Greece and Portugal and higher than in the Czech Republic. Wages are higher than in other former communist states but the quality of production and firms' export successes attest to Slovenia's competitiveness.

Main Industries The composition of economic activity in Slovenia resembles that in Western countries to a much greater extent than is true for other parts of Eastern Europe. Agriculture accounts for only 4% of GDP, the smallest share among the central European countries. The country's farmers are very productive, with large surpluses of maize, wheat, sugar beet and potatoes being produced. Manufacturing makes up 28% of GDP, while services contribute the remainder. Slovenia's manufacturers have developed an excellent record in exploiting niche markets abroad and the external sector is very important to the overall health of the economy. Generally, multinational companies prefer to base big new plants in countries with large potential domestic markets. However, Slovenia's stock of direct investment compares well with other central European countries. On a per capita basis, it is higher than Poland's. Slovenia is starting to sell of it largest companies. If all goes according to plan, a huge string of sales should occur between mid-2002 and the end of 2003. The country's tourist sector had almost two million visitors in 2001 and showed growth of 3%. The main problem for tourism is that of denationalisation. Many hotels were family-owned before World War II and later nationalised. Now, the original owners want them back but the process is extremely complicated. The government intends to spend much more on promotion of tourism in hopes of establishing its reputation in this sector. As a crossroads between East and West Europe, the country is rapidly developing its motorways, ports and rail systems.

Energy Slovenia has some coal, but must import most of its primary energy. It is for this reason that the country usually runs a trade deficit.

	1999	2000	2001
Inflation (% change)	6.1	8.9	8.4
Exchange rate (per US$)	181.77	222.66	242.75
Interest rate (% per annum, lending rate)	12.4	15.8	15.1
GDP (% real growth)	5.2	4.6	3.0
GDP (Billion units of national currency)	3,648.4	4,035.5	4,566.2
GDP (US$ million)	20,071.6	18,124.5	18,810.4
GDP per capita (US$)	10,162.8	9,208.1	9,589.6
Consumption (Billion units of national currency)	2,086.9	2,284.3	2,606.8
Consumption (US$ million)	11,481.1	10,259.2	10,738.7
Consumption per capita (US$)	5,813.2	5,212.2	5,474.7
Population, mid-year ('000)	1,975.0	1,968.3	1,961.5
Birth rate (per '000)	8.8	8.6	8.4
Death rate (per '000)	9.9	9.9	9.9
No. of households ('000)	636.6	636.8	637.3
Total exports (US$ million)	8,604.0	8,732.9	9,251.5
Total imports (US$ million)	9,952.0	10,106.8	10,143.5
Tourism receipts (US$ million)	953.0	1,160.0	1,263.1
Tourist spending (US$ million)	539.0	567.0	619.4

Average household size 2001 (persons)	3.09					
Urban population 2001 (%)	52.3					
Age analysis (%) (2001)	*0-14*	15.8	*15-64*	69.9	*65+*	14.3
Population by sex (%) (2001)	*Male*	48.5	*Female*	51.5		
Life expectancy (years) (2001)	*Male*	72.0	*Female*	79.4		
Infant mortality (deaths per '000 live births) (2001)	6.0					
Adult literacy (%)						

TRADING PARTNERS

Major export destinations 2001 (% share)		Major import sources 2001 (% share)	
GERMANY	26.4	GERMANY	18.8
ITALY	12.6	ITALY	17.5
CROATIA	8.7	FRANCE	10.2
AUSTRIA	7.5	AUSTRIA	8.1

Solomon Islands

Area (km²) 29,790

Currency Solomon Island dollar (SI$ = 100 cents)

Location The Solomon Islands extend some 1,400km from Bougainville (part of Papua New Guinea) in the north-west to the Santa Cruz islands in the south-east. Although the terrain varies significantly, typical landscapes are mountainous with dense tree cover. The capital is Honiara.

Head of State HM Queen Elizabeth II

Head of Government Allan Kemakeza (2001)

Ruling Party The government is formed by the People's Action Party (PAP).

Political Structure The Solomon Islands are an independent member of the Commonwealth, in which the Crown is represented by a Governor-General. Legislative authority is vested in the 50-member unicameral Parliament, which is elected by universal adult suffrage for a term of up to four years. The prime minister is elected from among the parliament's members, by secret ballot.

Last Elections Parliamentary elections were last held in December 2001. The PAP won 20 seats, the Association of Independent Members took 13 seats and the Solomon Island Alliance for Change claimed 12 seats. Minor parties took the few remaining seats. Kemakeza was then elected prime minister by parliament.

Political Risk Militants detained the prime minister in 2000 and violence became widespread during 2001. The government elected in December 2001 faces the challenge of rebuilding an economy that is almost devastated. Further, the incomplete collection of weapons and insecure law and order conditions are serious concerns. Compensation has also been a major burden on government finances since 2000. Guadalcanal islanders have been waging a growing campaign for restoration of their traditional lands and removal of squatters. Ethnic tensions between indigenous people of the two main islands, Guadalcanal and Malaita, have been growing. A peace accord negotiated in October 2000 was eventually finally implemented in 2001 and may help to ease the tension.

International Disputes There are no international disputes.

Economy The economy shrank by 3% in 2001, the third consecutive year in which there has been a contraction. GDP is expected to fall by 5% in 2002 and to stagnate in 2003. Inflation was 7% in 2001 and will rise to around 8% in 2002. The forecast is for prices to rise by 6% in 2003. Poor economic management and delays in starting the reconstruction process kept the economy depressed in 2001. The government's fiscal position deteriorated greatly in 2001, resulting in a deficit of about 8% of GDP. This was caused mainly by the rise in the number of government employees, the adverse impact on general revenue collections of a weaker economy and import duty and tax remissions. By the end of 2001, payments to public servants, transfers to provincial governments for education and health and payments to utilities were all delayed. Repairs to infrastructure damaged during the ethnic tension could not be started. No employee contributions were made to the Solomon Islands National Provident Fund (NPF) for the year. In addition, the government defaulted on international debts and domestic debts held by local commercial banks and the NPF.

Main Industries Major export-oriented business related to fisheries, copra, cocoa, palm oil and gold remained closed in 2001. Timber exports increased for the first three quarters of 2001, before stalling after exporters and the government disagreed over log valuations. These supply disruptions, together with generally weaker world prices, led to a substantial fall in exports during 2001, which was a major factor behind the decline in GDP. The finance sector is under great strain due to increased non-performing assets. Maintenance of stable and efficient financial intermediation will remain crucial during the reconstruction period for sustainable economic development. Insurance will be very difficult to obtain for any future venture, particularly in mining, and this will create an added hurdle to investors seeking to restart closed operations. However, some encouraging recent economic developments should be noted, notably in the recommencement of fresh fish exports and sales of tinned fish.

Energy Most of the country's fuel needs are met from firewood or similar sources. All oil has to be imported.

	1999	2000	2001
Inflation (% change)	8.3	6.0	7.0
Exchange rate (per US$)	4.84	5.09	5.31
Interest rate (% per annum, lending rate)	14.5	12.7	
GDP (% real growth)	-1.3	-14.0	-3.0
GDP (Million units of national currency)	1,761.1	1,506.3	1,628.8
GDP (US$ million)	364.0	296.0	307.0
GDP per capita (US$)	872.7	687.9	692.6
Consumption (Million units of national currency)	508.4	883.0	933.1
Consumption (US$ million)	105.1	173.5	175.9
Consumption per capita (US$)	251.9	403.3	396.8
Population, mid-year ('000)	417.1	430.3	443.3
Birth rate (per '000)	39.0	38.7	38.5
Death rate (per '000)	5.0	4.9	4.7
No. of households ('000)	65.7	67.8	69.6
Total exports (US$ million)	146.0	93.0	84.0
Total imports (US$ million)	110.0	125.0	108.0
Tourism receipts (US$ million)	6.0	7.0	6.3
Tourist spending (US$ million)	9.2	6.4	6.5

Average household size 2001 (persons)	6.44				
Urban population 2001 (%)	20.3				
Age analysis (%) (2001)	*0-14*	42.7	*15-64*	54.2	*65+* 3.0
Population by sex (%) (2001)	*Male*	51.4	*Female*	48.6	
Life expectancy (years) (2001)	*Male*	67.5	*Female*	70.1	
Infant mortality (deaths per '000 live births) (2001)	22.1				
Adult literacy (%) (1997)	62.0				

TRADING PARTNERS

Major export destinations 2001 (% share)		Major import sources 2001 (% share)	
JAPAN	20.9	AUSTRALIA	28.8
SOUTH KOREA	18.8	SINGAPORE	18.3
PHILIPPINES	11.9	USA	7.1
THAILAND	9.1	NEW ZEALAND	4.9

Somalia

Area (km^2) 630,000

Currency Somali shilling (SSh = 100 cents)

Location Somalia occupies the entire eastern tip of the Horn of Africa, with Kenya to its west, Ethiopia to the northwest and Djibouti to the north. Its northern coastline follows the Gulf of Aden, while its eastern coast lies on the Indian Ocean. Somalia's terrain is mixed, with plains toward the Indian Ocean coast but with hills and mountains in the north. Soil quality is poor and a large proportion of the population is nomadic. The capital is Mogadishu.

Head of State Abdiqasim Salad Hassan (2000)

Head of Government Hassan Abshir Farah (2001)

Ruling Party Main parties are the two factions of the United Somali Congress, the Somali National Movement, the Somali Democratic Movement and the Somali Patriotic Movement.

Political Structure The Republic of Somalia was ruled from 1969 until January 1991 by Maj.-Gen. Siyad Barre, who seized power in a coup and created a socialist state. The constitution was suspended from 1969 until 1991, when it was reintroduced in its unaltered form. A ruinous inter-ethnic feuding followed Barre's removal in 1991, and the situation eventually deteriorated into full-scale guerrilla war. Hassan has been appointed by an interim-parliament formed in 2000 as a result of the peace conference of Djibouti. This National Assembly has 245 members appointed by clan chiefs. Hasan is recognised by most factions, but is not supported by Somaliland and the region of Puntland. De facto, the state is an anarchy without any governmental structures.

Last Elections The elections held in April 1996 were of no real significance since the results were immediately disputed and fighting resumed with even greater intensity. By 1999, Somalia appeared to be breaking apart into two countries. One is southern Somalia with its capital in Mogadishu. The other is Somaliland in the north with its capital in Hargeisa. In June 2001, a huge majority of this breakaway state voted in favour of independence from the rest of Somalia.

Political Risk The president's forces control no more than half of the capital. Abdullahi Sheikh Ismail is the leader of a loose alliance of warlords who control most of Somalia. The northwest of the country has unilaterally declared its independence and is known as the Republic of Somaliland (previously British Somaliland). Its rulers object to the peace process because they fear that a reunited Somalia will try to reclaim it. Somaliland has a basic government, although it has not been recognised by the international community. Fighting continues in the south but Somaliland has been at peace for three years. Another breakaway state, known as Puntland, has been established north of Mogadishu.

International Disputes The severe deterioration in Somalia's internal situation in recent years has placed strains on its relationships with neighbouring countries. Ethiopia, which has a historical fear of a strong Somalia, supports the warlords in the country. Formally, Somalia maintains a claim against Ethiopia for the return of the Ogaden region, the vast triangular desert area that comprises the whole southeast of the country. The Kenyan border is also in doubt but this claim, too, will have to await the restoration of some form of government in Somalia. Somaliland maintains good relations with Ethiopia while Saudi Arabia is a firm supporter of the transitional government in Mogadishu.

Economy Somalia's traders have been doing remarkably well and their economic success is undermining the power of some of the small fiefs created by the war. Malnutrition is widespread and water supplies in much of the country do not operate. Growth in the war-devastated south is nil but in the north (in Somaliland) there is more progress with trading, small-scale manufacturing and farming all recovering.

Main Industries Agriculture is the most important sector, with livestock accounting for about 40% of GDP and about 65% of export earnings. Nomads and semi-nomads, who are dependent upon livestock for their livelihood, make up a large portion of the population. After livestock, bananas are the principal export; sugar, sorghum, corn and fish are products for the domestic market. The small industrial sector is based on the processing of agricultural products and accounts for 10% of GDP. Food processing, hides, wool and leather products are the main areas of industrial activity. In the north, in Somaliland, farmers produce frankincense (an aromatic oil), mangoes, henna and other exotic products. The country may have deposits of precious stones. The recent discovery of high-quality emerald deposits bears this optimism out.

Energy Somalia has no proven oil reserves, and only 200 billion cu ft of proven natural gas reserves. Somalia currently has no hydrocarbon production. Somalia's petroleum consumption was an estimated 4,000 bbl/d in 2000.

	1999	2000	2001
Inflation (% change)			
Exchange rate (per US$)	2,588.71	2,613.08	2,620.00
Interest rate			
GDP (% real growth)			
GDP			
GDP (US$ million)			
GDP per capita (US$)			
Consumption			
Consumption (US$ million)			
Consumption per capita (US$)			
Population, mid-year ('000)	9,794.1	10,097.0	10,893.0
Birth rate (per '000)	52.1	52.0	51.9
Death rate (per '000)	18.0	17.7	17.4
No. of households ('000)	2,000.4		
Total exports (US$ million)			
Total imports (US$ million)			
Tourism receipts (US$ million)			
Tourist spending (US$ million)	9,794.1	10,097.0	10,893.0

Average household size 2001 (persons)						
Urban population 2001 (%)	28.0					
Age analysis (%) (2001)	*0-14*	47.8	*15-64*	49.8	*65+*	2.4
Population by sex (%) (2001)	*Male*	49.7	*Female*	50.3		
Life expectancy (years) (2001)	*Male*	46.9	*Female*	50.0		
Infant mortality (deaths per '000 live births) (2001)	115.2					
Adult literacy (%) (1995)	24.1					

TRADING PARTNERS

Major export destinations 2001 (% share)		Major import sources 2001 (% share)	
UNITED ARAB EMIRATES	47.4	DJIBOUTI	27.9
YEMEN	24.5	KENYA	12.7
OMAN	10.2	INDIA	9.8
THAILAND	2.9	BRAZIL	6.4

■ South Africa

Area (km²)   1,184,825

Currency   Rand (R = 100 cents)

Location   South Africa shares borders with Namibia in the northwest, Botswana and Zimbabwe in the north, Mozambique in the northeast and Swaziland in the east. Apart from the sovereign enclaves of Lesotho and Swaziland, it includes various "independent republics" which have no international recognition. The climate is warm and generally dry, but is well suited to agriculture; there are also vast areas of bush and scrub. The capital is Pretoria.

Head of State   President Thabo Mbeki (1999)

Head of Government   Thabo Mbeki (1999)

Ruling Party   The African National Congress (ANC) leads the government.

Political Structure   A full system of universal suffrage was introduced for the first time in 1994, thus ending the apartheid system under which only white electors had the vote. The "homelands" where black citizens were officially confined under apartheid were effectively disbanded. The executive president is elected by universal suffrage for a 5-year term of office. A new constitution was agreed in May 1996. Parliament has two chambers. The National Assembly has 400 members, elected for a 5-year term by the proportional representation. The National Council has 90 members, elected for a 5-year term by the provincial parliaments.

Last Elections   The country's second non-racial parliamentary election took place in June 1999. The ANC won 66% of the vote and 266 seats. The Democrat Party garnered 10% of the vote and 38 seats, while the Inkatha Freedom Party won 9% of the vote and 34 seats.

Political Risk   Only one other large country (Brazil) has an income distribution more unequal than South Africa's. The top 10% of South Africa's income earners receive almost half of total income. This inequality contributes to the level of violence in the country with frequent murders, car hijackings and bombings. High rates of crime discourage investors and are a major reason for the rising rate of emigration of white South Africans. With a serious shortage of skilled labour, the country can ill afford to loose these trained workers. The government argues that strong intelligence agencies are needed to fight crime, especially the organised sort. That is the rationale for the increased spending on South Africa's "intelligence support" groups. However, the increased influence of domestic spying and intelligence agencies comes at a time when legislative oversight is particularly weak. This development very much bothers civil rights groups both within the country and outside.

International Disputes   Political violence and economic crisis in Zimbabwe have undermined South Africa's calls for continent-wide good governance and created greater doubt among investors about the region's stability. Economic cooperation with several neighbouring countries is also hampered by the fact that South Africa's economy is so much larger than those of its rivals.

Economy   GDP grew by 2.2% in 2001. Growth of 2.3% is expected in 2002 and 3% in 2003. Inflation was 5.7% in 2001 and will rise to 8.1% in 2002. In 2003, prices are forecast to increase by 5.2%. The South African economy's moderately impressive performance in recent years has been underpinned by sound financial policies. Authorities are working to lower the country's exposure to short-term foreign debt. By the fourth quarter of 2001, the country's Reserve Bank had reduced its short-term debt to less than US$10 billion. This compares with debts of more than US$23 billion two years previously. Some progress has also been made in the field of structural reforms. Several legislative amendments aimed at improving the efficiency of the labour market and creating new jobs have been approved since 2000. A free-trade agreement with the EU is now in effect. The government is also moving forward with the restructuring of state-owned enterprises and has announced a policy framework for accelerating the process. Despite these efforts, investment and economic growth will need to rise significantly if substantive progress is to be made in lowering unemployment. More reforms are necessary to make the labour market more competitive, to ensure that investment increases employment and that privatisation and continued trade liberalisation raise productivity growth and labour demand over time.

Main Industries   The government's new policy framework has lain to rest fears that it is not serious about privatisation. The plan places a strong focus on strengthening the regulatory mechanisms to oversee liberalised industries such as energy, transport and telecoms. There are also moves to improve corporate governance and ensure better ethics. The South African government owns hundreds of companies but the main thrust of its privatisation programme is on telecommunications, the electric utility company, a large transport group and a big defence company. The expansion of manufacturing is driven in part by the growth of black-owned businesses. Tourism is the sector benefiting most from the end of apartheid. South Africa, Zimbabwe and Mozambique will soon sign an agreement to create a 40,000 sq km cross-border conservation zone. Overseas (non-African) tourist arrivals have been on the rise in recent years but a fall has occurred first as a result of the problems in Zimbabwe, the high crime rate and more recently after the terrorist attacks on the US in 2001. Agriculture is an important earner of foreign exchange though it accounts for only 4% of GDP. South Africa's large mining sector offers diamonds, iron ore, copper, manganese, limestone and chrome but it is gold that dominates. South Africa is the third leading coal exporter in the world, and coal is the country's second largest foreign exchange earner after gold. South Africa also has a highly developed synthetic fuels industry, which takes advantage of the country's abundant coal resources and offshore natural gas and condensate production. The country has little oil but prospects for sustained natural gas production received a major boost in 2000 with the discovery of offshore reserves close to South Africa's border with Namibia.

Energy   With the exception of offshore gas reserves in Mossel Bay, development of known reserves of conventional oil and natural gas has been slow. Exploration efforts are concentrated on South Africa's west and south coasts. In 1998, the offshore Oribi field began production. Oribi, which is 140km offshore, is currently producing 18,000 bbl/d. Production at South Africa's second field, Oryx, began in 2000. South Africa's prospects for sustained natural gas production received a major boost in 2000 with the discovery of offshore reserves close to South Africa's border with Namibia.

	1999	2000	2001
Inflation (% change)	5.2	5.4	5.7
Exchange rate (per US$)	6.11	6.94	8.61
Interest rate (% per annum, lending rate)	18.0	14.5	13.8
GDP (% real growth)	2.1	3.4	2.2
GDP (Million units of national currency)	802,840.0	887,795.0	967,118.0
GDP (US$ million)	131,408.9	127,927.5	112,335.7
GDP per capita (US$)	3,085.3	2,955.9	2,556.0
Consumption (Million units of national currency)	503,172.1	555,453.8	607,837.4
Consumption (US$ million)	82,359.2	80,038.5	70,603.4
Consumption per capita (US$)	1,933.7	1,849.4	1,606.5
Population, mid-year ('000)	42,592.4	43,278.0	43,949.1
Birth rate (per '000)	26.0	25.6	25.1
Death rate (per '000)	12.9	14.2	15.6
No. of households ('000)	9,558.1	9,750.4	10,015.0
Total exports (US$ million)	26,706.5	29,982.6	29,284.3
Total imports (US$ million)	26,695.5	29,695.3	28,405.1
Tourism receipts (US$ million)	2,526.0	2,012.4	1,779.3
Tourist spending (US$ million)	1,806.0	1,602.8	1,407.4

Average household size 2001 (persons)	4.44				
Urban population 2001 (%)	50.6				
Age analysis (%) (2001)	*0-14*	34.1	*15-64*	60.9	*65+* 5.0
Population by sex (%) (2001)	*Male*	48.4	*Female*	51.6	
Life expectancy (years) (2001)	*Male*	48.3	*Female*	51.0	
Infant mortality (deaths per '000 live births) (2001)	58.8				
Adult literacy (%) (1998)	84.4				

TRADING PARTNERS

Major export destinations 2001 (% share)

USA	13.1
UNITED KINGDOM	12.5
GERMANY	9.2
JAPAN	7.0

Major import sources 2001 (% share)

GERMANY	15.2
USA	11.4
UNITED KINGDOM	8.5
JAPAN	5.8

South Korea

Area (km²)   98,445

Currency   Won (= 100 jeon)

Location   The Republic of Korea (South Korea) is located about 500km off the coast of mainland China, and forms the entire southern half of the Korean peninsula. There are many hundreds of small islands to the south, most of them uninhabited. The territory is mixed in character, with considerable mountainous areas. Consequently, most of the largest settlements are on the southern and eastern coasts, the capital city of Seoul being the notable exception. The capital is Seoul.

Head of State   Kim Dae-jung (December 1997)

Head of Government   Chang Sang (2002)

Ruling Party   The government is formed by the Democratic Party (MD) and the United Liberal Democrats (JMY).

Political Structure   South Korea has a prime minister but real power lies with the executive president. The National Assembly has 273 members, elected for a 4-year term, 227 members in 2-seat constituencies and 46 members by proportional representation.

Last Elections   Elections to the National Assembly were held in April 2000. The Grand National Party received 39% of the vote and 133 seats. The MD received 36% of the vote and gained 115 seats. The JMY captured 10% of the vote and 17 seats. In December 1997, Kim Dae-jung won the presidency. In July 2002, Chang Sang, the country's first female prime minister, was appointed by the president.

Political Risk   Over the past few years, the steady expansion of powers in the office of the president has raised concerns about the health of the country's democracy. There are good reasons for these fears. South Korea has a long history of purges, incarcerations, rigged elections and harsh national-security laws. Much has changed, but by Western standards, the government remains oppressive - particularly in the economic sphere. As Seoul opens up to international market forces, repeated conflicts and problems will occur. However, without a serious breakdown in democracy, these problems will be short-lived.

International Disputes   Relations with North Korea deteriorated significantly during 2001 and 2002. In July 2002, the two countries engaged in a naval gun battle which left several sailors dead. The clash is likely to prevent any improvement between the two Koreas as well as with the US, for some time. The immediate reason for the clash was a dispute over an extension of a land boundary between North and South. In 1996, South Korea and Japan opened discussions to resolve a dispute over three tiny islands in the Sea of Japan, which both countries claim.

Economy   GDP should grow by around 5% in 2002 and 5.5% in 2003. Inflation should be about 2% in 2002 and around 1.8% in 2003. The modest growth that occurred in 2001 was driven mainly by private consumption, in contrast to the broad-based domestic and external demand expansion in 2000. Because of the weak earnings outlook in the ICT sector, and sluggish private spending, companies had little incentive to invest in new plant and equipment in 2001. Export growth began to slow in the first quarter of 2000 and continued decelerating through the middle of 2001, bottoming out in the fourth quarter of the year. Consumption increased in 2001 by 3.7%, a much lower rate than in 2000. This helped support the labour market, and unemployment fell by the end of 2001. One reason for the relative strength of consumption in 2001 was the fact that the corporate sector had, after the financial crisis, generally engaged in significant cost cutting as part of the restructuring process. As a result, firms were not forced to make large-scale layoffs during this downturn. In addition, a high level of liquidity in the financial system, along with low loan demand from the corporate sector, led to increased credit availability for consumers. In the future, the government's traditional focus on supporting exports and investment may shift toward consumption. Manufacturing is now highly export oriented as well as cyclical in nature, and most investment is concentrated in this subsector. In response, the government has begun to utilise tax policy to stabilise consumption. Less dependence on export industries and on investment in plant and equipment will have an impact not only on the composition of GDP but also on the volatility of the equity market.

Main Industries   Although hit hard by the global economic downturn in terms of a large deceleration in export growth, Korea did not experience as severe a shock as economies that are heavily dependent on exports of information and communications technology (ICT) products. This is because Korea has a more diversified industrial base. Manufacturing growth decelerated sharply as a result of weaker orders for ICT products, which account for roughly half the exports of goods and services. As a result, industrial production growth slowed in the first half of 2001. In the second half of the year, external demand led to stronger growth in the automotive sector, helping offset some of the weakness in demand for ICT products. With a substantial depletion of inventories over much of the year and some improvement in domestic demand conditions, industrial production showed an upturn in the second half of 2001. Growth in the construction sector returned, to around 3.5%, from a 3.7% contraction in 2000. This was due to public spending on ports and roads as well as an upswing in residential building construction. Growth in the services sector remained resilient in 2001, although it was slower than in 2000, due to fairly brisk demand for recreational activities, hotel and restaurant services, communications services and increased trade in construction materials.

Energy   With no domestic reserves, South Korea must import all of its crude oil. Oil makes up the largest share of South Korea's total energy consumption, though its share has been declining in recent years. Petroleum accounted for 58% of primary energy consumption in 1999. South Korea consumed just over two million barrels a day of oil (bbl/d) in 2001, down from a high of 2.4 million bbl/d in 1997, all of which was imported. South Korea is the sixth largest oil consumer and fourth largest crude oil importer in the world. South Korea's total reliance on oil imports has led to a policy of securing and diversifying the country's oil supply. South Korea has both a short-term and a long-term approach to fulfilling its oil needs. In the short term, it has developed a strategic petroleum reserve. Strategic stocks are roughly equivalent to a 90-day supply, and are expanded in proportion to consumption levels. In the long term, the country is pursuing equity stakes in oil and gas exploration around the world. South Korea has 19 overseas exploration and production projects in 12 countries.

	1999	2000	2001
Inflation (% change)	0.8	2.3	4.3
Exchange rate (per US$)	1,188.82	1,130.96	1,290.99
Interest rate (% per annum, lending rate)	9.4	8.5	7.7
GDP (% real growth)	10.9	8.8	2.0
GDP (Billion units of national currency)	482,744.2	521,959.2	545,013.3
GDP (US$ million)	406,070.0	461,518.7	422,166.9
GDP per capita (US$)	8,626.2	9,729.1	8,818.4
Consumption (Billion units of national currency)	266,321.8	290,838.7	306,310.2
Consumption (US$ million)	224,022.0	257,160.9	237,267.7
Consumption per capita (US$)	4,758.9	5,421.1	4,956.1
Population, mid-year ('000)	47,074.2	47,436.9	47,873.7
Birth rate (per '000)	13.4	13.3	13.2
Death rate (per '000)	5.7	5.7	5.8
No. of households ('000)	13,868.6	14,138.0	14,413.1
Total exports (US$ million)	143,686.0	172,268.0	150,439.0
Total imports (US$ million)	119,752.0	160,481.0	141,098.0
Tourism receipts (US$ million)	6,802.0	6,058.3	6,293.8
Tourist spending (US$ million)	3,975.0	4,779.7	4,711.8

Average household size 2001 (persons)	3.36				
Urban population 2001 (%)	82.4				
Age analysis (%) (2001)	*0-14* 21.5		*15-64* 71.2		*65+* 7.3
Population by sex (%) (2001)	*Male* 50.4		*Female* 49.6		
Life expectancy (years) (2001)	*Male* 71.5		*Female* 78.8		
Infant mortality (deaths per '000 live births) (2001)	7.4				
Adult literacy (%) (1997)	97.2				

TRADING PARTNERS

Major export destinations 2001 (% share)

USA	20.9
CHINA	12.1
JAPAN	11.0
HONG KONG, CHINA	6.3

Major import sources 2001 (% share)

JAPAN	18.9
USA	15.9
CHINA	9.4
SAUDI ARABIA	5.7

Spain

Area (km^2) 504,880

Currency Euro (= 100 cents)

Location Spain occupies the greater part of the Iberian peninsula with coastal orientations in all four directions; eastward into the Mediterranean, south and west into the Atlantic, and north into the Bay of Biscay. Its only neighbours are Portugal, which it surrounds on both its land borders, and France. It is a co-administrator of Andorra. The climate is varied, with mountain ranges and high plateau and severe heat in the south. The territory also includes the Balearic islands (in the Mediterranean), the Canary Islands and the Moroccan enclaves of Ceuta and Melilla. The capital is Madrid.

Head of State HM King Juan Carlos (1975)

Head of Government Jose Maria Asnar (1996)

Ruling Party The Popular Party heads a coalition with the support of three regional parties.

Political Structure Spain is a constitutional monarchy in which the King plays a relatively modest political role, although he is active in trade promotion. Modern democracy dates from only 1975, when Franco died. The 1978 Constitution created a 350-member Congress of Deputies (Lower House) elected for four years, and an appointed Senate. The administrative regions have been extensively reorganised since the late 1970s to create 17 autonomous regions, including Andalucia, Catalonia and the Basque country.

Last Elections Elections were held in March 2000. The conservative People's Party of Jose Maria Asnar won a majority with 183 seats, giving Asnar a comfortable surplus in the 350-member chamber. The Socialist Party took 125 seats.

Political Risk After the terrorist attack on New York in 2001, Spaniards hoped that their own Basque terrorists might rethink their use of violence. However, a resumption of attacks in 2002 suggests that those hopes were premature. The prime minister complains often about the lack of international support for his tough stand against the Basque terrorists and against the Basque Nationalist party that governs the region and, allegedly, condones the attacks. The government has had some success in its appeals with better cooperation from Belgium, France and the US but this has not been enough to slow the pace of the terrorist activities. The prime minister insists that he can defeat the terrorists with tough action by police and courts. He has outlawed Batasuna, the political arm of the terrorists, but his tactics have created some divisions within the Socialist Party in Spain.

International Disputes Spain's only territorial dispute within the EU concerns the sovereignty of Gibraltar. The two EU countries resumed discussions on the issue in July 2002. The EU is pressing both countries to end Gibraltar's status as a tax haven in any deal they eventually conclude. The most likely outcome is thought to be an agreement that the UK and Spain would share sovereignty, but Gibraltar would be given a great deal of autonomy. Spain has occasionally had conflicts with other EU member states and other countries over alleged over-fishing in the North Sea. Madrid also faces a territorial claim from Morocco for the Spanish enclaves of Ceuta and Melilla, and for three small islands off the coast which still form part of Spain.

Economy Spain's GDP grew by 2.8% in 2001. Growth in 2002 is expected to be 2.3% and in 2003 GDP should rise by 3.2%. Prices increased by 3.2% in 2001 and are expected to rise by 2.3% in both 2002 and 2003. The pace of domestic demand has slowed even though the country's macroeconomic policy stance has remained supportive. Monetary conditions in Spain eased markedly in the period leading up to and following the adoption of the euro, but have been relatively relaxed in the period since then. With higher inflation than in most other euro area countries, real interest rates are still low and credit growth has remained very rapid. Spain's balanced budget target should still be achievable since the official revenue projections were very cautious. Uncertainties about the scale of the slowdown in activity are large. This will depend on developments in the external environment, which may become even less favourable in the near term, and on the behaviour of households and businesses, whose confidence may decline further. Spain's Stability Programme aims at keeping the general government account in slight surplus (0.25% of GDP) between 2002 and 2004 and at reducing the general government debt by seven percentage points of GDP. In addition to maintaining a small surplus, which should allow sufficient room for manoeuvre to counter adverse shocks, the programme provides for a further cut in the personal income tax as of 2003. Officials foresee continued brisk growth of capital expenditure to boost infrastructure development, while further restraint on current expenditure is planned in order to reduce total public expenditure as a percentage of GDP.

Main Industries Industry is centred in the east (Barcelona) and the north (Bilbao), which are home to a wide range of consumer goods as well as the heavy, capital-intensive industries that once dominated those regions. Major industries include electronics, steel, chemicals, fertilisers, food, wine and tobacco products, leather goods and timber products. Most important, however, is the car industry. Entirely foreign-owned but Europe's third largest, Spanish carmakers manufacture around two million cars per year. Unemployment has become a serious political issue for manufacturers with trade unions arguing that the unemployment fund, which is financed by employers, has a large surplus while 40% of the jobless get nothing. Agriculture continues to be a very important sector, but water shortages plague many farmers. Fruits, nuts, olives, tomatoes and peppers are the main export products. The government substantially reduced its involvement in the telecommunications and energy industries. Competition in both industries is much more vigorous now, although there are numerous charges of unfair practices. Tourism, which employs over 10% of the labour force, is a key economic sector but earnings fell after 11 September 2001.

Energy Oil plays a major (albeit decreasing) role in the energy industry. In the 1970s, oil accounted for 73% of Spain's primary energy consumption. That percentage has now fallen to less than 60% and will fall further as natural gas becomes more important. In 2001, Spain consumed about 1.5 million barrels per day (bbl/d) of oil, 99% of which was imported. Spain's largest producing area is in the Mediterranean Sea, with the Casablanca complex producing about 4,000 bbl/d. Because of state regulation of the industry, the country has avoided developing the excess refining capacity that characterises some other countries in southern Europe. Spain's total crude oil refining capacity stands at 1.3 million bbl/d.

	1999	2000	2001
Inflation (% change)	0.9	1.1	1.1
Exchange rate (per US$)	0.94	1.09	1.12
Interest rate (% per annum, lending rate)	3.9	5.2	5.2
GDP (% real growth)	4.1	4.1	2.8
GDP (Billion units of national currency)	565,481.0	608,787.0	650,193.0
GDP (US$ million)	602,949.8	528,804.5	581,820.2
GDP per capita (US$)	15,296.9	13,400.7	14,727.8
Consumption (Billion units of national currency)	352,395.0	353,106.5	1.0
Consumption (US$ million)	375,744.7	306,715.3	337,035.7
Consumption per capita (US$)	9,532.7	7,772.6	8,531.5
Population, mid-year ('000)	39,416.6	39,461.0	39,504.9
Birth rate (per '000)	9.1	9.0	9.0
Death rate (per '000)	9.4	9.5	9.7
No. of households ('000)	12,392.2	12,458.4	12,497.4
Total exports (US$ million)	109,964.0	113,325.0	115,155.0
Total imports (US$ million)	144,436.0	152,870.0	153,607.0
Tourism receipts (US$ million)	32,497.0	36,426.4	27,391.5
Tourist spending (US$ million)	23,968.0	24,657.5	21,502.3

Average household size 2001 (persons)	3.17				
Urban population 2001 (%)	77.7				
Age analysis (%) (2001)	*0-14*	14.9	*15-64*	68.1	*65+* 17.0
Population by sex (%) (2001)	*Male*	48.9	*Female*	51.1	
Life expectancy (years) (2001)	*Male*	75.2	*Female*	82.2	
Infant mortality (deaths per '000 live births) (2001)	5.2				
Adult literacy (%) (1998)	97.2				

TRADING PARTNERS

Major export destinations 2001 (% share)

FRANCE	19.1
GERMANY	11.7
PORTUGAL	9.6
UNITED KINGDOM	8.8

Major import sources 2001 (% share)

FRANCE	17.0
GERMANY	16.0
ITALY	8.4
UNITED KINGDOM	7.0

Sri Lanka

Area (km^2)   65,610

Currency   Rupee (Rs = 100 cents)

Location   Sri Lanka lies in the Indian Ocean, some 80km off the southern coast of India. Most of the island is forested, although the soil is ideally suited to agriculture. The climate is humid and tropical. The capital is Colombo.

Head of State   Chandrika Bandaranaika Kumaratunga (1994)

Head of Government   Ratnasiri Wickremanayake (2000)

Ruling Party   The government is formed by the United National Party (EJP).

Political Structure   The Democratic Socialist Republic of Sri Lanka, which has been independent in its present form since 1978, is a member of the Commonwealth. The country elects an executive president who serves a 6-year term. The president appoints a cabinet in accordance with the 225-seat parliament. The parliament has 225 members, elected for a 6-year term, 196 members elected in multi-seat constituencies and 29 by proportional representation. The country's politics are dominated by ethnic differences; Tamils in the north and east want their own independent republic.

Last Elections   Elections to parliament were held in December 2001. The EJP won 109 seats while the Bahejana Nidasa Party (BNP) 77 seats. The remaining seats were dispersed among five parties. Presidential elections held in December 1999 gave Kumaratunga the presidency with 51% of the vote. She defeated Ranil Wickremesinghe, who received 43% of the ballots.

Political Risk   The bloody ethnic conflict waged by the Tamil Tigers has continued for 20 years. The Tigers want a "homeland" for the Hindu, Tamil-speaking minority which make up about 17% of the country's population. In July 2001, the Tigers attacked the country's only international airport, dealing a serious blow to the country tourist industry.

International Disputes   The UK decided in 2001 to brand the Tamil Tigers as a terrorist organisation. The move prevents them from running their overseas headquarters in London and may deprive them from an important source of money. The expansion of the war on terrorism may further constrain the Tigers, but this group is not a primary focus of the effort. Relations with India have stabilised following that country's intervention in the mid-1980s to quell the growing violence.

Economy   Sri Lanka's economy grew by a meagre 0.4% in 2001 while inflation soared to over 14%. Prices are expected to rise by 8.5% in 2002 and 6% in 2003. With improvements in the external environment, the economy is likely to turn around in the second half of 2002, but the key for the first half of the year is to stop the decline in macroeconomic performance and to focus on stability. Export production will continue to sag for the first half of 2002, as the country's main foreign markets emerge from the current economic downturn. The expected break in the drought should lead to improved performance in the agriculture and hydropower sectors. In 2002, the recovery should be modest, with GDP expanding by 3.5%, and with potential for higher growth in 2003 if a stable macroenvironment is in place. Slower money supply growth is needed to contain inflation. A key concern is to control the fiscal deficit in order to eliminate pressure for monetary expansion to fill the financing gap. The government's commitment to privatisation of state-owned enterprises will help bring the overall deficit down to 8.5% of GDP in 2002, which should fall further in 2003. A stable macroeconomic environment should attract higher rates of investment, leading to a widening of the current account deficit as capital import growth accelerates. The recovery in exports, which are forecast to grow by 7% in 2002, will be more than matched by import growth.

Main Industries   The country's poor performance is largely due to external factors, with the slowdown in global growth dampening demand for the country's manufactured exports, high oil prices increasing the costs of production and shipping, and a serious drought lowering agricultural yields and hydropower generation. However, tourist arrivals plummeted in 2001 as a result of the civil war, while a hefty war-risk insurance surcharge on ships docking at the country's ports damaged the shipping industry. Receipts from privatisation increased for the year, but this is due to the government receiving the second US$25 million instalment from Emirates Airlines for its stake in Sri Lankan Airlines in early 2001, rather than a reflection of progress in the privatisation programme. In fact, the budget had included the planned sale of a 20% stake in Sri Lanka Telecommunications that was expected to raise US$250 million, but the sale was not completed due to globally depressed telecoms prices.

Energy   Sri Lanka produces no oil, and consumes about 70,000 barrels per day, all of which is imported. The country's commercial energy consumption consists of oil (76%) and hydroelectricity (24%). In addition, Sri Lanka consumes large amounts of non-commercial fuel, specifically biomass, nearly all of which is wood. Biomass consumption is increasing by about 3% annually. Overall, biomass accounts for about 55% of Sri Lanka's total energy consumption. Biomass is consumed mainly by households, and Sri Lanka has, in the past, run successful wood stove programmes. The government controls the price of petroleum and electricity. In addition, utilities are subsidised and power is sold at below-market rates.

	1999	2000	2001
Inflation (% change)	4.7	6.2	14.2
Exchange rate (per US$)	70.64	77.01	89.38
Interest rate (% per annum, lending rate)	14.7	16.2	19.4
GDP (% real growth)	4.3	6.0	0.4
GDP (Billion units of national currency)	1,106.0	1,257.6	1,400.1
GDP (US$ million)	15,657.3	16,331.8	15,664.3
GDP per capita (US$)	848.4	876.2	832.3
Consumption (Billion units of national currency)	790.4	906.2	1,024.0
Consumption (US$ million)	11,189.6	11,767.9	11,456.2
Consumption per capita (US$)	606.3	631.3	608.7
Population, mid-year ('000)	18,455.0	18,639.3	18,821.6
Birth rate (per '000)	17.4	17.4	17.3
Death rate (per '000)	6.2	6.2	6.3
No. of households ('000)	3,431.9	3,436.6	3,415.3
Total exports (US$ million)	4,594.1	5,430.2	4,817.4
Total imports (US$ million)	5,960.7	7,177.4	6,100.0
Tourism receipts (US$ million)	275.0	230.9	186.8
Tourist spending (US$ million)	219.0	206.9	188.3

Average household size 2001 (persons)	5.45					
Urban population 2001 (%)	24.0					
Age analysis (%) (2001)	0-14	26.0	15-64	67.3	65+	6.7
Population by sex (%) (2001)	Male	49.5	Female	50.5		
Life expectancy (years) (2001)	Male	69.6	Female	75.6		
Infant mortality (deaths per '000 live births) (2001)	21.1					
Adult literacy (%) (1997)	90.7					

TRADING PARTNERS

Major export destinations 2001 (% share)

USA	40.1
UNITED KINGDOM	11.0
GERMANY	4.5
BELGIUM	3.9

Major import sources 2001 (% share)

INDIA	9.9
SINGAPORE	6.5
HONG KONG, CHINA	6.3
CHINA	6.0

St Kitts

Area (km^2) 261

Currency East Caribbean dollar (EC$ = 100 cents)

Location St Kitts and Nevis comprises the islands of St Christopher and Nevis, situated in the northern Leeward Islands, in the Eastern Caribbean. The two are separated by a 3-km maritime strait, and are mountainous and densely forested. The climate is equable, although subject to storms in the autumn months. The capital is Basseterre.

Head of State HM Queen Elizabeth II

Head of Government Dr. Denzil Douglas (1995)

Ruling Party St. Kitts-Nevis Labour Party (SKNLP)

Political Structure St Kitts (St Christopher and Nevis) has been a fully independent member of the Commonwealth since 1983. The Crown is represented by a Governor-General who appoints the prime minister and cabinet in accordance with the wishes of parliament. The unicameral National Assembly consists of a speaker, three senators appointed by the Governor-General, and 11 members who are elected by universal suffrage for a term of five years. The island of Nevis has a separate 8-member legislature and a cabinet with certain internal powers.

Last Elections Elections to the National Assembly were held in March 2000 when the SKNLP won eight seats in the Assembly. The Concerned Citizens' Movement took two seats and the Peoples Action Movement received the remaining seat. In August 1998, Nevis held a referendum on secession from the federation. Although 62% backed secession, a two thirds majority was needed and the referendum failed.

Political Risk Local drug barons are very influential in the country and occasionally challenge government authority. The existing political system is also under stress from secessionists on the island of Nevis. Such a move is within the constitutional powers of the Nevis cabinet and could create major problems. Parliamentarians in Nevis claim that their island is being poorly treated by St. Kitts. Nevis contributes almost 40% of the federation's tax revenue but receives only a fifth of all government spending.

International Disputes St. Kitts's banking system has been under pressure from Western nations to strengthen its regulations to control money laundering. In 2001, the international commission to address problems of money laundering refused to remove the islands from its list of countries where regulations were inadequate.

Economy GDP grew by 1.8% in 2001 and prices rose by 2.1%. Traditionally, the islands' economy has depended on the growing and processing of sugar cane but this industry has been contracting as world prices have declined. The government is actively pursuing a programme designed to revitalise the faltering sugar sector. Most food must be imported. Tourism, export-oriented manufacturing and offshore banking activity have become the driving forces in the economy. Banking in particular has benefited from recent legislative changes. The government is also working to improve revenue collection in order to provide more funding for social programmes. Living standards, however, are still low in comparison with those in neighbouring countries. St. Kitts depends on the UK for almost all its exports and foreign exchange earnings and its economic prospects are therefore extremely vulnerable to conditions in the latter country.

Main Industries Nevis's economy is based on tourism and offshore financial services, while St. Kitts's economy is larger and more diversified. Tourism, although only marginally developed, has considerable potential. It is typically one of the fastest growing sectors of the economy but suffered significantly after 11 September 2001. Tourist facilities were also damaged in late 1999 when a hurricane hit the island. Agriculture contributes more than 50% of GDP, and is spread around the coastal areas. Bananas, copra and cotton are the main export products but sugar cane is the dominant product. Manufacturing consists mainly of light industries (mainly textiles) and the processing of agricultural commodities. Neither St. Kitts nor Nevis has any significant indigenous resources.

Energy The islands have no fuel except timber. They rely on imports from Venezuela and Mexico for most of their energy needs.

	1999	2000	2001
Inflation (% change)	3.4	2.1	2.1
Exchange rate (per US$)	2.70	2.70	2.70
Interest rate (% per annum, lending rate)	11.5	11.0	11.4
GDP (% real growth)	3.7	7.5	1.8
GDP (Million units of national currency)	822.7	886.8	926.0
GDP (US$ million)	304.7	328.4	343.0
GDP per capita (US$)	7,812.4	8,643.0	9,025.3
Consumption (Million units of national currency)	518.8	671.4	690.9
Consumption (US$ million)	192.1	248.7	255.9
Consumption per capita (US$)	4,926.5	6,544.2	6,733.9
Population, mid-year ('000)	39.0	38.0	38.0
Birth rate (per '000)	22.7	22.4	22.0
Death rate (per '000)	8.6	8.6	8.6
No. of households ('000)	8.8	8.5	8.4
Total exports (US$ million)	24.2	26.0	28.0
Total imports (US$ million)	170.0	178.0	179.9
Tourism receipts (US$ million)	70.0	84.4	73.3
Tourist spending (US$ million)	6.3	6.9	7.5

Average household size 2001 (persons)		4.49				
Urban population 2001 (%)		34.3				
Age analysis (%) (2001)	*0-14*	28.9	*15-64*	66.9	*65+*	4.1
Population by sex (%) (2001)	*Male*	49.6	*Female*	50.4		
Life expectancy (years) (2001)	*Male*	68.2	*Female*	73.9		
Infant mortality (deaths per '000 live births) (2001)		17.6				
Adult literacy (%) (1997)		90.0				

TRADING PARTNERS

Major export destinations 2001 (% share)		Major import sources 2001 (% share)	
USA	65.3	USA	43.5
UNITED KINGDOM	15.1	TRINIDAD AND TOBAGO	16.5
CANADA	6.5	CANADA	8.2
GERMANY	2.5	UNITED KINGDOM	8.2

St Lucia

Area (km^2)   616

Currency   East Caribbean dollar (EC$ = 100 cents)

Location   St Lucia, situated in the Windward Islands of the Eastern Caribbean some 32km north of St Vincent and 40km south of Martinique, is no more than 40km long at its greatest extent, yet its important strategic role has made it much sought after over the years. This is due partly to its record as a safe harbour during the annual hurricane season which afflicts other parts of the region. The capital is Castries.

Head of State   HM Queen Elizabeth II

Head of Government   Kenny Anthony (1997)

Ruling Party   St. Lucia Labour Party (SLP)

Political Structure   St Lucia, a member of the Commonwealth, is one of the Windward Islands group which favours political integration with Dominica, Grenada and St Vincent and the Grenadines. Parliament consists of two chambers. The House of Assembly has 17 members, elected for a 5-year term in single-seat constituencies. The Senate has 11 appointed members.

Last Elections   In elections held in December 2001, the SLP won 14 of the 17 seats in the island's legislature. The United Workers Party took three seats.

Political Risk   The island's heavy dependence on its banana crop as the main earner of foreign exchange renders it especially vulnerable to protectionist disputes and abrupt price movements. St Lucia is also subject to hurricanes and volcanic activity.

International Disputes   There are no international disputes.

Economy   GDP increased by 0.5% in 2001 while inflation was 2.5%. The island's National Development Corporation is working hard to develop tourism and promote St. Lucia as an investment location. It has plans for development of 600 acres of government land, formerly used as a US military base. The site will be converted into golf courses and include several major resorts. Despite these efforts, earnings from bananas are the only source of income for entire communities in some parts of St. Lucia. The island has more than 10,000 small farms that depend on the fruit. Annual exports exceed 70,000 tonnes but are falling as St Lucia's competitive position is eroded. Though foreign investment in manufacturing and information processing is rising, the pace of diversification is too slow. The island has recently opened a dedicated container terminal at Vieux Fort and has established a free-trade zone there. The intention is to offer transhipment connections for Central and South America, Europe and West Africa.

Main Industries   Agriculture accounts for 12% of the GDP but over 40% of all employment. Industry makes up a third of GDP and services contribute the remainder. Tourism is growing rapidly and attracts over 200,000 visitors a year, mainly from the US and the UK. However, the growth of tourism is restricted only to the larger resorts and its benefits have been spread unevenly. St Lucia has forests, sandy beaches, minerals (pumice), mineral springs and geothermal potential. Though foreign investment in manufacturing and information processing is rising, the island's industrial base depends heavily on the production of bananas. St Lucia is the largest supplier of bananas in the Windward Islands. Production, however, has been falling and production costs are about three times higher than in Central and South America.

Energy   St Lucia has no indigenous energy resources and relies on imports for all fuel requirements.

	1999	2000	2001
Inflation (% change)	3.5	3.6	2.5
Exchange rate (per US$)	2.70	2.70	2.70
Interest rate (% per annum, lending rate)	10.5	10.5	10.5
GDP (% real growth)	3.5	0.7	0.5
GDP (Million units of national currency)	1,820.2	1,893.2	1,955.0
GDP (US$ million)	674.2	701.2	724.1
GDP per capita (US$)	4,435.2	4,553.1	4,582.7
Consumption (Million units of national currency)	985.4	1,007.2	1,044.3
Consumption (US$ million)	365.0	373.0	386.8
Consumption per capita (US$)	2,401.0	2,422.4	2,448.0
Population, mid-year ('000)	152.0	154.0	158.0
Birth rate (per '000)	23.6	23.3	23.0
Death rate (per '000)	5.6	5.5	5.5
No. of households ('000)	31.1	31.7	32.5
Total exports (US$ million)	81.3	101.0	102.9
Total imports (US$ million)	347.2	381.0	384.7
Tourism receipts (US$ million)	311.0	331.6	233.7
Tourist spending (US$ million)	30.9	35.4	31.6

Average household size 2001 (persons)		4.86				
Urban population 2001 (%)		38.1				
Age analysis (%) (2001)	*0-14*	30.8	*15-64*	64.2	*65+*	5.1
Population by sex (%) (2001)	*Male*	49.4	*Female*	50.6		
Life expectancy (years) (2001)	*Male*	70.9	*Female*	76.2		
Infant mortality (deaths per '000 live births) (2001)		13.2				
Adult literacy (%) (1997)		82.0				

TRADING PARTNERS

Major export destinations 2001 (% share)		Major import sources 2001 (% share)	
USA	33.7	USA	26.8
UNITED KINGDOM	26.2	BRAZIL	22.1
FRANCE	22.3	TRINIDAD AND TOBAGO	15.2
BARBADOS	7.3	UNITED KINGDOM	7.4

St Vincent and the Grenadines

Area (km²)   389

Currency   East Caribbean dollar (EC$ = 100 cents)

Location   St Vincent, a 30-km island, is the main island in a group of some 100 islets which extend for more than 60km through the Grenadines group in the Windward Islands. Other islands in the Grenadines are part of the state of Grenada. St Vincent itself is about 160km west of Barbados and 34km southwest of St Lucia. The capital is Kingstown.

Head of State   HM Queen Elizabeth II

Head of Government   Ralph Gonsalves (2001)

Ruling Party   Unity Labour Party (ULP)

Political Structure   St Vincent and the Grenadines has been a Commonwealth member since gaining independence from the UK in 1979. The Crown is represented by a Governor-General who appoints the prime minister in accordance with the wishes of parliament. The unicameral National Assembly consists of six appointed senators and 15 members who are elected by universal suffrage for a term of five years.

Last Elections   Elections to the National Assembly were held in March 2001 when the ULP took 12 seats with 58% of the vote. The New Democratic Party won three seats. Ralph Gonsalves of the ULP became prime minister.

Political Risk   The political scene has become more contentious in recent years but no significant changes in policy are imminent. The islands are apparently a transhipment point for illicit drugs destined for the US and Europe.

International Disputes   The international commission to strengthen standards against money laundering refused to remove St. Vincent from its list of violators in 2001.

Economy   GDP rose by 0.3% in 2001 and prices increased by 0.9%. Unemployment is thought to be around 20% or higher. Central government expenditures increased by 2.5 percentage points of GDP from 1999 to 2001 partly due to an increased wage bill. Public investment has roughly halved to 7% of GDP due to capacity constraints and the slow disbursements of external funds. The external current account deficit is estimated to have doubled to around 16.5% of GDP in 2001 due largely to a decline in banana export volumes, higher imports and a slowdown in tourism receipts and remittances. The deficit was financed mainly by private capital flows. Public sector debt has increased from 49% of GDP in 1998 to 73% of GDP in 2001 following the takeover of private and other non-government guaranteed debt.

Main Industries   Farming accounts for 12% of GDP but productivity is low. Approximately a quarter of all workers are employed in the agricultural sector. Industry makes up 19% of GDP and services account for the remainder. Aside from bananas, other agricultural exports include arrowroot, coconuts, cocoa and spices, while cassava and vegetables are grown for the domestic market. In recent years, the economy of St. Vincent and the Grenadines has diversified from bananas into services, mainly tourism, telephone and Internet-based marketing, and offshore financial services. However, the rate of economic growth has slowed in recent years, reflecting mainly contraction in the construction sector as major public sector projects were completed. The pace continued to slow in 2001 due to the impact of a severe drought on agriculture and a slowdown in tourism resulting partly from the 11 September terrorist attacks. Manufacturing centres on the processing of raw materials for domestic use, but a range of light activities including woodworking and furniture and clothing are also flourishing. Most growth in recent years has been in the tourist industry. Tourism has great potential and a few large hotels have opened since 2000. As of end-2001, the offshore financial centre comprised 10,075 international business corporations, 896 trusts, 38 banks, 35 registered agents, 5 mutual funds and 1 insurance company.

Energy   St Vincent and the Grenadines have no indigenous fuels except for firewood, and the country imports nearly all its requirements. However, hydroelectric power accounts for three quarters of all electricity generation.

	1999	2000	2001
Inflation (% change)	1.0	0.2	0.9
Exchange rate (per US$)	2.70	2.70	2.70
Interest rate (% per annum)	12.5	11.8	11.0
GDP (% real growth)	4.3	1.8	0.3
GDP (Million units of national currency)	891.0	910.0	911.0
GDP (US$ million)	330.0	337.0	337.4
GDP per capita (US$)	2,920.4	2,956.5	2,883.8
Consumption (Million units of national currency)	593.4	569.3	571.3
Consumption (US$ million)	219.8	210.8	211.6
Consumption per capita (US$)	1,945.0	1,849.5	1,808.5
Population, mid-year ('000)	113.0	114.0	117.0
Birth rate (per '000)	19.2	18.9	18.5
Death rate (per '000)	5.9	5.8	5.8
No. of households ('000)	26.6	27.1	27.3
Total exports (US$ million)	48.6	47.2	41.5
Total imports (US$ million)	200.8	162.7	185.9
Tourism receipts (US$ million)	77.3	81.7	56.8
Tourist spending (US$ million)	8.7	8.7	8.0

Average household size 2001 (persons)	4.21					
Urban population 2001 (%)	55.9					
Age analysis (%) (2001)	*0-14*	34.0	*15-64*	61.7	*65+*	4.3
Population by sex (%) (2001)	*Male*	49.4	*Female*	50.6		
Life expectancy (years) (2001)	*Male*	70.9	*Female*	74.3		
Infant mortality (deaths per '000 live births) (2001)	15.2					
Adult literacy (%) (1997)	82.0					

TRADING PARTNERS

Major export destinations 2001 (% share)		Major import sources 2001 (% share)	
FRANCE	40.7	FRANCE	21.6
USA	11.8	USA	13.8
UNITED KINGDOM	10.3	TRINIDAD AND TOBAGO	11.9
GREECE	9.5	SINGAPORE	11.9

◼ Sudan

Area (km^2) 2,505,815

Currency Sudanese pound (S£ = 100 piastres)

Location Sudan, the largest country in Africa, lies in central northeast Africa where it shares borders to the north with Egypt, to the east with Eritrea and Ethiopia, to the south with Kenya, Uganda and the Democratic Republic of the Congo (formerly Zaire), and to the west with the Central African Republic, Chad, and to a small extent Libya. Very little of its terrain is suitable for cultivation, except for a limited area around the River Nile and its tributaries, the Atbara, the Blue Nile and the White Nile. The capital is Khartoum.

Head of State President Omar Hassan Ahmad Al-Bashir

Head of Government President Omar Hassan Ahmad Al-Bashir

Ruling Party The government is dominated by the National Congress Party.

Political Structure The elected regime was overthrown in 1989 and the leaders of the coup have dominated Sudanese politics since then. The president is elected for a 5-year term by the people. The National Assembly has 400 members, 275 directly elected for 4-year terms in single-seat constituencies and 125 indirectly elected by national conference.

Last Elections Presidential elections took place in December 2000 when Al-Bashir was returned to office with 87% of the vote. Elections to the National Assembly were held at the same time and the National Congress Party captured 355 seats.

Political Risk A war between Sudan's Arabic-speaking, Muslim north and the black African, Christian and animist south has simmered for most of the past 45 years. Numerous international human rights organisations have accused the Sudanese government of financing wide-scale human rights abuses with oil revenues, including the mass displacement of civilians living near the oil fields. The Sudan People's Liberation Army (SPLA), the main southern rebel group, has declared that it considers oil installations a "legitimate military target", as oil development has provided the Sudanese government the financial resources to expand its war effort. In November 2001, southern rebels claimed to have ambushed an army convoy and stated that such attacks would continue until "oil exploration, exploitation and development come to a halt". At least one million people have been killed and another 1.5 million displaced and vulnerable to starvation. Khartoum decided to break off all negotiations with the rebels in 2002.

International Disputes Worn down by a decade of sanctions, Sudan is seeking removal from the US list of states that sponsor terrorism. In 1998, two weeks after US Embassies in Nairobi, Kenya and Dar es Salaam, Tanzania were bombed, the US attacked a suspected chemical weapons facility located in Sudan. After a Khartoum-backed assassination attempt on Egypt's Hosni Mubarak in 1995, relations with Cairo have been frozen. The US has imposed an embargo on Sudan, forbidding investment. Kenya, Uganda, Ethiopia and Eritrea have all provided assistance to the SPLA.

Economy Sudan is among the world's poorest countries. GDP grew by 5.3% in 2001 and prices increased by 5%. Exports have grown sharply since 1999, and the merchandise trade balance has turned from negative to positive in 2001. The government announced that Sudan was aiming to accelerate and broaden the country's privatisation programme. Khartoum also is moving to cut costs, reduce subsidies on gasoline and benzene and scale back support to state-owned enterprises. These moves should help to bring the budget closer into balance. In 2000, Sudan opened its Red Sea Free Trade Zone, designed to encourage foreign direct investment. Despite its economic progress, Sudan still faces developmental obstacles, including a limited infrastructure and an external debt of around US$16 billion, representing a debt-to-GDP ratio of about 128%.

Main Industries Traditionally, its economy has been mainly agricultural - a mix of subsistence farming and production of cash crops such as cotton and gum arabic. Farming is the main source of income for the great majority of the population but has been severely disrupted by the war. Sugar, wheat, millet and sorghum are grown for domestic consumption, while groundnuts and oilseeds are some of the main export crops. Cattle are herded, mainly by nomads, in the desert. With the start of significant oil production (and exports) beginning in late 1999, however, Sudan's economy is changing dramatically, with oil export revenues now accounting for around 70% of Sudan's total export earnings. Sudan no longer relies on expensive imported oil products, which has helped the country's trade balance, while foreign investment has started to flow into the country (US$7 billion in 2001). However, Sudan's infrastructure has suffered from years of under-investment, which in part reflects a weak tax effort. A 1,500-km underground pipeline has been finished to carry oil from the south to Port Sudan in the north. Foreign companies expect to pump 150,000 barrels a day but the security of the pipeline remains paramount. Manufacturing accounts for only about 5% of GDP. Cement, timber processing, textiles and leather goods being the main products.

Energy In 2001, Sudan's estimated proven reserves of crude oil stood at 262.1 million barrels. Crude oil production averaged 209,000 barrels per day (bbl/d) during 2001, and has been rising steadily. Oil production for 2002 is forecast to reach 219,000 bbl/d. By 2003, oil output could reach 290,000 bbl/d or higher, with plans to reach 450,000 bbl/d by 2005. In 2001, in recognition of Sudan's growing significance as an oil exporter, OPEC granted the country observer status at OPEC meetings.

	1999	2000	2001
Inflation (% change)	16.0	8.0	5.0
Exchange rate (per US$)	252.55	257.12	258.70
Interest rate			
GDP (% real growth)	7.7	9.7	5.3
GDP (Billion units of national currency)	2,628.1	2,929.3	3,237.0
GDP (US$ million)	10,406.2	11,392.7	12,512.6
GDP per capita (US$)	358.5	386.3	404.0
Consumption (Billion units of national currency)	2,265.0	2,516.1	2,660.9
Consumption (US$ million)	8,968.6	9,785.8	10,285.7
Consumption per capita (US$)	308.9	331.8	332.1
Population, mid-year ('000)	29,029.9	29,490.0	30,975.0
Birth rate (per '000)	35.3	34.8	34.2
Death rate (per '000)	11.8	11.6	11.4
No. of households ('000)	4,719.0	4,824.7	5,103.2
Total exports (US$ million)	585.3	731.0	855.9
Total imports (US$ million)	1,719.1	1,953.0	2,192.7
Tourism receipts (US$ million)	2.0	6.0	5.9
Tourist spending (US$ million)	35.0	37.4	32.4

Average household size 2001 (persons)		6.11				
Urban population 2001 (%)		37.0				
Age analysis (%) (2001)	*0-14*	40.6	*15-64*	56.3	*65+*	3.1
Population by sex (%) (2001)	*Male*	50.0	*Female*	50.0		
Life expectancy (years) (2001)	*Male*	55.1	*Female*	57.9		
Infant mortality (deaths per '000 live births) (2001)		79.9				
Adult literacy (%) (1997)		53.3				

TRADING PARTNERS

Major export destinations 2001 (% share)		Major import sources 2001 (% share)	
CHINA	46.2	CHINA	11.8
JAPAN	14.4	SAUDI ARABIA	8.7
SOUTH KOREA	5.5	GERMANY	8.1
SAUDI ARABIA	5.3	UNITED KINGDOM	7.1

Suriname

Area (km^2) 163,820

Currency Suriname guilder (Sf = 100 cents)

Location Suriname is located on the northeastern Atlantic coast of South America, where it is flanked in the west by Guyana, in the east by French Guiana and in the south by Brazil. The major settlements are on the coast. Further inland, the dense jungle gives way to a high sierra where the only cultivable crop is balata, a rubbery sap obtained from certain trees. The capital is Paramaribo.

Head of State Runaldo Ronald Venetiaan (2000)

Head of Government Runaldo Ronald Venetiaan (2000)

Ruling Party The government is formed by New Front for Democracy.

Political Structure The Republic of Suriname gained its independence from the Netherlands in 1975 and has close ties to that country today. A protracted civil war led to a succession of coups and counter-coups but the situation had eased by the mid-1990s, following another military coup. The executive president is chosen by an electoral college based on the parliament which, in turn, is elected by popular vote for a 5-year term. The National Assembly has 51 members, elected every five years by proportional representation per district.

Last Elections In general elections held in May 2000, Ronald Venetiaan, and his New Front coalition received 47% of the vote and 25 seats. The Millennium Combination won 15% of the votes and 10 seats. The remainder of the seats were scattered among several parties.

Political Risk The country's legal system is very weak and easily influenced by drug barons.

International Disputes Suriname has territorial claims against its two neighbours, Guyana and French Guyana although neither is being pressed hard at present. In both cases the disputes arise from 19th-century uncertainties as to the course of rivers through impenetrable jungle; Suriname is claiming about 8,000 sq km from French Guiana and some 20,000 sq km from Guyana.

Economy GDP rose by 3.4% in 2001, while inflation was 50%. The improved rate of growth has resulted largely from stabilisation measures that the government took in late 2000. Most important was the devaluation of the official exchange rate by 47%. The large devaluation brought the exchange rate to a level that was much more consistent with economic fundamentals and therefore more credible. Officials have also sought to increase government revenues by raising the rates of excise tax on cigarettes and tobacco. This was accompanied by a removal of subsidies on most foodstuffs and petroleum and increased electricity and water tariffs. In order to mitigate the impact of the devaluation and the other fiscal measures, the government awarded lump sum increases to civil service salaries and pensions. The country's hyperinflation, which has been a constant problem for several years, began to fall in 2002 as fiscal policies have belatedly been tightened. During 2001, the government cleared a significant fraction of its arrears and worked on improving the maturity profile and average terms of its debts. Relations with the Netherlands have frequently been difficult and this has shut out many foreign investors. However, there has been some improvement in the ties between the two countries since 2001. Investors are nevertheless hesitant to contemplate projects in a country where the legal system is being seriously undermined and drug-runners wield considerable influence.

Main Industries Agriculture makes up 16% of GDP, industry accounts for 32% and services contribute 52%. Agriculture is viable only along the coastal regions where the terrain is more accessible. Products range from sugar and banana plantations to rice (the staple crop) and vegetables. Commercial fishing is growing in importance. Further inland, timber and forestry are found. In the high sierras, balata (a form of ersatz rubber) is extracted from trees. Suriname has an abundance of natural resources including: timber, hydropower potential, fish, shrimp, bauxite, iron ore, and small amounts of nickel, copper, platinum and gold. However, the economy is dominated by the bauxite industry, which accounts for around 15% of GDP and more than 65% of export earnings in recent years. After reaching over US$400 per tonne in early 2000, the international price of alumina (which accounts for two thirds of Suriname's recorded exports) had slumped to around US$150 per tonne in late 2001. If alumina prices remain weak in 2002, Suriname's export earnings will decline, thereby tending to push the external current account into deficit and eroding the central bank's stock of international reserves. The country's gold fields support many freelance miners but most these are Brazilians, many of them heavily armed. Other industries include lumbering, food processing and fishing.

Energy Suriname has immense and largely unrealised hydroelectric potential in its upland jungle areas, as well as some oil resources offshore.

	1999	2000	2001
Inflation (% change)	98.8	59.1	50.2
Exchange rate (per US$)	859.44	1,322.47	2,178.50
Interest rate (% per annum, lending rate)	27.3	29.0	25.8
GDP (% real growth)	5.0	2.9	3.4
GDP (Million units of national currency)	540,515.0	803,893.0	1,185,678.0
GDP (US$ million)	628.9	607.9	544.3
GDP per capita (US$)	1,512.6	1,457.7	1,289.7
Consumption (Million units of national currency)	507,789.8	767,482.1	1,163,187.9
Consumption (US$ million)	590.8	580.3	533.9
Consumption per capita (US$)	1,421.0	1,391.7	1,265.3
Population, mid-year ('000)	415.8	417.0	422.0
Birth rate (per '000)	19.6	19.2	18.8
Death rate (per '000)	6.0	6.0	6.0
No. of households ('000)	84.8	84.5	84.5
Total exports (US$ million)	450.0	435.0	402.2
Total imports (US$ million)	486.0	550.0	476.2
Tourism receipts (US$ million)	53.0	57.7	60.4
Tourist spending (US$ million)			

Average household size 2001 (persons)	4.94				
Urban population 2001 (%)	74.8				
Age analysis (%) (2001)	0-14	32.3	15-64	62.5	65+	5.3
Population by sex (%) (2001)	Male	49.4	Female	50.6	
Life expectancy (years) (2001)	Male	68.3	Female	73.5	
Infant mortality (deaths per '000 live births) (2001)	26.7				
Adult literacy (%) (1997)	93.5				

TRADING PARTNERS

Major export destinations 2001 (% share)		Major import sources 2001 (% share)	
USA	26.1	USA	34.3
NORWAY	15.9	NETHERLANDS	16.2
FRANCE	9.9	TRINIDAD AND TOBAGO	12.6
NETHERLANDS	7.7	NETHERLANDS ANTILLES	8.1

Swaziland

Area (km^2)   17,365

Currency   Lilangeni (L = 100 cents)

Location   Swaziland is a landlocked state in southern Africa, bordered in the east by Mozambique and on all other sides by South Africa. Four rivers ensure a satisfactory flow of irrigation to the lowlands; higher up the land turns to mountain ranges. The climate is tropical but pleasant. The capital is Mbabane.

Head of State   HM King Mswati III (1986)

Head of Government   Barnabas Sibusiso Dlamini (1996)

Ruling Party   All political parties are banned under the 1978 constitutional amendments.

Political Structure   The Kingdom of Swaziland, an independent member of the Commonwealth, is the only absolute monarchy in sub-Saharan Africa. All political activity has been banned since 1973, when King Sobhuza II took "supreme power". His successor, the current king, has relaxed the rules a bit. He appoints the prime minister and cabinet directly and they answer to him rather than to the 65-member House of Assembly or the 30-member Senate. Current practice is for 55 members of the House of Assembly and 10 Senators to be elected by the 40 traditional tribal communities, with the King appointing all the others.

Last Elections   Non-party elections took place in September and October 1998. As a result of those elections, Barnabas Dlamini was reinstated as prime minister after a 1-year absence.

Political Risk   Swaziland is one of the few countries outside the Middle East that continues to be dominated by tribal loyalties. Opponents of the current regime, who are led by Swaziland's Federation of Trade Unions, have faced evictions from their homes and an increasing level of violence. Nowhere in the country is more than a short bus ride from richer, more democratic, South Africa. The Swazis who stay at home are becoming more and more dissatisfied with their brand of pluralism.

International Disputes   Swaziland has asked South Africa to open negotiations on reincorporating some nearby South African territories that are populated by ethnic Swazis or that were long ago part of the Swazi Kingdom.

Economy   GDP grew by 1.6% in 2001 and prices rose by 7.5%. Swaziland's growth has been slowing, owing mainly to a weakening economic climate in South Africa. There is virtually no growth in per capita incomes in the country and levels could even begin to drop soon. Unemployment is presently running at around 30%. The government budget (including grants) has moved to a deficit estimated at 4.5% of GDP, owing largely to an increase in the wage bill (stemming from the full-year impact of a 15% pay raise in 2000) and larger subsidies to publicly-owned firms. A relaxation of foreign exchange controls is expected, along with a reduction in the company income tax rate in line with the rate in South Africa. Although Swaziland is regarded as a middle-income country with a per capita GDP of US$1,340, adult per capita consumption for the poorest 40% of its population is equivalent to US$230 or less. Moreover, Swaziland's HIV prevalence is estimated at 22.5% of the population aged 15-49.

Main Industries   The agricultural sector is the most important area of the economy for most of the population, supporting subsistence crops such as sugar cane, cereals and fruit, as well as cash crops such as pineapples and cotton. Other farm products include maize, tobacco, rice, citrus, pineapples, corn, sorghum, peanuts, cattle, goats and sheep. Exports of sugar and forestry products are the main earners of hard currency. Roughly 60% of the workforce is employed in agriculture. Productivity is very low, however, and farming makes up only 16% of GDP. Farmers suffer from overgrazing, soil depletion and drought. Farm expansion is hobbled by the fact that the king owns most land "in trust" for the nation, and can evict tillers on a whim. Exporters of sugar and some other products are in danger of losing their easy access to the US market because new laws that put restrictions on trade unions violate international conventions. Manufacturing makes up 40% of GDP. Exports of manufactures are few with most of the production being destined for domestic consumption. Major activities include brewing, timber products, textiles and various crafts. The stability of the country's banking system remains a concern. Mining has declined in importance in recent years as high-grade iron ore deposits were depleted and health concerns cut world demand for asbestos. The country earns much of its foreign exchange from the weekend visits of South Africans who come for gambling and the wildlife, and from remittances by Swazis working in South Africa's mines and factories.

Energy   Swaziland depends almost entirely on South Africa to meet its energy needs. However, it has an ample supply of hydroelectric power, but otherwise few natural energy resources, all of which have to be imported.

	1999	2000	2001
Inflation (% change)	5.9	9.9	7.5
Exchange rate (per US$)	6.11	6.94	8.61
Interest rate (% per annum, lending rate)	15.0	14.0	12.5
GDP (% real growth)	3.5	2.2	1.6
GDP (Million units of national currency)	8,410.0	9,673.0	10,654.0
GDP (US$ million)	1,376.5	1,393.8	1,237.5
GDP per capita (US$)	1,395.1	1,382.8	1,164.2
Consumption (Million units of national currency)	5,030.6	5,605.4	6,254.0
Consumption (US$ million)	823.4	807.7	726.4
Consumption per capita (US$)	834.5	801.3	683.4
Population, mid-year ('000)	986.7	1,008.0	1,063.0
Birth rate (per '000)	34.9	34.4	33.9
Death rate (per '000)	17.1	18.9	20.8
No. of households ('000)	157.5	161.8	171.4
Total exports (US$ million)	803.2	852.0	811.5
Total imports (US$ million)	1,071.7	1,124.0	1,032.0
Tourism receipts (US$ million)	35.0	36.7	32.4
Tourist spending (US$ million)	45.0	38.0	31.7

Average household size 2001 (persons)	6.23				
Urban population 2001 (%)	26.7				
Age analysis (%) (2001)	*0-14*	43.5	*15-64*	53.9	*65+* 2.7
Population by sex (%) (2001)	*Male*	48.0	*Female*	52.0	
Life expectancy (years) (2001)	*Male*	40.8	*Female*	41.5	
Infant mortality (deaths per '000 live births) (2001)	90.8				
Adult literacy (%) (1997)	77.5				

Sweden

Area (km^2) 449,790

Currency Swedish krona (SEK = 100 ore)

Location Sweden occupies the eastern and southern section of the Scandinavian peninsula which runs southwest from the Arctic Circle to meet with Denmark across the narrow sea channel which gives access to the Baltic from the North Sea. With a predominantly hilly and mountainous terrain, but without oil resources like Norway, it relies heavily on its heavily forested hills for much of its revenues. The main population centres are in the south and east. The capital is Stockholm.

Head of State HM King Carl XVI Gustaf (1973)

Head of Government Göran Persson (1996)

Ruling Party The Social Democratic Party leads a minority coalition with the Left Party and the Environment Party.

Political Structure Sweden is a constitutional monarchy in which the King appoints the prime minister on the basis of parliamentary advice. Legislative authority is vested in a unicameral 349-seat Parliament (Riksdag), which is elected by universal suffrage for a term of four years. Sweden became a full member of the EU in January 1995 - having been in the European Monetary System for many years. In 1998, parliament voted to join the Schengen accord which allows for border-free traffic within the EU.

Last Elections General elections in September 1998 were a setback for Persson and the ruling Socialist Party. The Socialists came away with 131 seats, down 20% from the result of the 1996 elections. Most of these losses were to the Left Party which saw its share of the vote double to 12%. The Socialist bloc, which includes the Social Democratic Party, the Left, the Greens and the Center, holds 208 seats in the parliament. The opposition Moderates and Christian Democrats both strengthened their presence in parliament.

Political Risk Repeated clashes between Swedish values and those of the country's immigrants have pushed the issue of immigration up higher on the political agenda. The growing number of problems between second-generation immigrants and their more tradition-minded parents is leading politicians to question Sweden's ability to integrate its ethnic minorities.

International Disputes Finland and Sweden disagree over the ownership of a group of islands in the Gulf of Bothnia, which Finland, the current owner, calls Ahvenanmaa and Sweden calls the Aaland Islands. The issue will not sour bilateral relations, however.

Economy The Swedish economy grew by 1.2% in 2001 and should see growth of 1.6% in 2002. In 2003, growth of 2.7% is forecast. Inflation was 2.6% in 2001 and is expected to be 2.3% in 2002. Prices are forecast to rise by 2.2% in 2003. The adverse external environment - especially in the high technology sector - impeded exports and has hurt consumer sentiment in Sweden. However, the weak krona improved the competitive position and, coupled with a supportive policy stance, should help the economy weather the downturn. The continued strength of employment and disposable income provides a sound basis for the growth of domestic demand. However, the incipient recovery is still somewhat fragile. It is especially vulnerable to the persistent weakness of the telecom sector, which contributed handsomely to productivity and export growth in recent years. Adverse confidence effects from declining asset markets could also inhibit the expected rebound in consumption. Moreover, large wage increases, low productivity growth and rigidities in product and labour markets could undermine the economy's supply response. Employment and participation rates in Sweden rose markedly and are now among the highest in the world, notably for women and older people. However, improvements in the functioning of the labour market are still needed. Wage growth must be restrained to reflect gains in productivity. The focus of active labour market policies is expected to shift gradually toward the long-term unemployed, job search support and improvements in the efficiency of programmes. Finally, the authorities hope to boost labour mobility by easing employment protection rules and by reducing housing market distortions. Meanwhile, the country's welfare model retains its popularity. The real test for the government may well be whether the welfare model of high taxes and generous benefits will cope with the next economic downturn better than it did in the 1990s.

Main Industries Agriculture accounts for 4% of GDP, while industry makes up 34% and services contribute the remainder. Farming is the main livelihood in large parts of the country, especially in the north; but elsewhere forestry and related products are the mainstays of the local economy. It is manufacturing, however, that dominates the Swedish economy. Sweden's large export sector, led by its engineering and forestry companies, has reaped the benefits of restructuring during the last decade. Manufactured exports fell sharply in 2002, however, with growth of just 1% expected after growth of 10% in 2001. Sweden is a leader in mobile phone usage and development of the mobile Internet. Biotechnology is another important emerging industry. The country's automotive trio (Volvo, Saab and Scania) have reorganised, consolidated some operations and sold off others in order to better compete in international markets. Similar tactics are being followed in the wood, newsprint and paper industries. As a result, the number of foreign-owned companies in Sweden continues to rise. Private consumption has been aided by sizeable real wage increases, declining unemployment, increased government transfers to households and rising asset prices, while investment is boosted by a combination of improved profit conditions, a healthy economic outlook and lower interest rates.

Energy Sweden has no indigenous fuels except for its hydroelectric energy, and its decision to shut down its nuclear power plants by the year 2010 is causing problems. In a normal year, about half of the country's electric power is produced by 12 commercial nuclear reactors.

	1999	2000	2001
Inflation (% change)	0.5	1.0	2.6
Exchange rate (per US$)	8.26	9.16	10.33
Interest rate (% per annum, lending rate)	5.5	5.8	
GDP (% real growth)	4.1	3.6	1.2
GDP (Billion units of national currency)	1,994.9	2,098.5	2,167.3
GDP (US$ million)	241,436.7	229,032.5	209,821.3
GDP per capita (US$)	27,256.3	25,834.9	23,649.1
Consumption (Billion units of national currency)	961.6	1,014.1	1,048.9
Consumption (US$ million)	116,386.6	110,687.0	101,551.2
Consumption per capita (US$)	13,139.2	12,485.5	11,445.9
Population, mid-year ('000)	8,858.0	8,865.2	8,872.3
Birth rate (per '000)	9.4	9.0	8.6
Death rate (per '000)	10.6	10.6	10.6
No. of households ('000)	4,349.2	4,365.8	4,381.7
Total exports (US$ million)	84,836.2	78,852.0	75,139.5
Total imports (US$ million)	68,620.7	72,632.2	62,670.2
Tourism receipts (US$ million)	3,894.0	4,608.2	3,704.5
Tourist spending (US$ million)	7,557.0	6,542.4	6,249.0

Average household size 2001 (persons)	2.03				
Urban population 2001 (%)	83.4				
Age analysis (%) (2001)	*0-14*	18.3	*15-64*	64.4	*65+* 17.3
Population by sex (%) (2001)	*Male*	49.4	*Female*	50.6	
Life expectancy (years) (2001)	*Male*	77.4	*Female*	82.4	
Infant mortality (deaths per '000 live births) (2001)	3.2				
Adult literacy (%) (1998)	99.0				

TRADING PARTNERS

Major export destinations 2001 (% share)

USA	11.2
GERMANY	10.0
UNITED KINGDOM	7.6
NORWAY	6.2

Major import sources 2001 (% share)

GERMANY	18.2
UNITED KINGDOM	8.3
NETHERLANDS	7.3
NORWAY	7.2

Switzerland

Area (km^2)   41,285

Currency   Swiss franc (CHF = 100 centimes/rappen)

Location   Centrally located in southern Europe, Switzerland's three official languages (French, German and Italian) reflect its three most important neighbours - although Austria to the east is also a major trade partner. Switzerland represents Liechtenstein at diplomatic level. The capital is Berne.

Head of State   President Kaspar Villiger (2002)

Head of Government   Kaspar Villiger (2002)

Ruling Party   Power is shared by the Christian Democrats (CVP), Radical Democrats (FDP) and Social-Democratic Party of Switzerland (SPS).

Political Structure   Switzerland is a federation of 20 cantons and 6 half-cantons which include German, French, Italian and Romansch speakers. The first three of these are official languages, while Romansch is a "semi-official" language. There is a high degree of political devolution. At the federal level, the executive president is elected every year from among the 7-member Cabinet. There is a 200-member Nationalrat (Lower House of Parliament).

Last Elections   Elections to the Nationalrat took place in October 1999. The Swiss People's Party/Democratic Centre Union received 23% of the votes and claimed 44 seats in the Lower House and 7 in the Upper House. The SPS took 23% of the ballots, 51 seats in the Lower House and 6 in the Upper House. The FDP won 20% of the vote, gaining 43 seats in the Lower House and 18 in the Upper House. The CVP received 16% of the vote, 35 seats in the Lower House and 15 in the Upper House. In May 2000, voters approved seven bilateral agreements that will strengthen the country's commercial relations with the EU.

Political Risk   For a country that has long been regarded as one of Europe's most secretive financial centres, the demands of the EU and the US that Swiss banks provide much more transparency in their dealings with foreigners is proving to be a difficult one.

International Disputes   Switzerland still does not recognise tax evasion as a crime and refuses to lift bank secrecy for fiscal crimes. This stance puts it at odds with other members of the OECD. The EU's proposed directive on the taxation of savings also envisages an exchange of information which will pose a serious challenge for Switzerland's bank secrecy law.

Economy   GDP rose by 1.3% in 2001. Growth will be just 0.8% in 2002 and 2.6% in 2003. Inflation was 1% in 2001 and the same rate is forecast for 2002 and 2003. The Swiss National Bank reacted swiftly to the significant weakening of inflation pressures associated with softer-than-expected economic activity and the sharp appreciation of the Swiss franc after 11 September 2001. As a result of the interest rate cuts, monetary conditions are currently expansionary. Nonetheless, inflation risks still appear very low. Fiscal policy is also supporting recovery, although its role is constrained. The Confederation's budget appears to be heading toward a deficit of CHF2-2.5 billion in 2002. Switzerland has a competitive export sector, including a vibrant financial services industry, which has adapted to the discipline of an upward trend in the real exchange rate for many years. It is likely that the externally-oriented sector will need to continue to live with such discipline in the future given the large balance of payments surplus. By contrast, vitality in the more sheltered domestic markets has been much less impressive and it is here that improved performance will be needed if the economy's growth potential is to be fulfilled.

Main Industries   Switzerland's agricultural sector is small and relatively inefficient. The country's 73,000 farmers derive 75% of their farming income from subsidies, and they benefit from one of the world's more protected markets. Tourism, especially winter sports, is one of the most important parts of the economy but has been hurt by the downturn in the industry after 11 September 2001 and intense competition from other tourist-based economies. Industrial production is expected to grow by 5.3% in 2002 but has been hit by a fall in investment, especially in the information technology industry. The ranks of Swiss corporations have also been swelled by a number of companies emerging from the country's medical technology sector which are capitalising on the country's traditional strengths in pharmaceutical and precision engineering. Switzerland remains the undisputed capital of the offshore private banking industry. It is under pressure from its neighbours to relax its laws on bank secrecy but that now appears to be unlikely. The country's large internationally active banks have suffered from the recent asset market volatility and the global economic slowdown. The domestically-oriented banks are well capitalised, but their lower level of underlying profitability makes them sensitive to the economic cycle. Government authorities hope to bolster the efficiency of the domestic banking system by further consolidation. The large insurance sector has a good track record, but strains are emerging following the terrorist attacks in the US and lower financial market returns. If lower returns persist, some institutions could face difficulties in meeting mandatory rates of return. A number of Swiss multinationals are among the world's leaders but generate the bulk of their profits outside the country. The overseas investments of these huge companies exceed the size of the domestic economy and are an important reason for the country's high standard of living. These companies are already well entrenched in the EU and the fact that Switzerland is not an EU member presents no problem for them as it does for small and medium-sized companies..

Energy   Switzerland has no indigenous fuel sources whatever, apart from its hydroelectric potential and is forced to rely on nuclear power to an unusual degree. All other fuels must be imported.

	1999	2000	2001
Inflation (% change)	0.8	1.6	1.0
Exchange rate (per US$)	1.50	1.69	1.69
Interest rate (% per annum, lending rate)	3.9	4.3	4.3
GDP (% real growth)	1.6	3.0	1.3
GDP (Million units of national currency)	388,568.0	404,392.0	416,748.0
GDP (US$ million)	258,674.6	239,449.6	246,945.7
GDP per capita (US$)	36,247.8	33,431.9	34,351.5
Consumption (Million units of national currency)	226,541.7	234,237.7	239,955.1
Consumption (US$ million)	150,811.6	138,697.4	142,186.4
Consumption per capita (US$)	21,133.1	19,364.9	19,778.9
Population, mid-year ('000)	7,136.3	7,162.3	7,188.8
Birth rate (per '000)	9.7	9.4	9.0
Death rate (per '000)	9.5	9.6	9.7
No. of households ('000)	3,121.1	3,141.8	3,164.1
Total exports (US$ million)	76,122.2	74,865.2	78,066.4
Total imports (US$ million)	75,437.9	76,070.3	77,070.5
Tourism receipts (US$ million)	7,739.0	8,268.2	7,077.5
Tourist spending (US$ million)	6,842.0	7,037.4	6,771.0

Average household size 2001 (persons)	2.28				
Urban population 2001 (%)	63.3				
Age analysis (%) (2001)	*0-14*	17.3	*15-64*	67.2	*65+* 15.4
Population by sex (%) (2001)	*Male*	48.8	*Female*	51.2	
Life expectancy (years) (2001)	*Male*	75.8	*Female*	82.2	
Infant mortality (deaths per '000 live births) (2001)	5.0				
Adult literacy (%) (1997)	99.0				

TRADING PARTNERS

Major export destinations 2001 (% share)

GERMANY	19.2
USA	10.6
FRANCE	9.9
ITALY	9.2

Major import sources 2001 (% share)

GERMANY	27.6
FRANCE	12.6
USA	10.9
ITALY	9.8

▪ Syria

Area (km^2)   185,680

Currency   Syrian pound (Syr = 100 piastres)

Location   Syria owes its unusual political influence to its position in the extreme northeast of the Mediterranean, where the Islamic Middle East meets with Israel on the one hand and secular Turkey on the other. Its Mediterranean coastline, in fact, is no more than 150km. More important is the country's long eastern and southeastern border with Iraq and Jordan, and that with Lebanon and Israel in the southwest. The climate is cool Middle Eastern, with occasional cold winters. The capital is Damascus.

Head of State   President Bashar al Assad (2000)

Head of Government   Mohammad Mustafa Miro (2000)

Ruling Party   Ba'ath Party leads the National Progressive Front coalition.

Political Structure   The country's 1973 Constitution calls for an executive president who is formally elected by universal suffrage every seven years. In principle, the president answers to a People's Assembly of 250 members who are elected for four years. However, the Alawite group has dominated Syrian politics since Hafez al Assad seized power in 1970. Most decisions are taken by the ruling Ba'ath Arab Socialist Renaissance party.

Last Elections   Elections to the People's Assembly were held in December 1998 when the Ba'ath Party and its allies won 167 of the 250 seats and went on to reform the existing coalition. Independents won the other 83 seats - the same number as in the previous elections. Hafez al Assad was reconfirmed as president after being approved in an uncontested national referendum in February 1999. He died in June 2000 and was replaced by his son.

Political Risk   Hafez Assad dominated his country for many years and groomed his son to succeed him. Bashar made some early gestures at reform but the old guard has now managed to rein in his efforts.

International Disputes   Syria demands that Israel withdraw to the line Syria held in 1967 before the 6-day war. Israel insists that the international frontier, demarcated by France and Britain in 1923, should be the boundary between the two countries. In 2001, Syria began to withdrawn some of its 35,000 troops from Lebanon but has not released its grip on its smaller neighbour. Syria's relations with Iraq have begun to improve after nearly two decades of hostility. Its relations with Turkey are occasionally tense because it claims the Hatay Province lying south of the two countries' 1921-1939 boundary.

Economy   GDP increased by 3.5% in 2001 and inflation was just 1%. With its rapidly rising population (around 2.5% per year), Syria's current growth rate is far below the estimated 5% rate the country is estimated to need in order to make significant economic progress. The largely state-owned economy continues to be hurt by low investment levels, fiscal imbalances and distortions (such as subsidies), an overvalued currency at the fixed exchange rate (for "essential" transactions), high levels of foreign debt, a hard currency shortage, falling exports, and other problems, including rapid population growth rates. According to the Syrian government, the country's unemployment rate is under 10%, although according to private analysts, the rate is more likely over 20%. Economists estimate that more than US$50 billion has been sent abroad by Syrians, rendering the country short of capital. Economic reforms are proceeding, but at a snail's pace. The style of the reforms also makes businessmen cautious rather than optimistic. The approach of the government has changed since Bashar took over from his father. A mild attempt at reforms was launched in 2000 and continues today. Initiatives included a slew of laws aimed at prodding the stalled economy into motion. Opposition is growing, however, mainly from those who have accumulated a huge amount of wealth by using the corrupt system. Foreign debt is another problem, although perhaps US$10 billion of the country's approximately US$21.2 billion debt is owed to the former Soviet Union and is considered unlikely to be repaid.

Main Industries   Farming, which is the main activity, is concentrated mainly on the Mediterranean coastline. Most of the eastern area of the country is arid uplands but there are extensive irrigation schemes in the northeast, along the Euphrates. Cotton and tobacco are cash crops, while wheat, barley and fruit are grown for the domestic market. Farmers hope their economic position will improve as a result of the government's promise to extend irrigation schemes and to pay them world prices for their crops. Private investors, with financial backing from the Gulf States, have been expanding into various sectors (textiles, pharmaceuticals, food-processing and other light industries), many built by wealthy Syrians from abroad. Tourism in recent years (at least prior to the 11 September 2001 terrorist attacks on the US) appeared to be growing as well, accounting for about 8% of Syria's GDP. Still, along with agriculture, foreign aid and remittances from Syrian workers abroad, Syria relies heavily on the oil sector - for around 55-60% of total export revenues. Foreign banks are being allowed to set up, but the state institutions that have monopolised banking since 1963 remain so inept that it can take weeks to transfer money between branches. Development of the manufacturing sector is constrained by a host of obstacles including export taxes, a shortage of credit and a corrupt and sluggish bureaucracy. Phosphates and asphalt are mined but the country has ample deposits of other natural resources that have yet to be developed.

Energy   Syria's oil industry faces many challenges in the years to come. Oil output and production continues to decline due to technological problems and depletion of oil reserves. Since peaking at 604,000 barrels per day (bbl/d) in 1996, Syria's oil output fell steadily, to an estimated 527,000 bbl/d in 2001, as older fields have reached maturity. Syrian oil production is expected to continue its decline over the next several years, while consumption rises, leading to a reduction in Syrian net oil exports. If this trend continues, it is feared Syria could become a net oil importer within a decade. Syria hopes to reverse this trend through intensified oil and natural gas exploration and production efforts, plus a switch from oil-fired to natural-gas fired electric power plants. Syria also has opened up new blocks for oil and natural gas exploration.

	1999	2000	2001
Inflation (% change)	-2.1	-0.6	1.0
Exchange rate (per US$)	11.23	11.23	11.23
Interest rate			
GDP (% real growth)	-2.0	2.5	3.5
GDP (Million units of national currency)	823,662.0	868,060.0	920,174.0
GDP (US$ million)	73,377.5	77,332.7	81,975.4
GDP per capita (US$)	4,639.2	4,795.8	4,866.5
Consumption (Million units of national currency)	575,866.0	579,627.0	631,865.4
Consumption (US$ million)	51,302.1	51,637.1	56,290.9
Consumption per capita (US$)	3,243.5	3,202.3	3,341.7
Population, mid-year ('000)	15,816.8	16,125.0	16,845.0
Birth rate (per '000)	30.1	29.9	29.8
Death rate (per '000)	4.2	4.1	4.1
No. of households ('000)	3,243.0	3,272.5	3,371.1
Total exports (US$ million)	3,463.7	4,250.0	4,356.7
Total imports (US$ million)	3,831.6	3,860.0	4,332.4
Tourism receipts (US$ million)	1,360.0	1,409.4	1,299.6
Tourist spending (US$ million)	630.0	631.0	535.3

Average household size 2001 (persons)	4.93				
Urban population 2001 (%)	55.0				
Age analysis (%) (2001)	*0-14*	42.7	*15-64*	54.3	*65+* 3.0
Population by sex (%) (2001)	*Male*	50.4	*Female*	49.6	
Life expectancy (years) (2001)	*Male*	70.3	*Female*	72.7	
Infant mortality (deaths per '000 live births) (2001)	23.2				
Adult literacy (%) (1997)	71.6				

TRADING PARTNERS

Major export destinations 2001 (% share)		Major import sources 2001 (% share)	
GERMANY	21.7	ITALY	8.1
ITALY	18.7	GERMANY	6.7
FRANCE	10.0	FRANCE	5.9
TURKEY	7.8	SOUTH KOREA	5.5

■ Taiwan

Area (km²)   35,990

Currency   New Taiwan dollar (NT$ = 100 cents)

Location   Taiwan is principally located on what was formerly known as the island of Formosa. This is a territory no more than 400km from north to south which lies between the South China Sea and the East China Sea about 200km off the coast of mainland China and about 700km north-east of Hong Kong. The capital is Taipei.

Head of State   President Chen Shui-bian (2000)

Head of Government   Yu Shyi-kun (2002)

Ruling Party   The government is formed by the Democratic Progressive Party (MCT) and non-partisans.

Political Structure   The president is elected for a 4-year term by the people. Parliament has two chambers. The Legislative Yuan has 225 members, 168 members elected for 3-year terms in multi-seat constituencies, 8 members representing the aboriginals, 41 members elected by proportional representation and 8 members representing the overseas Chinese elected by proportional representation. When necessary, a National Assembly with some constitutional tasks has to be elected by proportional representation on an ad hoc basis.

Last Elections   The presidential election was held in March 2000. Chen Shui-bian received 39% of the ballots, James Soong got 38% and Lien Chan received 23%. Elections to parliament took place in December 2001. The MCT took 87 seats in the Yuan, the Nationalist Party won 68 seats and the People First Party claimed 13 seats. The remainder was divided among three smaller parties.

Political Risk   A growing number of Taiwanese believe that the island is adrift, lacking political leadership and facing diminished economic prospects. Meanwhile, China continues to attract not only Taiwanese investment but Taiwanese immigration. In a move that will step up an already factious political battle, the island's main opposition party now backs the idea of establishing a confederation with China. Another emerging problem is the degree of corruption and organised crime. Rapid growth has allowed people with highly questionable backgrounds to enter commercial and political life. More than a quarter of all council members are reported to have gangland backgrounds.

International Disputes   Taiwan's complicated relationships with the US and China should become clearer over the next several years. However, the removal of some of these ambiguities will not necessarily represent a move towards a more peaceful region. The Bush administration in the US is gradually embracing a closer political and military relationship with Taiwan than any US administration since the late 1970s. The first response of Beijing has been to increase the number and accuracy of missiles in the provinces facing Taiwan - 600 are expected to be deployed by 2005. Domestic opinions about the relationship with mainland China are tied in part to the strength of the economy. As times become harder, more people believe that Taiwan should cast its lot with China. There has been a steady rise in the number of Taiwanese who are ready to accept the "one country, two systems" arrangement, but Hong Kong's experience with this approach has also created many sceptics.

Economy   GDP should increase by a modest 2.3% in 2002 but growth should accelerate to 4.8% in 2003. Prices will rise very little in 2002 and increase by 1.6% in 2003. The investment outlook is constrained by uncertainty over information technology exports and the movement production facilities to the mainland. Both trends should grow as external demand conditions improve, but the relocation investment to the mainland and associated high unemployment rates are structural features of the island's economy that restrict growth potential in the medium term. The process of restructuring will require Taiwan to become a provider of high value-added services to the region, rather than a manufacturing hub. Furthermore, greater integration within the Association of South-East Asian Nations (ASEAN) and, possibly, the countries of South Asia may open up new markets for the country. This development would be a more fruitful approach than exclusive reliance on mainland China, where Taiwan faces stiff competition from Hong Kong.

Main Industries   Much of the slowdown stemmed from the slump in exports of information technology products and the transmission of the export slowdown to private consumption and gross fixed investment. The economy's information technology exports account for more than 50% of exports of goods and services. The poor trade performance and associated recession in manufacturing pushed all components of domestic demand growth into negative territory in the second half of 2001. The severity of the downturn was exacerbated by a rising inventory-to-shipment ratio, indicating that the downward adjustment of stocks had not been large enough to adjust to falling sales. This partly explains why industrial production contracted over most of 2001. In the services sector, employment relative to that in industry increased by roughly 2% of the total labour force. However, employment growth in services did not fully offset the shrinkage of employment in manufacturing. Good weather contributed to a strong performance in the agriculture sector. Agriculture still provides the major source of employment, with production of sugar, yams, rice, tea and bananas, as well as vegetables and fruit.

Energy   Taiwan's current crude oil production is under 1,000 bbl/d. Most oil imports come from the Persian Gulf, though West African countries also are important suppliers for Taiwan. To ensure against a supply disruption, Taiwan's refiners are under a regulatory requirement to maintain stocks of no less than 60 days of consumption. Taiwan's government has announced plans to further liberalise the petroleum sector. Taiwan's legislature passed the Petroleum Administration Act in September 2001, which will permit the eventual sale of a majority stake in the Chinese Petroleum Corporation (CPC), a government-operated firm, to take place by mid-2004. Foreign firms will be allowed to acquire stakes in CPC on an equal basis with domestic investors. Despite the lack of formal ties between Taipei and Beijing, the two countries have developed a cooperative relationship in the field of energy. CPC and Beijing's state-owned China National Offshore Oil Corporation signed a deal to explore a 5,939-sq mile area in the Tainan Basin of the Taiwan Strait. Geologists have reportedly identified several structures considered worthy of exploration, and the two firms have expressed interest in forming a joint venture company to carry out exploratory drilling in the area.

	1999	2000	2001
Inflation (% change)	0.2	1.3	
Exchange rate (per US$)	32.22	33.50	32.85
Interest rate			
GDP (% real growth)	5.4	5.9	-1.9
GDP (Billion units of national currency)	9,276.5	10,363.3	9,271.6
GDP (US$ million)	287,884.0	309,385.0	282,239.0
GDP per capita (US$)	12,978.5	13,861.0	12,561.0
Consumption (Billion units of national currency)	5,662.6	6,176.2	5,955.8
Consumption (US$ million)	175,732.0	184,382.8	181,301.5
Consumption per capita (US$)	7,922.4	8,260.7	8,068.8
Population, mid-year ('000)	22,181.6	22,320.5	22,469.5
Birth rate (per '000)	15.0	15.0	14.9
Death rate (per '000)	5.7	5.7	5.8
No. of households ('000)	6,431.0	6,576.0	6,732.9
Total exports (US$ million)	121,496.0	147,777.0	122,505.0
Total imports (US$ million)	110,957.0	139,927.0	107,274.0
Tourism receipts (US$ million)	3,571.0	3,605.1	3,013.1
Tourist spending (US$ million)	5,635.0	6,184.8	5,472.5

Average household size 2001 (persons)	3.39					
Urban population 2001 (%)	77.5					
Age analysis (%) (2001)	*0-14*	20.7	*15-64*	70.6	*65+*	8.7
Population by sex (%) (2001)	*Male*	51.1	*Female*	48.9		
Life expectancy (years) (2001)	*Male*	75.4	*Female*	71.7		
Infant mortality (deaths per '000 live births) (2001)	5.9					
Adult literacy (%)						

▪ Tajikistan

Area (km^2)   143,100

Currency   Somoni (1S=1000 roubles)

Location   Tajikistan, almost the southernmost point of the former Soviet Union, is a predominantly Muslim state which borders on Afghanistan and China in the south. But for the Hindu Kush, a narrow tongue of Afghan territory, it would also meet Pakistan. In the west it borders on Uzbekistan and in the north-east on Kyrgyzstan. With a mainly dry climate but with well-irrigated soil, it produces cotton and similar crops. The capital is Dushanbe.

Head of State   Imamali Sharipovich Rakhmonov

Head of Government   Yakhiye Azimov (1996)

Ruling Party   The government is formed by the People's Democratic Party of Tajikistan (HDKT).

Political Structure   Tajikistan declared its independence from the Soviet Union in August 1991. A civil war followed when ex-communists from the west of the country deposed an alliance of Islamists and secular democrats from the east. Parliament has two chambers. The Assembly of Representatives has 63 members, elected for a 5-year term - 22 by proportional representation and 41 in single-seat constituencies. The National Assembly will have 33 members, 25 elected for a 5-year term by local deputies and 8 appointed by the president. The National Assembly has yet to be constituted.

Last Elections   The country held its first parliamentary election in March 2000. The HDKT won 30 seats while the communists took 13 seats. Non-partisans claimed another 15 with the remainder being divided among smaller parties. Presidential elections were held in November 1999, when Rakhmonov, a former chairman of the Supreme Soviet, was re-elected as head of state with 97% of the vote.

Political Risk   Tajikistan is a country of regional and ethnic conflicts. The successful conclusion of the peace process that began with the peace agreement of 1997 marking the end of the civil war was of crucial importance to stability and the country's potential to continue its economic recovery. A sharp economic division between the wealthy north of the country and the politically dominant south continues to plague the country. In 2000, Tajikistan became the only state in the region to have legalised an Islamic opposition party.

International Disputes   Tajikistan's one million Uzbeks were left out of the latest peace agreement and have little to lose by continuing to resist the present government. They are supported by Uzbekistan. Islamic insurgents in Tajikistan have carried out frequent raids in neighbouring Uzbekistan and Kyrgyzstan and are supported by the country's Islamic politicians. Russian troops continue to be based in Tajikistan today, long after conclusion of the peace agreement.

Economy   2001. The agriculture sector, which accounts for about 20% of GDP and more than half total employment, performed very well. Despite continued drought, it recorded an 11% expansion, fuelled mainly by a 35% increase in cotton production, which stemmed from an increase in both planted and irrigated areas and from the low-base effect of low output in 2000. The economy is highly dependent on foreign trade, with exports equivalent to 70% of GDP. Cotton and aluminium are responsible for over 80% of export earnings, rendering the economy extremely vulnerable to terms-of-trade shifts caused by fluctuations in international prices and, indeed, the prices of these two major exports deteriorated considerably in 2001: cotton, for example, fell by 35%. In addition, production of goods for export was severely hampered by a 2-month closure of the railway connection between Tajikistan and the Russian Federation - the country's major trading partner. Some conservative estimates put the loss of export earnings at about US$8 million, approximately 1% of total exports. Imports increased, but at a slower rate than in 2000. Wheat and power imports rose as a result of the drought.

Main Industries   Tajikistan's impressive growth has been led by a substantial increase in aluminium production. However, other industry subsectors languished, so while overall industrial production rose by 14.1%, industrial output (excluding aluminium) shrank by 5% in

Energy   Tajikistan has the lowest per capita GDP in the former Soviet Union. However, its economy has performed reasonably well. GDP is expected to rise by 6% in 2002 and 5% in 2003. The pace of inflation should slow with prices rising by around 10.5% in 2002 and 7.6% in 2003. The government derives its main revenues from sales taxes on cotton and aluminium (37% of the revenue base), as well as from excise and customs duties. The tax base of the private sector is very narrow, and neither personal nor corporate income tax yet plays a significant role. Economic growth, in which the driving force is rising capital-intensive aluminium production, has so far failed to have much of an impact on formal sector employment or the level of poverty. While the official unemployment rate fell to 2.8% in 2001 from 3.3% in 2000, unofficial estimates put the unemployment or underemployment rate much higher, at over 30%. Burdened by many non-performing loans, mostly extended in the form of direct credits to state-owned enterprises, or privatised enterprises with strong state connections, the banking sector remains paralysed. Lending to the private sector is at a virtual standstill.

	1999	2000	2001
Inflation (% change)	27.6	32.9	38.6
Exchange rate (per US$)	1.24	1.82	2.40
Interest rate			
GDP (% real growth)	3.7	8.3	10.0
GDP (Billion units of national currency)	1.3	1.8	2.6
GDP (US$ million)	1,086.0	991.0	1,084.0
GDP per capita (US$)	180.5	162.4	175.0
Consumption (Billion units of national currency)	1.0	1.4	1.9
Consumption (US$ million)	835.8	753.0	805.8
Consumption per capita (US$)	138.9	123.4	130.1
Population, mid-year ('000)	6,015.4	6,103.7	6,195.2
Birth rate (per '000)	27.1	26.1	25.3
Death rate (per '000)	6.5	6.4	6.3
No. of households ('000)	1,349.3	1,353.7	1,343.5
Total exports (US$ million)	666.0	792.0	580.0
Total imports (US$ million)	663.0	674.0	775.0
Tourism receipts (US$ million)			
Tourist spending (US$ million)	6,015.4	6,103.7	6,195.2

Average household size 2001 (persons)	4.54				
Urban population 2001 (%)	27.5				
Age analysis (%) (2001)	*0-14* 40.1		*15-64* 55.4		*65+* 4.5
Population by sex (%) (2001)	*Male* 49.8		*Female* 50.2		
Life expectancy (years) (2001)	*Male* 60.9		*Female* 69.0		
Infant mortality (deaths per '000 live births) (2001)	54.4				
Adult literacy (%) (1997)	98.9				

TRADING PARTNERS

Major export destinations 2001 (% share)

NETHERLANDS	29.8
RUSSIA	16.1
UZBEKISTAN	13.4
TURKEY	11.5

Major import sources 2001 (% share)

UZBEKISTAN	12.9
RUSSIA	11.1
KAZAKHSTAN	7.6
UKRAINE	5.4

■ Tanzania

Area (km^2)   939,760

Currency   Tanzanian shilling (Tsh = 100 cents)

Location   Tanzania is located on the central east African coast bordering the Indian Ocean, and comprises the mainland territory of Tanganyika and the islands of Zanzibar and Pemba. Tanganyika is bounded in the north by Uganda and Kenya, in the west by Rwanda, Burundi and the Democratic Republic of the Congo (formerly Zaire), and in the south by Zambia, Malawi and Mozambique. The capital is Dar es Salaam.

Head of State   President Benjamin Mkapa (1996)

Head of Government   Fredierick Sumaye (1996)

Ruling Party   The government is formed by the Revolutionary Party of Tanzania (CCM).

Political Structure   The Republic of Tanzania is an independent member of the Commonwealth, whose executive president is elected for a maximum of two 5-year terms by popular vote. Legislative authority is vested in a unicameral National Assembly, which serves for a 5-year term. The 274-member Assembly includes 232 directly elected with 37 seats allocated to women nominated by the president and five seats are allocated to members of the Zanzibar House of Representatives. Zanzibar has its own House of Representatives of 59 members, which legislates on internal matters. Until 1992 the CCM was the only legal political party.

Last Elections   Elections to the National Assembly were held in October 2000. The Revolutionary Party of Tanzania (CCM) won 244 seats. The remaining seats are scattered among several parties. Presidential elections were held in October 2000. Benjamin Mkapa was declared the winner with 71% of the vote.

Political Risk   There are deep divisions between Islamic and Christian communities. Many voters on Zanzibar's two islands would prefer independence from the mainland but tensions have eased under Mkapa's leadership. The country has repaired its ties to international donors, leading to a resumption of aid.

International Disputes   Tanzania has a disagreement with Malawi over the ownership of territorial water rights in Lake Nyasa (called Lake Malawi by Malawi) where their borders meet. The issue remains technical, however, and has not caused major strains.

Economy   Tanzania's GDP rose by 5.1% in 2001 and is forecast to increase by 5.5% in 2002 and 6% in 2003. Inflation was 5.2% in 2001. Prices should rise by 4.4% in 2002 and 3.9% in 2003. Under the current budget, the deficit for 2002 is expected to increase to 3.1% of GDP. The revenue-to-GDP ratio is expected to be 12.2%, while government expenditures will increase from 13.4% of GDP in 2001 to 15.3% in 2002. Import tariffs are being consolidated and simplified and tariffs will be reduced on all trade within the Southern African Development Community. Private investors now receive generous tax breaks and profits can be repatriated. Foreign banks are welcome and the power of trade unions has been tempered. Structural reforms to deepen financial and capital markets are expected to provide additional resources for private sector investment. The country's low levels of saving are the main drag on growth but dilapidated infrastructure (poor roads, costly electricity and inadequate water) also push up the costs of doing business. Other problems include a bloated bureaucracy and a culture that thrives on petty corruption. Tanzania remains one of the world's poorest countries.

Main Industries   Agriculture is the backbone of the economy, accounting for almost half of GDP and providing a livelihood for 85% of the population. Farming is subject to frequent droughts and flooding but the country has huge fertile zones which are still untouched and could be a major food producer if its farming system can be better organised. Agricultural output rose in 2001 thanks to good rainfalls. The mainland's leading exports include: coconuts, coffee, tea, cotton and groundnuts, while Zanzibar is a worldwide supplier of spices. Although the country's traditional exports fell by 3% in 2001, non-traditional exports grew by nearly 40%. The latter mainly reflects the production of new gold mines and a resumption of fish exports to EU countries. Imports were slightly lower than in 2000 because of sharp declines in capital goods and food imports - after the completion of major investment projects in the mining sector and recovery from drought, respectively Tanzania is rich in mineral deposits, including gold and diamonds. Investors from Australia, Canada and South Africa are all putting money into the mining sector. Spending on exploration is beginning to fall but investment in mining has risen substantially since 1998. The country has huge potential for tourism, with bigger herds of wildlife in better game parks than its neighbour, Kenya. The government aims to increase the total number of visitors to more than half a million in the next few years.

Energy   Tanzania relies exclusively on imports for its oil needs. While foreign oil prospectors have invested more than US$242 million in search of oil in Tanzania without success since 1981, the government in Dar es Salaam continues to encourage oil exploration in the country. State-owned Tanzania Petroleum Development Corporation has signed several joint venture agreements with foreign oil exploration companies in recent years. Experts have long suspected that there are considerable hydrocarbon reserves off Tanzania's coast. Tanzania plans to develop two offshore gas fields to provide fuel for power generation. Gas from these fields will be transported to Dar es Salaam by a 160-mile (250-km) pipeline, where it will be used to generate electricity. The pipeline could be extended to the Kenyan port city of Mambasa to supply gas for industrial usage and power generation.

	1999	2000	2001
Inflation (% change)	9.0	6.2	5.2
Exchange rate (per US$)	744.76	800.41	876.41
Interest rate (% per annum, lending rate)	21.9	21.6	20.3
GDP (% real growth)	3.5	5.1	5.1
GDP (Billion units of national currency)	6,432.9	7,225.7	7,992.3
GDP (US$ million)	8,637.6	9,027.5	9,119.3
GDP per capita (US$)	262.2	269.3	262.2
Consumption (Billion units of national currency)	5,667.4	6,069.6	6,435.8
Consumption (US$ million)	7,609.8	7,583.1	7,343.4
Consumption per capita (US$)	231.0	226.2	211.1
Population, mid-year ('000)	32,942.0	33,517.0	34,785.0
Birth rate (per '000)	39.6	39.1	38.5
Death rate (per '000)	13.2	13.2	13.1
No. of households ('000)	6,127.9	6,254.9	6,515.8
Total exports (US$ million)	543.1	663.2	687.3
Total imports (US$ million)	1,556.4	1,523.5	1,750.3
Tourism receipts (US$ million)	733.0	715.6	542.0
Tourist spending (US$ million)	550.0	569.1	543.7

Average household size 2001 (persons)	5.36				
Urban population 2001 (%)	33.3				
Age analysis (%) (2001)	*0-14*	45.8	*15-64*	51.7	*65+* 2.6
Population by sex (%) (2001)	*Male*	49.5	*Female*	50.5	
Life expectancy (years) (2001)	*Male*	50.1	*Female*	52.1	
Infant mortality (deaths per '000 live births) (2001)	74.9				
Adult literacy (%) (1997)	71.6				

TRADING PARTNERS

Major export destinations 2001 (% share)

INDIA	14.8
BELGIUM	9.5
JAPAN	7.8
GERMANY	7.5

Major import sources 2001 (% share)

SOUTH AFRICA	13.3
UNITED KINGDOM	6.3
KENYA	6.2
INDIA	5.9

■ Thailand

Area (km^2) 514,000

Currency Baht (Bt = 100 satangs)

Location Thailand, although the largest state in the Indo-Chinese peninsula, has access to the sea only in the far south. With Myanmar accounting for almost all of its shoreline with the Bay of Bengal, its access to that sea is limited to a long but narrow (150-km wide) isthmus to the south which eventually links up with Malaysia. Its more extensive coastline is on the Gulf of Thailand, where it borders Cambodia in the east. In the north-east it shares a border with Laos. The capital is Bangkok.

Head of State HM King Bhumibol Adulyadej (1946)

Head of Government Thaksin Shinawatra (2001)

Ruling Party The government is formed by a 3-party coalition led by the Thai Love Thai Party (TLT).

Political Structure The National Assembly has two chambers. The House of Representatives has 438 members, elected for a 4-year term, 100 members by proportional representation and 338 members in multi-seat constituencies. The Senate has 200 members elected in single-seat constituencies. Only non-partisans are allowed to run for office.

Last Elections General elections to the House of Representatives were held in January 2001. The TLT won 248 seats and the Democratic Party took 128 seats. The remainder were scattered among several minor parties. The TLT appointed Thaksin Shinawatra as prime minister. The Election Commission disqualified some victors on grounds of vote fraud. The Senate was previously made up of appointed members and has yet to be re-constituted.

Political Risk As a result of successive deficit-spending measures to stimulate the economy and support finance sector restructuring, public debt rose substantially. Total public debt outstanding amounted to about Bt2.9 trillion at the end of 2001, equivalent to around 57% of GDP. In 1996, prior to the financial crisis, the ratio of public debt to GDP was 15%. If debt continues to escalate, it could pose risks over the medium term, as an increasing debt service burden will constrain public expenditure options. Dangers of a much different type are posed by Thailand's huge drugs and sex industries. Infection rates for HIV began to soar in the late 1990s.

International Disputes Thailand's relations with Myanmar are strained owing to the influx of drugs and amphetamines from its neighbour. Similar problems exist with Laos. Western governments have pressured Thailand to take an even more stringent stand against these outlaws.

Economy Real GDP should rise by 2.7% in 2002 and 3.5% in 2003. A negligible price rise is expected in 2002 along with inflation of 2.7% in 2003. On a variety of indicators, the economy's external financial vulnerability is improving. By the end of 2001, total external debt fell to US$69 billion, from US$80 billion at the end of 2000. The reduction in debt was largely due to the liquidation of private sector foreign exchange liabilities. The baht depreciated from an average of 40 to the US dollar in 2000 to an average of 44.5 to the US dollar in 2001, which was broadly in line with the depreciation of other regional currencies against the US dollar. In the face of the weakening external demand, domestic demand recovery is crucial to economic growth. The government plans deficit-spending measures to support domestic demand. In 2002, a budget deficit equivalent to 3.8% of GDP was targeted. The new measures include higher spending on a public health programme, a village and urban revolving fund, a tourism promotion programme, a debt-suspension programme for farmers and housing credit support for government officials. The proportion of non-performing loans (NPLs) - defined as loans for which payment is at least three months overdue - had decreased to about 10% of the total by the end of 2001, down from about 18% at the end of 2000. To overcome a variety of obstacles to debt restructuring and to promote efficient management of NPLs, the government established the Thai Asset Management Company (TAMC) in 2001. By January 2002, the TAMC took over approximately US$16 billion in NPLs, mostly from state-owned banks. By the end of 2002, the TAMC is expected to have restructured about 70% of this debt. Thailand has been slower than expected to resolve the problems associated with the region's last crisis. This applies in particular to the issue of NPLs. Another issue that troubles analysts is concern over the country's willingness to exit from some of those industries where competitiveness had previously depended on an overvalued currency and cheap wages.

Main Industries Expansion of industrial output (which accounts for about 44% of GDP) decelerated to 1.3% in 2001 from 5.3% in 2000. The manufacturing production index, which covers about 63% of overall value added in manufacturing, rose by only 1.1%, a decline from 3.3% in 2000. The capacity utilisation rate slipped to 53.3%, from 56% in 2000. The slowdown in activity was most evident among export-oriented industries, including electronics. However, domestic-oriented industries, such as vehicles and parts, beverages and ornaments, fared somewhat better. Growth in services (accounting for about 48% of GDP) moderated to 2.3% in 2001 from 4% in 2000, and was broadly in line with the general pace of economic activity. Virtually all subsectors experienced difficult conditions. Tourist arrivals dropped in the wake of the 11 September 2001 events in the US, and a moderation in consumption spending was felt in the retail sector and in other services activities. Growth in the agriculture sector (which accounts for about 8% of GDP) fell to only 1.5% in 2001, from 4.8% in 2000, partly due to the sluggish performance in production following a reduction in the area planted to rice and cassava.

Energy Thailand has 516 million barrels of proven oil reserves. In 2001, Thailand produced about 175,027 barrels per day (bbl/d) of oil. Of that production, about 114,027 bbl/d was crude oil. Most of the remainder was natural gas liquids. Oil consumption fell during the Asian financial crisis, but moved back up to 715,000 bbl/d in 2001. Part of the reason consumption has not recovered fully is that the government has been raising taxes on petroleum products, which is intended to promote conservation and to reduce oil imports. Despite the industry's financial problems, there have been a number of significant recent oil discoveries, most notably offshore in the Gulf of Thailand. The country's modest proven oil reserves rose in 2001, from 352 million barrels in January 2001 to 516 million barrels by the end of the year.

	1999	2000	2001
Inflation (% change)	0.3	1.5	1.7
Exchange rate (per US$)	37.81	40.11	44.43
Interest rate (% per annum, lending rate)	9.0	7.8	7.3
GDP (% real growth)	4.4	4.6	1.8
GDP (Billion units of national currency)	4,632.1	4,904.7	5,099.6
GDP (US$ million)	122,499.0	122,276.0	114,774.0
GDP per capita (US$)	2,002.8	1,985.0	1,851.4
Consumption (Billion units of national currency)	2,836.8	3,004.4	3,132.5
Consumption (US$ million)	75,020.2	74,901.2	70,500.1
Consumption per capita (US$)	1,226.6	1,215.9	1,137.2
Population, mid-year ('000)	61,163.3	61,600.7	61,991.9
Birth rate (per '000)	19.1	18.8	18.5
Death rate (per '000)	6.1	6.2	6.2
No. of households ('000)	15,503.6	15,662.3	15,709.2
Total exports (US$ million)	58,440.3	69,056.8	64,223.0
Total imports (US$ million)	50,342.0	61,923.9	62,057.7
Tourism receipts (US$ million)	6,695.0	6,105.6	4,940.3
Tourist spending (US$ million)	1,843.0	2,116.9	1,767.2

Average household size 2001 (persons)	3.93				
Urban population 2001 (%)	22.0				
Age analysis (%) (2001)	0-14	24.8	15-64	69.3	65+ 6.0
Population by sex (%) (2001)	Male	49.9	Female	50.1	
Life expectancy (years) (2001)	Male	67.6	Female	73.5	
Infant mortality (deaths per '000 live births) (2001)	22.4				
Adult literacy (%) (1997)	94.7				

TRADING PARTNERS

Major export destinations 2001 (% share)		Major import sources 2001 (% share)	
USA	20.3	JAPAN	22.4
JAPAN	15.3	USA	11.6
SINGAPORE	8.1	CHINA	6.0
HONG KONG, CHINA	5.1	MALAYSIA	5.0

■ Togo

Area (km^2)   56,785

Currency   CFA franc (= 100 centimes)

Location   Togo is a narrow strip of land stretching north from the Atlantic coast of West Africa. It meets the Gulf of Guinea between Ghana in the west and Benin in the east. With a tropical climate, but with lower elevation than either Benin or Burkina Faso, the country has substantial agricultural capabilities. The capital is Lomé.

Head of State   President Gnassingbe Eyadema (1967)

Head of Government   Agbeyome Messan Kodjo (2000)

Ruling Party   The Rally of the Togolose People (RTP)

Political Structure   Although Togo has a non-executive president, he has retained significant powers during periods of unrest. The president is elected by popular vote and serves a 5-year term. The National Assembly has 81 members, elected for 5-year terms in single-seat constituencies.

Last Elections   Parliamentary elections were held in March 1999, when the RTP gained 79 of the 81 seats. The main opposition parties boycotted the elections. Presidential elections took place in June 1998. Eyadema was returned to office with 52% of the vote.

Political Risk   With a low level of personal spending power, but with substantial natural resources and commodities, Togo is a high-risk but potentially high-reward market for importers.

International Disputes   Togo's relations with its neighbours are frequently tense. The country demands the return of two areas of Ghana, the northern reaches of the Volta River in the east of the country and the southern coastal area around Lomé, which formed part of the former German Togoland. These areas were awarded to Ghana in 1919 in a partition between France and the UK, the two major colonial powers. The issue remains unresolved despite UN mediation and there have been accusations of maltreatment of minorities on both sides.

Economy   Growth was 2.7% in 2001, while inflation was 6.8%. The Togolese economy has performed poorly for the past several years and there is little prospect that this trend can be reversed in the short term. Low tax revenue, unrestrained expenditure and the suspension of external assistance have led to slippages in fiscal performance. The overall deficit has continued to increase and reached the equivalent of 5.8% of GDP in 2001. At end-2000, non-performing loans amounted to 42% of total claims and 7.4% of GDP. Delays in implementing structural reforms have also weakened the financial situation of public enterprises and the banking sector.

Main Industries   Agriculture is the dominant sector in Togo, accounting for more than 40% of GDP. Agriculture employs 60% of the workforce with the majority of the population depending on the cultivation of subsistence crops such as cassava, manioc and vegetables. Palm kernels, cocoa and copra are the main exports. The impact of and the loss of incentives for cotton producers since 2000 has hurt farmers. This was due to a decline in producer prices and delays in payments by the government monopoly in charge of cotton seed marketing. Moreover, the continued deterioration of the Togolese phosphate company's financial situation resulted in a sharp decline in phosphate production. Manufacturing activity is constrained by weak domestic demand and low levels of capacity utilisation, and growth in the services sector is modest. Progress in the implementation of the privatisation programme has been mixed. In 2000, the authorities signed a concession agreement with an international private group to take over the distribution and sales of electricity. This agreement is now operational. In addition, the authorities recently took steps to accelerate the privatisation of the banking sector, and progress has been made in the reform of the telecommunications and postal services. However, the reform of the remaining key public enterprises has been slow.

Energy   Togo has limited domestic fuel resources, apart from firewood, and is forced to import nearly all of its requirements from abroad. Electricity generation is of a low order and there is little exploitation of the country's hydroelectric potential. In 2000, the authorities signed a concession agreement with an international private group to take over the distribution and sales of electricity. This agreement is now operational.

	1999	2000	2001
Inflation (% change)	4.5	-2.5	6.8
Exchange rate (per US$)	615.70	711.98	733.04
Interest rate			
GDP (% real growth)	2.9	-1.9	2.7
GDP (Million units of national currency)	874,856.0	869,216.0	922,586.0
GDP (US$ million)	1,420.9	1,220.9	1,258.6
GDP per capita (US$)	313.1	263.7	259.3
Consumption (Million units of national currency)	752,200.0	820,000.0	851,290.1
Consumption (US$ million)	1,221.7	1,151.7	1,161.3
Consumption per capita (US$)	269.2	248.8	239.3
Population, mid-year ('000)	4,538.5	4,629.0	4,853.0
Birth rate (per '000)	39.9	39.5	39.1
Death rate (per '000)	13.7	13.5	13.4
No. of households ('000)	741.0	767.9	821.4
Total exports (US$ million)	391.4	362.9	226.1
Total imports (US$ million)	596.7	565.0	354.8
Tourism receipts (US$ million)	6.0	6.4	4.8
Tourist spending (US$ million)	2.0	2.1	1.4

Average household size 2001 (persons)	6.03				
Urban population 2001 (%)	33.9				
Age analysis (%) (2001)	*0-14*	45.9	*15-64*	50.9	*65+* 3.1
Population by sex (%) (2001)	*Male*	49.4	*Female*	50.6	
Life expectancy (years) (2001)	*Male*	50.9	*Female*	53.1	
Infant mortality (deaths per '000 live births) (2001)	76.9				
Adult literacy (%) (1997)	53.2				

TRADING PARTNERS

Major export destinations 2001 (% share)		Major import sources 2001 (% share)	
GHANA	22.4	FRANCE	18.5
BENIN	16.9	CANADA	6.3
BURKINA FASO	10.4	ITALY	5.9
PHILIPPINES	6.3	COTE D'IVOIRE	5.6

■ Tonga

Area (km²)   699

Currency   Pa'anga (T$ = 100 seniti)

Location   Tonga lies in the south-east of the important South Pacific Group which also includes Vanuatu, Fiji and the Solomon Islands. Its nearest major neighbour is New Zealand, more than 1,500km to the south. The capital is Nuku'alofa.

Head of State   HM King Taufa'ahau Tupou IV (1961)

Head of Government   Prince Lavaka Ata Ulukalala (2000)

Ruling Party   There are no official political parties in Tonga at present, although unofficial groupings exist.

Political Structure   The Kingdom of Tonga is a constitutional monarchy and an independent member of the Commonwealth. The King, who exercises full executive powers, is assisted by a 10-member privy council, or cabinet. Legislative powers are held by a 30-member unicameral Legislative Assembly. Apart from the King, the privy council and nine hereditary nobles, the Assembly includes nine members elected by universal adult suffrage. The issue of constitutional reform sharply divides members of the Assembly.

Last Elections   Elections to the nine available seats in the National Assembly were held in March 2002. The nine successful candidates belong to the democratic Human Rights and Democracy Movement.

Political Risk   Popular support for constitutional reform has periodically received a boost as instances of misconduct and corruption in the administration have become prevalent.

International Disputes   There are no international disputes.

Economy   Growth is slowing as GDP rose by only 3% in 2001. Even lower rates are expected in the future with growth of 2.9% in 2002 and 2.6% in 2003. Meanwhile inflation remains high. Prices rose by 7% in 2991 and should increase by 10% in 2002. The forecast is for inflation of 5% in 2003. The fiscal situation deteriorated in 2001 largely due to the civil servants' pay rise a shortfall in non-tax revenues and substantially increased spending to support certain ailing public enterprises. The wages' share of current expenditures reached 57% and the current budget was in deficit at about 0.5% of GDP. As of mid-2001 the assets of the Tonga Trust Fund which is held offshore and maintained separately from the budget and official foreign reserves fell steeply due to weak management. Credit to non-financial public enterprises more than doubled. The effectiveness of monetary policy remained constrained by the weakness of the balance sheet of the central bank which placed increased reliance on credit ceilings. Net private transfers from Tongans living abroad continued to be the major source of foreign exchange at about four times the value of exports. To improve fiscal performance the government has already begun to consider the extensive range of tax and tariff exemptions.

Main Industries   The general economic slowdown in recent years largely reflects slow growth in agriculture and tourism. Although there was a sharp decline in primary sector growth to 1.3% in 2001, the secondary sector grew by 5.4%, driven mainly by handicrafts manufacture, breadfruit production and processing of agricultural products. Activity in the construction and quarrying subsectors was also up by 9% as a result of several large aid-funded and private sector projects. The services sector as a whole expanded by 3.8% in 2001, but the performance of the subsectors displayed considerable variation. The commerce, hotels and restaurant subsector contracted by 2%, after significant expansion in 2000 due to millennium celebrations and conferences. The government administration and community services subsector, which accounts for some 18% of GDP, grew by 10% due mainly to a 20% pay rise for civil servants. Most other services subsectors recorded modest growth. The most promising industry in the country is tuna fishing, primarily for export, with more modest prospects in agriculture and tourism.

Energy   All of Tonga's fuel requirements, except for fuel wood, have to be imported at present.

	1999	2000	2001
Inflation (% change)	3.9	5.3	7.0
Exchange rate (per US$)	1.60	1.76	2.12
Interest rate (% per annum, lending rate)	10.3	10.7	9.9
GDP (% real growth)	3.1	6.2	3.0
GDP (Million units of national currency)	237.0	261.0	277.0
GDP (US$ million)	148.2	148.4	130.4
GDP per capita (US$)	1,512.3	1,499.2	1,304.4
Consumption (Million units of national currency)	121.1	189.3	195.1
Consumption (US$ million)	75.7	107.7	91.9
Consumption per capita (US$)	772.8	1,087.4	918.6
Population, mid-year ('000)	98.0	99.0	100.0
Birth rate (per '000)	25.2	24.9	24.6
Death rate (per '000)	6.1	6.0	5.9
No. of households ('000)	20.1	20.2	20.0
Total exports (US$ million)	12.0	11.0	13.0
Total imports (US$ million)	72.7	86.0	94.0
Tourism receipts (US$ million)	9.0	11.4	8.2
Tourist spending (US$ million)			

Average household size 2001 (persons)	4.91				
Urban population 2001 (%)	38.6				
Age analysis (%) (2001)	0-14	34.5	15-64	52.5	65+ 13.0
Population by sex (%) (2001)	Male	51.3	Female	48.7	
Life expectancy (years)					
Infant mortality (deaths per '000 live births) (2001)	38.8				
Adult literacy (%)					

TRADING PARTNERS

Major export destinations 2001 (% share)

JAPAN	51.1
USA	34.2
NEW ZEALAND	4.4
AUSTRALIA	1.6

Major import sources 2001 (% share)

NEW ZEALAND	32.9
FIJI	22.1
AUSTRALIA	11.1
THAILAND	8.1

Trinidad and Tobago

Area (km^2) 5,130

Currency Trinidad and Tobago dollar (T$ = 100 cents)

Location Trinidad is the most southerly island in the West Indies group, and lies just off the northern coast of Venezuela. Tobago, 32km northeast of Trinidad, is the more popular area for tourism, but there are also numerous small islands. The climate is warm, with a dry spring and a wet and often stormy autumn. The capital is Port-of-Spain.

Head of State President Arthur Napoleon Raymond Robinson (March 1997)

Head of Government Basdeo Panday (1995)

Ruling Party The United National Congress (UNC) leads a coalition with the National Alliance for Reconstruction (NAR).

Political Structure The Republic of Trinidad and Tobago is an independent member of the Commonwealth. The executive president is elected by parliament for a term of five years. Legislative power rests with the bicameral parliament, which consists of a 31-member Senate and a 36-member House of Representatives. The House is elected by universal suffrage for five years while the Senate is appointed - 16 members by the prime minister, six by the leader of the opposition and nine by the president. Tobago, the smaller of the two islands, has been independent from the UK since 1987 and has its own 12-member House of Assembly with some autonomous powers. In Tobago, politics run to quite a different agenda from those of Trinidad and the political complexion is very different.

Last Elections In presidential elections held in March 1997, Robinson took 67% of the popular vote. Elections to the House of Representatives were held in December 2001. The Indian-based United National Congress (UNC) won 18 seats and the People's National Movement (PNM) which is mainly black and has nearly always ruled, won the other 18 seats.

Political Risk The ethnic split between Indians who support the UNC and blacks who support the PNM continues. Three of Panday's own ministers have charged him with corruption, and defections from his party, the UNC, have left him with a minority in parliament. There are also differences between the citizens of Tobago and those of Trinidad. Politicians on Tobago suggest that there is a growing disparity in social services and are calling for secession.

International Disputes There are no international disputes.

Economy The economy grew by 4.5% in 2001 while prices rose by 2.5%. Once an economy of "boom and bust" depending on the fortunes of oil, Trinidad and Tobago is now entering a period of more stable growth as it shifts towards the utilisation of its expanding gas reserves. The country's per capita income is one of the highest in the Caribbean. Growth of about 4-5% is predicted in 2001. Fiscal policy remains expansionary. Though the central bank reports an overall surplus equivalent to 1.3% of GDP, a more realistic estimation is that the fiscal balance is in deficit. Without the windfall gains in oil revenues that benefited Trinidad and Tobago in 2000, that deficit would have reached an even higher level. Unemployment remains high, running at about 12.8%. Since 1995, Trinidad and Tobago has received foreign direct investment of more than US$5 billion and these inflows are expected to accelerate during the first half of this decade. A series of steps to promote exports (liberalisation of the trade and foreign exchange market and a change in the tax regime) have been introduced with modest success.

Main Industries Output of the petroleum sector (which consists of exploration and extraction of gas and oil, refining, petrochemical production and asphalt production) increased by 1% in 2001. Trinidad is also enjoying a natural-gas boom, with US$4 billion invested since 1998. The country's move from oil to liquid natural gas has spawned a growing petrochemical industry to make use of this resource. Meanwhile, the growth momentum of the non-petroleum sector was sustained. Robust growth rates were experienced in construction, distribution and transport, storage and communication sectors, with growth rates ranging from 7% to 9%. Growth in the construction sector, by 8%, reflected a significant increase in off-budget capital expenditures by the central government. Many manufacturers cater for local consumer needs, including textiles, food products, textiles and clothing. In the agricultural sector, output grew by 2.5%, reversing a 2-year cumulative decline of 17.5%. The increase was achieved despite flooding in late 2000 and problems with cocoa production. Farming is important on the islands with sugar, citrus fruits and copra being grown for export, while rice, coconuts, yams and bananas are produced for the domestic market. The non-oil sector now contributes 75% of GDP.

Energy Trinidad and Tobago is by far the Caribbean's largest producer of oil and gas, with oil production averaging about 140,000 barrels per day. Oil production, however, is slowly declining. Crude oil reserves, at an estimated 716 million barrels, are expected to last only another decade. In 2000, the country produced 490 billion cu ft of natural gas. Natural gas reserves, at an estimated 23.5 trillion cu ft, are expected to last for about 60 years. Both natural gas and oil exploration activities in Trinidad and Tobago continued at a fast pace in 2001 and into 2002. New discoveries of natural gas are eventually expected to push reserves up by another 100 trillion cu ft. Already, Trinidad and Tobago has become one of the major natural gas development centres in the world. Gas is expected to surpass oil as the main revenue earner for the country in the near future. Gas is used for electricity and petrochemical production, as well as heavy and light industry.

	1999	2000	2001
Inflation (% change)	3.4	5.6	2.5
Exchange rate (per US$)	6.30	6.30	6.23
Interest rate (% per annum, lending rate)	17.0	16.5	
GDP (% real growth)	6.8	4.8	4.5
GDP (Million units of national currency)	43,090.0	48,526.0	52,435.0
GDP (US$ million)	6,840.9	7,702.8	8,412.2
GDP per capita (US$)	5,305.9	5,948.1	6,421.5
Consumption (Million units of national currency)	25,407.3	29,282.8	32,796.4
Consumption (US$ million)	4,033.6	4,648.2	5,261.6
Consumption per capita (US$)	3,128.6	3,589.3	4,016.5
Population, mid-year ('000)	1,289.3	1,295.0	1,310.0
Birth rate (per '000)	13.8	13.7	13.6
Death rate (per '000)	5.9	6.0	6.0
No. of households ('000)	271.6	270.2	269.4
Total exports (US$ million)	2,803.9	4,654.7	4,964.4
Total imports (US$ million)	2,740.6	3,308.4	3,672.3
Tourism receipts (US$ million)	241.0	225.5	191.0
Tourist spending (US$ million)			

Average household size 2001 (persons)	4.79				
Urban population 2001 (%)	74.3				
Age analysis (%) (2001)	*0-14*	27.5	*15-64*	66.0	*65+* 6.5
Population by sex (%) (2001)	*Male*	49.6	*Female*	50.4	
Life expectancy (years) (2001)	*Male*	72.3	*Female*	77.0	
Infant mortality (deaths per '000 live births) (2001)	13.2				
Adult literacy (%) (1997)	97.8				

TRADING PARTNERS

Major export destinations 2001 (% share)

USA	57.3
JAMAICA	7.0
FRANCE	4.2
BARBADOS	3.9

Major import sources 2001 (% share)

USA	35.2
VENEZUELA	14.5
COLOMBIA	5.5
GERMANY	4.6

▧ Tunisia

Area (km^2)   164,150

Currency   Tunisian dinar (TD = 1,000 millimes)

Location   Tunisia, one of the smaller but more influential states in North Africa, lies on the Mediterranean coast with Algeria to its west and Libya to the east. Equally important, however, is its proximity to Italy (a sea voyage of only 200km from Tunis to Sicily) or to France, the governing power until 1956. The country's fertile northern soil enjoys adequate irrigation from numerous rivers; in the south, however, it gives way to desert terrain. The capital is Tunis.

Head of State   President Gen. Zine el-Abidine Ben-Ali (1987)

Head of Government   Mohamed Ghannouchi (1999)

Ruling Party   Rassemblement Constitutionnel Democratique (RCD)

Political Structure   The Republic of Tunisia became independent from France in 1957 and was ruled until 1981 as a 1-party state by the Parti Socialiste Destour. Now known as the Rassemblement Constitutionnel Democratique, the party still rules the country with little opposition. The executive president is elected for a maximum of three 5-year terms by universal suffrage, although in practice he has always stood unopposed. The Chamber of Deputies has 182 members, elected for a 5-year term in single-seat constituencies. 34 seats are guaranteed to the opposition.

Last Elections   Presidential elections were held in 1999, when Gen. Ben-Ali was re-elected with 99% of the vote. Elections to the National Assembly took place at the same time. The RCD received 92% of the votes and controls parliament as well as municipalities. The six legal opposition parties are virtually weightless compared with Ben Ali's RCD.

Political Risk   Tunisia's political risks stem not from economics but from the people's dissatisfaction with their government and the threat of Islamic fundamentalism. Tunisians enjoy their economic prosperity; but Ben-Ali has become a very unpopular president. Dissent is growing as charges of corruption persist.

International Disputes   The rise of Islamic fundamentalism in neighbouring countries has increased tensions. Tunisia also has a maritime boundary dispute with Libya. Malta and Tunisia are discussing the commercial exploitation of the continental shelf between their countries, particularly for oil exploration.

Economy   Tunisia's economy grew by 5% in 2001 and is expected to increase by 3.8% in 2002 and 6.4% in 2003. Prices rose by 1.9% in 2001. Inflation is forecast to be 3.4% in 2002 and 3% in 2003. This rather strong performance is the result of gradual economic liberalisation, prudent macroeconomic policies and Tunisia's integration into the world economy. Prices have remained under control thanks to tighter monetary policies despite higher food and energy costs. However, despite significant job creation, high labour force growth has left the unemployment rate roughly unchanged over this period at around 15%. Targets for the budget deficit have been comfortably met, as supplementary spending on petroleum price supports were more than offset by higher tax revenues. The external current account deficit is expected to rise to 3.8% of GDP owing to a combination of factors. These include a rising investment rate, a deterioration in agricultural trade, a slowdown in the growth of tourism receipts and the rise in oil prices. Structural reforms have been proceeding at a cautious but steady pace. Though per capita income is only US$2,000, Tunisia does not face the serious income inequalities that exist in other North African countries.

Main Industries   Agriculture accounts for 13% of GDP and production rose rapidly in recent years. The bulk of the country's population depends on farming, which takes place mainly along the northern coasts and valleys. Cereals such as wheat and barley, and olives, vines and citrus fruits produce heavy exportable crops. Further inland, farming is limited to cattle herding. Industry contributes 28% to GDP and is the focus of an ambitious programme of privatisation. Tunisia began reducing tariffs against EU manufactured goods in 1996, but overall trade protection remains high and significant restructuring is still needed to meet the challenges of free trade with the EU. In the past, weak lending practices and banking supervision resulted in the accumulation of a large stock of non-performing loans. However, banking sector reforms and public enterprise restructuring have succeeded in reversing this trend.

Energy   Tunisia produced only 82,000 barrels per day of oil in 2001 and levels are falling. Meanwhile, domestic petroleum demand is increasing rapidly, and the country became a net oil importer in 2000 for the first time in over 20 years. Because Tunisia's refining capacity is low, the country exports crude oil, and imports refined products. Currently, Tunisia has over 300 million barrels in proven oil reserves, with estimated recoverable reserves significantly higher than that. The government is placing its hopes in the development of new, smaller fields in cooperation with independent, foreign companies. Foreign oil companies plan to spend US$120 million on exploration in Tunisia during 2002, compared with just US$86 million in 2000.

	1999	2000	2001
Inflation (% change)	2.7	3.0	1.9
Exchange rate (per US$)	1.19	1.37	1.44
Interest rate (% per annum, commercial lending rate)	5.9	5.9	
GDP (% real growth)	6.1	4.7	5.0
GDP (Million units of national currency)	24,671.5	26,685.0	28,779.0
GDP (US$ million)	20,798.4	19,468.4	20,003.3
GDP per capita (US$)	2,228.4	2,063.1	2,094.6
Consumption (Million units of national currency)	14,179.6	15,356.1	16,671.3
Consumption (US$ million)	11,953.6	11,203.3	11,587.7
Consumption per capita (US$)	1,280.8	1,187.2	1,213.4
Population, mid-year ('000)	9,333.2	9,436.5	9,549.9
Birth rate (per '000)	18.7	18.6	18.6
Death rate (per '000)	6.6	6.5	6.5
No. of households ('000)	1,944.8	1,981.4	2,002.3
Total exports (US$ million)	5,871.8	5,850.2	6,491.6
Total imports (US$ million)	8,474.4	8,566.9	10,055.3
Tourism receipts (US$ million)	1,560.0	1,630.7	1,371.6
Tourist spending (US$ million)	239.0	249.9	211.7

Average household size 2001 (persons)	4.76				
Urban population 2001 (%)	66.0				
Age analysis (%) (2001)	*0-14*	29.6	*15-64*	64.0	*65+* 6.4
Population by sex (%) (2001)	*Male*	50.4	*Female*	49.6	
Life expectancy (years) (2001)	*Male*	69.3	*Female*	71.8	
Infant mortality (deaths per '000 live births) (2001)	27.0				
Adult literacy (%) (1998)	67.0				

TRADING PARTNERS

Major export destinations 2001 (% share)		Major import sources 2001 (% share)	
FRANCE	28.5	FRANCE	26.3
ITALY	22.3	ITALY	18.5
GERMANY	12.3	GERMANY	9.8
BELGIUM	5.3	SPAIN	4.3

▪ Turkey

Area (km^2)   779,450

Currency   Turkish lira (TL)

Location   With control over both banks of the Bosporus, Turkey controls access to the Black Sea. The country has a land border with Greece and Bulgaria to the west. In the southeast it meets with Syria and Iraq, while the eastern border meets with Iran and in the northeast it borders Georgia and Armenia. The capital is Ankara.

Head of State   Ahmet Necdet Sezer (2000)

Head of Government   Bülent Ecevit (1999)

Ruling Party   Democratic Left Party (DSP) leads a coalition with the National Action Party and the Motherland Party.

Political Structure   Turkey's president is elected by popular vote for seven years by parliament. The country has a unicameral 550-seat Grand National Assembly with 550 members, elected for a 5-year term by mitigated proportional representation with a barrier of 10%. Although Islam is dominant, the country has been secular since 1919. The Kurdish Democracy Party was banned in 1994 after a series of terrorist attacks.

Last Elections   General elections to the Grand National Assembly were held in May 1999. The Democratic Left won 136 seats closely followed by the National Action Party with 130 seats. The Virtue Party (previously known as the Welfare Party) took 110 seats. The big surprise was the emergence of the right-wing National Action Party, which was not represented, in the previous parliament.

Political Risk   For years Turkey has complained about the EU's failure to put the Kurdistan Workers' Party (PKK) on its list of terrorist organisations. In 2002, just when the European Commission was ready to make this move, the PKK announced that it has "fulfilled its missions" and had been dissolved. It now aims to reorganise as the Kurdistan Freedom and Democracy Congress. Ankara argues that this is just a tactical ploy and that the PKK still keeps around 5,000 men under arms in northern Iraq.

International Disputes   Relations with Greece are much improved after a tense period in 1996 and 1997. Greece supports Turkey's aspirations to join the EU and the Greek prime minister is popular in Turkey. The issue of Cyprus, which has been divided into Greek and Turkish parts since 1974, is the only subject of major concern between the neighbouring countries. Turkey has accused Iran of supporting the country's rebel Kurds. Turkish suppression of Kurdish militants has also led to disputes with Iraq and Syria which, along with Iran, have Kurdish minorities of their own. Syria also demands the return of Hatay Province, Turkey's southernmost province. Relations with Israel are another source of problems. In 2002, the Turkish army quietly signed a US$600 million agreement with Israel to modernise its fleet of tanks. However, Israel's subsequent invasion of Palestine provided a good opportunity for Turkey's pro-Islamic opposition parties to condemn the deal. If relations become too close, however, the Turkish government faces a strong backlash from its own Muslims.

Economy   The Turkish economy contracted by 6.2% in 2001 but should grow by 3.6% in 2002. Growth in 2003 is forecast to be 4.7%. Inflation was 54% in 2001. Prices are expected to rise by 49% in 2002 and 27% in 2003. Aside from the country's troubled banking system, Turkey's economy suffers from two macroeconomic defects which have also contributed to its recent problems. These are the large current account deficit and the inability to contain inflation. The growing external imbalance resulted from an unsustainable boom in demand, exacerbated by the impacts of higher world oil prices and the weakening of the euro. Inflation has remained clearly above targets, indicating problems in reducing expectations to levels consistent with wage moderation and the preservation of Turkish competitiveness. Turkey's latest agreement with the IMF makes it the world's largest debtor to that institution. So far, developments in 2002 have been promising and the foundations for a recovery in domestic demand are now in place.

Main Industries   Agriculture accounts for 14% of GDP, industry is responsible for 30% and services contribute the remainder. Much of the population works in agriculture, cultivating grapes, fruit, barley, cotton and other products. Turkey's tourist sector is looking forward to a renewed boom with the aid of the sharp currency devaluation that has damaged most other sectors. Tourism revenues in 2001 were forecast to be US$10-11 billion but ended up less than 70% of that target. Ambitious plans have been announced to restructure the banking sector, which has triggered two recent financial crises. New accounting standards, along with a US$150 million recapitalisation scheme, are being implemented. In addition, bank owners agreed to inject another US$750 million to strengthen the banking system. Industrial production contracted by 10% in 2001 but is expected to grow by 2.5% in 2002 and 43.5% in 2003. In this sector, the textile industry is Turkey's largest producer and exporter. Turkey's textile producers are generally very modern and highly competitive. The removal of quotas on exports to the EU - which is part of the country's recent agreement - has improved growth prospects. The global phase-out of textile quotas called for in the Uruguay Round also increases this sector's potential. The country has recently announced an ambitious programme of privatisation although most of industry remains under state control. In the telecommunications sector, Turkey expects to install 2-2.5 million additional lines per year, raising telephone density from 25% in 1995 to 40% by 2005.

Energy   Energy consumption is growing much faster than its production, making Turkey a rapidly growing energy importer. Also, Turkey currently is experiencing significant energy shortfalls. This will necessitate billions of dollars worth of investments in coming years. Despite the growth in the private sector in recent years, developments in the Turkish energy sector are still heavily influenced by the central government. Turkish oil consumption has increased in recent years, and this trend is expected to continue, with growth of 2-3% annually in coming years. Oil provides around 43% of Turkey's total energy requirements, but its share is declining (as the share of natural gas rises). Around 90% of Turkey's oil supplies are imported, mainly from the Middle East and Russia. Turkish imports from Saudi Arabia have declined in recent years as Iraqi oil supplies have gradually increased. Turkey's port of Ceyhan is a major outlet for Iraqi oil exports. For several years, it has been reported that as much as 100,000 bbl/d of oil and oil products were being smuggled into Turkey via tanker truck, mainly from northern Iraq. This "border trade" costs the Turkish treasury millions of dollars in lost tax revenue.

	1999	2000	2001
Inflation (% change)	64.9	54.9	54.4
Exchange rate (per US$)	418,783.00	625,218.00	1,225,590.00
Interest rate (% per annum, lending rate)	82.0	33.0	
GDP (% real growth)	-4.7	7.4	-6.2
GDP (Trillion units of national currency)	81,929.9	125,158.1	181,802.8
GDP (US$ million)	195,638.0	200,183.2	148,339.0
GDP per capita (US$)	3,087.1	3,111.9	2,272.1
Consumption (Trillion units of national currency)	57,828.7	92,001.8	132,120.7
Consumption (US$ million)	138,087.5	147,151.5	107,801.7
Consumption per capita (US$)	2,179.0	2,287.5	1,651.2
Population, mid-year ('000)	63,373.0	64,328.0	65,287.7
Birth rate (per '000)	22.3	21.7	20.9
Death rate (per '000)	6.4	6.3	6.3
No. of households ('000)	15,482.0	15,777.0	16,011.2
Total exports (US$ million)	26,588.0	26,571.5	28,537.1
Total imports (US$ million)	40,692.0	53,498.9	46,340.6
Tourism receipts (US$ million)	5,203.0	7,684.0	5,522.6
Tourist spending (US$ million)	1,471.0	1,496.0	1,225.3

Average household size 2001 (persons)		4.08				
Urban population 2001 (%)		75.2				
Age analysis (%) (2001)	0-14	29.9	15-64	64.6	65+	5.5
Population by sex (%) (2001)	Male	50.8	Female	49.2		
Life expectancy (years) (2001)	Male	67.6	Female	72.8		
Infant mortality (deaths per '000 live births) (2001)		40.7				
Adult literacy (%) (1997)		83.2				

TRADING PARTNERS

Major export destinations 2001 (% share)		Major import sources 2001 (% share)	
GERMANY	17.9	GERMANY	12.5
USA	10.0	ITALY	8.2
ITALY	8.3	USA	7.2
UNITED KINGDOM	7.8	RUSSIA	7.0

■ Turkmenistan

Area (km^2) 488,100

Currency Manat (introduced November 1993). Russian roubles are also used.

Location Turkmenistan is located in the far south of the former Soviet empire, bordering Iran and Afghanistan in the south and the Caspian Sea in the west, with Uzbekistan and Kazakhstan to the north. The terrain is dominated by the Kara-Kum desert, and the climate is accordingly arid for most of the year. The capital is Ashkhabad.

Head of State President Saparmurat Niyazov (October 1990)

Head of Government Saparmurat Niyazov

Ruling Party Democratic Party of Turkmenistan (DPT)

Political Structure Turkmenistan declared its independence from the Soviet Union in October 1991. Despite the country's strong economic performance in recent years (due mainly to greater exports of oil and natural gas), it is still ruled by the Communist Party, albeit under the new name of the Democratic Party of Turkmenistan. The 1991 Constitution allows for an executive president, who is the Chairman of the Supreme Soviet, and who was first elected by that body, although he was subsequently confirmed by popular vote. In a subsequent referendum, he was named president for life. In practice, the country is a 1-party state. Turkmenistan has two parliamentary chambers. The Majlis (Assembly) has 50 members, elected for a 5-year term in single-seat constituencies. The People's Council has as members the 50 members of the Majlis, 50 directly elected members and additional executive and judicial officials.

Last Elections In accordance with the wishes of President Niyazov, a referendum held in 1994 approved the decision to abolish the 1997 elections. Ominously, the official reports of the poll declared that 99% of the electorate voted in favour. The last elections to the Majlis were held in December 1999. The DPT was the only allowed party and won all seats.

Political Risk Despite the country's impressive economic performance (mainly due to exports of oil and natural gas) economic and political reform is stifled under the autocratic leadership of Niyazov. Turkmenistan is also regarded as one of the world's most repressive and abusive governments by human rights groups. The president is the target of frequent criticism for having indulged in an expensive building programme of palaces and retreats, while much of the capital is without basic necessities. International lenders have occasionally suspended sector loans to the country in protest at Niyazov's anti-democratic policies.

International Disputes Turkmenistan has a dispute with Azerbaijan over ownership of several Caspian sea oil fields.

Economy Turkmenistan is believed to be one of the poorest countries in all of central and east Europe. GDP grew by 10% in 2001 but the pace is slowing. Growth of 6% is anticipated in 2002 with a forecast of 4.8% for 2003. Inflation continues to be a problem with prices rising by 15% in 2001. A similar rate of increase is expected for 2002 while the forecast for 2003 is that inflation will be about 11.6%. Turkmenistan has benefited from positive developments in external circumstances which to a large extent determine the economic performance and prospects of its export-dependent economy. The continued economic upturn in the Russian Federation and Ukraine and in other Commonwealth of Independent States economies sustained export demand. Natural gas exports rose because of fuller capacity utilisation of a new pipeline to Iran. The government has adopted a 3-pronged overall economic policy framework: a transition strategy that accords to the state the leading role in economic development a gradual approach to economic liberalisation and privatisation and a special emphasis on minimising social costs by subsidising the provision of basic necessities and services. Within this framework the government is also pursuing the twin goals of industrial diversification and self-sufficiency in food and other basic goods. As part of the diversification strategy some public sector investment and foreign exchange earnings have been used for establishing textile and garment manufacturing plants often in collaboration with Turkish partners. These joint ventures are now exporting to the US and Europe.

Main Industries The value of industrial output, which consists mainly of oil and gas production, registered an impressive growth rate of 27% in 2001. However, transport bottlenecks continued to impose a binding constraint on further expansion of energy product exports. Cotton exports, the other major revenue earner for the economy, also increased, in their case by 7%, and were helped by a 10% larger harvest than in 2001 (according to official figures). The superior quality of Turkmenistan's cotton fibre and the higher share of processed and value-added cotton exports partly mitigated the impact of a fairly sharp decline in average international cotton prices. Aided by favourable weather conditions and continued policy support, wheat production registered growth of 18% and contributed to a 23% rise in agricultural output. The emergence of a small export surplus in cereals testified to the success of the government's policies to diversify agriculture away from a cotton monoculture and to generate self-sufficiency in grain production. The services sector has lagged behind industry and agriculture, as a result of weak development in private financial and retail trade activities. Transport and construction, which remain largely in government hands, showed growth of 4% and 7%, respectively, during January-October 2001, compared with the same period in 2000.

Energy Turkmenistan is important to world energy markets because it contains over 100 trillion cubic feet of proven natural gas reserves, the third largest in the world. It also borders the Caspian Sea, which contains major oil and natural gas reserves. Nearly seven billion cubic metres (bcm) of gas were exported in 2001. Natural gas production increased to 51.3 bcm, a rise of 9% over the 2000 level. Of this, 37.3 bcm were exported, 11% more than in the previous year. Oil production also rose, by 12%. The country currently produces 51 bcm of gas, representing the utilisation of only half its installed production capacity. In 2002, the production target for gas is 72 bcm, a near 40% increase over 2001's level. Similarly, with expanded capacity coming on-stream at the Turkmenbashi oil refinery in 2002, a marked increase in production and exports of refined oil products can be expected. Moreover, exports of natural gas, oil and other basic commodities to the northern and western regions of Afghanistan, which border Turkmenistan, are likely to strengthen over the medium term.

	1999	2000	2001
Inflation (% change)	23.5	8.0	15.0
Exchange rate (per US$)	5,200.00	5,200.00	5,200.00
Interest rate			
GDP (% real growth)	16.0	17.6	10.0
GDP (Billion units of national currency)	17,127.7	22,377.4	28,307.4
GDP (US$ million)	3,293.8	4,303.3	5,443.7
GDP per capita (US$)	744.0	957.7	1,193.0
Consumption (Billion units of national currency)	6,095.1	7,800.1	12,694.9
Consumption (US$ million)	1,172.1	1,500.0	2,441.3
Consumption per capita (US$)	264.8	333.8	535.0
Population, mid-year ('000)	4,427.2	4,493.4	4,563.1
Birth rate (per '000)	27.6	27.1	26.6
Death rate (per '000)	6.9	6.8	6.6
No. of households ('000)	862.7	878.2	901.1
Total exports (US$ million)	1,340.0	2,700.0	2,560.0
Total imports (US$ million)	1,478.0	1,785.0	2,105.0
Tourism receipts (US$ million)	71.0	118.8	117.3
Tourist spending (US$ million)			

Average household size 2001 (persons)	5.12				
Urban population 2001 (%)	45.0				
Age analysis (%) (2001)	0-14	37.2	15-64	58.5	65+	4.3
Population by sex (%) (2001)	Male	49.5	Female	50.5	
Life expectancy (years) (2001)	Male	63.3	Female	70.0	
Infant mortality (deaths per '000 live births) (2001)	40.4				
Adult literacy (%) (1996)	99.7				

TRADING PARTNERS

Major export destinations 2001 (% share)

IRAN	20.4
UKRAINE	15.4
AZERBAIJAN	10.4
SWITZERLAND	8.0

Major import sources 2001 (% share)

USA	12.0
UKRAINE	10.4
UNITED ARAB EMIRATES	7.0
RUSSIA	6.7

■ **Tuvalu**

Area (km^2) 25

Currency Australian dollar (A$ = 100 cents)

Location Tuvalu is a group of nine coral islands and atolls formerly known as the Ellice Islands and located in the South Pacific to the north of Fiji, south of Kiribati and east of the Solomon Islands. With a total land area of just 25 sq km, and with hardly any of its land reaching more than four metres above sea level, the islands are mainly suitable only for coconut growing. The capital is Funafuti.

Head of State HM Queen Elizabeth II

Head of Government Koloa Talake (2001)

Ruling Party The government is formed by the non-partisans.

Political Structure Tuvalu, an independent special member of the Commonwealth since 1978, is formally ruled by the British monarch acting through a Governor-General. In practice, all executive power is exercised by a prime minister and cabinet which are elected from the parliament. The parliament of Tuvalu has 13 members, 12 members elected for a 4-year term in four double- and four single-seat constituencies and one ex-officio member.

Last Elections At the last elections in March 1998, only non-partisans were elected.

Political Risk About 1,000 Tuvaluans work in Nauru in the phosphate mining industry. However, Nauru has begun repatriating Tuvaluans as phosphate resources decline and this will present additional problems for Tuvalu's politicians. The island's political structure appears able to cope with the frequent disagreements that erupt in the country without resorting to drastic political action. However, the tiny economy continues to be vulnerable to external factors and this may eventually feed into the political sphere.

International Disputes Tuvalu has a compensation claim for £2 million against the UK. If paid, this sum would represent 29 years' worth of foreign exchange revenues.

Economy In 2001 GDP grew by 4% and is expected to rise by 3% in both 2002 and 2003. Inflation is falling with prices rising by just 1.8% in 2001 and 1.5% in 2002. Prices are forecast to rise by 2.1% in 2003. Prior to 2001 net income from overseas had been augmented significantly by returns from the Tuvalu Trust Fund (TTF) but these returns were smaller in 2001 due to weakness in overseas financial markets. The expectation of further windfall gains encouraged a 2001 budget that explicitly broke with the post-independence tradition of fiscal prudence by planning operating expenditures of A$2.3 million in excess of estimated revenues. The actual budget outcome for 2001 was estimated to yield an overall budget surplus of A$2.5 million equivalent to about 20% of GDP. Total revenues were 11% above the original budget estimate because of unexpectedly high tax and fishing licence revenues. However revenues from interest dividends and telecommunications licence fees were lower than the budget estimate. In an effort to reduce the disparity between household income in Funafuti and the outer islands the government is implementing an Island Development Program. This aims to decentralise administration improve public service delivery promote small business development and encourage the sustainable augmentation of financial resources for outer island development.

Main Industries Growth was led by the public sector, with public administration rising by close to 5% and construction continuing its recent expansion due to government- and donor-funded projects. Road improvement on the main island of Funafuti was the most significant of these projects and stimulated growth in mining and quarrying. Other sectors grew at more modest rates of around 2%. GNP in 2001 substantially exceeded GDP because of estimated remittances from Tuvalu's seafarers of A$2.6 million, fishing licence fees of A$6.1 million, telecommunications licence fees of A$0.31 million and revenues from leasing out Tuvalu's Internet domain address (".tv") of A$1.6 million. In 2002, the construction of a new A$7 million government office building and a new hospital began, while road reconstruction continues. New school classrooms are to be built on two of the outer islands. A slight increase in public sector employment is projected as existing vacancies are filled. These developments will stimulate private sector activity, which is otherwise constrained by remoteness from markets and poor international transport links.

Energy Tuvalu has no oil or gas, and apart from firewood all energy requirements are imported.

	1999	2000	2001
Inflation (% change)	1.0	5.0	1.8
Exchange rate (per US$)	1.55	1.72	1.94
Interest rate			
GDP (% real growth)	3.0	3.0	4.0
GDP (Million units of national currency)	9.0	9.7	10.3
GDP (US$ million)	5.8	5.6	5.3
GDP per capita (US$)	527.4	469.9	442.0
Consumption (Million units of national currency)	6.1	6.8	6.9
Consumption (US$ million)	4.0	3.9	3.6
Consumption per capita (US$)	359.5	328.2	295.8
Population, mid-year ('000)	11.0	12.0	12.0
Birth rate (per '000)	22.6	22.3	22.0
Death rate (per '000)	8.6	8.5	8.4
No. of households ('000)	1.3	1.5	1.6
Total exports (US$ million)			
Total imports (US$ million)			
Tourism receipts (US$ million)			
Tourist spending (US$ million)	11.0	12.0	12.0

Average household size 2001 (persons)	7.99					
Urban population 2001 (%)	53.2					
Age analysis (%) (2001)	*0-14*	34.5	*15-64*	52.5	*65+*	13.0
Population by sex (%) (2001)	*Male*	51.2	*Female*	48.8		
Life expectancy (years)						
Infant mortality (deaths per '000 live births) (2001)	25.7					
Adult literacy (%)						

TRADING PARTNERS

Major export destinations 2001 (% share)

GERMANY	29.7
UNITED KINGDOM	21.8
SWEDEN	18.8
FIJI	10.9

Major import sources 2001 (% share)

FIJI	61.3
AUSTRALIA	15.3
VIETNAM	7.6
NEW ZEALAND	7.2

■ Uganda

Area (km^2)   236,580

Currency   New Uganda shilling (Ush = 100 cents)

Location   Uganda is a landlocked country in central east Africa, bordered in the east by Kenya, in the south by Rwanda, Tanzania and the shore of Lake Victoria, in the north by Sudan and in the west by the Democratic Republic of the Congo (formerly Zaire). The country has a mountainous terrain with ample rainfall, and has numerous large rivers that converge in the Lake Victoria complex to the south. The capital is Kampala.

Head of State   President Yoweri Museveni (1986)

Head of Government   Apolo Nsibambi (1999)

Ruling Party   The government is formed by the National Resistance Movement (NRM), the Democratic Party (DP), Uganda National Rescue Front and Uganda People's Congress (UPC).

Political Structure   Uganda is an independent member of the Commonwealth ruled by an executive president who is assisted by a cabinet. The National Parliament has 292 members, 214 are elected without party-label in single-seat constituencies, while 78 members are elected from special interest groups. The current president, Yoweri Museveni, came to power in the military coup of 1986 and suspended all political parties.

Last Elections   Presidential elections were held in March 2001. Museveni received 69% of the vote and was re-elected. Parliamentary elections were held in June 2001, though only non-partisan candidates were allowed to participate.

Political Risk   The country's political stability remains shaky, in part because of its poor relations with its neighbours. Kenyan and Sudanese raiders have killed many and severely disrupted farming in border regions. Museveni has disarmed many Ugandan rebels but his army is unable to guard the country's borders from foreign incursions. In Kampala, corruption that reaches the ministerial level hinders Museveni's efforts to keep the economy on track.

International Disputes   Until the middle of 2001, Uganda troops were involved in the Congo but most have now been withdrawn. Following Kabila's assassination, the UN condemned Uganda for the invasion and has called for sanctions against the country. In response, Museveni has threatened to withdraw from the Lusaka accord which had been agreed in an effort to bring peace to the Congo.

Economy   Uganda's GDP increased by 4.9% in 2001 and should grow by 5.8% in 2002 and 6.3% in 2003. Inflation was 4.6% in 2001 and will be 0.2% in 2002. In 2003, prices are expected to rise by 5.5%. The promising outlook is attributed to prudent macroeconomic policies and a modest number of structural reforms that have helped to achieve broad-based economic growth. The economy depends to a substantial degree on coffee, tea and cotton, the three main export crops. Coffee production, alone, accounts for more than half of GDP. This great dependence is expected to pose a serious problem in the future as new and more efficient coffee producers enter world markets. Critics are concerned about standards of living and the severe regional disparities in the incidence of poverty. While tax administration has improved revenue performance, it is imperative that the government implement additional measures, including steps to combat smuggling and enforce penalties for tax evasion.

Main Industries   Agriculture accounts for more than 40% of GDP, but its share is falling. Farm output is a major earner of foreign exchange, with coffee, tea and cotton being especially important. The main products for the domestic market are plantains, bananas, cassava, sweet potatoes, potatoes, sorghum and maize. Most farming is on a subsistence basis. Manufacturing accounts for just a fifth of GDP but its share rose steadily over the past few decades. Much of the sector is engaged in the processing of raw materials for the domestic market, though there has been rapid expansion in the production of consumer goods. There are a few heavy industrial manufacturers producing steel and cement in and around the capital. The financial sector remains weak and poorly regulated. Tourism has much to offer, though hotels and marketing are primitive. The number of international visitors is beginning to recover after a drop in 2001. Uganda has numerous mineral deposits. The country's largest single foreign investment is in the development of its cobalt reserves in the Rwenzori foothills. Rehabilitation of copper mines closed in the 1970s is also underway.

Energy   Although Uganda has no proven oil or gas resources, some exploration is taking place, and there are signs that the western Rift Valley may contain hydrocarbon deposits. The landlocked country is dependent on the importation of all oil products in their refined form. Oil accounts for more than 80% of Uganda's commercial energy needs.

	1999	2000	2001
Inflation (% change)	-0.2	6.3	4.6
Exchange rate (per US$)	1,454.83	1,644.48	1,755.66
Interest rate (% per annum, commercial lending rate)	21.5	22.9	22.7
GDP (% real growth)	8.1	4.0	4.9
GDP (Billion units of national currency)	8,411.1	9,193.2	10,061.2
GDP (US$ million)	5,781.5	5,590.4	5,730.7
GDP per capita (US$)	271.1	256.7	248.2
Consumption (Billion units of national currency)	7,053.4	7,974.0	8,380.1
Consumption (US$ million)	4,848.3	4,849.0	4,773.2
Consumption per capita (US$)	227.4	222.7	206.8
Population, mid-year ('000)	21,323.6	21,778.0	23,085.0
Birth rate (per '000)	50.5	50.5	50.6
Death rate (per '000)	19.2	18.6	17.9
No. of households ('000)	3,938.0	4,078.1	4,383.5
Total exports (US$ million)	518.6	460.6	456.8
Total imports (US$ million)	1,342.0	1,516.1	1,593.5
Tourism receipts (US$ million)	149.0	152.0	105.1
Tourist spending (US$ million)	141.0	107.9	112.2

Average household size 2001 (persons)	5.34				
Urban population 2001 (%)	14.6				
Age analysis (%) (2001)	0-14	49.7	15-64	48.1	65+ 2.2
Population by sex (%) (2001)	Male	49.6	Female	50.4	
Life expectancy (years) (2001)	Male	44.4	Female	45.8	
Infant mortality (deaths per '000 live births) (2001)	96.9				
Adult literacy (%) (1997)	64.0				

TRADING PARTNERS

Major export destinations 2001 (% share)

BELGIUM	16.8
NETHERLANDS	14.1
GERMANY	7.4
USA	5.9

Major import sources 2001 (% share)

KENYA	43.3
INDIA	6.8
SOUTH AFRICA	6.4
UNITED KINGDOM	5.6

■ Ukraine

Area (km^2) 603,700

Currency Hryvnia (Hr)

Location Although far from being the largest of the former Soviet states, Ukraine has a large part of its finest agricultural land. Situated to the west of the former empire, it borders on Poland, Slovakia and northern Romania in the west, on Belarus in the north, and on Russia in the east and south, where it meets the Black Sea. There are innumerable rivers, including the Dnepr and its tributaries. The capital is Kiev.

Head of State President Leonid Kuchma (July 1994)

Head of Government Anatoly Kinakh (2001)

Ruling Party The government is formed by independents and reformists.

Political Structure The country has an executive president who is elected by universal suffrage for a 5-year term. Parliament has 450 members, elected for 5-year terms, 225 members by proportional representation and 224 in single-seat constituencies.

Last Elections The last elections to the Supreme Soviet were held in March 2002. The centre-right alliance, Our Ukraine, took 112 seats, the Communist Party of Ukraine claimed 66 seats and the pro-presidential party, For a United Ukraine got 102 seats. Presidential elections took place in November 1999 and Kuchma was returned to power with 56% of the vote. In April 2000, Ukrainians voted overwhelmingly in favour of strengthening the power of the president, at the expense of parliament.

Political Risk The murky state of politics in Ukraine keeps investors uncertain and risks high. Opposition candidates managed to get into parliament in the general election of March 2002, though one candidate was murdered. All the pro-presidential candidates did well as the president's camp pulled voters from prisons, the armed forces, the civil service and state-run factories. In practice, the situation in Ukraine is much worse than the results of the latest election might suggest. Businesses close to the president, Leonid Kuchma, are generally above the law.

International Disputes There are allegations that Kuchma personally authorised illegal sales of air-defence systems to Iraq valued to more than US$100 million. The US accuses Ukraine of providing much more assistance to Iraq to further the latter's search for weapons of mass destruction. Ukraine was remodelled so extensively under Josef Stalin, that it retains a large number of political and ethnic anomalies. Relations with Poland, from which a large part of its territory was snatched, are now warm. In 1997, Ukraine and Russia signed a political treaty in which Moscow acknowledged, for the first time, the borders of a sovereign Ukraine. Ukraine's goal of joining the World Trade Organisation now seems unlikely.

Economy GDP increased by 9.1% in 2001. Forecasts call for growth of 5% in 2002 and 4% in 2003. Inflation was 12% in 2001. Prices should rise by 7.6% in 2002 and 9.4% in 2003. The continued economic recovery has been made possible by considerable idle capacity, improved competitiveness of the Ukrainian economy in the wake of the real exchange rate depreciation in 1998-1999 and the strengthening of domestic demand as a result of wage and pension increases. Ukraine's external current account surplus narrowed from 4.75% of GDP in 2000 to 3.5% in 2001. The competitiveness of the economy was preserved, as the real effective exchange rate has remained broadly stable since mid-2000. As a result of the debt-rescheduling agreement in 2001, the debt-service burden was moderated. Ukraine has also started to benefit from transfers, including World War II compensation payments, and from increasing inflows of FDI, albeit from a comparatively low base. With the National Bank of Ukraine continuing its extensive purchases of foreign exchange on the inter-bank market, Ukraine's official gross international reserves increased to US$3.1 billion at end-December 2001, equivalent to almost eight weeks of imports, and net international reserves turned positive, reaching US$1.1 billion.

Main Industries Despite a good performance in 2001, Ukraine's agricultural sector continues to pose serious problems for the government. Production fell by 80% during the 1990s and has still not returned to the levels recorded in 1990. Before the end of the Cold War, Ukraine accounted for nearly half of all farm output in the Soviet Union. Poor harvests have led to social unrest and aroused fears about political stability. Today, millions of tiny vegetable plots account for the bulk of production while the large, factory farms produce little. As much as 95% of fruit and vegetables produced in the country are home grown. The main stumbling block to agricultural reform is the pattern of land ownership. The government's programme of reforms for other sectors has not been much more effective. There has been little headway on privatisation, tax reform, bankruptcy laws, or energy sector restructuring. Ukraine seeks foreign investment, but its bureaucratic laws, policy bungles and general lack of progress scares many would-be investors away. In the meantime, more Ukrainian industry is being taken over by Russian buyers. Russian investors have bought a series of companies including a US$70 million aluminium smelter, an oil refinery, and a television and radio station. Ukraine is rich in minerals, but has failed to use this natural wealth for its economic gain. The country has the world's largest supply of titanium, the third largest deposits of iron ore (more than 200 million tonnes) and 30% of the world's manganese ore.

Energy Ukraine has 395 million barrels of proven oil reserves, the majority of which are located in the Dnieper-Donets basin in the eastern part of the country. Although the pace of exploration has picked up, oil production has tapered off since independence. Since 1992, when Ukraine produced 95,000 barrels per day (bbl/d), production has been on the decline, dipping to 84,000 bbl/d in 2000. The government calculates that oil production was unchanged in 2001 at 84,000 bbl/d. At this level of production, Ukraine's oil production volumes satisfy only about 25% of the country's domestic needs, making Ukraine highly dependent on foreign oil supplies. Although Ukraine's oil consumption has dried up dramatically since independence - dropping 57% from 813,000 bbl/d in 1992 to 346,000 bbl/d in 2000 - the country's consumption still far outstrips its production capacity. Ukraine imports the majority of its oil from Russia, with lesser amounts coming from Kazakhstan. With a highly developed oil pipeline system, Ukraine plays an important role as a transit country for Russian oil exports to Europe. Ukraine has an excellent opportunity to play a major role in bringing increased oil exports from Azerbaijan and Kazakhstan to European oil markets. Rather than seeking to import Caspian Sea region oil for domestic consumption, Ukraine is hoping to reap tariffs for Caspian oil transiting its territory as it heads westwards.

	1999	2000	2001
Inflation (% change)	22.7	28.2	12.0
Exchange rate (per US$)	4.13	5.44	5.37
Interest rate (% per annum, lending rate)	55.0	41.5	32.3
GDP (% real growth)	-0.2	5.9	9.1
GDP (Million units of national currency)	130,442.0	170,070.0	201,927.0
GDP (US$ million)	31,580.7	31,261.5	37,587.7
GDP per capita (US$)	636.5	635.4	772.1
Consumption (Million units of national currency)	66,968.9	107,981.8	131,437.0
Consumption (US$ million)	16,213.5	19,848.8	24,466.3
Consumption per capita (US$)	326.8	403.4	502.6
Population, mid-year ('000)	49,613.1	49,201.7	48,680.9
Birth rate (per '000)	8.6	8.5	8.3
Death rate (per '000)	14.9	15.1	15.2
No. of households ('000)	18,753.9	18,693.7	18,718.4
Total exports (US$ million)	11,582.0	14,573.0	16,265.0
Total imports (US$ million)	11,846.0	13,956.0	15,775.0
Tourism receipts (US$ million)	3,200.0	3,042.3	3,415.2
Tourist spending (US$ million)	3,083.5	2,361.1	3,247.3

Average household size 2001 (persons)	2.63					
Urban population 2001 (%)	71.6					
Age analysis (%) (2001)	*0-14*	17.6	*15-64*	68.2	*65+*	14.2
Population by sex (%) (2001)	*Male*	46.3	*Female*	53.7		
Life expectancy (years) (2001)	*Male*	62.7	*Female*	73.5		
Infant mortality (deaths per '000 live births) (2001)	15.0					
Adult literacy (%) (1996)	98.8					

TRADING PARTNERS

Major export destinations 2001 (% share)

RUSSIA	23.5
ITALY	6.3
USA	4.8
TURKEY	4.7

Major import sources 2001 (% share)

RUSSIA	31.6
GERMANY	11.6
TURKMENISTAN	8.2
BELARUS	5.0

■ United Arab Emirates

Area (km^2)   75,150

Currency   UAE dirham (= 100 fils)

Location   The United Arab Emirates (UAE) is a confederation of nominally independent states which form a crescent running along the southern Persian (Arabian) Gulf coast of Saudi Arabia - although its eastern edge also incorporates an access to the Gulf of Oman. With the main land area of Oman to the east, and with the enclave which is the urban capital of Oman lying at its extreme eastern tip (in the Straits of Hormuz), the UAE occupies a position of immense strategic importance. The capital is Abu Dhabi.

Head of State   Zayd ibn Sultan al Nahayan of Abu Dhabi

Head of Government   Maktum bin Rachid al Maktum of Dubai

Ruling Party   There are no legal political parties in the United Arab Emirates.

Political Structure   The UAE is a federation of seven emirates - Abu Dhabi, Dubai, Sharjah, Ajman, Fujairah, Ras al-Khaimah and Umm al-Qaiwain. Political power is concentrated in Abu Dhabi, which controls the vast majority of the UAE's economic and resource wealth. The two largest emirates - Abu Dhabi and Dubai - provide over 80% of the UAE's income. In 1996, the UAE's Federal National Council approved a permanent constitution. The establishment of Abu Dhabi as the UAE's permanent capital was one of the new framework's main provisions.

Last Elections   There have been no elections to any of the UAE's bodies in recent decades.

Political Risk   The royal families in the seven Emirates are gradually being forced to cede more and more of their power to the private sector. The process is likely to accelerate in the future but at some point the sheiks will probably try to draw a line. The political fallout from such a dispute could undermine the UAE's economic and foreign policy. All the emirates are concerned about the high percentage of foreign workers residing in the UAE and are trying to reduce this number. At mid-2002, expatriates accounted for 91% of the total national workforce. Analysts predict that the share will reach 95% by 2010. Foreign workers have transferred substantial sums of money from the UAE to family members in Egypt, India, Pakistan, Sri Lanka, the Philippines, Bangladesh and Jordan. Religious extremism is another concern but the government treats its critics very carefully, locking up only a few and admonishing the rest.

International Disputes   The UAE and Iran continue to dispute the ownership of three islands, Abu Musa and the Greater and Lesser Tunb Islands, which are strategically located in the Strait of Hormuz. All three islands were effectively occupied by Iranian troops in 1992. The Mubarak field, which is located six miles off Abu Musa, has been producing gas-rich oil since 1974. Although Iran remains a continuing concern for officials in Abu Dhabi, they have chosen not to escalate the territorial dispute. Iran is one of Dubai's major trading partners, accounting for 20-30% of Dubai's business. Relations between Saudi Arabia and the UAE also showed some signs of strain in 1999, due to Saudi development of the Shaybah oil field, with estimated reserves of 14 billion barrels of crude oil. The UAE and Saudi Arabia do not have a precisely defined border in the sparsely populated desert separating them, and the Shaybah field straddles territory claimed by both governments.

Economy   With per capita incomes exceeding US$20,000, the standard of living in the United Arab Emirates is one of the highest in the world. GDP grew by 5% in 2001 and is forecast to rise by 3.6% in 2002 and 2.9% in 2003. Prices rose by 2.2% in 2001 and will increase by 2.3% in 2002. In 2003, inflation is expected to be 1.9%. The anti-terrorist campaign has raised the heat on smuggling and money laundering, lucrative staples of the UAE's free-wheeling economy. Like other Gulf States, the UAE is trying to restrict the employment of foreign workers. As the number of foreigners grows, fears that they may demand more rights increases proportionally. Vast reserves of oil and gas, combined with easy access to a variety of sea routes, allow the country to earn great wealth while avoiding many of the conflicts plaguing other countries in the Gulf region. The UAE also has one of the more diversified economies among the major oil-producing Persian Gulf states. This diversity has helped to cushion the economic impact of the collapse of crude oil prices. Nevertheless, oil and derivative products account for about 75% of the UAE's total exports.

Main Industries   In recent years, the UAE undertook several projects to diversify its economy and to reduce its dependence on oil and gas revenues. The non-oil sectors of the UAE's economy presently contribute more than two thirds of the UAE's total GDP, and about 30% of its total exports. The federal government has invested heavily in sectors such as aluminium production, tourism, aviation, re-export commerce and telecommunications. As part of its strategy to further expand its tourism industry, the UAE is building new hotels, restaurants and shopping centres, and expanding airports and duty-free zones. In 2002, Dubai announced the construction of the world's largest luxury housing estate to cost over US$3 billion. Dubai has become a central Middle East hub for trade and finance, accounting for about 70% of the Emirates's non-oil trade. However, its flourishing transit trade through its ports has suffered from the general spending caution in the region, plus the steep rises in insurance rates. For its part, Abu Dhabi plans to develop an offshore financial and commodity trade centre on Saadiyat Island, which will include storage facilities, a port, a freight centre and a financial and insurance centre to facilitate trading. Agriculture also makes up only a small portion of the UAE's economy.

Energy   The UAE contains proven crude oil reserves of 97.8 billion barrels, or slightly less than 10% of the world total. Abu Dhabi holds 94% of this amount, or about 92.2 billion barrels. Dubai contains an estimated 4 billion barrels, followed by Sharjah and Ras al-Khaimah, with 1.5 billion and 100 million barrels of oil, respectively. Most of the UAE's oil fields have been producing since the 1960s or early 1970s. Proven oil reserves in Abu Dhabi have doubled in the 10 years to 2001, mainly due to significant increases in rates of recovery. Abu Dhabi has continued to identify new finds, especially offshore, and to discover new oil-rich structures in existing fields. Under the UAE's constitution, each emirate controls its own oil production and resource development. The UAE's natural gas reserves of 212 trillion cu ft (Tcf) are the world's fifth largest after Russia, Iran, Qatar and Saudi Arabia. Over the last decade, natural gas consumption in Abu Dhabi has doubled, and is projected to reach four billion cu ft per day (bcf/d) by 2005. The development of natural gas fields also results in increased production and exports of condensates, which are not subject to OPEC quotas.

	1999	2000	2001
Inflation (% change)	2.1	1.4	2.2
Exchange rate (per US$)	3.67	3.67	3.67
Interest rate			
GDP (% real growth)	3.9	5.0	5.0
GDP (Million units of national currency)	201,846.0	249,229.0	247,850.0
GDP (US$ million)	54,961.5	67,863.6	67,488.1
GDP per capita (US$)	19,920.8	23,098.6	21,857.3
Consumption (Million units of national currency)	86,185.5	89,126.5	96,231.8
Consumption (US$ million)	23,467.8	24,268.6	26,203.4
Consumption per capita (US$)	8,505.9	8,260.2	8,486.5
Population, mid-year ('000)	2,759.0	2,938.0	3,087.7
Birth rate (per '000)	15.9	15.8	15.8
Death rate (per '000)	3.7	3.8	3.9
No. of households ('000)	466.0	475.1	482.5
Total exports (US$ million)	35,527.0	45,934.0	46,447.2
Total imports (US$ million)	33,230.6	38,139.3	40,259.4
Tourism receipts (US$ million)			
Tourist spending (US$ million)			

Average household size 2001 (persons)		6.18				
Urban population 2001 (%)		85.9				
Age analysis (%) (2001)	0-14	26.1	15-64	72.8	65+	1.1
Population by sex (%) (2001)	Male	67.3	Female	32.7		
Life expectancy (years) (2001)	Male	73.9	Female	78.2		
Infant mortality (deaths per '000 live births) (2001)		11.2				
Adult literacy (%) (1997)		74.8				

TRADING PARTNERS

Major export destinations 2001 (% share)		Major import sources 2001 (% share)	
ASIA	33.6	USA	6.8
JAPAN	29.2	GERMANY	6.7
SOUTH KOREA	10.5	JAPAN	6.6
INDIA	5.4	FRANCE	6.4

United Kingdom

Area (km^2) 244,755

Currency Pound sterling (£ = 100 pence)

Location Lying off the coast of western continental Europe between the Atlantic Ocean and the North Sea, the UK consists mainly of two distinct land masses. The larger incorporates England, Scotland and the Principality of Wales, and the smaller consists of Northern Ireland - actually, the northwestern part of the island of Ireland. The capital is London.

Head of State HM Queen Elizabeth II

Head of Government Tony Blair (1997)

Ruling Party Labour Party

Political Structure The UK is considered to be a constitutional monarchy even though it has no written constitution. The non-executive monarch rules through an elected House of Commons (the lower House of Parliament), and this is supplemented in an advisory capacity by a House of Lords (Upper House). Northern Ireland has been ruled directly from London since the abolition of the Stormont Parliament in the early 1970s. However, English laws are not automatically applicable in Northern Ireland or in Scotland, where other rules sometimes apply. A historic change occurred in 1997, when Scotland voted heavily in favour of a referendum creating a Scottish parliament. England and Scotland have shared the same monarch since 1603 and Scotland has been ruled by the British Parliament since 1707. The new Scottish Parliament, which consists of 129 members, opened its first session in 2000.

Last Elections Elections to the House of Commons took place in June 2001. Labour took 413 seats while the Conservatives captured 166 seats. The Liberal Democrats claimed 52 seats with minor parties taking the remainder. The first elections to the Scottish parliament were held in May 1999 and gave Britain's ruling Labour Party a majority.

Political Risk In the aftermath of 11 September 2001, the UK has introduced a wave of anti-terrorist legislation but many observers are unsure of the laws' long-term consequences. Under the new anti-terrorism laws, foreigners can be detained indefinitely without trial.

International Disputes British warplanes, along with its American allies, continue to conduct patrols over Iraq. The only intra-EU territorial dispute concerns the long-running debate with Spain about the return of Gibraltar. The two EU countries resumed discussions on the issue in July 2002. The EU is pressing both countries to end Gibraltar's status as a tax haven in any deal they eventually conclude. The UK promises that any agreement will be subject to the approval of Gibraltar's people. The most likely outcome is thought to be an agreement that the UK and Spain would share sovereignty, but Gibraltar would be given a great deal of autonomy.

Economy The economy grew by 2.2% in 2001 and growth of 2% is expected in 2002. In 2003, the economy should expand by 2.8%. Inflation was 2.1% in 2001. Forecasts call for prices to rise by 2.4% in 2002 and 2.5% in 2003. If the rate of growth slips too far, fiscal measures on both the tax and on the spending side will be used to provide a significant demand stimulus, so that the slowdown should be less severe than in most other European OECD countries. With household sentiment remaining upbeat and interest rates low, consumption has cushioned weak export and investment demand. Unemployment and inflation have remained low. Growth is expected to return to a solid pace soon, boosted by the turnaround in international trade and supported by rapidly expanding public expenditure. While sound monetary and fiscal policies have contributed to greater macroeconomic stability, and should continue to do so, imbalances between internal and external demand have been building up and some deep-seated structural problems remain to be settled. In particular, it is important for structural policy to succeed in enhancing human capital and work incentives, raising competitive pressures and improving public infrastructure.

Main Industries While the country's macroeconomic performance has been good, concerns about growing domestic and external imbalances have heightened. To date, most of the private services sector has continued to grow relatively strongly, and construction activity has strengthened, contrasting sharply with weakening activity in the internationally-exposed industries, especially in parts of manufacturing. While the high-tech industries have been disproportionately hit by the slowdown in global demand in 2002, the persistent strength of sterling against the euro has continued to put pressure on the more traditional manufacturing industries. It has severely squeezed output, profit margins and employment in manufacturing. The volume growth of imports has consistently outpaced that of exports, and the trade deficit has widened further in 2002. One counterpart of this emerging imbalance has been the sharp fall in the household savings ratio since 1997, as macroeconomic stability, including sustained low inflation and strong gains in wealth have reduced the appetite for saving. This has been associated with buoyant private consumption underpinned by strong household confidence, which was bolstered by falling interest rates, rapidly rising house prices and vigorous after-tax income growth. Despite the job losses in manufacturing, total employment has continued to expand. Lately, this has been helped by the first rise in public sector employment in two decades. Agriculture is of limited importance, despite the fact that the country is fully self-sufficient in most basic products. Farms tend to be larger than the European average.

Energy The UK holds about five billion barrels of proven oil reserves, almost all of it located in the North Sea. Most of the country's production comes from basins east of Scotland. The northern North Sea (east of the Shetland Islands) also holds considerable reserves, and smaller deposits are located in the North Atlantic Ocean, west of the Shetland Islands. There are over 100 oil and gas fields currently on-stream, and several hundred companies are active in the area. In December 2000, the British government gave approval to four new projects that will result in US$1.5 billion in new investment in the British North Sea. The UK has Europe's largest onshore oilfield, Wytch Farm. Estimated reserves are 500 million barrels. Exploration is active in the area, and it is hoped that even smaller fields at nearby locations will also be economically viable.

	1999	2000	2001
Inflation (% change)	2.3	2.1	2.1
Exchange rate (per US$)	0.62	0.66	0.69
Interest rate (% per annum, lending rate)	5.3	6.0	5.1
GDP (% real growth)	2.1	3.0	2.2
GDP (Million units of national currency)	901,269.0	944,913.0	989,254.0
GDP (US$ million)	1,458,229.6	1,429,669.7	1,424,094.0
GDP per capita (US$)	24,566.8	24,040.9	23,915.9
Consumption (Million units of national currency)	560,978.0	595,668.6	615,303.3
Consumption (US$ million)	907,647.7	901,256.9	885,768.2
Consumption per capita (US$)	15,291.2	15,155.3	14,875.4
Population, mid-year ('000)	59,357.6	59,468.2	59,545.9
Birth rate (per '000)	11.5	11.2	10.9
Death rate (per '000)	10.7	10.6	10.6
No. of households ('000)	24,083.0	24,272.0	24,556.8
Total exports (US$ million)	268,193.0	281,564.0	267,349.0
Total imports (US$ million)	317,959.0	334,396.0	320,973.0
Tourism receipts (US$ million)	20,223.0	23,148.4	19,251.7
Tourist spending (US$ million)	35,631.0	36,384.5	34,301.0

Average household size 2001 (persons)	2.45				
Urban population 2001 (%)	89.5				
Age analysis (%) (2001)	*0-14*	19.0	*15-64*	65.6	*65+* 15.4
Population by sex (%) (2001)	*Male*	49.3	*Female*	50.7	
Life expectancy (years) (2001)	*Male*	75.5	*Female*	80.5	
Infant mortality (deaths per '000 live births) (2001)	5.2				
Adult literacy (%) (1998)	99.0				

TRADING PARTNERS

Major export destinations 2001 (% share)		Major import sources 2001 (% share)	
USA	15.9	USA	14.0
GERMANY	11.6	GERMANY	11.8
FRANCE	9.6	FRANCE	7.7
NETHERLANDS	7.3	NETHERLANDS	6.2

■ Uruguay

Area (km^2)   186,925

Currency   New Uruguayan peso (= 100 cent simos)

Location   Uruguay, the smallest republic in South America, lies on the central Atlantic coast between Argentina in the south and west, and Brazil in the north. With an equable climate and with generally adequate rainfall despite occasional droughts, the area consists largely of grassy plains with lush forests in some parts. The capital is Montevideo.

Head of State   President Jorge Luis Batlle Ibáñez (2000)

Head of Government   President Jorge Luis Batlle Ibáñez (2000)

Ruling Party   Colorado Party leads a coalition with the National (Blanco) Party.

Political Structure   Uruguay has an executive president who is elected every five years, together with a 99-member House of Deputies and a 31-member Senate. The political system was effectively suspended from 1973, when a military dictatorship took over the country, until 1985, when civilian rule was restored.

Last Elections   Presidential elections took place in November 1999 when Ibáñez won office with 54% of the vote. Elections to the House and Senate occurred in October 1999. The Christian-Democratic Party received 39% of the vote earning them 40 seats in the House and 12 in the Senate. The Colorado Party got 31% of the vote giving them 31 seats in the House and 10 in the Senate. The National Party received 21% of the vote which accorded them 22 seats in the House and 7 in the Senate.

Political Risk   Uruguay's small economy leaves it extremely vulnerable to economic shocks and disruptions in either of its larger neighbours, Argentina and Brazil.

International Disputes   A short section of boundary with Argentina is in dispute. The same applies to two short sections of the boundary with Brazil - the Arroyo de la Invernada (Arroio Invernada) area of the Rio Cuareim (Rio Quarai) and the islands at the confluence of the Rio Cuareim (Rio Quarai) and the Uruguay River. Uruguay is a full member of the Mercosur common market with Brazil, Argentina, and Paraguay (Chile and Bolivia are associate members).

Economy   Uruguay's economy contracted by 3.1% in 2001 and a further contraction of 1.7% is expected in 2002. In 2003, growth of 3% is forecast. Prices rose by 4.4% in 2001. Inflation is expected to be 7.1% in 2002 and 9.4% in 2003. Uruguay has one of the highest standards of living and most equitable distributions of wealth in Latin America but it has been hurt badly by the deteriorating economy of its larger neighbour, Argentina. However, the government reacted promptly to the fall in foreign investment inflows and the related financial difficulties. In the first quarter of 2002, Uruguay lost its investment-grade credit rating (meaning that it must pay more to borrow). The president soon persuaded congress to pass emergency measures including spending cuts and new taxes. The aim is to cut the budget deficit from 4.2% of GDP in 2001, to 2.5% in 2002 and to zero by 2004. In return, the IMF quickly approved loans to help the country through the present crisis. The government has also promised other reforms, such as broadening the tax base, ending state monopolies in energy and telecoms, and inviting private companies to run roads and airports. The loss-making state mortgage bank will also end subsidised loans and be restructured. Because most of Uruguay's debt is in US dollars, a prolonged slide in the value of its currency has almost doubled the debt since 1998. By early 2002, the level of debt had reached 65% of GDP. Even with the austerity measures, the government fears that further currency weakening could lift the debt to 65% of GDP by 2004. The country also suffers from persistently high unemployment rates associated with the rigidities in the labour market and in labour legislation. Unemployment is presently around 14% in the urban sector. Private consumption continued to suffer as a result of falling income, rising unemployment and poor expectations.

Main Industries   Agriculture's share in GDP amounts to just 8% and the share has been falling in recent years. Farms, however, are very productive. The sector's main products include wheat, rice, corn, sorghum; and livestock. Cattle herding is the main farming activity and the biggest single source of foreign exchange. In 2001, there was an outbreak of foot-and-mouth disease, which halted Uruguay's meat exports but that has now been vanquished. The country weakening currency also helps exporters. In industry, plans to privatise a wide range of companies are moving ahead after government beat back an anti-privatisation referendum in 2001. In addition to the government's privatisation plans in the energy sector, the government has recently sold, or intends to sell, concessions for cellular telephone networks, a container terminal at the Port of Montevideo, a major private toll road between Montevideo and the resort town of Punta del Este, and a new US$40-million airport for Punta del Este. Partial privatisation of the state telecom company as well as the national railroad, are also proceeding. Manufacturing, which accounts for almost a fifth of GDP, includes various agro-processing industries such as meat processing, wool and hides, sugar, textiles, wine, footwear and leather apparel. Other industries manufacture industrial components and industrial intermediates such as vehicle tyres, cement, plywood and petroleum products and a range of more sophisticated consumer goods. Mineral extraction is of little significance in comparison with most other South American economies. Uruguay has iron ore, dolomite, marble and granite.

Energy   Uruguay has no fossil fuel resources and only a small amount of hydroelectric power (compared to its neighbours), and thus relies heavily on imports to meet its energy needs. About 60% of total energy consumption in 1999 came from imported sources. Uruguay imports 43,000 barrels of oil per day (bbl/d). The role of natural gas in Uruguay's energy sector is expected to grow over the next few years. Approximately 850 megawatts (MW) of new gas-fired generating capacity is expected to be installed in Uruguay over the next 10 years. Present plants using oil are to be converted to dual use (oil and gas). Gas will come from new pipelines linking gas-rich Argentina to Uruguay.

	1999	2000	2001
Inflation (% change)	5.7	4.8	4.4
Exchange rate (per US$)	11.34	12.10	13.32
Interest rate (% per annum, lending rate)	53.3	49.1	51.7
GDP (% real growth)	-2.8	-1.3	-3.1
GDP (Million units of national currency)	237,143.0	242,636.0	247,583.0
GDP (US$ million)	20,913.4	20,053.2	18,588.6
GDP per capita (US$)	6,456.8	6,157.7	5,676.8
Consumption (Million units of national currency)	173,360.0	179,327.0	184,905.0
Consumption (US$ million)	15,288.4	14,820.9	13,882.7
Consumption per capita (US$)	4,720.2	4,551.0	4,239.7
Population, mid-year ('000)	3,239.0	3,256.6	3,274.5
Birth rate (per '000)	17.4	17.2	17.1
Death rate (per '000)	9.4	9.3	9.3
No. of households ('000)	1,265.4	1,256.4	1,277.6
Total exports (US$ million)	2,237.1	2,294.7	2,069.1
Total imports (US$ million)	3,356.8	3,465.8	3,525.1
Tourism receipts (US$ million)	653.0	668.1	526.4
Tourist spending (US$ million)	280.0	295.1	249.6

Average household size 2001 (persons)	2.60					
Urban population 2001 (%)	91.5					
Age analysis (%) (2001)	*0-14*	23.8	*15-64*	63.5	*65+*	12.7
Population by sex (%) (2001)	*Male*	48.7	*Female*	51.3		
Life expectancy (years) (2001)	*Male*	71.3	*Female*	78.7		
Infant mortality (deaths per '000 live births) (2001)	14.2					
Adult literacy (%) (1997)	97.5					

TRADING PARTNERS

Major export destinations 2001 (% share)		Major import sources 2001 (% share)	
BRAZIL	23.6	ARGENTINA	23.1
ARGENTINA	18.2	BRAZIL	19.1
USA	8.8	USA	11.4
PARAGUAY	3.6	CHINA	4.5

USA

Area (km^2)   9,363,130

Currency   US dollar (US$ = 100 cents)

Location   The US is a federation of 50 states which spans the land mass between the Pacific Ocean and the northern Atlantic. As such, it occupies most of the North American continent, extending from the Alaskan enclave in the west to Maine in the extreme northeast. In the north it borders on Canada, and in the south with Mexico. The west and southwest consist mainly of mountain ranges. The capital is Washington, DC.

Head of State   President George Bush (2001)

Head of Government   George Bush (2001)

Ruling Party   The Republican Party controls the government; Republicans hold a majority in the House of Representatives but Democrats control the Senate.

Political Structure   The US has an executive president, elected for a 4-year term of office by universal suffrage, who then selects and directs his own cabinet ("Administration"). The US Congress comprises a 435-member House of Representatives, half of whom are elected every two years, and a 100-member Senate, which serves for six years but a third of which is re-elected every two years. The country has a strong federal structure, and devolves its legal and fiscal system to a considerable extent.

Last Elections   Elections to the House and Senate were held in November 2000. In the House, the Republican Party received 49% of the vote and won 221 seats while the Democrats took 47% of the vote and 212 seats. Two seats went to non-partisans. In the Senate, the vote was evenly split and the two both captured 50 seats. In presidential elections held in November 2000, the Republican, George Bush, defeated Al Gore despite the fact that Gore won the popular vote. One Republican later became an independent, giving the Democrats control of the Senate.

Political Risk   The US dollar is under pressure and most analysts agree that it is still overvalued. Meanwhile, the trade deficit continues to set new records. These problems are hurting the performance of the stock market. A wave of corporate scandals and financial misdealing further undermines investors' confidence. The voters have lost some of the confidence in the present administration and if consumer spending falls further, the country's weak economic recovery will be jeopardised.

International Disputes   The government's decisions to reject the Kyoto Treaty, its unease with the new International Court, the decision to proceed with an anti-missile system and a number of other policies have created tensions with European allies. Relations with Cuba also remain tense. Meanwhile, the administration's policy in the Middle East remains confused and ineffective. Relations with Iraq and Iran are especially poor and an invasion of the former may be in the works.

Economy   GDP grew by just 1.2% in 2001 and should increase by 2.3% in 2002. In 2003, growth of 3.4% is expected. Inflation was 2.8% in 2001 and will be 1.4% in 2002. In 2003, prices are forecast to rise by 2.4%. After seven years of strong growth (averaging 4% per year), the downturn in the US economy was sharp but occurred in several stages. The first stage was in the autumn of 2000 when signs of the end of the ICT bubble appeared, bringing with it more moderate investment increases and worsening inventory problems. The second stage of the downturn came in the spring of 2001 as growth ground to a halt, with further shrinkage in the manufacturing sector caused by absolute declines in durables purchases, especially of ICT-related goods, by consumers, businesses and foreigners. There were signs that the deceleration was bottoming out over the summer, but as more evidence became available, it became clear that the weakness was by no means over, as labour-market outcomes deteriorated and consumer confidence dropped sharply. The final stage began on 11 September with the terrorist attacks in New York and Washington. Output fell in the second half of 2001 and recovered only marginally in 2002. Despite the downturn, there is evidence that the rise in long-term trends in productivity, which was observed during the second half of the 1990s has been maintained during the course of the present slowdown. Actual productivity growth in the non-farm sector has slowed for cyclical reasons, rising by only 1.75% in the year to the third quarter of 2001. This, however, represents one of the best performances in a period of major economic slowdown since the 1960s, supporting the view that productivity trends are better now than in a generation.

Main Industries   The country's manufacturing sector bore the brunt of the recession. Manufacturing is highly diversified and accounts for more than a quarter of GDP. The sector boasts activities which range from heavy goods such as steel and motor vehicles to high-technology, aircraft, light engineering and consumer products. The country's vaunted high-tech industries have suffered greatly during the present recession and investment in high-tech products continues to be weak today. A number of older industries such as steel, textiles, clothing and assembly-based operations have passed through a painful period of contraction and restructuring, and some are still in trouble today. The government's efforts to protect its troubled steel industry have sparked a major trade dispute with the EU. Agriculture accounts for 2% of GDP and is predominately large scale and generally efficient. The US is a major exporter of foodstuffs and processed foods. Nevertheless, the government plans to offer substantially more generous subsidies to the farmers. The move will make the US programme of agricultural support almost as protectionist as the much-criticised Common Agricultural Policy of the EU.

Energy   During 2001, the US produced around 8.1 million barrels per day (MMBD) of oil, of which 5.9 MMBD was crude oil, and the rest natural gas liquids and other liquids. Total oil production in 2001 was down sharply (around 2.5 MMBD, or 24%) from the 10.6 MMBD averaged in 1985. For 2001, top oil producing areas included the Gulf of Mexico, Texas onshore, Alaska's North Slope, California, Louisiana, Oklahoma and Wyoming. Domestic oil exploration and development spending by major US oil companies also rebounded during 2001 from the deep cuts made during the oil price collapse of 1997/1998. Improved technology and new or increased offshore production in the Gulf of Mexico (including at deepwater areas beyond the continental shelf) also could help matters. In 2000, deepwater production in the Gulf of Mexico for the first time surpassed shallow water production.

	1999	2000	2001
Inflation (% change)	2.2	3.4	2.8
Exchange rate (per US$)	1.00	1.00	1.00
Interest rate (% per annum, lending rate)	8.0	9.2	6.9
GDP (% real growth)	4.2	4.1	1.2
GDP (Billion units of national currency)	9,268.6	9,872.9	10,208.1
GDP (US$ million)	9,268,600.0	9,872,925.0	10,208,125.0
GDP per capita (US$)	34,296.5	36,188.4	37,079.1
Consumption (Billion units of national currency)	6,284.1	6,773.9	6,979.8
Consumption (US$ million)	6,284,084.0	6,773,883.1	6,979,780.4
Consumption per capita (US$)	23,252.9	24,829.1	25,352.8
Population, mid-year ('000)	270,249.0	272,820.1	275,306.4
Birth rate (per '000)	14.0	13.7	13.4
Death rate (per '000)	8.5	8.4	8.4
No. of households ('000)	102,803.0	103,794.0	104,999.9
Total exports (US$ million)	702,098.0	781,125.0	730,803.0
Total imports (US$ million)	1,059,440.0	1,259,300.0	1,180,150.0
Tourism receipts (US$ million)	74,881.0	84,479.0	68,447.7
Tourist spending (US$ million)	59,351.0	62,152.6	58,008.5

Average household size 2001 (persons)		2.63			
Urban population 2001 (%)		77.3			
Age analysis (%) (2001)	0-14	21.2	15-64	66.2	65+ 12.6
Population by sex (%) (2001)	Male	48.9	Female	51.1	
Life expectancy (years) (2001)	Male	74.4	Female	80.2	
Infant mortality (deaths per '000 live births) (2001)		7.2			
Adult literacy (%) (1997)		99.0			

TRADING PARTNERS

Major export destinations 2001 (% share) **Major import sources 2001 (% share)**

CANADA	22.4	CANADA	18.7
MEXICO	13.9	MEXICO	11.3
JAPAN	7.9	JAPAN	11.0
UNITED KINGDOM	5.6	CHINA	9.3

■ Uzbekistan

Area (km^2)   447,400

Currency   Som

Location   Uzbekistan, one of the southernmost of the former Soviet republics, runs southeast in a broad sweep, from the dried-out Aral Sea to the Afghan border in the south and the Tajikistan border in the east. Kazakhstan remains to the north; a further finger of land extends eastward to meet Kyrgyzstan. The land is mostly desert or at best plain, and the climate is warm and mainly dry. The capital is Tashkent.

Head of State   President Islam Karimov (1990)

Head of Government   Utkur Sultonov (December 1995)

Ruling Party   The government is formed by the People's Democratic Party (CDP).

Political Structure   Uzbekistan, a predominantly Sunni Muslim state, has an executive president who is directly elected by universal suffrage for a term of eight years (recently extended from five years). He answers to a National Assembly with 250 members, elected for a 5-year term, 83 members directly and 167 members by the local councils. Most parties are excluded.

Last Elections   Presidential elections took place in January 2000, when Karimov was returned to office with 92% of the vote. Elections to the Supreme Soviet were held in December 1999. The CDP took 48 seats, the Fatherland Progress Party won 20, the Self Sacrifice Party received 34 and the remainder was divided among minor parties.

Political Risk   Islamic extremists have lost influence and power since the Allied war in neighbouring Afghanistan. There are constant concerns about drug trafficking, however. Neighbouring Tajikistan was shaken by an attempted coup in November 1998 and officials accused Uzbekistan of supporting the rebels. The country's high dependence on exports of two major products, gold and cotton, make it vulnerable to adverse movements in world prices or the vagaries in the weather, as was the case for cotton in 2000. The government has sought to prop up its Soviet-style command economy with subsidies and tight controls on production and prices. Although this gradualist reform strategy has helped the country to avoid the dramatic economic contraction and drastic decline in living standards recorded in many other countries in the Commonwealth of Independent States, thus far it has failed to bring about much-needed structural changes.

International Disputes   In 1999, Uzbekistan's relations with Tajikistan became strained when Tajik guerrillas based in Uzbekistan began to conduct raids across the border. In 2000, Uzbek border guards advanced 5km into Kazakhstan and held the territory for several days.

Economy   Uzbekistan is one of the poorest areas of the former Soviet Union with more than 60% of its population living in poverty-ridden rural communities. GDP has been growing in recent years but the pace is slowing. Growth is expected to be just 2.2% in 2002 but is forecast to improve to about 3% in 2003. Inflation continues to be high with prices rising by 27% in 2001 and roughly 22% in 2002. The forecast is for inflation of 13.5% in 2003. Official statistics show that registered unemployment at end-2001 was the same as 12 months earlier namely 0.4% of the workforce. Actual unemployment however is estimated to be much higher and hidden unemployment in the rural sector has been rising. The 2002 state budget which envisages a fiscal deficit of 2% of GDP is to be financed from privatisation revenues short-term government bonds and credits from the central bank amounting to 0.5% of GDP. The budget includes social assistance to support vulnerable population groups that are likely to be affected by the liberalisation measures. The positive stimulus from exchange rate depreciation may encourage non-traditional exports and help the economy diversify its export base away from cotton and gold. However a current account deficit of 1-2% of GDP is forecast for 2002-2003 as imports are likely to rise faster with investment activity picking up in response to an improved policy environment.

Main Industries   Growth of industrial output accelerated to 8.1% in 2001 from 5.8% in 2000. Production of automobiles surged, mainly as a result of better capacity utilisation at UzDaewooAuto, a joint venture. Production of natural gas and ferrous metals also rose, while output of oil and gas condensate decreased. Due mainly to growing private activity, the services sector grew by 14.2% in 2001, marking a slight improvement over the 13% recorded in 2000. Retail trading has contributed noticeably to the expansion of the sector over the past few years as a result of small-scale privatisation. This growth was achieved despite government restrictions on consumer goods imports. A slump in international cotton and gold prices in 2001 hurt export earnings, exposing the vulnerability of the economy to fluctuations in commodity markets. The fall in commodity prices forced the government to continue its policy of import compression and import substitution, to prevent external financing requirements from rising further. A programme of structural reforms is also being implemented in line with the government's plans for exchange rate unification and for further liberalisation of price and procurement policies in the cotton-growing sector.

Energy   Uzbekistan is estimated to contain 594 million barrels of proven oil reserves, with 171 discovered oil and natural gas fields in the country. The Bukhara-Khiva region contains over 60% of Uzbekistan's known oil fields, including the Kokdumalak field, which accounts for about 70% of the country's oil production. In addition, the Fergana region contains another 20% of the country's oilfields, and the Ustyurt plateau and the Aral Sea have been targeted for further exploration. Oil deposits in Kokdumalak, Shurtan, Olan, Urgin and south-Tandirchi (all in southwestern Uzbekistan) are being developed rapidly. From 65,500 barrels per day (bbl/d) in 1992, Uzbekistan increased its oil production to 161,000 bbl/d in 1998. In 1996, Uzbekistan became a net oil exporter. However, Uzbekistan's oil and gas condensate production has been declining in the past few years as existing fields are exhausted faster than new commercial reserves are discovered.

	1999	2000	2001
Inflation (% change)	29.1	25.0	27.2
Exchange rate (per US$)	124.63	236.61	403.98
Interest rate			
GDP (% real growth)	4.3	3.8	4.5
GDP (Million units of national currency)	2,123,734.6	3,245,551.9	4,644,592.6
GDP (US$ million)	17,041.0	13,717.0	11,497.0
GDP per capita (US$)	722.9	572.9	473.0
Consumption (Million units of national currency)	1,747,464.6	2,608,314.6	3,666,021.0
Consumption (US$ million)	14,021.8	11,023.8	9,074.7
Consumption per capita (US$)	594.8	460.4	373.3
Population, mid-year ('000)	23,574.3	23,941.8	24,306.2
Birth rate (per '000)	23.2	22.6	22.1
Death rate (per '000)	6.0	6.0	5.9
No. of households ('000)	4,116.9	4,237.1	4,356.3
Total exports (US$ million)	2,710.0	2,324.0	2,655.0
Total imports (US$ million)	2,841.0	2,810.0	2,715.0
Tourism receipts (US$ million)	15.0	17.7	10.0
Tourist spending (US$ million)	23,574.3	23,941.8	24,306.2

Average household size 2001 (persons)	5.69					
Urban population 2001 (%)	36.9					
Age analysis (%) (2001)	*0-14*	37.2	*15-64*	58.2	*65+*	4.6
Population by sex (%) (2001)	*Male*	49.7	*Female*	50.3		
Life expectancy (years) (2001)	*Male*	66.4	*Female*	72.2		
Infant mortality (deaths per '000 live births) (2001)	38.4					
Adult literacy (%) (1997)	99.0					

TRADING PARTNERS

Major export destinations 2001 (% share)

RUSSIA	16.7
UKRAINE	5.6
ITALY	4.9
TAJIKISTAN	4.3

Major import sources 2001 (% share)

RUSSIA	12.1
SOUTH KOREA	11.5
GERMANY	6.9
KAZAKHSTAN	5.1

Vanuatu

Area (km^2)   14,765

Currency   Vatu (V = 100 centimes)

Location   Vanuatu, which was formerly run as an Anglo-French condominium under the name New Hebrides, consists of about 80 islands in the south-west Pacific located about 1,000km west of Fiji. Most of the islands are uninhabited and many are active volcanoes. The country has a moderate tropical climate, and is occasionally susceptible to cyclones. The capital is Port Vila.

Head of State   President John Bani (1999)

Head of Government   Edward Natapei (2001)

Ruling Party   A coalition led by the Union of Moderate Parties (UMP) leads the government.

Political Structure   The Republic of Vanuatu is an independent member of the Commonwealth. The executive president is elected for a 5-year term by an electoral college, which includes not only the Parliament but also the presidents of the numerous regional councils. These councils enjoy a considerable degree of regional autonomy. The 52 members of the unicameral national Parliament are elected by universal adult suffrage.

Last Elections   Parliamentary elections were held in April 2002. The UMP won 15 seats while the Party of Our Land (socialist) took 14 seats. Other representatives in the Parliament include the Vanuatu National United Party (8 seats), non-partisans and several smaller parties.

Political Risk   Regional and outer island development has been a long-standing and challenging objective for governments in Vanuatu. Outside the major towns of Port Vila and Luganville, infrastructure is poor and government services rarely available. There is a critical need to bring these regions and outer islands into the economy to ensure support there. Corruption among politicians is a perennial problem. Language differences are another source of tension. Some political groups are predominantly French-speaking, while others are English- speaking.

International Disputes   Vanuatu claims the Matthew and Hunter Islands east of New Caledonia.

Economy   After growing by 4% in 2001 GDP is expected to rise by just 0.7% in 2002 and 1.9% in 2003. Inflation was only 2% in 2001 but will increase. Prices are expected to rise by 4.5% in 2002 and 4% in 2003. Government revenues fell below forecast levels in 2001 as the economic slowdown reduced import duties and VAT collections. Revenues from Internet gambling and the Asset Management Unit's sale of public assets failed to live up to expectations. As a result of the deteriorating fiscal position the government reduced spending on recruitment of new staff and introduced other restrictions. Poor export performance resulted in a deterioration of the trade balance. Nevertheless international reserves remained comfortable covering about 5.7 months of imports. To strengthen the fiscal position through a broadening of the tax base the government recently established a Revenue Review Committee to prepare a strategic tax policy framework. The intention was to lift the ratio of revenues to GDP from the current level of 22-23% to 27%. However none of the major recommendations made by the committee in mid-2001 has yet been implemented. The government is aiming to achieve GDP growth of 4.5% over the medium term by encouraging private including foreign investment. Accordingly the Foreign Investment Act was amended in 2001 to promote investment from overseas. The high level of international reserves and prospects of a rebuilding of export revenues during 2002 mean that a stable exchange rate and a sustainable balance-of-payments position should be achievable over the medium term.

Main Industries   The economy contracted slightly during 2001, a key factor being the loss of agricultural production following two damaging cyclones early in the year. Copra exports fell by nearly 50%; exports of kava and beef also weakened. Tourism also performed poorly, particularly in the last few months of the year. Output of the industrial and services sectors has stagnated, largely because of reduced wholesale and retail trade. Industry accounts for around 13% of GDP and tends to centre on the processing of food products, notably canned or frozen meat, or timber products. All other manufactures are imported.

Energy   Vanuatu has no indigenous oil, gas or coal resources and will remain dependent for the foreseeable future on imports for its energy requirements.

	1999	2000	2001
Inflation (% change)	2.0	2.0	2.0
Exchange rate (per US$)	129.07	137.64	145.31
Interest rate (% per annum, commercial lending rate)	10.3	9.9	9.1
GDP (% real growth)	-2.5	2.5	4.0
GDP (Million units of national currency)	27,622.1	29,455.6	32,985.8
GDP (US$ million)	214.0	214.0	227.0
GDP per capita (US$)	1,178.9	1,151.0	1,193.0
Consumption (Million units of national currency)	18,961.2	19,789.8	21,416.6
Consumption (US$ million)	146.9	143.8	147.4
Consumption per capita (US$)	809.3	773.3	774.6
Population, mid-year ('000)	181.5	185.9	190.3
Birth rate (per '000)	33.0	32.6	32.3
Death rate (per '000)	5.8	5.7	5.5
No. of households ('000)	31.5	32.6	34.0
Total exports (US$ million)	25.8	29.6	15.0
Total imports (US$ million)	95.6	57.0	80.0
Tourism receipts (US$ million)	56.0	47.2	42.6
Tourist spending (US$ million)	9.0	8.4	8.8

Average household size 2001 (persons)		5.71				
Urban population 2001 (%)		20.3				
Age analysis (%) (2001)	*0-14*	41.2	*15-64*	55.5	*65+*	3.3
Population by sex (%) (2001)	*Male*	50.1	*Female*	49.9		
Life expectancy (years) (2001)	*Male*	67.1	*Female*	70.1		
Infant mortality (deaths per '000 live births) (2001)		30.1				
Adult literacy (%) (1997)		64.0				

TRADING PARTNERS

Major export destinations 2001 (% share)		Major import sources 2001 (% share)	
INDONESIA	36.2	JAPAN	26.4
GREECE	16.0	AUSTRALIA	16.5
JAPAN	12.6	SINGAPORE	14.7
THAILAND	11.4	GERMANY	10.9

◼ Venezuela

Area (km^2) 912,045

Currency Bolivar (= 100 centimos)

Location Venezuela, perhaps the most oil-rich state in South America, lies on the northeast Atlantic and Caribbean coast of the continent, with Brazil to the south, Colombia to the west and Guyana to the east. Much of the south and west of the country comprises the high sierras of the Guiana highlands, and in the northwest the land rises again to the Sierra Nevada. Elsewhere, there are low forested areas, especially along the Orinoco River which winds slowly northeast through the country. The capital is Caracas.

Head of State President Hugo Chavez (1999)

Head of Government Hugo Chavez (1999)

Ruling Party The Movimiento Quinta República (MVR) leads a coalition.

Political Structure President Chavez has made important changes in the political structure. A 131-member Constituent Assembly rewrote the 1961 constitution, and the new constitution passed overwhelmingly in a December 1999 public referendum. The new constitution increases the presidential term from five years to six and allows the president to run for re-election. National Assembly has 165 members, elected for a 5-year term. The country has an extensively devolved political structure, with 20 autonomous states and 72 dependencies.

Last Elections Hugo Chavez of the MVR was re-elected as president in July 2000, winning a landslide victory and another six years in office. The former coup leader took 59% of the vote, compared to 37% for his main rival. Elections to the National Assembly took place in July 2000. The MVR received 76 seats, the Democratic Action Party won 29, the Movement towards Socialism won 21 seats and the remainder were dispersed among several factions.

Political Risk Venezuela's bungled coup attempt in April 2002 suggests just how confused the country's political and economic fortunes have become. Hugo Chávez, the country's president, has hung on to power for now. Many, however, believe that in the future he can either stay in power or he can seek to further his revolutionary aims. He cannot, however, attempt both. Riots, demonstrations and pressure on Chávez have continued unrelentingly in the months since the attempted coup. Anti- Chávez sentiment runs deep within the military.

International Disputes Venezuela has an outstanding territorial dispute with Guyana over an area of land deep in its interior, but this is largely dormant. There have been tensions in the country's relationship with Colombia, which claims that Venezuela has aided Colombian rebels trying to bring down the Colombian government.

Economy Venezuela's economy grew by 2.7% in 2001 but is expected to contract by 0.8% in 2002. Growth in 2003 should be 1.3%. Prices rose by 12.5% in 2001 and will increase by 20.8% in 2002. In 2003, another 20.2% increase is forecast. Chávez's policies have prompted massive movements of capital out of the country. In February 2002, the Venezuelan currency band was abandoned. The bolivar was floated, and by mid-year the currency was worth about 20% less than it was before the float. In order to generate more revenue, the government imposed a new hydrocarbons law in November 2001. Royalty rates on oil production have been increased from 16.6% to 30% (the global average is a reported 7.1%). The state-owned oil company must also hold a 51% stake in any new exploration and production agreement. FDI flows have been relatively large, but are still not sufficient to compensate for the capital flight that Chávez's policies have produced. Attempts to diversify the economy and reduce its dependence on oil have not been successful.

Main Industries Agriculture is fragmented and lacking in investment. Half the country's 500,000 farms occupy just 1.6% of the arable land. At the other end of the scale, just 1% of the farms account for over 46% of the land. When elected, Chávez promised a radical land reform and issued a decree in November 2001 to speed this up. Now, both the landowners and the landless have turned to violence. The resultant disruptions have stopped investment in agriculture and reduced production. The sector produces cotton, coffee, cocoa, rice, sugar, tobacco and bananas both for domestic consumption and for export. Meat production is of an unusually high order. Oil dominates the economy, accounting for more than three quarters of total Venezuelan export revenues, about half of total government revenues and about one third of gross domestic product. Venezuela's 2002 budget had been based on a selling price of US$18.50 per barrel for its crude oil. Confronted with falling world prices, that figure has now been revised downwards. Manufacturing includes several heavy, energy-intensive industries such as steel and aluminium. The government has banned privatisation of social security, healthcare and the state oil company, and previously-planned privatisations, for instance, in the electricity sector, have stalled.

Energy Venezuela is home to the Western Hemisphere's largest conventional proven oil reserves at 77.7 billion barrels, as of January 2002. Substantial heavy oil and bitumen deposits are not included in this total. In 2001, Venezuela produced an estimated 3.1 million barrels per day (bbl/d), from 2000 production figures. Of this total, about 476,000 bbl/d were consumed domestically, while the remaining 2.6 million bbl/d were exported. Since his election, Chávez has maintained a policy of strict adherence to OPEC quotas. This requires producers to shut production, filling storage facilities, reducing production at existing fields and reducing investment and total production capacity. The 2002 OPEC quota of 21.7 million bbl/d for Venezuela is its lowest since 1991. Venezuela operates one of the Western Hemisphere's largest refining systems and is one of the world's largest oil refiners. Domestic refinery capacity is about 1.3 million bbl/d, with significant additional holdings in Curaçao, the US and Europe.

	1999	2000	2001
Inflation (% change)	23.6	16.2	12.5
Exchange rate (per US$)	605.72	679.96	723.67
Interest rate (% per annum, lending rate)	32.1	25.2	22.5
GDP (% real growth)	-6.1	3.2	2.7
GDP (Billion units of national currency)	62,577.0	82,450.7	90,421.0
GDP (US$ million)	103,310.6	121,258.2	124,948.5
GDP per capita (US$)	4,315.7	4,969.4	5,025.6
Consumption (Billion units of national currency)	41,579.7	50,289.5	59,275.4
Consumption (US$ million)	68,645.4	73,959.5	81,909.9
Consumption per capita (US$)	2,867.6	3,031.0	3,294.5
Population, mid-year ('000)	23,938.2	24,400.8	24,862.6
Birth rate (per '000)	24.2	23.8	23.3
Death rate (per '000)	4.7	4.7	4.7
No. of households ('000)	5,010.6	5,116.6	5,190.2
Total exports (US$ million)	20,190.0	31,802.0	31,462.4
Total imports (US$ million)	14,063.7	16,212.7	18,022.0
Tourism receipts (US$ million)	656.0	765.0	830.7
Tourist spending (US$ million)	1,646.0	2,039.7	2,213.3

Average household size 2001 (persons)	4.77				
Urban population 2001 (%)	87.4				
Age analysis (%) (2001)	*0-14*	33.6	*15-64*	61.9	*65+* 4.5
Population by sex (%) (2001)	*Male*	50.3	*Female*	49.7	
Life expectancy (years) (2001)	*Male*	70.7	*Female*	76.5	
Infant mortality (deaths per '000 live births) (2001)	19.5				
Adult literacy (%) (1997)	92.0				

TRADING PARTNERS

Major export destinations 2001 (% share)		Major import sources 2001 (% share)	
USA	43.7	USA	32.4
NETHERLANDS ANTILLES	13.7	COLOMBIA	5.6
BRAZIL	3.6	ITALY	4.3
COLOMBIA	2.8	BRAZIL	4.3

▦ Vietnam

Area (km^2)   329,565

Currency   New dông (= 10 hào = 100 xu)

Location   Vietnam is located on the South China Sea coast of the Indo-Chinese peninsula. The country follows the coast for more than 2,000km from the Chinese border in the north to the far south where it joins Cambodia on the Gulf of Thailand. There is also a western border with Laos. The climate is tropical and extremely humid. The capital is Hanoi.

Head of State   President Tran Duc Luong (1997)

Head of Government   Phan Van Khai (1997)

Ruling Party   Communist Party of Vietnam (CPV)

Political Structure   The influence of the communist party remains dominant despite attempts at economic and political reform. The country has a semi-executive president who has until recently been elected from single-candidate lists, and a 498-member National Assembly which is formally vested with all legislative power. In practice, the CPV controls the armed forces and the judiciary.

Last Elections   At the last elections in May 2002, only a few groups dominated by the Vietnamese Fatherland Front (VFF), a front of the Communist Party of Vietnam, were allowed to participate. Others participants included selected organisations and affiliates, and some non-partisans. In all, 51 seats were won by non-party candidates with the remainder of more than 400 seats going to the VFF. The National Assembly choose Phan Van Khai and Tran Duc Luong to be the country's Prime Minister and President.

Political Risk   Although Vietnam passed a constitutional amendment in 2001 that puts the private sector on an equal footing with state-owned enterprises, there is still much ideological ambivalence about the move. The government promised donors in 2001 that it would sell over 300 state companies but only half that number has been sold so far. Even if the programme goes according to schedule, the government intends to preserve a substantial public sector. Private firms are barred from "sensitive" industries including infrastructure and defence.

International Disputes   Vietnam is involved in an ongoing territorial dispute with other regional states over the potentially hydrocarbon-rich Spratly Islands. Vietnam, China, the Philippines, Brunei, Taiwan and Malaysia all make claims to the Spratly Islands. Vietnam and China clashed over territorial rights in 1999, preventing planned exploration in the South China Sea. Vietnam settled its dispute with Thailand in 1997 with an agreement that defines each country's boundaries in the Gulf of Thailand. The agreement ends 20 years of conflicting boundary claims in the 2,507 sq mile overlapping area and clears the way for exploration and production of hydrocarbons.

Economy   GDP should grow by around 5.3% in 2002 and 7% in 2003. Inflation is forecast to be 4.9% in 2002 and 3.7% in 2003. Domestic demand was the main source of economic expansion in 2001 led by strong growth in investment stemming from low interest rates the continuing creation of a large number of small and medium-scale enterprises an increase in government capital spending and a rise in FDI inflows. Investment's strong growth offset the deceleration in consumption which rose by only 4.9% in 2001 due to the decline in rural incomes associated with the weakening performance of the agriculture sector. The urban unemployment rate fell somewhat from 6.4% in 2000 to 6.3% in the first seven months of 2001. The gradual shift in labour from agriculture continued and was directed mainly toward the services sector. The lower than expected fiscal deficit in 2001 gives room for phasing in some of the costs of implementing reforms in banking and the public sector in 2002-2004. By some estimates the capital cost of such reforms could come close to 3-4% of GDP each year.

Main Industries   The agriculture sector recorded weaker growth than expected in 2001. The moderate 2.3% increase was due to a 1.7% decrease in rice output, a fall in the price of agricultural goods and estimated growth of 5% in fisheries, the best-performing subsector. However, the deceleration in agriculture was more than offset by a strong performance in industry and construction. Growth in industry was estimated at 9.7% in 2001, on the back of manufacturing and construction strength. Manufacturing is estimated to have increased by 9.2% while construction recorded a robust performance of 13%, due to the implementation of infrastructure projects, urban development projects in major cities, particularly Hanoi and Ho Chi Minh City, and a real estate boom. Within industry generally, the foreign-invested subsector grew at its lowest rate in recent years, namely 12.1%. Non-state activities grew by 20.3% in 2001, partly due to the vigorous impact of the Enterprise Law, which streamlined administrative procedures for doing business. The Law abolished 145 out of 400 licences in 2000, and government decree no. 30 issued that year required 60 licences to be abolished in 2001. In 2001, services sector growth was estimated at 4.4%. Wholesale and retail trade maintained its modest improvement of 3.3%. Real estate services were the leading area, strengthening by an estimated 8% due to the buoyant real estate market. The easing of procedures for issuing land-use certificates, the granting of permission to buy land to overseas Vietnamese and the recognition of Vietnam as one of the safer countries in the region all promoted land transactions. As a result, land prices in major urban centres such as Hanoi and Ho Chi Minh City increased by three or four times during the year.

Energy   Vietnam has 600 million barrels of proven oil reserves, and further discoveries are likely. Crude oil production averaged over 288,000 bbl/d in 2000 and almost 357,000 bbl/d during the first nine months of 2001. Production grew rapidly in recent years, from only 175,000 bbl/d as recently as 1996. The country has six operating oil fields. Most oil exploration and production activities occur offshore in the Cuu Long and Nam Con Son Basin. Vietnam currently has no operating oil refineries - therefore almost all of its oil production is exported. Export markets include Japan (the largest importer of Vietnamese oil), Singapore, the US and South Korea. Vietnam had net exports of an estimated 133,000 bbl/d of oil in 2000, and oil exports are one of the country's largest foreign currency earners.

	1999	2000	2001
Inflation (% change)	4.1	-1.7	0.1
Exchange rate (per US$)	13,943.20	14,167.70	14,725.20
Interest rate (% per annum, lending rate)	12.7	10.6	9.4
GDP (% real growth)	4.2	5.5	4.7
GDP (Billion units of national currency)	397,278.2	429,668.9	457,590.9
GDP (US$ million)	28,492.6	30,327.4	31,075.4
GDP per capita (US$)	358.3	375.8	380.1
Consumption (Billion units of national currency)	274,553.0	289,207.5	310,280.9
Consumption (US$ million)	19,690.8	20,413.2	21,071.4
Consumption per capita (US$)	247.6	252.9	257.8
Population, mid-year ('000)	79,531.3	80,705.6	81,750.0
Birth rate (per '000)	21.0	20.7	20.4
Death rate (per '000)	6.8	6.6	6.5
No. of households ('000)	15,271.5	15,544.0	15,821.6
Total exports (US$ million)	11,540.0	14,448.0	15,100.0
Total imports (US$ million)	11,636.0	15,636.0	16,000.0
Tourism receipts (US$ million)	470.6	685.3	430.8
Tourist spending (US$ million)	79,531.3	80,705.6	81,750.0

Average household size 2001 (persons)	5.19				
Urban population 2001 (%)	19.9				
Age analysis (%) (2001)	0-14	32.7	15-64	62.0	65+	5.3
Population by sex (%) (2001)	Male	49.4	Female	50.6	
Life expectancy (years) (2001)	Male	66.3	Female	71.0	
Infant mortality (deaths per '000 live births) (2001)	36.2				
Adult literacy (%) (1997)	91.9				

TRADING PARTNERS

Major export destinations 2001 (% share)

JAPAN	17.3
AUSTRALIA	7.7
CHINA	7.6
USA	7.3

Major import sources 2001 (% share)

SINGAPORE	13.6
CHINA	11.9
JAPAN	11.5
SOUTH KOREA	11.2

Western Samoa

Area (km²)   2,840

Currency   Tala (W$ = 100 sene)

Location   Western Samoa consists of nine islands, of which the two largest are Savai'i and Upolu, lying in the South Pacific north of Tonga and some 2,400km north of New Zealand. The country has a pleasant climate, although it is susceptible to cyclones. The capital is Apia.

Head of State   HH King Susuga Malietoa Tanumafili II (1962)

Head of Government   Tuilaepa Sailele Malielegaoi (1998)

Ruling Party   Human Rights Protection Party (HRPP)

Political Structure   Western Samoa, an independent member of the Commonwealth, has a constitutional monarch who may dissolve the 49-member Fono (Parliament) at any time and who appoints the prime minister on the recommendation of the Fono. A system of full universal voting was introduced in December 1990, prior to the country's first fully franchised elections. However, the voting mechanism was changed in 1993 to extend the life of the parliament from three years to five. The head of state is presently appointed for a life term. In future, the head of state will be elected for a 5-year term by the parliament.

Last Elections   Legislative elections were last held in March 2001. The Human Rights Protection Party (HRPP) won 23 seats, the Samoan National Development Party (SNDP) won 13 seats and independents captured the remainder.

Political Risk   The country is reasonably stable in political terms but is isolated and subject to occasional typhoons and active volcanism.

International Disputes   There are no international disputes.

Economy   GDP increased by 5% in 2001 and a similar pace is forecast for both 2002 and 2003. Inflation was only about 1.5% in 2001 and will reach 3% in 2002. Economic performance has benefited in recent years from reforms introduced in the 1990s. Total export revenues strengthened by about 20% in 2001 due to a surge in exports of fresh fish and garments. Imports were about 31% higher than in 2000 with non-oil private sector imports accounting for most of the rise. Foreign exchange reserves dropped and provided about 4.8 months of import cover at the end of the year compared with 6.4 months in the previous year. As a proportion of GDP external public debt declined from 64.8% to 60.2% at the end of fiscal year 2001 (ending 30 June). Tax revenues rose by 11.5% compared with the previous year as a result of continued rapid GDP and import growth. The government's major short-term policy challenge is to ensure macroeconomic stability while facilitating growth-promoting structural change and investment. An expansionary fiscal policy and an accommodative monetary policy stance were major factors in the rapid economic expansion of 2001 and careful monitoring is needed to avoid undesirable pressures on the balance of payments and inflation. In fiscal year 2002 an overall deficit of 1.5% of GDP is budgeted as the government continues to implement a strategy of current surpluses and development expenditures funded by external concessional loans. Total revenues and grants are projected to rise by 3.2% compared with 2001. Stronger exports and private remittances are expected to prevent any deterioration in the current account balance as a result of import growth.

Main Industries   Manufacturing, construction, transport and communications, electricity and water, and hotels and restaurants all performed well in 2001. However, agriculture declined by about 16% as subsistence production fell and efforts to diversify production for export remained unsuccessful. Fishing continued its expansion with the introduction of new, larger fishing vessels. In contrast, tourist arrivals were down somewhat because of the impact of the 11 September 2001 events. For example, September arrivals were nearly 12% lower than the corresponding monthly arrivals in the previous year, but because spending per tourist was higher, gross tourism earnings strengthened. Provided that external shocks can be avoided, the economy should be driven mainly by ongoing and new construction products in 2002-2003. The expansion of the fishing fleet and of agricultural production will also contribute. Stronger agriculture will have a beneficial impact on the poor, who reside mainly in rural areas. Manufacturing will continue to register strong growth as garment production strengthens and copra-processing activity recovers somewhat. However, a slowdown in tourism-related sectors is expected.

Energy   Apart from firewood, the country is entirely dependent on imports for its fuel requirements.

© Euromonitor International 2002

	1999	2000	2001
Inflation (% change)	0.3	1.0	1.5
Exchange rate (per US$)	3.01	3.29	3.48
Interest rate (% per annum, commercial lending rate)	11.5	11.0	9.9
GDP (% real growth)	3.5	6.8	5.0
GDP (Million units of national currency)	706.0	772.0	846.0
GDP (US$ million)	234.3	234.9	243.2
GDP per capita (US$)	1,343.0	1,326.0	1,353.6
Consumption (Million units of national currency)	315.6	453.7	497.2
Consumption (US$ million)	104.7	138.1	143.0
Consumption per capita (US$)	600.4	779.3	795.5
Population, mid-year ('000)	174.5	177.2	179.7
Birth rate (per '000)	28.7	28.5	28.3
Death rate (per '000)	5.8	5.8	5.7
No. of households ('000)	35.7	36.0	36.2
Total exports (US$ million)	20.4	14.2	15.5
Total imports (US$ million)	115.4	105.6	129.0
Tourism receipts (US$ million)	38.1	38.6	34.0
Tourist spending (US$ million)	4.4	4.1	4.1

Average household size 2001 (persons)		4.92				
Urban population 2001 (%)		21.7				
Age analysis (%) (2001)	*0-14*	38.1	*15-64*	57.4	*65+*	4.5
Population by sex (%) (2001)	*Male*	52.0	*Female*	48.0		
Life expectancy (years) (2001)	*Male*	61.6	*Female*	64.9		
Infant mortality (deaths per '000 live births) (2001)		27.4				
Adult literacy (%) (1997)		98.0				

TRADING PARTNERS

Major export destinations 2001 (% share)		Major import sources 2001 (% share)	
AUSTRALIA	63.7	USA	29.5
INDONESIA	11.9	NEW ZEALAND	17.9
USA	11.6	AUSTRALIA	13.5
AMERICAN SAMOA	2.2	FIJI	13.0

▪ Yemen

Area (km^2)   527,968

Currency   Yemeni riyal (= 100 fils)

Location   The Republic of Yemen, which took its present form in 1990, occupies the entire southern tip of the Arabian Peninsula, controlling the strategically important access from the Arabian sea through the Gulf of Aden, to the Red Sea. With Saudi Arabia to its north and Oman to the northeast, it faces Djibouti, Ethiopia and Somalia across the Gulf of Aden. The capital is Sana'a.

Head of State   President Ali Abdullah Saleh

Head of Government   Abdul-Qader Bagammal (2001)

Ruling Party   The government is formed by the General People's Congress (MSA).

Political Structure   The current state of Yemen was the result of a federation in May 1990, when the Republic of Yemen was formed by the union of the Yemen Arab Republic (North Yemen) with the People's Democratic Republic of Yemen (South Yemen). In 1994, the southern states declared their own secession from the federation. However, the rebellion was crushed and by mid-1995 the country appeared to be stabilising. The president is elected for a 7-year term by the people. The parliament (or Assembly of Representatives) has 301 members, elected for a 6-year term in single-seat constituencies. In February 2001, a national referendum was held in which voters agreed to the postponement of parliamentary elections until 2003. The referendum also extended Saleh's possible time in office until 2013. This voting, like previous ones, was accompanied by violence.

Last Elections   Presidential elections occurred in September 1999 when Saleh received 96% of the ballots. Parliamentary elections took place in March 1997. The MSA won 187 of the 301 seats in the House of Representatives while the Islah Party, which was the junior coalition partner in the outgoing parliament, won 53 seats. Independents captured 54 seats and two opposition parties took the remaining seats. The election was boycotted by the main opposition Yemen Socialist party, some of whose leaders launched the bid that triggered the civil war, and three other parties.

Political Risk   Prior to 11 September 2001, Yemen had become a centre of anti-American activity and terrorism. The government, however, is trying to cooperate in the anti-terrorist campaign. Authorities have threatened all their religious academies with closure and have deported many foreign students. The academies, which are thought to have trained as many as 25,000 extremists, have gone underground and still pose a danger to Yemen and to other countries.

International Disputes   Relations between Yemen and the US were tense following the attack on the American navy in Yemen's main port. The situation has now improved but the government lacks full control over much of its territory and many Muslim extremists are still functioning. Yemen and Saudi Arabia have resolved their long-standing border dispute. In a treaty signed in June 2000, the two governments agreed on the delineation of sections of their common border which had been in dispute since the 1930s.

Economy   Yemen's economy grew by 3.3% in 2001 while inflation was 11.9%. Yemen's economy has been negatively affected in 2001/2002 by declining prices for its oil exports, its largest source of hard-currency revenues. Remittances from Yemenis working in the wealthier countries of the Persian Gulf also have declined. Concerns about security and project risk in Yemen have heightened in recent months as a result of the terrorist attacks of 11 September 2001. Expenditure growth remains broadly in line with GDP except for a surge in petroleum subsidies, especially diesel. Yemen remains one of the poorest countries in the world, with a per capita income of only US$500. Fiscal policy aims to keep the non-oil deficit below 15% of GDP. Structural reforms that are planned will focus on further tax reform, including the introduction of a value-added tax, civil service reform and the restructuring of public financial institutions.

Main Industries   Income from oil accounts for approximately 40% of Yemen's total government revenues and is the country's main source of foreign currency. Most of the population, however, is engaged in subsistence agriculture, with sorghum, millet, sesame and other cereals being the most popular crops. Yemen's government continues to implement an economic reform programme which includes banking reform, privatisation of state-run industries, major infrastructure investment and reduction or elimination of government subsidies, including wheat, flour, gasoline and electricity. The government has said that it will encourage private investment in agriculture, fisheries and oil, and sell off its stake in companies throughout the Yemeni economy. Some companies will be offered for tender or auction, while others will be sold by private subscription. The government also stresses that it is seeking both foreign and local investors. State-owned businesses cited as candidates for privatisation include farm and agricultural cooperatives, construction companies, power stations, public housing facilities, refineries, the state's petroleum retail network, shipping companies and the state telecommunications company. Progress toward privatisation, however, has been slow.

Energy   Yemen's oil output, which averaged 452,521 barrels per day (bbl/d) in 2001, provides the country's main source of hard currency revenue. The country contains proven oil reserves of four billion barrels. Reserves are concentrated in five areas in the north. Yemen currently has a crude refining capacity of 130,000 bbl/d from two ageing refineries. With natural gas reserves of 16.9 trillion cu ft, Yemen has considerable potential as a natural gas producer and exporter. However, there is currently no production of natural gas in Yemen, and the gas which is extracted as a by-product of oil production is reinjected.

	1999	2000	2001
Inflation (% change)	8.0	10.9	11.9
Exchange rate (per US$)	155.72	161.72	168.67
Interest rate (% per annum, lending rate)	22.0	14.3	
GDP (% real growth)	3.7	5.1	3.3
GDP (Million units of national currency)	1,135,134.0	1,447,948.0	1,474,296.0
GDP (US$ million)	7,289.7	8,953.5	8,740.6
GDP per capita (US$)	413.8	494.3	450.5
Consumption (Million units of national currency)	750,546.0	953,623.0	944,989.6
Consumption (US$ million)	4,819.9	5,896.8	5,602.5
Consumption per capita (US$)	273.6	325.6	288.8
Population, mid-year ('000)	17,617.9	18,112.0	19,401.0
Birth rate (per '000)	50.5	50.0	49.4
Death rate (per '000)	9.4	9.0	8.7
No. of households ('000)	3,089.1	3,216.9	3,493.9
Total exports (US$ million)	2,440.4	4,078.8	3,676.7
Total imports (US$ million)	2,008.4	2,323.7	2,354.8
Tourism receipts (US$ million)	60.1	76.0	68.0
Tourist spending (US$ million)	75.2	90.2	108.1

Average household size 2001 (persons)	5.63				
Urban population 2001 (%)	35.7				
Age analysis (%) (2001)	*0-14*	47.9	*15-64*	49.7	*65+*	2.4
Population by sex (%) (2001)	*Male*	50.2	*Female*	49.8		
Life expectancy (years) (2001)	*Male*	60.1	*Female*	62.3		
Infant mortality (deaths per '000 live births) (2001)	64.9				
Adult literacy (%) (1997)	42.5				

TRADING PARTNERS

Major export destinations 2001 (% share)   **Major import sources 2001 (% share)**

INDIA	19.0	SAUDI ARABIA	12.3
THAILAND	17.2	UNITED ARAB EMIRATES	8.9
CHINA	11.5	USA	7.3
SOUTH KOREA	11.1	FRANCE	6.0

▪ Zambia

Area (km^2) 752,615

Currency Zambian kwacha (Kw = 100 ngee)

Location Zambia is a landlocked country lying in the centre of Central Southern Africa. It borders in the south on Zimbabwe, Botswana and Namibia. In the north are the Democratic Republic of the Congo (formerly Zaire) and Tanzania, in the west is Angola and in the east is Malawi. The country has a varied terrain, ranging from mountain ranges to the lowlands of the Zambezi, Luapula, Kafue and Luangwa rivers. The climate is subtropical, but humidity is not excessive. The capital is Lusaka.

Head of State Levy Patrick Mwanawasa (2002)

Head of Government Levy Patrick Mwanawasa (2002)

Ruling Party Movement for Multiparty Democracy (MMD)

Political Structure The executive president is elected by universal suffrage for a 5-year term, and answers to a National Assembly. The National Assembly has 159 members, 150 members elected for a 5-year term in single seat-constituencies, 8 appointed members and the Speaker.

Last Elections Presidential and parliamentary elections both took place in December 2001. Mwanawasa, leader of the MMD, defeated Anderson Mazoka of the United Party for National Development. In the parliamentary elections, the MMD won 69 seats, the United Party for National Development won 49 seats and the United National Independence Party claimed 13 seats. The remainder were distributed among several parties.

Political Risk Many international observers complained that the elections in 2001 were rigged and unfair. Deaths due to HIV/AIDS are seriously undermining both the public and private sector's administrative capacity and technical skills. The press is tightly controlled and corruption is rife. The government has spent more on building villas for visiting African heads of state than it spends on fighting the disease.

International Disputes Relations with Angola are tense after Zambia supported the rebel group, UNITA, in it losing cause in Angola. Zambia and the Democratic Republic of the Congo (formerly Zaire) are unable to agree on their mutual border in the area of Lake Mweru. Zambia has also had shaky relations in the past with neighbouring Mozambique, but most of the underlying problems have been smoothed over for now.

Economy GDP increased by 5% in 2001 and inflation was 22.5%. The government's strategy for development hinges critically on the copper sector and is subject to considerable uncertainty. In 2001 and 2002, several mining companies have informed the government that the viability of their investment plans is threatened by low copper prices. The key policy challenge facing Zambia is to sustain the gains made in 2000 and 2001 in raising the rate of economic growth, in the face of these considerable uncertainties in the mining sector. Given the difficulties in the copper sector, the government is keen to diversify the Zambian economy. Private sector investment will continue to be encouraged, particularly into export-oriented agriculture, light manufacturing, small-scale mining and tourism. However, even with rapid implementation of reforms, it is unlikely that growth in the non-mining sectors will offset the expected lower performance of the copper sector. The main macroeconomic targets for the period 2002-2004 are to achieve real GDP growth of at least 4% a year; realise a substantial deceleration of inflation to single digits by 2003; and build up gross international reserves.

Main Industries Zambia's agricultural sector contributes 17% to GDP. It is rich in agricultural potential and has a good rainfall pattern, other than in the southern part of the country, which is prone to drought. The country is one of Africa's most highly urbanised, with over 40% of the population living mostly in eight cities. The rural population is scattered over a large area and farms tend to be comparatively large. Farming centres on maize, vegetables and livestock, mainly for domestic consumption. Sugar, tobacco and cotton are produced for export. Despite weak agricultural production, Zambia's economic performance during 2001 was impressive. Growth was led by the mining, construction, wholesale and retail trade, and manufacturing. Export performance was strong, reflecting a 27% increase in copper export volumes. Non-traditional exports rose by 13% as a result of strong performance by horticulture and floriculture. Tourism earnings also rose sharply, partly on account of the solar eclipse. This strong export performance was more than offset by the increase in imports, particularly for the metal sector, leading to a current account deficit of about 1.9 percentage points of GDP more than anticipated. The higher metal imports were financed by private sector capital inflows. The banking industry was strengthened by injections of new capital in some bank, the liquidation of two others and closer supervision of the entire system. Progress was also made in the petroleum sector reform programme. In particular, the state-owned Zambia National Oil Company (ZNOC) was put under receivership, and international consultants were appointed to prepare a valuation. Mineral extraction involves mainly copper, the single most abundant deposit in Africa, which generally accounts for around 75% of Zambia's foreign exchange earnings. The mines, however, are in poor condition.

Energy Zambia has no indigenous oil or gas reserves, though it has some coal. The country is obliged to depend on imports for most of its fuel needs. The vast bulk of its electricity derives from hydroelectric sources.

	1999	2000	2001
Inflation (% change)	26.8	26.1	22.5
Exchange rate (per US$)	2,388.02	3,110.84	3,610.93
Interest rate (% per annum, commercial lending rate)	40.5	38.8	46.2
GDP (% real growth)	2.2	3.6	5.0
GDP (Billion units of national currency)	7,479.5	10,074.6	13,147.6
GDP (US$ million)	3,132.1	3,238.5	3,641.0
GDP per capita (US$)	347.5	353.2	375.2
Consumption (Billion units of national currency)	4,666.0	6,441.4	8,747.0
Consumption (US$ million)	1,953.9	2,070.6	2,422.4
Consumption per capita (US$)	216.8	225.8	249.6
Population, mid-year ('000)	9,012.3	9,169.0	9,705.0
Birth rate (per '000)	43.0	42.6	42.1
Death rate (per '000)	20.1	19.7	19.3
No. of households ('000)	2,173.3	2,197.2	2,295.6
Total exports (US$ million)	693.1	819.0	889.3
Total imports (US$ million)	811.7	731.0	791.1
Tourism receipts (US$ million)	85.0	60.9	53.3
Tourist spending (US$ million)			

Average household size 2001 (persons)	4.17				
Urban population 2001 (%)	43.8				
Age analysis (%) (2001)	*0-14*	47.7	*15-64*	50.0	*65+* 2.2
Population by sex (%) (2001)	*Male*	49.9	*Female*	50.1	
Life expectancy (years) (2001)	*Male*	42.2	*Female*	41.3	
Infant mortality (deaths per '000 live births) (2001)	83.4				
Adult literacy (%) (1997)	75.1				

TRADING PARTNERS

Major export destinations 2001 (% share)

SOUTH AFRICA	23.8
SWITZERLAND	8.5
MALAWI	7.3
THAILAND	7.1

Major import sources 2001 (% share)

SOUTH AFRICA	65.1
ZIMBABWE	6.6
UNITED KINGDOM	3.2
TANZANIA	2.9

▨ Zimbabwe

Area (km^2)   390,310

Currency   Zimbabwe dollar (Z$ = 100 cents)

Location   Zimbabwe is a landlocked country lying in east-central southern Africa. It is separated from the Indian Ocean by Mozambique - a factor which proved crucially awkward during the decades of civil war in that country. In the north it borders on Zambia, in the southwest on Botswana and in the south on South Africa. The climate is dry and tropical, yet there is usually enough water thanks to the numerous large rivers which flow through the country. The capital is Harare.

Head of State   President Robert G. Mugabe (1987)

Head of Government   President Robert G. Mugabe

Ruling Party   Zimbabwe African National Union-Patriotic Front (ZANU-PF)

Political Structure   Zimbabwe, an independent member of the Commonwealth, has an executive president who is elected by universal suffrage for a 6-year term and presides over a single-chamber House of Assembly. The Assembly's 150 members, who also serve for six years, include 120 elected members, 10 tribal chiefs, 8 provincial governors appointed by the president, and 12 other presidential appointees. In 1999, the president announced his intention to form a commission to draw up a new constitution.

Last Elections   In parliamentary elections held in June 2000, Mugabe's ZANU-PF coalition was returned to power but with only a slim majority. The opposition Movement for Democratic Change swept most urban areas, winning 57 of the country's 120 constituencies. The ZANU-PF coalition received just over 50% of the vote and 62 seats. A total of 37 court challenges to the results in various constituencies were subsequently made, most to no avail. In March 2002, presidential elections were held. The violence-marred poll returned Mugabe to power with 56% of the vote. He defeated Morgan Tsvangirai, leader of the Movement for Democratic Change.

Political Risk   In order to implement his policy of land distribution, Mugabe has commanded some 2,900 white farmers to stop farming. Meanwhile, Zimbabwe is facing its worst food shortage in 60 years, caused by drought and several years of violent harassment of the nation's white farmers. The government itself estimates that nearly seven million of the country's 13 million people will be without adequate food in a few months.

International Disputes   The country's relations with virtually all Western countries have seriously deteriorated as a result of Mugabe's policy of confiscating farmland. Zimbabwe has also been suspended from the Commonwealth. Relations with several African countries are strained.

Economy   Zimbabwe's economy contracted by 8.4% in 2001 while inflation was 77%. With the contraction in 2001, the cumulative decline in real per capita GDP since 1997 is 23%. Expansionary monetary policies have pushed inflation toward triple-digit levels and created an asset price bubble. Poverty and unemployment are rising, and food shortages - stemming from price controls on main commodities and foods, crop destruction, drought and floods, and the lack of foreign exchange - are serious. Zimbabwe's economic and social problems are spilling over to other countries in the region in the form of increased illegal immigration, weakened investor confidence and financial market turmoil.

Main Industries   With its fertile lands, Zimbabwe was traditionally regarded as the breadbasket of southern Africa. In normal times, the sector accounts for 20% of GDP with production being equally divided between black- and white-owned farms. However, Mugabe's policy of land confiscation has devastated the farm sector. White farmers who defy the latest edit will face jail terms. In all, 95% of commercial farmland has been slated for redistribution. Roughly 60% of all commercial farmers must stop work. Another 35% have only received preliminary notices of confiscation by the end of June 2002. Black farm workers - approximately two million people in all - face destitution. In normal times the country's white farmers account for well over a third of exports and a quarter of formal sector employment. The manufacturing sector is small but was growing rapidly until credit dried up and the Zimbabwean dollar plummeted. Most firms still cater mainly to the domestic market and exports are modest. Tourism has great potential but the number of visitors has dropped off sharply as a consequence of the present unrest. The mining sector is especially important to the economy, producing gold, silver, asbestos and copper but exports of these minerals have also suffered from the government's erratic policies on exchange rates. Many banks are very weak and have almost stopped lending.

Energy   The bulk of Zimbabwe's energy needs are met by importing petroleum from South Africa, although the country does have some coal and uses this for electricity generation. About a third of Zimbabwe's electricity comes from hydroelectric resources.

	1999	2000	2001
Inflation (% change)	58.5	55.9	76.7
Exchange rate (per US$)	38.30	44.42	55.05
Interest rate (% per annum, commercial lending rate)	55.4	68.2	38.0
GDP (% real growth)	-0.7	-5.1	-8.4
GDP (Million units of national currency)	210,409.0	314,330.0	506,216.0
GDP (US$ million)	5,493.5	7,076.7	9,195.2
GDP per capita (US$)	476.0	606.4	7,315.2
Consumption (Million units of national currency)	135,782.6	200,042.2	349,221.5
Consumption (US$ million)	3,545.1	4,503.6	6,343.5
Consumption per capita (US$)	307.2	385.9	5,046.5
Population, mid-year ('000)	11,541.2	11,669.0	1,257.0
Birth rate (per '000)	36.6	36.2	35.7
Death rate (per '000)	17.9	17.9	17.8
No. of households ('000)	3,194.3	3,190.1	3,230.0
Total exports (US$ million)	1,419.4	1,989.0	1,873.2
Total imports (US$ million)	1,684.6	2,365.0	2,777.4
Tourism receipts (US$ million)	202.0	155.5	125.0
Tourist spending (US$ million)	80.2	103.4	95.2

Average household size 2001 (persons)	3.66					
Urban population 2001 (%)	36.0					
Age analysis (%) (2001)	*0-14*	42.3	*15-64*	54.9	*65+*	2.8
Population by sex (%) (2001)	*Male*	49.1	*Female*	50.9		
Life expectancy (years) (2001)	*Male*	43.3	*Female*	42.5		
Infant mortality (deaths per '000 live births) (2001)	57.4					
Adult literacy (%) (1997)	90.9					

TRADING PARTNERS

Major export destinations 2001 (% share)   **Major import sources 2001 (% share)**

UNITED KINGDOM	7.5	SOUTH AFRICA	44.6
GERMANY	6.9	MOZAMBIQUE	4.6
SOUTH AFRICA	5.6	GERMANY	3.5
JAPAN	5.4	UNITED KINGDOM	3.4